MW01156130

A
TORAH
COMMENTARY
FOR OUR
TIMES

A
TORAH
COMMENTARY
FOR OUR
TIMES

VOLUME III: NUMBERS AND DEUTERONOMY

HARVEY J. FIELDS

Illustrations by
GIORA CARMI

UAHC PRESS · New York, New York

Library of Congress Cataloging-in-Publication Data
(Revised for volume 3)

Fields, Harvey J.
    A Torah commentary for our times.

    Includes bibliographical references.
    Contents: v. 1. Genesis—v.2. Exodus and
Leviticus—v. 3. Numbers and Deuteronomy.
    1. Bible. O.T. Pentateuch—Commentaries. 2. Bible.
O.T. Pentateuch. I. Karmi, Giyora, ill. II. Title.
BS1225.3.F46 1990   222'.1077   89-28478
ISBN 0-8074-0511-6 (v. 3)

This book is printed on acid free paper
Copyright © 1993 by Harvey J. Fields
Manufactured in the United States of America
10 9 8 7

Feldman Library

THE FELDMAN LIBRARY FUND was created in 1974 through a gift from the Milton and Sally Feldman Foundation. The Feldman Library Fund, which provides for the publication by the UAHC of selected outstanding Jewish books and texts, memorializes Sally Feldman, who in her lifetime devoted herself to Jewish youth and Jewish learning. Herself an orphan and brought up in an orphanage, she dedicated her efforts to helping Jewish young people get the educational opportunities she had not enjoyed.

In loving memory of my beloved wife Sally
"She was my life, and she is gone;
She was my riches, and I am a pauper."

"Many daughters have done valiantly,
but thou excellest them all."

Milton E. Feldman

For
SYBIL

partner, wise critic, eyes,
and love of my life

Contents

THE TORAH PORTIONS OF DEUTERONOMY

Acknowledgments

With this volume of *A Torah Commentary for Our Times* completed, I look back upon the past five years of research, study, and writing with great satisfaction. Pondering the unique and profound interpretive tradition of Torah throughout Jewish history has transformed me. "How incredible!" I have often muttered to myself as amazement and pride congealed at the discovery of a new and novel jewel of wisdom offered by commentators. Their humanity, art, and reverence continue as a challenge, a model of intellectual and spiritual excellence. Orchestrating their arguments and differing opinions, "speaking" with them, sometimes through them, leaves me enriched and a whole lot wiser—I hope.

Thanks to hundreds of students who have studied Torah with me during these past years. They have all helped to shape the form and substance of these pages. It was Aron Hirt-Manheimer who urged this project upon me. I am indebted to his wise advice, critical suggestions, and constant friendship. I am also deeply grateful to Rabbi Howard I. Bogot, Rabbi Shelton Donnell, and Rabbi Steven Z. Leder for their thoughtful reading and reactions to this volume. My work here has been blessed by the devoted and careful editing of Annette Abramson and by the production expertise of Stuart L. Benick.

My wife, Sybil, has sifted each volume of this commentary with her keen understanding of Jewish tradition and her devotion to clarity and excellence. I dedicate this volume to her out of gratitude, respect, and love.

Harvey J. Fields

TREASURES OF TORAH

"Words of Torah," say the ancient rabbis, "are like golden bowls. With golden bowls, the more you polish and rub them, the more they shine and brighten the faces of those who look at them. So it is with words of Torah. The more they are studied, explored for meaning, discussed, and used as a guide for action, the more they brighten the faces of those who love them." (*Avot de-Rabbi Natan* 31:34b)

Within Jewish tradition, "enlightenment" and "wisdom" are synonymous with knowing and practicing the words of Torah. The author of Psalm 19:8–9 has this in mind when commenting: "The Torah of God is perfect, renewing life; the teachings of God are enduring, making the simple wise; the laws of God are just, rejoicing the heart; the commandments of God are clear, giving light to the eyes."

This view of Torah as the vital source of Jewish enlightenment and the guide for ethical and ritual behavior is established within the Torah itself. Moses constantly reminds the Israelites that God has made a covenant, a sacred agreement, with them. The teachings and commandments of Torah have been given to them so that they may become a "holy" people. Indeed, the possession, understanding, and practice of Torah justifies Jewish existence. Moses warns the Israelites: "See, I set before you this day life and prosperity, death and adversity. . . . Choose life—if you and your offspring would live—by loving *Adonai* your God, heeding God's commands, and holding fast to God." (Deuteronomy 30:15–20)

It is not surprising that the study and interpretation of Torah became an obsession of Jews. Rabbinic commentators see in its tales, history, poetry, and laws more than an ordinary library of information. They compare Torah to a "lifeline," praise it as "the medicine of life," refer to it as a "map of existence," or as "fine wine that strengthens and soothes the spirit." The Torah, they say, "adds beauty to Israel." It prevents evil thoughts from seizing and distorting human powers for goodness, truth, justice, and love. For the Jewish people, Torah is a spiritual "homeland." Those who study and practice its teachings are never alienated from themselves or from their people.

Contemporary interpreter Rabbi Jacob Neusner does not exaggerate when he defines Judaism as the unique expression of Torah. Bearing in mind centuries of comment, passion, and intellect devoted to understanding Torah, Neusner concludes that "Judaism consists of the religious tradition enshrined in the holy books, expressed by the holy words, deeds, way of living, principles of faith, subsumed under the word 'Torah.' " (*Song of Songs Rabbah* 1:15; *Numbers Rabbah, Shelach,* 17:6; *Sifre Deuteronomy, Ekev,* 82b; *Pesikta de-Rav Kahanah* 102a; *The Way of Torah: An Introduction to Judaism,* p. 91)

These attributions of power and meaning to Torah all demonstrate its essential role in the history and destiny of the Jewish people. Each generation of Jews has evolved its understanding of itself through its struggle to decipher and apply the values and laws of Torah to its time. In our own age, as we have amply seen in Volumes One and Two of *A Torah Commentary for Our Times,* the exciting challenge of grappling with the meanings of Torah goes on. In this third and final volume, we turn attention to the Torah books of Numbers and Deuteronomy, where we encounter that continuing effort.

Reviewing Genesis, Exodus, and Leviticus

The first book of Torah, Genesis, deals with "origins." It presents the beginnings of life, humanity, the covenant with Abraham, and Isaac and Jacob establishing the relationship of the Jewish people to its land and God. The book ends with Joseph leading the family of his father, Jacob, to the safety and shelter of Egypt.

Exodus chronicles the rebirth of the Israelites. Joseph dies, his contributions to Egypt's survival forgotten by a new pharaoh who enslaves the Israelites. In the darkest moment of their captivity, Moses arises to lead them out of Egypt. Liberated, they live in the Sinai desert, where they are given the Torah; organize themselves as a community; and build a sanctuary. Punctuating the narrative of Exodus are the constant complaints of the people about living conditions in the desert. While Moses ascends Mount Sinai to bring them the Torah, they betray him and God by building a golden calf. God threatens to punish them with destruction for their breach of faith. Moses intervenes and saves them.

The Book of Leviticus contains directions for guiding the people and the priests in offering sacrifices to God. While it reads like a manual of ritual discipline, it includes an articulation of ethical commandments matched only by the Ten Commandments found in Exodus and Deuteronomy. Interpreters encounter many challenges in making Leviticus relevant to their times. Their discussions range from questions about the meaning of prayer and sacrifice to concerns about sin, ancient diseases, slander, and scapegoating. Within its dense rules about the slaughter of sacrifices and care for those afflicted with disease, interpreters discuss care for the poor, justice for the oppressed, and the challenge of creating a society based on the moral precept of "love your neighbor as yourself."

The Book of Numbers

In contrast to the first three books of the Torah, *Bemidbar,* literally translated as "in the desert," but commonly known as "Numbers," is a narrative of the Israelite people's forty years of wandering across the Sinai desert. The name "Numbers" is attached to the book because the first four of its thirty-six chapters deal with taking a census, or "numbering" the people, just one month after their liberation from Egypt.

Numbers captures the young community emerging out of oppression and organizing its leadership, institutions, and resources for reconquering its homeland. In a way, the book reveals the people of Israel during its difficult and awkward years of adolescence. Camping in forty different places, they face the natural obstacles of a barren and hostile desert. As a new and evolving community they forge laws with which to govern themselves and a military readiness for repossessing their land.

Like Exodus, Numbers combines narration with legislation. Concern for the purity of the community and its special relationship to God is addressed by laws dealing with nazirites, the suspected adulteress, oaths, blessings of priests, wearing of fringes, inheritance of land, the ritual offering of the red heifer, and concern for the safety of those guilty of manslaughter. All of these laws are meant to prepare the people for their administration and possession of the land of Israel.

Ironically, the tales woven into Numbers often feature the theme of rebellion. The people are constantly complaining about their plight in the desert. They question the leadership of Moses and Aaron, at times even demanding a return to Egypt. They whine about the tasteless manna, gripe about the lack of water. When Moses sends spies into the Land of Israel to bring back a report meant to guide the people in conquering the land, the majority of the scouts spread the lie that victory over its inhabitants will be impossible. At another point, Korah and his followers foment a rebellion against Moses and Aaron. Exasperated by the people's lack of faith, even Aaron and Moses turn against God. As a result of complaining and disloyalty, the entire generation freed from Egypt, including Moses and

Aaron, is condemned to die in the wilderness. Only Joshua and Caleb are permitted to survive and lead the new generation of Israelites into the Land of Israel.

The story of Balak, king of Moab, calling upon Bala'am son of Beor in Pethor to curse the Israelites seems to rescue the demoralized people. The foreign prophet, promised great wealth by Balak if he will pronounce the destruction of the people, refuses to be bought. Instead, he praises them. Three times he blesses them, predicting that "no harm is in sight for Jacob, no disaster in view for Israel" and concluding: "How beautiful are your tents, O Jacob, your dwellings, O Israel."

Numbers concludes with a rush of preparations for reconquering the Land of Israel. A new census is taken. A detailed description of sacrifices for holy days is given. Division of the land is discussed along with the rights of women to inherit. The book concludes with Moses and the people standing on the steppes of Moab at the Jordan River near Jericho in readiness for the journey and battles ahead.

Through the generations, interpreters of Numbers have dealt with a number of issues. Attention is given to the meaning of "counting" the Israelites, to the peculiar ceremony for examining the claim against a suspected adulteress, to the significance of nazirite vows. Commentators examine grievances of the Israelites, probe the spies' report about the Land of Israel, ask about the justification of Korah's rebellion against Aaron and Moses, and pose the question: Why was Moses, so devoted a servant of God, not allowed to crown his career of leadership by bringing the people into the Land of Israel?

Matters of ritual and law also attract the attention of interpreters. They explore the importance of *tzitzit*, or "fringes," commanded to be worn by Israelites; probe the peculiar ceremonies surrounding the sacrifice of the *parah adumah,* or "red cow"; review the dangers of fanaticism raised by Pinchas's execution of Zimri and a Midianite woman; and grapple with the importance of the process of justice in society.

The discussion of these issues within this volume illustrates the wide variety of views held by interpreters of the Torah, who often clash with one another. An insight overlooked for centuries may be discovered and "polished up" for a "new" argument by a contemporary commentator. As sifted and critically discussed by interpreters, the trials facing the Israelites as they trek across the wilderness for forty years, maturing as a people, are still relevant. In many ways, Numbers reflects the uncertain and adventurous human journey of every generation.

The Book of Deuteronomy

As commentators have noted for centuries, the Book of Deuteronomy differs in its structure and in the character of its language. The English title "Deuteronomy" is derived from the Greek word that means "second law," which is the translation of the Hebrew expression *mishneh ha-Torah* (Deuteronomy 17:18), or "a repetition of the law." The Hebrew name for the book is taken from its second word, *devarim,* meaning "words." Those various titles of the book provide a clue into its style and contents.

Commenting on the unique nature of the Book of Deuteronomy, Nachmanides notes that "in this book Moses explains to the generation that is about to enter and conquer the Land of Israel many of the commandments that he believed required repetition and elaboration . . . as in the many instances against idolatry. He repeats the laws to impress the people with the serious consequences of not observing them." Don Isaac Abravanel agrees with Nachmanides. However, he adds another dimension, claiming that "Moses composed the Book of Deuteronomy on his own, commenting and interpreting what he understood to be God's purpose in giving the commandments to the people of Israel."

Both Nachmanides and Abravanel locate what seems to differentiate Deuteronomy from the other books of the Torah. Its narrative and laws are all a part of a personal reflection of Moses. The leader is portrayed at the end of his career. A new generation of Israelites, led by Joshua and Caleb, is poised to enter the Land of Israel. Moses gathers them together and for the last time addresses them. Deuteronomy contains his final three speeches to the people. It is a collection of his recollections, reflections, and interpretations forged over forty years.

In the first speech Moses reminds the people of their experience at Mount Sinai and of God's warnings against idolatry. He tells them that their parents were not allowed to enter the land because of their constant unfaithfulness to God.

In the second speech he repeats the Ten Commandments and many of the laws already found in Exodus. Loyalty to God's commandments, Moses promises, will assure the people's survival; unfaithfulness will bring punishment and destruction. Ritual and ethical commandments are treated with equal importance. Observing the Sabbath; caring for the poor, the stranger, and the hungry; not cooking a kid in its mother's milk; dispensing justice in the courts; caring for trees in time of war; prohibitions against wearing cloth woven of a mixture of linen and wool; marriage and divorce; and appropriate and inappropriate sexual relations are among the varied subjects Moses interprets for the people.

In his final speech Moses speaks of the *berit*, or "covenant," that God made with the people at Mount Sinai. He reminds them that it applies to all generations of Israelites and that all its commandments are possible for anyone to fulfill. They are "in your mouth and in your heart, to observe." He warns against rejecting the covenant, telling the people: "I have put before you life and death, blessing and curse. Choose life—if you and your offspring would live—by loving *Adonai* your God, heeding God's commands, and holding fast to God."

Deuteronomy concludes with a record of the end of Moses' life. He blesses the people with words of poetry and then calls Joshua forward to receive the authority of leadership. At one hundred and twenty years of age, Moses ascends Mount Nebo in the land of Moab. From there he can see the Land of Israel. He dies on Mount Nebo, but his burial place is unknown. "Never again," says the Torah, "did there arise in Israel a prophet like Moses—whom *Adonai* singled out, face to face. . . ."

As we might suspect, commentators engage in their exploration and study of Deuteronomy with the same critical vigor we have seen demonstrated in their interpretations of the other books of Torah. They rivet their attention on such subjects as the fair dispensation of justice, the tension between arrogance and gratitude, sin and repentance, and evil and goodness in the world. The regulations for the slaughter of animals, care for the environment, returning lost property, and the responsibility of handing on leadership from one generation to the next—all concern them. So does the interpretation of the *Shema*, what we can mean by "loving God," and how to understand Moses' claim that the people of Israel is an *am segulah,* or "a treasured people."

Hidden treasures

While Deuteronomy repeats many of the laws and commandments found in the earlier books of the Torah, interpreters do not overlook the significant variations in text or the drama of this book as the last teachings of Moses to his people. The artistry and differing style of Moses' testimony and motives provide a lively and compelling insight into some of the most important aspects of Jewish tradition.

It was Rabbi Pinchas, living in fourth-century Babylonia, who drew a comparison between looking for lost money and searching for the meanings and lessons of Torah.

It is strange, he said, how human beings will kindle hundreds of wicks and lamps to find a few coins that have been lost. So much effort and determination for such a small reward! So much work for so little profit!

However, continued Rabbi Pinchas, there is an important message here. If you seek after an understanding of the words of Torah, as if they were lost and hidden treasures, you will be greatly rewarded. Light many hundreds of wicks and lamps. For the Torah is a treasure that provides life in this world and in the world to come. Its exploration invigorates the mind and challenges the intellect and spirit to pursue deeds of goodness, justice, and love. (*Song of Songs Rabbah* 1:9)

THE
TORAH
PORTIONS
OF
NUMBERS

PARASHAT BEMIDBAR
Numbers 1:1–4:20

The second book of the Torah, Exodus, concludes with a description for setting up the sanctuary on the first day of the first month of the second year after the Israelites leave Egypt. The fourth book of the Torah, known in Hebrew as *Bemidbar,* or "in the desert," or in English as Numbers, begins with God commanding Moses to take a census of the entire Israelite community. The commandment is given on the first day of the second month of the second year after the Israelites' departure from Egypt. All males over the age of twenty are counted, and it is reported that there is a total of 603,550. This number excludes 22,000 Levites, who are exclusively responsible for all services of the sanctuary and are to camp around the sanctuary at all times. After counting all firstborn Israelite males over the age of one month, Moses is instructed to compare their number of 22,273 with the total of 22,000 Levites and to charge a redemption tax for the additional 273. It is to be paid to Aaron and his sons for service to the sanctuary. Moses also lists and counts the Kohathites separately from the Levites since the Kohathites are responsible for lifting and carrying the sacred objects of the sanctuary. They are not to be present when the sanctuary is either dismantled or set up.

OUR TARGUM

· 1 ·

One month after setting up the sanctuary "in the desert" *(bemidbar),* Moses is instructed by God to number all Israelite males over the age of twenty, all who are able to bear arms. The census is taken according to the tribal houses of the Israelites: Reuben; Simeon; Judah; Issachar; Zebulun; the sons of Joseph, Ephraim and Manasseh; Benjamin; Dan; Asher; Gad; and Naphtali. Moses and Aaron register all the males. Their total is 603,550.

The Levites, the sons of Levi, are not counted in the census since they do not bear arms but are exclusively responsible for the sanctuary and its

rituals. They are commanded to camp around the sanctuary at all times and to assist Aaron the priest in all the rituals.

· 2 ·

Moses counts the Levites from the age of one month. The total comes to 22,000. He also numbers the firstborn males among the Israelites. That total comes to 22,273.

God tells Moses that the Levites will carry out the work of the sanctuary and free the rest of the Israelites from such ritual responsibilities. However, since there are an additional 273 firstborn Israelites, a special tax of five shekels per head is to be paid as a donation, freeing them from their sanctuary duties. The money is given to Aaron and his sons to be used at their discretion.

· 3 ·

Dismantling and preparing the sanctuary for movement from place to place is to be done, exclusively, by Aaron and his sons. All objects of the sanctuary, the screens, curtains, ark, bowls, lampstands, are to be covered with dolphin skin or special cloths.

· 4 ·

Moses and Aaron are told to take a count of the Kohathites, the descendants of Kohath, one of the three sons of Levi. Those between the ages of thirty and fifty are assigned to lift and carry the sanctuary parts when they are moved from place to place.

THEMES

Parashat Bemidbar contains two important themes:

1. The meaning of *midbar*, or "desert," in Jewish tradition.
2. The significance of counting the Israelites.

PEREK ALEF: *Why Does So Much of Such Importance in Jewish History Happen in the Midbar—in the Desert?*

In 1838–1839, the famous Scottish artist David Roberts (1796–1864) journeyed throughout the Middle East. His pictures and personal diary are valuable records of what he saw and experienced. Traveling by foot and camel caravan through the Sinai desert, Roberts and his party encountered searing heat by day and shivering cold at night. His diary describes the ragged peaks, the black, rugged, desolate summits, "the dark frowning front of Mount Sinai," and the barren desert.

Commenting on his climb through the pass toward Mount Sinai, Roberts says, "Although I had crossed the most rugged passes of the Alps and made from Chamouny the whole circuit of Mount Blanc, I never found a path so rude and difficult as that which we were now ascending." Another member of his party writes, "I had never seen a spot more wild and desolate." (David Roberts; Nachman Ran, editor, *The Holy Land,* Wellfleet Books, New York, 1982, pp. V-27 - V-35)

Those who have traveled through the triangular-shaped Sinai peninsula, situated between Egypt's Gulf of Suez and the Gulf of Eilat, know its variegated landscape. In the north, along the Mediterranean Sea, one finds endless stretches of high, shifting sand dunes. Further south are jagged limestone cliffs and mountains relieved by vast rocky plateaus. In the southern area are tall granite mountains, valleys, and gorges eroded from the melt of winter rains and snow and imbedded with rich veins of copper and turquoise. Even today, there are fewer than one hundred thousand inhabitants in this arid and unfriendly region.

It is into the desolate landscape of the Sinai desert that the newly liberated Jewish people wander and remain for forty years. Students of Jewish history and Torah literature have constantly asked through the centuries, "Why did they stay so long?" Why after bitter years of Egyptian oppression did Moses not lead them directly to the Land of Israel? Indeed, why is the Torah given to the people of Israel in such a hostile environment rather than in the comfort of the Promised Land flowing with milk and honey? Finally, why does the Torah devote the entire book of *Bemidbar* and much of Deuteronomy to the Israelites' struggle for survival in such an inhospitable place?

Torah commentators offer various answers.

In our own times, historian and Israeli statesman Abba Eban suggests that the liberated Israelites were locked in the Sinai for strategic reasons. They had intended to return to the land of their ancestors, but they were few in number and incapable of taking on the Philistine armies, which controlled the shorter, more direct, northern route to Canaan, or the Canaanite armies along the Negev border. Eban explains that it took forty years of wandering "from oasis to oasis" before they were strong enough to reconquer their land. (*My People: The Story of the Jews,* Random House, New York, 1984, pp. 15–16)

While he does not disagree with Eban's observation, Israeli historian Nachman Ran sees more in the desert experience than a forced period of wandering and building strategic strength. The desert experience, says Ran, was a time of nation building and religious development. "To a people whose entire living generation had seen only the level lands of Egypt, the Israelite march into this region of mountain magnificence, with its sharp and splintered peaks and profound valleys, must have been a perpetual source of astonishment and awe. No nobler school could have been conceived for training a nation of slaves into a nation of freemen or weaning a people from the grossness of idolatry to a sense of the grandeur and power of the God alike of Nature and Mind." (*The Holy Land,* p. V-27)

For Ran, the *midbar* is a "school" where the Israelites mature out of slavery and idolatry into a free, powerful people. Within its unique, barren, and dangerous environment they learn respect for the wonders of nature and the importance of each person to the community. No longer slaves, they must now bear the burden of their survival. Their desert journey teaches them mutual dependence and loyalty to one another and to the ethical and ritual commandments that are meant to uplift life with sacred meanings. In Egypt they were condemned to live by the will of others. In the *midbar* they become free human beings responsible to God and to themselves for every choice they make.

Other commentators believe that the experience of the Israelites in the desert toughened them for all the trials they would face in the future. They suffer hunger and thirst, are attacked by enemies seeking to destroy them, and are forced to endure discomfort and constant danger. Their suffering strengthens their will to survive. It gives birth to a conviction that, no matter how oppressed or beaten, they will ultimately emerge victorious over those who threaten their destruction.

This desert experience later becomes a model for Jewish behavior. During times of persecution Jews would look back upon their wanderings across the hostile Sinai desert. Recalling its trials and triumphs, they would draw inspiration and determination to overcome all forces set against them.

Rabbi Akiba stretches this lesson about the importance of Israelite suffering in the desert to include another dimension. Their trials and suffering, he says, "allowed them to merit receiving the priceless gift of Torah." Akiba's assertion is a bold one: The experience of pain and disappointment brings special rewards. (*Sanhedrin* 101a)

Writer Helen Keller, blind and deaf from childhood, may have been saying the same thing when she commented, "I thank God for my handicaps for, through them, I have found myself, my work, and my God." Her rewards grew out of her striving to surmount her disabilities.

Sometimes the reward of our own suffering is a greater appreciation of the pain of others and the determination to do something to relieve it. Bearing distress often enlarges our sympathy. It provides a new wisdom and perspective from which to disarm violence and injustice with the pursuit of compassion, truth, cooperation, and peace. One of Akiba's best friends, Simeon ben Azzai, might have had this in mind when he taught that "the reward for doing a mitzvah is the opportunity to do another mitzvah. (*Avot* 4:2)

On the other hand, Akiba may have had in mind the reward, or sense of satisfaction, that

comes from suffering for the sake of a righteous cause. Jews have often been persecuted for loyalty to their faith and people. Akiba himself was tortured and died a martyr's death at the hands of the Romans. Yet, even in the midst of his agony, he whispered to his students, "Now I understand the words, 'You shall love *Adonai* your God with all your heart, all your soul, and all your power.'" In the midst of his painful death, he reached the conclusion that his reward for suffering was the knowledge that he was giving his life for the sake of his people and faith.

Why in the wilderness?

Philosopher Philo explains that the Torah was given in the wilderness because cities are filled with corruption, luxury, idolatry, and other evils. He also argues that, for one to be pure and ready to receive the Torah, one must be separated from all the vices of the city. (On the Decalogue, I)

Torah was given in the desert to teach that we must consider ourselves open like the midbar *in order to learn Torah.* (Nedarim 55b)

Just as the desert contains nothing but layers of sand, so, too, the human body is composed of nothing but dust. But, just as the desert was transformed into a holy place by the appearance of the Divine Presence, so, too, with human beings. They become a source of greatness if they allow their spiritual spark to dominate their actions. (Rabbi Mordechai Katz, Lilmod Ul'lamade: From the Teachings of Our Sages, *Jewish Education Program Publications, New York, 1978, p. 129*)

Several early rabbinic commentators disagree with Akiba's claim that the Israelites were rewarded for their suffering in the desert with the gift of Torah. Instead they argue that God deliberately chose the desolate *midbar* as the most appropriate environment for giving the Torah. In supporting their contention, they cite a number of reasons.

The barren *midbar*, say the rabbis, belongs to no one. It is no-man's-land. For that reason God selects it as the best place for giving the Torah because the Torah is for all peoples. Like the desert, the Torah is open and free, accessible to everyone. It is neither a secret doctrine nor an exclusive one. Anyone at anytime is welcome to accept it and make it one's own. This, say the rabbis, explains why the Torah is given in no-man's-land. It is a gift to all human beings. (*Mechilta, Bachodesh* and *Yitro*)

Another teacher suggests that the Torah was given in the *midbar* and not in the Land of Israel to prevent arguments among the people of Israel. Had it been given in the territory of one tribe, that tribe might have said, "Look at us. We are superior to all other tribes since the Torah was given on our land." To prevent such claims and the jealousy and misunderstandings that might have resulted from them, God presents the Torah to the people of Israel in the *midbar,* which belongs to no one. In this way they are taught that no Jew is superior to another and that all Jews have responsibility for carrying out the commandments of the Torah. (*Numbers Rabbah, Chukat,* 19:26)

Other commentators believe that the Torah was given in the wilderness of Sinai to teach that, as the desert is open to all influences, those who wish to make the Torah their own must also be open to all its various teachings. In other words, the best students are not those who close their minds or have no patience for the views of others but rather those who make themselves like the desert. They are receptive to new ideas, willing to consider new perspectives. They take time to examine and experiment with novel views, unafraid to try innovative suggestions. "If people are not as free as the desert," one interpreter says, "then they are not worthy to receive the Torah." (*Pesikta de-Rav Kahana* 107a)

Modern interpreter Rabbi M. Miller of Gateshead, England, claims that "of all the places in the world, it was just in a place of drought and desolation, of barrenness and blackness, that God was welcomed with honor." Miller's view is that the desert was the appropriate place for the spiritual message of Torah because the desert is not corrupted by previous growth and development. It remains desolate, wild and pure, without need of alteration.

Miller's point is that "the Torah is given to those who make themselves as a wilderness, who purge themselves of impure influences and desires, of all aspirations and interests that are incompatible with the spirit of the Torah." Such influences, he explains, may include selfishness, the urge to covet what others possess, the corruption of friends or family, vicious habits, impatience, or cruelty to others. All of these influences block the attainment of "higher levels of moral and spiritual greatness." Preconceived ideas and prejudices blind us to new ideas and cripple us with dangerous habits. (*Shabbat Shiurim,* 5729, pp. 215–221)

Rabbi Miller's contention that the giving of the Torah in the desert contains a significant spiritual and ethical lesson is shared by Rabbi Morris Adler. However, Adler makes a different point. He argues that we live "in a desert age." The "voice of God does not sound clear and true in such a time." Confusion over right and wrong, faith, and reason prevails. In such a time it feels as if God were absent.

The reminder that the Torah was given in such a wilderness, says Adler, teaches that "there is no human condition . . . so dark that it can completely shut out God." Quite the opposite is the case. "God speaks, and sometimes . . . speaks most clearly in the wilderness." Often, explains Adler, people find themselves in difficult situations, overwhelmed by worries, stress, and pain. They are treated unjustly and feel themselves "succumbing to a sense of hopelessness." Precisely at such times it is helpful to remember that God gave the Torah in the desert, not in the lush land of milk and honey. "Whatever your particular desert, I say to you, 'Listen. Listen, for even there God speaks. . . .'" (*The Voice Still Speaks,* Bloch Publishing Company, New York, 1969, pp. 265–269)

Peli

Expanding Adler's insight, Pinchas H. Peli sees the desert as a metaphor, describing the psychological and spiritual realms of human existence.

There is a "wilderness" within each person, a "desert" where selfish desires rule, where one looks out only for one's own needs. No person is ever satisfied in the desert. There is constant complaining about lack of food and water, the scorching hot days and bitter cold nights. Anger, frustration, disagreements, and hunger prevail. The Torah is given in the desert, Peli argues, "to conquer and curb the demonic wilderness within human beings." The lesson here is that, "if human beings do not conquer the desert, it may eventually conquer them. There is no peaceful coexistence between the two. . . ." (*Jerusalem Post,* June 1, 1985, p. 17)

Why does so much of such importance in Jewish history happen in the desert? As we have seen, there are many answers to that question. One more suggests itself.

According to Jewish tradition, when you see the *midbar,* you are to say, "Be praised *Adonai* our God for the wondrous works of creation." The wilderness has always inspired awe and respect. Its quiet is mysterious and invites contemplation. One goes to the wilderness, as Moses did, to find new perspectives on life, to deepen spiritual awareness, and to gain clearer insights into moral concerns. Perhaps that is why the desert plays such a significant role in Jewish tradition. The *midbar* is the place where liberated Israelites receive the Torah, clarify their strategies for entering the Promised Land, and bond together as a people ready to face their uncertain future.

PEREK BET: *Why Count the Israelites?*

Bemidbar, or the Book of Numbers, opens with a date. We are told that, on the first day of the second month in the second year following the Exodus from Egypt, Moses was commanded to gather the Israelites together. A year has passed since they were liberated. They have wandered in the desert and stood together at Mount Sinai to receive the laws of God. Now, on the first day of the second month, a year after leaving Egypt, Moses is told to take a census of the people.

Interpreters who study the words of the instruction given to Moses call attention to their peculiarity. The words *seu et rosh* may be translated "take a census," but literally they mean "lift up," or "mark the head." As a result, their true meaning remains unclear.

Furthermore, commentators point out that this census at the beginning of Numbers differs from another census previously mentioned in Exodus 30:12–15. There we are given no precise date of the counting. Instead Moses is told to record the names of each person twenty years or older and to require payment of a half-shekel as an offering to God. By contrast, in the census of Numbers, no payment is mentioned or required.

Several questions arise: Why this numbering of the Israelites a year after the Exodus? What is the meaning of the words *seu et rosh?* Why does the Torah provide two versions of the census? What, if any, is the relationship between them?

For purposes of clarity, let's begin by answering the last question first. Early rabbinic commentators maintain that God commands Moses to number the people of Israel at least four times: once just after leaving Egypt (Exodus 12:37); another time after they build the golden calf; once again to protect them from the spread of a plague (Exodus 30:11); and a year after they depart from Egypt and are wandering in the desert (Numbers 1:1ff.)

Why are the people counted so many times?

The answer, say the rabbis, is to demonstrate God's love for the people of Israel. God, they explain, is like a king who possesses a fabulous treasure. He adores it. Each day he takes it in his hands and caresses it. He counts it to make sure that nothing is lost. So it is, say the rabbis, with the people of Israel. God loves to count them and, with each counting, declares, "I have created all the magnificent stars of the universe, yet it is Israel who will do My will." (*Numbers Rabbah* 2:19)

Rashi

Building upon this interpretation, Rashi explains that each census is a sign both of God's love for and reliance upon the people of Israel.

Just as we count those things or persons important to us and "count" upon them to care for us and, if necessary, defend us, so God counts upon every Jew to be a partner in the task of *tikkun olam*, or "improving and enhancing the world." Each census is a loving analysis of God's agents—or of God's "treasure." What we have here is a sign that God not only loves us but needs us. God is "counting" upon us to carry out our part of the covenant-partnership. (Commentary on Numbers 1:1)

Rashi's grandson, Rashbam, disagrees. He contends that the census has nothing to do with God's love for the Jewish people. Instead he argues that the counting of all those over the age of twenty years is a strategic matter. "They are preparing to enter the Land of Israel and require an army ready to go forth into battle." The census is taken to determine how many soldiers are eligible for the military challenge facing them. (Commentary on Numbers 1:1)

Ramban (Nachmanides)

Agreeing with Rashbam's view, Nachmanides explains that the census is an illustration of the Torah's warning against relying upon miracles. The people must fight to reclaim their land. It will not be handed to them by a miracle. The census is a means of organizing and enlisting them. It makes it clear that victory depends on each of them and on the coordination of their talents and efforts.

People are assets: rules for successful companies
Treat people as adults. Treat them as partners; treat them with dignity; treat them with respect. Treat them—not capital spending and

---

automation—as the primary source of productivity gains. These are the fundamental lessons from excellent companies. . . . In other words, if you want productivity and the financial reward that goes with it, you must treat your workers as your most important asset. (Thomas J. Peters and Robert H. Waterman, Jr., In Search of Excellence, *Harper and Row Publishers, Inc., New York, 1982, p. 238)*

Rabbi Jacob J. Weinstein enlarges Rashbam's interpretation. He points out that the census was "a model for large scale administrative competence." Moses asks for and records the name of each person. He organizes the census by tribe, separating the responsibilities of the Levites, who care for the services and security of the sanctuary. Each tribe, organized by family groups, is divided into four sections and assigned its own standard with a special identifying symbol.

What we have in the census is not simply a call-up for military service but the creative organizing of a community. The census is a practical necessity. It enables the Israelites to identify individual talents and abilities—the important assets of leadership required for victory. Through the process of counting the people, Moses is building an organizational structure and creating a design and purpose to Israelite society, even as it wanders in the Sinai desert. (*The Place of Understanding,* Bloch Publishing Company, New York, 1959, pp. 97–99)

Seu et rosh
Nachmanides notes that the words seu et rosh, *usually translated "take a census," literally translate as "lift up the head. . . ." These words are meant to teach us that "we are to honor those who are pious and generous and criticize those who are not." (Commentary on Numbers 1:1)*

Rabbi Pinchas teaches that there is a secret meaning in the words seu et rosh. *They are also the words used by an executioner who says, "Take off so and so's head." In the Torah these words teach that, if the people of Israel are*

> *worthy in good deeds, they will keep their heads and live; if not, they will loose their heads and die.* (Numbers Rabbah *1:11*)

In contrast with the practical organizing function of a census, Nachmanides suggests a psychological purpose. The people of Israel know their history. The patriarch Jacob has led them to Egypt with only seventy people. There they suffer oppression, sickness, plague, and death. To bolster their morale and build a sense of confidence in their strength, Moses calls for a census. Through it he demonstrates to them that, while they went to Egypt with only 600 people, they are now a force of 603,550 ready to defeat any army that threatens them.

Furthermore, Nachmanides explains, the census is conducted by Moses in a special manner. Instead of just numbering the people, those taking the poll are instructed by Moses "to do so in a manner that will give honor and importance to each person." Thus, says Nachmanides, Moses tells the poll takers, "Do not ask the head of each family for the number of people in the family. Rather, invite each person to pass before me. Take down that person's name, and let each one feel honored to be part of the census." By numbering each person, Moses encourages pride and feelings of self-worth. (Commentary on Numbers 1:45)

Leibowitz

Contemporary interpreter Nehama Leibowitz underscores the importance of Nachmanides' approach. She points out one of the great social dangers of our times: political, social, economic, and religious ideologies "that subject the individual to the mass and see the individual as a cog in the machine of the state, assuming that if one human being is destroyed there is always another one to take his place." Instead, Leibowitz continues, "Nachmanides emphasizes that the census was personal and individual . . . impressing on us the value and critical worth of each and every

soul, which is a unique creation of God and a world of its own." (*Studies in Bemidbar*, World Zionist Organization, Jerusalem, 1980, pp. 12–15)

Each is important
They are not just like animals or material objects, but each one has an importance of his own like a king or priest. Indeed, God shows special love toward them, and this is the significance of mentioning each one of them by name and status. They were all equal and individual in status. (Isaac ben Moses Arama, Akedat Yitzhak*)*

The census brings home the message to each and every one. Each sees that one does not stand alone but is a part of the totality of things. Yet, the entire world is dependent on each individual. . . . By being counted, we know our place in and our worth to the community at large. (Yehuda Nachshoni in Studies in the Weekly Parashah, *quoting the view of Shaloh from his* Shenei Luchot ha-Berit*)*

Hirsch

Rabbi Samson Raphael Hirsch argues that the census was more than a means of bolstering Israelite morale or of assuring each person's importance to the community. It is not enough, Hirsch points out, to have your name listed on a register or to take your place in a line behind a standard.

In Hirsch's view, the significance of the census is twofold.

First, as indicated in Exodus 30:12, a mandatory payment of a half-shekel is required from every person for the upkeep of the sanctuary. "Through this contribution," explains Hirsch, we learn that "a Jew is only 'counted' as belonging [to the people] by *doing something* for the sanctuary."

Payment of the half-shekel as a tax is the way

in which each Israelite demonstrates support for the community. The funds are pooled and used to finance schools and synagogues, to care for the aging, and to provide for the poor and homeless, the sick and needy. A Jew is "counted" upon by the community for support and is only a part of the census—of those who count—when *doing something* to benefit the entire community.

Second, Hirsch sees more than a lesson of community responsibility and generosity in the ancient Israelite census. He notes that the census is arranged as a valuable model of community organization. "The individuals first group themselves into families, the families into tribes, and finally the tribes into one common 'house of Israel.' "

Hirsch points out that, while each individual is unique, so, too, are the family and the tribe. All are linked "by a common inner factor, and each one of them must feel itself to be . . . a concrete and important part of this unity." In the census each person stands out with a name, family connections, and tribal affiliation, yet each feels a part of the whole community. "The greatest diversity of tribal and family specialties . . . and dispositions was diligently and carefully nurtured," explains Hirsch, yet "every tribe in its specialty and every family in its own peculiarity have to work at the common task of the house of Israel. . . ."

The census, therefore, is a model of community responsibility for the people of Israel and all humanity. Essentially, it underscores not only the importance of preserving and promoting individual rights and creativity but also strengthens the bonds of family, diverse religious, social, political, and economic associations as the means of ensuring a secure human future. Hirsch concludes that "every member of the family is counted by name, so that each one joins the whole, conscious of the importance of his personality to the nation." (Commentary on Numbers 1:1–2)

For Jewish interpreters the ancient census of the Israelites a year after the Exodus from Egypt was much more than an ordinary numbering of people. They elaborated upon its method and meanings, underscoring lessons about the role and responsibilities of each individual to family, nation, and all of humanity. Their creative views provide us with lasting insights to ponder.

QUESTIONS FOR STUDY AND DISCUSSION

1. Do problems, suffering, and hardships really help to "strengthen" a person or a people? What have they contributed to Jewish survival throughout the ages?

2. Poet T.S. Eliot, using the metaphor of the desert, once referred to contemporary society as a "wasteland." Would you agree? Why would Jewish tradition claim that the Torah was given in the desert, in a "wasteland"? What do we learn about coping with modern life from the ancient experience of the Israelites in the desert?

3. What are the lessons we can draw from the census of the Israelites? How can they be applied to our responsibilities to family, community, nation, and the whole human family?

PARASHAT NASO
Numbers 4:21–7:89

Parashat Naso concludes the census begun in the first chapters of Numbers with a counting of the Gershonites, Merarites, and Kohathites and a description of their work in the sanctuary. It also includes instructions for removing from the Israelite camp those suspected of disease or those who may have become impure by touching a dead body. Moses explains how to seek forgiveness for wrongdoing and what to do if a husband suspects his wife of adultery. The practices of the nazirite are repeated together with a description of the ritual for completing a nazirite vow. The portion concludes with the threefold priestly blessing for the people of Israel and with a description of the offerings brought by the twelve tribal chieftains to the sanctuary dedication ceremony.

OUR TARGUM

·1·

Moses takes a census of the Gershonite clans. Recording those between the ages of thirty and fifty, he notes a total of 2,630. They are responsible for carrying the sanctuary coverings, hangings, cords, accessories, and the altar. Ithamar, Aaron's son, is to supervise their work.

Moses also counts Merarite clan members between the ages of thirty and fifty. Their duties, like those of the Gershonites, have to do with moving the sanctuary. Under the direction of Ithamar, they are to carry the planks, bars, posts, sockets, pegs, and cords. The Merarites total 3,200.

Moses also records the number of Kohathites, whose work is connected with transporting parts of the sanctuary. Their total is 2,750, bringing the number of Levites caring for the sanctuary to 8,580.

·2·

The people are told that anyone who has an oozing open sore or who may have touched a corpse is to be removed from the Israelite camp.

·3·

Moses instructs the people that, if one person wrongs another, confession and restitution are required. If one steals property, its worth plus 20 percent is to be restored to the owner. If the owner has died, restitution is to be made to the sanctuary priest along with a ram offering of repentance. Such offerings belong to the priests.

·4·

Moses informs the people that, when a husband is jealous and suspects his wife of unfaithfulness, but there is no witness to prove his accusation, she is to be brought before the sanctuary priest. He will uncover her head and ask her to place her hands upon the altar of the meal offering. He is then to prepare a mixture of water, earth, and ashes from the meal offering. This mixture, known as the "water of bitterness," is meant to induce a trance.

The priest will then say to her: "If no man has had intercourse with you and you have not been unfaithful to your husband, be immune from this water of bitterness. If you have been unfaithful, then may God curse you with sagging thighs and belly."

After the priest writes the curse, the woman will drink the water of bitterness. If she falls into a trance, she is guilty; if she does not, she is innocent.

·5·

Moses reminds the people that those who vow to be nazirites are not to cut their hair or drink wine or any other intoxicants. Nor are they to have contact with a corpse. Contact with a corpse annuls the nazirite vow. The vow may, however, be resumed by shaving the head on the seventh day and by bringing offerings of turtledoves, pigeons, and a lamb to the sanctuary priest.

The nazirite term concludes with a sacrifice of a male lamb in its first year, a ewe lamb in its first year, a ram, a basket of unleavened cakes with oil mixed in, and unleavened wafers spread with oil, along with meal and libation offerings. The nazirite delivers these offerings, shaves his or her hair, and places the offerings upon the altar. The priest then places the shoulder of the ram and one unleavened cake and wafer into the hands of the nazirite. He waves them before the altar, accepting them as a donation. Upon conclusion of this ritual, a person is considered a former nazirite and may drink wine.

·6·

Moses gives Aaron and his sons the formula for blessing the people: May *Adonai* bless and guard you. May *Adonai* deal kindly and graciously with you. May *Adonai* bestow favor upon you and grant you peace.

·7·

On the day after the sanctuary is completed, Moses consecrates it and all its furnishings. During each of the subsequent twelve days, the tribal chieftains bring a special offering to the Levites for use in the sanctuary.

·8·

After the sanctuary dedication, whenever Moses wishes to speak with God, he enters and listens to the voice reaching him from above the ark cover between the two lionlike cherubim.

THEMES

Parashat Naso contains two important themes:

1. Eliminating suspicion and restoring trust.
2. Abstention as a way to holiness.

PEREK ALEF: *The Case of Suspected Adultery: Can We Move from Suspicion to Trust?*

The Book of Proverbs contains a number of valuable insights into human behavior. About "patience" and "jealousy" it teaches: "Patience results in much understanding; impatience results in foolishness. A calm disposition assures physical health, but jealousy rots the bones." (14:29–30) By drawing a parallel between impatience and jealousy, Jewish tradition provides a context in which to understand the case of a *sotah*, a wife suspected by her husband of adultery.

What does the Torah tell us?

Two situations are described. The first is the case of a wife who has had sexual relations with another man and keeps the matter a secret from her husband. The husband suspects her, but he has no witness. His jealousy grows against her. What shall he do? The second situation is of the wife who has not had sexual relations with another man. Her husband, however, suspects her. Though he has no witness, he is wild with jealousy. How is she to be protected from the "foolishness" of her husband?

Within ancient society, such cases were handled through "tests" or "ordeals." For example, the Babylonian *Code of Hammurabi* (about 1750 B.C.E.) states that a wife suspected by her husband of infidelity is to prove her innocence by throwing herself into a river. If she survives, she is innocent; if she drowns, she was guilty. Other cultures also record harsh measures for suspected wives. They could be thrown out of the house by their husbands, divorced, publicly humiliated, beaten, or killed. Some societies used trials by fire or, as in the Torah, the drinking of a ritual mixture prepared by priests.

Clearly, women suffered at the hands of jealous husbands, and their treatment was often cruel. There was, however, no similar "trial" for husbands who might be suspected, justly or unjustly, by their wives of infidelity. Such "equal" justice did not exist in ancient times. However, the Torah does offer a significant advancement in the protection of women. So do its interpreters.

In *Sotah,* an entire section of the Talmud dealing with the subject of a "suspected adulteress," rabbinic authorities carefully prescribe a process that a jealous husband must follow. If he suspects his wife of having an affair with a specific man, the husband must warn her in the presence of two witnesses about meeting secretly with him. Then, only if he has two witnesses who testify that she secretly spent time enough to have sexual relations with the man, can her husband request that she be forced by the court to drink the "water of bitterness." The case may not be heard by a local court, but it must be taken to the Supreme Court, or Sanhedrin, in Jerusalem. Only the Supreme Court has the power to order a wife to drink the "water of bitterness." However, if the man has been unfaithful to the woman, either before or after their marriage, or if she is disabled, he has no right to bring such charges against her. (*Mishnah Sotah* 1:1–4)

So many conditions (e.g., the warning about a specific man; the presence of two witnesses to testify to the time spent secretly with that specific man; the husband's record of fidelity; the necessity to hear the case before the Supreme Court in Jerusalem) were spelled out that women were protected from the fury of jealous husbands who might treat them unjustly. Even a woman under suspicion could not legally be thrown out of her home, divorced, or physically harmed. Rabbinic law assured her right to a fair inquiry and trial.

Protecting women
In ancient times, the life of a wife suspected of being unfaithful could be terminated abruptly without investigation. Judaism, however, re-quired that a very thorough investigation be made before any action could be taken. This requirement was intended to safeguard the woman's good name and to protect her from merciless prosecution. (Sefer ha-Hinuch, Mitzvot 365–367)

By the time the Temple is destroyed and the Supreme Court, or Sanhedrin, ceases to function in 70 C.E., the use of the ordeal of the "water of bitterness" for the *sotah* is no longer practiced. For many commentators, however, other questions about the treatment of the suspected adulteress remain. Why would a wife, or for that matter a husband, become unfaithful? How should jealousy, envy, anger, and abuse be handled by courts of law? What is so unique about the relationship of husband and wife that the matter of suspected adultery requires not only an elaborate ceremony of proof but also attention from a Supreme Court in Jerusalem?

In exploring these questions, the rabbinic commentators speculate on what might cause a wife to seek a sexual relationship with a man other than her husband. Quoting the wisdom of Proverbs: "A person who commits adultery is devoid of sense; only a self-destructive person does such a thing," the rabbis draw a parallel between "insanity" and "infidelity." In another discussion they boldly declare that "every moral lapse is also a mental one." In other words, no person sins without losing a grasp on reality. Harmful decisions are made by those who fail to understand the consequences of their actions.

Specifically, the rabbis suggest that there is no difference between a man using a woman as a prostitute or a woman having an extramarital affair. Both, say the rabbis, "have lost their reason." They are choosing a course of action without rationally calculating the dreadful consequences for themselves and their loved ones. Neither men nor women indulge in sexual relationships outside of marriage unless "a spirit of folly possesses them." (*Sotah* 3a; *Numbers Rabbah* 9:6)

By placing the behavior of a husband or wife who commits adultery or may be suspected of marital infidelity into the category of "folly" or "loss of reason," the rabbis seek to expose the *cause* of the trouble. For them the issue is not simply the adultery but the factors precipitating it. What could lead a person to seek love and sex outside of marriage? Could it be loneliness, constant arguments, serious differences of interest, abuse, insensitivity, or mental instability? Understanding causes introduces the possibility of curing the problems. It opens opportunities for seeking reconciliation between husband and wife.

Rabbi Meir and his wife, Beruriah, known as a woman of great wisdom, serve as a model of mutual respect and caring. Rabbi Meir makes several psychological observations about human behavior and marriage. Teaching students during the second century C.E., he observes that there are three kinds of personalities: the type of person who sees a fly fall into his cup, flicks it out, and drinks the contents of the cup (such a man may see his wife gossiping with neighbors and relatives, male and female, and, because he trusts her, leaves her alone); the type of person who sees a fly fluttering over his cup and immediately throws away the contents of the cup without tasting them (such impulsive behavior is evil; it is typical of a person who will suddenly decide, without cause, to divorce his wife); and the third type of person who finds a dead fly in his cup, takes it, sucks it, and then drinks the contents of the cup. Such a crude person, observes Rabbi Meir, will, without protest or warning, allow his wife to become intimate with her servants, go out into the marketplace dressed immodestly, and wash herself where men bathe. In his lack of caring or genuine commitment to her, he will callously use her and then find a reason to discard her.

On the treatment of wives

A husband should advise his wife to be modest; he should be flexible, not domineering; he should never resort to force or terror; he should not promote domestic strife by constantly arguing and criticizing; he should not speak out of jealousy but out of commitment and love; he should be easygoing, always honoring his wife above himself. In this way he will never drive her away or into immorality. (Based on Num-

bers Rabbah *9:2; also Y. Nachshoni, Studies in the Weekly Parashah, Bemidbar, Mesorah Publications Ltd., Jerusalem, 1989, pp. 945–948)*

Rabbi Meir's point is that temperament and neglect can drive a wedge between husband and wife. If a husband observes his wife entering into inappropriate relationships or a wife feels abandoned or compromised by her husband's relationships with other women, such misunderstandings require open and immediate discussion between husband and wife. Their feelings must be expressed. Unless they care enough about each other to articulate what bothers them and what they deem acceptable behavior, suspicions will eventually drive husband and wife to acts of immorality. Rabbi Meir uses the example of the *sotah* as an opportunity to explore and explain the challenges facing the fragile relationship of marriage. (*Numbers Rabbah* 9:12)

Peli

While modern commentator Pinchas Peli does not disagree with Rabbi Meir's psychological observations or with the causes of stress between husband and wife, he does offer a different view about the strange ceremony of the "water of bitterness." He speculates that "it is possible that Torah devised the best way under the circumstances to save this marriage by removing the mutual psychological distrust" between husband and wife. That is to say that "the *sotah* ceremony is an extreme remedial measure for a troubled marriage. . . . Jealousy, overpossessiveness, and similar emotions can be destructive and explosive in any husband-wife relationship. The *sotah* ritual brings to us one painful remedy." (*Jerusalem Post* May 28, 1988, p. 22)

Peli's point is that sometimes bitterness, suspicion, anger, and pain nearly destroy a marriage. In such situations one needs to drink the "water of bitterness" to restore trust, mutual respect, and understanding. Radical "medicine" is the only cure. In ancient times that meant the wife's submission to the ritual for a suspected adulteress. In our own time it can mean that both husband and wife seek counseling and learn how to drain the bitterness of misunderstanding from their relationship, restoring their love and trust for each other.

The issues raised in the case of the *sotah* in ancient times are significant today, not only for husbands and wives, but for all relationships based on mutual commitment. Friendships, business partnerships, and family ties are also ruined by suspicion, selfishness, and misunderstanding. How do we repair and strengthen such relationships? Ironically, those who neglect faltering relationships may find themselves drinking a home-cooked brew of the "water of bitterness."

PEREK BET: *The Case of the Nazirite: Can Abstention Guarantee Holiness?*

The Torah assigns several different categories of responsibility for the people of Israel: chieftains of tribes, priests, carriers of the ancient *mishkan,* or "sanctuary." All these jobs are designated by God and passed on from generation to generation. By contrast, the Torah informs us that any person, male or female, can freely choose to become a nazirite.

Becoming a nazirite entails a commitment of service for a minimum of thirty days. One is prohibited from cutting one's hair, drinking or eating grapes, raisins, vinegar, grape husks, or grape kernels. Like a priest, a nazirite is forbidden contact with a dead body. According to the Torah, "throughout one's term as a nazirite one is consecrated to God." (Numbers 6:8)

Commentators disagree on the role and institution of the nazirite in Jewish tradition. Nine chapters and sixty sections of the *Mishnah* and one hundred and thirty pages of *Gemara* in the Talmud present varying and often contradictory views on the subject. Even now, interpreters of Torah both praise and condemn the *Torat Nazir,*

or the "Nazirite's Code of Behavior," while few Jews actually practice it.

 Rashi

On the basis of *Targum Yonatan,* Rashi explains that the word *nazir,* or "nazirite," comes from the root meaning "to separate oneself" and refers to those students of Torah who "keep themselves separate from the ways of the common people." Extending Rashi's view, David Kimchi praises the nazirites for providing "a way for young people to distance themselves from worldly pleasures and passions." Others approve of the practice, especially of abstaining from wine, because it allows one "to serve God with a clear mind." (See Rashi, Kimchi, and *Tze'enah u-Re'enah* on Numbers 6:1ff.)

In his eleventh-century book of philosophy and ethics, *Hovot ha-Levavot,* "Duties of the Heart," Bachya ben Joseph ibn Pakuda praises nazirite practice and discipline. He argues that God places human beings on earth to test their souls and to make them as pure as angels. They battle for such purity against all physical needs, temptations, and desires. Often worldly pleasures appear harmless, but frequently they lead to excesses that overwhelm our powers of reason and seduce us into habits of self-destruction.

Nazirites, explains Bachya, are "physicians for the souls of human beings." Serving as models of abstention, they teach moderation. "All people," Bachya continues, "should work only enough to support themselves and to avoid being a burden on others; they should limit their conversation and restrain their envious eyes and ears. They should control hunger, should be satisfied with a single meal each day, viewing it as necessary medicine, and should fast one day during each week." The commitment of the nazirite leads people to appreciate this modest way of life.

Bachya's championing of the nazirite and the life of abstention is supported by commentator Moshe Chaim Luzzatto in his popular seventeenth-century textbook, *Mesillat Yesharim,* "Pathway of the Righteous." "True abstinence," explains Luzzatto, "means making use of only those things that some natural demand has rendered indispensable." For example, we need to nurture our body with a minimum of liquid each day. One should drink only the minimum required. Such control is not for the average person, however, but rather it is the gift of a disciplined spiritual minority capable of seeking holiness before God.

Luzzatto describes the ideal behavior of such a minority. This minority holds itself aloof from society, does not look beyond its own needs, ignores and disdains all pleasures of life. Seeking solitude and saintliness, it chooses to do more than the laws of Torah require. Luzzatto concludes that the nazirites are revered teachers and sources of inspiration because of their exemplary behavior.

Other commentators disagree, finding the nazirites' life of abstention nothing less than "sinful." Rabbi Eleazar Ha-Kappar, who lived during the second century and was a good friend of Rabbi Judah who composed the *Mishnah,* held that, by abstaining from wine and denying themselves the enjoyments of life, nazirites neglected the commandments of Torah and were "sinners." This, Rabbi Eleazar points out, explains why, at the conclusion of their nazirite vow, they must bring a sin offering to the sanctuary. Having deliberately abstained from the potential joys that God prepares for all human beings, they must seek forgiveness. This, remarks Rabbi Eleazar, is why God demands such an offering. (*Ta'anit* 11a)

Demonstrating strong disapproval of nazirite vows, which are meant to deny the pleasures of life, rabbinic authorities living in the Land of Israel during the second and third centuries argue that such vows are self-destructive. They are compared to "taking a sword into your own hand and thrusting it into your heart." Rabbi Yitzhak teaches that, if you are present at the time another person is considering such a vow, you must shock him to his senses by asking: "Are not all the restrictions and laws of Torah enough for you? Why do you insist on restraining yourself from that which the Torah permits you to enjoy?" Others claim that, when each human being

comes before God on the Day of Judgment, God will ask, "Why did you deny yourself pleasure from all that your eyes beheld?" (Jerusalem Talmud, *Nedarim* 9:1; 30:3)

> **Judaism on asceticism**
> *Not a single one of the 613 positive and negative commandments of the Torah defining the orthodox [traditional] norm of Jewish life as developed by the rabbis enjoins any form of asceticism or mortification. . . . There is but one public fast day—the Day of Atonement— a solemn day of searching one's soul. . . . It is to be noted that the nazirites were not pledged to celibacy. The renunciation of a normal sex life was never regarded as a virtue in Judaism.* (Abba Hillel Silver, Where Judaism Differed, Macmillan, New York, 1956, pp. 195, 198– 199)

Rambam (Maimonides)

Philosopher and commentator Moses Maimonides also opposes the choice of abstinence and self-denial. "The Torah," he writes, "advocates no mortification of the body. Its intention was that a person should follow nature, taking the middle road. One should eat in moderation and live uprightly and faithfully within the society of others not in the deserts and mountains. One should not afflict the body by wearing wool and hair. Because the Torah forbids such abstention from the joys of life," concludes Maimonides, "it warns us with the example of the nazirite."

In his classic discussion of Jewish law, the *Mishneh Torah,* Maimonides, on the subject of the nazirite, warns against the self-righteous tendency of concluding that all forms of bodily pleasure lead to sin and, therefore, should be avoided. He counsels that if people foolishly decide, because passion, envy, and pride are evil, to separate themselves from others and abstain from eating meat, drinking wine, marrying, living in comfortable homes, or wearing fine clothing, they should be told that they are choosing "an evil path." Our tradition, argues Maimonides, "forbids us from denying to ourselves any of the joys permitted by Torah." (*Shemonah Perakim and Mishneh Torah, Deot* 3:1)

The chasidic teachers frowned upon the nazirite practice of self-denial or abstinence. Human beings, they taught, were born to enjoy life, to breath in the sweet fragrances of flowers, taste crisp, delicious delicacies, wonder at the magic of majestic mountains and green forests, and fulfill the powerful surge of sexual desires in the mysterious realm of love. For the Chasidim, enjoying life was a way of praising God. Rabbi Pinchas Shapiro of Koretz holds that "joy atones for sins because it is the gift of God." Rabbi Moshe Leib of Sassov comments that "joy is better than tears . . . for it breaks through all the gates of heaven."

Rabbi Baruch of Medzibozh, grandson of the Ba'al Shem Tov, the founder of Chasidism, captures Jewish tradition's enthusiasm for all the delights of life and its disdain for withdrawal or self-denial when he comments that "one should take into one's heart three things: the love of God, the love of Israel, and the love of Torah. One does not need to engage in ascetic practices. It is sufficient for the average person to understand that in all things, physical and material, there is holiness." (*Sefer ha-Hasidut,* p. 60a)

Modern commentator Simeon Federbush is critical of the nazirites, not simply for their rejection of "worldly privileges and possessions," but also for their "antisocial attitude toward the community." Federbush condemns the practice of nazirites because it "separates one from the benefits of life" and removes one from "striving for the perfection of the human race." He argues that "any chain is only as strong as its weakest link. If one denies oneself to provide for one's own wants, who will take care of the needs of others? . . . Those who are occupied with ascetic indulgence will have no concern for the needs of their neighbors." (*Ethics and Law in Israel,* p. 166, quoted in B.S. Jacobson, *Meditations on the Torah,* Sinai Publishing, Tel Aviv, 1956, p. 213)

Learning to limit one's appetites
*Sforno points out that the self-denial of the nazirite is limited. "One is told to refrain from drinking wine only; one is not allowed to cause pain and suffering to oneself by other restrictions or self-affliction. The Torah aims at decreasing desires, not eliminating them entirely." In learning to limit one's appetites, one becomes "holy to God." (*Y. Nachshoni,* Studies in the Weekly Parashah, Bemidbar, p. 956)*

Aharon Halevi, the author of *Sefer ha-Hinuch,* approaches the case of the nazirite from a positive but guarded perspective. Human beings, he explains, are born with great spiritual and intellectual potentials that are placed within frail bodies full of passions and drives. The challenge of each person is to control the demands and temptations of the body and to rise toward holiness. By abstaining from wine and not cutting their hair, nazirites overcome vanity and begin a climb toward holiness. They work at ruling their inclination for self-indulgence and seek to place themselves in a position where they can pay scrupulous attention to what the Torah and God demand. However, says Halevi, nazirites must be warned against going too far and dangerously tipping the delicate balance toward the soul at the expense of the body. Like Maimonides, Halevi emphasizes moderation, yet he praises nazirites for their choice to seek the will of God. (*Mitzvot* 368–377)

Ibn Ezra

Ibn Ezra seizes the notion of "overcoming vanity" through abstinence and claims that nazirites symbolize by their self-denial the important virtues of self-control and discipline. He points out that the word *nazir* is actually associated with the Hebrew word for "crown" and stands for those who, like powerful monarchs, rule their dangerous passions and destructive temptations by constantly curbing them. While ibn Ezra may not have understood the power of addiction to smoking, drinking, and drugs, it is clear that he sees in the vow and discipline of the nazirite a means of achieving "control" over such deadly influences.

Sixteenth-century interpreter and philosopher Moses Isserles takes ibn Ezra's explanation to a logical conclusion. Also citing Maimonides' ideal of "the middle road," or moderation in all human choices, Isserles points out that nazirites are to be praised for realizing that they "have a weakness for worldly pleasures" and difficulty "diverting their evil inclinations from extremes to the middle way." By taking on the nazirite vow, such people push themselves to excessive self-denial and then "find the way back to the ideal of moderation." In other words, nazirites realize their impulse for indulgence and choose to overcome it by training themselves in self-denial. Eventually they master their inclinations and achieve the satisfaction that comes from living a life of moderation.

Jewish tradition remains deeply divided over whether to praise or condemn the nazirites' abstention from wine and the cutting of hair and their refusal to touch a dead body. On the face of it, the nazirite vow and practice seem remote from any modern application. Yet debating whether to praise or criticize the nazirite tradition may miss the essential meaning of the nazirite commitment and behavior.

Perhaps, for moderns, the real lesson to be drawn from the example of the nazirite deals with the challenge of introducing the discipline of "yes, I will" or "no, I will not" into our lifestyles. Temptations of alcohol, drugs, smoking, overworking, and overeating are everywhere. Reviewing the Torah's description of the nazirite vows and practice may offer a powerful symbolic message. For example, the decision to abstain from wine may signal the dangers of addiction and the necessity of cultivating a clear mind. The command against cutting hair may teach that egocentric concern for how one looks and for fashion and exterior style do not replace inner substance and quality of character. The nazirite's prohibition against touching a dead body may imply not a rejection of the inevitability of death but an acceptance that the most holy or pure occupation is to work for every cause that preserves and promotes life.

Unraveling the meaning of the nazirite's vow raises serious questions, not only on abstinence and the enjoyment of life's gifts, but also on fundamental considerations for controlling our needs and shaping our desires to benefit ourselves and our community and to serve God.

QUESTIONS FOR STUDY AND DISCUSSION

1. How does Jewish tradition "protect" wives from the jealous abuse of husbands? What other safeguards can you add? What about the rights of husbands?

2. Is it responsible to "excuse" immoral behavior by citing "mental instability" as its cause? How can individuals and the justice system function "fairly" if the system takes into consideration "mental" causes for antisocial behavior?

3. Does the nazirite, who abstains from wine, the cutting of hair, and the touching of a corpse, achieve a greater sense of holiness? What does Jewish tradition teach about achieving a "spiritual" nearness to God? What divides Jewish commentators on this issue? What standards of behavior can one choose today to achieve Maimonides' ethical life of the "middle of the road," or moderation?

4. Rabbi Judah taught that, "in the spring when we see the beautiful trees swaying in the breeze, we should stop to recite a prayer. We

should say, 'Be praised, O God, for creating a world where nothing is lacking, a world filled with beauty to delight the human heart.' " (*Eruvin* 43b) Do you agree that a positive acknowledgment of the gifts of life is superior to abstinence and self-denial as a means of encouraging people to appreciate human existence and avoid self-destructive habits?

PARASHAT BEHA'ALOTECHA
Numbers 8:1–12:16

Parashat Beha'alotecha contains instructions for installing the *menorah* in the sanctuary and for consecrating the priests and Levites. It also describes the procedure to be followed by any Israelite who misses bringing the Pesach sacrifice, and it includes a description of the Israelites' journey through the desert. When the people complain about their diet of manna, Moses asks God, "Why have You laid the burden of all this people upon me?" He is counseled to appoint seventy experienced elders and officers to share leadership and the spirit of prophecy with him. Among the appointed are Eldad and Medad, who are filled with enthusiasm. Despite Joshua's complaint about them, Moses defends their right to act as prophets. Miriam and Aaron criticize Moses for his marriage to a Cushite woman. Miriam is punished with leprosy. Both Aaron and Moses plead on her behalf. After being excluded from the camp for seven days, she is cured.

OUR TARGUM

·1·

The commandment to install the seven-branched *menorah,* or "candelabrum," is repeated here. (See Exodus 25:37; 27:21.)

·2·

Moses calls the Levites to the sanctuary and consecrates them to help the priests with the sacrifices. They are selected from the Israelite community and take the place of the firstborn who would otherwise be designated for the sanctuary work. The career of the Levites extends from the age of twenty-five to fifty, when they retire.

·3·

Moses tells the people what to do if they are defiled by touching a corpse, or if they are on a long journey at the time specified for the Pesach festival (the fourteenth day of Nisan at twilight). Since, in both situations, they are unable to offer the Pesach sacrifice, provision is made for them to bring the sacrifice to the sanctuary a month later. At that time they are to eat it with unleavened bread and bitter herbs, observing the event as if it were Pesach. Furthermore, Moses informs the people that strangers residing among the Israelites shall observe all the rituals and laws of Pesach without discrimination.

·4·

A cloud covers the sanctuary during the day, and a cloud of fire covers it at night. When the cloud lifts, the Israelites break camp and journey onward through the desert. God instructs Moses to create silver trumpets to be blown by Aaron's sons, the priests, on four occasions: (1) to signal the beginning of a journey; (2) to gather the people; (3) to call them to battle; and (4) to announce the celebration of a sacrifice, a festival, or a joyous occasion.

·5·

On the twentieth day of the second month in the second year after the Exodus from Egypt, Moses and the people begin their journey through the desert toward the Land of Israel. The tribes carry their individual banners as they march in order. Moses invites Hobab, son of his father-in-law, Jethro, to join the journey, but Hobab declines. With the ark in front of them, the people set out, and Moses declares: "Advance, O

Adonai!/May Your enemies be scattered,/And may Your foes flee before You!"

·6·

Traveling through the desert, the people complain to Moses about the lack of meat, and they complain about their mundane diet of manna. God warns them to stop their ungrateful griping, but they persist in protesting. Overwhelmed by their criticism, Moses asks God: "Why have You dealt ill with Your servant? Why have I not enjoyed Your favor? Why have You laid the burden of all this people upon me? Did I conceive all this people? Did I bear them, that You should say to me, 'Carry them in your bosom as a nurse carries an infant,' to the land that You have promised on oath to their fathers? . . . I cannot carry all this people by myself, for it is too much for me. . . ."

God instructs Moses, as Jethro had counseled him earlier (see Exodus 18:13–27), to appoint elders and officers with whom to share leadership. God provides food enough for the people and places the spirit of prophecy upon the seventy appointed leaders. Two of these, Eldad and Medad, continue to speak in the spirit of prophecy, seeming to challenge the authority of Moses and Aaron. Joshua, Moses' trusted attendant, reports the matter to Moses, who refuses to restrain them. He tells Joshua, "Would that all *Adonai*'s people were prophets!"

·7·

Later Miriam and Aaron speak out publicly against Moses because of his marriage to a Cushite woman. They question their brother's integrity, saying, "Has God spoken only through Moses? Has not God spoken through us as well?"

God summons Miriam and Aaron and explains that, while *Adonai* speaks to other prophets through visions, *Adonai* speaks to Moses plainly, directly, and without riddles. For criticizing her brother, Miriam is punished with leprosy. When Moses and Aaron intervene on her behalf, God orders her excluded from the camp for seven days.

THEMES

Parashat Be-ha'alotecha contains two important themes:

1. Understanding and responding to complaints.
2. Understanding the motives of others before criticizing them.

PEREK ALEF: *Responding to Murmuring and Complaints*

Just after the people of Israel are liberated from Egyptian slavery, they approach Moses with complaints about conditions in the wilderness. (See Harvey J. Fields, *A Torah Commentary for Our Times*, Volume II, *Parashat Beshalach*, "*Perek Bet*," UAHC Press, New York, 1991, pp. 36–39.) Moses responds by requesting God to provide them with water and food. They are given manna each day with a double portion on Fridays so that they will not have to work at collecting it on the Sabbath. Fresh water is also supplied in abundance.

Now, two years later, after receiving the commandments at Mount Sinai and building their sanctuary, the Israelites once again raise their voices with bitter complaints. They protest about their living conditions in the desert. As a result of their behavior, God punishes them with fire throughout the camp. Seeing this, Moses intervenes, and the fire ceases.

The complaints, however, are just beginning. Joining with the non-Israelites who have accompanied them out of Egypt, the people wax nostalgic, deceiving themselves about the conditions under which they had lived in Egypt. "If only we had meat to eat! We remember the free fish we used to eat in Egypt, the cucumbers, the melons, the leeks, the onions, and the garlic. Now our stomachs are shriveled. There is nothing at all! Nothing but this manna to look to." (Numbers 11:4–6)

Interpreters of Torah ask two questions about the grievances and grumblings of the people: What caused them? What might have been an appropriate response by Moses?

Rashi

Rashi offers an excuse for the people. He suggests that they are exhausted from their first three-day journey. Upset, even angry, that Moses is pushing them along and not allowing them time to rest, they raise their voices in protest. Cranky and tired, they whine like children, recalling easier times when all their needs for food and comfort had been provided by others. (Commentary on Numbers 11:1)

Ramban (Nachmanides)

Nachmanides agrees with Rashi. He explains that the people have justifiable reasons for their complaints. Moses has taken them from the familiar surroundings of Mount Sinai, where they had camped for two years, to a desolate wilderness, where they are uncertain about the future. Frightening questions confront them: Are they safe from enemies? Will there be sufficient food and water? Who will provide it? Their anxiety is painful. It confuses them. All their murmurings, says Nachmanides, grow out of their mental anguish and self-pity. "They react like others under duress and compulsion." (Commentary on Numbers 11:1)

Nachmanides, however, does not offer his explanation as an excuse or justification for the people's reaction. Instead, he sees self-centered demands as a lack of faith. He condemns the Israelites for their refusal to trust in God. Rather than giving thanks for all they enjoy, they are ungrateful, even disloyal. Instead of trusting that they are in safe hands with Moses and God, they

gripe about food and offer false and exaggerated comparisons between their lives as slaves in Egypt and their existence as a free people. Fixed on nostalgic and erroneous perceptions of the past, they become mired in bitter criticisms, making them incapable of sharing a vision and strategy for their future. (Commentary on Numbers 11:4–6)

Hirsch

Rabbi Samson Raphael Hirsch offers a different viewpoint. The Israelites, he argues, suffer not from nostalgia but from boredom. All their needs are met. They enjoy a near perfect situation in the wilderness. Each day they are given manna and plenty of fresh water. Nothing is lacking. Nonetheless, comments Hirsch, they "feel themselves buried alive."

"The people," he continues, "were as if in mourning over themselves. They look on themselves as already dead." With all their needs met, their Torah given, their sanctuary complete, their lives "offer them no compensation, remain worthless and without meaning in their eyes." Frustrated at having no new goal, challenge, or mission, they begin murmuring against Moses and God.

Hirsch imagines them saying to Moses, "It is not nourishment that we lack . . . what we lack are the tasty, stimulating foods that excite the appetite. We miss the change of diet so necessary for health. The complete monotony, the unvarying sameness of our food makes it unbearable." The Israelites, Hirsch maintains, are desperately seeking a way out of boredom. They want excitement, stimulation, and variation of foods and experiences. Their complaints to Moses evolve from their need for new challenges, visions, and opportunities. (Commentary on Numbers 11:1–11)

They were confused . . .
The children of Israel witnessed the revelation at Sinai and had certainly become uplifted by

that event, but the inspiration soon wore off. After a while, instead of remaining transformed by that experience into a holy people, capable of becoming a light unto the nations, their memories are of Nile smorgasbords, big kiddushim, *and fancy bar mitzvahs with open bars and Viennese tables. At Sinai the vision was sharp and vivid, but the desert muted these visions and replaced them with an obsession for the materialistic. The Jews felt bereft and empty, and so they complained, not even certain themselves of what they really wanted. (Rabbi Shlomo Riskin,* Jerusalem Post, *May 27, 1990)*

Peli

Pinchas Peli echoes Hirsch's viewpoint but turns it critically upon the Israelites. "Bored with the affluent life, they are seeking ever new thrills and new cravings to titillate and stimulate them. Too demoralized to look towards the future, they turn to the past. . . . Their memory is very selective indeed. They do not remember the torture and humiliation of slavery. They do not remember the joys and excitement of liberation. All they remember is the fish they ate in Egypt."

Peli's point is clear. Like Hirsch he believes that the complaints of the Israelites rise out of their dissatisfaction with the near perfect status quo of the community. What remains unclear is whether Peli and Hirsch mean to suggest that human beings simply cannot tolerate perfection. (See *Jerusalem Post,* June 15, 1985.)

Why did they complain?
The cry of the rebels was for meat and variety, not for food as such, for there was no hunger among the people. . . . Satiety, boredom, lack of challenge, and the inconveniences of nomad existence were seeds of discontent as potent as want and poverty. (W. Gunther Plaut, The Torah: A Modern Commentary, *UAHC Press, New York, 1981, p. 1095)*

Bad will be the day . . .
Bad will be the day for human beings when they become absolutely content with the life that they are living, with the thoughts that they are thinking, with the deeds that they are doing; when there is not forever beating at the doors of their souls some great desire to do something larger, which they know they were meant and made to do because they are still, in spite of all, the children of God. (Philip Brooks)

In contrast to those who explain the grievances of the Israelites as expressions of their anxiety or boredom, Samuel, who was the head of the academy of learning in Nahardea, Babylonia, during the third century, hints at another reason. He calls attention to the words used by the Israelites in their complaint. What did they mean, he asks, when they cried out, "We remember the free fish we ate in Egypt"?

In response, Samuel speculates that by "free fish" the Torah is hinting at forbidden sexual relations. In other words, the real complaint of the Israelites derives neither from their recollection of delicious foods nor from their boredom with manna. What they resent, according to Samuel, is the Torah's curtailment of various behavioral norms (e.g., the Torah forbids sexual relations out of wedlock, especially with members of the family, including sexual intercourse with parents, siblings, aunts or uncles, grandparents, stepparents, or in-laws). This kind of regulation that would radically change their behavior, explains Samuel, is the reason the people stood at the door of their tents murmuring against Moses and God.

Samuel's students amplify his observation, maintaining that the people resent the manna because it identifies those who have indulged in forbidden sex! How so? The manna, they claim, fell before the tents according to the needs of each family. If a man commits adultery and a child is born, then an extra portion of manna falls in front of *his* tent. At that point everyone knows that he has fathered a child out of wedlock. For this reason, the people rise against Moses. The law and manna change their way of life, forcing upon them a new moral code. They bitterly resent being held accountable for their ethical actions. (*Yoma* 75a)

Rabbi Meir Simcha Ha-Cohen (1845–1926), author of the commentary *Meshekh Hochmah*, suggests that not only the moral laws of Torah cause the early Israelites to rebel. They also object to other restrictions, especially those that regulate what they may or may not eat. The laws of *kashrut* forbid the eating of pork and certain other meat products and define how animals are to be slaughtered. Ha-Cohen claims that the Israelites protest because they want to eat meat without restrictions as they did in Egypt. "Stop making matters difficult for us," they gripe to Moses. "Let us eat whatever we desire."

Rabbi Reuven P. Bulka agrees with Ha-Cohen's observation, pointing out that "one of the essential ingredients of the Torah's life-style is that it proposes self-control for fulfillment's sake. Judaism is a disciplined life-style in which the discipline itself is seen as the necessary ingredient for bringing fulfillment." Applying this view to our Torah portion, Bulka writes, "It is, perhaps, this element of control that was brought forth in the disciplined supply of food afforded by the manna. Rebellion against this became rebellion against the entire Jewish life-style. The rebels rejected control. Instead, they demanded a life of instant gratification." (*Torah Therapy: Reflections on the Weekly Sedra and Special Occasions,* Ktav, New York, 1983, pp. 83–84)

Rabbi Jacob Weinstein views the matter differently. He rejects finding fault with the complaining Israelites. Instead, he argues for compassion and an appreciation of their difficult situation. The people are desperate, fearful, and uncertain about their future. What we have here, says Weinstein, is an indication of "how present difficulties cast a retroactive glow of delight over the past and suffuse old woes and mute old indignities." To put it another way, our perspective of the past is influenced by our experience in the present. The Israelites did what many people in similar circumstances do. They idealized the past because they were so frightened about the uncertainties of the future. (*The Place of Understanding,* p. 103)

Rabbi Morris Adler strongly disagrees with Weinstein. He refuses to excuse the Israelites for their complaints. Instead, he believes that what we have in this Torah report is an example of how "memory can be a dangerous thing." Human beings distort and change history to suit their prejudices. The Israelites "did not remember the lashes . . . the brutal hand of the oppressor. . . . They remembered the food they used to eat, the security they used to have . . . their memories became an accusation against Moses . . . a source of their resentment, and they brought tragedy upon themselves. They became the generation of the wilderness, destined to wander forty years, but never to arrive, never to inherit because they lacked the spirit." (*The Voice Still Speaks,* p. 297)

Interpreters through the ages provide a number of explanations for the constant complaining of the Israelites. In doing so they expose some significant reasons for political and social protest in every age. The Torah text, however, also deals with the reaction of Moses to the protesting people. Hearing their complaints, Moses voices a few of his own. Feeling lonely, isolated, and besieged, he asks God: "Why have You dealt ill with Your servant, and why have I not enjoyed Your favor, that You have laid the burden of all this people upon me?" According to the Torah, God responds by telling him to appoint seventy elders and officers, people of experience, to share the burden of leadership with him.

Once before, Moses' father-in-law, Jethro, gave him similar advice. (See *A Torah Commentary for Our Times,* Volume II, *Parashat Yitro,* pp. 42–47.) Moses followed it and was helped in caring for the people. Now, perhaps, as rabbinic tradition suggests, those leaders are dead, having been put to death because of their involvement in the building of the golden calf. So Moses again bears the burden of leadership alone and discovers that it is too much for him. The complaints of the people make this clear. To lead them, he requires the wise counsel and assistance of those who can help him ease their anxieties and nurture their creative energies for the benefit of their community.

The Torah is suggesting a model for leadership. The most productive way to handle complaints is not to whine before God nor to grumble that "the task is too much for me." Such negativity leads to certain defeat. Instead, Moses is told to face his troubles with others, to shape the future by gathering around him those with whom he can share the burdens of leadership and a vision for the future.

Rabbi Judah identifies the moment of complaining as one of the ten trials of the Israelites in the desert. In each trial, the survival of the people is at stake, and a lesson is learned. In this case, the trial teaches the moral of "collaboration." Trials are best confronted and creatively solved when they are shared. (*Eruvin* 15b)

PEREK BET: *Why Do Miriam and Aaron Protest against Moses?*

After the appointment of the seventy leaders, the people journey from Kibroth-hatta'avah to Hazeroth in the Sinai desert. We are told that, while camping at Hazeroth, "Miriam and Aaron spoke against Moses because of the Cushite woman he had married." They said, "Has *Adonai* spoken only through Moses? Has God not spoken through us as well?" (Numbers 12:1–2)

What prompts Moses' sister and brother to protest against him? Why does it appear to be a public matter rather than a private, "in-the-family" discussion?

Some commentators express surprise at this story, claiming that there is no apparent explanation for Miriam's and Aaron's criticism of Moses. Others argue that the explanation is clearly offered in the text. Are we not told, they point out, that Moses' sister and brother condemn him for his marriage to a Cushite woman and for acting as if God speaks exclusively through him? Those maintaining that there is no apparent explanation for Miriam's and Aaron's criticism respond that, while the Torah text provides a hint of an explanation, it does not offer any evidence that Moses claimed to speak "exclusively" for God. Neither are we given an identity for the Cushite woman he married.

Given this justified difference of opinion, how do we make sense of this Torah story? Why do Miriam and Aaron speak against their brother? Why is Miriam more severely punished for doing so?

Seeking explanations for these complexities in this Torah story, the author of *Targum Onkelos* explains that Miriam and Aaron criticize Moses for having separated himself from his beautiful wife, Zipporah. Furthermore, since the Torah mentions Miriam before Aaron, this must mean that she took the lead and provoked Aaron against Moses. For that reason she deserves a more severe punishment.

Rashi agrees with this explanation but raises a question: Since there is no evidence in the text, how does Miriam know that Moses has separated from his wife, Zipporah?

Rashi answers his own question with a view expressed by Rabbi Nathan, a teacher who lived in Babylonia during the second century. Rabbi Nathan traces the roots of the confrontation involving Aaron, Miriam, and Moses to the story of Eldad and Medad. Miriam, he explains, happens to be standing next to Zipporah when she hears the report of the prophesying in the camp by Eldad and Medad. Because she is aware that Moses always separates himself from her when the word of God comes to him, Zipporah cries out, "Oh, their poor wives! Their husbands will abandon them just as Moses stays away from me."

Upon hearing Zipporah's remark, explains Rabbi Nathan, Miriam reports the matter to Aaron. Without investigating the truth of the accusation, Miriam and Aaron rush to judgment. They embarrass Moses, publicly confronting him with what they believe is the insensitive and unfair desertion of his wife.

Using Rabbi Nathan's creative addition to our Torah story, Rashi concludes that Miriam is punished for wrongfully accusing Moses of being insensitive to his wife and for speaking disrespectfully against her brother in public. (Commentary on Numbers 12:1)

Objecting strongly to these creative inventions and additions by Onkelos, Rabbi Nathan, and Rashi, interpreter Joseph ibn Kaspi charges them with subverting the meaning of the Torah text. "I am shocked," he says, "at these ancients, who are so much more perfect than I . . . and who explain a Torah text by the very opposite of its written meaning or substitute a word or add phrases that change its meaning."

Kaspi goes on to contend that this Torah text means only that Moses took another Cushite woman besides Zipporah as his wife. "He did so for reasons of his own, and it is not right for us to pry into his business or his motives. . . . It is [also] unacceptable to suggest, as do Onkelos, Rabbi Nathan, and Rashi, that Moses became a celibate. He was no Franciscan, Augustine, or Carmelite monk!"

Kimchi also registers strong objections to those who invent additions to the Torah text. How does he account for the public criticism of Moses by Miriam and Aaron?

Kimchi claims that the words of the Torah text mean that Miriam and Aaron object to Moses' marriage to *another* Cushite woman. Kimchi explains that Moses is already married to Zipporah, who is a Cushite. Without seeking to understand his motives for marrying an additional woman, Miriam and Aaron criticize him. They leap to conclusions. They mistakenly assume, insists Kimchi, that, as prophets, they are the equals of Moses; they, therefore, believe they comprehend his reasons for marrying again. In truth, says Kimchi, they criticize him without justification and out of ignorance. Consequently, they are punished. (Commentary on Numbers 12:1ff.)

Given Kimchi's explanation, one wonders if he is not as guilty as Onkelos, Rabbi Nathan, and Rashi of inventing additions to the Torah text to explain the protest of Miriam and Aaron against Moses.

In contrast to Kimchi, Jacob ben Isaac Ashkenazi, author of *Tze'enah u-Re'enah,* a commentary for women, suggests two possible reasons for Miriam's and Aaron's condemnation of Moses. Ashkenazi speculates that their criticism, "He married a Cushite woman!" stems from their conviction that Moses considers himself superior to his people. Miriam and Aaron, suggests Ash-

kenazi, are upset that, rather than finding a wife among the Israelites, Moses seeks out and marries a Cushite. Ashkenazi, perhaps worried about some intermarriages in his own community, claims that Miriam and Aaron ask Moses accusingly, "Are none of your own people's women good enough for you?"

They object to his marrying a Cushite woman . . .
Philosopher Martin Buber holds that "the reason for the 'talk against Moses' is his wife." Miriam "takes the lead" because "this is a family affair. . . . What the brother and sister reproach Moses with is conditioned not by a general tendency to keep the blood pure but by the concept that continuation of the gift of prophecy . . . would be unfavorably affected by the alien element." (Moses, Harper and Row Publishers, Inc., *New York, 1958, pp. 167–168)*

In addition, writes Ashkenazi, there may be another explanation for Miriam's and Aaron's complaint against Moses. Perhaps, Ashkenazi speculates, they are outraged over Moses' treatment of Zipporah, his wife. They may have overheard him tell her, "I am occupied with important work on behalf of the community and have no time for you." Consequently, they could conclude that Moses is neglecting her and even refusing to have sexual relations with her. The Torah's explanation, "because of the Cushite woman," might therefore be understood as an expression of concern for Zipporah's well-being. This also, argues Ashkenazi, may account for the reason Miriam and Aaron decide to speak out publicly against their brother. (*Tze'enah u-Re'enah* on Numbers 12:1)

They slandered Moses . . .
One who slanders another in secret will not be forgiven. One who slanders a member of one's family will find no forgiveness. . . . We are told that Miriam and Aaron slandered Moses for marrying a Cushite woman. . . . Was she

not Zipporah . . . different from all other women by her dark skin, her kind words, and her good deeds? . . . And were not the Israelites also called by God Cushites, as in the phrase, "Are you not like the Cushites to Me, O children of Israel?" (Pirke de-Rabbi Eliezer 53)

Leibowitz

After reviewing various explanations of the criticism of Moses by Miriam and Aaron, Nehama Leibowitz concludes that this Torah story is about the dangers of slander and gossip. She comments that "the desire to make the great person small, to blacken the reputation of the famous, to belittle the character of the good person, and minimize any symptom of human greatness is prevalent among the small-minded, those who prey on human weakness, those who themselves fail to achieve any heights of greatness or heroism."

Leibowitz suggests that this was precisely the human weakness of jealousy that filled Miriam and Aaron. It drove them to speak "against Moses." "Evidently," explains Leibowitz, "the Torah did not wish to prohibit merely explicit gossip about people in general and the spiritual leaders of our generation in particular. It wished to prohibit any kind of talk or gossip disparaging of others."

Citing Bachya ben Joseph ibn Pakuda, the author of the ethical text *Hovot ha-Levavot,* "Duties of the Heart," Leibowitz warns: "Should one of your friends be superior to you . . . in deeds . . . do not allow your evil inclination to say, 'Stir up the opinion of others against him. Find fault with him. Spread lies to diminish his good reputation.' Instead, say to your evil inclination, 'Remember what happened to Miriam and Aaron when they spoke against Moses.' " (*Studies in Bemidbar,* pp.132–133)

Because the story of Miriam and Aaron speaking against Moses does not clearly spell out their motives, Torah interpreters become inventive in suggesting their own. Little wonder that this ancient story continues to excite debate. Is it jealously or concern for Moses' role as a leader that leads his brother and sister to protest his marriage to the Cushite? No one can be sure. However, each of the differing explanations of our interpreters raises serious ethical questions about human behavior and the resolution of conflict. Once again, the Torah text invites controversy and focuses upon continuing moral issues.

QUESTIONS FOR STUDY AND DISCUSSION

1. Interpreters suggest several reasons for the Israelites' complaints about their situation. They fear the uncertainty of the future, are spoiled and resist change, are bored and lack challenge, are obsessed with materialistic desires and seek new thrills. They resent the restraints of ethical laws and idealize their bitter past. Which of these "reasons" provides the best explanation for their complaints to Moses and to God? How should human beings at various stages in their lives appropriately express such complaints? What is the most helpful way of dealing with such complaints? Why is it important for leaders to "share," as Moses did, the protestations of their constituents rather than bear the burden alone?

2. It is a serious matter to invent or read into the Torah text meanings that may have not been intended by the original author or authors. It is like lifting out of context what another person has said. Note how Joseph ibn Kaspi takes Onkelos, Rabbi Nathan, and Rashi to task for "subverting" the Torah text with additions and interpretations. Would you agree with him? Why? Which interpreter makes the most sense in explaining what led Miriam and Aaron to protest against Moses?

3. The author of Proverbs 10:18 claims that the person "who slanders another is a fool." Rabbinic tradition teaches that "a slanderer deserves to be stoned." (*Arakin* 15b) How would you define "slander"? Why do you think the rabbis find slandering another person a serious sin? Why do you think Jewish tradition considers slander a capital offense? (See *Tosefta Peah* 1, 2.)

PARASHAT SHELACH-LECHA
Numbers 13:1–15:41

Parashat Shelach-Lecha describes how the twelve spies, each representing a tribe of Israel, scout the Land of Israel. After forty days they return. Ten of them report that the land is fruitful, but its cities and countryside are filled with powerful warriors—giants. Two of the spies, Caleb and Joshua, disagree. They urge the people to conquer the land. Hearing the divided report, the people protest against Moses and Aaron, telling them, "Let us go back to Egypt." God threatens to abandon the people for their disloyalty and to create a new people for Moses to lead. Moses pleads with God to pardon the people, pointing out that God's reputation is at stake. He argues that, if the people are destroyed, it will appear that God freed them from Egypt to crush them in the desert. The people are told that, because of their lack of faith, they will die before entering the Land of Israel, and only after forty years of wandering in the desert will their children conquer the land. Offerings to be presented at the sanctuary are described, as is the treatment of the *ger,* or "stranger," who resides among the Israelites. The Israelites are warned that the penalty for gathering wood on the Sabbath is death by stoning. They are commanded to attach a blue cord or thread to the fringes at the corners of their garments as a reminder of their responsibility to fulfill all the commandments of Torah.

OUR TARGUM

· 1 ·

God instructs Moses to send twelve spies, one from each tribe, to scout the Land of Israel. "See what kind of country it is," they are told. They are instructed to investigate its cities, people, soil, and forests and "bring back some of the fruit of the land."

The scouts spend forty days exploring the land. Before they return they stop in the valley of Eshkol near Hebron, where they cut a cluster of grapes and gather some pomegranates and figs. Upon their return, they show the fruits to the Israelites, proving that the land they scouted is indeed flowing "with milk and honey." However, ten of the spies frighten the Israelites. After displaying the fruit of the land, these ten tell stories of the powerful people, the large fortified cities, and the dangerous inhabitants.

The report terrifies the community. Caleb, however, seeking to assure the people, says, "Let us by all means go up [to the land], and we shall gain possession of it, for we shall surely overcome it."

Spreading even more fear, the ten spies claim that the country "is one that eats up its inhabitants. All the people we saw are giants," they say. "We looked like grasshoppers to ourselves, and so we must have looked to them."

The entire community of Israelites turns on Moses and Aaron, shouting at them, "Why is *Adonai* taking us to that land to fall by the sword? Our wives and children will be carried off! . . . Let us head back for Egypt."

At that point, Joshua and Caleb tell the community that the land is "exceedingly good" and that, with faith in God, the people will conquer it. Rejecting their counsel, the people threaten to pelt them with stones.

God tells Moses that, since the people have no faith, they will be destroyed. "I will provide you with a nation far more numerous than they!" Moses, like Abraham, responds by challenging God. "What will the Egyptians say when they see that God has freed the people only to kill them? What will the nations conclude about God's power when it becomes known that God is powerless to bring them into the Promised Land?" (For Abraham's challenge to God, see Genesis 18:16–33.)

Moses pleads with God to forgive the people for their lapse of faith. Agreeing, God declares, *"Adonai!* Slow to anger and abounding in kindness; forgiving iniquity and transgression . . ."

The people are told that for their lack of faith they will wander for forty years and that the entire generation of those who were freed from Egypt will die in the desert. Only their children, led by Caleb and Joshua, will go up to conquer the land.

Despite what they hear, the people declare that they have changed their minds and are now ready to conquer the land. Moses warns that they will not succeed. Defiantly, they attack and are shattered by the Amalekites and Canaanites at Hormah.

· 2 ·

Moses instructs the people about the offerings by fire that they are to bring to the sanctuary. The people are advised to seek forgiveness for sins committed unintentionally by bringing sacrifices. Those who deliberately sin, however, will be punished.

Moses also tells them that the *ger,* "stranger" or "convert," is to be treated like an Israelite: "The same ritual and the same rule shall apply to you and to the stranger who resides among you."

·3·

Journeying through the wilderness, an Israelite is discovered gathering wood on the Sabbath. Because he has broken faith with the commandment to observe the Sabbath, he is put to death by stoning.

·4·

Moses is told to instruct the Israelites to attach a cord of blue [a dye made from the blood of a rare mollusk] to the fringes at the corners of their garments. The fringes are to remind the people "to observe all the commandments and to be holy to God."

THEMES

Parashat Shelach-Lecha contains two important themes:

1. The sin of the spies in not separating fact from fiction and truth from falsehood.
2. The meaning of wearing *tzitzit,* or "fringes."

PEREK ALEF: *What Was the Sin of the Spies?*

The Torah provides us with two versions of the story of the spies sent to scout the Land of Israel. *Parashat Shelach-Lecha* (Numbers 13:1–14:45) contains a much more extensive account than does *Parashat Devarim* (Deuteronomy 1:19–45). Both versions, however, agree that twelve tribal leaders are sent to explore the land.

The spies return to the people in the wilderness after a forty-day journey and bring back ripe fruits. Ten of the twelve scouts report that it is "a land that flows with milk and honey," *but* it is also a land of the Anakites, or "giants." "We felt like grasshoppers in their sight," they say. They report that it is also the land of the Amalekites, enemies of the Israelites.

Joshua and Caleb disagree with the ten other scouts, urging the people to go up and conquer the land.

In panic, the people protest to Moses: "Let us go back to Egypt." Angered by the report of the spies and by the reaction of the people, God punishes them with forty years of wandering in the desert, a year for each of the forty days of the spies' journey. The people are told that not one of the generation liberated from Egypt will enter the Land of Israel. Only their children, led by Joshua and Caleb, will victoriously enter the land.

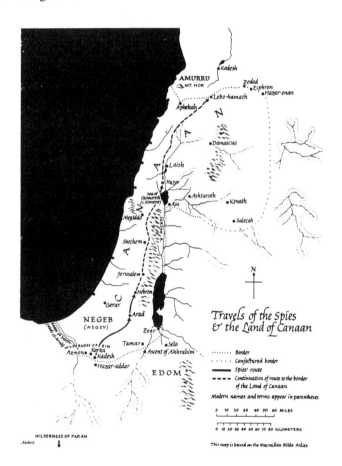

Travels of the Spies & the Land of Canaan

········· Border
· · · · · Conjectured border
——— Spies' route
- - - - Continuation of route to the border of the Land of Canaan

Modern names and terms appear in parentheses

0 10 20 30 40 50 60 MILES
0 10 20 30 40 50 60 70 80 KILOMETERS

This map is based on the Macmillan Bible Atlas

Clearly something drastic has happened! The people who suffered long years of Egyptian slavery are condemned to wander in the wilderness for forty years and to die there. What causes this catastrophe? What do the spies either say or do to bring on such severe punishment? What is their sin?

As we may imagine with so significant an event, there are a variety of views among Torah interpreters.

An author of an early rabbinic interpretation suggests that the spies, like Miriam, engage in the sin of slander. (See the discussion in *Parashat Beha'alotecha, "Perek Bet."*) Instead of remembering Miriam's punishment for publicly criticizing Moses, the spies return from their journey and, immediately and publicly, speak slanderously about the Land of Israel. They tell the people: "It is a land that eats up its inhabitants," meaning that the land is difficult to farm, its soil is of poor quality, and its air is polluted, bringing ill health. For their deliberate slander of the land, they and the generation accepting their report are punished. (*Numbers Rabbah* 16:2)

In his study *Moses as a Political Leader,* Aaron Wildavsky suggests that the sin of the spies is more serious than slander. The people have left Egypt with the promise of conquering the Land of Israel. This is their goal. The spies, says Wildavsky, return and take advantage of the people's anticipation of their report to "discredit the entire enterprise." That is their sin.

They conspire to convince the people that God is leading them not to a land of opportunity and plenty but to disaster. Reporting that the cities of the land are protected by high walls and guarded by powerful giants, they strike fear into the hearts of the people. They destroy their dreams and willingness to go forward to conquer the land. Because the spies kill the hopes of their people, they and their generation are condemned to wander and die in the wilderness. (University of Alabama Press, 1984, pp. 114–118)

Isaac Arama suggests that the sin of the spies was their rejection of the Land of Israel. "It is this rejection of the Land of Israel," argues Arama, a fifteenth-century commentator living in Spain during the reign of Ferdinand V and Isabella I, "that explains our tribulations and exile. . . . We shall never recover our spiritual and physical balance until we return to it." Since the spies

scorn and spurn the land and rally the people to tell Moses to take them back to Egypt, they are all condemned to die in the desert. Because of their disloyalty to the land, they are unworthy of reconquering it and rebuilding their nation.

Chasidic teacher Yitzhak Meir of Ger views the matter differently. He comments that the sin of the spies is not their plan to undermine the expectations of the people to settle the land but their actual carrying out of the plan after their scouting mission. Human beings, observes Rabbi Meir of Ger, are not held responsible for evil thoughts or for evil plans. They sin when they translate their evil plans into the reality of deeds. This is the sin of the spies. With their unfavorable report they turn a whole nation away from its goal of conquering their land. (A.Z. Friedman, *Wellsprings of Torah,* 2 vols., Judaica Press, New York, 1969, p. 306)

Other commentators also accuse the spies of misleading the people. For example, Sforno explains that, when they mention the Anakites, or "giants," they mean to suggest that the climate of the land is so polluted that only the strongest among them will survive. When they claim that they felt like "grasshoppers," the spies are deliberately exaggerating the physical size of their enemies to frighten the people.

Peli

By observing that "it is a land that eats up its people," modern commentator Pinchas Peli argues that the spies are conducting a "demoralizing campaign," deliberately deceiving the people with lies about the land they have just scouted. (*Torah Today,* B'nai B'rith Books, Washington, D.C., 1987, pp. 169–172)

Leibowitz

Ramban (Nachmanides)

"The spies," comments Nehama Leibowitz, "knew their job well. First they sing the praises of the Promised Land, aware that a lie to succeed must have a modicum of truth in it to give it an appearance of objectivity. They knew how to pass from an apparently objective report to a subjective expression of opinion." For instance, they tell the people, "We came to the land you sent us to; it does indeed flow with milk and honey, and this is its fruit." Then they say, "But we saw giants there." It is for the sin of inciting the people to fear about going up to conquer the land, for lying to them, for misleading them with deliberate exaggerations, and for not separating fact from fiction that the spies are punished. (See *Studies in Bemidbar,* pp. 135–146.)

Rabbi Menachem M. Schneerson agrees that the sin of the spies is in their deception of the people. However, he points out that they also mislead themselves. They are pious and good and worry about the spiritual life of their people. However, they fear, explains Schneerson, that the people will enter the Land of Israel and become so busy with materialistic concerns, with work, feeding their families, building their homes, creating entertainments for themselves, and caring for their communities that they will have "progressively less time and energy for the service of God."

That, explains Schneerson, is what they mean when they said, "It is a land that eats up its inhabitants." Their sin is in misleading the people and themselves with "their opinion . . . that spirituality flourishes best in seclusion and withdrawal." The spies, concludes Schneerson, "were wrong. The purpose of a life lived in Torah is not the elevation of the soul: It is the sanctification of the world . . . taking possession of the Land of Israel and making it a holy land." (*Torah Studies,* Lubavitch Foundation, London, 1986, pp. 241–242)

Nachmanides disagrees with most of these interpretations. The spies, he contends, do not present any false facts, nor do they exaggerate what they saw. They show the people the fruit of the land, and they tell the truth about it. Their fault, argues Nachmanides, is in misunderstanding the purpose of their mission and in their manner of reporting about it.

They are sent, Nachmanides points out, on a "reconnaissance mission" with the task of bringing back strategic details on how best to conquer the land. Since Moses is preparing for war, their assignment is to return with details about the land and its people, which will guarantee victory. The entire future of the people depends upon their report.

Their sin, says Nachmanides, is the tone in which they deliver their information. Upon their return they begin speaking in glowing, positive terms about the wonderful fruit of the land; then, however, they turn negative. Using the word *efes,* or "but," they declare, "But the people of the land are powerful." That evaluation, concludes Nachmanides, "signifies something negative, beyond human capability, something impossible to achieve under any circumstances." It produces fear. Quite obviously it is the negative presentation by the spies that panics the people and causes them to reject conquering the Land of Israel.

The positive versus the negative
Rabbi Abraham Chill notes that the spies were confronted with the negative dangers of conquering the land as opposed to the positive consequences victory would bring. They were faced with a positive versus a negative choice. "The tosafot *deal with this enigma," says Chill, "by reasoning that, if one is confronted by the necessity to make a choice, the preference should be for positive thinking. . . . The dynamics of*

positive thinking should supplant the debilitation of negative defense." (The Sidrot, *Geffen Publications, Jerusalem, 1983, p. 132*)

Nachmanides also accuses the spies of withholding valuable information. Moses asks them to determine whether their enemies are few or many. The scouts never furnish those crucial numbers. Furthermore, they compound their sin by seeking to undermine Moses' authority. Instead of delivering their report privately to him, they present it publicly to the people. Afterwards, adds Nachmanides, the ten spies go from tent to tent, spreading more of their "evil report." It is the withholding of information and the deliberate undermining of Moses' authority that result in their punishment. (Commentary on Numbers 13:1–14:2)

Contemporary interpreter Rabbi Morris Adler suggests another reading of the spies' behavior. Their sin is the "subversion" of the people by the deliberate misuse of their position and power. Adler reminds us that the spies are not ordinary Israelites. They are carefully chosen leaders, "whose words carried great weight." The people rely upon their judgment and trust them. When they lie about what they have seen, they destroy the people's confidence.

This story, says Adler, is a lesson of how "the prominent, the highly educated, the well-placed . . . undermined the morale of the people in a way that was just short of a brutal military assault. They breached the wall of the people's confidence; they brought panic and disillusionment as surely as if the enemy's legions had actually trampled upon the Israelites. This," explains Adler, "was the kind of subversion that these princes in Israel practiced, and the result was almost the annihilation of the entire people."

Why did the spies, these leaders of their people, engage in such subversion? Adler believes that they were pleased with the status quo of the desert. They opposed change. Everything was provided: food, water, shelter. Life was good enough for them. They did not want to take on the burden of conquering the Promised Land

nor the risk of losing the power and security they already possessed. That was their sin, Adler concludes. They wanted to pull down the blinds on all the pain and sorrow of the world and live in the security of their own safe desert. They chose to subvert the dream of achieving the Promised Land, where justice, freedom, and peace would prevail for all. (*The Voice Still Speaks,* pp. 301–305)

Adler's view of the spies' intentions is supported by one of the earliest comments on their mission. Rabbi Simeon ben Yochai (second century C.E.) told his students that "the spies went up to the Land of Israel with evil thoughts and returned with evil thoughts." In other words, before they began their reconnaissance mission, they had already reached conclusions on what they would tell the people. What they would see or hear would not alter their opinions. On the contrary, they would use examples that supported their preconceived ideas, rejecting all others. That was their sin. They failed themselves and their people by closing their minds, by refusing to scout the land without prejudice or narrow-mindedness. (*Sotah* 35a; also Rashi on Numbers 13:26)

Why were they possessed with such preconceived notions? What might have caused the spies, these leaders of Israel, to bring back such a negative report? Why panic the people about conquering the land? A clue might be found in the last observation they share with the Israelites about the people of the land. In a moment of rare candor they say, "All the people that we saw in it are men of great size; we saw the Nephilim there—the Anakites are part of the Nephilim—*and we looked like grasshoppers to ourselves,* and so we must have looked to them."

The spies reveal their low self-esteem. "We looked like grasshoppers to ourselves," they say, indicating little respect for their capabilities. They see themselves as weaklings, powerless, without strength or imagination to overcome their enemies. Their lack of self-respect breeds self-contempt and fear of others.

Psychologist Erich Fromm observes that "the affirmation of one's own life, happiness, growth, and freedom is rooted in one's capacity to love."

We love productively only when we learn to love ourselves.

We can only conquer "Promised Lands" when we have regard for our talents and believe in our creative powers. The sin of the spies grows from their failure of self-love and self-respect. Perhaps that explains their punishment. Unable to appreciate themselves, they are condemned to wander and die in the desert. Only Joshua and Caleb, who refuse to see themselves as "grasshoppers," are worthy of entering the Promised Land.

PEREK BET: *The Meaning of Wearing Tzitzit, or "Fringes"*

The Torah tradition concerns itself with nearly every aspect of human existence, including clothing. For example, it forbids women from dressing as men, men from dressing as women, and either from wearing *sha'atnez*, a garment made of a mixture of wool and linen. (Deuteronomy 22:5, 11) Of particular importance is the commandment on wearing *tzitzit*, or "fringes." It is not only found in our Torah portion but also in Deuteronomy 22:12.

Moses instructs the Israelites to wear *tzitzit* on the corners of their garments "throughout the generations." Each fringe is to include a *petil techelet*, or "blue thread." As for the purpose of the *tzitzit*, Moses tells the people: "Look at it [the fringe] and recall all the commandments of God and observe them, so that you do not follow your heart and eyes in your lustful urge. Thus

you shall be reminded to observe all My commandments and to be holy to your God. I *Adonai* am your God, who brought you out of the land of Egypt to be your God: I, *Adonai* your God." (Numbers 15:39–41)

Throughout the centuries Jewish men have been placing *tzitzit* on the four corners of a garment known as a *talit katan*, a "small prayer shawl," worn either over or under a shirt, and upon the four corners of the *talit* worn at prayer. The mitzvah to wear *tzitzit* is considered so important by the rabbis who composed the first prayers of the synagogue that they included it as one of four paragraphs recited each morning and evening after the *Shema*, the declaration of God's unity.

The *petil techelet*, however, did cause problems. Apparently the blue dye from which it was made either became impossible to acquire or the secret of its manufacture was lost. Some scholars speculate that it was made from the blood of a rare mollusk called *chilazon*, living off the coast of the Land of Israel. When the mollusk could no longer be found, the rabbis did not abandon the making and wearing of *tzitzit*. Instead, they deliberately overlooked the prescription of Torah and decreed that the fringe could be made without the *petil techelet*.

Clearly, they believed that wearing *tzitzit*, even without the *petil techelet*, was of great significance. As a matter of fact, both Rabbi Simeon ben Yochai and Rabbi Meir teach that "carefully fulfilling the mitzvah of wearing *tzitzit* guarantees seeing the face of God!" Others claim that "the mitzvah of wearing *tzitzit* is equal in importance to all of the commandments." (*Menachot* 43a; also Jerusalem Talmud, *Berachot* 1:2; *Nedarim* 25a)

What prompts such an evaluation? Why does Jewish tradition attach such importance to wearing *tzitzit*?

Rashi

Commenting on the word *tzitzit*, Rashi notes that its numerical value is 600 (*tzadei* = 90, yod = 10, tzadei = 90, yod = 10, tav = 400) and that the fringe is tied with eight threads and five knots. Together the full numerical equivalent comes to 613, which is the number of commandments Rabbi Simlai, in the fourth century, found in the Torah.

Later Jewish tradition refers to these 613 commandments by the acronym *TaRYaG Mitzvot* (tav = 400, resh = 200, yod = 10, gimel = 3). Together they total 613 and are understood to be divided between 165 positive commandments and 365 negative commandments. Rashi maintains that wearing the *tzitzit* and "looking upon it [the fringe]" remind one of the obligation to fulfill all 613 commandments of Torah. (Commentary on Numbers 15:37ff.; also *Makot* 23b)

Rashi's observation is drawn from a view expressed by earlier rabbinic commentators. They hold that, when Jews look upon the *tzitzit*, they are reminded of the commandments, and "looking leads to remembering them, and remembering leads to doing them." Since the performance of every mitzvah is important, the *tzitzit* function as a powerful symbol stimulating Jewish behavior. When worn and seen, they are a sign pointing to the carrying out of the commandments. (*Numbers Rabbah* 7:5)

In some communities Jews, while putting on the *talit* with its fringes, recite the following mystical prayer, capturing the symbolic meaning of the *tzitzit:* "For the purpose of unifying God's name . . . and in the name of all Israel, I wrap myself in this *talit* and *tzitzit*. So let my soul and my 248 limbs and 365 veins [which is 613] be wrapped in the light of the *tzitzit*. . . . Through the fulfillment of this commandment may my soul, spirit, holy spark, and prayer be saved from all distractions. . . . And may the doing of this commandment be considered by God as important and fulfilling as all the particulars, details, and intentions of the 613 commandments that depend upon it."

Noting that the Torah commandment for wearing *tzitzit* includes the instruction to "look at it [the fringe] . . . so that you do not follow your heart and eyes in your lustful urge," the rabbis comment that the meaning of the *tzitzit* is more than a symbolic reminder to observe the commandments. It functions, as well, to preserve ethical and, particularly, sexual purity. "The heart and eyes tend to mislead the body." Our senses require direction and discipline, say the rabbis. That is the purpose of the *tzitzit*. They save those who wear them from evil temptations. (*Numbers Rabbah* 7:6)

The *tzitzit*, however, do not have magical powers. Pinchas Peli explains that the *tzitzit* "are not a talisman, an amulet to guard the person who wears them from demons and evil spirits." Instead the fringes represent "the inner conscience of the religious person."

Peli tells the talmudic story of the man who once hired a prostitute. She prepared a tempting room with seven beautiful beds in it. Lying naked on the bed, she invited him to join her. As he took off his clothing, his *tzitzit* struck him in the face, and he fell to the floor. When she inquired what was wrong, he told her that in seeing the *tzitzit* he had been reminded of his ethical duty. "They testify that I am doing something wrong!" he told her. Upon seeing how his faith functioned in his life, the woman decided to study and become a convert to Judaism. ("Torah Today" in the *Jerusalem Post*, June 18, 1986; *Menachot* 44a)

People, comments Peli, are absentminded, careless, forgetful of their obligations, and easily tempted into dangerous behavior. They often follow their eyes and hearts without calculating the consequences of what they are doing to themselves and others. The commandment to wear fringes is given to counter such tendencies, to alert us to our ethical and religious obligations.

In his discussion of the *tzitzit*, Professor Yeshayahu Leibowitz, brother of Torah commentator Nehama Leibowitz, draws a distinction between "ethical" and "religious" obligations. In an ethical decision, Leibowitz argues, a person relates to another as a human being and relates to treating that person as a human being with no criteria other than that it feels right or wrong. One might say, "I will do unto others as I would like them to do unto me," or one might ask, "If everyone did what I am about to do, would the world be a just, kind, and peaceful place?"

On the other hand, religious decisions, explains Leibowitz, place a person before God and require that one live in accordance with the commandments because that is what God demands. Rather than asking, "Does it feel right or wrong?" or "Is this what I would want others to do?" the only question one asks is: "What does God require of me?" *Tzitzit,* concludes Leibowitz, remind us not to go astray by following the whim of our heart or eyes. They are a powerful reminder of a Jew's religious obligations to God. (*Weekly Parashah,* Shmuel Himelstein, translator, Chemed Books, Brooklyn, New York, 1990, pp. 138–141)

Leibowitz's view that the *tzitzit* remind the people of Israel's obligations to God agrees with an early rabbinic observation that the fringes are an insignia of the people's liberation and relationship to God. Before the Exodus, say the rabbis, the people were forced to wear badges of slavery, emblems indicating that they were the property of Pharaoh. The badges were a form of humiliation. Like the "yellow star" forced upon Jews by the Nazis, they identified the people as objects of scorn and targets for hatred and brutality.

Once liberated, the people are commanded to wear *tzitzit.* The fringes are a badge of freedom. They symbolize the liberation of the Jews: Jews will never again be slaves to other human beings and will serve only God. (*Menachot* 43; also *Shabbat* 57a)

David Wolfson, an early Zionist leader, provides another meaning for *tzitzit.* When Theodor Herzl asked him to make the preparations for the First Zionist Congress in Basle, Switzerland, in 1897, Wolfson sought colors and a flag that would unite delegates from all over the world. He was faced with the problem of choosing a flag to decorate the congress hall. Wolfson relates: "Then it flashed upon my mind; but we do have a flag indeed! It's white and blue: the *talit* in which we wrap ourselves during prayer. This *talit* (with its *tzitzit*) is our coat of arms, our emblem. Let us take out the *talit* and unfurl it before the eyes of Israel, before the eyes of all nations." (See B.S. Jacobson, *Meditations on the Torah,* p. 223.)

Today, *tzitzit* continue to be prized by Jews as a symbol of their historic covenant with God and as a badge of freedom and national existence. Looking at the fringes recalls ethical and ritual responsibilities. They are a reminder that the Jew, as a servant of God, must confront temptation and confusion between right and wrong behavior in light of what the 613 mitzvot of Jewish tradition demand. *Tzitzit* remain a proud badge of Jewish identity and commitment.

QUESTIONS FOR STUDY AND DISCUSSION

1. Most commentators seek an answer to the question: "What was the sin of the ten spies who returned from the Land of Israel?" Of all the different responses, which makes the most sense to you? Why?

2. Isaac Arama claims that the sin of the spies was their rejection of the Land of Israel. One of the first ministers of religion in the new State of Israel, J.L. Maimon, declared in 1951 that "anyone who spreads an evil report about the Land of Israel—even if it is true—is a spy." Is it wrong to criticize one's nation? Is it a sign of disloyalty? Is it disloyal for a Jew to "spread an evil report" about the State of Israel?

3. Modern philosopher Rabbi Abraham Joshua Heschel comments: "*A real symbol* is a visible object that represents something invisible; something present representing something absent. . . . The purpose of ritual art objects in Judaism is not to inspire love of God but to enhance our love of doing a mitzvah. . . ." How does the wearing of *tzitzit,* or "fringes," fulfill Heschel's definition of a Jewish religious symbol? How do the Shabbat candles, the *Havdalah* spice box, the *matzah* eaten at Pesach, the *mezuzah,* or the *lulav* and *etrog* waved during Sukot services "enhance our love of doing a mitzvah"?

PARASHAT KORAH
Numbers 16:1–18:32

Parashat Korah tells of the rebellion of Korah, Dathan, Abiram, and On against the leadership of Moses and Aaron. With 250 respected leaders of the community, they accuse Moses and Aaron of acting "holier" than the other Israelites. Hearing their complaint, Moses instructs them to bring offerings to the sanctuary on the next day and tells them that God will demonstrate who is to be trusted as leader of the community. The next morning the leaders of the rebellion and their followers are punished. Some are swallowed when the earth opens; others are killed by fire or plague. The community then accuses Moses and Aaron of bringing death upon the people. God threatens to destroy the entire people, but Moses orders Aaron to place an offering on the altar, which is meant to save the people from harm. Moses then organizes the priesthood to be headed by Aaron and his descendants. They, along with the tribe of Levi, are to be responsible for managing all gifts donated to the sanctuary. Unlike other tribes of Israel, Levites are not given any territory. They are given offerings as payment for their work in the sanctuary.

OUR TARGUM

·1·

Korah, the great grandson of Levi, along with Dathan, Abiram, and On, descendants of Reuben, and 250 elected leaders of the community organize a rebellion against Moses and Aaron. "All the people are holy," they complain. "Why then do you raise yourselves above God's congregation?"

Stunned by their accusation, Moses challenges Korah and his followers to bring fire pans and incense with them to the sanctuary the next morning. "God will make known who is holy and who is not," he says.

Turning to Korah, Moses questions his motives. "You have been given special duties in the sanctuary and opportunities for leadership. Why do you now seek the priesthood that God has given to Aaron?"

When Moses asks Dathan and Abiram to meet with him, they refuse. "For what reason should we meet with you?" they say. "You have brought us out of a land flowing with milk and honey to die in this wilderness. Do you now also need to demonstrate your power over us? We will not come." Stunned, Moses prays to God, "Pay no regard to their words. I have never taken anything from them nor wronged them."

·2·

The next morning Moses and Aaron meet with Korah and his followers in front of the sanctuary. Each is carrying a fire pan with red hot coals and incense on it. By that time Korah has organized the entire community against Moses and Aaron.

God speaks to Moses and Aaron, telling them to withdraw from Korah and the community because they are about to be destroyed. Moses and Aaron plead to God on behalf of the people, asking, "If one person sins, will You be angry with the whole community?"

God tells Moses to order the people to withdraw from the area around the tents of Korah,

Dathan, and Abiram. Then, as the people look on, Moses announces, "If these people die by a natural death, it will mean that I have not been designated by God to lead you. If they are swallowed by the earth opening up, that will be a sign that God has sent me to lead you." At that point, the earth opens and swallows Korah, Dathan, Abiram, and their families, as well as their 250 followers.

·3·

Moses orders Aaron's son, Eleazar, to collect all the fire pans and beat them into sheets to be used as plating for the altar. The bright plating is to remind all Israelites that only Aaron's descendants may serve as priests.

·4·

The day after Korah's rebellion, the Israelites bitterly accuse Moses and Aaron of bringing death upon their community. Hearing the accusation, God tells Moses and Aaron, "Remove yourselves from this community that I may annihilate them in an instant." Seeing that a plague is breaking out among the people, Moses tells Aaron to place a fire pan on the altar to gain forgiveness for the people. When the plague ends, 14,700 are dead.

·5·

Moses asks the chief of each of the twelve tribes to deposit a staff inside the sanctuary. Each chief is to write his name on his own staff. Aaron's name is to be inscribed on the staff of Levi. The next day, upon entering the sanctuary, Moses notices that Aaron's staff has sprouted blossoms and almonds. After the staffs are returned to the tribal chiefs, Moses returns Aaron's staff to the sanctuary as a warning to those who might in the future rebel against God.

·6·

Aaron and his sons are commissioned as *kohanim*, or "priests," to oversee all rituals of the sanctuary. The Levites are to help them, but the Levites are to have no contact with the altar or other sacred objects. All offerings are to be given to the priests for their use, and tithes (a tenth of the products harvested) are to be designated for the Levites as payment for their service to the sanctuary.

Neither the *kohanim* nor the Levites are to be given land holdings.

THEMES

Parashat Korah contains two important themes:

1. The difference between just and unjust disputes.
2. Magic and miracles in Jewish tradition.

PEREK ALEF: *Korah's Rebellion: A Deadly Dispute*

Appearances can at times deceive us into believing we understand what we see or read. This seems to be the case with the data we are given about the rebellion led by Korah, Dathan, Abiram, and On against Moses and Aaron. At first, this appears to be a single story about a protest organized by these leaders and 250 followers. However, as most modern biblical scholars point out, the truth may be that the Torah report is an edited version of at least two different stories.

Untangled, there is first the report of Korah, the son of Izar, son of Kohath, who was the son of Levi. Korah protests the appointment of Aaron and his family as priests, suggesting that Moses is unjustly singling out his brother for privileges that belong equally to other descendants of Levi, including Korah himself. Mocking Moses, Korah publicly denounces him with the accusation: "You have gone too far! For all the community are holy, all of them, and *Adonai* is in their midst. Why then do you raise yourselves above God's congregation?"

Clearly, Korah's intent is to undercut Moses' authority and gain the priesthood for himself and his family. In response, Moses asks Korah, "Is it not enough for you that the God of Israel has set you apart from the community of Israel and given you access . . . to perform the duties of God's Tabernacle . . . ? Yet you seek the priesthood too!"

Woven into this battle over the priesthood is a second protest led by Dathan, Abiram, and On against Moses. They accuse him of promising the people a land flowing with milk and honey but instead exposing them to death in the desert.

Like Korah, they seem intent on stirring up a rebellion against Moses' leadership.

In both stories, Korah, Dathan, Abiram, and On are joined by 250 chieftains, "respected leaders." These chieftains are not identified by name, nor are we given any reasons for their rebellion against Moses and Aaron. As participants in the protests, however, they are put to death by fire at the same time that Dathan, Abiram, and Korah are swallowed up by the earth.

Several questions remain unanswered about the protests led by Korah, Dathan, and Abiram. What were these protests really about? For example, the author of Psalm 106, after making the observation that "those who act justly and who do right at all times are happy" (Psalms 106:3), then offers a judgment about Dathan's and Abiram's rebellion against Moses and Aaron: "There was envy of Moses in the camp, and of Aaron, the holy one of God./The earth opened up and swallowed Dathan, closed over the party of Abiram./A fire blazed among their party, a flame that consumed the wicked." (Psalms 106:16–18) Is the Psalmist correct? Was it "envy" that fueled the dispute or were there other more significant motives among the ancient Israelites?

Unfortunately, the Torah text leaves us guessing as to the real causes of the rebellions led by Korah, Dathan, and Abiram. That absence of information, however, does not inhibit later commentators from developing their own theories. As we have seen previously in our studies of Torah, the absence of details and descriptive facts is often an invitation to imaginative speculation and invention. Faced here with the need to explain the dramatic punishments and the deaths of Korah, Dathan, and Abiram, commentators offer us a rich variety of explanations.

Early rabbinic interpreters suggest that Korah draws support from the 250 tribal chiefs by using "persuasive words." He is a clever and effective public speaker, arguing his cause in a compelling way. People are moved by his soothing tone of voice and the convincing ways in which he presents his claims and arguments. His style, inflections, and rich vocabulary sway the people into believing that his claims against Moses and Aaron are just.

Other rabbinic commentators add that Korah's attack on Moses and Aaron grows out of frustrated ambition and the claim that he has been robbed of privileges guaranteed by family position. How is this so? Interpreters point out that Amram, father of Moses and Aaron, was the brother of Izhar, Hebron, and Uzziel. Korah was the eldest son of Izhar. Yet, when leadership appointments over the people of Israel are made, Korah sees Moses and Aaron receiving high appointments as sons of his eldest uncle. He also watches Elizaphan, the eldest son of Uzziel (the youngest brother of Amram) elevated to prince of the Kohathites. Angered that, as the firstborn of Izhar (the second eldest brother after Amram), he is being bypassed by Moses' appointment of Elizaphan, Korah raises an angry voice of public protest. "I am the next in age!" he claims. "The appointment is rightfully mine. Moses is acting unjustly. Should the son of the youngest of my father's brothers be superior to me?"

Korah misleads the people

To foment his rebellion, Korah spends all night going from tribe to tribe accusing Moses and Aaron of wrongdoing. He carefully crafts his speech for each audience, but his message always makes the same point: "I am not like Moses and Aaron, who want to attain fame and power for themselves. I want all of us to enjoy life." He wins the support of the people by misleading them. (Numbers Rabbah *18:10*)

Many commentators sympathize with Korah's argument. They maintain that in bypassing Korah, the eldest son of the second eldest brother of Amram, and elevating Elizaphan, the eldest

son of the youngest brother of Amram, Moses breaks with the tradition of appointing the eldest before the youngest, setting off a deeply emotional family dispute. Korah's pride is hurt; his expectations are shattered. Feeling cheated of his rightful inheritance, he is justified in leading a rebellion against Moses and Aaron.

Other interpreters disagree, pointing out that, while Korah's disappointment may be understandable, his public repudiation of Moses and Aaron is irresponsible. For his behavior he deserves the punishment he receives. On the basis of the Torah's claim that Korah publicly impugns the authority of Moses, these interpreters offer some creatively inventive examples. They claim that, to embarrass Moses, Korah waves his finger at him and asks, "Since the Torah claims that *tzitzit* must be made with a blue thread, does it mean that a person wearing a shirt made of blue threads need not wear *tzitzit?*" On another occasion, Korah asks, "If a house is filled with Torah scrolls that contain all the words inside a *mezuzah,* does the house require a *mezuzah* on the door?" By raising apparent contradictions within the Torah, Korah seeks to ridicule Moses and Aaron. Korah's ultimate target, say these interpreters, is the Torah itself. In mocking Moses over inconsistencies within the Torah, Korah derides not only the Torah but God, the source of Torah. (*Numbers Rabbah 18:1–4*)

Other commentators claim that Korah goes further than scorning the Torah. He actually distorts its meanings. Walking among the Israelites, he points out that the Torah laws are difficult, suggesting that they are even unjust. Seeking to stir the emotions of the people against Moses and Aaron, Korah tells them about a poor widow and her daughter who have been harassed constantly by Moses and Aaron with one legal claim after another. She is about to plow, and they tell her, "According to the Torah you cannot plow. . . ." When she is ready to cut the wool of her animals, Aaron claims that the Torah gives him the right to collect his priestly tax on the first of the wool. Smiling cynically, Korah concludes, "You see they are exploiting our poor and needy." (*Midrash Shocher Tov* on Psalms 1:1)

These imaginative interpretations by rabbinic commentators seek to explain why Korah was punished with death for his rebellion. But what of Dathan, Abiram, and the 250 leaders of the community? How do we account for their being swallowed alive by the earth?

Some of the early rabbinic interpreters argue that it was a matter of association with the wrong neighbor. Dathan and Abiram happen to pitch their tents near Korah and his family. They hear Korah's constant criticism of Moses and Aaron and are convinced that Korah's cause is just. As a result of their friendship they join his rebellion and, in the end, are punished along with Korah. From the experience of Dathan and Abiram we are taught, "Woe to wicked people, and woe to their neighbors."

Other commentators argue that they are punished for much more than simply "associating with bad neighbors." Dathan and Abiram "invite punishment with their mouths" and with their "stubbornness." When Moses asks them to join him for a discussion about their differences, they refuse. As he approaches their tents, hoping that his show of humility will convince them to change their minds, they rebuke him and seek to humiliate him. In doing so, they foment rebellion among the people. For their "insolence" and "contentiousness" they are destroyed along with Korah. *(Numbers Rabbah* 18:4,5,12; also *Midrash Tanchuma* on *Korah)*

Unlike the early rabbinic interpreters who invented a background of events to explain why Korah, Dathan, and Abiram deserve their punishment, other commentators seek the reasons for their deaths within the Torah account itself.

Ibn Ezra

Abraham ibn Ezra explains that the whole episode is an ugly political dispute over the changes Moses initiates concerning the rights of firstborn males. Moses alters those rights when he appoints the Levites, in place of the firstborn, to care for the sanctuary sacrifices. Many of the people, argues ibn Ezra, believe that he introduces this change to benefit his own clan. Afterwards, explains ibn Ezra, Moses appoints his brother, Aaron, and Aaron's sons to preside over the Levites. This upsets the Levites who had assumed they would control the sanctuary, without taking orders from others.

Ibn Ezra explains that Dathan and Abiram join the rebellion because they feel that Moses is taking privileges away from their tribe (Reuben) and giving more power to the tribe of Joseph. Korah, who is also firstborn, organizes all this discontent into the rebellion against Moses and Aaron, telling them: ". . . all the community are holy, all of them. . . . Why then do you raise yourselves above God's congregation?" This rebellion, ibn Ezra concludes, is fueled by the anger of the firstborn. Korah accuses Moses of discrimination and of robbing the rights of the firstborn in order to take those rights and privileges for himself and his family.

Ramban (Nachmanides)

Many commentators disagree with ibn Ezra's conclusions. Nachmanides, for instance, notes that Korah's mutiny does not occur at the time when Moses appoints the Levites or confers special responsibilities upon Aaron and his family for service in the sanctuary.

Rather, says Nachmanides, Korah organizes his protest when the spies return from the Land of Israel with their troubling and divided reports and after the people bitterly complain about the difficult conditions of life in the desert. "Korah," Nachmanides points out, "finds the opportune moment to pick his quarrel with Moses and his policy. He assumes that the people will side with him because of their frustration and discomfort."

According to Nachmanides, this emphasis on the psychological readiness of the people to attack Moses and Aaron also explains the defiant behavior and accusations of Dathan and Abiram. They not only refuse to meet with Moses for a discussion of their grievances, but they distort historical fact to inflame the people against him. Lies become stepping stones to personal advantage. Publicly Dathan and Abiram ask Moses, "Is it not enough that you brought us from a land flowing with milk and honey to have us die in the wilderness. . . ?"

Cleverly they distort the past. Suddenly Egypt, which is associated with oppression, slavery, and starvation, is glorified as "a land flowing with milk and honey." Because they take advantage of the confusion and fears of the people, perverting the truth and misleading them, Dathan and Abiram are punished. (Commentary on Numbers 16)

Two different views on "holiness"
Philosopher Martin Buber suggests that "both Moses and Korah desired the people to be . . . the holy people. But for Moses this was the goal. In order to reach it, generation after generation had to choose again and again . . . between the way of God and the wrong paths of their own hearts; between life and death. . . . For Korah, the people . . . were already holy . . . so why should there be further need for choice? Their dispute was between two approaches to faith and to life." (Moses: The Revelation and the Covenant, *Harper and Row Publishers, Inc., New York, 1958, pp. 189–190)*

Leibowitz

On the basis of the discussion in *Pirke Avot* 5:17, Nehama Leibowitz reaches still another conclusion about why Korah, Dathan, Abiram, and the company of 250 leaders are punished so severely for their rebellion. *Pirke Avot* states that there are two kinds of disputes: one that is pursued for a "heavenly" or good cause and one that is pursued for selfish reasons. As an example of the first, the rabbis cite the arguments between the great teachers Hillel and Shammai, which were always over matters of ethical or ritual principle. On the other hand, the chief example of "selfish" and unworthy controversy is that of Korah and his followers.

Leibowitz writes that Korah and his followers "were simply a band of malcontents, each harboring [individual] personal grievances against authority, animated by individual pride and ambition, united to overthrow Moses and Aaron, hoping thereby to attain their individual desires." Eventually, "they would quarrel among themselves, as each one strove to attain selfish ambitions. . . ." They deserve their punishment, argues Leibowitz, because all their motives were self-serving, meant to splinter and divide the Jewish people. (See *Studies in Bemidbar*, pp. 181–185.)

Rabbi M. Miller agrees with Leibowitz's views on Korah and the 250 leaders. However, citing a sixteenth-century commentary of Rabbi Judah Loew ben Bezalel, known as the Maharal from Prague, Miller maintains that Dathan and Abiram had no justifiable, legitimate grievances for joining Korah's rebellion. Rather, they "split the people out of sheer delight in mischief." They enjoyed "degrading the great, in denying value to any other human being. . . ." What drove them was "a love of evil for its own sake . . . the unadulterated joy of hearing the denigration of others." (*Sabbath Shiurim*, Feldheim, New York, 1979, pp. 245–252)

The importance of law
Rabbi Shlomo Riskin suggests that "the conflict between Moses and Korah reflects a tug of war within the human spirit. . . . Korah denies the importance of the laws. He says, 'Who needs this system of do's and don'ts, you shalls and you shall nots? We're holy already.' Certainly this perspective was attractive to every Israelite who wanted to be left alone. Who wants to be told what to do and what not to do? If I want to commit adultery, who are you to tell me I shouldn't?" (Jerusalem Post, *July 1, 1989)*

One other interpretation of Korah's rebellion and God's destruction of all its participants ought to be considered. Korah, Dathan, Abiram, and the other leaders make the claim that "all the people are holy." In doing so, they call into question the authority of Moses and Aaron to make communal decisions. While they advocate the holiness of each person, they do not take the next step. They do not call for a vote of each person or anything resembling democracy. Their dispute is over *who* will lead and who will make decisions for the community and is meant to put those powers into their hands.

Their mutiny raises a significant tension that is both political and religious. When Korah attacks Moses and Aaron with the claim "all the people are holy" and with the question "Why do you raise yourselves above God's congregation?" he is focusing on the common confusion between individual freedom and the limits to individual freedom that living in society imposes. As an individual, I would like to be free to walk anywhere I wish; as a member of society, I must restrict my wanderings at the fence of my neighbor's property. But living within a community demands that I must often sacrifice personal liberty, comforts, pleasures, and possessions for the well-being of others.

This dispute between Korah, Dathan, Abiram, and the 250 leaders on one side and Moses and Aaron on the other is about who will decide what is right for the community and who will define the accepted law and practice of society. Will it be left to the designated interpreters of Torah (Moses and Aaron) or to the whim of rabble-rousers (Korah and his followers)? Will it be a community ruled by the loudest voice with the most might or by the laws of Torah, publicly open to all?

It seems apparent from the punishment of Korah and all the followers of his rebellion that the Torah tradition promotes a rule of law even when it curbs the absolute freedom of the individual to pursue self-interest. Korah's rebellion is condemned, not only because it was self-serving, but also because it perpetuated a false and dangerous notion that society can exist without any limitations on individual liberty. For society to function, the rights of individuals must be limited, and leaders must be given special powers and responsibilities within the context of law.

Rav Huna, a leader of Babylonian Jewry for forty years during the third century, underscores this bias when he comments that, if one listens to the earth at the place where Korah and his followers were swallowed, one hears them saying over and over again, "Moses and his Torah represent the truth. We are liars." Individual rights are guaranteed and protected by law. They crumble when society lapses into a tyranny of individuals claiming, as Korah did, "I am holy, so I have the right to do whatever I wish." (See *Baba Batra* 74a.)

Jewish commentators are critical of Korah, Dathan, Abiram, and their followers. All agree that their rebellion grew out of evil, self-centered motives and that they deserved the punishment they received. For modern readers, the ancient tale and its interpretations remain a valuable source of lessons about the differences between a just and an unjust dispute and about the definition of a just and free society.

PEREK BET: *Magic and Miracles in Jewish Tradition*

After Korah, Dathan, Abiram, and their followers publicly question and criticize the leadership of Moses and Aaron, Moses challenges them to bring pans of fire and incense to the sanctuary. Moses commands the people to separate themselves from the rebels. He declares that God will make known who has the authority to lead the people. "By what happens in the morning," Moses says, "you will know that it was *Adonai* who sent me to do all these things."

The next morning the people assemble. According to the Torah, they watch as the earth miraculously opens, swallowing Korah, Dathan, Abiram, and their families, households, and possessions. All is lost inside the smoldering earth. Soon a fire blazes forth killing all 250 of Korah's followers. The entire community witnesses this gruesome scene.

Later in our *parashah*, Moses commands each of the twelve tribal chieftains to bring a staff for deposit in the sanctuary. The next day he discovers that Aaron's staff has miraculously sprouted, producing blossoms and almonds! Despite the wonder, however, the people of Israel continue to complain about their conditions.

Miraculous events are reported in many different places within the Torah. Ten plagues are sent to punish the stubborn Pharaoh. The Red Sea aparts before the fleeing Israelites and drowns the pursuing Egyptians. Manna is sent to feed the wandering Israelites on their journey through the desert. Water flows from a rock when Moses strikes it. In *Parashat Balak* a donkey speaks to her master.

How are we to understand such incidents that defy the known laws of nature? Are Jews expected to accept such wonders on faith? If one rejects as "impossible" or questions the reliability of such miracles, are the authority of Torah and its meaning diminished? If the Torah contains miracle stories like the earth opening and swallowing up Korah, Dathan, and Abiram, can we conclude that it is more a work of fiction than of profound religious truth?

It should not surprise us that Torah interpreters have struggled with such questions for many centuries. Early rabbinic commentators accept the descriptions of miracles within the Torah as a matter of faith. They take for granted that, if the Torah reports them and they were witnessed by others, such incidents are credible.

Yet, how can events like manna falling from heaven, an animal speaking, a sea opening, the earth swallowing Dathan and Abiram possibly be *rationalized* within the scheme of the laws of nature? How can one account for such miracles?

Facing that question, early Jewish interpreters suggest that such miracles were planned by God at the very creation of the heavens and earth. These events described in the Torah are not interruptions of natural law. Rather, they are *programmed* into creation to occur at precisely the historic moment when they are necessary. We can understand miracles, therefore, as pre-programmed "natural" events. (*Avot* 5:6)

However, the rabbinic acceptance of this theory about miracles is combined with blunt skepticism. "Miracles cannot be cited as proof for any argument," say the rabbis. "In danger, one must not rely on a miracle." Similarly, Yannai warns that one should "never depend on a miracle." Nachman ben Jacob teaches, "Miracles occur, but food is rarely provided by them." (*Yevamot* 121b; *Kiddushin* 39b; *Shabbat* 32a,52b)

Rambam (Maimonides)

Philosopher and commentator Moses Maimonides actually bases his proof of God's governing power over all nature on the reality of miracles. Taking the Torah as a reliable source of information about the world, Maimonides argues: "We might be asked, 'Why has God inspired a certain person and not another?' 'Why has God revealed Torah to one people and not another?' 'Why has God's power been revealed through one prophet and not another?' We answer all such questions," explains Maimonides, "by saying: 'That is God's will. That is God's wisdom . . . and we do not understand why God's will or wisdom determined any of these things.'" In essence, Maimonides contends that, while the miracles reported in Torah raise questions, they also demonstrate God's mysterious and wonderful power over all nature. (*Guide for the Perplexed,* pp. 199–200)

Nachmanides suggests that great miracles like the parting of the Red Sea teach human beings to appreciate "the hidden miracles" around them. He explains that "everything that happens in our affairs, private or public, is miraculous." Life itself is a wonder-filled gift! (See comments on *Balak.*)

Seventeenth-century Jewish philosopher and interpreter Baruch Spinoza offers a very different view on biblical miracles. Believing that nothing can violate the laws of nature, Spinoza rejects miracles as ignorant "prejudices of an ancient people," who believe that God intervenes in nature for their benefit. This accounts for the way in which stories like the punishment of Korah, Dathan, and Abiram are presented. They are distorted, says Spinoza, by the innocent but false assumptions and opinions of events that the early Hebrews could not understand or explain. (*Theological-Political Treatise,* R.H. Elwes, translator, Dover Publications, New York, 1955, pp. 82–93)

Spinoza's rejection of miracles is disputed by

modern philosopher and commentator Martin Buber. He writes that "the concept of miracle" described within the Torah "can be defined at its starting point as an abiding astonishment." Such "astonishment" is a natural occurrence. Furthermore, says Buber, "the great turning points in religious history are based on the fact that again and ever again an individual and a group attached to [that individual] wonder and keep on wondering at a natural—or historical event—at something that intervenes fatefully in the life of this individual and this group." The point of "astonishment" comes in the realization that one grasps the "cause" of the miraculous event and is permitted "a glimpse of the sphere in which a sole power, not restricted by any other, is at work."

Placed in the context of our Torah portion, the earth opening up to swallow Korah, Dathan, and Abiram is an astonishing miracle in which one sees the "power" of God "at work." Experiencing the miracle, one knows the certainty of God's existence and "power." The miracle is a window into God's presence. (See *Moses*, pp. 74–78.)

Belief in miracles

Every miracle can be explained—after the event. . . . Every miracle is possible, even the most absurd, even that an ax floats. . . . In fact nothing is miraculous about a miracle except that it comes when it does. The east wind has probably swept bare the ford in the Red Sea hundreds of times and will do so again. . . . But that it did this at a moment when the people in their distress set foot in the sea—that is the miracle. (Franz Rosenzweig, The Star of Redemption, *William H. Hallo, translator, Beacon Press, Boston, 1972, pp. 93–94)*

Rabbi Mordecai M. Kaplan, the philosopher who inspired the creation of the twentieth-century American movement of Reconstructionist Judaism, disagrees with Buber and also rejects most traditional explanations of biblical miracles. "In our day, when humanity has achieved marvels of control over nature by a technology that assumes the uniformities of natural law, belief in miracles that contravene natural law is a psychological impossibility for most people." Kaplan dismisses the arguments of those who point out that the miracles of the Torah did not occur privately but were witnessed by many people. Today's science challenges "the credibility of miracles," he writes, repudiating them as factually inaccurate. (*Questions Jews Ask: Reconstructionist Answers,* Reconstructionist Press, New York, 1956, pp. 155–156)

Peli

Pinchas Peli does not argue for the "credibility of miracles" but maintains that each one mentioned within the Torah contains an important lesson. "Korah's spectacular downfall," for example, "was to serve as a warning. It was meant to call our attention to the differences between authentic, responsible leadership and illusory, appealing rhetoric." The report of the miraculous process of growth of the blossoms and almonds on Aaron's staff is meant "to teach us that true leadership is not necessarily demonstrated by the ability to produce immediate results . . . with instant cures to all problems. Even the leader chosen by God in a miraculous act cannot skip the several stages in the growth of an almond. The orderly sequence must be followed. First sprouts, then blossoms, and only then the finished product." ("Torah Today" in the *Jerusalem Post,* June 29, 1985)

It is apparent that Jewish interpreters approach the subject of miracles from varying points of view. Some are skeptical; others find profound symbolic and spiritual meanings; still others dismiss miracles as figments of primitive imagination, unworthy of contemporary consideration. "Miracles," Nehama Leibowitz comments, "cannot change human minds and hearts. They can always be explained away." (*Studies in Bemidbar,* p. 231)

There can be no doubt, however, that the Torah's miracle stories are intriguing. The mystery they embody seems to attract our attention and underscore their importance. We read them with fascination, wondering about their meaning and sensing that they contain secrets we should try to fathom. It is, after all, nearly always the extraordinary, not the ordinary, that captures our attention, challenging us to unravel its hidden, illusive code and message. Could this explain the miracles mentioned in the Torah? Are they meant as powerful invitations—bait for tempting, bending, and stretching the human mind, imagination, and heart—into new realms of reasoning and faith?

QUESTIONS FOR STUDY AND DISCUSSION

1. Is there a difference between the rebellion of Korah and that of Dathan and Abiram? Are there modern parallels to their protests? What did they do, according to our interpreters, to justify such serious punishment?

2. Korah claims that Moses and Aaron are acting as if they were more "holy" than others among the Israelites. How do the various interpreters explain this accusation? What do individuals and societies learn today from their points of view?

3. David Ben-Gurion, the first prime minister of Israel, once said: "In Israel, to be a realist, you must believe in miracles." What did he mean? How does such an observation apply to some of the stories about miracles in the Torah?

PARASHAT CHUKAT
Numbers 19:1–22:1

Parashat Chukat begins by describing the ritual slaughter and sacrifice of the *parah adumah,* or "red cow," by Eleazar the priest, and the ritual cleansing for those who touch a corpse. Miriam, the sister of Moses and Aaron, dies at Kadesh. Again the people complain that they have no water to drink. God tells Moses to take his rod and order a rock to bring forth water. Angry at the complaining people, whom he calls "rebels," Moses strikes the rock with his rod. Water pours out. The people drink and water their animals. God informs Moses that because of his anger he will not be allowed to lead his people into the Land of Israel. Moses asks the king of Edom for permission to pass through his land. The king refuses, and the Israelites take another route. When they reach Hor, Aaron dies, and his priestly authority is passed on to his son, Eleazar. The people mourn Aaron for thirty days. Afterwards they are attacked by the Canaanites, whom they conquer with God's help. However, the people continue to complain to Moses: "Why did you make us leave Egypt to die in the wilderness?" God sends snakes among the people to bite them for their disloyalty. Moses begs forgiveness for them when they admit their wrongdoing. God tells Moses to place a *seraph* figure—a snake made of copper—on his staff. When the people see it, they will be healed. The Israelites are later attacked by the Amorites and the people of Bashan and Og. In each battle the Israelites emerge victorious, conquering towns and acquiring large territories.

OUR TARGUM

·1·

Moses and Aaron are told that the ritual for preparing and cleansing water to remove the sins of the people is to begin with the slaughter and sacrifice of a *parah adumah,* or "red cow." The animal must have no defect and must never have worn a yoke. After its slaughter, Eleazar the priest is to sprinkle its blood seven times in front of the sanctuary and then burn all its flesh. Ashes from the red cow are to be kept and added to water used to purify the Israelites.

·2·

Those who touch a corpse are unclean for seven days. On the third and seventh day they may purify themselves with the water from the ritual of the red cow.

·3·

After the Israelites arrive at Kadesh in the wilderness of Zin, Miriam, the sister of Moses and Aaron, dies and is buried there.

·4·

The community is without water and complains to Moses and Aaron asking, "Why did you make us leave Egypt to bring us here to die in this desolate desert?" Angry at the people's ingratitude, Moses and Aaron pray to God, who tells them to gather the people together before a rock from which water will flow. When the people, whom Moses calls "rebels," gather in front of the rock, Moses takes his rod and strikes the rock. Water pours out. There is enough to satisfy not only the people but their flocks as well. However, Moses and Aaron are told that because of their anger they will not be allowed to enter the Land of Israel. The place of this incident is named Meribah, which means "quarrel."

· 5 ·

Seeking friendship, Moses sends messengers to the king of Edom to ask permission for the Israelites to pass through his land on their way to the Land of Israel. He promises the king that the Israelites will not take food or drink as they cross his territory. The king refuses, threatening to launch a war against the Israelites if they enter his land.

· 6 ·

Moses is told by God to bring Aaron and his son, Eleazar, to the top of Mount Hor. There Moses removes and gives Aaron's priestly garments to Eleazar. Aaron dies on the mountain, and the Israelites mourn for thirty days.

· 7 ·

Moving through the Negev, the Israelites are attacked by the Canaanites. With God's help, the Israelites defeat their enemies.

· 8 ·

Near the Sea of Reeds the people complain again to Moses about their lack of bread and water. They question his taking them out of Egypt. God punishes their rebellious behavior by sending snakes to bite and kill them. Realizing what they have done, they plead for Moses to intervene. God tells Moses to fashion a *seraph*—a copper snake—and place it on his staff. When the people see the staff, they are healed.

· 9 ·

The Israelites, attacked by the Amorites and the people of Basham and Og, are victorious, conquering towns and acquiring large territories.

THEMES

Parashat Chukat contains two important themes:

1. The mystery and meaning of rituals.
2. The reason Moses and Aaron are not allowed to enter the Land of Israel.

PEREK ALEF: *The Parah Adumah: What Is the Meaning of This Strange Ritual?*

The ceremony of the *parah adumah,* or "red cow," must have been an intriguing and important ritual to the early Israelites. According to the Torah, and later reports in the Talmud, the priests are to search for a cow with a perfect red coat—a perfect cow that has never worn a yoke or been used for work. Upon finding such a cow, the priest slaughters it outside the sanctuary, sprinkles some of its blood seven times in the direction of the sanctuary, and then builds a fire. He throws the cow's remains into the fire along with a piece of cedar wood and hyssop tied together with a red string. After the cow has completely burned, its ashes are divided into three parts: one for use in purifying those who

have touched a corpse; one to be kept outside the sanctuary for safekeeping; and one for use in the future to be mixed with the ashes of another red cow. Some reports indicate that, from the time of Moses until the Temple is destroyed by the Romans in 70 C.E., only nine such red cows were used for this special ceremony.

And how did the purification ceremony using the ashes of the red cow work?

A ritually pure person would mix together a jar of fresh spring water with some ashes from the red cow. The water would then be sprinkled on a ritually impure person during the third or seventh day of impurity. At the setting of the sun on the seventh day, the person would become pure again. (*Yoma* 2a, 14a, 42b–43b; *Sotah* 46a; *Niddah* 9a; *Nazir* 61b; *Megillah* 20a; *Kiddushin* 25a, 31a, 62a; see also Abraham Chill, *The Mitzvot: The Commandments and Their Ra-*

tionale, Bloch Publishing Co., New York, 1974, pp. 348–349)

This strange ceremony has puzzled many interpreters. Why, they have asked, do the ashes of a red cow contain the power to purify those who touch a corpse? Why is this ceremony so important? What is its meaning and power?

Apparently, non-Jews also were baffled by this ceremony of the red cow. The famed Rabbi Yochanan ben Zakkai, head of the Sanhedrin at the time of the destruction of the Temple, was once asked by a non-Jew to explain the ritual. "Do you really believe that some ashes from a red cow purify a person who has touched a corpse? Are you not practicing magic?" he challenged.

Rabbi Yochanan answered the man by comparing the ritual of the red cow to the commonly practiced ritual among non-Jews for curing an insane person. "Don't you expose the mad person to the smoke of roots and sprinkle water upon him in order to cure him? Are not both ceremonies similar?" asked the rabbi.

Later, Rabbi Yochanan's students, who had overheard the conversation, said to him, "Appealing to common sense, you provided the non-Jew with a simple answer. Now share with us the real meaning of the ritual of the red cow."

Rabbi Yochanan responded by telling them that there is no explanation. The ritual is commanded by God. It is set out within the Torah law. That is what justifies its observance, not some rational interpretation. (*Pesikta de-Rav Kahana* 4:7)

Rabbi Isaac, possibly a student of Rabbi Yochanan, agrees, claiming that even wise King Solomon could not fathom the reasons for the ritual of the red cow. This view is shared by Rabbi Joshua of Siknin, who explains that the ritual of the red cow is one of four "laws of Torah" for which there is no rational explanation. (*Yalkut Shimoni* 759; *Numbers Rabbah* 19:5)

Ramban (Nachmanides)

In contrast, Nachmanides criticizes those who are satisfied with saying "there is no explanation

of this ritual" and offers an explanation of his own. Pointing out that most human beings, like Adam, make mistakes and are sinful, Nachmanides holds that their corpses are impure, and those who touch them become impure. In order to remove this impurity, water mixed with the ashes of the red cow must be sprinkled upon them. The ritual purifies them by removing from them the association with sin. (Commentary on Numbers 19:2)

Rabbi Joseph Becor Shor provides another interpretation for the ritual of the *parah adumah.* He explains that the ritual is meant to prevent Jews from sinning by contact with corpses. It is a natural tendency to cling to loved ones who have died and, occasionally, to want to caress and embrace their dead bodies, if only for a final time. Shor holds that, to warn Jews against this tendency or against the practice in some societies of worshiping the dead or wearing garments made from their skin or bones, the Torah declares contact with a dead body defiling.

Leibowitz

A sprinkling by waters mixed with ashes from the red cow is the only rite for purification from such sin. The ritual possesses both educational and purifying powers. It not only purifies from sin, but it also functions as a dramatic reminder that Jews are forbidden to touch or venerate the bodies of their dead. (See Nehama Leibowitz, *Studies in Bemidbar,* pp. 233–235.)

Purifying polluted water
Analyzing the ritual of the red cow, research chemist Dr. Robert Kunin writes that "our biblical ancestors were well aware of water pollution and were also aware of technology capable of treating such polluted water. . . . A chemist analyzing this ritual carefully soon realizes that the mixture of ashes is a mixture of granular and powdered activated carbon and bone char—a mixture of virgin carbonaceous adsorbents capable of removing practically all known toxins, viruses, and pollutants, in-

cluding radioactivity. It should be noted that the components of the ash and the basic method of treating water as described in Numbers is essentially the only method currently approved by the United States government. ("The Mystery of the Red Heifer," Dor le Dor, *Spring 1985, pp. 267–269)*

Obadiah Sforno offers a symbolic explanation. He points out that the priest takes cedar wood, identified with pride because the cedar tree stands tall, and hyssop, identified with humility because it is a fragrant low-growing plant, along with a red scarlet thread, identified with sinfulness, and throws all three into the fire consuming the red cow. The ashes, which combine *pride, humility,* and *sinfulness,* are then mixed with water for the purification ritual.

For Sforno, the power associated with the red cow ritual pulls the sinner back from the evil of pride toward the ideal of humility. The mixture of ashes and water provides a method for repentance. Specifically, if arrogance pushes one to neglect the laws of Torah by touching a corpse, that one then requires purification. The ritual for this purpose is composed of symbolic messages. By being sprinkled with the mixture of ashes from the red cow, cedar wood, hyssop, and a scarlet thread, the sinner who has allowed pride to rule is purified and reminded to pursue humility and more moderate paths of behavior. (Commentary on Numbers 19:1–10)

Hirsch

Rabbi Samson Raphael Hirsch also maintains that the meaning of the ritual of the *parah adumah* is symbolic. Yet his interpretation differs significantly from that of Sforno. For Hirsch, the ritual represents "the proclamation of the public conviction of the possibility of freedom from sin,

the ability of mastering all physical temptations and allurements, proclaiming the fact of the moral power of the human will. . . ." In other words, human beings can correct their wrongdoing; there is a way out of the harm and hurt they do.

How does Hirsch reach such a conclusion?

He begins by pointing out that the red cow exemplifies the "animal nature" of human beings—all of the unmastered, uncontrolled powers each person possesses. Such powers, Hirsch argues, are expressed in behavior that is self-destructive and often abusive of others. For example, driven by uncontrolled anger, a person will lash out at loved ones, hurting them and damaging future relationships.

In slaughtering a red cow that has never worn a yoke, symbolizing our unrestrained powers, Hirsch explains, we achieve "full mastery over the animal." Uncontrolled inclinations and ambitions are put to the service of free will. In offering the red cow that has never worn a yoke outside the sanctuary, the ancient Israelites celebrate taking control of their "animal side" and freely choosing to direct the expression of its powers. They demonstrate that they are free to shape the moral decisions that affect their lives and society.

Yet, continues Hirsch, free-choosing human beings are subject to the same physical laws of disintegration and death as "the rest of the physical-organic world." Human beings are born and die. They "touch" death constantly, and doing so makes them impure. Hirsch states that it contaminates them and sets limitations on them—the limitations of the human animal.

The ritual of the *parah adumah* enables human beings to overcome such contamination and go beyond the boundaries of life and death. That is its meaning and power. Hirsch maintains that mixing the "ash" of the slaughtered red cow, which symbolizes the triumph over the animal within us, with the "living water" demonstrates that each human being is endowed with a "never dying immortal spiritual being. . . ." By controlling and guiding human powers for creativity, justice, and love, the human being defies death and achieves immortality. The ceremony of the red heifer celebrates our power to live beyond the mysterious doors of death. (Commentary on Numbers 19:1–10)

No person, however sinful, is lost
I believe that this ritual of the red heifer,
strange though it may seem, preserving within
it seemingly primitive elements, dramatizes ef-
fectively and vividly how the Jew and Judaism
look upon human beings. Here is an instru-
ment for cleansing the impure, for no person is
hopeless . . . there is no person who has fallen
so low, who has so completely expelled from
[within] the image of God. . . . No person,
therefore, has to stagger through life crushed
and oppressed by the burden of guilt, to be
perpetually and eternally doomed by one error
or by a series of mistakes. There is an opportu-
nity through religious belief to start anew.
(Morris Adler, The Voice Still Speaks, *p. 333)*

In contrast to Hirsch's inventive symbolic interpretation of the ritual of the *parah adumah,*
modern biblical scholar Jacob Milgrom maintains
that this ancient ritual is meant to purge the
individual and sanctuary of wrongdoing. It is a
ceremony of ethical cleansing.

Ancient Jews, explains Milgrom, believed that
acts of immorality affected more than just those
involved in them. There are consequences of
wrongdoing that infect and pollute the entire
community. Milgrom describes three categories
of such sins: individual wrongdoings committed
inadvertently, communal sins committed inadvertently, and deliberate wrongdoings committed with design. In all cases, these sins have a
contaminating effect, not only upon the guilty
individuals, but also upon the community and
sanctuary. Asking forgiveness through sacrifices
and prayers, even repairing the wrong through
apology or restitution, is not enough to purify
what is soiled by wrongdoing.

For the ancients, says Milgrom, the ritual of
the *parah adumah* alone has the power to remove
or exorcise such sinfulness. "By daubing the altar
with blood or by bringing it inside the sanctuary,
the priest purges the most sacred objects and
areas of the sanctuary on behalf of the person
who caused their contamination by physical impurity or inadvertent offense." In other words,
the person and the community corrupted by
wrongdoing are restored to a state of purity and

can then go on without the burden of guilt.
(Jacob Milgrom, editor, *JPS Torah Commentary:
Numbers,* Jewish Publication Society, Philadel-
phia, 1989, pp. 438–447)

As we have seen, Torah interpreters do not
agree on the meaning of the *parah adumah* ritual.
The significance of the selection and sacrifice of
a pure red cow that has never worn a yoke and
the unique mixture of ashes, combining cedar
wood, hyssop, and the red thread with water,
remains a mystery. Contemporary scholar David
I. Kertzer seeks a solution by pointing out that
purification rituals often "separate members from
the rest of the world." They make them feel
unique by unifying them "as a solidarity unit."
(*Ritual, Politics, and Power,* Yale University Press,
New Haven, 1988, pp. 17–18)

Does the ritual of the red cow signify communal bonding, like induction ceremonies where
one drinks or eats special foods or circumcision
as a sign of the covenant? Such rituals can provide participants with a unique identity, distinguishing them from "the rest of the world."

Clearly, the ritual of the red cow functions as
a means of reentry into the sacred community
for one who has broken the taboo of touching a
corpse. Separation from the community and the
sanctuary is a serious matter. Wrongdoers, those
who break the law or transgress appropriate practices of the group, feel banished; they require a
way back into the comfort of community solidarity. A ritual like the *parah adumah* guarantees
their return, their acceptance back into full-group
membership and participation.

The original meanings of each element of the
parah adumah ceremony elude understanding.
One matter, however, is clear: All interpreters
agree that the ritual sprinkling of the mixture of
ash and water removes the sinner's contamination and allows reentry into the sanctuary of the
people. In this way, this ceremony, like ritual
circumcision and the laws of *kashrut,* preserves
the "solidarity" and "sanctity" of the Jewish people. The ritual serves Jewish survival.

PEREK BET: *Decoding the Sin and Punishment of Moses and Aaron*

As the mysterious ritual of the *parah adumah*
challenges commentators, so, too, does the harsh

punishment of Moses and Aaron described in this *parashah*.

The people arrive at Kadesh in the wilderness of Zin. Miriam, the sister of Aaron and Moses, dies and is buried there. Again the people "join against" Moses and Aaron, blaming the two brothers for bringing them to die in the desert. "Why did you make us leave Egypt to bring us to this wretched place? . . . There is not even water to drink!"

Moses and Aaron turn to God and are instructed: "You and your brother Aaron take the rod and assemble the community, and before their very eyes order the rock to yield its water. Thus you shall produce water for them from the rock and provide drink for the congregation and their beasts."

The two leaders assemble the people in front of the rock, and Moses speaks to them: "Listen, you rebels, shall we get water for you out of this rock?" Then he raises his hand and strikes the rock twice with the rod. Water flows out for the entire community. The people drink and water their animals.

God, however, is not finished with Moses and Aaron. They are told: "Because you did not trust Me enough to affirm My sanctity in the sight of the Israelite people, therefore, you shall not lead this congregation into the land that I have given them." God gives the complaining Israelites water while publicly humiliating Moses and Aaron.

What have they done to deserve such severe punishment? How can these two devoted leaders of their people for nearly forty years now be sentenced to die in the desert, without ever seeing the Promised Land? And, if Moses, who held the staff and spoke to the Israelites, did something wrong, why is Aaron also punished?

These questions bother Jewish interpreters. How can a God of justice inflict such a sentence upon loyal leaders?

Some commentators are sympathetic to Moses. Early rabbinic interpreters see some justification for Moses' actions. Not only do the people rally against Moses, they also taunt him as he stands before the rock. "You claim to be a miracle worker," they tell him. "We know your tricks. You are standing before a rock that you have prepared for a magic display of your powers. If you want to prove yourself, move to that rock

over there, to the one chosen by us, not by you!" Furious at their insults, Moses loses his temper. He calls them *hamorim,* which means "rebels," or "fools." He strikes the rock, but only a trickle of water comes forth. The people laugh at him. Making fun of him, they say, "Moses, is this all you can do? Is this your big miracle? This is not even enough water for a few babies, and we need enough for thousands." Embarrassment and anger swell within him. He pauses, then he strikes the rock again, producing a powerful gush of water.

These rabbinic interpreters reconstruct the situation: The people exasperate Moses. Embarrassed and ashamed, he loses patience. He becomes justifiably angry. However, the Israelites are also at fault, not just Moses. His punishment is only partially warranted. This also seems to be the conclusion of the Psalmist who, reflecting on this incident, writes: "They [the people of Israel] provoked anger at the waters of Meribah/and Moses suffered on their account,/because they rebelled against God/and he spoke rashly." (*Numbers Rabbah* 19:9; also Psalms 106:32–33)

Other early rabbinic commentators disagree with this explanation. They point out that both Moses and Aaron are guilty of arrogance. Their instruction is to *speak* to the rock, not *strike* it. Instead, Moses publicly strikes it not once, *but twice!* In doing so, Moses implies a lack of faith in God to bring forth water. For this reason he is told, "Because you did not trust Me enough to affirm My sanctity in the sight of the Israelite people, therefore, you shall not lead this congregation into the land that I have given them." (*Numbers Rabbah* 19:10)

Rambam (Maimonides)

Moses Maimonides claims that God punishes Moses because of his exasperation with the complaints and quarreling of the Israelites. Extreme anger is his downfall; intelligence and impatience condemn him. Instead of remaining even-tempered, Moses flies into a rage. He insults the people by calling them "rebels." In doing so, he fails as a leader and as a model for their own behavior. Maimonides argues that Moses should have exercised moderation by being more understanding of the Israelites' frustrations and more accepting of their criticism, including their baseless accusations. Instead, he allows anger to control him, insults the people, flies into a rage, calls them names, and forcefully shatters the rock. Such an extreme response, says Maimonides, deserves punishment. (*Shemonah Perakim* 4)

The sin was raising the rod
Rabbi Samson Raphael Hirsch explains that the sin of Moses grew out of his deep disappointment with the people. He is stunned that after forty years he still must carry his staff to prove his credibility. For that reason he speaks "in words of deep reproach . . . and in passionate agitation struck the rock." It was, Hirsch insists, "the impulsive vehement raising of the rod . . . in which the wrong consisted." (See commentary on Numbers 20:10–12 in The Pentateuch, *L. Honig and Sons Ltd., London, 1959, pp. 368–370.)*

On anger
Anger kills the foolish person. (Job 5:2)

Loss of temper leads to hell. (Jonathan ben Eleazar in Nedarim *22a)*

Anger deprives a wise person of wisdom, and a prophet of vision. (Simeon ben Lakish in Pesachim *66b)*

Anger begins in madness and ends in regret. (Abraham Hasdai, Ben ha-Melek ve-ha-Nazir *30: 1230)*

Peli

Aaron does nothing
Pinchas Peli writes that Aaron is condemned because he watches silently while his brother flares out of control. He does nothing to pacify him, nor does he speak out to defend the Israelites. "Aaron could have pointed out to Moses

---

his error and requested him to stop. . . . Through not protesting, he became an accomplice and was penalized accordingly. (Torah Today, pp. 177–179)

Nachmanides takes issue with Maimonides' explanation. Accusing Maimonides of adding "nonsense to nonsense," Nachmanides points out that nowhere in the Torah text does it say that either Moses or Aaron is angry with the people. Quite the opposite, says Nachmanides. It is the people who are angry. Over and over again they complain about their situation, demonstrating a lack of faith in God.

As for Moses and Aaron, Nachmanides maintains that their sin lies in misleading the Israelites. They speak carelessly to the people. Gathering them before the rock, they declare, "Listen, you rebels, shall *we* get water for you out of this rock?" rather than "shall *God* get water for you out of this rock?" Their words imply that it is their power, not God's, that will cause water to gush forth.

This deliberate deception of the people, argues Nachmanides, is the serious wrongdoing of Moses and Aaron. They seduce the people, and perhaps themselves, into thinking that the water pours from the rock at their command or by their skill. Nachmanides concludes that Moses and Aaron deserve criticism and condemnation for two reasons: They take matters into their own hands, giving the impression that they have little confidence in God, and, by calling attention to themselves, they fail to "sanctify" God's power before the people. For these reasons they are not permitted to lead the people into the Promised Land. (Commentary on Numbers 20:1–13)

Rabbi Levi Isaac of Berdichev, a famed chasidic teacher of the seventeenth century, extends Nachmanides' assessment. Always supportive of the people of Israel, he maintains that the two leaders are punished for *how* they express their criticism.

Levi Isaac explains: "There are two types of criticism. One makes use of kind, understanding words, uplifting others by reminding them that they are created in God's image and that their good deeds bring God much pleasure. . . . When criticism is then given, it does not tear a person down but strengthens the will of the person to accept and fulfill the commandments of Torah." The second kind of criticism, says Levi Isaac, "is harsh. It demeans people, makes them feel bad about themselves, and means to shame them into fulfilling the commandments of Torah."

Moses and Aaron are punished because as leaders of their people they criticize with needlessly harsh words. They shame them by calling them *hamorim,* or "rebels." Instead of building up their pride, reminding them that they are made in the image of God, they rebuke them with a nasty slur and insult. Their lack of understanding and support for their people brings about their punishment. (See David Blumenthal, *God at the Center,* Harper and Row, San Francisco, 1987, pp. 118–119.)

Lack of humility leads to violence
In all the sins of Moses, whether we consider the murder of the Egyptian, the breaking of the commandments, or the striking of the rock, there are the common elements of anger and violence, of unbridled self-will, and of temporarily ignoring God. The sin of Moses at Meribah is thus characteristic of the man, one of a series, and serious. Why serious? Serious because civilization depends on humility. Without a sense of limits that flows from the awareness of a moral law and an ethical God, every brutality, every corruption, every atrocity becomes possible. (Rabbi Norman D. Hirsch, "The Sin of Moses," CCAR Journal, *October 1965)*

Modern commentator Aaron Wildavsky sees Moses' failure differently. "At Meribah," he writes, "Moses substitutes force for faith. In his hands, the rod reduces a divinely ordered act to a trickster's shenanigans. But the import runs deeper. If Moses' strongest leadership quality has been his ability to identify with the people, then the lack of faith at Meribah is a double one. Moses not only distances himself from God by doubting the adequacy of God's work but also distances himself from the people by assuming power that was God's."

It is ironic, says Wildavsky, that Moses, who

in this instant "rebels" against God's command, calls the people "rebels." In fact, "Moses was guilty of the worst form of idolatry—self-worship." When he says to the people, "Listen, you rebels, shall *we* get water for you out of this rock?" and then strikes the rock, he leaves the impression that he, not God, is responsible for the miracle of producing water. In doing so, Moses rebels against God. He assumes the role of God by suggesting through his behavior that the power to perform miracles is in his hands and in the rod. "Spiritually," concludes Wildavsky, "he has gone back to slavery, as if to replace Pharaoh." It is, then, for the sin of *idolatry*—self-worship—that Moses is punished. (*Moses as a Political Leader,* pp. 155–158)

As we have seen, there are a number of views about why Moses and Aaron deserve the punishment they receive. The Torah text seems to leave the matter unclear. For that reason commentators from every age have sought to solve the riddle. In all their explanations, however, they may have missed an obvious clue. Modern interpreter Rabbi Morris Adler suggests that the Torah text is deliberately vague because it means "to teach us by indirection, as it so often does, the great truth that the sins of leaders are not necessarily overt, blatant, obvious; that the important failings of great leaders could be subtle yet deep, unclear yet destructive."

Adler's thesis is a significant one. Few leaders, he points out, are corrupt criminals. Instead, they fall prey to "more invisible temptation." They seek the approval of the people by bending the truth, by blurring principle, by compromising their independent decision-making for financial support. They make judgments not on the basis of what is true but on how it will be received. Placing themselves on pedestals, they ask, "What are the newspapers saying about me?" and not "What is the right policy to support?"

"So," says Adler, "the Torah does not spell out the sins of the leader . . . but is purposely vague and uncertain. Maybe there was a moment of pride . . . of anger . . . a careless word. . . . Maybe he failed to apply the wisdom of his mind to today and was satisfied with repetitions of insight taken from remote yesterdays."

Perhaps the message of this Torah portion is

that, just as we are unclear about what sin brought about the punishment of Moses and Aaron, so it is with most leaders—most people. It is not the gross and obvious sins that spell defeat but rather "the subtle and intangible and impalpable corrosions" that prevent them from entering the Promised Land. (*The Voice Still Speaks,* pp. 341–345)

QUESTIONS FOR STUDY AND DISCUSSION

1. Some commentators argue that ritual and religion are matters of faith and should not be subject to reason. "Some matters," they say, "must be accepted on blind faith." How does such an argument relate to the ritual of the *parah adumah*? How does this argument relate to other Jewish rituals? Is a certain amount of "blind faith" justifiable or dangerous? Is "blind faith" necessary for religion (and science) to flourish?

2. Several interpreters suggest symbolic meanings for the ritual of the red cow. Which makes the most sense? Which carries the most meaning? How do other rituals like circumcision, the Pesach seder, going to the *mikveh,* and wearing a *talit* convey powerful messages for modern Jews?

3. Biblical interpreter Samuel David Luzzatto observes that "Moses committed one sin, but the commentators charge him with thirteen and more . . . everyone invents a new offense for him." Which of the many "sins" suggested by the commentators make the most sense? Why?

4. Rabbi Shlomo Riskin writes: "That Moses could not enter the Holy Land was not so much a result of his own failure as it was a result of the nation's shortcomings." How would you assess the pressure of the Israelites on Moses? Is Riskin correct in his assessment, or was Moses solely to blame for his wrongdoing? Would you blame society or the environment for the failings of individuals?

PARASHAT BALAK
Numbers 22:2–25:9

Parashat Balak takes its title from Balak son of Zippor, king of Moab. Afraid that the Israelites will attack his nation, Balak sends messengers to invite Bala'am ben Beor, a well-known pagan prophet, to come and curse the people of Israel. At first, God forbids Bala'am to grant Balak's request. Then the seer is sent but told that he must say only what God commands. On the way, Bala'am's donkey sees an angel standing before her and refuses to go forward. Bala'am beats her. After the donkey protests that she is being mistreated, Bala'am himself sees the angel. Fearful, he asks if he should return home, but the angel tells him to continue, warning once again that he is to say only what God commands. On three occasions King Balak asks Bala'am to curse the Israelites, but each time the seer blesses them. Furious, Balak tells Bala'am to return home. In parting, the seer predicts that Israel will soon "smash the brow of Moab." Later, when the Israelites camp in Shittim, they have sexual relations with Moabite women and offer sacrifices to the Moabites' god. As a result they are punished with a plague. When Pinchas, son of Eleazar the priest, witnesses an Israelite entering a tent with a Moabite woman, he takes a spear and kills both of them. His action ends the plague after 24,000 Israelites have died.

OUR TARGUM

· 1 ·

Fearing that the Israelites will attack his country, Balak son of Zippor, king of Moab, sends messengers to Bala'am son of Beor in Pethor, a town located on the Euphrates River in ancient Mesopotamia. Bala'am is known as a pagan prophet with special powers to bless and curse. Balak promises to pay him richly for cursing the people of Israel. When Balak's messengers tell Bala'am what their king wants, Bala'am asks them to stay the night while he considers the offer.

During the night, God tells Bala'am, "Do not go with them. You must not curse that people, for they are blessed." The next morning, Bala'am tells the messengers that he cannot accept Balak's offer. When these messengers report Bala'am's response, Balak sends other messengers who, as Balak instructs them, promise Bala'am anything he wishes. Bala'am listens to the offer and declares: "Though Balak were to give me his house full of silver and gold, I could not do anything . . . against the command of God."

Later that night, God tells Bala'am to go with the messengers but to say only what God commands.

· 2 ·

Bala'am sets out for Moab on his donkey. Along the way, an angel holding a sword appears in front of the donkey, blocking her way. The donkey swerves off the road. In anger, Bala'am beats her. Again the angel appears before the donkey. The donkey presses against a fence, hurting Bala'am's foot. Bala'am beats her with a stick. When the angel appears for a third time, the donkey sits down, refusing to move. Bala'am beats her again.

Finally, the donkey speaks, complaining to Bala'am, "Why are you beating me? Am I not the donkey you have been riding for many years? Have I behaved this way before?"

At that moment, the angel, with the sword drawn, appears to Bala'am and reveals that, had the donkey not turned aside, he would have killed Bala'am. Fearing the angel, Bala'am tells him, "I will turn back if that is what you wish." The angel answers, "Go with Balak's servants, but say only what I tell you."

· 3 ·

When Bala'am arrives, Balak asks why he refused to come the first time he was invited. Bala'am answers, "I can say only the word that God puts into my mouth."

Bala'am orders Balak to build several altars and prepare sacrifices for them. Standing next to the sacrifices, Bala'am praises the Israelites, declaring, "How can I damn whom God has not damned? . . . May my fate be like theirs."

Hearing this praise, Balak cries, "What have you done to me?" He then takes Bala'am to Pisgah, a high place where he builds seven altars. But, again, instead of cursing the Israelites, Bala'am blesses them, predicting, "No harm is in sight for Jacob, . . . *Adonai* their God is with them."

Furious, Balak takes Bala'am to the peak of Peor. On seeing the Israelites camping below, the pagan prophet declares: "How fair [beauti-ful] are your tents, O Jacob,/Your dwellings, Israel!/. . . Blessed are they who bless you,/Cursed are those who curse you!"

Exasperated with Bala'am, Balak once again seeks to bribe him into cursing the Israelites. Bala'am responds, claiming he can say only what God has commanded. He then speaks a final blessing, promising that the Israelites will triumph over all their enemies, including the people of Moab.

· 4 ·

While camping at Shittim, the Israelites have sexual relations with the women of Moab and begin worshiping their idols. God punishes them with a plague. As an Israelite is taking a Moabite woman into his tent, Pinchas, son of Eleazar the priest, attacks them with a spear and kills them. The plague ends after 24,000 Israelites are dead.

THEMES

Parashat Balak contains two important themes:

1. God's mysterious and wonderful presence in history.
2. Encountering the unknown future.

PEREK ALEF: *Bala'am and His Strange Book*

The Talmud justifiably calls this Torah portion the "Book of Bala'am." Bala'am, identified as the son of Beor from Pethor, a town along the Euphrates River in what is now Syria, is the main character of the drama. The Torah, however, provides no background information about him. We are told only where he comes from and that Balak, the king of Moab, says of him: "He whom you bless is blessed indeed, and he whom you curse falls under the curse." (*Baba Batra* 15a)

This "Book of Bala'am" raises several important questions: Who is Bala'am? What are his powers? Is he an enemy or a friend of the Jewish people? Does God really speak to him and appear to his donkey? How significant are these events in which Moses is not even mentioned and in which the main characters are non-Jews?

The first interpretations of Bala'am's powers and intentions are found in the Hebrew Bible. In Numbers 31:8 we find that, after their victory over the Midianites, the Israelites, without explanation, "put Bala'am son of Beor to the sword."

A reason for the punishment may be found in Deuteronomy 23:4–6, where we are informed that "no Ammonite or Moabite shall be admitted into the congregation of *Adonai;* none of their descendants, even in the tenth generation . . . because they did not meet you with food and water on your journey after you left Egypt, and because they hired Bala'am son of Beor, from Pethor of Aram-naharaim, to curse you.—But *Adonai* your God refused to heed Bala'am; instead, *Adonai* your God turned the curse into a blessing for you, for *Adonai* your God loves you.—" This view of Bala'am as a Moabite, a hired diviner who intends to curse and harm Israel but whose scheming is reversed by God, is repeated in Joshua 13:22, 24:9–10; Micah 6:5; and Nehemiah 13:2.

Early rabbinic interpreters also share this negative view of Bala'am. In discussing him, Rabbi Eliezer and Rabbi Yochanan agree that the blessings he speaks about Israel are not his but those that God puts into his mouth. Eliezer argues that an "angel" places them there; Yochanan disagrees. They are extracted, he says, with a "hook." Bala'am speaks the blessings against his will. Even God must force them out of his mouth. (*Sanhedrin* 105b)

Rabbi Abba ben Kahana agrees with Yochanan, declaring that Bala'am was one of three people pronounced "despicable" by God. The others are Cain, who murders his brother Abel, and Hezekiah, whose self-centered boasting leads to Israel's destruction by Babylonia. Rabbi Abba ben Kahana says that Bala'am is the "vilest of sinners" because he intends to curse and injure the people of Israel. Other rabbinic interpreters label him a "money changer" because he sells his advice, including curses and blessings, to leaders of nations.

Some rabbinic interpreters speculate that Bala'am is directed by Satan and that he hates the Israelites more than Balak because they never seek his advice. He also doubts God's promise to protect them. Summing up the early rabbinic view of Bala'am, one commentator says, "He possesses three qualities: an evil eye, a haughty spirit, and a greedy soul." (*Numbers Rabbah* 20:6–11)

Peli

Bala'am perverts his gifts

Claiming that Bala'am is responsible for helping to lure the Israelites into whoring with the Moabites, modern interpreter Pinchas Peli comments: "God grants human beings various degrees of talent in different areas of creativity; it is they themselves who are responsible, however, for putting this latent gift to the right use. Many waste their gifts; others pervert their use. Bala'am was among the latter. . . . After uttering some of the most lofty songs in praise

of Israel, Bala'am proceeds to offer their enemies some of the most sinister pieces of advice on how to go about destroying Israel and its 'goodly tents'; behind their backs, he plots their annihilation through the lure of fertility goddesses." (Jerusalem Post, *July 19, 1986, p. 22*)

Ibn Ezra

Following early rabbinic tradition, ibn Ezra claims that Bala'am is a deceptive schemer, a dangerous man. He substantiates his accusation by pointing out that Bala'am never tells Balak's messengers that God will not permit him to curse the Israelites. He allows them to believe that he is willing to damn the king's enemies. Moreover, Bala'am orders Balak to build altars and make sacrifices without telling Balak that God will permit him only to bless the Israelites. Bala'am withholds information and distorts the truth. He seeks to take advantage of the king's fears for his own financial gain.

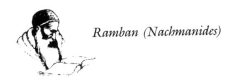

Ramban (Nachmanides)

Nachmanides agrees with ibn Ezra's observation but sees in it something much more sinister than "financial gain." He claims that "it was God's original desire that Bala'am go with the messengers and bless the Israelites . . . for God wanted Israel blessed by a prophet of the nations." In failing to make clear his intentions to the messengers, Bala'am creates the false impression "that God has given permission to curse the people. . . ." Consequently, "when they see that God does not curse the Israelites," they may assume "that God has had a change of mind and is fickle. . . ." For Nachmanides, Bala'am is a dangerous person because he not only fails to tell Balak's messengers that he can only bless Israel, but he has no scruples in misleading others about God's true intentions. (Commentary on Numbers 22:20)

Hirsch

Rabbi Samson Raphael Hirsch offers a very different view from that of Nachmanides. For Hirsch, Bala'am's faith in God evolves, as does his willingness to do God's will. When Bala'am first agrees to go with Balak's messengers, "his mind is still obscured by the obsession that he would be able to achieve the purpose desired by Balak and himself." That purpose is to curse Israel. However, after he sees that "God cannot be influenced by means of sorcery," his intentions shift.

Realizing that he cannot damn the people, Bala'am "becomes a vehicle for the will of God." With experience, his faith in God becomes more profound. He becomes more open to hearing and doing God's will. At that point, Hirsch concludes, "It is not a question of God putting a word into his mouth against his will, *in spite of himself,* as heretofore, but of the spirit of unconstrained prophecy informing his utterances." (Commentary on Numbers 22:22, 24:1–2)

Leibowitz

Nehama Leibowitz shares Hirsch's view that Bala'am may have begun with sinister intentions toward Israel, but he evolves into a person whose faith in God increases with experience and proximity. She points out that Bala'am ascends from a "common sorcerer to a prophet 'who hears the words of God.'" First, explains Leibowitz, Bala'am asks Balak to build altars and offer sacrifices. His purpose is to invoke "divine aid through magical means, striving to accommodate the divine will to his interests rather than to achieve closer communion" with God. Finally, after two experiences of blessing Israel "against his will," Bala'am "leaves

all his schemes and wholeheartedly gives himself up to the divine prophetic urge."

Bala'am was a convert
Modern biblical scholar and archeologist W.F. Albright concludes that "Bala'am was really a North-Syrian diviner from the Euphrates Valley, that he became a convert to Yahwism [Israel's faith], and that he later abandoned Israel and joined the Midianites in fighting against the Yahwists." (W. Gunther Plaut, The Torah: A Modern Commentary, *pp. 1184–1185)*

Unlike some earlier commentators, Leibowitz boldly claims that Bala'am is a "prophet," not a diviner, sorcerer, or magician for hire. Like Hirsch, she applauds Bala'am's spiritual growth and evolution from a man who sees less than his donkey to a person who achieves "pure prophecy." To those who question whether "prophecy" is a power given to non-Jews as well as Jews, Leibowitz quotes modern Israeli scholar Ephraim E. Urbach. He concludes that in Jewish tradition "prophecy is not the exclusive gift of Israel. . . . On the contrary, prophecy . . . was given at the outset to all human creatures." (*Studies in Bemidbar,* pp. 282–327)

Philosopher Martin Buber takes issue with Nehama Leibowitz. Bala'am, he argues, never reaches "pure prophecy." A prophet, explains Buber, never foretells "a fixed, unchangeable future." Prophets do not predict what will happen tomorrow. Instead, "they announce a present that requires human choice and decision." It is a present "in which the future is being prepared" but whose outcome depends upon the work and decisions of human beings.

Bala'am, Buber explains, is not "commissioned," not "sent" by God. He fails to make decisions on his own. Rather, "God makes use of him." Bala'am may have the potential to be a prophet and take initiative, but he never fulfills that potential. He remains detached and aloof from others. He never engages others. Instead, he announces God's words, exercising no will of his own. He speaks about tomorrow but does not participate in making the choices and decisions that will shape the future. Consequently, he remains a common magician. (*Moses,* pp. 170–171)

Modern biblical and literary critic Robert Alter extends Buber's view of Bala'am. Pointing out that the "Book of Bala'am" contains "high comedy," Alter observes that Bala'am, a seer who cannot see, is cast ironically into a story about seeing! For comic relief the author treats us to the sideshow of a donkey with better vision than that of her owner. Bala'am, the most renowned of all magicians, is exposed as a pagan professional. He claims he has the power to manipulate God but ends up being controlled and maneuvered by God.

This entire story, Alter argues, is meant to demonstrate the flaws of paganism. "Paganism, with its notion that divine powers can be manipulated by a caste of professionals through a set of carefully prescribed procedures, is trapped in the reflexes of a mechanistic worldview while, from the biblical perspective, reality is in fact controlled by the will of an omnipotent God beyond all human manipulation." For the pagan, knowledge of the world and how to dominate it are consigned to expert magicians or seers like Bala'am. That explains why Balak is willing to pay him such a high price to curse Israel. By contrast, the Torah puts forth the view that no human being can truly comprehend, and certainly not manipulate, God's will. God's will is beyond understanding, too awesome to be grasped. (*The Art of Biblical Narrative,* Basic Books, New York, 1981, pp. 104–107)

The "Book of Bala'am" is more than an example of the Torah's art. It reveals early Jewish views about sorcery and magic and contains a critique on professional prophets who made their living either cursing or blessing the enemies or allies of their rulers. In this ancient story about a seer who cannot see and whose donkey understands more of God's will than he does, pagan notions about manipulating God are ridiculed and condemned. The tale seems to make the point that human history and Israel's history are in the power of an unfathomable God. No person can fully understand God's intentions. Often what is perceived as a curse turns into a blessing, and what seems to be a benefit sours into a disappointment.

PEREK BET: *Decoding Bala'am's Poetry and Blessings*

The "Book of Bala'am" contains not only a moving narrative about a pagan prophet summoned to curse the people of Israel but also some very beautiful poetry. Balak, the king of Moab, fears that the Israelites will "lick clean" his land and fortunes. Bala'am, he hopes, will predict their destruction. Yet each time Bala'am prepares to curse Israel, his words become blessings. His pronouncements rise with poetic rhythm and power to praise the very people Balak wants him to curse.

Modern biblical commentators differ on the time Bala'am's poetry was composed. Some believe that the poetic sections reflect a time different from that of the Torah narrative. They speculate that these "poetic descriptions date from the time of Saul and of David" and echo national aspirations meant to demonstrate Israel's superiority over surrounding pagan peoples.

Other interpreters disagree, arguing that the narrative and poetry of the story of Bala'am "form an organic unity." Still others point out that the narrative portion and the poetic portions may have been independent of each other at one point but were later fused "by a single editorial hand," thus producing "a new artistic creation." (See Julius A. Bewer, *The Literature of the Old Testament,* Columbia University Press, New York, 1962, pp. 13–14; Yehezkel Kaufmann, *The Religion of Israel,* Schocken Books, New York, 1972, pp. 84–91; and Jacob Milgrom, *JPS Torah Commentary: Numbers,* pp. 467–468.)

This disagreement on the time and authorship of Bala'am's poetry may never be settled. Unfortunately, there are no existing documents that can move the discussion beyond speculation. That, however, does not remove the challenge of interpreting the meaning of Bala'am's poetry about the people of Israel. Each of the three poems contains puzzling and enchanting expressions.

In the first, Bala'am says of the Israelites:

As I see them from the mountain tops,
Gaze on them from the heights,
There is a people that dwells apart,
Not reckoned among the nations.

(Numbers 23:9)

What does this verse mean?

Rashi

Rashi, working with the literal translation of the original Hebrew, suggests that Bala'am is predicting a secure future for the people of Israel. He means to say: "I look at your origins [mountain tops] and see that you are strongly rooted in your ancestors [heights]. You are distinguished [dwell apart] by your Torah traditions, and because of them you will not suffer the fate [be reckoned] of extinction but will survive and prosper."

Hertz

Rabbi Joseph H. Hertz agrees with Rashi, interpreting the phrase "a people that dwells apart" to mean that "Israel has always been a people isolated and distinguished from other peoples by its religious and moral laws and by the fact that it has been chosen as the instrument of a divine purpose." His understanding of the meaning of "not reckoned among the nations," however, differs from that of Rashi. Hertz quotes the work of Marcus Jastro, a modern student of Hebrew and other ancient Middle East languages, who notes that *yitchashav,* or "reckon," may be better translated as "conspire." Thus the verse means that "Israel is a people that dwells alone; *it does not conspire against the nations.*" (*The Pentateuch and Haftorahs,* Soncino Press, London, p. 674)

Hertz's interpretation may reflect the mood of late nineteenth- and early twentieth-century England rather than the accurate intention of the Torah text. He seems to be saying that, while Jewish tradition differs from other religious expressions, it is not hostile toward other peoples or cultures. Worried about anti-Semites, who claim that Jews believe themselves to be "superior" to other religious and cultural groups, Hertz seizes the words of Bala'am to prove that such claims are false.

Rabbi Samson Raphael Hirsch also seems uncomfortable with Bala'am's statement, ". . . I see them from the mountain tops . . . a people that dwells apart." Hirsch maintains this statement means that Bala'am has a "panoramic view" of the Jewish people "in a future time." That view, says Hirsch, means Israel "will live in an insulated land without much intercourse with other nations." It will sustain "its 'internal' national mission as a national social body and will not seek its greatness as a nation among nations." In other words, the people of Israel does not seek "control of the world," as anti-Semites claim. Rather, Jews seek only a peaceful, cooperative coexistence with other peoples and nations. (Commentary on Numbers 23:9)

Each of the above interpretations finds the Torah's description of Israel as "a people that dwells apart,/Not reckoned among the nations" perplexing and disturbing. It raises fundamental questions about the definition and nature of Jewish existence. Are Jews a nation like other nations, or are they a religious group without national aspirations? Within Bala'am's poetic praise, Jewish commentators locate some of their painful ambivalence and their serious concerns about the harmful misunderstandings of Jews and their tradition promulgated by anti-Semites.

These views, however, seem imposed upon the poetic words of Bala'am. The question remains: Can we uncover what Bala'am, or the author of these poems ascribed to him originally, had in mind?

Perhaps in the simplest terms they mean that the people of Israel "dwells apart" in a sacred covenant relationship with God, and, because of that covenant, it is judged differently by itself and by others. When Bala'am looks upon the people, he sees in their traditions and values a uniqueness worthy of blessing.

Bala'am's second poem of blessing includes the following verses:

No harm is in sight for Jacob,
No woe in view for Israel.
Adonai their God is with them . . .

Lo, a people that rises like a lion,
Leaps up like the king of beasts,
Rests not till it has feasted on prey
And drunk the blood of the slain.

(Numbers 23:21, 24)

Nachmanides offers a different reading of the Torah text. He believes: "No harm is in sight for Jacob,/No woe in view for Israel" is not an accurate translation of the original Hebrew. He insists that the Hebrew word *aven*, translated above as "harm," means "wrongdoing," and the Hebrew word *amal*, translated as "woe," denotes "deception." Thus, argues Nachmanides, the phrase should read "No wrongdoing [among the people of] Jacob,/No deception [among the people of] Israel."

Nachmanides perceives that Bala'am is not predicting the future but making a judgment about the character of the Israelites. Because they do not engage in falsehood, cheating, or deliberate harm to others, God is with them. Therefore, they merit protection from their enemies and, like the lion, the "king of beasts," will be victorious over all who attack them. (Commentary on Numbers 23:21,24)

Early rabbinic tradition provides a different interpretation of the phrase "a people that rises like a lion,/Leaps up like the king of beasts." This phrase, say the rabbis, captures the unique and surprising quality of the Jewish people. "One moment they are asleep, neglecting the Torah and its mitzvot; the next moment they awake and rise 'like a lion.' They read the words, 'Hear, O Israel; *Adonai* our God, *Adonai* is One,' and set out to apply the ethics of their Torah tradition to every aspect of their business dealings and relationships with others." They are animated by their faith and commitment to God. As a result of such behavior, explain the rabbis, Bala'am understood that he and the five kings of Midian, Evi, Rekem, Zur, Hur, and Reba, (Numbers

31:8) would be defeated. Inspired by their moral way of life, the people of Israel would rise up like a lion and not rest until its enemies were crushed. (*Numbers Rabbah* 20:20)

Bala'am's third poem of praise for the Israelites includes the following phrases:

How fair are your tents, O Jacob,
Your dwellings, O Israel!
Like palm groves that stretch out,
Like gardens beside a river,
Like aloes planted by *Adonai*,
Like cedars beside the water;
Their boughs drip with moisture,
Their roots have abundant water. . . .

God who freed them from Egypt
Is for them like the horns of the wild ox.
They shall devour enemy nations,
Crush their bones,
And smash their arrows.

(Numbers 24:5–7, 8)

Rashi interprets the verse "How fair [beautiful] are your tents, O Jacob" with an imaginative speculation about what Bala'am sees as he gazes down at the Israelite tents. Rashi supposes that Bala'am "notices that their tents are not directly facing one another." From this, Rashi suggests that the Israelites are following a unique moral principle that guarantees privacy for each home. They situate their dwellings so that one cannot look into the private space of another. Each home is guaranteed its seclusion and solitude.

Elaborating on Rashi's explanation, Nehama Leibowitz comments that "Bala'am, who had been reared among the idolatrous and immoral practices of his home country, is here praising the purity and chastity characteristic of the Jewish people." The term *tovu*, or "fair," says Leibowitz, means "perfection in all respects—beauty and charm, simplicity and purity." What Bala'am sees, Leibowitz concludes, is a remarkably "perfect" people—pure in every way. (*Studies in Bemidbar*, pp. 290–296)

Rabbi Joseph H. Hertz elaborates on this idealization of the Israelites. He argues that Bala'am "is swept away in rapt admiration of the Israelite encampments and homes arrayed harmoniously and peacefully, a picture of idyllic happiness and prosperity." Citing what some rabbinic interpreters have made of Bala'am's poetic words, Hertz explains that "the 'tents' are the 'tents of Torah,' and the 'dwellings' (literally, 'homes') are the synagogues." He concludes by declaring, "There loomed up before Bala'am's mental vision the schoolhouses and synagogues that have ever been the source and secret of Israel's spiritual strength." (*The Pentateuch and Haftorahs,* p. 678)

To suggest that Bala'am somehow sees the future institutions of Jewish life, its schools and synagogues, is a rather farfetched idealization. Yet his poetic words, "How fair are your tents, O Jacob,/Your dwellings, O Israel!" are found inscribed on many synagogue walls and, as the first words of the *Pesukei de-Zimra,* or "Verses of Praise," begin the Jewish worship service. While Bala'am may have meant them as praise for the people of Israel, they have come to embody the enthusiasm of Jews for their synagogues, schools, and homes.

Modern interpreter Jacob Milgrom views the phrases of Bala'am's poetry not as praise for Jewish institutions but as a prediction of Israel's future. The poet, says Milgrom, suggests that their tents will be set out in a lush garden environment "beside the water," recalling the Garden of Eden. The garden will be filled with sweet-smelling aloe trees, tall cedars with boughs that drip moisture, and roots fed by "abundant water." The people will enjoy victory over their enemies. "God who freed them from Egypt" will crush their foes and "smash their arrows." This prediction for a people living in an arid land, fearful of enemies all about them, is reassuring. It provides hope for the future.

One common thread unites Bala'am's three poems: anxiety about the future, the fear of unknown dangers ahead. Bala'am's poems deal directly with the apprehensions of a people whose history has been uncertain and filled with anxiety. The first poem defines the Israelites as unique among the nations, protected when they fulfill their covenant with God. The second promises triumph over those plotting Israel's destruction. The third poem transforms Israel into a people enjoying an ideal existence of safety and abundance in the Garden of Eden.

In our times, concern for security and dreams of prosperity continue as central themes not only for Jews but for all human beings. Peace with justice remains elusive. Greed and hostility still endanger our human family. Politicians, fortune-tellers, fanatics, and religious frauds still promise more than they can deliver. Perhaps that explains why Bala'am's ancient poetic art retains its power and captures our imagination.

QUESTIONS FOR STUDY AND DISCUSSION

1. What accounts for the negative view of Bala'am by so many commentators?

2. Philosopher Martin Buber argues that Bala'am never reaches "pure prophecy." What does he mean? What is the significance of the distinction he makes? What does critic Robert Alter add to Buber's conclusions about Bala'am?

3. Rabbi W. Gunther Plaut writes: "At its worst, the setting apart of the Jew has meant ghettoization, disenfranchisement, anti-Semitism, and, finally, the Holocaust. At its best, it has signified the attempt to render an entire people holy. . . ." How do those who interpret Bala'am's poetic phrase "There is a people that dwells apart" define its meaning?

4. In Bala'am's third poem, water is a recurring theme. How is it used? Why? Compare its use in Bala'am's poem with its use in Genesis 2:8–10; Psalms 1:3; Jeremiah 17:8, 31:11; and Isaiah 58:11.

PARASHAT PINCHAS
Numbers 25:10–30:1

Parashat Pinchas elaborates on the incident at the end of *Parashat Balak:* Pinchas, son of Eleazar, kills Zimri son of Salu and Cozbi daughter of Zur, a Midianite, who have entered a tent to have sex. Pinchas's zealousness saves the Israelites from a plague. God rewards him with a covenant of peace and his descendants with the office of the priesthood for all time. Moses tells the people to crush the Midianites for their "trickery" in seducing the Israelites into idolatry and whoring with their women. After the plague, Moses and Aaron take a census of the entire Israelite community. The total number of Israelites is 601,730. Moses also announces the division of the land, providing larger tribes with greater holdings and smaller tribes with lesser ones. Each person is assigned a lot of equal size, except for the Levites who are not given land but are compensated monetarily for their work in the sanctuary. During the taking of the census the case of the daughters of Zelophehad—Mahlah, Noah, Hoglah, Milcah, and Tirzah—arises. They claim that, because their father has died and left no sons, they should have the right to inherit his holdings. God confirms their claim and instructs Moses to announce that, if a man dies without leaving a son, a daughter will inherit his property. Moses is told to climb to the top of Mount Abarim to see the Land of Israel, and he is informed that he will die there. When Moses requests that his successor be chosen, God tells Moses to appoint Joshua. Moses is to instruct Joshua to present himself to Eleazar the priest, who will consult the Urim for important decisions and instructions regarding the community. The *parashah* concludes with a description of the offerings to be presented daily, on the Sabbath, on new moons, for Pesach, Shavuot, Rosh Hashanah, Yom Kippur, and for each of the days of Sukot, including the eighth day, or Shemini Atzeret.

OUR TARGUM

·1·

Elaborating on the final incident in *Parashat Balak*, the Torah informs us that Pinchas, son of Eleazar the priest, zealously kills Zimri son of Salu and Cozbi daughter of Zur, a Midianite, for entering a tent to have sexual relations. According to the Torah, Midianite women are leading the Israelites into whoring and idolatry. Pinchas rushes forward to punish Zimri and Cozbi for their sin. Because Pinchas has displayed such zeal, God rewards him with a covenant of peace and bestows upon his descendants the office of the priesthood for all time.

Moses is told to attack and defeat the Midianites because, through prostitution, they have sought to lure the Israelites into worshiping their idol-god, Ba'al-peor, and have caused a severe plague upon the people.

·2·

After the plague, Moses and Aaron take a census of the Israelites above the age of twenty-seven who are able to bear arms. They total 601,730.

·3·

God gives Moses directions for dividing the Land of Israel among the tribes. The tribes are to receive land proportional to their size, and the individuals are to receive lots of equal size. The Levites, who number 23,000, are not to receive land since they are to receive monetary compensation for their service to the sanctuary.

·4·

The daughters of Zelophehad—Mahlah, Noah, Hoglah, Milcah, and Tirzah—approach Moses with the claim that they deserve to inherit their father's land since their father has died without leaving a male heir. God informs Moses that

their cause is just and that he must transfer their father's share to them. Furthermore, the right of all daughters to inherit land when there is no male heir is established as a law of Torah.

·5·

God tells Moses to climb the heights of Abarim. From there he will see the Land of Israel, but he, like Aaron, will not be permitted to lead his people there because he disobeyed God's command at the Waters of Meribath-kadesh.

Moses requests that God appoint a successor so the "community may not be like sheep that have no shepherd." God tells Moses to choose Joshua son of Nun and to commission Joshua before all the people. Moses is also to instruct Joshua to consult with Eleazar the priest on all matters concerning the community. Joshua is to follow the instruction Eleazar receives when he seeks direction from the Urim (these "lights" attached to the breastplate of the High Priest, a jewel for each of the tribes, were believed to be a sacred means of divination).

·6·

Moses describes the offerings to be brought to the sanctuary and to be presented daily, on Sabbaths, new moons, Pesach, Shavuot, the "day when the horn is sounded" (Rosh Hashanah), Yom Kippur, and each day of Sukot, including the eighth day (Shemini Atzeret).

THEMES

Parashat Pinchas contains two important themes:

1. The dangers of fanaticism.
2. Concern for the rights of women.

PEREK ALEF: *Pinchas: Dangerous Fanatic or Hero of Faith?*

The incident of Pinchas's spearing and killing of Zimri son of Salu, of the tribe of Simon, and Cozbi daughter of Zur, a tribal head of the Midianites, raises serious moral questions.

As the Torah states, the Israelites are whoring with Midianite women, who are also enticing them into the worship of their idol, Ba'al-peor. God commands Moses to put to death all the ringleaders who have led the people into wrongdoing. At that moment, Zimri and Cozbi publicly parade past Moses and enter a tent with the intention of having sexual relations. Pinchas, son of Eleazar son of Aaron, is furious. He takes his spear, rushes into the tent, and stabs both of them. The incident concludes with God rewarding Pinchas with a *berit shalom,* "a covenant of peace," and his descendants with the priesthood for all time.

Did Pinchas do the right thing? Should he be praised or condemned for his zeal, rewarded or punished for killing Zimri and Cozbi? Since Pinchas seems to benefit from breaking the commandment "You shall not murder," how do we explain the apparent contradiction?

Early rabbinic tradition is divided on whether or not Pinchas's act is justified. Some commentators point out that Moses, who is present in the camp, sees Zimri and Cozbi walk past him into the tent but does not signal others to punish them. Without speaking up or suggesting a hearing or trial, Pinchas rushes to execute Zimri and Cozbi. Pinchas does not consult with Moses, who is the highest authority of law within the community, but takes the law and power of prosecution into his own hands.

Rav, head of the Sura Academy, and Samuel, head of the Nahardea Academy in Babylonia, differ strongly in their assessment of Pinchas's actions. Rav condemns him. He holds that Pinchas sees what Zimri and Cozbi are doing and says to Moses, "Did you not teach our people when you came down from Mount Sinai that any Israelite who has sex with a non-Israelite may be put to death by zealots?" Moses, says Rav, listens to Pinchas and responds, "Let God who gave the advice execute the advice!"

Clearly Rav finds fault with Pinchas for his

fanaticism. "Why are you making the judgment and carrying it out?" he asks, criticizing him for failing to follow Moses' instruction. Rav argues that, although Pinchas may have acted within the law, he should have allowed God "to execute" its provisions rather than doing it himself.

On the other hand, Samuel, who often disagrees with Rav, praises Pinchas for his zeal. Samuel claims that this is a case where God's law is being publicly desecrated, and, therefore, Pinchas is correct, even heroic, for his decisive action. Furthermore, says Samuel, it is permissible in this case for Pinchas to ignore Moses' warning or authorization since the action taken by Pinchas is clearly meant to support the law that prohibits such prostitution and idolatry.

> ### The demands of God
> *Pinchas "saw in Zimri's act an open breach of the covenant, a flagrant return to the practices that the compact at Sinai had forsworn. There was no precedent in the brief history of the people to determine how to deal with such a religious and moral emergency. . . . Pinchas's impulsive deed was not merely a kind of battlefield execution but reflected his apprehension that the demands of God needed human realization and required a memorable and dramatic example against permissiveness in the religious realm. (W. Gunther Plaut,* The Torah: A Modern Commentary, *p. 1195)*

Rabbi Barpazzi raises the possibility that Moses and others in the camp were upset with Pinchas's fanatical behavior and were ready to punish him by excluding him from the community. They were bothered by his circumvention of Moses' authority, by his self-righteous assumption that he did not need the permission of the community, or of the courts, for his zealous behavior. However, just as they were ready to punish Pinchas with excommunication, says Rabbi Barpazzi, God intervened and announced that the actions of Pinchas were praiseworthy and would be rewarded with "a covenant of peace" and that the priesthood would be given to his decendants. With that, his critics fell silent.

Rabbi Barpazzi seems to be suggesting the possibility that, while Pinchas did the right thing by taking the law into his own hands, he erred in the way in which he acted. He should have consulted with Moses and, perhaps, others. His actions would have been more just had he gained the community's consent rather than acting alone. (Jerusalem Talmud, *Sanhedrin* 9:7, 11, 82a)

Still other interpreters claim that Pinchas acted only when he saw that Moses was neglecting his duty by not carrying out the laws of the Torah. Perhaps, these commentators claim, Moses was weak from long years of stressful leadership or so old that he forgot the laws forbidding sexual relations between Israelites and non-Israelites. Given the situation, and the danger of punishment by God to the entire people for Moses' neglect, Pinchas took matters into his own hands, saving the people from catastrophe. For that reason, these interpreters maintain that Pinchas was entirely justified and was rewarded by God. These teachers conclude that Pinchas's decisive actions teach one to be "fierce as a leopard, swift as an eagle, fast as a hart, and strong as a lion in doing God's will." (*Numbers Rabbah* 20:24; *Avot* 5:23)

Rambam (Maimonides)

Moses Maimonides agrees with this view and includes it in his *Mishneh Torah*. He writes that "a Jew may be put to death by zealots if he is found having sexual intercourse with a non-Jewish woman or prostitute." He points to the example of Pinchas, stating that "zealots are justified in killing such a person only if they catch him during the act itself. Should they kill him afterwards, however, they are to be charged with murder." ("Illicit Relations," 124–125)

> ### Kanaim pogeim bo
> *Translated literally,* kanaim pogeim bo *means that zealots may take justice into their own hands and may execute a transgressor on the spot. There are, to be sure, many halachic*

"legal" fences that serve to limit implementation of this principle. First, punishment may be meted out only while the act is actually in the course of being performed. According to some authorities, the usual hatra'ah, *or "warning," must be administered. More significantly, the rule that applies is:* halachah ve-ein morin ken; *while the punishment is justified, no one may be instructed to carry it out. Nevertheless, a person who acts in accordance with this principle acts in accordance with* halachah. *(J. David Bleich,* Contemporary Halachic Problems, *Volume II, Ktav, New York, 1983, pp. 273–274)*

Differing from Maimonides, Turkish-born (16th century) commentator Rabbi Moshe ben Chaim Alshekh suggests that Pinchas's zeal may not have originated in the pure motive of defending the ethical laws of Torah. Rather, his stabbing of Zimri and Cozbi is a deliberate act meant to prove he is worthy of the priesthood and of passing on that privilege to his descendants.

According to Alshekh, Pinchas realizes his claim to the priesthood is flawed. His father, Eleazer son of Aaron, is not yet a priest at the time of his birth. Technically, Pinchas is not automatically in line to inherit his father's office. "He therefore decides to risk his life and, armed with the mitzvah of killing Zimri, hopes to wipe out what appears to him a stain on his character, namely, not being a priest though his father was a priest."

Alshekh believes Pinchas has an ulterior motive for his demonstration of zeal. He rushes forward to punish Zimri and Cozbi, not out of a sense of outrage at their public insult to God and Torah, but because he wishes to attract Moses' attention and secure the office of the priesthood for himself and his offspring. His act, therefore, must be denounced. (Commentary to Numbers 25:1)

Hirsch

Commentator Rabbi Samson Raphael Hirsch disagrees with Alshekh's argument. He justifies

and praises Pinchas's act as "not merely an external forward rush but the result of his deep inner feeling that made a betrayal of God's affairs feel like a treachery against one's own self." Zimri, he explains, is not an ordinary Israelite. He ranks as a "prince, as one who should set the example as a pattern of noble moral purity" for his people. His public act of entering a tent with the intention of having sexual intercourse with a Midianite woman "derided God . . . Torah and Israel." It debased the Jewish people and faith.

In the face of Zimri's outrageous public behavior, argues Hirsch, someone is needed to restore the people's faith in God and to demonstrate Israel's commitment to God's commandments. Pinchas understands this and believes that, unless he acts, the people will forfeit their relationship with God and "thereby their own future existence." Pinchas's conviction and "honest brave act," Hirsch concludes, save "the soul of his nation for faithfulness to God and to God's Torah." For this reason God rewards him with a covenant of peace and his descendants are designated as priests for all time. (Commentary on Numbers 25:6–15)

The danger of the true believer
The fanatic is perpetually incomplete and insecure. He cannot generate self-assurance out of his individual resources—out of his rejected self—but finds it only by clinging passionately to whatever support he happens to embrace . . . he easily sees himself as the supporter and defender of the holy cause to which he clings. And he is ready to sacrifice his life to demonstrate to himself and others that such indeed is his role. He sacrifices his life to prove his worth. . . . Passionate hatred can give meaning and purpose to an empty life. Thus people haunted by the purposelessness of their lives try to find a new content not only by dedicating themselves to a holy cause but also by nursing a fanatical grievance. (Eric Hoffer, The True Believer, *Harper and Row, New York, 1966, pp. 80, 92)*

Hirsch's contemporary Rabbi Naphtali Zvi Judah Berlin, author of the Torah commentary *Ha-*

Emek Davar, suggests that, while Pinchas's zeal may reflect deep conviction, it also reveals sinister and disturbing motives. People who are ready to murder, terrorize others, and destroy for a cause are often filled with hatred, bitter suspicions, and the poison of prejudice. As a result, their acts of vengeance against others are often followed by self-destructive acts. Feelings of guilt and regret lead them to target themselves or those close to them for punishment.

Berlin imagines that Pinchas, despite his courageous act of leadership and his demonstration of commitment to God's Torah, is deeply disturbed by his zealous, impulsive behavior. Despite the fact that his motives are pure, he remains agitated for taking the law into his own hands without consulting Moses and for not taking Zimri before the judges and courts of his day.

This, Berlin comments, explains why God gives him "a covenant of peace." It is not a reward for his impulsive behavior but a cure for it. This "covenant" is meant to calm him, "that he should not be quick-tempered or angry. Since the nature of his act, killing with his own hands, tended to leave his heart filled with intense emotional unrest, God provides a means to soothe him so that he can cope with his situation and find peace and tranquility of soul." Clearly, Berlin is troubled by Pinchas's zeal, finding in it signs of psychological disturbance that require the "healing" of God's "covenant of peace." (Discussion of Numbers 25:11–12)

Reviewing the variety of interpretations of Pinchas's behavior reveals deep differences of opinion about his execution of Zimri and Cozbi. Some applaud his action; others deplore it, leaving modern readers of the Torah with the continuing challenge of answering the question: Was Pinchas a dangerous fanatic or a genuine hero of faith?

PEREK BET: *Women's Rights: What Does the Torah Say?*

In preparing the people to enter the Land of Israel, Moses assigns portions of land to each family according to the listing of their tribes. The inheritance of property is to pass through fathers and sons from one generation to the next.

Hearing this, the five daughters of Zelophehad, whose tribe is Manasseh, one of Joseph's sons, rise in protest before Moses. Standing in front of the *mishkan,* where all official meetings of the community are held, they tell Moses and the leaders of the community that the law of inheritance from father to sons is unjust. "Our father was not one of Korah's disloyal faction, but he died in the wilderness, and he has left no sons. We ask that his name not be lost but that his portion be given to us, his daughters."

Moses consults with God and is told that their plea is justified. He announces to the community: "If a man dies without leaving a son, his property is to be transferred to his daughter." Obviously, the daughters of Zelophehad win a significant victory for women's rights.

But do they?

In the final chapter of Numbers (36:1–13), the tribal leaders of Manasseh issue a counterprotest. Approaching Moses, they accuse him of cheating them of their tribal lands. Since each tribe will receive a portion of land according to its size and that land will be passed from father to son, the area of the tribal land will remain the same. However, if the daughters of Zelophehad are given their father's land and marry out of the tribe of Manasseh, that land will pass from father to son into another tribe. "Our allotted portion will be diminished," the tribal heads tell Moses.

According to the Torah, God informs Moses that the leaders of the counterprotest have a just cause. To solve the dilemma, the daughters of Zelophehad are told they can marry only within their tribe, and the people of Israel are informed that "no inheritance of the Israelites may pass over from one tribe to another . . . every daughter . . . who inherits a share must marry someone from a clan of her father's tribe. . . ." (Numbers 36:7–8) While women win the right to inherit, it is clearly subservient to the higher principle of preserving the size and borders of tribal lands.

Interpreters of Torah raise several questions about this incident concerning the daughters of Zelophehad: Why were these women given such deferential treatment? What was the motivation for their treatment? Why did Moses turn to God for a decision rather than make it immediately on his own? Did the women really win a "victory"? What roles are considered appropriate for women within the Jewish community and within society?

Modern commentator Jacob Milgrom contrasts ancient Israelite practices of inheritance with those of their neighbors. He finds that the right of daughters to inherit property from their fathers is upheld in Sumerian law a thousand years before the Torah is written. The practice is common throughout Mesopotamia, in communities along the Mediterranean coast, and in the laws of ancient Egypt well before the liberation of the Israelites. Later Greek law also stipulates the right of daughters to inherit equally with sons.

In the face of such "equality" of treatment, Milgrom asks, "How then are we to explain the fact that the Bible gives women no inheritance rights except in the case where there are no sons?" In other words, why does the Torah appear to discriminate against women, especially a woman's right to inherit the land and property of her parents?

Milgrom suggests that, in contrast to ancient Israel's neighbors in Mesopotamia and Egypt where "centralized urban societies" already existed, the early Torah laws of the Israelites reflect a nomadic-clan structure. In such a society "the foremost goal of its legal system was the preservation of the clan." Equity between members of the tribe or family preserves peaceful relationships and strengthens cooperation between all persons.

This explains why the pleas of both Zelophehad's daughters and the leaders of the tribe of Manasseh are considered just. Both uphold the principle of preserving the clan. Zelophehad's daughters argue that, if they are not given the right to inherit, their father's name will be lost—his properties absorbed without identity. The leaders counter that, if the daughters marry outside the tribe, the clan will lose its rightful land holdings. The Torah's solution solves both problems. The daughters will inherit their father's property, thereby preserving his name; tribal lands will not be diminished because the daughters must marry within their tribe.

This solution, however, does not give daughters equality with sons in the area of inheritance.

Both the Torah and the Talmud make it clear that under normal circumstances, where there are sons and daughters, inheritance of property is from father to sons. Women share the lot of their husbands; they do not inherit from their fathers. (*JPS Torah Commentary: Numbers,* pp. 482–484)

Milgrom's sociological explanation of the nomadic and tribal laws of inheritance in ancient Israel and their comparison to such laws in other ancient societies clearly aid in understanding the reasons behind the Torah's laws of inheritance. What about the place of women in the rest of the Torah tradition? How do the interpreters of Torah view the protesting daughters of Zelophehad and their demand for equal rights within society?

Peli

Contemporary interpreter Pinchas Peli writes that these women "are not presented as private individuals but as genuine representatives and spokeswomen of all members of their sex. The case they pleaded is not regarded as a personal claim for land appropriation but rather as an outcry of women against discrimination and second-class citizenship." Citing insights from early rabbinic commentaries, Peli praises the five daughters of Zelophehad for their wisdom and approach to the problem facing them.

The rabbis, for instance, point out that, when the daughters hear Moses announce the laws of inheritance, they realize they are not included. Instead of immediately rushing forward and loudly challenging him, the Torah says that "they drew near." In other words, they demonstrate patience. They organize themselves, discuss the matter, formulate an approach, and then calmly "draw near" to Moses with their concerns.

According to Simeon ben Lakish, founder of a third-century academy for Torah study in Tiberias, they do not take their case directly to Moses. Instead, they discuss the matter with the tribal chiefs of tens, of fifties, hundreds, and thousands. Showing honor to each of them, the daughters ask that the officers consider the matter before they take it to their superiors. Finally, having patiently pursued their claim within the judicial process, "they draw near" to Moses.

Other rabbinic interpreters also claim that the five daughters chose their tactics and words of protest with great care. While they believe that the Torah law is unfair to them and to others, they demonstrate constant loyalty to Moses, to their people, and to the Torah. They draw the contrast between their father who had remained loyal to Moses and other Israelites who had followed Korah. Furthermore, they deliberately use words that clarify the distinction between them and those who had said to Moses: "Give us a captain, and we shall return to Egypt." Echoing that statement, they tell Moses, "Give us an inheritance in the land." In this way, say the rabbis, the daughters demonstrate their superior commitment to their people and to the Land of Israel. Instead of abandoning the Promised Land, they merely demand their just inheritance within it. (*Numbers Rabbah* 16:10–12)

Peli concludes from his review of early rabbinic commentaries that the daughters of Zelophehad "in their superb wisdom . . . chose a suitable place, a proper time, and the proper approach" to lobby Moses regarding the law of inheritance. He writes: "In their arguments in favor of women's rights . . . they made Moses see what he had overlooked before. In truth, says the Talmud, Moses was supposed to have written that daughters get their rights along with sons. It was, however, a special privilege granted to the daughters of Zelophehad that this should be written into the Torah as a result of their painful and powerful protest." (*Baba Batra* 119a; "Torah Today," *Jerusalem Post*, July 20, 1985)

Women more pious than men
The women of Israel were always more pious than the men: We see that they did not want to give their earrings for the golden calf. Also, when the spies came, the women did not agree with them. Thus, all the men died in the desert and never reached the Land of Israel, but the wives did. (See Numbers 26:64; Tze'enah u-Re'enah on Numbers 27:1.)

Rabbi Samson Raphael Hirsch sees much more than the issue of land inheritance in the incident between Moses and the five daughters of Zelophehad. Hirsch contends that the heart of the matter in question is the loss of the family name. He points out that the daughters do not only say, "Give us an inheritance of land," but rather they offer an explanation for their request. They plead with Moses, "Let not our father's name be lost. . . ."

The perpetuation of the family name is their just cause, says Hirsch. It is the reason why the Torah determines that "the daughter has a right of inheritance only if there is no son or descendant of one." For, in such a case, the family name would disappear. To safeguard against such a danger, "If there is no son and no descendant of a son, then the daughter or her descendant is the heiress." (Commentary on Numbers 27:1–4)

Hertz

Caring for daughters
The rabbis, while denying the daughters a share in the inheritance where there are sons, still make ample provision for their maintenance and support, as long as they remain unmarried. The cost and provision of such maintenance constitute the first charge upon the estate of the deceased. In case the estate was small, the principle was laid down: "The daughters must be supported, even if the sons are reduced to beggary." (J. H. Hertz, The Pentateuch and Haftorahs, *p. 692)*

Modern commentator Rabbi W. Gunther Plaut cites the daughters of Zelophehad as an example of the treatment of women during the biblical period. He observes: "While the Torah records a number of laws in which men and women are treated equally (for instance, as regards reverence for parents; punishment in cases of incest; and dietary observances), it is on the whole male-oriented. The male has rights the female does not enjoy. She is to be wife and mother, invested with inherent dignity, to be sure, but by law and social order relegated to a second-class status comparable to that of minors." Regarding the case of Zelophehad's daughters, Plaut concludes that they "are accorded special treatment—but only so long as they fulfill the primary purpose of preserving the integrity of tribe and land (Numbers 36:6), reflecting the fact that men always remained members of their tribe, while women might in effect join another tribe by marriage." (*The Torah: A Modern Commentary*, pp. 1218–1219)

As Plaut points out, the traditional Jewish view of women places them in a "second-class status." While some early rabbinic authorities hold that women are gossips, envious, gluttonous, lazy, quarrelsome, and weak-willed, others argue that they are more pious than men, more merciful, hospitable, sensitive to the needs of others, and wiser. Yet all are agreed that women may not act as witnesses; nor as judges; nor be counted as a part of the *minyan,* the "ten men required for worship"; nor sit with men during worship. Furthermore, every married woman, according to Moses Maimonides, is obligated "to wash the face, hands, and feet of her husband; mix for him his cup of wine; prepare his bed; and stand and serve him. . . ." Regarding the doing of mitzvot, women are exempt from all commandments that must be fulfilled within certain boundaries of time, such as the putting on of *tefilin* or worshiping three times daily. (See *Genesis Rabbah* 18; 45; *Avot* 2:8; *Shabbat* 33b; *Kiddushin* 30b; *Megillah* 14b; *Berachot* 6b; *Niddah* 45b; *Yad ha-Hazakah, Ishut* 21:3.)

While such a degraded view of women undoubtedly reflects the era and sensibilities of the premodern period, it is precisely this view that early Reform Jews in the nineteenth century rejected. In 1837, Abraham Geiger spoke out for the equality of the sexes proclaiming, "Let there be from now on no distinction between duties for men and women . . . no assumption of the spiritual inferiority of women . . . no institution of the public service, either in form or content, that shuts the doors of the temple in the face of women; no degradation of women. . . ."

Nine years later at the Breslau Rabbinical Conference, a paper presented called for the equality of women in all religious duties, declaring that both sexes share equal responsibilities toward rearing children and that women are as obligated as men to pursue Jewish education. While it would be over one hundred years until the first women were ordained as rabbis or cantors, women played significant roles of leadership within the Reform Jewish community. (W. Gunther Plaut, *The Rise of Reform Judaism: A Sourcebook of Its European Origins,* UAHC, New York, 1963, pp. 252–255)

Contemporary traditional Jews have also responded to changing attitudes about women. Few Orthodox Jews demand of their wives the service defined by Moses Maimonides. Indeed, Rabbi Eliezer Berkovits, a leading Orthodox scholar, goes so far as to declare that such practice "is incompatible with the status that the woman had in the ethos of Judaism . . . our self-respect would not allow us to accept this kind of service from our wives, or even from any other human being." Referring to the case of Zelophehad's daughters, Berkovits comments that "notwithstanding the biblical law of inheritance, today in Orthodox Jewish families, wives do inherit their husband's property and daughters inherit together with sons." However, Berkovits makes it clear that women within traditional Judaism still suffer disabilities and inequalities and that these must be solved by seeking legally "valid possibilities" within the structure and interpretation of Jewish law. He warns that it is not only the status of women that is at stake but also the capacity of traditional Judaism to meet the requirements of the modern era. (From *Contemporary Jewish Ethics,* Menachem Marc Kellner, editor, Sanhedrin Press, New York, 1978, pp. 355–373)

Today women are assuming roles of leadership in every area of social, political, religious, business, and professional life. Equal numbers of men and women are working in information services as managers, administrators, and financial experts. As many women as men are starting new businesses, entering scientific professions, and attending liberal Christian and Jewish seminaries.

In such an age, women will also play an equal role in defining Jewish tradition and practice.

During biblical times it was the daughters of Zelophehad who challenged and altered an unjust law of Torah. Standing up for their rights, they extended fair treatment for others. Today, as both men and women struggle to define their rights and responsibilities, they will undoubtedly strengthen and revitalize some of the most significant ethical values and practices of Jewish tradition.

QUESTIONS FOR STUDY AND DISCUSSION

1. Two great teachers of Jewish tradition, Rav and Samuel, disagree on the justification of Pinchas in killing Zimri and Cozbi. What is the moral basis for their arguments? How do other commentators divide on this moral issue?

2. How would you apply the ancient talmudic principle *kanaim pogeim bo* to the incident of Pinchas's killing of Zimri and Cozbi? Does it protect against fanatics taking the law into their own hands? Could such a principle be applied on an international basis between hostile nations and peoples?

3. The Torah labels both the claim of the daughters of Zelophehad and the counterprotest of the tribal leaders of Manasseh as "just." Is the solution offered by the Torah a fair one?

4. Professor Paula E. Hyman comments: "Within the framework of traditional Judaism, women are not independent legal entities. Like the minor, the deaf-mute, and the idiot, they cannot serve as witnesses in Jewish courts. . . . They do not inherit equally with male heirs; they play only a passive role in the Jewish marriage ceremony; and they cannot initiate divorce proceedings. . . . What Jewish feminists are seeking . . . is not more apologetics but change, based on acknowledgment of the ways in which Jewish tradition has excluded women from entire spheres of Jewish experience and has considered them intellectually and spiritually inferior to men." (From "The Other Half: Women in the Jewish Tradition," in *Conservative Judaism*, Summer 1972) How are the modern movements within Jewish life dealing with what "Jewish feminists are seeking"?

PARASHAT MATOT-MAS'EY
Numbers 30:2–36:13

Parashat Matot-Mas'ey is one of seven designated Torah portions that, depending upon the number of Sabbaths in a year, is either read as two separate portions or combined to assure the reading of the entire Torah. While this volume will combine them, it will present an interpretation on each of their most important themes.

Parashat Matot reports the laws, given to the Israelites, for making vows. It also contains a description of the Israelites' war against the Midianites, including the distribution of the booty. The Torah portion concludes with Moses resolving a request by the Gadites and Reubenites for the lands of Jazer and Gilead.

Parashat Mas'ey recounts forty years of *mas'ey,* or "journeys," by the Israelites from Egypt to the Land of Israel. Moses provides instructions for conquering the land, defining its borders, and dividing it among the tribes. He also defines provisions for setting up six cities of refuge where those accused of manslaughter may go for safety and a fair trial. The Book of Numbers concludes with a counterprotest regarding the daughters of Zelophehad (see the discussion in *Parashat Pinchas*) and a further clarification of the Torah's laws of inheritance.

OUR TARGUM

·1·

Moses presents God's laws regulating vows. All vows must be fulfilled. However, when a woman makes a vow as a minor or as a wife, her promise is good only if her father or husband offers no objection to it. By contrast, the vow of a widow or divorced woman is binding upon her.

·2·

Moses commands the Israelites to organize war against the Midianites, who, with the Moabites, had lured the people into prostitution and the worship of Ba'al-peor, when they were camped at Shittim. (Numbers 25:1–9) The Israelites destroy the Midianite towns, capturing booty and many female captives and their children. Moses is furious with the chieftains, reminding them of their battle orders to slay every male. He commands them to carry out the order and to destroy every male among the children and every Midianite woman who has had sexual relations.

Warriors who have killed a person or touched a corpse are told to stay out of camp for seven days and cleanse themselves and their booty through rituals of water and fire. The priests and family heads inventory the booty, dividing it between the warriors and sanctuary.

· 3 ·

The Reubenites and Gadites, who own great numbers of cattle, approach Moses with the request to settle the lands of Jazer and Gilead on the east side of the Jordan River. They claim that these lands are better suited for cattle than the lands allotted to them inside the borders of Israel. While these lands have been conquered by the Israelites, they have not been designated as part of their inheritance.

Moses strongly objects. He accuses them of abandoning their people just when they are poised to enter their land, comparing their actions with the disloyalty shown by their fathers who had scouted the Land of Israel and returned with false reports. The Reubenites and Gadites pledge to act as shock-troops and lead the battle for conquering the Land of Israel and to keep their hereditary holding in the land. Convinced of their integrity, Moses assigns them the lands of Jazer and Gilead.

· 4 ·

Parashat Mas'ey records the names and locations of Israelite camps and journeys from the Exodus through forty years in the desert to the steppes of Moab at the Jordan River near Jericho. The Exodus begins on the fifteenth day of the first month, *Nisan*. Forty years later on Mount Hur, Aaron dies at the age of 123. When the people reach the steppes of Moab, near the Jordan River and the city of Jericho, Moses tells them to enter

the Land of Israel, overwhelm its inhabitants, destroy their idols, and demolish their cult sanctuaries. Afterwards, they are to divide the land by tribal lots.

Moses informs the Israelites that the southern border of their land is from the southern tip of the Dead Sea to Kadesh-barnea in the middle of the Negev desert and to the Mediterranean Sea just south of what today is Gaza. The western boundary is the coast line of the Mediterranean Sea. The northern boundary is to run eastward from what today is near the Israel-Lebanon border to near Mount Hermon close to Damascus, Syria. The eastern border is to stretch south from near Damascus to the Sea of Galilee and from there along the Jordan River and Dead Sea.

Moses informs the people that the land inside these borders is to be divided between nine and one-half tribes, reminding them that the tribes of Reuben, Gad, and the half-tribe of Manasseh have been given their portion in land east of the Jordan River.

where one person who unintentionally murders another may flee, finding safety and a fair trial.

·5·

The people are also told to assign special towns and lands to the Levites and to choose six cities

·6·

The family heads of the clans of Manasseh and Joseph complain to Moses about his allotment to the daughters of Zelophehad. They point out that, if these daughters marry men from another tribe, the tribal lands will pass into that tribe and not remain within the allotment given to Manasseh and Joseph. God informs Moses that their claim is just. To solve the problem of allowing daughters to inherit from their fathers, Moses decrees that every daughter who inherits a share of land must marry someone from a clan of her father's tribe. In this way the tribal portions will remain the same. Following this law, the daughters of Zelophehad marry men within their clans.

THEMES

Parashat Matot-Mas'ey contains two important themes:

1. Caring for yourself or others.
2. Justice for one who accidently harms another.

PEREK ALEF: *"Are Your Brothers to Go to War While You Stay Here?"*

Parashat Matot raises significant moral questions concerning the petition of the Reubenites and Gadites to settle the conquered lands of Jazer and Gilead on the eastern side of the Jordan River. The tribal leaders approach the aging Moses, Eleazar the priest, and the other heads of the community during the crucial months preceding the battle for the Land of Israel. They explain that the area of Jazer and Gilead is cattle country, and they are ranchers with many cattle. "Favor us," they say, "by giving us this land; do not move us across the Jordan."

Moses is infuriated by their request. Sensing betrayal, he angrily tells them: "Are your brothers to go to war while you stay here? Why will you turn the minds of the Israelites from crossing into the land that *Adonai* has given them?" Pausing, he continues by accusing them of the same sort of treason practiced by their ancestors. "That is what your fathers did when I sent them from

Kadesh-barnea to survey the land. After going up to the valley of Eshkol and surveying the land, they turned the minds of the Israelites from invading the land that *Adonai* had given them. . . . And now you, a breed of sinful men, have replaced your fathers."

It is a stinging denunciation, but the Reubenites and Gadites hold their ground. Responding to Moses' charge, they request only enough time to build sheepfolds for their flocks and towns for their children. Afterwards, they are willing to serve in the vanguard of the Israelites' battle for the land and remain until "everyone of the Israelites is in possession of his portion." They also assure Moses that they will make no claim on any land west of the Jordan River.

Moses accepts their promise, warns them against breaking it, and tells them: "Build towns for your children and sheepfolds for your flocks, but do what you have promised."

Criticizing the request of the Gadites and Reubenites, the early rabbis comment on their explicit greed and link them to Korah, Goliath, and Bala'am, who acted unscrupulously to accumulate their wealth only to lose it. They argue that the petition brought before Moses by the Gadites and Reubenites is self-serving. It is the work of people "who love their money" and are willing to sacrifice the welfare of their people to protect their own narrow interests. In fact, say the rabbis, "they separate themselves from their people because of their concern for possessions."

In drawing the parallel between the Gadites and Reubenites to Bala'am, Goliath, and Korah, rabbinic interpreters suggest that they all suffer defeat for the same reason. They "snatch their wealth" by using strength, power, manipulation, and devious means. They are out for themselves, are inconsiderate of others, and will use any means to increase their riches. Their wealth is temporary, say the rabbis. It goes as quickly as it comes because it is not the "gift of God." Because of their greed, they lose it all within two centuries when they are exiled by the invading troops of Assyria.

The rabbis' charge, however, goes even further. They point out that the Gadites and Reubenites prove how foolish they were by their priorities. When Moses criticizes them for seeking land on the east side of the Jordan River before they have helped conquer the Land of Israel, they answer, "We will build here sheepfolds for our flocks and towns for our children."

Their response, claim the rabbis, reveals their priorities. Rather than speaking first about towns for their children and families, they emphasize building sheepfolds for their flocks. They show greater concern for their cattle than for human beings, more attention to their possessions than to their own flesh and blood. Moses, they conclude, is fully justified in denouncing them. (*Numbers Rabbah* 12:7–9)

Jewish historian Josephus Flavius, who lived during the first century (37 C.E. to 100 C.E.), agrees with this harsh rabbinic assessment of the Gadites and Reubenites. Moses, he writes, understands that they are seeking a strategy for securing their wealth on the east side of the Jordan River, not participating in the Jewish people's conquest of their land. For that reason he is justified, argues Josephus, in labeling them "arrogant cowards" because "they had a mind to live in luxury and ease while all the rest were laboring with great pains to obtain the land they were desirous to have." Josephus condemns them for pursing self-interest and neglecting responsibility to the common good of their people. (*Antiquities of the Jews,* IV, 5, A.L. Burt Co., New York, n.d.)

Peli

Modern commentator Pinchas Peli agrees, claiming that the Gadites and Reubenites represent a serious "separatist" threat to the Jewish people. "Moses' concern," Peli writes, "was . . . with the ethical implications of the seceding of the two tribes from a war that should be fought by all of Israel. The conquest of *Eretz Yisrael* was not incumbent only on those people who planned to live on the land. It was, in the eyes of Moses, the culmination of the drama of redemption that should be acted out in full by all the tribes that came out of Egypt."

According to Peli, however, Moses also worries about "the effect that the step taken by Reuben and Gad might have on the morale of the people." He scolds them with sharp language, calling them "a brood of sinful men," and linking them to the "slanderous spies" whose reports were designed to frighten an earlier generation from going up to conquer the Land of Israel. Their request to remain on the east side of the Jordan River undermines the unity of the people and threatens to deplete their strength just when it is most required. Moses, says Peli, understands that a divided people will not be victorious over its enemies. Their request is nothing less than treason. For that reason he severely reprimands them. (*Torah Today,* pp. 189–193)

Ramban (Nachmanides)

Nachmanides sympathizes with Moses' suspicion of the Gadites and Reubenites but maintains that their true intentions are misunderstood. Moses, he writes, is guilty of overreaction. Rather than patiently hearing them out, he rushes to condemn them. He "suspects that they are only suggesting that they stay on the east side of the Jordan because they are afraid of the people in the land of Canaan."

That explains, says Nachmanides, why Moses accuses them of a failure of nerve and of acting like their ancestors who, out of fear, spread lies that the people inhabiting the land are "giants" and would overwhelm the Israelites in battle. Nachmanides is critical of Moses and points out that the intention of the Gadites and Reubenites was never to abandon the effort to conquer the land but to enlarge the inheritance of the tribes by settling in desirable lands east of the Jordan River. Justifying his observation, Nachmanides quotes them as telling Moses: "We will hasten as shock-troops in the van of the Israelites until we have established them in their home. . . . Nor will we claim any share with them on the other side of the Jordan and beyond, having received our share on the east side of the Jordan." (Numbers 32:17–19)

Nachmanides' argument is that the Gadites and Reubenites came before Moses "with a request, not a confrontation." They were seeking, not only what was best for them, but also what they believed would be best for all Israelites. Their plan would give their people more, not less, land. Had Moses taken the time to hear them out instead of instantly condemning them, their real intentions would have been clear.

Moses is criticized
Our sages declare that Moses offends God by describing the Israelites as "a band of sinners" and was punished accordingly . . . in that one of his descendants became a priest to heathen worship. . . . It teaches us . . . if someone has a quarrel with another person, he should not in anger insult the ancestors of that person . . . there even exists an ancient ban against speaking ill of those already sleeping in the ground, even when there are justified reasons for doing so. (Yitzhak Magriso, Me'am Lo'ez on Numbers 32:14–15)

Abravanel

Abravanel agrees with Nachmanides and probes for an explanation of Moses' confusion and indignant response. What accounts, he asks, for Moses' immediate and angry answer to the Gadites' and Reubenites' request to settle their families and cattle east of the Jordan River? He discovers an explanation in the first words they speak to the aging leader. They say to him: "It would be a favor to us if this land were given to your servants as a holding; do not move us across the Jordan." (Numbers 32:5)

Their mistake, says Abravanel, is in putting the matter of their crossing the Jordan in negative terms. In doing so, they confuse Moses, leading him to assume that they fear the battle ahead and are seeking a way to avoid helping conquer the Land of Israel. Had they simply said: "We are ready to join in conquering the land and will be satisfied if you allow us to inherit this land east of the Jordan," Moses would not have misunderstood their motive. Their fault was in the carelessness of their presentation, in the thoughtlessness of their words. (Commentary on Numbers 32:5)

Abravanel's contemporary Isaac Arama believes that Moses should have apologized for his hasty, false assumptions about the Gadites and Reubenites. However, he argues that their motives were deeply divided and thus confused Moses. On the one hand, they were ready to fight alongside the Israelites; on the other hand, they would have been pleased to be excluded and allowed to remain east of the Jordan with their families. They alternated with ambivalence between loyalty to the people and a willingness to forgo their tribal inheritance in the Land of Israel. They knew that their people's destination for forty years was to inherit and live in the Land of Israel, but they also "wished to stay abroad because they had found territory that suited their cattle, as if they had come to this destination to accommodate their animals with choice pasture."

This serious confusion about their motives

accounts for the ambivalence Moses senses in their request, leading him to accuse them of treason. Their own lack of clarity about their goals and their destination leaves them incapable of articulating a direction. They become prisoners of their own ambivalence, unable to determine what they want because they do not know what they want. Little wonder that Moses did not comprehend their true intention. The Reubenites and Gadites hardly understood it themselves. (See *Akedat Yitzhak* on Numbers 32:1–27.)

The controversy continues

According to Rabbi Simcha Zissel of Kelm, the petition of these two and a half tribes not to cross the Jordan because of cattle boils down to a desire for money. Now it doesn't take a great flight of the imagination to relate the cattle and grazing lands of those days to the cattle and grazing lands of today. Why do Jews continue to live outside Israel—on the other side of the Jordan or the other side of the Atlantic? Because they've found good grazing lands for their cattle, and it's a shame to give it up. But even if the descendants of Gad and Manasseh petitioned someone today about their choices, we could very well assume that Moses would say today what he said then: "Why should your brothers go out and fight while you stay here?" (Comment on Numbers 32:6 by Rabbi Shlomo Riskin, Jerusalem Post, *July 21, 1990)*

In contrast to the explanations of Abravanel and Isaac Arama, Rabbi Moshe ben Chaim Alshekh excuses the Gadites' and Reubenites' request, arguing that it was motivated by generosity and realism, not by confusion. He points out that Gad and Reuben "seek to convince the tribal leaders that by their choice everybody will wind up having more land." "The reason they stress that they would *first* build enclosures for their cattle and then provide for their children is to convince Moses that the safety of their children is not their primary concern." Their first priority is to benefit their people.

Supporting his argument, Alshekh writes: "When Moses realizes that the intention of these tribes has been sound, that they have only erred in their semantics, having been imprecise in the use of language, he instructs Eleazar and Joshua that they should not be harassed for their decision to ultimately reside east of the Jordan River." As with Abravanel, Alshekh identifies the problem as one of "semantics." However, rather than blaming the Gadites and Reubenites for carelessness and confusion of goals, he dismisses the matter, saying that, once Moses understands the true intention of their request, "he accepts the fairmindedness of the Reubenites and Gadites and that his suspicions had not been based on fact." (Commentary on Numbers 32:20)

The differing views over the motives of the Gadites and Reubenites in asking to inherit lands east of the Jordan River and to remain in them until they build enclosures for their cattle and cities for their children raise significant moral questions about the division between responsibility to oneself and family and responsibility to one's community. The clash of Moses with the Gadites and Reubenites over interests and intentions is a common and continuing one.

Zugot

Hillel captures the dilemma with three hard questions: "If I am not for myself, who will be for me? But, if I am only for myself, what am I? And, if not now, when?" (*Avot* 1:14)

PEREK BET: *Cities of Refuge: Justice for Unintentional Homicide*

Parashat Mas'ey presents a revolutionary approach to providing justice for those who have committed involuntary manslaughter, meaning that they have unintentionally murdered another person. It suggests that in such accidents guilty parties may escape avenging relatives by going immediately to one of six *arei miklat*, or "cities of asylum." Within those cities, three of which are located in the Land of Israel (Hebron, Shechem, and Kedesh) and three east of the Jordan River (Bezer, Ramoth, and Golan), those who have committed involuntary manslaughter are to find safety and justice from those seeking to avenge the death of their loved ones.

How did these *arei miklat,* or "cities of asylum," function?

The Torah and rabbinic law provide us with some answers. During the biblical period, relatives of murder victims, whether premeditated or unintentional, had the right to find and execute those who were guilty of killing their loved ones. Those whose crime was committed by accident, however, had the right to save themselves from the revenge of families by going immediately to one of the six cities of asylum. All roads leading to these cities had to be clearly marked with signs pointing the way. In addition, roads were to be straight, level, and in good condition. No obstacle was to stand in the way of those seeking asylum.

Upon arrival at the city gate, unintentional murderers presented themselves to elders who offered hospitality. Once rested, they were taken to a court where it was determined whether they were guilty of premeditated murder or involuntary manslaughter. If judged guilty of premeditated murder, they were put to death; if guilty of unintentional homicide, they were allowed to live rent- and tax-free in the refuge city during the lifetime of the incumbent High Priest. After the death of the High Priest, they could return to their home cities, without fearing harm from avengers. (Numbers 35:9–34; Deuteronomy 4:43, 19:8–10; Joshua 20:7; *Makot* 10a–b, 13a)

Modern commentator Rabbi W. Gunther Plaut speculates that the "institutionalization of such asylum may be the earliest of its kind . . ." and points out that "the distinguishing features of the biblical provisions are the restriction of asylum to the unintentional slayer and the connection of the institution with the death of the High Priest." Plaut claims that the notion of the cities of asylum arose out of the need to end family feuds by taking the process of law out of the hands of private individuals and emphasizing the role of "public law enforcement."

For Plaut, the *arei miklat* serve three different

purposes. They are meant to protect unintentional murderers from the passion of avengers, to punish them, and "to contain and isolate the sin that had been committed." He suggests that the isolation of sin is the most important, explaining that "the killing of a human being, though it occurred without evil intent, was a moral injury to the total community" because the people of Israel have "a special God-relationship that was founded on zealous regard for the sanctity of every life." (*The Torah: A Modern Commentary,* pp. 1249–1250)

Rabbi Jacob ben Isaac Ashkenazi of Yanof, author of *Tze'enah u-Re'enah,* supports Plaut's view, maintaining that the *arei miklat* are a means of containing the sin of murder. He writes that each murder, intentional or unintentional, banishes God's Presence from the world because each human being is made in the image of God. When that image is destroyed, God's Presence is sent into exile. By contrast, the High Priest through his saintly function in the sanctuary brings God's Presence into the world. This is why, explains Rabbi Jacob, the unintentional killer is confined to the city of asylum until the High Priest dies. Those who diminish God's Presence "should not go into the world," should not contaminate it with their sin while the High Priest who labors to bring God's Presence into the world is alive. (Commentary on Numbers 35:25)

Hirsch

Rabbi Samson Raphael Hirsch amplifies the point made by Rabbis Plaut and Jacob concerning the sacredness of life by emphasizing the special relationship between the people, the Land of Israel, and God. He writes that "the land is only given on the condition of every human life being respected and being unassailably sacred to the Torah. One drop of innocent blood shed and no notice taken of it drops a stitch in the bond that connects the land with the nation and both with God."

Rambam (Maimonides)

Regulations for the arei miklat

The city of asylum should not be large or small, but average; it is to be established only at a place that affords marketing possibilities and water resources; if there is no water, it has to be installed; it has to be established as a place that attracts settlement in its environment. (Moses Maimonides, Mishneh Torah, *"On Homicide," 8:8)*

Unlike Plaut and Jacob, Hirsch does not look upon the asylum cities as places for the containment of those who "contaminate" the world through their sin of unintentional homicide. Instead, he sees them as providing opportunities offering forgiveness and rebirth. Hirsch argues that, just as when we are born, we are "set in the world as a permanent surrounding"; "consigning the unintentional murderer to a *miklat*-city is similarly a second confining birth. The *miklat*-city is henceforth the whole world to the one who is relegated to it."

According to Hirsch this "rebirth" within the *miklat*-city is not a form of punishment but a chance to find "a life there." For that reason, says Hirsch, the town "should be of medium size . . . not enclosed by a wall, provided with water and food markets . . . all national classes must be settled there." It must have teachers, students, people of science, of spiritual and intellectual quality. According to Jewish tradition, students must be allowed to follow their teacher if he is guilty of unintentional murder, and a teacher must be given the freedom to follow a student.

Quoting from the description of the *arei miklat* in Deuteronomy 19:5, Hirsch emphasizes that unintentional murderers are to "flee to one of these cities *and live*." For that reason, the *arei miklat* are to be environments for "rebirth," nurturing places where human beings can enjoy the company of others, pursue their talents, and grow

both spiritually and intellectually. Despite the fact that the manslayer is confined to such cities until the death of the High Priest, they are not *prisons*. They "must form," concludes Hirsch, "a complete world on a small scale." (Commentary on Numbers 35:6–12)

Medieval commentator Aharon Halevi does not agree with Hirsch's point of view, stressing that asylum cities are meant as punishment places for those who cause the death of others. "Their crime is great because it corrupts the entire world. Our teachers say that a person who commits a premeditated murder will not be saved from death even though he may have observed all the other commandments of Torah. . . . Therefore, a person who has unintentionally caused the death of another deserves the punishment of exile because he has been the agent for a terrible accident. The punishment of exile is comparable to death in a social sense because he is separated from his loved ones and home. He is sent to live among strangers." (*Sefer ha-Hinuch,* 410)

Halevi's view reflects the opinion of some early rabbis who compare the "exile" of Adam from the Garden of Eden to the "exile" of the unintentional murderer to one of the *arei miklat*. Yet the punishment is mixed with compassion. The rabbis point out that Adam ate from the Tree of Knowledge of Good and Bad even though he had been told, "In the day that you eat from that tree, you will die." (Genesis 2:17) Yet God did not put him to death. Instead, say the rabbis, God demonstrates compassion and expels him from the Garden of Eden.

The lesson to be learned here, continue the rabbis, is that human beings are to show compassion upon "the fate of one who commits murder in error. Such a person is to be protected from avengers and exiled from his own home to cities of refuge. . . . Furthermore, you are to establish resting places on the direct roads leading to them, and at each resting place and along the way there are to be signs reading 'To the cities of asylum' so that the person will know how to get there." (*Numbers Rabbah* 23:13)

Rabbi Yitzhak Magriso, author of *Me'Am Lo'ez,* also stresses the compassion shown by Jewish tradition toward the unintentional murderer by creating the *arei miklat*. Their purpose, he maintains, is "to prevent the blood avenger from killing him." Rabbi Magriso adds that the "reason given for the killer having to stay in the city of refuge until the death of the High Priest is that the relatives of the murdered person would then relent. By mourning for the death of a great person, their own anguish would cool since they would come to realize that all human beings die sooner or later, even the greatest of their generation."

Rabbi Magriso recognizes the apparent inequity in connecting liberation from the city of refuge to the death of the High Priest. After all, one unintentional murderer might be confined to the city of asylum for many years while another might be required to stay for no more than a day should the High Priest die just after his assignment to the city by the court. Such disparity in the length of sentences raises questions about the fairness of linking them to the life of the High Priest. Indeed, members of a grieving family whose loved one has been killed could ask: "What kind of justice is this?"

"The answer," argues Rabbi Magriso, "is that, while there are no scales for measuring which willful murder is more terrible and which is less terrible, in the case of unintentional killings there are differences. There may be an inadvertent killing that is close to deliberate murder; for instance, when someone kills another while chopping wood. If he had looked about him, he would have seen the man standing there, and he would not have hit him. By carelessly swinging the ax to split the wood, he hit the man in the head and killed him.

"On the other hand, if the victim was far away and the metal part of the ax flew out of the other's hand and killed him, his guilt is less; in fact, the killing is considered entirely inadvertent.

"God knows the relative guilt of such inadvertent killings. . . . Accordingly, if one killed another accidentally, this could take place close to the High Priest's death, and his punishment would be correspondingly light. While, if it was close to a deliberate killing, it would take a long time before the High Priest died, and the killer's punishment would be correspondingly harsh." (Commentary on Numbers 35:9–15)

Clearly, Rabbi Magriso is establishing the principle that, because the accidental death has a variety of causes, some through carelessness, others through pure coincidence, the release from punishment ought also to be based upon "coincidence" or "fate." The death of the High Priest presents such a happenstance. No one can know the precise timing. It can be considered "God's will," not the intervention of any human being. For that reason, the "timing" of release from one of the arei miklat, no matter how close or far from the sentence, cannot be questioned.

Don Isaac Abravanel provides a more psychological explanation of the link between the High Priest's death and the end of exile in the arei miklat for the unintentional murderer. He points out that, when the High Priest died, the entire people "trembled and repented for his sins." The sense of sorrow was great. So was the feeling about the uncertainties of life itself. "It could, therefore, be assumed," explains Abravanel, "that the avenger of a person accidentally killed would, under the sad circumstances of the High Priest's death, reconsider his anger, calm himself, and no longer seek to execute vengeance for the killing of a member of his family. . . . Then it would be safe for the accidental murderer to leave the asylum city and return home." (Commentary on Numbers 35:25)

While some interpreters claim that the arei miklat are set aside as places of punishment or as a means of containing the "sin of murder" from spreading through the society, most Jewish teachers stress that they are meant to save the person who has committed unintentional murder from death by individuals who might take the law into their own hands and to provide a place where such a person can live a protected and productive life. The asylum cities are not "prison cities" or "penal colonies." Quite the opposite. The arei miklat are meant to be "rebirth" places where a person tormented by the shame and guilt of having accidentally taken a life would be able to surmount anguish and rebuild a creative human existence.

QUESTIONS FOR STUDY AND DISCUSSION

1. The request of the Gadites and Reubenites for settlement on the east side of the Jordan River troubles Moses. Is a person's first loyalty to his family or to his people? Are there times when we must put aside self-interest for the good of our nation and our people? What are the criteria for such a decision? What can we learn from the example of the Gadites and Reubenites?

2. Several commentators criticize Moses for his reaction to the petition of the Gadites and Reubenites. Could he have listened more sensitively and clarified their fears or desires? Should he have demonstrated more patience and understanding? Was he wrong in linking their behavior to their dead ancestors, who could not defend their reputations? Which of the interpreters explains best Moses' reaction?

3. Some interpreters argue that the *arei miklat* were created to keep the murderer from mixing in society with the result that he could meet members of the family of the person who had died at his hand. Such a meeting could cause great sadness or provoke great anger, leading to his own death at the hands of a family avenger. Is isolation a justified response to accidental murder? Is murder a crime that demands a different level of punishment? Why?

4. How would you compare the treatment of those guilty of accidental murder today with the treatment suggested by the Torah and our interpreters?

THE
TORAH
PORTIONS
OF
DEUTERONOMY

PARASHAT DEVARIM
Deuteronomy 1:1–3:22

Parashat Devarim begins a series of speeches by Moses to the Israelites. They are about to enter the Land of Israel. Moses will die in Moab on Mount Nebo. He reminds the people that they will take possession of the land given to Abraham, Isaac, and Jacob. He recalls the time when he was unable to lead them by himself and how God told him to appoint wise leaders to assist him. Moses also recounts sending scouts to explore the land, resulting in a divisive report that frightened the people with predictions of defeat. Because of the scouts' lies and the people's lack of faith, their whole generation was not allowed to enter the land. Only Caleb and Joshua son of Nun, who brought back a positive report, would lead the new generation of Israelites into the Land of Israel. Moses then recounts their route of travel from Kadesh-barnea southward to Ezion-geber, then northward skirting Edom and Moab to Kedemoth and Heshbon, and their victorious battles with Sihon king of Heshbon and Og king of Bashan.

OUR TARGUM

·1·

In Hebrew, this Torah portion, like the fifth and final book of the Torah, Deuteronomy, is called *Devarim,* or "words," because it contains the last "words" or speeches of Moses to the Israelites. Addressing them from Mount Nebo, overlooking the Land of Israel, Moses commands the people to enter and recover the land promised to Abraham, Isaac, and Jacob. He notes that their borders are to extend from the Mediterranean Sea on the West, to Lebanon on the North, and to the Euphrates River on the East.

·2·

Recalling their forty years of desert wandering, Moses reminds the people of their bickering and complaining. He admits that he was incapable of bearing the burden of their leadership by himself and thus appointed wise judges and experienced

tribal leaders to assist him. He commanded them to hear all differences of opinion among the people and to judge each case fairly and impartially. Matters too difficult for the judges were to be referred to him.

· 3 ·

Moses reminds the people that, when they reached Kadesh-barnea, about fifty miles south of Beersheba, he commanded them to go forth and conquer the Land of Israel. When they suggested that spies be sent to scout the land, he agreed. When the scouts returned, ten of the twelve brought back a report that exaggerated the strength of the people of the land and frightened the Israelites. Sulking in their tents, the people refused to go forward, fearing they would be defeated. As a result of their lack of faith, God punished the whole generation by condemning them to die by the sword of the Amorites before reaching the Promised Land.

Only Caleb and Joshua the son of Nun, who brought back a positive report urging the people to conquer the land, were now privileged to lead a new generation into the Land of Israel.

· 4 ·

Moses traces the Israelites' forty-year march through the wilderness. He recalls his warning not to fight the descendants of Esau, who live in Seir, nor to harass the Moabites. Thirty-eight years of wandering passed during their journey from Kadesh-barnea to the wadi Zered. During that period the older generation had died.

Moses instructs the new generation to go to war with Sihon king of Heshbon and Og king of Bashan if they refuse to allow the Israelites to pass peacefully through their countries. When the kings refuse to allow such passage, they are defeated by the Israelites. Their conquered lands are divided among the tribes of Reuben, Gad, and the half-tribe of Manasseh.

Moses concludes this part of his speech by commanding Joshua to conquer the Land of Israel, without fear of its inhabitants.

THEMES

Parashat Devarim contains two important themes:

1. The art of making judgments.
2. The responsibility of leaders and followers.

PEREK ALEF: *Decide Justly in All Cases*

The fifth book of the Torah, *Devarim,* Hebrew for "words," or Deuteronomy, Greek for "repetition of the Law," presents a series of speeches by Moses to the Israelites as they are about to enter the Land of Israel. In his speeches, Moses traces the Israelites' forty-year trek through the desert.

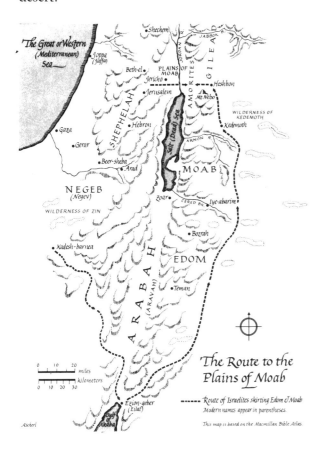

The Route to the Plains of Moab

----- Route of Israelites skirting Edom & Moab
Modern names appear in parentheses.

This map is based on the Macmillan Bible Atlas.

Some scholars claim that *Devarim* was written by an unknown prophet during King Josiah's reign (715–640 B.C.E.) and served as the basis of his consolidation and reformation of the ancient Jewish state. (See II Kings 22–23.) Others dispute this theory, arguing that the text is the work of Moses, that it mirrors the language and laws found within the books of Exodus, Leviticus, and Numbers, and that it presents his last teachings to the people just before his death on Mount Nebo.

While the dispute about dating and authorship persists, the artistry of *Devarim* is acknowledged by all students of Torah. It contains not only reports about the early history and traditions of the Israelites but also a valuable record of the ethical values and laws that guided their society.

Near the beginning of our Torah portion Moses recalls a moment of crisis when he realized that he, by himself, could not lead the Israelites. He remembers saying, "I cannot bear your disputes and bickering by myself." To aid him, he appoints "wise, discerning, and experienced" tribal leaders and judges. "I charged them to hear out the people and to decide justly between them, Israelites or strangers. I commanded them to be impartial in judgment, hearing out low and high alike. I told them to fear no person in rendering a judgment because judgment is God's." (Deuteronomy 1:16–17)

In commenting on the difficult burden of making judgments, the early rabbis, many of whom were presiding court judges, compare the responsibility to dealing with fire. "If you come too close, you will be burnt; if you stray too far, you will be cold. The art of making judgments," they conclude, "is finding the right distance."

Perspective is critical in rendering fair decisions. Independence of outlook and a delicate balance of viewpoint and attitude are essential for arriving at good judgments. Yet how does one achieve independence combined with a balanced viewpoint and attitude? How does one screen out prejudice, bias, and the inclination to favor one person over another?

In his presentation to the Israelites, Moses suggests three significant rules for making judgments: "hear out" those with conflicting views; do not "show partiality to low or high, Israelites or strangers"; and "fear" no one when you are ready to render your decision. Using these guidelines, interpreters of Torah elaborate on the art of achieving justice in human relationships. *(Mechilta* on *Yitro)*

Rabbi Berechiah, quoting his teacher Rabbi Hanina, remarks that "those making judgments must possess seven attributes. They must be wise, understanding, full of knowledge, able, reverent, truthful, and despise corruption." Because for centuries each Jewish community functioned with its own *dayanim,* or "judges," who dealt with all personal and communal problems (e.g., disputes between husbands and wives, children and parents, business partners; business claims; matters of inheritance; ritual matters), it was critical that the reputation of *dayanim* be beyond reproach. Berechiah's seven attributes offer a high standard for judges and others called upon to render judgments. (*Deuteronomy Rabbah* 1:10)

Rabbi Hanina, a wealthy trader and physician who built the second-century academy in the city of Tzporin, or Sepphoris, in the Galilee, also comments about "hearing" a dispute properly. "A judge must not hear the arguments of one person before the arrival of the other person with whom he has a disagreement. Nor should one person seek to pressure the judge into hearing him before the other party is present." A fair, impartial hearing is one where the opponents can correct or object to the impression or facts being presented. To allow a hearing with only one of the parties present could prejudice the judgment. "Hearing," therefore, means listening to both parties together. (*Sanhedrin* 7b)

Within Jewish law, however, "hearing" means even more. If, for instance, one appearing before a judge wishes to bring more evidence or enlarge one's arguments, one must be permitted to do so. A judge must be patient even if the parties are long-winded or the case is tedious. Disputants must not be cut off; they should be heard to the end without intermission. The judge should also ask questions, seeking to "go behind words" and "get to the truth." "Hearing" means paying attention to nuances, inflections, and possible manipulation of facts.

Rabbinic law is also sensitive to how those who make judgments use their eyes. Judges should not look at only one of the disputants. If they do, they may give the impression that one is more important than the other or that one's argument, clothing, gestures, or physical appearance is more pleasing than that of the other. Such an impression could lead to the assumption that the judge is showing favoritism even before a decision is announced. It may also result in a person's leaving a hearing with the conclusion that "the judge's eyes were constantly on my opponent. He favors him. He never paid any attention to me." (*Shulchan Aruch*; *Or ha-Chaim*)

Commenting on the "appearance" of partiality, Rabbi Moshe ben Chaim Alshekh warns against allowing the dress of disputants to influence judgment. "Because one is dressed in fine clothing, the latest fashion, is no reason to favor that person. A person should not go away from a hearing saying, 'Had I worn better clothing, the judge would have heard my case with greater respect and sympathy.'"

Nor, says Alshekh, should judges fear that their reputations will be weakened if, after hearing all the arguments, they decide to refer the dispute to others or to a higher authority. To admit one's inability to reach a fair, knowledgeable judgment is not a sign of weakness but of strength, claims Alshekh. Furthermore, there are times when it is impossible to reach impartial conclusions or when the person called upon to hear the case may not be expert enough to comprehend all of the information necessary for fair and wise judgment. (Commentary to Deuteronomy 1:17)

Commentator Jacob ben Isaac Ashkenazi of Yanov notes that "showing partiality" is not simply a matter of how judges "hear" a dispute but also how they speak to those arguing before them. "If a judge speaks pleasantly to one person and rudely to the other," Ashkenazi warns, "he may influence the emotional state of both disputants, encouraging one and discouraging the other. In fact, such a demonstration of partiality may make it more difficult for the parties to present their cases, especially for the one who assumes that he, for whatever reason, is disliked by the judge. Pressuring or signaling displeasure with disputants may influence the way in which they present facts. . . . [It may] cause them to become so confused that they neglect important elements of their case. Judges, therefore, must do nothing to indicate their preference between contestants." (*Tze'enah u-Re'enah* on Deuteronomy 1:17)

Judging others

Judges should see themselves as if a sword were hanging at their necks and as if hell were open at their feet. They should know whom they are judging and that God will punish judges who depart from the strict line of justice. . . . Whenever judges render true decisions, it is as if they had put right the whole world. . . . (Sanhedrin *7a; also* Tur, Choshen Mishpat *8)*

*Rabbi Akiba teaches: Do not allow sentimentality in making judgments. (*Mishnah Ketubot *9:2)*

Zugot

Rashi

*Hillel says: Do not judge another person until you have put yourself in that person's place. (*Avot *2:5) To which Rashi adds: Do not harshly condemn another for falling into temptation until you have been tempted by similar circumstances and have overcome them.*

*Joshua ben Perachyah says: "Judge all people by giving them the benefit of the doubt." Quoting the chasidic teacher Rabbi Bunum, Rabbi Isaac Unterman comments: "It is always good to give everyone the benefit of the doubt. If the person is really innocent, then you acted correctly and in accordance with the truth. If, on the other hand, the person is guilty, your act is not irrevocable." (*Pirke Aboth, *p. 45)*

Hertz

Rabbi Joseph H. Hertz, quoting a story from the Babylonian Talmud, emphasizes the care judges must take to demonstrate impartiality. Samuel, a revered scholar and judge, was crossing a stream on a narrow plank. A stranger, seeing that the rabbi could use some help, reached out, took his hand, and brought him safely to the other side of the stream. Upon learning the man's name, Samuel realized that the man was scheduled to appear before him for judgment in a few days.

"Friend," Samuel told him, "by your kind favor you have disqualified me as the judge in your dispute."

Favors, even innocent kindness, charity, or the appearance of gestures of generosity, must not be accepted by those making judgments. The integrity of a judge must be above reproach.

The issue of "partiality" also pertains to strangers and noncitizens. Hertz points out that Jewish law makes it clear "there must be no difference between an Israelite and the resident alien." Equal respect and treatment in court is to be given to all persons. They are to be heard and judged on the merit of their case, not by their national, ethnic, religious, or racial heritage. Jewish tradition recognizes how easy it is to discriminate against those whose language, customs, religious beliefs, or skin color may be different. It warns against establishing one standard of justice for citizens and another for strangers. (*The Pentateuch and Haftorahs*, pp. 738–739)

Hirsch

Interpreter Samson Raphael Hirsch quotes the ancient Torah commentary *Sifre,* which makes the point that those engaged in judgment should "not be quick in giving it but should give each individual case repeated consideration even if it is quite similar to cases that have previously arisen on several occasions." Hirsch emphasizes the danger in reaching quick decisions based on first impressions. Often, there is a tendency to hear the opening arguments and rush to judgment on the basis of previous cases. In making such assumptions, judges overlook critical individual circumstances that should be considered in arriving at just decisions. For that reason, Jewish law demands that each case be heard with care for all its details and that "no preliminary opinion of the case should be formed."

Hirsch also raises the delicate issue of threats against judges by those whose cases they are hearing. According to our Torah portion, judges should "fear no person" when it comes to rendering a decision because "judgment is God's."

What in practical terms does this mean? Should a judge risk his life, or the lives of his family members, by pronouncing a decision that could encourage an act of violence?

Rambam (Maimonides)

Basing his conclusion on our Torah portion's commandment to "fear no person, for judgment is God's," Maimonides says, "It is the judge's duty to render judgment without any thought of the injury the evildoer may cause him." The judge must not say, "I fear this person because he may kill my son or burn my wheat or destroy my plants." (*Sefer ha-Mitzvot,* Negative Commandments #276)

Hirsch agrees with Maimonides, arguing that "in giving judgment you are doing the work of God." He explains that "it is not your affair, which you can decide in accordance with your own ideas; it is God's justice, which is to be made actual through you. Therefore, you are not to hold back your just judgment out of the slightest fear." Quoting the Talmud, Hirsch concludes, "Every judge who by his verdict makes true justice into an actual accomplished truth is considered as if he had participated in God's work of creation." (Commentary on Deuteronomy 1:17)

The emphasis of Jewish tradition upon hearing and judging disputes justly is not simply for judges. The guidelines also apply to all engaged in hearing arguments and helping others solve disputes: friends, couples, parents, children, business partners, colleagues, students, teammates—all who must inevitably deal with the clashing opinions or claims of others. If a third party listens with patience to both sides, does not cut off discussion but asks questions that clarify matters, pays attention to the nuances of each party's claim, and strives to treat both disputants equally, there is a good chance that a reasonable settlement will be reached.

The ethical rules for judging the arguments of others, identified by our Torah portion and expanded upon by our commentators, offer a wise path to justice. Since making judgments about the claims of others is "dealing with fire," these important guidelines may save us from being burned.

PEREK BET: *The Spies: Another View*

Several times within Deuteronomy Moses addresses the people and reviews past incidents. Recalling their history, especially their forty years of wandering in the desert, is an important function of his role as leader. He connects them to their roots, emphasizing their unique identity and experience as a people that has endured slavery and has faced the challenges of creating a community of laws and traditions in a desolate desert. In speaking to them about their history, he is preparing them for their future in the Land of Israel. Each incident becomes a lesson meant to strengthen them for the trials ahead.

It is particularly curious that, when Moses retells the story of sending twelve spies to scout the Land of Israel, his version in Deuteronomy (1:19–45) differs completely from the version we have already discussed in *Parashat Shelach-Lecha.* (Numbers 13:1–14:45)

In *Parashat Shelach-Lecha,* God commands Moses to send a leader from each tribe to scout the Land of Israel. They are instructed to return with information about the geography, people, fortifications, soil, and forests of the land, along with some samples of its fruit. When the scouts return at the end of forty days, they report that the land "flows with milk and honey" but warn that its peoples are giants and its cities well fortified. They spread fear among the people, telling them, "We cannot attack the people who inhabit the land for they are stronger than we."

Only Caleb and Joshua disagree, advising Moses and the people to go forward and take control of the land.

Frightened by the other scouts, the people protest to Moses and Aaron, "Why is *Adonai* taking us to that land to fall by the sword? . . . Let us head back to Egypt." For their faithlessness and fomenting of panic among the people, God punishes the spies by extinguishing their entire generation over the next forty years. Only their children, led by Caleb and Joshua, will enter the Promised Land.

In the Numbers version of the story, the spies are blamed for the people's fear and faithlessness. Their distinguished tribal leaders have misled the people with false reports and exaggerations. "You shall bear your punishment," Moses tell them.

The version of the spy story found in this Torah portion differs significantly. Moses recalls the journey of the people to Kadesh-barnea from Mount Horeb, where he had given them the Ten Commandments. According to Moses' recollection, they are camped on the edge of the Land of Israel, ready to conquer it. The people approach him and say: "Let us send men ahead to check the land for us and bring back word on the route we shall follow and the cities we shall come to."

Moses agrees and selects twelve spies. After touring the land for forty days, they return, declaring, "It is a good land that *Adonai* our God is giving to us." The people, however, do not listen to the report. Instead, they refuse to follow God's command to conquer the land. They complain about conditions in the desert and "sulk in their tents." In response to their lack of faith, God punishes them by announcing that none of them, except Caleb and Joshua, will enter the Land of Israel. "Because of you," says Moses, "God was also angry with me, forbidding me from entering as well."

In this recollection by Moses, it is not God who commands Moses to send the spies but the people, who come to Moses, demanding the spies make the journey. In addition, it is not the spies who are at fault for misleading the people by telling them of giants among the Amorites, but it is the people who misconstrue their report. Indeed, it is the people, not the spies, who "have no faith in *Adonai* your God, who goes before you on your journeys. . . ."

In Numbers, the spies are guilty of misleading the people. They cause a crisis of faith in the community and bring death to their generation. In Deuteronomy, it is not the spies but the people who bear responsibility for the catastrophic episode.

What accounts for these two very different versions of the same event? Do we have here a major contradiction of fact and content within the Torah? Are we dealing here with the failing memory of an aging Moses?

Rashi explains that, in Deuteronomy, in his last speeches to the people of Israel, Moses deliberately indicates how disappointed he was with their ancestors' request that spies be sent into the land. Quoting an earlier interpretation from the *Sifre,* Rashi claims that Moses was upset with the people because "they come before him as an unruly crowd, the young people pushing aside their elders, showing no respect for one another or for him."

Rashi also says that Moses tried and failed to placate them with a parable. He told them: "There was a man who said to a friend of his, 'Sell me your donkey.' When the friend agreed, the buyer asked, 'Will you sell it to me on trial?' Again the friend agreed. Then the buyer asked, 'May I try it out in the mountains, take it out in the hills?' Once again the friend agreed. Finally, the buyer, realizing that his friend had total confidence in the donkey, said, 'I shall take the donkey without any trials.' "

Rashi explains that, after reciting the parable, Moses told the people, "I agreed to send the spies, hoping that you would see that I had total confidence in God and in the land, but you did not! You failed to reconsider your request to send spies. Little wonder that catastrophe followed."

According to Rashi and the *Sifre,* it is the people who force Moses to send the spies, and it is the people who bring ruin to themselves by their lack of faith in the report of Caleb and Joshua. In Moses' Deuteronomy recollection, argues Rashi, he makes clear that accusation against the people. (Commentary on Deuteronomy 1:19–24)

The author of the early rabbinic commentary *Tanna Debe Eliyahu* extends the indictment. Claiming that the people were ungrateful, he points out that, although Moses leads them out of Egypt, provides them with silver and gold booty from the Egyptians, and delivers them from Pharaoh's pursuing army at the Red Sea, they remain stubborn and unfaithful. Distrusting Moses and God, they not only complain bitterly about conditions in the desert but also demand that Moses send spies into the Land of Israel.

The author of *Tanna Debe Eliyahu* illustrates his interpretation by presenting his version of the confrontation between the people and Moses. Reading between the lines of Moses' recollection, he puts his own words into Moses' mouth, claiming that, in addition to what the Torah records of his speech, Moses also told the people: "Each one of you approached me, not just a few of you, but all adults and children, demanding that the spies be sent." In other words, it was the people who should bear the blame for sending the spies.

The author of *Tanna Debe Eliyahu* further maintains that, although they saw the fruit of the land, the grapes, the figs, and the pomegranates, they remained defiant, refusing to go forward and conquer the land. Thus they were punished and prevented from entering the Land of Israel. (29:27, pp. 144–146)

Who is responsible for evil?

Rabbi Judah Aryeh Loeb Alter in his commentary Sefat Emet *asks: Why did Moses agree to send the spies but then blame the people for sending them? Because, answers Rabbi Loeb, the people pressured Moses, forcing him to send them. Their insistence infected him, teaching that the sins of people can infect their leaders as well. (See A.Z. Friedman,* Wellsprings of Torah, *pp. 369–370.)*

Jerusalem was destroyed only because the people did not speak out and criticize one another for their wrongdoings. (Shabbat 119b)

Rabbi Jonah teaches: "Those who refuse to listen to criticism or to give it will die," meaning that "criticism" is the only way out of wrongdoing. (Commentary on Proverbs 15:10)

In his book, The Abandonment of the Jews: America and the Holocaust, 1941–1945 *(Pantheon, New York, 1984), author David S. Wyman examines the failure of leaders of the Western world to rescue Jews from extermination in Nazi death camps, raising the*

---

question of responsibility for speaking out in the face of evil. He writes: "Roosevelt, Churchill, and the Pope might have made clear to the Nazis their full awareness of the mass-murder program and their severe condemnation of it. If, in addition, Roosevelt and Churchill had threatened punishment for these crimes and offered asylum to the Jews, the Nazis at least would have ceased to believe that the West did not care what they were doing to the Jews. That might possibly have slowed the killing. And it might have hastened the decision of the SS, ultimately taken in late 1944, to end the extermination." (See pp. 331–340.)

The punishment suffered by the wise who refuse to take part in the government is to live under the government of bad leaders. (Plato)

A demonstration will not solve the problem of poverty, the problem of housing, the problem in the school. But, at least, the demonstration creates a kind of constructive crisis that causes a community to see its problem and to begin moving toward acting on it. (Martin Luther King, Jr.)

Rabbi Moshe ben Chaim Alshekh argues that the people are not only unfaithful and defiant, but they deliberately deceive Moses. They lead him to believe that they require a strategic plan for conquering the land and for that reason are demanding a spy mission. Alshekh writes that the people also insist that the report of the spies not be given to Moses but to them, signaling their distrust of Moses as a leader. The people, Alshekh concludes, must, therefore, bear full responsibility for their deception of Moses and for rejecting his leadership. They cannot blame the spies for their punishment and exclusion from the Land of Israel. Their dishonesty and subterfuge led to disaster. (Commentary on Deuteronomy 1:7)

Modern Israeli commentator Nehama Leibowitz stresses the same point. Making reference to the interpretive work of biblical critic David Hoffman, Leibowitz explains the differences between the versions of the spy story in Numbers and in Deuteronomy. In Numbers, "Moses speaks as a historian recounting the events as they took place." In Deuteronomy, "He is delivering a moral discourse urging the people to learn the lesson of history.

"In his criticism of the people," Leibowitz writes, "Moses recalls that it was the people who initiated the idea of spying out the land. . . . He does so to be able to draw a moral, to emphasize the direct responsibility of their ancestors for their actions. They had wanted to send the spies in the first place, and their responsibility for what happened afterwards was even greater." Moses, says Leibowitz, "wishes to stress this point forcefully upon the descendants of that generation."

Leibowitz

Following this line of reasoning, Leibowitz also points out that "in the earlier account the spies appear as slanderers and misleaders of the people." However, "in the recounting of this incident . . . the main responsibility for the slander is no longer attached to the spies. Moses speaks of the people and accuses the Israelites as a whole and them alone."

Leibowitz concludes: "The Torah here wishes to teach us an important lesson. Human beings are put to the test by God at every moment of their existence . . . the ears hear and the heart is seduced. The question becomes: Is the listener who is misled by the seducer free from all moral responsibility? The Torah makes each person responsible for his or her actions. The listener has a choice of turning a deaf ear to evil and misleading words. Choice belongs to each of us. We have the duty to resist. . . . Each of us has to be his or her own leader, responsible for every action, and not just a cog in the vast machine called society." (*Studies in Devarim*, World Zionist Organization, Jerusalem, 1980, pp. 16–25)

In their distinction between the two versions of the spy mission into the Land of Israel, Jewish commentators raise critical ethical questions about human responsibility in the face of evil. They emphasize that it is not only the leaders who bear the guilt for the injustices and wrongdoings of society. Ordinary citizens are to be held accountable as well. Moses, they claim, meant to teach that lesson in his review of Israelite history.

The lesson remains an important one today. As British statesman Edmund Burke commented: "All that is necessary for the triumph of evil is that good people do nothing."

QUESTIONS FOR STUDY AND DISCUSSION

1. What are the rules the Torah and Jewish commentators lay down for making "just" judgments between disputing parties? How can these rules be applied to making judgments in arguments between family members, friends, and business associates?

2. Jewish law teaches that "a person who accepts money for acting as a judge renders verdicts that are valueless, and a person who accepts pay for testifying as a witness also renders valueless testimony." (*Mishnah Berachot* 4, 6) Given what the Torah and interpreters say about "showing partiality," what is wrong with accepting "pay" or a small gift for judgments and testimony?

3. In our Torah portion, Moses blames the Israelites for asking to send spies into the Land of Israel and for believing their report of doom about the impossibility of conquering it. Is that a fair accusation? Should the people or the leaders—including Moses and Aaron—bear the guilt? Who is really at fault?

4. In 1943, when the occupying Germans announced the roundup of the Jews of Denmark, an extraordinary rescue operation was set into motion, involving the Danish people and the Swedish government. Jews were hidden and then secretly ferried across to Sweden, where they remained in safety until the

end of the war. Of the 8,000 Jews of Denmark, only 400 were rounded up by the Nazis; 51 of them died in the Theresienstadt concentration camp. Is it possible for ordinary people to make a difference in the face of evil? Clearly, the Danish people did. What other examples are there? What do they have in common?

PARASHAT VA'ETCHANAN
Deuteronomy 3:23–7:11

Parashat Va'etchanan continues Moses' speeches to the Israelites just before his death. He pleads with God to allow him to enter the Land of Israel, but he is refused. He warns the people against falling into idolatry; reminds them to observe all the commandments given to them; and recalls their awesome experience at Mount Horeb, where they received the Ten Commandments. Moses also sets aside Bezer, Ramoth, and Golan as refuge cities for those who commit unintentional homicide. Proclaiming that God made a covenant with the Israelites at Mount Horeb, Moses recites the Ten Commandments. The people are overwhelmed and ask Moses to recite the rest of the commandments, promising to obey them. Afterwards, Moses tells them, "Hear, O Israel: *Adonai* is our God, *Adonai* is One. You shall love *Adonai* your God with all your heart and with all your soul and with all your might." Warning them against repeating their rebelliousness at Massah, Moses tells them, "Do what is right and good in the sight of *Adonai,* that it may go well with you. . . ." Finally, Moses informs the Israelites that they are not to spare the people who occupy their land nor intermarry with them. The Israelites are God's chosen and treasured people who will be loved by God if they remain loyal to God's covenant and commandments.

OUR TARGUM

·1·

Moses continues his last speeches to the Israelites while they are camped in a valley near Beth-peor on the east side of the Jordan River. He tells of pleading with God to allow him to enter the Land of Israel and of his disappointment at being refused. God instructs Moses to view the land from Pisgah, a high place on the east side of the Jordan River, and to advise Joshua about conquering the land.

· 2 ·

Moses tells the Israelites that God has given them laws and commandments by which to live when they enter the Land of Israel. They are to observe them faithfully and to teach them to their children. That will prove that they are a "wise and discerning people . . . a great nation."

He reminds the people of the time they stood with him at Mount Horeb (Sinai). The mountain was "ablaze with flames to the very skies, dark with the densest clouds," and God "commanded you to observe the Ten Commandments" and avoid making or worshiping idols. Moses warns them that failure to observe God's commandments will result in their being driven from their land and scattered among the nations. If they search for God with their hearts and souls, God will not fail them or forsake the covenant made with their ancestors.

Moses speaks of the unique relationship between God and the Jewish people. God spoke to them out of the fire at Mount Horeb, liberated them from bondage, and gave them the Land of Israel. "Know therefore this day and keep in mind that *Adonai* alone is God in heaven above and on earth below; there is no other. Observe God's laws and commandments . . . that you may long remain in the land that *Adonai* your God is giving you for all time."

· 3 ·

Moses sets aside three cities—Bezer, Ramoth, and Golan—as refuge places where those who have committed unintentional homicide may flee for justice.

· 4 ·

Moses continues by declaring that "God made a covenant with us at Horeb . . . out of the fire." He then repeats God's words to the people, the Ten Commandments: (1) I *Adonai* am your God who brought you out of the land of Egypt, the house of bondage. (2) You shall have no other gods beside Me. You shall not make for yourself a sculptured image. . . . (3) You shall not swear falsely by the name of *Adonai*. . . . (4) Observe the Sabbath day and keep it holy. . . . (5) Honor your father and your mother. . . . (6) You shall not murder. (7) You shall not commit adultery.

(8) You shall not steal. (9) You shall not bear false witness against your neighbor. (10) You shall not covet.

Recalling the revelation at Mount Horeb, Moses reminds the people of their fear of the fire and their request that he receive the Ten Commandments for them. He agreed and warned them to follow God's commandments. He told them, "Do not turn aside to the right or to the left: follow only the path that God has given you."

Moses then instructs them: "Hear, O Israel: *Adonai* is our God, *Adonai* is One. You shall love God with all your heart and with all your soul and with all your might. Take to heart these commandments. . . . Impress them upon your children. . . . Recite them when you are at home and when you are away. . . . Bind them between your eyes . . . inscribe them on the doorposts of your house."

To parents he adds, "When your child asks, 'What is the meaning of these laws and commandments?' explain: 'We were slaves to Pharaoh in Egypt and God freed us . . . that we might be given the land promised to our ancestors. We are to observe these commandments for our survival.'"

·5·

Moses speaks of the Israelites entering the Land of Israel and dislodging the Hittites, Girgashites, Amorites, Canaanites, Perizzites, Hivites, and Jebusites. He cautions the Israelites against intermarriage with these foreign people, reminding them that "God chose you to be a treasured people. . . ." Those who observe the commandments will be rewarded and those who do not will suffer destruction.

THEMES

Parashat Va'etchanan contains two important themes:

1. Deciphering the meaning of the *Shema.*
2. Loving God.

PEREK ALEF: *Can We Decipher the Meaning of the Shema?*

Of the 4,875 verses in the Torah, one stands out as the code of faith for Jews. Since the time of the Temple in Jerusalem, the words *Shema Yisrael, Adonai Elohenu, Adonai Echad,* "Hear, O Israel: *Adonai* is our God, *Adonai* is One," have been recited twice daily by pious Jews. They are among the first words taught to a young child and the last words recited at the time of death. Jewish martyrs have proudly pronounced them against forces of tyranny, and, through the centuries, they have constituted the most universally known Hebrew phrase in Jewish tradition.

Hertz

In evaluating the words of the *Shema,* Rabbi Joseph H. Hertz, once the Chief Rabbi of the British Empire, writes: "Throughout the entire realm of literature . . . there is probably no utterance to be found that can be compared in its intellectual and spiritual force, or in the influence it exerted upon the whole thinking and feeling of civilized humanity, than the six words that have become the battle cry of the Jewish people for more than twenty-five centuries." (*Authorized Daily Prayer Book,* Bloch Publishing Co., 1948, p. 269)

Rabbi W. Gunther Plaut, author of *The Torah: A Modern Commentary,* characterizes the *Shema* as "a precious gem . . . a diamond set into a crown of faith and proven true and enduring in human history." (pp. 1369–1370)

Despite these testimonials to the importance of the *Shema,* commentators of Torah raise questions about its meaning. And, as with other portions of Torah, they differ in their interpretations.

Rabbi Pinchas ben Hama claims that the Israelites first said the *Shema* as they were standing at Sinai; the early rabbis teach that it is an affirmation of the Jewish people's partnership with God. Other rabbis argue that the phrase "*Adonai* our God" means "God is our Source." In other words, human beings derive from God and are made "in the image of God." (*Deuteronomy Rabbah* 2:31, 35)

Rashi

Rashi offers a different approach. Living in eleventh-century France, in a world of conflicting faiths, he hopes that in time human thought will evolve to the point where all human beings embrace one notion of God and achieve peace. For him the words "Hear, O Israel: *Adonai* our God, *Adonai* is One" translate into "Hear, O Israel: *Adonai,* whom we recognize as our God, will one day be accepted by all people as One, and their belief in one God will unite us as one human family."

In this view, Rashi reflects the perspective of the *Alenu* prayer recited at the conclusion of Jewish worship services. In the words of Deuteronomy 4:39, the *Alenu* declares: "Know therefore this day and keep in mind that *Adonai* alone is God in heaven above and on earth below; there is no other." *Alenu* then continues with the hope that all evil will be ended, that the world will be "perfected under God's rule," and that all human beings will acknowledge that "God is One." (Zechariah 14:9)

In *Gates of Prayer: The New Union Prayerbook* (Chaim Stern, editor, Central Conference of American Rabbis, New York, 1975, p. 620), a more modern version of the *Alenu* mirrors Rashi's interpretation: "Eternal God, we face the morrow with hope made stronger by the vision of Your kingdom, a world where poverty and war are banished, where injustice and hate are gone. Teach us more and more to share the pain of others, to heed Your call for justice, to pursue the blessing of peace. Help us, O God, to gain victory over evil, to bring nearer the day when all the world shall be one."

Rambam (Maimonides)

For Maimonides the *Shema* is not a statement of hope that all human beings will eventually agree that "God is One" but a theological declaration that "the Cause of all existence is One." In his "Thirteen Principles of Faith," Maimonides declares that God's unity is eternal and unique, that God creates all that is and continues to create all that will be, and that God has no body or form. In other writings, he holds that God's power may not be compared to any other power known to human beings. "God is not subject to physical limitations or definitions. . . . God's power is endless."

The *Shema*, says Maimonides, affirms the unity of all that exists and will exist. God's power embraces everything. It is the primary Cause uniting the countless stars of the cosmos; the green globe of earth with its complex web of life; and the yesterday, today, and tomorrow of humanity. In the declaration of the *Shema*, Jews acknowledge that God is not mortal, not limited by human frailties, and not a symbol reducible

to stone, wood, or artistic images. God, Maimonides argues, is the One Power that creates all that is. (See Philip Cohen, *Rambam on the Torah*, Rubin Mass Ltd., Jerusalem, 1985, pp. 146–147.)

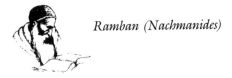

Ramban (Nachmanides)

Nachmanides sees in the words of the *Shema* a very personal statement by Moses. He points out that, in most other cases where Moses uses the words "Hear, O Israel," he follows them with "*Adonai your* God," not with "*Adonai our* God." Why, asks Nachmanides, does Moses in this particular situation choose to say *our* God?

Nachmanides speculates that Moses is concerned with appearances. God has liberated the people from slavery, has provided for their needs in the desert, and has given them the Ten Commandments. Now, in reminding the people of all God has done, Moses does not want to exclude himself. In declaring God's unity with words of the *Shema*, he makes it clear that he is including himself as a witness to God's goodness and power.

> שְׁמַע יִשְׂרָאֵל, יְהֹוָה אֱלֹהֵינוּ, יְהֹוָה אֶחָד.
> Hear, O Israel: *Adonai* is our God, *Adonai* is One.

Nachmanides bases his interpretation on the actual Torah text. In the Torah text, the last letter, *ayin*, of the first word of the *Shema* and the last letter, *dalet*, of the last word are enlarged. Combined, the letters spell the word *ed*, meaning "witness." In reciting the *Shema*, Jews bear "witness" to God's unity and power. (Comments on Deuteronomy 6:4)

Rabbi Abraham Samuel Benjamin Sofer, a nineteenth-century Hungarian interpreter, also calls attention to the way in which the *Shema* is worded. The verse, says Sofer, could have been written "Hear, O Israel: *Adonai* is our God and is One." Instead, the word *Adonai* appears twice. Why?

Sofer speculates that Moses meant to teach that all human experience comes from God. What we know as good and evil, our moments of joy and sadness, all our successes and disappointments, and our good or bad fortune—all are derived from God. At times, Sofer explains, there is a tendency to believe, as did many other early religious traditions, that there are gods for good and gods for evil. Contradicting this assumption, Moses tells the people: "Hear, O Israel: *Adonai* our God provides all the goodness we experience, and *Adonai* our God is the author of the harsh judgments we endure. *Adonai* is One." (See discussion in B.S. Jacobson, *Meditations on the Torah*, p. 271.)

Contemporary commentator Rabbi Shlomo Riskin holds a view close to Sofer's. Carefully analyzing the Hebrew words *Shema Yisrael, Adonai Elohenu, Adonai Echad,* he notes that two words are used for God. The first is *Adonai;* the second is *Elohenu.* Early Jewish tradition, says Riskin, associates God's qualities of mercy and love with the word *Adonai* and God's qualities of judgment with *Elohim.* (*Elohenu* means "our God.")

Riskin maintains that, when Moses first spoke the words of the *Shema,* he meant to clarify a significant problem faced by the Israelites and by all people as well: the problem of understanding God's unity and the way God works in our lives and in the universe. "When things go smoothly," Riskin writes, "when one feels a warm glow of love, success, and good health, one naturally attributes this to the good, compassionate nature of God *(Adonai).* But, when sudden tragedy strikes, the death of a loved one, national calamity, an earthquake, one feels the awesome and inexplicable power of God *(Elohim).* The holy *Zohar* teaches that this seeming split in God's character is a result of our imperfect vision. If we could see more clearly, we'd understand that everything God does is done for the good of humanity. Perhaps we can't always perceive it, but how can a finite creature be expected to fathom the Infinite Will?"

The message of the *Shema,* Riskin adds, "is that, if our eyes (and ears) were truly opened, we would comprehend that everything in the world, both the things we think of as being clearly good and those other things that frighten us with their might, emerges from a compassionate and loving God; in other words, '*Adonai* is One.'" Within Jewish tradition, Riskin concludes, we teach that "just as we praise God for the good so must we praise God for the evil. If we truly understand what the *Zohar* teaches, then we will understand that there is no evil." (*Jerusalem Post,* week of August 12, 1989, p. 23)

What the Shema is for and against
The Shema "*is against the plurality of small gods and half-gods and no gods; it is against the fragmentizing idolatry of worshiping a part for a whole. . . . It is a unity against the duality that would neatly package life into good and evil compartments and assign evil to a lesser scapegoat god, leaving to the chief god the dignity of presiding over unalloyed good. . . .*"

The Shema "*is for the common parenthood of God . . . the unity of humanity. It is for that diversity found in a family. . . . The Shema says: Hear, thou! God is One; therefore, God's children must be one.*" (Jacob J. Weinstein, The Place of Understanding, *Bloch Publishing Co., New York, 1959, pp. 126–127*)

"*Hear, O Israel . . .*" means that every Jew is a member . . . of a community that extends not only in many lands but throughout history.

"*Adonai our God . . .*" means whatever be our condition . . . we will not . . . deny life, despair of the ultimate vindication of righteousness. . . .

"*Adonai is One . . .*" means this is not a universe in which evil has a chance of winning. . . . The ultimate authority, the final sovereign is not the force of army and legion but the God who in time will assert sovereignty. (Morris Adler, The Voice Still Speaks, *pp. 372–373*)

Can we truly believe, however, that "there is no evil" and that this is the message of the *Shema?* Rabbi Leo Baeck, leader of German Jewry during the Holocaust years, probes this significant question. "The Jewish spirit has always sought to grasp the oneness of all reality. All reality, whether unfolding itself in one sphere or in the other, expresses one great unity to the Jewish spirit. . . . Only the One God exists, and, therefore, there is only one order, no matter how manifold its appearances, how contradictory its representations. . . . Within every thing, therefore, there exists an inner reality—unique, one, concealed, unfathomable, infinite, eternal—that is its foundation. . . . Everything proceeds from the One God; everything returns to the One God." (*This People Israel: The Meaning of Jewish Existence,* Albert H. Friedlander, translator, Jewish Publication Society, Philadelphia, 1965. pp. 7, 14, 23)

Baeck's view seems to differ from Riskin's. It is not that there is "no evil" or suffering. Quite the contrary. The suffering of human beings and the evil they experience is real and from God. "Suffering becomes a test of human power to overcome afflictions," says Baeck. He concludes, "The wisdom of Judaism—its very history so devised it—is that it sees life as a task imposed upon human beings by God. Suffering is part of that task; every creative individual experiences it. Through suffering human beings experience those conflicts that give tragic significance to their will to fulfillment." In other words, not only is evil real but in the battle against it human beings test their strength. In reciting the *Shema,* Jews set their energies toward resolving conflicts and transforming them "into unity and harmony." (*The Essence of Judaism,* Schocken Books, New York, 1948, pp. 136–138)

While Baeck does not deny the "reality" of evil, his solution argues that God, who is all-powerful and all-knowing, actually causes evil so that human beings will be tested to triumph over it. Modern Jewish philosopher Rabbi Mordecai M. Kaplan disagrees. He points out that, if we say that God is responsible for evil, then we must accept that God brought on all the atrocities of history and that God is responsible for earthquakes, famine, floods, and other natural catastrophes. Such a conclusion, argues Kaplan, makes God into an evil monster!

Instead, Kaplan believes that we can resolve this difficult problem by "assuming that God's omnipotence [all-powerfulness] is not an actually realized fact at any point of time but a potential fact." If we take into consideration that God is eternal (exists forever), then it is possible to understand "that the evil that now mars the cosmos will ultimately be eliminated" by human beings who, as God's creation, are seeking to "reduce the amount of evil in the world." Evil, therefore, is not, as Baeck says, deliberately and knowingly placed by God in our lives or in the universe as a test for human beings, but, rather, it represents an obstacle to the good that God is seeking to achieve.

Kaplan clarifies his point by answering the question: "Why did God make polio?" He writes: "God did *not* make polio. God is always helping us human beings to make this a better world, but the world cannot at once become the kind of world God would like it to be. When human beings make use of the intelligence God gives them, they learn more and more of the laws of health, by which all kinds of illness can be prevented or cured." In this way, concludes Kaplan, human beings help God eliminate the "evil that now mars the cosmos." For Kaplan, the *Shema* is an expression of the special partnership between God and the Jewish people in the battle against suffering and in the triumph of good over evil. (*Questions Jews Ask,* pp. 115–120)

Rabbi David Hartman also speaks of the *Shema* as an expression of the partnership between the Jewish people and God. He writes: "In reciting the *Shema,* we hear God addressing the community. The emphasis, so to speak, is 'Hear, O Israel: study, reflect, and be attentive to the revelatory message of Torah.' It is the moment of commitment of the community to God and to God's Torah. In the *Shema* . . . one captures the felt immediacy of the revelatory moment of Sinai. God invites the community to enter into the covenant."

Hartman's explanation places Moses in the position of using the words of the *Shema* to remind the people of their experience with God at Mount Sinai, where they received the Ten Commandments. Since that time, Hartman says, Jews recall standing at Sinai when they recite Moses' words. In saying the *Shema* they reenter the covenant of ritual and ethical mitzvot, pledging themselves to God "who commands a total way of life." (*A Living Covenant,* The Free Press,

New York, 1985, pp. 164–165)

Rabbi Jacob ben Isaac Ashkenazi of Yanof, author of *Tze'enah u-Re'enah,* compares reciting the *Shema* to receiving a cherished love letter. "When you say the *Shema,*" he writes, "it should be as if you are reading a letter from the king, which was written to you only today and which you cherish. You listen to each and every word. So should you pay careful attention to each and every word of the *Shema.*" (Comment on Deuteronomy 6:6)

Throughout the centuries, Jews have recited the *Shema* as the most important expression of their faith. They have regarded the words as "love letters," but they have also argued over their meanings, deciphering various messages as if these words contained clues to understanding their relationship to God. Today, the explorations and debates continue. The declaration of Jewish faith remains a source of inspiration and challenge.

PEREK BET: *Is It Possible to Love God?*

In defining "love," psychologist Erich Fromm asserts that it is "an activity, not a passive affect; it is a 'standing in,' not a 'falling for.'" Fromm goes on to explain that "the active character of love can be described by stating that love is primarily *giving,* not receiving. . . . Giving is the highest expression of potency [power]. In the very act of giving, I experience my strength, my wealth, my power. This experience of heightened vitality and potency fills me with joy. I experience myself as overflowing, spending, alive. . . . Giving is more joyous than receiving, not because it is a deprivation, but because in the act of giving lies the expression of my aliveness." (*The Art of Loving,* Harper and Row Publishers, Inc., New York, 1974, pp. 18–19)

Following the statement of the *Shema* in Deuteronomy 6:4, Moses commands the Israelites: "You shall love *Adonai* your God with all your heart and with all your soul and with all your might." This commandment is a cornerstone of Jewish tradition. It is recited together with the *Shema* at worship and is considered by rabbinic tradition as one of the 613 mitzvot, the commandments of Jewish practice.

The statement, however, raises serious questions. Given Erich Fromm's definition of love, is it possible to love God? What could Moses have meant by this commandment? Can "love" for either a human being or God be commanded? How is such love expressed?

Early rabbinic interpreters also struggled with these questions. In the *Tanna Debe Eliyahu* (pp. 139–141), they claim that the mitzvah "to love God" is "the most important commandment of the Torah" and that it entails causing others to love God. For instance, if one studies Torah and acts honestly and fairly in business dealings, then others will say: "Look at the caring and ethical behavior of those who say they love God. Seeing the direct results of such love, they will be inspired to become lovers of God and to teach their children to study Torah and follow its commandments."

Furthermore, say the rabbis, loving God means making no distinction between the way Jews deal with Jews and the way Jews deal with non-Jews. To love God means to treat every human being with respect and to act honestly, justly, and kindly to all. Those who, by their actions, show their love for God set an example for others. It is God's influence on their lives that makes them witnesses to God's power.

Another issue raised by rabbinic commentators is the distinction between loving and fearing God. To show this distinction, they relate the story of a king with two servants. One loved the king; the other feared him. Once the king went on a year-long voyage. The servant who loved him started a beautiful garden, tended it carefully, and, when the king returned, presented him with heaping platters of fruits. The king was delighted and filled with gratitude. Seeing the grateful response of the king, the servant who feared him quickly found some dry fruits and brought them before him. Realizing that this gift was an afterthought, the king was displeased.

To love God means to know the joy of "generosity." Love leads to giving, to sharing one's creativity with another. Fear cripples our capacity to share. It drains our energies from positive efforts to efforts to protect and serve the self. In the act of loving we concentrate all our efforts to provide thoughtful contributions. We use our talents to create "heaping platters of fruits." Loving God, say the ancient rabbis, is like all true loving, an expression of joyful and creative gratitude. (*Yoma* 86a)

Rashi also seeks to define the meaning of loving God. On the basis of comments in the *Sifre,* he argues that the Torah itself offers an explanation: To the commandment "to love God" it adds the words "with all your heart, with all your soul, and with all your might." "With all your heart" means we should serve God with all our powers for goodness, compassion, and charity, as well as with our powers for competition, success, and physical strength. "With all your soul" means we should be ready to give our lives, if necessary, for the principles of our faith. "With all your might" means we should be willing to use our property and wealth to perform acts of charity that promote the survival of our people. Rashi concludes that "lovers of God" see the commandments of Torah as neither antiquated nor out of touch with reality; they see them as always relevant and challenging to their times. (Commentary on Deuteronomy 6:4–6)

While Maimonides agrees with the rabbis of the *Tanna Debe Eliyahu* and Rashi on many points, he clearly views the commandment "to love God" from another perspective. Charity and compassion are sufficient. For him, "loving God with all your heart" is an intellectual commitment. It is a matter of study and critical contemplation. "In the act of contemplation," Maimonides argues, "you come closer to understanding God and to reaching that stage of joy where love of God is bound to follow."

Maimonides has in mind the study of not only the commandments of Torah but also the sciences, including philosophy. "Love of God depends upon knowledge," he says. "Therefore, we should devote ourselves to understanding and becoming knowledgeable in the skills and sciences through which we develop appreciation of God and of our ethical responsibilities. It is only when we comprehend the real nature of our world and universe that we can penetrate the wisdom of God and attain to the love of God."

Loving God, however, is more than the pursuit of knowledge about Torah and "the nature of our world." Recalling the work of Abraham, the founder of Jewish tradition, Maimonides points out that Abraham took upon himself the teaching to potential converts of the Jewish view of God and morality. In this way he brought them to a love for the one God and welcomed them as a part of the Jewish people. "He made God beloved of many people." For Maimonides it is not enough to study or perform the mitzvot with devotion. Loving God means reaching out to those without faith and bringing them in as converts to Judaism. (*Mishneh Torah, Teshuvah* 3, 6, 10; *Sefer ha-Mitzvot,* Positive Commandments #3)

 Luzzatto *Leibowitz*

Loving God

Those who set God before them and are exclusively concerned with doing God's pleasure and observing God's commandments will be called lovers of God . . . the love of God is not a separate commandment but an underlying principle of all the commandments. The love itself cannot be the subject of a command. (Samuel David Luzzatto. See Nehama Leibowitz, Studies in Devarim, *p. 65.)*

*Psychologist Erich Fromm observes that "the basis for our need to love lies in the experience of separateness and the resulting need to overcome the anxiety of separateness by the experience of union. The religious form of love, that which is called the love of God, is, psychologically speaking, not different. It springs from the need to overcome separateness and to achieve union." (*The Art of Loving, *p. 53)*

The only way to attain to a real fear and love of God, to a genuine longing for God through worship, to a comprehension of God is through prayer offered with self-sacrifice and burning enthusiasm. (Rabbi Kalonymus Kalmon, as quoted in Louis Jacobs, Hasidic Prayer, *Schocken Books, New York, 1978, p. 20)*

An individual unable to pray is permitted to engage in telling jokes to awaken a sense of love in his mind. Perhaps, the individual will then say: "If I have laughter from such nonsense, how much more should I appreciate the delights God has given me." As a result, such a person will recite the prayers in love and awe. (Maggid of Meseritch. See Louis Jacobs, Hasidic Prayer, *p. 51.)*

Bachya ben Joseph ibn Pakuda, the author of *Duties of the Heart,* agrees with Maimonides that one achieves a love of God through "contemplation and study" and that the love of God is expressed by reaching out to instruct and welcome converts. He differs, however, in his emphasis. "This love," he writes, "requires that a person should contemplate the basis and principles of the commandments . . . [such contemplation] will bring much delight."

Pakuda argues that worldly concerns often prevent a person from such "contemplation" and "delight." To overcome the stress and temptations of daily concerns and the pursuit of riches, which prevent us from achieving the "love of God," he maintains that we must "retreat from worldliness, from the pleasures of the material world, and from physical desires." Those who seek the true love of God must "commune with God in solitude, dedicate themselves to God alone, trusting, craving, and serving God without any other interests." (See chap. 3; also B.S. Jacobson, *Meditations on the Torah,* pp. 263–274.)

Modern commentator Rabbi W. Gunther Plaut rejects Pakuda's notion of retreating from the world to commune "with God in solitude" as the means to loving God. Instead, Plaut returns to the suggestion of the early rabbinic interpreters that the love of God is expressed through mitzvah-deeds. "It is our attention to the mitzvot that will make us as well as others aware of the One in whose name they are performed, and, the greater our devotion and concentration upon the mitzvah and its Giver, the more likely we will be to enter into the context of pure love. . . ." Plaut concludes: "Each mitzvah done in the right spirit is an act of loving God. It can be done

everywhere and anywhere, wherever the opportunity for mitzvot exists, and it is, therefore, not exclusively the consequence of spiritual contemplation." (*The Torah: A Modern Commentary,* pp. 1370–1371)

Peli

Pinchas Peli agrees with Plaut's emphasis on doing mitzvot as the primary expression of our love for God. He maintains, however, that, while the love of God results "from the awareness of the oneness of God," it is proven in the way it influences us to set an example for others.

Peli calls attention to Moses' command "to take to heart these words that I command you this day. Teach them diligently to your children. . . ." He explains that "the teaching with which we are concerned here is not done by passing on information or by preaching or issuing orders but by personal example, which by its sheer sincerity and passion should be qualified to impress our children or students. . . ." Peli writes, "Your children will be taught by the fact that you yourself practice your religion. . . . Action and thought must go together in the life of the truly religious person." ("Torah Today," in the *Jerusalem Post,* August 10, 1985, p. 10)

Defining the meaning of love and the way it is expressed among human beings continues as a major subject of debate among students of human behavior. Is love a matter of trust, mutual respect, a sense of responsibility for one's self and others, a means of surmounting the fear of loneliness, a biological drive to maintain human survival? Is it a magical, awesome gift of God? And, if it is difficult to explain the meaning of love among human beings, the notion of loving God is equally perplexing.

For that reason, Jewish commentators continue the struggle of deciphering Moses' command to the Israelites: "You shall love *Adonai* your God. . . ." In all their discussions, however, they fail to recognize that love is not static, but dynamic. It evolves, grows, matures. The love expressed by a child is not the same as that felt by a young adult or that achieved by an elderly person who has a life filled with experience. Love is a construct of many feelings: respect, knowledge, loyalty, caring, mercy. It is expressed in uplifting the needy, in the pursuit of justice, in the nurturing of others, in the warmth of an embrace, and in the passion shared by two human beings.

Perhaps Moses, the wise and aged leader of the Israelites, understood that love is not a single expression but rather a mysterious and wonderful gift evolving from human beings and expressed in a variety of ways. That understanding may account for his command: "You shall love *Adonai* your God with all your heart, with all your soul, and with all your might." Moses may have meant that the love of God is achieved only when we develop our emerging powers of mind (heart), spirit (soul), and physical strength (might). Love of God grows, changes, and ripens. As with love among human beings, it is the achievement of a lifetime, not of a moment. For that reason, Moses commands that its cultivation be given the highest priority in every aspect of our lives.

QUESTIONS FOR STUDY AND DISCUSSION

1. Rabbi Milton Steinberg observes: "In proclaiming the oneness of God . . . the prophets . . . were bent on establishing the principles that reality is an order, not an anarchy; that humanity is a unity, not a hodgepodge; and that one universal law of righteousness holds sway over all human beings." (*Basic Judaism,* Harcourt Brace, 1947, pp. 42–43) Given the discussion of the *Shema* by our interpreters, what is the continuing importance of monotheism set forth by Moses and the prophets of Judaism?

2. Rabbi Leo Baeck comments: "In Judaism, love towards God is never a mere feeling; it belongs to the sphere of ethical activity." (*The Essence of Judaism,* p. 129) Do the interpreters of Moses' statement "You shall love *Adonai* your God . . ." agree? Which definition of the "love of God" makes most sense? Why?

3. Given Moses Maimonides' views on loving God, should Jews proselytize?

PARASHAT EKEV
Deuteronomy 7:12–11:25

Parashat Ekev continues the speeches of Moses to the Israelites. He tells them that, if they maintain their covenant with God by observing all the commandments, God will make them fruitful and victorious over their enemies. Reminding them of their forty years of wandering through the wilderness, Moses tells them: "God subjected you to the hardship of hunger . . . then gave you manna . . . in order to teach you that human beings do not live on bread alone. . . ." He then warns them that after settling in their land and enjoying its fruits, they should not arrogantly assume: "My own power and the might of my own hand have won this wealth for me." Nor, continues Moses, should they conclude that it is for their virtue that God allows them to defeat their enemies and conquer their land. Rather, it is punishment of the inhabitants for idolatry, and it is God's fulfillment of the covenant made with Abraham, Isaac, and Jacob. Moses recalls the disloyalty of the people; how they built the golden calf when he was receiving the Ten Commandments on Mount Horeb; how they rebelled at Kadesh-barnea; and how he intervened with God to save them, granting them another set of the tablets on which the Ten Commandments were engraved. Moses recounts the death and burial of Aaron. He also tells the people that God wants them to "cut away the thickening about their hearts," observe the commandments, and learn from their history how God freed them from Egyptian slavery and led them through the desert. If you keep the commandments, Moses promises, God will dislodge all nations before you. No one will stand before your power.

OUR TARGUM

· 1 ·

Continuing his speeches to the Israelites before they enter the Land of Israel, Moses warns them that "if you obey these laws and observe them faithfully" God will keep the covenant made with Abraham, Isaac, and Jacob. He informs the people that their land will be fruitful and without disease, and he tells them they will be victorious over their enemies.

He reminds the people of their journey through the wilderness. God, Moses explains, tested them with hardships to determine if they would keep the commandments. They received manna to eat, "in order to teach you that human beings do not live on bread alone, but they may live on anything that *Adonai* decrees."

Moses cautions the Israelites against arrogance, advising that, when eating from the land, "give thanks to *Adonai* your God for the good land that has been given you."

He warns: "When you have eaten your fill, and have built fine houses to live in, and your herds and flocks have multiplied, and your silver and gold have increased, and everything you own has prospered, beware that you do not grow boastful and forget *Adonai* your God—who freed you from the land of Egypt, the house of bondage; who led you through the . . . wilderness . . . who fed you with manna." Be careful not to say: "My own power and the might of my own hand have won this wealth for me. Remember that it is *Adonai* your God who gives you the power to get wealth, in fulfillment of the covenant that God made on oath with your ancestors (Abraham, Isaac, and Jacob), as is still the case."

· 2 ·

Moses also warns the Israelites: After you have been victorious over your enemies, do not say that "God has enabled me to occupy this land because of my virtues." Moses points out that God has enabled the Israelites to possess the land by dispossessing their enemies because of their "wickedness." God has also given them the land in fulfillment of the covenant with Abraham, Isaac, and Jacob.

·3·

Recalling the time when he climbed Mount Horeb [Sinai] and brought back the Tablets of the Covenant with the Ten Commandments, Moses reminds the Israelites that their ancestors built a golden calf. He tells the people that God said to him: "I see that this is a stiffnecked people. Let Me alone and I will destroy them and blot out their name from under heaven, and I will make you a nation far more numerous than they."

Moses reports that after shattering the Tablets of the Covenant, he sided with the people, arguing with God: "Do not annihilate Your very own people. . . . Else the country from which You freed us will say, 'It was because *Adonai* was powerless to bring them into the land that was promised them, and because God hated them, that God brought them out to have them die in the wilderness.' " (See discussion of parallel text in *A Torah Commentary for Our Times,* Volume II, *Parashat Ki Tisa,* Exodus 30:11–34:35, pp. 77–85.)

Moses relates that God gave him new Tablets of the Covenant with the Ten Commandments and told him to resume the journey toward the Land of Israel. Moses also recounts the death and burial of his brother, Aaron.

·4·

"And now, O Israel, what does *Adonai* your God demand of you?" Moses eloquently asks the people. God, he declares, demands that they keep the commandments. "Mark, the heavens to their uttermost reaches belong to *Adonai* your God, the earth and all that is on it! Yet it was to your ancestors that *Adonai* was drawn in love for them, so that God chose you, their direct descendants, from among all peoples."

For those reasons, Moses continues, "Cut away the thickening about your hearts and stiffen your necks no more. For *Adonai* your God is God supreme . . . upholding the cause of the fatherless and the widow, befriending the stranger . . . with food and clothing. You too must befriend the stranger. . . . You must revere *Adonai* your God."

THEMES

Parashat Ekev contains two important themes:

1. Arrogance and gratitude.
2. "Circumcising" the heart.

PEREK ALEF: *Warning against Arrogance*

Moses raises important ethical considerations in these speeches to the people before they enter the Land of Israel and before he goes to die on Mount Nebo. Recalling their difficult years of wandering through the desert, he tells them that God has tested us with hunger, long days of hot sun, and long cold nights. All that we were given to eat was manna. The years were filled with harsh trials.

Moses, however, does not focus only on the past. He worries about the future. He foresees a time when the Israelites will be comfortable, prosperous, and secure in their land. They will have defeated all their enemies and will be enjoying a flourishing economy. He wonders what the state of their spiritual health will be in such a future era of victory and abundance. Unsure of what they will choose to do, Moses presents them with four guidelines:

Guideline One: Remember the hardships of your past and how you were tested for forty years in the desert to teach you that human beings do not live on bread alone but on what God commands.

Guideline Two: God is bringing you into a good land where you will lack nothing. When you have eaten your fill, give thanks to *Adonai* your God for the good land that has been given you.

Guideline Three: When you are satisfied, have built fine houses, and have increased your herds, gold, and silver, beware of your heart growing haughty, of forgetting God's commandments, of saying: "My power and the might of my own hand have won this wealth for me!"

Guideline Four: After you have defeated your enemies and you occupy the land, do not say to yourselves: "God has enabled me to occupy this land because of my virtues."

Several commentators note Moses' concern as expressed in his guidelines and ask: Why this anxiety about how the Israelites will deal with their future victories and prosperity? Why does Moses focus on their response to success?

Early rabbinic interpreters provide a clue in their discussion of *Guideline Two* in which Moses commands the people: "When you have eaten your fill, give thanks to *Adonai* your God for the good land that has been given you." Explaining this guideline, talmudic commentators point out that it was the catalyst that led the rabbis of the Great Assembly in Jerusalem to create the *Birkat ha-Mazon*, the blessing recited at the end of each meal. Concerned with fulfilling their "debt" to God, they reasoned that "whoever eats and enjoys fruits from God's world without pronouncing a prayer of gratitude steals God's property."

Rabbinic interpreters believed that Moses was deeply worried about the Israelites after their entering the Land of Israel. He feared they would settle in their land, enjoy its fruits, and conclude that they owed nothing to God. Moses presumed they would forget about all that God had done for them and reach the conclusion that they alone were responsible for their harvest of plenty.

For this reason, say the rabbis, Moses warns the Israelites not to eat without pronouncing blessings of thanksgiving, not to enjoy the fruits of the land without acknowledging God with words of gratitude. He compares "eating" and "drinking" without reciting a prayer of thanks to "stealing." (*Berachot* 33a–35a)

Rabbi Nachman and Rabbi Yochanan connect ingratitude not only to the dangers of "stealing from God" but also to "forgetting" and "denying" God. Moses, they argue, is concerned that the Israelites will enter the land, enjoy great prosperity, and forget all the commandments God has given them. Surrounded by abundance, they will grow arrogant and deny God's claim on them. Such "forgetting" will lead to abandon-

ing both their moral and ritual traditions. It will bring an end to the sacred society they are seeking to create. (*Berachot* 49b and *Sotah* 4b)

Ramban (Nachmanides)

Nachmanides also underscores the importance of Moses' emphasis upon "remembering." He claims that the Israelites, about to conquer the Land of Israel and enjoy its fruits, will assume that they alone have brought about all of their victories and are responsible for the bountiful harvests of their fields. Such a conclusion will be logical. After all they are strong men, people of courage and determination. They will have prevailed in war, and the produce of the land will convince them that they alone are the creators of their destiny. For that reason, says Nachmanides, Moses instructs them: "When you are about to say, 'My power and the might of my own hand have won this wealth for me!' *remember*. . . ."

Nachmanides points out that, for Moses, "remembering" is an antidote to arrogance. He explains that the great leader understands the tendency of human beings to take credit for their accomplishments and victories. Self-congratulations are always a dangerous temptation. So Moses warns them to recall their history and cool their pride by remembering that it is God who liberated them from the slavery of Egypt, where they had no power; and it is God who sustained them in the desert wilderness, where they were helpless and hungry. When they are dwelling in comfortable homes, celebrating the bounty of harvests and their wealth, they are advised to recall that it is God who gives the power to accumulate riches. And, when they are about to boast of their victories and gloat about their virtues, they are to recall that it is God who gave them the power to destroy their enemies.

The dangers of pride
The people of Israel are compared to a vine to teach us that just as a vine has large and small clusters of grapes, the larger ones hanging lower

than the smaller ones, the greater a person is (the heavier his wisdom), the profounder his humility.

King Solomon teaches that pride causes a person to speak dishonestly. It forces a person to deviate from the truth and to make accusations that are unfounded. God weeps over those who are filled with pride. (Bachya ben Asher, Kad ha-Kemach, Encyclopedia of Torah Thoughts, Charles B. Chavel, translator, Shilo Publishing House, Inc., New York, 1980, pp. 130–136)

Nachmanides maintains that such recollections, precisely at the moment of celebration, place pride into perspective. They moderate human claims to glory and the dangers of self-centered flattery. History humbles human beings. It prevents arrogant assumptions about human power by setting victories and defeats into the larger and more mysterious context of all life. In his warnings to the Israelites, Moses seeks to teach them that all their bountiful harvests, their wealth and amazing triumphs are not the work of their hands alone but are gifts of God. (Comments on Deuteronomy 8:18–9:4)

By bread alone

Human beings do not live from physical bread . . . but only by God's power, which went forth at the time of creation and which caused bread to come into existence. It is from this spiritual essence that human beings live because it is the food that provides nourishment for the soul. (From Likutei Torah, as found in A.Z. Friedman, Wellsprings of Torah, p. 387)

Rabbi Moshe ben Chaim Alshekh agrees with Nachmanides. He comments that "the person who enjoys exceptional wealth and apparent good fortune" must deal with powerful temptations. It is difficult, he explains, not to "incline toward arrogance" and "the feeling that one is the architect of one's own good fortune independent of God." The danger of such feelings, says Alshekh, is that they often lead a person away from following God's commandments.

The process of moving away from God's commandments, Alshekh argues, "is gradual, almost imperceptible in its progress." It begins "by observing the commandments with the expectation of some material reward. Next, one eats without giving thanks or credit to God. Finally, one takes the credit for successes and bounty and then rejects God and turns to idol worship." Moses, says Alshekh, understood these dangers, and this explains his guidelines to the people. (Commentary to Deuteronomy 7:4–8:14)

Leibowitz

Modern commentator Nehama Leibowitz echoes the conclusions of both Nachmanides and Alshekh. She points out that Moses' observations focus on the tendency of human arrogance and the resulting dangers in forgetting human reliance upon God. "In blindness," she writes, "human beings tend to detect the guiding hand of God only when it is visible in miracles, as had been the case with Israel during the whole of their progress through the wilderness. They fail to see the hidden miracles performed for them continually, even when the world around them . . . seems to be going on as usual."

Moses, Leibowitz seems to be saying, is intent on warning the Israelites against such "blindness." He is anxious that they retain their sense of awe about the world and their unique history. This explains his reminder to them of God's power at work in their past. "Recollection of visible miracles," she concludes, "is designed to open our eyes to the hidden ones that are the foundation of the whole Torah . . . to awaken our faith in the direct intervention of God." (See *Studies in Devarim*, pp. 90–96.)

Rabbi Morris Adler sees in Moses' guidelines something beyond that suggested by previous commentators. He suggests that the awareness that "human beings do not live on bread alone" is "the highest objective of all religious enterprise and aspiration." Adler argues that, in this "great primary statement," Moses is claiming that human beings are "not only body, but also mind."

They are capable of thought and do not realize their potential unless their intellectual powers are awakened to ask questions and seek answers. "Intellectual curiosity is one of the most stirring and significant aspects of human life. . . . When this capacity develops to its fullest, you get scientific knowledge; you get the understanding of the world about us. . . ."

Moses seeks to stress the importance of the human mind by warning the Israelites that feeding the body bread is not enough. Human beings require intellectual nourishment as well. Education must be given highest priority in human affairs because it is the way the intellect is cultivated and evolves.

Adler, however, believes that, when Moses warns "human beings do not live on bread alone," he also means to emphasize that human beings are seekers both of good and of faith. They cannot live without exercising their sense of justice, their sensitivity to what is right and fair. Nor can they exist without acknowledging that "there is mystery in this world; there are vistas of which our limited human understanding can have only the faintest and vaguest of comprehension."

Moses, Adler seems to be suggesting, means to counter the arrogance of those who declare, "My own power and the might of my own hand have won this wealth for me," or who assume that their victories and harvests are of their own proud making. He senses the dangers of their "moral callousness," their selfish concerns, their "loss of obligation" to use their talents and abilities to benefit others, and their impaired understanding that human beings are "dependent upon cosmic forces" that sustain all life. Through his warnings, Adler argues, Moses is urging upon the Israelites the wisdom of gratitude and humility that ultimately leads to responsibility. "True gratitude," he concludes, "always flowers in obligation."

Nearly all of our commentators see in Moses' guidelines significant lessons. They single out arrogance and pride as dangers that lead to moral insensitivity, corruption, and the denial of God. Moses, they believe, is suggesting that the antidote to arrogance is both gratitude and the power of recollection. Our interpreters extend his view, concluding that an appreciation of history puts all human accomplishments into perspective. It roots us in gratitude and a sense of obligation for the gifts of God.

PEREK BET: *Cutting Away Thickness about the Heart*

In these speeches to the Israelites, Moses not only recalls the past but speaks eloquently about the challenges of the future. He recalls how he climbed Mount Sinai to bring the Ten Commandments to their parents' generation and how they rebelled by building a golden calf. Then he recounts his intervention to save the people and his return to Sinai to bring them a second set of the tablets, having shattered the first upon seeing them dancing around their golden idol.

All that history, says Moses, is a prelude to obligations for the future. Having reminded the people of how easily, after just forty days, their parents had given up on him and enthusiastically donated their gold to create an idol, Moses puts a hard question to them: "And now, O Israel, what does *Adonai* your God demand of you?"

He allows no pause between the rhetorical question and his answer. "Only this," he tells them, "to revere *Adonai* your God, to walk only in God's paths, to love and serve *Adonai* your God with all your heart and soul, keeping God's commandments and laws, which I enjoin upon you today, for your good." Seeking to enlarge their understanding of God, perhaps to break the dangerous tendency toward reducing God to an object or an idol, Moses points his finger to the heavens. "Behold, the heavens and infinite stars, the earth and everything on it belongs to God." In other words, God is greater than any *thing* a human being might make, even greater than the sum of all the wonderful aspects of creation. God is the Source of everything in the heavens and on the earth.

Yet, Moses does not conclude his description of God with this observation about God's creation of all aspects of the cosmos. He stretches the imagination of the Israelites by declaring, "And with it all, God was drawn in love to your ancestors and chose you, their direct descendants, from among all peoples."

One can sense the satisfaction and pride felt by the Israelites listening to Moses. His declaration makes them feel special, selected for privileges denied to others. It is satisfying to believe that God "loves" them and will protect and provide for them. "To be chosen by God," one can almost hear the Israelites whispering to one another, "means to be designated from all that exists in the heavens and on the earth for special treatment! We're the lucky ones!"

Moses, however, does not allow the people time to relish such conclusions. Instead he uses tough language to stun them into another dimension in their relationship to God. He tells them, "Cut away the thickening about your hearts and stiffen your necks no more. For *Adonai* your God is God supreme . . . the great, the mighty, and the awesome God, who shows no favor and takes no bribe, but upholds the cause of the fatherless and the widow, and befriends the stranger, providing them with food and clothing.—You too must befriend the stranger, for you were strangers in the land of Egypt. . . . Love, therefore, *Adonai* your God, and always keep God's charge, laws, rules, and commandments."

It is a powerful statement. Moses intends to stir the Israelites before him. He uses the language they know in an entirely novel way. They are familiar with the commandment to circumcise their newborn infant sons, but now Moses is commanding them to "circumcise their hearts." What can he mean? Does Moses really have in mind some kind of grizzly ritual of cutting flesh?

Within Jewish tradition, circumcision, which consists of "cutting away" the foreskin of the penis and exposing the glans, is not only a surgical procedure. From the time of Abraham it has also been a ritual for identifying a Jew with the *berit,* or "covenant," between the Jewish people and God. The ceremony is called *berit milah,* or the "covenant of circumcision." Traditionally, the ritual is performed on the eighth day after the birth of males, or as a part of the male conversion ceremony, in fulfillment of the Torah's commandment: "Every male among you throughout the generations shall be circumcised . . . that shall be the sign of the covenant between Me and you." (Genesis 17:9–14)

While circumcision of the penis is a "mark" of being a Jew and has been a significant force for Jewish identity and survival, one wonders why Moses draws a parallel between "circumcising" the penis and the heart. A clue may be found in the speeches of the prophet Jeremiah to the leaders and people of Jerusalem during the reign of King Josiah (639–609 B.C.E.). Seeing the unjust treatment of the poor and outraged by the corruption of the rich and the absence of morality throughout Judean society, Jeremiah calls the people to return to their faith. Speaking in the name of God, he commands them: "Circumcise your hearts to *Adonai.* Cut away the thickening about your hearts, people of Judah and inhabitants of Jerusalem, lest My anger break forth like fire and burn, with none to quench it, because of your wicked acts." (Jeremiah 4:1–4)

Commenting on Jeremiah's message, modern interpreter Rabbi Sheldon Blank writes that the "symbol" of Jeremiah's concern is the "uncircumcised heart." He explains that "biblical psychology localizes feelings and emotions in the body and looks to the heart as the organ of comprehension—an uncircumcised heart is 'a closed mind.'" Blank points out that Jeremiah draws an analogy between the human heart and a field where crops are planted. "A farmer does not plant an untilled land that weeds have taken over. To make the soil productive, first he plows it and rids it of weeds. So it is with human beings; the human mind as well must be cleared of noxious growth and made receptive. Only then can ideas strike root and grow. This," Blank concludes, "is the obvious meaning of the figure in its first appearance: the uncircumcised heart is the unreceptive mind." (*Jeremiah: Man and Prophet,* Ktav, New York, 1961, pp. 193–207)

According to Blank and other modern interpreters, Jeremiah warns the people of Judah that, unless they change their ways and "return" to carrying out the commandments of Torah, they will encounter "disaster after disaster." Their nation will be destroyed by nations sweeping in from the north. "Wash your heart clean," the prophet admonishes them. But all he encounters is stubbornness, "the unreceptive mind." As a result, he complains bitterly in the name of God: "For My people are stupid,/They give Me no heed;/They are foolish children,/They are not intelligent,/They are clever at doing wrong;/But unable to do right." (Jeremiah 4:14, 22)

Jeremiah's definition of the uncircumcised heart is moral insensitivity. It is acting cleverly; conniving to cheat others; taking advantage of them; oppressing the poor, homeless, and hungry; turning away from those who require healing and help. The uncircumcised heart is a form of stubbornness that leads to callous and cruel treatment of others.

The cure for such a hard heart is to "circumcise" it, to "cut away the thickening" that causes the insensitivity and produces the "closed mind" and the inability to choose right from wrong. Yet, how is that to be accomplished? How do you prevent the heart from hardening again into dangerous and selfish habits? Jeremiah suggests that the human heart, or "mind," must be nurtured like a crop-bearing field. It requires plowing, constant weeding, and seeding. For Jeremiah "circumcising the heart" begins with the acknowledgment of God's covenant with Israel. By conscientiously integrating the commandments of Torah into every aspect of what we do, we uplift our awareness of good and evil, of what improves the quality of human society, and of what harms the common good. The sensitive heart for Jeremiah is synonymous with a wise, just, and caring heart.

to restore understanding, seeing, hearing, and sensitivity.

How shall that be done? Rashi suggests that the remedy for dissolving the membrane that, from neglect, grows around the heart is constant study, self-scrutiny, and performance of the ethical and ritual mitzvot of Torah. This, presumably, is what Moses means when he shocks the Israelites with the words: "Circumcise your hearts." Study of Torah, says Rashi, is the way Jews "cut away the thickness" about their hearts. (Comments on Exodus 6:10 and Deuteronomy 10:16)

Rashi may have had in mind a comment by Rabbi Avira or Rabbi Yehoshua ben Levi, both of whom identify the "thickening about the heart" with the *yetzer ha-ra,* or the human "inclination for wrongdoing." The *yetzer ha-ra* is our tendency to self-centeredness, to weighing all decisions by how they will benefit us. It is evident in our uncaring attitude about the feelings and needs of others. The rabbis claim that unless the *yetzer ha-ra* is carefully balanced by the *yetzer ha-tov,* our "inclination for doing good," it will clog the heart, causing an "occlusion." It will prevent us from doing the will of God. Moses, the rabbis conclude, understands this danger and, therefore, cautions the Israelites to remove the "occlusion," or *yetzer ha-ra,* from their hearts. (*Sukah* 52a)

Rashi

Jeremiah's use of Moses' command to the Israelites to "cut away the thickening about your hearts" also seems to form the basis of Rashi's interpretation. He argues that Moses is telling the Israelites to "remove the closure and cover on your hearts that prevent My words from gaining entrance." Rashi does not identify how the heart, which for him is the center of human affection and intelligence, is covered and closed. What he makes clear is that, once a person's heart is sealed, God's wisdom cannot enter; God's words of Torah are locked out. Whatever barrier is blocking access to the heart must be cut away

Hirsch

Make your heart obedient . . .
Rabbi Samson Raphael Hirsch suggests that by telling the Israelites "to circumcise their hearts," Moses meant "to make your heart obedient to yourself and to your God . . . to do away with the intractability, the insubordination of your heart, to bring your heart with its feelings and desires under your mastery . . . [and] not to allow yourselves to be detracted from the service of God by any uncontrolled thinking or willing and by no stubbornness and self-willed obstinacy." (Comment on Deuteronomy 10:16)

Rambam (Maimonides)

Moses Maimonides sees in Moses' statement a warning against "obstinacy" or "stubbornness." He argues that the whole purpose of the Torah is to put human desires and creativity into human hands. Freedom of choice is given to us. The Torah helps direct our choices. It encourages us to realize that we make mistakes; stubbornness and selfishness often overwhelm our best intentions and confuse us.

Moses, says Maimonides, understood this. For that reason he warned that the Israelites would settle in their new land and sink into self-centered obstinacy. They would forget about God, who had liberated them from slavery. They would abandon God's Torah and commandments, making decisions based on selfishness and greed rather than on the Torah's laws of justice, kindness, and love. Maimonides maintains that, sensing the danger, Moses commands them to "circumcise their hearts." By this he meant: In making decisions, keep your hearts open to the teachings of Torah, to the anguish of others, to the mistakes you will make and the need to rectify them. (*Guide for the Perplexed* 33)

Not satisfied with Maimonides' rational interpretation, some chasidic rabbis suggest that Moses was not referring to human stubbornness or the painful plight of others when he told the Israelites to "circumcise the thickening about your hearts and stiffen your necks no more." Instead, say these chasidic teachers, Moses suspected that the Israelites would begin to question the Torah and its commandments. They would raise doubts about the ethical behavior commanded, pointing out that by following the Torah we must give charity to the poor and, therefore, take less for ourselves. Questions, say the chasidic rabbis, can lead to dangerous answers and choices. Proof that Moses realizes this lies in his statement, "Circumcise the thickening about your hearts," which when punctuated with some minor adjustments means, "If you wish to circumcise the thickening about your heart and your neck, then ask no more questions."

Supporting their view, these chasidic interpreters recall how Rabbi Shneur Zalman of Liadi was constantly besieged for answers to difficult questions about the meaning of various Torah commandments. Wherever he traveled, Jews would crowd about him. As he finished his prayers in the synagogue, they would approach him with their most difficult questions. One day, when he apparently recalled Moses' speech to the Israelites, he told them, "Ask no more questions! Instead, join with me in singing this melody. Hum it if you do not know the words." As the people sang, their spirits were renewed and their minds cleared. They were able to look upon the Torah and uncover answers for their questions. (See S. Y. Zevin, *A Treasury of Chasidic Tales*, Volume Two, Mesorah Publications, New York/Hillel Press, Jerusalem, 1980, pp. 512–515.)

The chasidic masters are concerned with the attitude of cynical rationalism, which assumes that if you ask enough of the right questions you will understand everything—all the mysteries of creation, heaven and earth, life and death. Such a presumption leads, they believe, to arrogance and dangerous assumptions of superiority and insensitivity. Moses, say the chasidic teachers, feared such attitudes. He identified them with what he called the "thickness about your heart." He knew that human beings are incapable of answering all questions and that there is much about our universe and ourselves that will always remain shrouded in mystery. So, say the chasidic teachers, he tells the Israelites: "If you wish to circumcise the thickening about your hearts and your neck, then ask no more questions. Be satisfied with what the Torah teaches and with the vast mysteries and wonders of life."

Clearly the command to "circumcise the heart" is a strange and baffling one. As we can see, interpreters reach a variety of opinions about its meaning. On the face of it, "cutting away the thickening about the heart" is a frightening, even grizzly, suggestion. Yet the aging Moses knows that he must attract the attention of the young Israelites as they ready themselves to follow Joshua into the Land of Israel. Perhaps that explains why he uses such a shocking metaphor. Human sensitivities for justice, truth, honesty, and kindness can easily be calloused. "See enough violence," psychologists observe, "and you begin to get used to it. You begin to tolerate it, even excuse it."

After leading his people for forty years, Moses knew their hearts and his. He understood human strengths and weaknesses and the dangers of anger, pride, self-centeredness, habit, callous insensitivity, and stubbornness. These needed to be "cut away," not unlike the foreskin, as a sign of the covenant between God and the Jewish people.

The purpose of the covenant between God and the Jewish people is to raise human life to levels of sacred behavior, justice, caring, honesty, and love. Anything that prevents Jews from such an accomplishment must be removed. Thus, Moses warns the Israelites with a powerful metaphor. Using the ritual of circumcision, he commands them: "Cut away the thickening about your hearts and stiffen your necks no more." Achieving the Promised Land requires heightened moral sensitivity and integrity.

QUESTIONS FOR STUDY AND DISCUSSION

1. The Book of Proverbs contains several warnings about pride and arrogance. We are told: "In the mouth of a fool is a rod of arrogance,/ But the lips of the wise protect them." (14:3) "Pride goes before ruin,/Arrogance, before failure./Better to be humble and among the lowly/Than to share spoils with the proud." (16:18–19) "A person's pride will humiliate him,/But a humble person will obtain honor." (29:23) Would you agree with these ancient observations? Why do Jewish commentators see dangerous ethical consequences in pride? Can the act of giving thanks curb arrogance? What else do our commentators suggest as antidotes to pride?

2. Our commentators define the "uncircumcised heart" as the unreceptive, thoughtless, and insensitive mind, clogged by habit and stubbornness. Chasidic tradition argues that the way to open such a mind is through quiet meditation or song, not through debating questions and answers. Would you agree? Are there other "better" means of "circumcising" the heart for the purpose of achieving sensitivity, compassion, and wisdom?

PARASHAT RE'EH
Deuteronomy 11:26–16:17

Parashat Re'eh continues Moses' speeches to the Israelites. Warning that they face the choice between a life of blessings or a life of curses, he urges them to observe God's commandments in the land west of the Jordan, where they will settle. He tells them to destroy all idolatrous altars and to worship at the place designated by God. Rules about sacrifices, tithes, and care for the Levites are discussed along with regulations for slaughtering and eating meat. Moses warns the people not to be lured into idolatry by false prophets, family members, or friends. He commands them not to disfigure themselves or eat anything harmful to their health. He clarifies which animals are permitted and which are forbidden for eating and details regulations for setting aside a tenth part of one's produce (tithe) for the stranger, fatherless, and widow. Moses also defines the sabbatical year as a time for canceling all debts and for extending care to the needy, promising that those who help the poor will be blessed with no regrets. In addition, he instructs the Israelites in the treatment of slaves and reviews the three Pilgrimage Festivals of Pesach, Shavuot, and Sukot.

OUR TARGUM

·1·

Moses declares that God is giving the Israelites a choice of making life a blessing or a curse. He urges them to choose the way of blessing by carrying out God's commandments. When they enter the Land of Israel, they are to pronounce a blessing at Mount Gerizim and a curse at Mount Ebal, located across from each other near Shechem. Moses emphasizes that when the people settle in the land, they are to destroy all sites of idol worship and bring their sacrifices, tithes, and gifts to the Levites in the place chosen by God.

Moses informs them that they may follow their desire to eat meat from any of the sheep and cattle given to them, including the deer and gazelle, but the blood is forbidden. It is to be poured on the ground like water. Offerings of flesh and blood may be burnt on the altar.

· 2 ·

Moses warns against adding or subtracting from the commandments. He cautions the Israelites not to be tempted to worship the gods of other nations, telling them that false prophets, diviners, and even family members and friends will seek to divert them from their faith. They should reject all invitations to idolatry. Those who mislead Israelites into idolatry, says Moses, are to be shown no pity. They are to be stoned to death for causing Israelites to stray from loyalty to God and the commandments of Torah.

· 3 ·

Moses tells them, "You are a people consecrated to *Adonai* your God: *Adonai* your God chose you from among all other peoples on earth to be God's treasured people." Reviewing the meaning of "God's treasured people" (see also *Parashat Shemini, A Torah Commentary for Our Times,* Volume II), Moses reminds them that they are forbidden to harm their bodies or to shave their heads when loved ones die. They may eat meat from the ox, sheep, goat, deer, gazelle, roebuck, wild goat, ibex, antelope, mountain sheep—animals that have cleft hooves and chew cud. All other meat is forbidden, including camel, hare, daman, and pig. Anything in the water with fins and scales is allowed. Clean birds are permissible, but the eagle, vulture, black vulture, kite, falcon, buzzard, raven, ostrich, nighthawk, sea gull, hawks of any kind, owl, pelican, buzzard, cormorant, stork, heron, hoopoe, and bat are forbidden. All winged swarming things are also forbidden, as is anything that has died a natural death. Also, they are not permitted to boil a kid in its mother's milk.

· 4 ·

Moses sets out rules concerning the yearly tithes, a tenth part of all the crops of the fields. He tells the people that they are to put aside their pro-

duce, or the value of their produce in cash, for their festival celebrations and for the Levites, who have no fields. Every third year the entire tithe is to be left for the Levite, the stranger, the fatherless, and the widow. Every seventh year they are to forgive all debts.

Expressing concern for the poor, Moses tells the Israelites, "Do not harden your heart and shut your hand against your needy kinsman. Rather, you must open your hand and lend him sufficient for whatever he needs. . . . Give to him readily and have no regrets . . . for in return *Adonai* your God will bless you. . . . For there will never cease to be needy ones in your land."

·5·

Furthermore, Moses deals with the treatment of Hebrew slaves: They must be freed after seven years; they must not be sent away empty-handed but given food from the flock, threshing floor, and vat; slaves who refuse liberation are to have an awl put through their ears at the doorpost, indicating they have chosen to be slaves forever.

·6·

Moses repeats the laws for celebrating the three Pilgrimage Festivals—Pesach, Shavuot, and Sukot. (See also *Parashat Emor, A Torah Commentary for Our Times,* Volume II, pp. 138–146.)

THEMES

Parashat Re'eh contains two important themes:

1. Slaughtering animals and eating meat.
2. The meaning of being an *am segulah,* "a treasured people."

PEREK ALEF: *Shechitah: Regulations for Slaughtering Animals and Eating Meat*

Addressing the Israelites about their future in the Land of Israel, Moses emphasizes the critical importance of observing all the mitzvot, or "commandments," of Torah. If the people do so, they will be blessed; if they do not, they will be cursed. The choice is theirs.

An important part of that choice has to do with what they eat. Moses predicts that once they settle in their land and begin to prosper, the people will have an urge for meat, saying, "I want to eat meat." Moses encourages them, "You may eat meat whenever you wish."

Earlier, when they were wandering through the desert, the only meat permitted for food was cut from animals sacrificed on the altar of the sanctuary. Aside from that, the people ate only the manna that was provided for them each day, with a double portion on Fridays for Shabbat. Now Moses presents a new possibility. When they settle the Land of Israel, they will be allowed to satisfy their craving for meat.

Moses makes it clear, however, that there are important limitations they must follow: "You

may slaughter any of the cattle or sheep that *Adonai* gives you, *as I have instructed you;* and you may eat to your heart's content in your settlements. . . . *But make sure that you do not partake of the blood.*" As the Torah makes clear in Leviticus 6:1–8:36, eating blood is forbidden. It must be removed from the animal, poured on the ground, and buried. Since it is considered the sacred substance of life, it may not be consumed. (See discussion in *Parashat Tzav, A Torah Commentary for Our Times,* Volume II, pp. 108–109.)

Moses also suggests that there exists a required means of slaughter. He tells the Israelites to slaughter meat "as I have instructed you." However, there is no record of such instructions in the Torah. Later, during the talmudic period, rabbinic leaders and interpreters set out rules for the *shechitah,* or the "ritual slaughtering," of animals and birds for food. (See *Hullin.*) These rules are to be carefully followed by the *shochet,* or "slaughterer," who is responsible for the preparation of meat for the Jewish community.

The *shochet* must study and become expert in slaughtering. His hands must be steady. The knife used for slaughter must be regularly examined for sharpness by passing it over a thread or fingernail. The knife must be clean, smooth, and without a dent or nick. It must be at least twice the length of the diameter of the animal's neck and not pointed at its end.

Before slaughtering, the *shochet* is to pronounce the blessing: "Be praised, *Adonai* our God, Ruler of the universe, who sanctifies us with commandments and commands us regarding the act of *shechitah*." Slaughtering is to be performed with a horizontal cut across the throat, severing the trachea and the esophagus. The knife must be drawn quickly back and forth with no *shehiyah*, "pausing"; *derasah*, "pressing"; *hachladah*, "burrowing"; *hagramah*, "cutting out"; or *agirah*, "tearing out." The *shochet* is to spill the blood of the animal upon the ground or upon a bed of dust, pronouncing the blessing: "Be praised, *Adonai* our God, Ruler of the universe, who sanctifies us with commandments and commands us to cover the blood with earth." (See Isaac Klein, *A Guide to Jewish Religious Practice*, Jewish Theological Seminary, distributed by Ktav, New York, 1979, pp. 307–312.)

What is the purpose of these carefully developed regulations regarding the slaughtering of animals?

Rambam (Maimonides)

In his *Guide for the Perplexed*, physician and philosopher Moses Maimonides discusses the importance of diet and the proper means of slaughter. Apparently aware of those who claim that a vegetarian diet is superior to one with meat, he counters that a balanced human diet requires "vegetables and the flesh of animals." He writes: "No doctor has any doubts about this."

Given the requirement for meat, Maimonides expresses concern about the manner of killing animals. Jewish tradition teaches us that the death of the animal should be as painless as possible. It is forbidden to torment the animal by cutting the throat in a clumsy manner, by sawing it, or by cutting off a limb while the animal is still alive. It is also prohibited to kill an animal with its young on the same day. . . . There is no difference in this case between the pain of a human being and the pain of other living beings since the love and tenderness of the mother for her young ones are not produced by reasoning, but by instinct, and exist not only in human beings but in most living beings." Maimonides adds: "For the same reason, the Torah commands us to let the mother bird fly away when we take her young, or her eggs . . . for when the mother bird is sent away, she does not see the taking of her young ones and does not feel any pain." (3:48)

In stressing compassion for animals, Maimonides uses the talmudic ethical category known as *tza'ar ba'alei chayim*, or concern for the "pain of living things." Nothing should be done that needlessly causes pain to an animal. The procedure of *shechitah*, which uses a razor-sharp knife on an area of the throat with very few sensory cutaneous nerve endings, insures that the incision itself causes no pain. With the instant severing of the carotid arteries and jugular veins, there is a massive loss of blood, resulting in unconsciousness within a few seconds. The procedure of *shechitah* has been recognized for centuries as the most humane method of slaughter now in use.

The concern of Maimonides and other commentators for the principle of *tza'ar ba'alei chayim*, the "pain of living things," is not simply a matter of compassion for animals. The same principle is applied to human relations. These laws are set out, says Maimonides, "with a view to perfecting us so that we should not acquire habits of cruelty and should not inflict pain needlessly, but [we] should be kind and merciful even with animals."

To eat or not to eat meat
Rabbi Judah Ha-Nasi declares that a person should be careful not to eat meat. Rabbi Yochanan says that our generation is physically weak, and, if a person has only one gold coin, he ought to buy meat with it. Rabbi Nachman says that our generation is so weak that a person should borrow money to buy meat so that he will be strong in doing God's service. (Tze'enah u-Re'enah, Devarim, p. 912)

Hirsch

Rabbi Samson Raphael Hirsch writes: "The eating of meat is one of the purposes for which God has given you your herds and your flocks." (Comment on Deuteronomy 12:21)

For the sake of self-discipline, it is far more appropriate for human beings not to eat meat. Only if they have a strong desire for meat does the Torah permit it, and even this only after the trouble and inconvenience necessary in order to satisfy the desire. Perhaps because of the bother and annoyance of the whole procedure, people will be restrained from such a strong and uncontrollable desire for meat. (Kelei Yakar, in Abraham Chill, The Mitzvot, *p. 400)*

Agreeing with Maimonides, Aharon Halevi of Barcelona observes in his *Sefer ha-Hinuch* that the "root purpose" of all these regulations about animals and their slaughter "is to teach us that our souls must be beautiful, choosing fairness and pursuing loving kindness and mercy. In training our souls to such behavior with regard to animals, which are not created other than to serve us . . . we train ourselves to do good for human beings and to watch over them lest they cross the boundary with regard to that which is proper and bring pain to others. This is the proper path for the holy, chosen people." (596)

The prevailing motive behind the regulations dealing with the slaughter of animals has to do with the effect that butchering other living beings has upon humans beings. Jewish teachers fear that taking the life of animals promotes insensitivity, even cruelty. To counter this danger, they insist upon blessings before and after the slaughter, care for the sharpness of knives, and the quickest, least painful method of death—all means of teaching compassion in the midst of animal slaughter.

Modern interpreter Rabbi Abraham Isaac Kook differs from this view. He argues that the slaughter and eating of animals is morally wrong and that the rules of *shechitah* do not represent a means of perfecting human behavior. Instead, they are a compromise with physical needs that one day will be overcome.

Kook maintains that at creation (see Genesis 1:24–28) human beings are told to be fruitful and multiply "and rule the fish of the sea, the birds of the sky, and all the living things that creep on earth." However, human beings are not commanded to slaughter animals for meat. While the eating of meat is allowed to Noah and the generations after him, Kook points out that the Israelites are permitted to eat meat slaughtered only for the purposes of sacrifices on the sanctuary altar at the time of their wandering through the desert. He also explains that the permission to eat meat mentioned in this Torah portion arose out of Moses' realization that the people could not control their appetite for it.

For that reason, says Rabbi Kook, rules for the compassionate slaughter of animals were created. They are meant to stress that, despite the human need for meat, killing animals is morally wrong—an act of cruelty and shame. Kook argues that the rules of *shechitah* will ultimately lead human beings to reject afflicting any pain on animals and, therefore, to abandon the consumption of meat. "These regulations will ultimately educate human beings. The silent protest will, when the time is ready, be transformed into a mighty shout and succeed in its purpose. The aim of *shechitah* is designed to reduce pain and to create a realization that one is not dealing with an inanimate object but with a living being." (See Nehama Leibowitz, *Studies in Devarim,* pp. 137–142.)

Rabbi Kook's view that the ideal relationship between human and animal species precludes the slaughter of animals and the eating of meat is one with which most vegetarians would agree. While Kook believed that humanity eventually would adopt that ideal and that the regulations of *shechitah* actually promoted such a conclusion, he did not argue against continuing the slaughter of animals or for a strictly vegetarian diet.

All the regulations of *shechitah* are part of Jewish ritual. They are meant to function within the lives of Jews as a means of bonding the community by sharing standards of behavior. They are meant to uplift ordinary moments into sacred ones. When the *shochet* pronounces a blessing before the act of slaughtering, or as the blood is covered with dust, he is reminded that his work—even the grizzly duty of putting an animal to death for the consumption of meat—must fulfill God's commandments. His skill must be placed in the service of compassion for the pain of animals and reverence for all life. In treating the slaughter of animals as ritual, Jewish tradition seeks to prevent it from becoming a cruel and callous function of human behavior.

Today, the technologies of animal slaughter and the health risks associated with meat consumption are major topics of controversy. Many argue that slaughter houses employing stun guns in an assembly-line killing of animals is extremely cruel; in comparison, the regulations and procedures of *shechitah* are far superior. They introduce important ethical and ritual considerations into the grim butchery of animals—of living beings.

PEREK BET: *Am Segulah: Can Israel Be God's "Treasured People"?*

Several times in the Hebrew Bible the people of Israel are referred to as God's *am segulah*, "treasured people."

In the third month after their liberation from Egypt, Moses climbs Mount Sinai. There, according to the Torah (Exodus 19:4–6), God tells Moses: "You have seen what I did to the Egyptians, how I bore you on eagles' wings and brought you to Me. Now then, if you will obey Me faithfully and keep My covenant, you shall be My *am segulah*, 'treasured possession,' among all the peoples . . . you shall be to Me a kingdom of priests and a holy nation."

In our Torah portion, *Re'eh,* Moses declares to the Israelites: "You are a people consecrated to *Adonai* your God: *Adonai* your God chose you from among all other peoples on earth to be God's treasured people." (Deuteronomy 14:2) In another speech to the people, Moses expands the idea, clearly indicating the mutuality of the commitment between God and the people of Israel. He says, "You have affirmed this day that *Adonai* is your God, that you will walk in God's ways, that you will observe God's laws and commandments and rules, and that you will obey

God. And *Adonai* has affirmed this day that you are, as God promised you, God's *am segulah*, 'treasured people,' who shall observe all God's commandments, and that God will set you, in fame and renown and glory, high above all the nations that God has made; and that you shall be, as God promised, a holy people to *Adonai* your God." (Deuteronomy 26:17–19)

This idea that God selects or designates the people of Israel as an *am segulah* remains a central belief in Jewish tradition. The prophet Malachi (3:17) uses the term. So does the Psalmist who, singing in the Jerusalem Temple, praises God for having "chosen Jacob—Israel—as a treasured possession." (135:3–4)

In daily, Shabbat, and festival worship, just before Jews recite the *Shema*, "Hear, O Israel: *Adonai* is our God, *Adonai* is One," they say: "Be praised, O God, who in love has chosen Israel as God's people." The identical notion is a part of the *aliyah* blessing chanted before the reading of the Torah: "Be praised, O God . . . who has chosen us from all peoples by giving us the Torah."

Clearly the idea of the people of Israel as a "chosen people," as an *am segulah*, a "treasured people," is central to Jewish faith. Yet, what does this assertion mean? How does the Torah understand it? How has it been interpreted throughout the ages?

Early rabbinic commentators speak of the mystery of love between God and the people of Israel. God, they say, discovers the oppressed and beaten people in Egypt, liberates them, leads them through the desert, and gives them the Torah at Mount Sinai. God's love for Israel is "eternal." It is a love of rescue and protection, a love of deep mutual affection and commitment. Quoting the Song of Songs as love poetry between God and Israel, the rabbis claim that God says of Israel, "My beloved is mine and I am my beloved's," and the people of Israel respond, "God is our God, and we are God's people."

This sense that God's mysterious and eternal love for Israel leads to its being chosen as an *am segulah* is expressed by Moses, who tells the people that they are "consecrated" to God, who has selected them not because they are powerful or because they are numerous but because God "loves" them. It is for that reason, Moses tells them, that God freed them from Egypt and made a covenant with them. (See *Exodus Rabbah* 99:1; *Tanna Debe Eliyahu*, p. 31; *Song of Songs Rabbah* 2:16, and Deuteronomy 7:6–11.)

The nature of love, whether between God and Israel or between human beings, cannot be explained. No one knows the secret of what attracts one person to another or what sustains a relationship through years of sad and happy times, through celebrations, achievements, disagreements, and disappointments. If the capacity and power of human love remain a riddle, so does the mystery of the relationship between God and human beings. The origins of life, the sources of human curiosity, and the urge to create, care, seek justice, and love are all beyond explanation. We are more sure of our astonishment than of our tentative theories. For many early rabbinic interpreters, God's choice of Israel as an *am segulah,* God's liberation of Israel from Egypt, and Israel's exile and return to its land could only be explained as an expression of such powerful and mysterious love.

Other rabbinic commentators, however, define the relationship, with a sense of humor, as one of mutual desperation. God and Israel treasure each other and love each other because they cannot do otherwise. These interpreters argue that at precisely the time Israel is wandering on the Sinai desert, God is searching for a people to accept the Torah. Each of the great nations of the world is asked if it will take the Torah, and each refuses, saying that the Torah's teachings are not suitable or compatible with its beliefs and culture. Finally, say these rabbis, God sees the tattered and desperate Israelites making their way across the desert. Lifting Mount Sinai over their heads, God asks threateningly, "Will you accept my Torah or be buried by this mountain?" Seeing that they have no choice if they wish to live, the Israelites respond: "It is a tree of life to all who grasp it. . . ."

For these rabbis, the Israelites choose life by choosing the Torah. It is a desperate choice of a desperate people singled out by a desperate God. God requires an *an segulah,* a "treasured people," not for special favors but for a special burden. They are to be responsible for carrying the Torah

and its commandments into the world. The survival of the world and all within it depends upon the truths of Torah and the loyalty of those who carry out its ethical and ritual commandments. Israel is beloved by God when it chooses to be God's partner and when it lives by Torah. To the extent that they "choose" to live by the commandments they guarantee their survival. (*Numbers Rabbah* 14:10; *Avodah Zarah* 2b–3a)

Rashi

Rashi offers his own interpretation of what it means for Israel to be called an *am segulah.* He suggests that the people of Israel are like a precious golden cup or gem among a larger collection of cups and gems belonging to a ruler. They are precious, special, but not exclusive. All peoples and nations belong to God, writes Rashi. No people, including Israel, can claim that it alone is God's people.

Israel's special relationship with God, Rashi holds, derives from its historical and mutual covenant and from its commitment within that covenant to abandon idolatry and pagan practices and to become a holy people through its practice of all the mitzvot of Torah. God chooses them for that purpose. They are a "treasured people" to God if they uphold their part of the covenant. (Comments on Exodus 15:5; Deuteronomy 14:2)

Ramban (Nachmanides)

Nachmanides connects Rashi's view with those of the Jewish mystics who speak of God's love for Israel and of Israel's love for God. They teach that *if* the people of Israel are loyal in carrying out the mitzvot, they are God's treasure, *am segulah,* or they are "a treasure in God's hand." Nachmanides agrees, emphasizing the conditional nature of the relationship. God loves Israel for its love, its attention, and its loyalty. Every mitzvah performed proves that loyalty. Love promotes love; loyal deeds engender loyal rewards. That is the test of love. It is demonstrated through the doing of mitzvot. Anything else is disloyalty. (Comments on Exodus 19:5)

Dangers and challenges

Israel was elected for the purpose of entering into a covenant relationship with the God of the whole world in order to be God's "kingdom of priests." Without the Torah, and without the commandments, the "chosen people" ceases to be a meaningful concept and is liable to degenerate into pagan notions of chauvinism and racism. (Jakob J. Petuchowski, Ever Since Sinai, *B. Arbit Books, Milwaukee, 1979, p. 64)*

Israel did not discover God. Israel was discovered by God. Judaism is God's quest for man. The Bible is a record of God's approach to Israel. . . . There is no concept of a chosen God, but there is the idea of a chosen people. The idea of a chosen people does not suggest the preference for one people over another. We do not say that we are a superior people. The "chosen people" means a people approached and chosen by God. The significance of this term is genuine in relation to God rather than in relation to other peoples. It signifies not a quality inherent in the people but a relationship between the people and God. (Abraham Joshua Heschel, God in Search of Man, *Farrar, Straus and Cudahy, New York, 1955, pp. 425–426)*

*In seeking to understand the contemporary meaning of being a "chosen people," Rabbi W. Gunther Plaut suggests: "Perhaps it is the destiny of the Jew today to maintain the possibility of minority and diversity . . . to be acculturated yet not assimilated; to be totally in this world yet also beyond it; to be loyal to nations of many countries yet the earth's true internationalists; to be the bearers of many cultures yet never to be known by them; to be acceptable yet never quite accepted for kodesh is invisibly engraved on the forehead of every Jew. (*The Case for the Chosen People, *Doubleday, New York, 1965, pp. 120–121)*

Philosopher Yehudah Halevi proposes a different view in his book, *The Kuzari.* He presents an imaginary discussion between a rabbi and the king of the Kuzars. Writing in eleventh-century Spain, Halevi advances the idea that the people of Israel are "the heart of the nations." When they are sick or suffer, all peoples are sick and suffer. They are an *am segulah,* a people "distinguished from other people by godly qualities, which makes them, so to speak, an angelic caste. Each of them is permeated by the divine essence . . ." with the result that "the human soul becomes divine. It is detached from material senses and joins the highest world, where it enjoys a vision of the divine light and hears the divine speech."

For Halevi, being a part of this "treasured people" is to sense God's influence and to be shaped by it. Living within "the divine light" brings wisdom and sensitivity, justice, and love to the human heart. Hearing "the divine speech" within one's mind opens the way to doing God's will by fulfilling the commandments of Torah.

Halevi's view of being a part of the "treasured people" does not promise a life after death in pleasant and beautiful gardens but rather a life "among angels on earth." The Jewish people are "the heart of the nations," Halevi argues. What they do, how they carry out the commandments of Torah has consequences not only for them but for the entire human family. (See *The Kuzari,* Schocken Books, New York, 1964, pp. 70–76, 109–115.)

Modern philosopher Martin Buber reflects Yehudah Halevi's view but adds his own emphasis. Calling the Jewish people a *res sui generis,* a unique people molded by their history and by "a great inner transformation" through which they became "an anointed kingdom" representing God, Buber seeks to define "the idea of election." He warns against the slogans of nationalism built on empty pride and dangerous assumptions about superiority. Buber maintains that the notion of Israel as a chosen people "does not indicate a feeling of superiority but a sense of destiny. It does not spring from a comparison with others but from the concentrated devotion to a task, to the task that molded the people into a nation."

"The prophets," Buber continues, "formulated that task and never ceased uttering their warning:

If you boast of being chosen instead of living up to it, if you turn election into a static object instead of obeying it as a command, you will forfeit it!" In specific terms, Buber challenges Zionists with the message that "Israel be a nation that establishes justice and truth in its institutions and activities" and that summons all peoples "to walk in the light of *Adonai.*"

For Buber, the people of Israel is no ordinary nation. The people have a mission, a prophetic purpose. They are to bring about the time when justice and compassion will rule all personal, national, and international endeavors and when humanity will be redeemed from cruelty, deceit, and war. The people of Israel is God's instrument to bring about such an era of understanding, truth, and peace. So is Zionism. "True Zionism," Buber concludes in an essay to Zionists in the Land of Israel and throughout the world, is "the desire to establish something like 'the city of the great king. . . .' We need 'Zionists of Zion' here and abroad." (*Israel and the World: Essays in a Time of Crisis,* Schocken Books, New York, 1963, pp. 223–224 and 258 ff.)

Differing with Buber and most of the interpretors on the meaning of Israel as an *am segulah* is the creator of the modern Reconstructionist movement, Rabbi Mordecai M. Kaplan. For Kaplan the concept of "being chosen" grows out of four "entirely unwarranted" assumptions: first, that Jews possess hereditary traits that make them religiously and ethically superior to others; second, that Jews were the first to receive these religious and ethical conceptions and ideals; third, that Jews possess the truest form of religious and ethical ideals; and fourth, that Jews have the historic task of teaching these ideals to the world.

Such assumptions, says Kaplan, are "unproved." He argues that "national traits" are more a product of "historical circumstances . . . geographic environment, and social institutions" than of "heredity." "For Jews to claim sole credit for having given mankind those religious and ethical concepts that hold out the promise of a better world smacks of arrogance." Few modern Jews, Kaplan continues, believe that they have "the truest form of truth" when it comes to religion or ethics. The idea that God selected Israel to "fulfill the mission of making God known to the nations" is not central to Jewish tradition

but is found only in "less than a dozen passages in the second part of Isaiah."

Kaplan advances the idea that each nation and people has a special "vocation." He writes: "No nation is chosen or elected or superior to any other, but every nation should discover its vocation or calling as a source of religious experience and as a medium of salvation to those who share its life. . . ." For the Jewish people this means using all of its traditions, historical experience, ethical wisdom, and culture to advance its survival and enrich all peoples with its unique way of life. (*The Future of the American Jew,* Macmillan, New York, 1948, pp. 211–130)

Kaplan's rejection of the idea of the Jewish people as "chosen," or as an *am segulah,* has received wide criticism. Scholars have pointed out that the concept is not confined to the prophetic pronouncements of Second Isaiah but is found sprinkled generously throughout the Torah, in other biblical writings, and in the Talmud and Midrash. Others claim that, except for Yehudah Halevi's interpretation of Israel as "the heart of the nations," the concept of *am segulah* has never been interpreted to mean that the people of Israel considered itself superior to other peoples. Instead, its meaning is precisely what Kaplan has in mind when he uses the term "vocation." In other words, the people of Israel has a special task, a responsibility, a unique role to play in the history of nations.

The business of Israel

The business of Israel is not to vaunt itself as the historical possessor of a priceless heritage but to live and serve and teach in the sight of all the world as becomes the bearers of a great name and of a glorious tradition . . . to live as seekers after God, doers of justice, ever fanatical for social righteousness, possessed of childlike purity of heart. Whether the heritage is to be carried on depends upon the life of the Jew today, here and everywhere upon the capacity of the individual Jew to give himself to those noble and consecrated ends of life. (Rabbi Stephen S. Wise, quoted in A Modern Treasury of Jewish Thoughts, *Sidney Greenberg, editor, Thomas Yoseloff, New York, 1964, p. 285)*

It is this "task" that modern interpreter Rabbi Leo Baeck attaches to the idea of being "chosen." Israel, he writes, "is elect if it elects itself." Baeck, like other commentators, sees the concept of being an *am segulah* as conditional. If the people obey God's commandments and are loyal to their covenant with God, they will survive and prosper as a "chosen" people. "Israel, though chosen by God, can remain so only if it practices righteousness; sin separates it from God," says Baeck. "Election," he continues, "is a prophetic calling of an entire people. This mission goes beyond Israel itself; it is an election for the sake of others . . . (as the prophet puts it) . . . 'I *Adonai* have called you in righteousness, and will hold your hand, and will keep you, and give you for a covenant of the people, for a light to the nations; to open the blind eyes, to bring out the prisoners from the prison, and them that sit in darkness in the prison house.' " (Isaiah 42:6ff.) Baeck concludes that "this classical idea, of which the essential core has been retained, could only have arisen from the consciousness of election." (*The Essence of Judaism,* pp. 65–68)

The majority of Jewish commentators seem to agree that the Jewish people in its covenant with God sensed that their relationship was more than self-serving. They bore the unusual task of being God's instrument for extending truth, justice, righteousness, compassion, and peace on earth among all peoples. The awareness of this responsibility grew in them and, as Baeck explains, became a "consciousness of election." Nothing in this view claims superiority. On the contrary, being an *am segulah* means the people of Israel must measure its existence by the values and demands of Judaism. To be chosen by God means to be responsible, not only for your own survival, but for the survival of all peoples.

Struggling to determine the meaning of being an *am segulah,* a "treasured people" of God, interpreters to this day must deal with the sig-nificant question: "What is the purpose of Jewish existence?" It is out of such exploration that ancient ideas are confronted and new understandings and responsibilities are born.

QUESTIONS FOR STUDY AND DISCUSSION

1. Why does Jewish tradition put such emphasis upon the manner in which an animal is slaughtered? Are there considerations beyond concern for the pain of animals?

2. The laws of *shechitah* are part of Jewish ritual. Ritual is meant to uplift life with special meanings, to enhance it with ethical values and sensitivities, and to celebrate it with joy. How do the rituals and regulations of *shechitah* perform such a function?

3. Some interpreters argue that the claim that the people of Israel is an *am segulah* leads to arrogance and feelings of superiority. How does the historic notion that being "a treasured people" means being selected for carrying out the commandments of Torah and for being "a light to the nations" answer this objection?

4. There are many contemporary thinkers who argue that surviving as a nation is sufficient and that no nation or people needs to justify its existence, traditions, or culture. Given Jewish history and experience, is mere survival enough? Do the people of Israel and all peoples need to think about life beyond the borders of their own self-interests? Can Yehudah Halevi's view of being an *am segulah* still motivate Jews to stretch their concerns beyond the survival of their people?

PARASHAT SHOFETIM
Deuteronomy 16:18–21:9

Parashat Shofetim opens with the command to appoint judges and legal officials to carry out justice within the society and with a warning against the worship of other gods. Two witnesses must be heard before a court can impose the death penalty. Cases of homicide, civil law, or assault too difficult to decide in one court must be transferred to a higher court. Regulations for choosing a king/leader are presented, including a warning that this leader should follow the laws of Torah faithfully. The offerings for priests are again set forth; also set forth is the difference between a true and false prophet. Cities of refuge for those guilty of manslaughter are described, with laws forbidding the movement of landmarks. The portion concludes with regulations to be observed during war and with assessments of communal responsibilities when the body of a murder victim is found beyond city limits.

OUR TARGUM

·1·

Moses tells the people to appoint judges in their settlements so that they may be governed with justice. These judges must show no partiality and are forbidden to take bribes. "Justice, justice shall you pursue, that you may thrive and occupy the land that *Adonai* your God is giving you."

A person may receive the death penalty only on the testimony of two witnesses. The testimony of one witness cannot be used to validate guilt. If witnesses give false testimony, they shall be punished. If a case dealing with homicide, civil law, or assault proves too complex for the court hearing it, it is to be sent to a higher court of priests or judges whose verdict must be carried out.

·2·

The people are forbidden to set up places for idols, to offer defective sacrifices, or to engage in moon or sun worship.

·3·

Upon entering the Land of Israel, the people may choose monarchy as a form of government. The king must not be a foreigner, may not keep many horses or send servants back to Egypt to purchase additional horses, may not have many wives nor amass silver and gold to excess. The laws of Torah, which he is to study throughout his life, will insure that he is humble and never arrogant toward his people.

·4·

Moses repeats that the levitical priests, the entire tribe of Levi, will not be allotted any land. They are to be given the shoulder, cheeks, and stomach of offerings; first fruits of new grain; wine; oil; and the first shearing of sheep. In this way they will be compensated for their service in the Temple.

He again warns the people against such forbidden religious practices as offering children to fire or following soothsayers, diviners, sorcerers, casters of spells, or those who claim to consult with spirits, ghosts, or the dead. Such people should be banished from the community.

·5·

Moses predicts that other prophets like him will rise to lead the people and that they should be followed. However, he warns the people not to follow those who speak in the name of other gods or those who make untrue predictions in God's name. He declares them "false prophets."

Preparing them to enter the land, Moses reviews the importance of establishing refuge cities for those accused of causing the accidental death of another person. He explains that if a person cutting wood swings an ax to cut down a tree and the ax-head flies off the handle killing a person, the unwitting killer should be allowed to flee to a refuge city for justice, spared from the revenge of the victim's relatives. In this way, explains Moses, innocent blood will not be shed.

He also forbids moving landmarks, a form of stealing property allotted by God to the people entering the Land of Israel.

·6·

Anticipating the wars for reconquering the land, Moses orders the priests to encourage the people with the following formula: "Hear, O Israel! You are about to join battle with your enemy. Let not your courage falter. Do not be in fear, or in panic, or in dread of them. For it is *Adonai* your God who marches with you . . . to bring you victory."

He continues by instructing them to exempt from battle those who have built a new home but not dedicated it, planted a vineyard but not harvested it, become engaged but not married, or are anxious and afraid.

The tactics of war also concern Moses. He tells the people that a town approached for attack must be offered terms of peace. If its citizens respond peaceably, they can be taken to serve as forced labor; if they do not surrender, the city should be besieged and everything in it taken as booty.

When you capture a city, says Moses, do not destroy its trees. You may eat their fruit, but you may not cut them down. Because trees are not human, they cannot withdraw before you. Only trees that do not yield fruit may be cut down and used for constructing siege mounds from which to attack the city.

·7·

Moses declares that when a dead body is found outside a city and the murderer is unknown, the elders and officials from nearby towns should measure the distance between each town and the corpse. When it is determined which city is nearest the corpse, its elders will sacrifice a heifer and declare: "Our hands did not shed this blood, nor did our eyes see it done," and they will be absolved of guilt.

THEMES

Parashat Shofetim contains two important themes:

1. The guarantee and pursuit of justice within the society.
2. Concern for trees and the ecological balance of the world.

PEREK ALEF: *"Justice, Justice Shall You Pursue"*

The pursuit of justice is one of the most frequently repeated concerns, not only of the Torah, but of Jewish tradition. The Israelites are commanded to use "just weights and honest measures" in their business dealings and to hear and "decide justly in disputes between any persons, Israelites or strangers." They are forbidden to take bribes or to favor persons in judgment because they are rich or poor.

Society is to pursue justice in dealing with social, political, and international matters. The prophet Amos declares in the name of God: "Let justice well up as waters, and righteousness as a mighty stream." Isaiah proclaims: "Seek justice, relieve the oppressed." The Psalmist poses the question, "Who is worthy to dwell in God's sanctuary?" and answers, "Those who live without blame, act justly, acknowledge the truth, do not slander others, harm others, hold grudges against their neighbors." The mother of Lemuel, king of Massa, advises her son: "Speak up for those who are silent, for the rights of the unfortunate. Speak out, judge justly, champion the poor and the needy." (See Leviticus 19:36; Deuteronomy 1:16; Amos 5:24; Isaiah 1:17; Psalms 15:2; and Proverbs 31:8–9.)

The emphasis of the biblical tradition upon the pursuit of justice influences later rabbinic teachers as well. Commenting on our Torah portion's command to appoint judges and for those judges to "pursue justice," Rabbi Simeon ben Gamaliel, who served as president of the Sanhedrin in the middle of the first century, C.E., warns his generation: "Do not ridicule or scorn the doing of justice for it is one of the foundations of the world. For the world is balanced on three things—on justice, on truth, and on peace." (*Deuteronomy Rabbah* 5:1; also *Avot* 1:18)

Other rabbinic commentators claim that the guarantee of justice in the courts and in all dealings between human beings is more important than all the sacrifices offered at the Temple in Jerusalem. Justifying their view, they quote a verse from Proverbs, which declares: "To do righteousness and justice is more desired by God than sacrifices." The rabbis maintain that sacrifices had value during the limited historical period of the Temple. By contrast, the doing of justice is always crucial to society's welfare.

To seek justice

To seek justice is to relieve the oppressed. But how else are the oppressed to be relieved if not by judging the oppressor and crushing the ability to oppress! History is not a Sunday school where the question is to forgive or not to forgive. The toleration of injustice is the toleration of human suffering. Since the proud and the mighty who inflict the suffering do not, as a rule, yield to moral persuasion, responsibility for the sufferer demands that justice be done so that oppression be ended. (Eliezer Berkovits, Man and God: Studies in Biblical Theology, *Wayne State University Press, Detroit, 1969)*

Rabbi Nachman offers an example of the importance of justice within society by singling out the accomplishments of King David. "He judged others justly, acquitting the blameless and condemning the guilty, making the robber restore his stolen property." As a result, the kingdom he built was a strong and secure one. People trusted one another and lived in cooperation and peace. (See Proverbs 21:3; *Deuteronomy Rabbah* 5:3.)

This emphasis upon justice within Jewish society is particularly evident within the early biblical and rabbinical judicial systems. *Parashat Shofetim* begins with Moses commanding the people to "appoint judges and clerks for your tribes, in all your settlements." Elders are to appoint judges for these courts and give them power to carry out hearings, trials, and judgments. If they, for any reason, cannot reach a decision, the case is to be turned over to a higher court of priests.

Rabbi Judah Ha-Nasi, author of the *Mishnah*, provides a description of the courts and cases before them. Each city had its local *bet din,* or "house of justice," comprised of three or seven judges with two levitical attendants. In Jerusalem there was a Small Sanhedrin of twenty-three judges and a Great Sanhedrin, which was not only the final arbiter of the law but also responsible for determining the religious calendar and defining matters of religious tradition. The Great Sanhedrin was comprised of seventy-one members, a number chosen because of God's command to Moses to choose seventy elders to help him with the leadership of the people. Adding Moses to the seventy, the rabbis held that the Great Sanhedrin should have a total of seventy-one members.

Rabbi Judah describes the work of each of these courts. The local *bet din* dealt with cases of property and personal injury. The Small Sanhedrin adjudicated criminal and capital cases. The Great Sanhedrin heard all exceptional matters and resolved those cases sent to it by the lower courts.

The system of justice also included regulations for appointing judges, examining witnesses, and hearing and deciding cases. Excluded from acting as judges were relatives, dice-players, those who loaned money on interest, pigeon-flyers, and those who sold produce grown during the sabbatical year. Relatives were also forbidden from serving as witnesses. Witnesses were to be examined one at a time without hearing the testimony of others so the court could compare their reports and reach a just decision.

In noncapital cases representatives were permitted to present arguments for dismissal or conviction in any order; in capital cases, however, the court first heard arguments for acquittal and then for conviction. The eldest judges were required to declare their opinion first when discussing a noncapital case. In capital cases, the youngest were required to speak first so that their opinions would not be influenced by the older judges.

A simple majority determined the verdict in noncapital cases; in capital cases a majority of one was sufficient for acquittal, but a majority of two was necessary for conviction. A higher court could reverse the decision of a lower court on noncapital matters, but in capital cases a higher court could only reverse a case from conviction to acquittal. Finally, the verdict on a noncapital case could be rendered on the same day as the hearing. In capital cases, if the verdict was acquittal, it could also be given on the same day, but if the court decision was conviction, the announcement could be made only the next day. Trials were never permitted on Shabbat or on festivals. (*Mishnah Sanhedrin* 1–5)

Clearly the issue of fair treatment in all cases was central to the Jewish court system of justice. Biased testimony and influence of one judge on another were to be avoided to guarantee fair trials. Decisions seemed to tilt toward acquittal and dismissal rather than conviction.

Commenting on the Torah's command to appoint judges who will promote justice, the *Sifre* emphasizes the importance of appointing judges with expert knowledge of the *halachah,* or "law," and with records of unquestionable integrity, honesty, and righteous behavior.

Rashi

Rashi notes that dispensing justice means not accepting bribes and never showing favor or preferential treatment to witnesses or those seeking judgment before the court. (Comments on Deuteronomy 16:18–20)

Several commentators ask the question: "Why does Moses repeat the word *tzedek,* or "justice," in his statement: "Justice, justice shall you pur-

sue, that you may thrive and occupy the land that *Adonai* your God is giving you"? Pointing out that the commandment could stand without the repetition since the Torah does not often repeat words, interpreters offer a number of explanations.

Some modern scholars suggest that the repetition is simply the way in which the ancient text forms an exclamation point or emphasizes an idea. By repeating the word *tzedek,* Moses underscores the importance of pursuing justice as a means of community survival.

Others argue that the term is repeated to convey the idea that the pursuit of justice is not only the responsibility of government, of judges within society, but also a mitzvah—an imperative—for each individual. One may not say, "Let the courts worry about right and wrong or justice and injustice. I will remain silent."

This may have been what Rabbi Aha meant when he quoted Rabbi Tanhum, son of Rabbi Hiyya, who said, "Though a person may be a scholar of Torah and a teacher of great renown, careful in observing all the ritual commandments, if such a person is able to protest wrongdoing and neglects to do so, he is to be considered cursed." Hearing this observation, Rabbi Jeremiah quoted Rabbi Hiyya who taught: "If a person is neither a scholar, nor a teacher, nor known for observing all the ritual commandments but stands up to protest against evil, such a person is called a blessing."

For rabbinic interpreters of Torah and for the prophets, the pursuit of justice in society was paramount. Correcting the evils originated by human beings was considered the highest ethical priority. Moses' repetition of "justice, justice" was understood to mean: "Don't be satisfied with observing wrongdoing. Stand up and protest against it!" (*Leviticus Rabbah* 25:1)

Why I protest
Author Elie Wiesel tells the story of the one righteous man of Sodom, who walked the streets protesting against the injustice of his city. People made fun of him, derided him. Finally, a young person asked: "Why do you continue your protest against evil; can't you see no one is paying attention to you?" He answered, "I'll

tell you why I continue. In the beginning I thought I would change people. Today, I know I cannot. Yet, if I continue my protest, at least I will prevent others from changing me." (One Generation After, *Random House, New York, 1970, p. 72)*

Set the example

Levi Isaac taught that the meaning of the commandment "Set judges . . . in all your settlements" is that you must set justice in your gates, your high places, which you carry out and which you assure with your deeds. Each Jew is to be an example of the doing of justice for God. (See David R. Blumenthal, God at the Center, *pp. 154–155.)*

The mandate to go out of your way to guarantee justice is also seen in a rabbinic discussion comparing Abraham to Job. Job suffers great personal agony. He loses his riches; he endures the death of his children. Seeking an explanation, justice from God, he asks: "Did I not feed the hungry, give drink to the thirsty, clothe the naked? Why has all this evil come upon me?"

The rabbis claim that God answers: "True, you did all those just acts, but don't count yourself as having fully pursued justice. Compare your deeds with those of Abraham. Where you invited hungry guests into your home and greeted them when they came to the door, he ran out to greet them and invited them inside. Where you gave meat to those who normally ate meat, Abraham gave meat to those who were unaccustomed to eating meat. Where you provided wine and beds for those who were accustomed to drinking wine and sleeping on cots, Abraham built roadside inns to provide for thirsty and tired travelers."

From the rabbinic point of view, Job's pursuit of justice is halfway. He sits and waits. He gives only what is required. He does what is right but does not extend himself to do more. By contrast, Abraham goes beyond what is necessary. He generously greets tired travelers and gives them hospitality. He is not content to help the needy; he wants to prevent the root causes of the difficulties they face. By building roadside inns, he makes the extra effort. He practices the double

emphasis of *tzedek, tzedek tirdof,* or "justice, justice shall you pursue." (*Avot de-Rabbi Natan 7*)

Simeon ben Lakish, who lived and taught in Tiberias during the third century C.E., interprets the repetition of *tzedek, tzedek* as a special lesson in judgment. Lakish urges caution and careful probing. The repetition of *tzedek,* he teaches, is to remind us to make the extra effort to review and examine the evidence by listening carefully to what is said and by seeking out deception. There should be no rush to judgment. (*Sanhedrin 32b*)

Other commentators claim that the repetition of *tzedek* attached to the verb *tirdof,* or "pursue," means to emphasize that there are two forms of justice that must be fulfilled: the *tzedek* of "righteous" action and the *tzedek* of "just compromise." For example, what should be done when two ships meet at the same moment at the entrance to a narrow waterway? Each claims that it arrived first and, therefore, should enter first. Each has *tzedek* on its side. However, if both enter the channel at the same time, they will crash and sink.

The rabbis conclude that in such a case the best solution is to effect a compromise. The repetition of *tzedek* teaches us that when two fully justified claims clash with each other, the just solution is for the parties to find a compromise between them. (*Torah Temimah.* See commentary on Deuteronomy 16:20.)

Rambam (Maimonides)

Moses Maimonides suggests an additional interpretation of the repetition of *tzedek.* It is there, he says, to emphasize the need to reach judgments through a process of consultation. Individuals and judges should not make decisions based on their own impressions. They should discuss a case thoroughly, review it carefully, listen to varying opinions and perspectives, and reach judgments with open eyes and minds. Pursuing justice means going out of your way to make sure that you have gathered all the facts, have consulted with all the experts, and have taken no short cuts. (Comment on Deuteronomy 16:20)

Obviously, the pursuit of justice is a critical and central concern of Jewish society. Within the Hebrew Bible and imbedded within rabbinic commentary, the accomplishment of justice is a requisite for truth and peace. Jews are commanded to pursue justice because no human community can survive without it. The cornerstone of Jewish ethics is to "be deliberate and careful in judgment" because "where justice is done, peace and truth prevail." (*Avot* 1:1; *Pesikta de-Rav Kahana* 140b)

PEREK BET: *Don't Destroy the Environment, God's Precious Gift!*

If the pursuit of justice discussed above is meant to preserve the delicate relations of human beings within society, Moses' instruction concerning the treatment of trees is meant to preserve the delicate relations of human beings to the environment of the earth. Moses tells the people: "When in your war against a city you have to besiege it a long time in order to capture it, you must not destroy its trees, wielding the ax against them. You may eat of them, but you must not cut them down." Then, as if to create sympathy for the trees, he adds the question: "Are trees of the field, like human beings, capable of withdrawing before you into the besieged city?" (Deuteronomy 20:19)

While the commandment deals specifically with cutting down trees during a siege, Jewish interpreters extend it to cover all forms of wasteful destruction under the principle of *bal tashchit,* or "do not destroy." (See discussion of this principle as it relates to the treatment of animals in *Parashat Re'eh.*)

Accordingly, they forbid shifting the course of a stream that could cause the roots of trees to dry up. When asked for the justification for such a law, the rabbis explain that our Torah portion forbids destroying trees, not only by chopping them down with an ax, but "by all means of destruction," including the diversion of water from their roots. Rabbinic commentators also extend Moses' prohibition of cutting down trees during a siege to a prohibition of cutting them

down during times of peace. Wasteful destruction is condemned. "Anyone who deliberately breaks dishes, tears clothing, wrecks a building, clogs up a fountain, or wastes food violates the law of *bal tashchit.* (*Hullin* 7b; *Tosafot Baba Kamma* 115b; *Avodah Zarah* 30b; *Kiddushin* 32a)

Aversion to vandalism
Rabbi Joseph Karo in his Shulchan Aruch *declares: "It is forbidden to destroy or to injure anything capable of being useful to human beings."* (Hilchot Shemirat Guf va-Nefesh 14)

Rabbi Robert Gordis comments: "The principle of bal tashchit *entered deep into Jewish consciousness so that the aversion to vandalism became an almost psychological reflex, and wanton destruction was viewed with loathing and horror by Jews for centuries."* (Congress Bi-Weekly, *April 2, 1971, p.10*)

Teach your children what we have taught our children—the earth is our mother. Whatever befalls the earth befalls the children of the earth. If human beings foul the ground, they foul themselves. This we know. The earth does not belong to humanity; humanity belongs to the earth. This we know. All things are connected like the blood that unites one family. All things are connected. Whatever befalls the earth befalls the children of the earth. Humanity did not weave the web of life; it is merely a strand in it. Whatever humanity does to the web, it does to itself. (Chief Seattle, as quoted in The Earth Speaks, *edited by Steve Van Matre and Bill Weiler, Institute for Earth Education, Warrensville, Illinois, 1983, p. 122*)

While all commentators seem to agree with the emphasis against wasteful destruction, there are differences of opinion on the justification for such a prohibition. The differences reveal at least two foundations for the Jewish concern about the environment.

Moses ibn Ezra, for example, takes a very pragmatic view about chopping down trees. He argues that fruit trees yield food; human beings require their produce for existence. Therefore, we are prohibited from cutting them down because, in doing so, we are injuring ourselves. "The life of human beings," he writes, "derives from trees." One does not destroy the environment because destruction of the environment results in self-destruction.

Hirsch

Rabbi Samson Raphael Hirsch agrees with this pragmatic—human-centered—approach. He emphasizes that "the tree of the field is the human being; the products of the soil are the condition for human existence." For Hirsch, as for ibn Ezra, destroying fruit trees or wasting precious resources endangers human life. It wastes that which we require for survival. God gave us the world to enjoy, with its fruits to nourish and sustain us. We are commanded "to rule the fish of the sea, the birds of the sky, the cattle, the whole earth," not to pollute its waters and air or waste its precious resources and beautiful forests. Such careless destruction endangers not only our planet but human life as well. (Comments on Deuteronomy 20:19)

A story about Honi Ha-Ma'agal, who lived during the first century C.E. in the Land of Israel, dramatically exemplifies the dependency of human beings on trees. Out walking one day, he sees an old man planting a carob tree. He asks him: "How long does it take for a carob tree to bear fruit?"

The old man replies, "Seventy years." Surprised, Honi asks: "Old man, do you expect to live another seventy years to eat from its fruits?" The old man laughs. "When I came into the world, I found carob trees planted by others. Now I am planting new ones for my children and their children." (*Ta'anit* 23a)

Contemporary environmentalists raise the same concern as the old man, seeing the need to plant fruit trees for the future. Restoring our planet's diminishing resources is a critical issue—one that affects our present and will certainly shape our future on earth. Destruction of tropical forests,

which contain between 50 percent and 80 percent of the earth's species and countless genetic materials for curing diseases and improving crops, endangers the future of life on earth. Lumbering without a policy of reforestation has reduced forests in the United States, Europe, Africa, and Asia, leaving huge expanses of land open to erosion. The burn-off of these lands introduces millions of tons of greenhouse gases and pollutants into the atmosphere.

The ethical concerns of Jewish commentators about preserving and replenishing the critical resources of the earth have clear implications for life on this planet. Caring about trees is a matter of life and death. Perhaps that was the motivation behind the teaching of Rabbi Yochanan ben Zakkai, a student of Hillel, who headed the Sanhedrin during the siege of Jerusalem by the Romans in 70 C.E. Rabbi Yochanan taught that if you are in the midst of planting a tree and are told that the Messiah, the messenger bringing a new era of peace to the world, has arrived, you must not stop planting. "First," says Rabbi Yochanan, "finish planting the tree, then go out and greet the Messiah."

In other words, the duty of insuring the future through replenishing the earth is more important than promises of peace, even if they are brought by the Messiah. Work done to preserve and protect the environment serves to promote human survival.

Blessings for trees
Rabbi Judah said: "When you go out during spring and see the trees budding, you should say, 'Be praised, O God, who has caused nothing to be lacking in the world and has created beautiful creations and beautiful trees from which human beings derive pleasure.'" (Berachot 43b)

When you see handsome or beautiful people or lovely trees, you should say: "Be praised, O God, who creates beautiful creatures in the world." (Mishnah Berachot 7:7)

Let us begin to think about the mystery of life and the links that connect us with the life that *fills the world, and we cannot but bring to bear upon our own lives and all other life that comes within our reach the principle of reverence for life. (*Albert Schweitzer*)*

There is, however, another interpretation of Moses' command against cutting down trees. Beyond justifying the prohibition from a pragmatic—human-centered—point of view, there is also a spiritual foundation for not destroying trees and the environment. Jacob ben Isaac Ashkenazi of Yanof, author of *Tze'enah u-Re'enah,* presents such a point of view. He suggests that there is good reason for the Torah text not only to forbid cutting down trees but to ask the question: "Are trees of the field, like human beings, capable of withdrawing before you into the besieged city?" It does so, says Rabbi Jacob, to focus attention on the sacred "life" within trees.

Jacob ben Isaac asks, "Why does the Torah compare a tree to human beings? Because, just as human beings have the power to grow within them, so do trees. And just as human beings bear children, so do trees bear fruits. When a human being is hurt, the painful cries are heard throughout the world, and when a tree is chopped down, its cries are heard from one end of the earth to the other." (Comment on Deuteronomy 20:19)

Using the tree as an example, Rabbi Jacob means to create a sympathy and awareness that all living things—human beings, animals, trees, or vegetation—are formed by God, the sacred Source of life. For that reason all existence must be respected and nurtured.

It is remarkable that Jewish tradition's concern for the environment originates in an ancient time when fears about exploiting or endangering the planet were remote. Nonetheless, Torah interpreters sensed the danger of damaging God's creation by polluting and wasting precious natural resources and potentials. They saw the earth as a gift to humanity and human beings as partners with God in sustaining the delicate ecological balance of earth. With the Psalmist they taught, "The heavens are the heavens of God; but the earth God has given to humanity." (Psalms 115:16)

QUESTIONS FOR STUDY AND DISCUSSION

1. Rabbi Ephraim Lunshitz, who died in Prague in 1619, asked, "Is it possible for a man to act justly, and yet unrighteousness can be involved in what he does?" Take the case of a businessman who secretly cheats by adjusting his scales so they will underweigh his product, at the same time providing an incentive to his customers by advertising that product at a better price than that of his competitors. How do the principles of justice discussed by the commentators apply to such a case?

2. Jewish tradition claims that without justice there can be no truth or peace in human society. Do you agree? What examples from history or contemporary life can you give to prove this ancient argument?

3. Rabbinic commentators claim that when God created the first human beings, all the trees in the Garden of Eden were placed before them. God said: "Behold all that I have created, how beautiful and excellent it all is! I have created it all for you. Think upon this. Do not corrupt or ruin My world for there will be no one to repair it after you." (*Ecclesiastes Rabbah* 7:28) What are the lessons we can learn from this ancient rabbinic warning?

4. Scientists have identified four major threats to the earth's environment: (1) destruction of forests and life species; (2) overpopulation; (3) global warming; and (4) waste disposal. Given the discussion about forbidding the destruction of trees, how do you think Jewish tradition deals with these "threats"?

PARASHAT KI TETZE
Deuteronomy 21:10–25:19

Parashat Ki Tetze contains a mixture of seventy-two commandments, dealing with such diverse subjects as the treatment of captives, defiant children, lost animals, birds' nests, roof railings, divorce, rights of aliens, loans, vows, protection of works, parental guilt, charity for the poor, regulations for inheritance, and fair weights and measures. The portion concludes with a warning to remember how the Amalekites attacked the weary Israelites in the desert.

OUR TARGUM

· 1

Moses sets out rules for the fair treatment of women captives. If they are taken as wives and then divorced, they are to be set free.

The rights of inheritance for the firstborn apply although a father may have multiple wives and many other children.

A disloyal and defiant son who does not obey his parents is to be brought for judgment before the town elders. If he is guilty, they are to stone him to death. A person put to death must be buried on the same day.

· 2 ·

If a neighbor's animal or garment is lost, it must be returned when it is found. If an animal has fallen on the road, it must be helped. One must not remain indifferent.

Men and women must not dress in each other's clothing.

If a bird's nest with fledglings or eggs is found, the mother bird must not be taken with her young.

Railings must be placed on roofs.

A vineyard must not be sown with a second kind of seed. One may not plow with an ox and ass together nor muzzle an ox while it is threshing. One may not wear garments mixed with the fibers of wool and linen. *Tzitzit,* or "fringes," are to be worn on the four corners of garments.

If a man marries a woman and later charges she was not a virgin, but her parents prove her virginity with stained sheets from the wedding night, the man is to be punished and fined for ruining the reputation of the woman. He may not divorce her. However, if the charges are true, she is to be stoned for bringing shame on the people of Israel.

The penalty for adultery is death. If a man has sex in a city with a woman engaged to another man, both are to be put to death—she because she did not cry out for help; he because he violated her. If, however, he rapes her in an open field, only he shall be put to death for he is like a murderer. If a man lies with a virgin who is not engaged and they are discovered, he is to marry her and he may never divorce her.

·3·

A man is not permitted to marry his father's former wife. Children of adulterous or incestuous relationships, along with Ammonites or Moabites, are not to be admitted to the people of Israel. Edomites, however, are to be considered as brothers and sisters.

All human waste is to be disposed of outside the camp.

Slaves seeking refuge must be taken in and treated kindly. Israelites are forbidden to become cult prostitutes, nor can money from whoring be used as gifts to the sanctuary.

·4·

It is forbidden to take interest from other Israelites but permissible to do so from foreigners. Promises must be fulfilled.

When entering your neighbor's vineyard or fields as a laborer, you may eat grapes and pluck ears of corn with your hands, but you may not place grapes in a container or cut grain with a sickle.

A man may not remarry a woman he has divorced, who then married another man who divorced her or died.

A newly married man is exempt from army service for one year.

When a loan is made to a neighbor, it is forbidden to enter his house to claim his pledge. If he is needy, the pledge must be returned to him at sundown. Abuse of needy, destitute laborers is forbidden. Wages should be paid by sundown of each day.

Uphold the rights of the stranger. Do not take a widow's garment as a pawn. Leave all sheaves overlooked during the harvest for the stranger, the fatherless, and the widow. Do not shake your olive tree twice or pick your vineyard a second

time. Instead, allow the needy to eat what is left after the harvest.

·5·

When a court renders a decision, the punishment of the guilty party is to be carried out before the innocent party. The punishment is not to exceed forty lashes.

When brothers live together and one of them dies leaving no son, it is the duty of a living brother to marry his brother's widow and to father a child in his brother's name. If the brother refuses, the widow may publicly declare: "He refuses to build up his brother's house."

You must employ honest weights and measures in all business dealings. Those who deal dishonestly are hateful to God.

Finally, Moses reminds the people how Amalek attacked the weak and weary Israelites on their journey through the desert. "Remember Amalek," he warns. "Blot out the memory of Amalek from under heaven."

THEMES

Parashat Ki Tetze contains two important themes:

1. A warning against indifference.
2. Marriage and divorce.

PEREK ALEF: *You Shall Not Remain Indifferent*

Parashat Ki Tetze contains seventy-two commandments, the largest number in any Torah portion. Among these are the obligation to return lost property and the responsibility to help those in need.

Regarding lost property, the Torah commands us to return anything we find that belongs to another person, be it an ox, a sheep, a garment—anything that may have been lost. The Torah adds the warning, "You must not remain indifferent." (Deuteronomy 22:1–3)

The Torah is also quite clear concerning the obligation to aid someone in need. Our responsibility is to help others with their burden. If, for example, while traveling along a road, we come upon the fallen ox or donkey of a friend, the Torah says, "Do not ignore it; you must help him raise it."

What obligations, however, do we have if the lost property belongs to an enemy or the animal in distress belongs to someone we dislike?

In a parallel passage found in *Parashat Mishpatim* (see Exodus 23:4–5), Moses makes it clear that the lost property of enemies must be returned and an animal in distress belonging to an enemy must be helped. Are we then to assume that the Torah teaches that we have the same ethical responsibility to both friends and enemies when it comes to returning lost property or offering help? Would not such a command contradict normal human emotions?

Early rabbinic interpreters insist that, whether the lost item belongs to one's enemy or friend, it must be returned. Furthermore, if the person finding the property makes a profit with it before returning it to the owner, that profit belongs to the owner and must be paid back when the lost property is restored. If the property cannot be returned and its care costs money, the owner must pay the amount when the property is restored. (*Baba Metzia* 26a–30a)

> *The status of lost property*
> Some found articles become the property of the finder immediately, and others have to be advertised.
>
> The following become the property of the finder: scattered fruits, scattered coins, small sheaves of corn lying in a public road, cakes of pressed figs, bakers' loaves, strings of fish, pieces of meat, fleeces of wool in their natural state. . . .
>
> The following found articles must be advertised so that the owner may repossess them: fruit in a vessel or an empty vessel; money in a purse or an empty purse; heaps of fruit; heaps of

coins; three coins, one on top of the other; small sheaves lying on private property; homemade loaves of bread; fleeces of wool that had been removed from a workshop. . . . If someone finds something in a store, it belongs to him; but, if he finds it between the counter and the storekeeper's seat, it belongs to the storekeeper. (Mishnah Baba Metzia 2:1, 2, 4)

For example, rabbinic interpreters tell of a man who, passing the door of Rabbi Hanina ben Dosa, accidentally left some of his hens. "We must not eat their eggs," Rabbi Hanina told his family. However, the eggs and hens quickly multiplied, and there was no place to keep them. So Rabbi Hanina sold them and purchased goats. Sometime later, the man who had accidently left his hens returned, asking about them. Rabbi Hanina inquired if he had some identification to prove his ownership. He did. Rabbi Hanina immediately gave him the goats.

They also tell of Rabbi Pinchas ben Yair who was once visited by men who brought with them two measures of barley. They deposited the barley with him and then apparently forgot about it. Rabbi Pinchas sowed the barley for several years, harvesting it and storing it. When, after seven years, the men returned, Rabbi Pinchas told them: "Take your storehouses filled with grain." (Ta'anit 25a; Deuteronomy Rabbah 3:5)

Leibowitz

Both incidents above emphasize not only the ethical responsibility of returning to others what they have lost but also the principle that the person finding lost property should not profit from it. In her discussion of both rabbinic stories, modern commentator Nehama Leibowitz points out an additional ethical dimension. "The mitzvah of restoring lost property . . . involves, not only the passive taking charge of the article until the owner claims it, but also an active concern with safeguarding a neighbor's possessions so that they remain intact and constitute something

worth restoring." Jewish law is clear about the obligation of returning that which has been lost. The finder must care for the property, may not profit from it, and, if it is invested, owes all earnings when it is restored. (*Studies in Devarim*, p. 214)

The issue of returning lost property raises other important considerations about the way human beings deal with one another and the trust required to make human society secure. Bachya ben Joseph ibn Pakuda argues that such ethical concerns relate to other matters raised by the Torah. Restoring property, says Bachya, is a fulfillment of the Torah's instruction to "love your neighbor as yourself." (Leviticus 19:18) Property is an extension of each individual. It is like the limb of one's body. Loving one's neighbors means taking care of all that is important to them as you would want them to safeguard all that is important to you. Returning lost property is a demonstration of love and concern for one's neighbors. (See Abraham Chill, *The Mitzvot*, pp. 452–454.)

Aharon Halevi in his *Sefer ha-Hinuch* extends Bachya's view, arguing that the commandment to return lost property is "fundamental" and that "all society depends upon it." It is not just a matter of one person taking care of another's possessions or of "loving" another. What is important here is the critical matter of "trust" among human beings. A society depends upon the faith people place in one another. Without people feeling that they can rely upon one another—that others are looking out for what belongs to me and that I must look out for what belongs to them—society collapses into suspicion, selfishness, and bitter contention. Whether people return or keep lost articles, says Halevi, is a significant indication of a society's health. (538)

You shall return it
A man once visited Rabbi Aaron of Chernobyl and told him about his nightmares. In one dream he picked up a wallet containing a fortune. When he pursued its owner in the crowd, he could not find him. With the funds he found he grew wealthy. On the other hand, the man who had lost the money fell on terrible

misfortune, losing his businesses and the trust of others. He died leaving his wife and children in poverty, with no one to support them and no one to finance the education of his children.

The man who had prospered told Rabbi Aaron of Chernobyl that he suffered from terrible recurring dreams about taking the wallet and being responsible for the harm its loss had brought upon others. He pleaded for the rabbi to advise him what to do.

The rabbi commanded him to find the family of the man, to give them half of what he had accumulated, and to see to it that the man's children were educated. When he did so, his recurring nightmares ceased. (S.Y. Zevin, A Treasury of Chasidic Tales, pp. 561–563)

What about returning that which you may have to go out of your way to rescue? If you have restored lost property once to its owner, must you do so again if you find it? What if the lost property belongs to an enemy? What if you find an enemy's property in danger? What obligations do you have?

Ramban (Nachmanides)

Nachmanides makes it clear that the mitzvah of returning lost property supersedes any inconvenience to the finder. The finder is obligated to announce the discovery of the lost item so that others will know he possesses it, and the loser's anxiety will be shortened.

Carrying out the mitzvah of restoring lost property applies to friends, strangers, and even to enemies. If one encounters a person whose property is in danger—a donkey who has fallen while carrying a heavy load, a runaway animal, or a broken vehicle—one's ethical responsibility is to help save the property. This applies also to the property of an enemy. Nachmanides puts it this way: "Assist others. Remember the bond of humanity between you and forget the hatred." (Comments on Deuteronomy 22:1–2)

Benno Jacob

Benno Jacob builds upon Nachmanides' interpretation. He explains that "when you see the animal of your enemy fallen on the road, it is natural for you to think, 'I will ignore it. I will not lend a helping hand. After all, why should I do a good deed for someone who hates me and has treated me badly?' But the Torah teaches us to overcome our hatred and to do everything possible to be of help."

Jacob sees the act of helping an enemy as a means of arriving at reconciliation. First, one sees the fallen animal and understands that help must be given. One is likely to say, "I'll help to relieve the pain of the animal." Yet, once involved, words of concern for the animal are exchanged. This leads to other words and finally to forgiveness between those who are angry with each other. In this way, the mitzvah of turning aside to aid an animal brings about renewed trust and friendship. (Comment on Exodus 23:4–5)

Peli

You must not remain indifferent

From the moment one notices an animal gone astray or an object lost by someone, one may not "hide oneself." Whether he is busy with something else or whether he chooses to get involved, a person is in fact involved and duty-bound to bring the object to his home, keeping it there safely until it can be returned to its owner. . . . While some legal systems require returning or handing over found property to the authorities, none enjoins the finder from ignoring the lost object in the first place. (Pinchas H. Peli, Jerusalem Post, September 7, 1985)

People often value possessions as much as life itself. Therefore, when they lose something that has a special distinction, they are likely to feel great pain as if a life has been lost. Those finding the lost object and failing to return it are contributing to the distress and mental anguish of others. (Rabbi Menachem ben Benjamin Recanati, 13th century, Italy, as found in Abraham Chill, The Mitzvot, *p. 454)*

Rambam (Maimonides)

Moses Maimonides comments: We are forbidden to shut our eyes to lost property; we must pick it up and return it to its owner. This prohibition is what is meant by the words: "You must not remain indifferent." (Sefer ha-Mitzvot, Positive Commandments #269)

Malbim

Nehama Leibowitz, basing her interpretation on that of Malbim, suggests that the command to turn aside and help an enemy whose property is in danger is an example of how the Torah deals with the real world. It does not present a world where all people get along with one another or rush to care for one another's property. Instead, it "takes into account the grim reality that people do not achieve the desired observance of 'you shall not hate others in your heart.'"

Leibowitz stresses that the Torah "lays down rules of behavior even for such an admittedly immoral situation where two people are hostile to each other, enjoining such acts of assistance as relieving the ass of an enemy of its burden and the returning of his lost property. These small deeds of goodwill," Leibowitz concludes, "would, it is hoped, eventually lead to the removal of hatred. . . ." Indeed, as Leibowitz

makes clear, the rabbinic commentators of the Talmud state the moral standard to be followed and the reason for it. "If you are faced with the situation of your friend requiring help with his animal and also your enemy, your first duty is to aid your enemy. For in this way we train and discipline our instincts." (*Studies in Shemot*, World Zionist Organization, Jerusalem, 1980, pp. 428–434; *Baba Metzia* 32b)

After the Torah clarifies the duty to return lost property or to keep it safe until it can be restored to its owner, it concludes with the words *lo tuchal le-hitalem*, or "you must not remain indifferent." Many interpreters point out that this phrase may also be translated literally as "you shall not hide" or "you shall not act as if you were blind."

This powerful phrase puts forth the ethical demand of Torah. Upon encountering a lost object, a fallen animal in pain under its burden, the property of friends or enemies in danger, one's duty is to help. We are not permitted to look the other way, to pass by without paying attention, or to continue with our business as usual. Hiding the truth from ourselves and not acting to help others is immoral. Indifference is intolerable. Responsible caring is at the heart of Jewish ethics.

PEREK BET: *Marriage and Divorce*

Parashat Ki Tetze discusses both the institution of marriage and the process of divorce. In the Torah, men choose their wives and have the right to divorce them. If a wife lies about being a virgin at the time of marriage, she may be stoned to death. If a woman "fails to please her husband because he finds something obnoxious about her," he may divorce her. There are few hints that affection is the basis of marriage relationships; there is no indication of mutuality or equal rights for women in choosing a husband or seeking a divorce. (See Genesis 24:67.)

In interpreting the Torah's description of marriage and divorce, the commentators raise significant questions. They inquire about the purpose of marriage, explore its emotional and legal consequences, and examine the appropriate conditions and rituals for divorce. As with other subjects, it is the interpreters who, over the centuries, unlock new understandings and initiate new rituals. In doing so, they adapt the commandments of Torah to new conditions of society and to new moral sensibilities. Marriage and divorce are important examples of such dynamic change and evolution within Jewish tradition.

After describing the creation of heaven and earth, the Torah reports that God comments, "It is not good for man to be alone. I will make a fitting helper for him." In answer to loneliness, God creates woman and declares: "A man will leave his father and mother and cling to his wife so that they become one flesh." Within this early description, the Torah advances the view that marriage provides mutual support, total trust, caring, and companionship. Husband and wife are "helpers" to each other; they are to be inseparable—"one flesh"—both physically and spiritually. Together they form a sacred new world through which they create a family. (Genesis 2:18–24)

Early rabbinic commentators stress the importance of marriage. Rabbi Akiba remarks that "a man who does not marry impairs the divine image," meaning that love and marriage are the will of God. Rabbi Jacob teaches that "he who does not have a wife lives without joy, without blessing, without a helper, without goodness, and without atonement. Some add, without Torah and moral protection." Rabba ben Ulla adds, "without peace." (*Genesis Rabbah* 17:2; *Yevamot* 62a–63b)

The author of the mystical commentary the *Zohar* underscores the centrality of marriage by claiming that, since finishing the creation of the world, God has been busy with creating "new worlds" by bringing together bridegrooms and brides. Since marriage perpetuates life and fills it with love, nothing has greater value. Marriage, concludes the author of the *Zohar*, keeps God in the world because God's Presence dwells in the love between husband and wife. (*Zohar* 1:89a; 3:59a)

While the Torah makes reference to "a man marrying a women," it does not describe any ceremony or ritual. Later rabbinic tradition defines three aspects of the marriage ritual: *sheduchin,* or "engagement"; *erusin,* or "betrothal";

and *nisuin,* or "marriage vows." Originally, these three rituals were celebrated at different times. Later, *erusin* and *nisuin* were merged into the wedding ceremony called *kiddushin,* or "holiness."

Just before the wedding ceremony a *ketubah,* or "written agreement" between husband and wife, is signed. The *ketubah* functioned throughout the centuries as a prenuptial agreement, spelling out the obligations assumed by the husband in marriage. These included support, food, clothing, shelter, and sexual relations. It also specified fixed financial arrangements should the couple divorce. Many Jews continue to use the ancient formulas for their *ketubah;* others choose a *ketubah* that is more egalitarian in its language, making clear the mutual responsibilities and commitments of husband and wife.

After signing the *ketubah,* the bride and groom are led to the *chupah,* or "wedding canopy," symbolizing the Jewish home they are about to establish. Beneath the *chupah,* the *birkat erusin,* or "betrothal blessing," is recited, including the blessing, "Be praised, O God, who sanctifies Your people Israel through the celebration of *chupah* and marriage." The groom then places a wedding ring of precious value, but without jewels, upon the bride's finger and says to her: "With this ring be consecrated to me as my wife in accordance with the law of Moses and the people of Israel." Among Reform, Conservative, and Reconstructionist Jews, brides often exchange a ring and a similar vow with their bridegrooms.

The exchange of rings is followed by the recitation of the *sheva berachot,* or "seven wedding blessings." These thank God for the creation of man and woman and the desire to perpetuate life; ask God to provide bride and groom with the happiness of Adam and Eve in the Garden of Eden; and express the hope that the rejoicing of bride and groom will soon be heard in the Land of Israel. The rabbi then presents the couple with their *ketubah,* and the ceremony is concluded by breaking a glass. According to some rabbis, breaking the glass commemorates the destruction of the Jerusalem Temple in 70 C.E. Others say that the ritual is meant to remind the bride and groom that they have obligations to the "shattered" within society, the poor, hungry, homeless, and helpless. Still others see in the ritual a symbolic expression of the triumph of truth, hope, and love over the persecution and suffering of the Jews throughout the ages.

All the prayers and rituals of *kiddushin* are meant to uplift and celebrate the love shared by bride and groom. However, the marriage ceremony is not only a public acknowledgment of their special love relationship, but it also marks the establishment of a Jewish home, which guarantees the Jewish future. Through their commitments to celebrate Shabbat and holy days, to maintain their Jewish community and the welfare of their people throughout the world, and to elevate their relationship through Jewish study and charity, bride and groom strengthen the Jewish people. Rabbinic interpreters understood that marriage was not only an institution through which human satisfaction might be achieved, but they praised it as one of the "most important ingredients of the magic potion that has strengthened the Jew to survive." (Trude Weiss-Rosmarin, quoted in *A Modern Treasury of Jewish Thoughts*, p. 149)

Despite such regard for the institution of marriage, however, rabbinic commentators were realists. They knew that some partnerships between husband and wife begin in rapture and happiness but end in disappointment and bitterness. Rabbi Akiba observes that "if a husband and wife are worthy, then God dwells between them. If they are not worthy, fire will consume them." Akiba, whose marriage to Rachel was one of passion, sacrifice, mutual support, and respect, may have been speaking from his own experience. He and Rachel endured hardship in order for him to acquire a Jewish education. Their devotion to each other was a model for their students. Akiba observed that without such shared priorities, without trust and an affection that accommodates differences, marriage turns into a battleground—into a consuming fire. (*Sotah* 17a)

Because Jewish tradition does not rule out incompatibility between husband and wife, it accepts the tragedy and necessity of divorce. "Many marry," comments a rabbinic teacher, "some succeed, some come to grief." Others express the matter of compatibility in a powerful image.

"When love is strong, a husband and wife can make their bed on the edge of a sword's blade. When love diminishes in strength, a wide, soft bed is never large enough." Couples may marry with great expectations, feeling that they share enthusiasms, mutual passion, and a will to create a home and family. Yet, with all their good intentions, differences surface. Stress from work and unresolved tensions often lead to great unhappiness and a decision to divorce. (*Numbers Rabbah* 9:4; *Sanhedrin* 7a)

The Torah treats divorce as an occurrence that must be regulated by law and the traditions of the community. The Torah says, "If a wife fails to please her husband, if he finds something obnoxious about her, he may write her a *sefer keritut,* or a *get,* as it is called in the Talmud, a "document of divorce." (Deuteronomy 24:1) Rabbinic commentators insist that a wife also has the right to initiate divorce if she is unhappy with her spouse. Grounds for initiating divorce by either husband or wife may be sexual or social incompatibility, distasteful feelings in the presence of the other person, infertility, one spouse's refusal to have children, a refusal to work or provide support, mental illness, a chronic disease that makes sharing physical intimacy impossible, unfaithfulness, conversion to another religion, abandonment, or abuse. (See Isaac Klein, *A Guide to Jewish Religious Practice,* Jewish Theological Seminary, distributed by Ktav, New York, 1979, chap. XXXIII, pp. 466–473.)

While the Torah speaks only of the husband giving his wife a "document of divorce," later rabbinic tradition defines the process of the divorce proceedings: The husband arranges for a *sofer,* or "scribe," to write a *get,* a document especially for the wife that includes the declaration: "I release you . . . to go and be married to any man you may desire. . . ." The *get* is given to the wife by the husband before two witnesses who sign it. Where distance separates a couple, the husband may send the *get* to his wife through an agent authorized by him to present it. For a divorce to be valid, both parties must agree willingly, without pressure, to give and to accept it. (*Shulchan Aruch* 140–141)

Despite the realistic acceptance of the necessity of divorce, Jewish interpreters underscore the tragedy it represents. "If a man divorces his wife," they teach, "even the altar of the Temple sheds tears." Rabbi Yochanan is more harsh in his judgment: "Whoever divorces his wife is hated by God!" Undoubtedly such commentators saw in divorce not only the sad defeat of all the hopes of bride and groom but also a severe blow to the vitality and future of the Jewish community. (*Gittin* 90b; *Avot de-Rabbi Natan* 30)

No marriage is without its periods of satisfaction and frustration. A medieval rabbi has observed that "the honeymoon lasts for a month, the troubles for a lifetime." Jewish tradition wisely counsels that husband and wife facing irreconcilable differences should seek counseling and the mending of their love. Marriage expert, author, and psychologist Dr. Aaron T. Beck writes that "mates need to cooperate, compromise, and follow through with joint decisions. They have to be resilient, accepting, and forgiving. They need to be tolerant of each other's flaws, mistakes, and peculiarities." Beck concludes that as these "virtues" are developed over time, "the marriage develops and matures." (*Love Is Never Enough*, Harper and Row Publishers, Inc., New York, 1988, p. 4)

With major changes in the roles of men and women in the workplace and in marriage, the mutual commitment to work at such maturation of love is critical. As a part of that process, Jewish tradition can play an important role. Celebrating sacred times and seasons together can bond a couple, as can shared commitments to enhance the community through volunteer service and charity. Love suffocates when it is not shared. It evolves into mutual satisfaction, support, and fulfillment when its power is allowed to flower in all our relationships.

The talmudic rabbis comment that "it is as hard to arrange and sustain a good marriage as it was for God to divide the Red Sea before the escaping Israelites." The recognition that love between husband and wife is truly an unfathomable mystery and a delicate gift is at the heart of Jewish tradition's view of marriage and divorce. To build their relationship into blessings remains the challenge of every husband and wife.

QUESTIONS FOR STUDY AND DISCUSSION

1. The Torah and nearly all of the commentators place great emphasis upon restoring lost property. Why is this important to the stability of a society? Are there other commandments that are equally critical?

2. Do you agree with those commentators who argue that when we reach out to help our enemies, it is likely we will end up as friends? Can you cite some examples from your own experience or from history?

3. If you were writing a *ketubah* today, what would you have a bride and groom pledge to do in their marriage to assure its success? If you were putting together a modern *get*, what would the divorce document say?

4. Commenting on the significance of Jewish commitment and practice as a means of strengthening a marriage, Benjamin Kaplan writes: "A religiously motivated home can bring a sense of belonging . . . it can be the major buffer in easing the tensions that beset couples . . . it can absorb the shocks and tempers . . . in this frightfully competitive society." (*The Jew and His Family*, Louisiana State University Press, Baton Rouge, 1967, p. 189) Do you agree? What advice would you give couples about Jewish celebrations in their homes and involvement in their Jewish community?

PARASHAT KI TAVO
Deuteronomy 26:1–29:8

Parashat Ki Tavo addresses the time when the Israelites will settle in the Land of Israel. Moses instructs them to place in a basket the first fruits they have harvested and present them, together with a prayer, to the priest at the sanctuary. Their prayer is to be a formula recalling they were slaves in Egypt, liberated by God, and given the land whose first fruits they now enjoy. They are also to set aside a tenth part of their yield for the Levite, the stranger, the fatherless, and the widow, and they are to keep all the commandments given to them. In this way they will be a treasured people to God. Moses and the elders tell them, when they have settled in the land, to write the commandments on large plastered stones and set them up on Mount Ebal, where they are also to build an altar to God. Then representatives of the tribes of Simeon, Levi, Judah, Issachar, Joseph, and Benjamin are to stand on Mount Gerizim to hear the blessing describing the good times that will come as a result of observing God's commandments. Facing them on Mount Ebal, representatives from the tribes of Reuben, Gad, Asher, Zebulun, Dan, and Naphtali are to stand to hear the curse resulting from disobeying the commandments. God promises the Israelites blessings of plenty, security, and peace if they observe faithfully the teachings of Torah. Curses of destruction, agony, want, and exile will befall them if they spurn the teachings of Torah. "Observe faithfully all the terms of this covenant," Moses warns, "that you may succeed in all that you undertake."

OUR TARGUM

· 1 ·

Moses instructs the people, when they enter the Land of Israel and complete their harvest, to take their first fruits in a basket for an offering at the sanctuary. When the priest places the basket on the altar, the people are to declare: "My father was a fugitive Aramean. He went down to Egypt with meager numbers and sojourned there. . . . The Egyptians dealt harshly with us. . . . We cried to *Adonai* . . . *Adonai* heard our plea. . . . *Adonai* freed us from Egypt . . . and gave us this land. . . . Wherefore I now bring the first fruits of the soil which You, *Adonai,* have given me."

In the third year, after setting aside a tenth of the yield for the Levite, the stranger, the fatherless, and the widow, the Israelites are commanded to declare: "I have cleared out the consecrated portion from the house; and I have given it to the Levite, the stranger, the fatherless, and the widow, just as You commanded me. . . . Look down from Your holy abode, from heaven, and bless Your people Israel and the soil You have given us, a land flowing with milk and honey, as You swore to our ancestors."

Moses reminds the people they are commanded to observe God's commandments faithfully. He tells them they are God's treasured people and, because of their faithfulness, God "will set you, in fame and renown and glory, high above all the nations . . . and you shall be, as God promised, a holy people to *Adonai* your God."

· 2 ·

Moses provides instruction for them after they have crossed the Jordan. They are to set up large stones on Mount Ebal, plaster them over, and write upon them all the commandments of the Torah. In addition, they are to build an altar to God of uncut stones for offerings.

Moses describes a special ceremony where representatives from the tribes of Simeon, Levi, Judah, Issachar, Joseph, and Benjamin will stand on Mount Gerizim while words of blessing are spoken. Representatives from the tribes of Reuben, Gad, Asher, Zebulun, Dan, and Naphtali will stand on Mount Ebal while the curse is spoken. The ceremony is to dramatize to the Israelites the critical importance of living according to the laws of Torah.

Among the curses mentioned are those directed at Israelites who make idols; insult their parents; move a neighbor's landmark; mislead a blind person; subvert the rights of the stranger, the fatherless, or the widow; practice improper sexual relations; hurt another in secret; accept a bribe; or fail to live according to the terms of the Torah.

Ignoring God's commandments, Moses says, will cause calamity, panic, and misfortune. Enemies will bring destruction. God will strike Israel with sickness, scorching heat, and drought. "The skies above you shall be copper and the earth under you iron . . . you will be wiped out." Furthermore, you will be driven into exile; others will harvest your fields; nothing you plant will succeed. "The cricket shall take over all the trees and produce of your land." Plagues and chronic diseases will afflict you. "You shall find no peace. . . . The life you face shall be precarious; you shall be in terror, night and day, with no assurance of survival."

Conversely, abundant blessings are promised to the people if they are faithful to the laws of the Torah. They will be blessed with victory over their enemies and plenty in their harvests and all their undertakings. "*Adonai* will make you the head, not the tail; you will always be at the top and never at the bottom . . . if you do not deviate to the right or to the left from any of the commandments that I enjoin upon you. . . ." Your children will be blessed, all your property will prosper, so will your basket of charity, all your comings and goings.

Because of your faithfulness to the commandments, Moses tells the people, "*Adonai* will open for you a bounteous store, the heavens, to provide rain for your land in season and to bless all your undertakings. You will be creditor to many nations, but debtor to none." These are the terms of the covenant Moses concludes with the Israelites.

THEMES

Parashat Ki Tavo contains two important themes:

1. Reliving history.
2. Facing the consequences of our actions.

PEREK ALEF: *The Drama and Meaning of Reliving History*

In these speeches to the Israelites in the desert, Moses focuses on the future when the people have already conquered the Land of Israel and are enjoying its harvests. At that time, he tells them, they are to take "every first fruit of the soil . . . put it in a basket and go to the place where God's name will be established." Once at the sanctuary, they will present the basket to a priest, saying: "I acknowledge this day before *Adonai* our God that I have entered the land that *Adonai* swore to our ancestors to give us."

As the priest takes the basket, the Israelites are to continue the ritual drama with the following declaration: *Arami oved avi. . . .* "My father was a fugitive Aramean. He went down to Egypt with meager numbers and sojourned there; but there he became a great and very populous nation. The Egyptians dealt harshly with us and oppressed us; they imposed heavy labor upon us.

We cried to *Adonai,* the God of our ancestors, and *Adonai* heard our plea and saw our plight, our misery, and our oppression. *Adonai* freed us from Egypt by a mighty hand, by an outstretched arm and awesome power, and by signs and portents. God brought us to this place and gave us this land, a land flowing with milk and honey. Wherefore I now bring the first fruits of the soil that You, O *Adonai,* have given me."

One can easily imagine participating in such a ritual: filling the basket with first fruits, presenting it at the sanctuary, and reciting the declaration. But what is the purpose of this ceremony?

Several commentators point out that the ritual of declaration constitutes one of the only prayers found in the entire Torah. Its meaning, however, is a matter of dispute.

Rashi

Some interpreters, including the author of the *Sifre* and Rashi, insist that the translation of *Arami oved avi* is "an Aramean sought to destroy my father," meaning that Laban, for whom Jacob worked twenty years, intended to destroy him. This interpretation, as we shall see, is followed by those who authored the first Pesach *haggadot.*

Rashi's grandson argues that the Aramean mentioned is not Laban but Abraham, who was born and raised in Aram-naharaim.

Ibn Ezra

Others, following Abraham ibn Ezra, point out that it makes no sense to identify Laban or Abraham as the Aramean. Instead, ibn Ezra claims Moses is referring to Jacob, whose mother had come from Aram-naharaim, who was persecuted there by Laban, and who fled from the oppression of famine into Egypt, where Joseph was in power and could assure the survival of Jacob's family.

Given the variety of interpretations of the words

Arami oved avi, the ritual prayer could mean: "My father was a fugitive (wandering or persecuted) Aramean," referring to Abraham or Jacob. Or the text could mean: "An Aramean sought to destroy my father." In other words, Laban schemed to destroy Jacob and his family. Most modern biblical scholars agree that the identification of either Abraham or Jacob as the "fugitive" Aramean is correct.

The *Mishnah* describes the colorful celebration of offering the first fruits at the Temple in Jerusalem. In each town throughout the Land of Israel, prayer groups would gather. They would celebrate during the evening; in the morning they would commence their pilgrimage to Jerusalem, led by a flute player, followed by an ox with horns overlaid with gold and a wreath of olive leaves on its head. When they reached Jerusalem, they sent messengers to the Temple and prepared their first fruits for offering. As they marched through the city, the people of Jerusalem would greet them, saying: "Welcome to Jerusalem." When they reached the Temple, the Levites would break into song.

Inside the Temple, holding their baskets, they would recite: "I acknowledge this day. . . . My father was a fugitive Aramean. . . . Wherefore I now bring the first fruits of the soil that You, *Adonai,* have given me." The long walk up to Jerusalem, the parade through the streets, the musical entrance into the Temple, and the drama of reciting their declaration with basket in hand must have made a powerful impression and filled them with memories for a lifetime. (*Bikkurim* 3)

Is this what Moses had in mind when he defined the ritual drama of the first-fruits offering? Did he envision a musical parade? Why was a fixed formula of declaration put into the mouth of the worshiper? Why wasn't the prayer a spontaneous declaration or a prayer of thanks to God for the abundant fruits of the harvest? Why was the prayer about the past, about suffering, misery, and oppression?

Moses Maimonides addresses such questions in his *Guide for the Perplexed.* (3:39) Offering the first fruits of the harvest, he says, is a way people "accustom themselves to being generous" and a means of "limiting the human appetite for more consumption, not only of food, but of property."

Maimonides views the ritual drama as an antidote to materialism and overindulgence. "People who amass fortunes and live in comfort," he observes, "often fall victim to self-centered excesses and arrogance. They tend to abandon ethical considerations because of increasingly selfish concerns." Bringing a harvest basket of first fruits and reciting the prayer "promotes humility."

Rambam (Maimonides)

Maimonides also points out that "it is essential . . . to recall previous experiences of suffering and distress in times of ease." Such recollections remind us that human experience is a mixture of successes and failures, of joys and disappointments. History, like the life of a human being, is complex and often frustrating. People often become cynical and abandon their hopes and dreams.

The triumph of freedom over oppression often evolves slowly through pain, setbacks, and strong determination. Jacob suffers, his children endure hunger and homelessness, his grandchildren and subsequent generations are oppressed, tortured, and enslaved in Egypt. Without faith in God's liberating power, the Israelites would not have achieved freedom. It sustained them through the darkest hours. In offering the first fruits with a declaration recalling their stormy history, the people underscore the importance of taking nothing for granted. This ritual, concludes Maimonides, "helps us keep God's miracles fresh in memory and perpetuate faith."

For Rashbam the ritual is much more than a means of recalling the past and the Jewish people's reliance upon God's miracles. Rashbam points out that each participant, standing inside the Temple with the basket of first fruits, becomes a part of a significant drama—a highly personal confession. Identifying with Abraham, the worshiper declares: "*My* father [Abraham] was a wandering Aramean." By this he means to say that "*my* parent, not someone else's but *mine*, was lost, and *my* relatives suffered in Egypt, were liberated, and fought to conquer the Land of Israel. They were victorious and I hold this basket of fruits because of God's help."

Rashbam believes that for the pilgrim this ritual is a life-transforming moment of identification with one's ancestors and with the truth that the fruits in the basket and the liberation from Egypt are not the accomplishments of human beings alone. It is God's will that transforms seed into fruits; it is God's will that frees the captive. Rashbam sees each participant in the Temple ritual arriving at this conclusion: "*My* parents came from a strange land where they were slaves to this good and prosperous land. Now, in gratitude, I am bringing the first fruits of the land to the Temple because I realize that this bounty is not of my doing, but I enjoy it through God's mercy." (Comments on Deuteronomy 26: 3–11)

Words count
Rabbi Aharon Halevi argues that the Israelites are commanded to recite the prayer "My father was a fugitive Aramean. . . . Adonai freed us from Egypt. . . . Wherefore I now bring the first fruits . . ." because "the mind and imagination of people are deeply impressed by what they say." This prayer "arouses the heart, prompting the minds of those who say it to believe that all they enjoy came to them from the God of the universe." (Sefer ha-Hinuch 606)

Against conceit
Rabbi Jacob J. Weinstein comments: "Each Israelite was religiously commanded to recall in the time of prosperity that his [her] father was a wandering Aramean, a hobo, a sojourner, a rootless and homeless refugee. The intention of this admonition was to curb the conceit of the self-made person. He [she] was reminded that it required more than industry, skill, ambition, and contriving to rise from poverty to affluence.

It required also the help of God. . . . True piety, philosopher Santayana said, is a sense of reverence for the sources of our being." (The Place of Understanding, *pp. 136–138)*

Modern philosopher Martin Buber comments that this declaration of the Israelite at the sanctuary is unique because it is a very personal, individual expression. Instead of saying, *"Our fathers were fugitive Arameans,"* one says, *"My father. . . ."* What we have here, says Buber, is a "merging of the people and the individual into one." The drama of the worship identifies the individual with Israel's history. It roots him in the past by allowing him to make the claim that he is a direct descendant *(my father . . .)* of those who came out of Egyptian slavery and forty years of desert wandering into the Land of Israel.

This identification is not casual. It deliberately links Jews to their historical experience and to the responsibilities of carrying out the commandments. Each year, explains Buber, the worshiper comes to the sanctuary and, in effect, says: "I as an individual feel and profess myself as one who has just come into the land, and, every time I offer its first fruits, I acknowledge who I am and renew my identity." (*Israel and Palestine*, Farrar, Strauss and Young, New York, 1952, pp. 3–5)

Buber's interpretation of the pilgrim's declaration as a means of identity with one's history may be compared to a similar declaration in the Pesach *haggadah.* After completing the narration of the liberation from bondage, which begins with the words "In the beginning our ancestors were idol worshipers" and includes a rabbinic commentary on the statement "My father was a fugitive Aramean," each person at the seder says: "In every generation a person is to see himself as if he were going out of Egypt. . . ." The drama of the seder, like the drama of presenting the basket of first fruits, bonds the individual to the Jewish people. Such rituals banish loneliness by placing us in the company of others who are celebrating shared ethical aspirations, heroes and heroines, tragedies and triumphs. Participating in the seder transports the individual back "home" to ancient ties of faith and tradition.

What about those who are not born into the people, whose past is non-Jewish but who convert to Judaism? Is it appropriate for converts to say *Arami oved avi,* "My father was a fugitive Aramean"?

According to the *Mishnah,* converts may bring their baskets of first fruits to the sanctuary, but they are forbidden to recite the prayer. The prayer includes statements that, for converts, are untrue: "I acknowledge this day before *Adonai* our God that I have entered the land which *Adonai* swore to our ancestors to give us," and "My father was a fugitive Aramean." Rather than recite a ritual prayer that is technically untrue, as one's birth parents were not Jews, the convert may bring the basket without saying the ancient prayer. From the *Mishnah*'s point of view, the ritual is not to be trivialized by inviting people to falsify their pasts. (*Bikkurim* 1:4)

The *Mishnah*'s view, however, is challenged by other authorities. Rabbi Judah claims that converts are not only permitted to say the words "My father was a fugitive Aramean," but they are also encouraged to recite all prayers that include the phrase "Our God and God of our ancestors, God of Abraham, God of Isaac, and God of Jacob." Rabbi Judah bases his view on the belief that Abraham was also a convert, and God promised to make him "father of a multitude of peoples." The promise, he argues, legitimately makes Abraham the "father" of all non-Jews who choose to become Jews, making it appropriate for them to address Abraham as their parent. (Jerusalem Talmud, *Bikkurim* 1:4)

In the eleventh century, Moses Maimonides signaled his agreement with Rabbi Judah. He ruled that it was permissible for converts to recite the prayers of the first fruits. His view became the acceptable practice of the Jewish community. Interestingly, this is the only case where Maimonides challenges the *Mishnah.* (*Mishneh Torah, Bikkurim* 4:3)

Later, a famous convert by the name of Obadiah wrote to Maimonides asking for a clarification of his ruling. "Should a convert," he asked, "recite prayers with the words 'Our God and God of our ancestors,' or 'who has commanded us,' or 'who has chosen us,' or 'who has brought us out of Egypt . . .?'"

Referring to Obadiah as "our teacher and master . . . the scholar and understanding one, the righteous convert," Maimonides answered: "You should recite all the prayers just as they are formulated in the liturgy. Change nothing! But, just as every born-Jew prays and recites benedictions, so you should do so whether in private or public as a leader of the congregation. . . . The reason for this is that Abraham our father taught all humanity. . . . Consequently, everyone who accepts Judaism until the end of all generations . . . is a descendant of Abraham. . . . There is absolutely no difference whatsoever between us and between you." (Jacob S. Minkin, *The World of Moses Maimonides,* Thomas Yoseloff, New York, 1957, pp. 375–376)

Leibowitz

Commenting on Maimonides' letter, modern interpreter Nehama Leibowitz concludes that "the letter utterly repudiates any racial theory that would evaluate human character in terms of ethnic origins. Maimonides well and truly bases human merit in the eyes of God upon our conduct and deeds."

Peli

Pinchas Peli agrees but widens the point of view. "By joining the Jewish religion, the convert joins the Jewish people and its history. Abraham, Isaac, and Jacob, to whom the land was promised, are also ancestors of the convert. [One] can rightly say, therefore, the full text of the first-fruits offering." (*Torah Today*, B'nai B'rith Books, Washington, D.C., 1987, pp. 227–228)

The ritual drama of the first-fruits offering was meant to express gratitude to God for liberation from bondage, for the Land of Israel, and for the bounty of the harvest. The ritual, however, is more than words of prayerful thanksgiving. The power of the experience on the individual was enormous. In recalling Abraham's struggle and the suffering of the Israelites, the worshiper

made Israelite history his or her own. The ceremony, for a born-Jew or a convert, confirmed the bond of the individual to the people of Israel. Through this ceremony one became a proud participant in Judaism's challenges and future.

PEREK BET: *Blessings and Curses; Who Is Responsible for Them? Are They Just?*

In these speeches by Moses to the Israelites, we find a powerful idea—an idea that has occurred earlier in the Torah. Some would argue that it is the greatest challenge put before the Israelites. They are told that if they faithfully observe the mitzvot, or the "commandments," they will be blessed. If they do not practice the mitzvot, they will be cursed. The choice is theirs.

This proposition of blessings and curses is also presented in Leviticus, *Parashat Behar-Bechukotai.* (See *A Torah Commentary for Our Times,* Volume II.) Now the Torah returns to it. This time, however, it is presented partially in the form of a ritual formula to be pronounced by tribal leaders and then proclaimed by the Levites to the people.

The ritual contains twelve curses, each beginning with the words "Cursed be the one who." The curses condemn (1) creating images; (2) insulting parents; (3) moving a landmark; (4) misleading a blind person; (5) subverting the rights of the stranger, the fatherless, and the widow; (6) having sexual relations with one's father's wife; (7) having sexual relations with animals; (8) having incestuous relations; (9) having sexual relations with one's mother-in-law; (10) secretly harming a neighbor; (11) accepting a bribe; and (12) failing to uphold the laws of Torah.

Conversely, Moses assures the people that if they observe faithfully all the commandments of Torah, they will enjoy four special blessings, each beginning with the words "Blessed shall you be." The blessings shall come upon the people (1) in their cities and in the country; (2) in the numbers of their children, herds, and produce; (3) in their basket and kneading bowl; and (4) in their comings and goings.

After articulating these curses and blessings, Moses adds a list of additional rewards if the Israelites observe all the commandments God has given them. These include victory over their enemies, productivity of their herds and crops, abundant prosperity, and leadership among all the nations.

Moses adds, if the people fail to practice the mitzvot, they will be punished with such catastrophes as calamity, frustration in all that they undertake, sickness, blight, skies that turn to copper and earth that turns to iron, destruction by their enemies, madness, blindness, dissolving of family ties, exile, ruthless rule by strangers, terrible famine, and a return to Egyptian slavery and oppression.

The Torah concludes these curses and blessings, these rewards and punishments, with the statement: "These are the terms of the covenant that *Adonai* commanded Moses to conclude with the Israelites. . . ."

One ponders these blessings and curses and asks: What did Moses think? Did he really believe that refusal to follow the commandments would bring about such frightful punishments? Or did he make the result of following the commandments so pleasant and the consequence of deliberate or careless rejection so calamitous because he believed that only "fear of God" would bring compliance? In our modern society, is there anything to be learned from this list of curses and blessings?

Knowledge brings responsibility
Rabbi Simeon ben Halafta taught that if one becomes knowledgeable of Torah and its commandments but then does not fulfill them, the punishment will be more severe.

Other rabbis teach that benefits, even peace, come into the world on account of the merits of those who live according to the commandments.
(Deuteronomy Rabbah *7:4,7*)

Several early rabbinic interpreters suggest that God actually rewards those who obey the mitzvot of the Torah. Rabbi Joshua of Siknin, in the name of Rabbi Levi, teaches that as a reward

God hears the prayer of those who carry out the commandments. Others suggest that the reward is success in business. Rabbi Jonathan holds that performing the mitzvot leads to the blessing of having children, the guarantee of rain in its season, and life after death (resurrection). Rabbi Abba ben Kahana speaks for many of the early rabbinic commentators when he declares: "If the people of Israel live by the laws of Torah, God will reward them in the world to come—in the life after death."

The idea of being rewarded in the world to come is a recognition of the harsh realities of human existence. The world we inhabit is imperfect. As biblical authors Job and *Kohelet* note, good people suffer, as well as evil ones. Those who live piously and generously often endure pain with no clear benefits or protection for their loyalty to God. In response to the difficult question of why some good people suffer and some evildoers seem to escape suffering, many rabbinic commentators suggest that God's blessings and curses await us in the world to come—in heaven. It is there we will know the true justice of God.

From the rabbinic interpreters' point of view, that does not mean that human beings have no role in determining their fate in the world to come. On the contrary, the choices we make in life influence God's final decree. The intention of the Torah's list of blessings and curses is to urge us to choose lives filled with mitzvah deeds so we will be assured of an eternity of blessing. (*Deuteronomy Rabbah 7:1–9*)

Rashi offers a significant correction of this early rabbinic position. Noting the double emphasis of the Torah's warning: "If you will listen, really listen [to the commandments] . . ." he explains that the intention is educational. The Torah means to help people understand that the road to performing the commandments may be difficult, especially in the beginning. Therefore, the people are promised blessings so they will be encouraged to take the first steps to carry them out. Once they are on the way to fulfilling the commandments and have discovered how pleasant it is to live by them, they will more easily embrace God's law. (Comment on Exodus 19:5)

Rashi's point seems to agree with that of Simeon ben Azzai: "Be as quick to obey a minor mitzvah as a major one and flee from transgression, for one mitzvah performed leads to another, and one transgression leads to another. Indeed, the reward of one mitzvah is another mitzvah, and the punishment of one transgression is another transgression." (*Avot* 4:2) Rashi, like ben Azzai, sees the list of blessings and curses as a pedagogic device, a means of urging the people to comply with the commandments of Torah.

Moses Maimonides agrees but points out that the Torah specifically promises relief from serious disabilities for those who carry out the commandments because "it is impossible for people to perform the service of God when they are sick, hungry, thirsty, or in trouble." The reward of good health enables people to move toward the great purpose of Torah, "the attainment of perfection of knowledge and becoming worthy to enter the world to come." The rewards are not simply incentives. They bring major benefits, allowing frail human beings the strength of good health and a long life in which to achieve knowledge and earn an entrance into heaven. (*Mishneh Torah, Teshuvah* 9)

Is it appropriate, however, to argue that rewards and blessings are guaranteed to those who observe the mitzvot and that punishment and curses are destined to fall upon those who refuse to follow the commandments of Torah? As we have seen, this appears to be the intent of the Torah text and many of its most important interpreters.

Contemporary Jewish philosopher Rabbi David Hartman explains Maimonides' view with a story about his father, a traditional Jew. Each year the family built a beautiful *sukah,* inviting friends to share the joy of the festival. One year, writes Hartman, "a sudden rainstorm forced our family to leave the *sukah,*" and "I cannot forget my father's explanation to his children as we left the *sukah.*" He told us, "God must be displeased tonight with the community of Israel. He does not welcome us into His 'canopy of peace.'" The rain, continues Hartman, "was seen as a sign of divine anger and rejection."

Hartman disagrees with his father's explanation that God deliberately sends curses and blessings upon human beings as a result of their observance or nonobservance of the commandments. As an alternative, he argues that the world in which we live is imperfect. Human beings make mistakes; they begin with a motive to help and sometimes end up hurting one another. They struggle to bring trust, justice, mercy, and love into human relationships but often fail. Best intentions crash into misunderstandings. Blessings turn to curses and plunge us into confusion.

That is reality, says Hartman. Jewish tradition teaches us to "be sober and careful when performing a mitzvah. God," he asserts, "will give you the protection needed to perform mitzvot, but belief in God's protection should not make you oblivious to real dangers. You must combine your trust in God's protective love with a healthy respect for reality," for a recognition that our best intentions sometimes are twisted into curses.

Does that mean we should not expect rewards for carrying out the mitzvot? Not so, says Hartman, believing that such expectations are critical. "To give up anticipation of reward in this world for mitzvot could destroy the vitality of the sense of personal relationship with God that animates covenantal religious life. . . . If we are taught to expect rewards for mitzvot also in this world, then sometimes we may be disappointed, but we will also attach greater significance to the joyful moments in our lives by seeing them as signs of divine approval." (*A Living Covenant*, pp. 184–194)

Rabbi Hartman's position is that the curses and blessings mentioned in our Torah portion are useful because they add urgency to our relationship with God. They help define the consequences of our actions although there are times when such consequences are beyond our understanding. Most of the time, however, the curses function as warning signs. They signal what we should not do. On the other hand, the blessings we enjoy remind us that God is pleased with our partnership.

Rabbi Abraham Joshua Heschel approaches the subject of our Torah portion from a very different point of view. The purpose of the Torah, he cautions, "is not to substitute for but to extend our understanding." It is meant "to extend the horizon of our conscience and to impart to us a sense of the divine partnership in our dealings with good and evil and in our wrestling with life's enigmas. Clearly one of these serious questions is: What does God want of me?"

Heschel answers that God wants our mitzvah deeds. "It is in *deeds* that human beings become aware of what life really is, of their power to harm and to hurt, to wreck and to ruin; of their ability to derive joy and to bestow it upon others; to relieve and to increase their own and other people's tensions. . . . The deed is the test, the trial, and the risk. What we perform may seem slight, but the aftermath is immense. An individual's misdeed can be the beginning of a nation's disaster. The sun goes down, but the deeds go on. . . ."

For Heschel, deeds have serious, sometimes unknown, and long-range consequences. They possess enormous power to bring blessings or curses, rewards or punishment, fulfillments or despair. But they are also the means through which human beings celebrate or reject their partnership with God. "With a sacred deed goes more than a stir of the heart. In a sacred deed, we echo God's suppressed chant . . . we intone God's unfinished song. God depends upon us, awaits our deeds."

So, says Heschel, does the future of our planet and species. "We stand on a razor's edge. It is so easy to hurt, to destroy, to insult, to kill . . . life." For that reason we must regard ourselves as "half-guilty and half-meritorious." If we perform one good deed, we move the scale toward blessing. One transgression and we move the scale into the realm of curses. "Not only the individual but the whole world is in balance. One deed of an individual may decide the fate of the world."

Heschel places the burden for rewards and punishments, blessings and curses, upon each individual. The long list of blessings and curses mentioned in the Torah is not there as a warning, as an incentive to action, or as a promise of eternal joy in heaven. The blessings and curses, says Heschel, define the harsh consequences of choices made by human beings who hold in their hands not only the fate of their personal lives but also the fate of the world. Through their mitzvah choices, human beings either banish God's Presence from their midst or become sacred instruments through which God's power for justice, goodness, mercy, and love enters and transforms the world. (*God in Search of Man,* chaps. 28, 34)

Moses places before the ancient Israelites a covenant with consequences. They have choices to make. By following the mitzvot, they can assure themselves of blessings; by rejecting them, they will reap a whirlwind of destruction. Their future does not depend upon blind fate. It depends upon them, upon their choices. We might say that God waits for their answer. Today, we might add, God waits for our answer.

QUESTIONS FOR STUDY AND DISCUSSION

1. Lawrence A. Hoffman, a modern scholar on ritual, explains that prayer is a form of art through which individuals bring order, integrity, hope, and vision into their lives. "When worship works, we are artists in the finest sense of affirming wholeness through the power of our traditional images of time, space, and history." (*The Art of Public Prayer,* Pastoral Press, Washington, D.C., 1988, pp. 148–151) Review the various interpretations of the pilgrim's prayer. How does the prayer fulfill Hoffman's definition of ritual?

2. In her book, *Choosing Judaism* (UAHC Press, New York, 1981), Lydia Kukoff, a convert to Judaism, offers this advice to those entering Jewish life: "Sometimes as I sit in our decorated *sukah,* or as I march around the synagogue on Simchat Torah carrying a Torah scroll, I think back to the time when I walked into those services 'cold.' I am so glad I didn't give up. Don't you give up either. Today it is all new to you. For now, just try to participate as much as you can. In time, you will find that it all belongs to you. You won't get there in a year, but twelve months later you'll be further along, and certainly

even further with each succeeding year." (p. 66) Compare this advice to that offered by Maimonides to the convert Obadiah.

3. Review the interpretations of blessings and curses for observance or nonobservance of the commandments. Are there contemporary consequences (blessings and curses) for observance or nonobservance of the ethical mitzvot of Torah?

4. Several commentators suggest that the enjoyment and personal satisfaction derived from doing a mitzvah leads to the doing of other mitzvot. As examples, the joy and love shared while observing Shabbat may inspire us to acts of charity, and the delight of celebrating a Pesach seder may lead to working for the liberation of people still oppressed. What are some other benefits (blessings) that may be derived from observing the mitzvot? What impact can the observance of ritual commandments have upon observance of ethical commandments?

PARASHAT NITZAVIM-VAYELECH
Deuteronomy 29:9–31:30

Parashat Nitzavim-Vayelech is one of seven designated Torah portions that, depending upon the number of Sabbaths in a year, is either read as two separate portions or combined to assure the reading of the entire Torah. While this volume will combine them, it will present an interpretation on each of their most important themes.

Parashat Nitzavim continues Moses' speeches to the Israelites just before they enter the Land of Israel. He tells them that God is making a covenant with them and, through them, with all future generations, fulfilling the promise made to Abraham, Isaac, and Jacob. The covenant will last, he warns, only if they do not worship other gods. If they forsake the Torah's commandments, devastation, plagues, and curses will afflict them. However, Moses promises that they will not be entirely forsaken. If they return to *Adonai* and take the blessings and curses seriously, God will forgive them and restore them to their land, allowing them another opportunity to conduct their lives according to the laws of Torah. God, says Moses, is setting the choice of life and death before them. They are told: "Choose life."

Parashat Vayelech begins with Moses' announcement that he is one hundred and twenty years old and no longer able to lead the people. He assures them that they will be successful in reconquering the Land of Israel and calls upon Joshua to succeed him as leader, promising that God "will not fail you or forsake you." He transmits the Torah to the priests, instructing the people to gather every seven years at the festival of Sukot to hear the reading of the Torah, which they are to study. Forecasting that the people will nonetheless abandon the laws of Torah, God gives Moses a poem to "confront them as a witness" to all they have been taught. (See Deuteronomy 32: 1–43.) Moses transmits the Torah to the Levites, asking them to place it in the Ark of the Covenant. Moses then calls the people together to hear the poem.

OUR TARGUM

· 1 ·

Parashat Nitzavim opens with Moses' announcement to the people: "You stand this day, all of you, before *Adonai* your God . . . to enter into the covenant of *Adonai* your God . . . as God swore to your ancestors, Abraham, Isaac, and Jacob. I make this covenant . . . both with those who are standing here with us this day . . . and with those who are not with us here this day."

Recalling the forbidden idolatry of other nations, Moses warns the Israelites that they must not turn to "fetishes of wood and stone, silver and gold." Those who do will be punished, especially those who say: "I shall be safe, though I follow my own willful heart." God will punish those who serve other gods with the misfortunes of disease, plagues, and devastation, like those brought upon Sodom and Gomorrah. Moses tells the people that when later generations ask, "Why were they punished with such terrible curses?" they will be told of Israel's unfaithfulness to the covenant.

Foreseeing such a time, Moses speaks of the Israelites' exile from their land, but he promises that God will ultimately restore them. God will open their hearts to the Torah's commandments, and they will be given "abounding prosperity" in all they do.

· 2 ·

"This commandment that I place before you," declares Moses, "is not too difficult for you, nor is it beyond reach. It is not in the heavens, that you should say, 'Who among us can go up to the heavens and get it for us and teach it to us, that we may observe it?' Neither is it beyond the sea, that you should say, 'Who among us can cross to the other side of the sea and get it for us and impart it to us, that we may observe it?' No, the Torah is very close to you, in your mouth and in your heart to observe it."

Lifting his voice, Moses pleads with the people. "See, I set before you this day life and prosperity, death and adversity. For I command you this day to love *Adonai* your God, to walk in God's ways, and to keep God's commandments. . . . I call heaven and earth to witness against you this day: I have put before you life and death, blessing and curse. Choose life . . . by loving *Adonai* your God and observing God's commandments."

· 3 ·

Parashat Vayelech opens with Moses informing the Israelites that he is one hundred and twenty years old and no longer capable of leading them. "Joshua will lead you," he says, calling upon the people to be strong and resolute against their enemies when they go forth to reconquer their land.

Speaking to Joshua before all the Israelites, Moses publicly transfers his authority to him, declaring: "Be strong and courageous, for it is you who shall go with this people into the land that *Adonai* swore to their ancestors to give them, and it is you who shall divide it among them. God will go before you. . . . Fear not. . . ."

·4·

Moses writes the Torah and gives it to the priests and to the elders of Israel. He instructs them to read it to the people every seven years at the time of the fall harvest of Sukot.

·5·

Moses is told by God that he will soon die and that he and Joshua should come to the Tent of Meeting. God tells them that after Moses dies, the people will forsake the Torah and worship false gods. God will abandon the people and punish them with evils and troubles. In the midst of all their sorrow, they will understand why they are suffering. "Surely," they will say, "it is because our God is not in our midst that these evils have befallen us." Moses informs them that he is giving them a poem to be read and studied at such a time. (See Deuteronomy 32:1–43; also *Parashat Ha'azinu*.)

About to die, Moses hands the Torah to the Levite priests, who place it in the Ark of the Covenant. He then speaks to the people, complaining that they are stiffnecked, and he asks that all the elders come forward so he can share with them the words of his poem.

THEMES

Parashat Nitzavim-Vayelech contains two important themes:

1. The meaning of *teshuvah,* or "repentance."
2. Passing leadership from one generation to the next.

PEREK ALEF: *Seeking and Achieving Teshuvah, "Repentance"*

The setting of our Torah portions, *Nitzavim* and *Vayelech,* is dramatic. Moses, grown old and weary, speaks for the last time to the people he has led for forty years through the desert. They are at the parting of the ways. The people will enter the Land of Israel, led by Joshua; Moses will die on Mount Nebo. What can Moses say in his final speech to the Israelites? What final message can he leave them with?

He decides to challenge them with the covenant they have made with God. It is a covenant, he reminds them, that is made not only with them but with all Jews for all times. Its conditions and commandments, he assures them, are accessible. These are not impossible to carry out. Moses urges them to be loyal to the covenant, warning that they will suffer great hardships and punishment if they reject it. "See, I set before you this day life and prosperity, death and adversity," he tells the people, pleading, "Choose life . . . by loving *Adonai* your God."

Woven into this moving appeal is a central theme of Jewish tradition: *teshuvah,* or "repentance." Moses encourages the Israelites to carry out the commandments of their covenant with God. While he warns them of the painful consequences of rejecting the commandments, he also leaves the door open for them to correct their mistakes or wrong decisions. Should they deliberately plunge into wrongdoing or err accidentally, says Moses, they can seek forgiveness. Human errors, selfish and harmful acts, shameful behavior—all can be rectified and will be forgiven by God.

Moses explains that even an arrogant person who believes he can break the law with impunity because God will protect him will be punished for abandoning the commandments but will also be given another chance. God does not abandon human beings. God wants human beings to right the wrongs they do, to feel regret for hurting others, and to improve their behavior. God, explains Moses, wants every human being to make *teshuvah,* or "repentance," returning to a life of performing mitzvah deeds defined by the Torah.

Many commentators point out that Moses uses a form of the verb *shuv,* or "turn," seven times within this last speech to the Israelites. (Deuteronomy 30) The repetition of the verb emphasizes Moses' message that *teshuvah* is desirable and possible. Failure to observe the commandments of the covenant may lead to punishment but not to God's abandonment. God does not turn away from any human being nor forsake any sinner. Instead, God waits for the repentance or return of every person. One can always make *teshuvah,* always "return" to God.

This view that the person who rejects God's commandments can seek forgiveness through *teshuvah* is also voiced by the prophets of Israel. For example, Isaiah declares, "Let the sinner give up doing wrong and . . . return to God." Jeremiah suggests that those who turn away from God's commandments will realize their mistakes and seek a new sensitivity for doing good. "Amend your ways and your doings," he instructs the people. Ezekiel speaks of "making a new heart and a new spirit" and doing God's will. Hosea tells his generation, "Return, O Israel, to *Adonai* your God." (Isaiah 56:6; Jeremiah 7:3, 26:13; Ezekiel 18:21; and Hosea 14:2)

It is not surprising, therefore, to find the concept of *teshuvah* as a central theme in Jewish thought and practice. Both the Torah and the prophets share the conviction that our mistakes, even our deliberate wrongs, should be forgiven through repentance. Most rabbinic interpreters agree. Rabbi Samuel ben Nachman, one of the renowned teachers of the third century C.E. in the Land of Israel, speaks for many when he observes, "The gates of repentance are always open." Another rabbinic teacher declares, "Just as a soiled garment can be made white again, so can the people of Israel make repentance and return to God." (*Lamentations Rabbah* 3.44. 9; *Exodus Rabbah* 23:10)

Great is teshuvah
Rabbi Hama ben Hanina taught: "Great is repentance for it brings healing to the world."

Rabbi Yonatan ben Eleazar taught: "Great is repentance for it prolongs life." (Yoma 86b)

The test of teshuvah
Rabbi Judah ben Ezekiel taught: "The test of repentance is refraining from sin on two occasions when the same temptation returns." (Yoma 86b)

The rabbinic tradition, however, adds a further dimension to correcting our errors through repentance. It claims that "if we begin to incline toward regretting the wrongs we have done, God moves within us, pushing us toward admitting and correcting our errors." Another interpreter claims that "God rushes toward all those who make repentance with compassion, mercy, and love." Rabbi Jassa agrees, arguing: "God says to us, 'Make an opening for repentance as large as the eye of a needle, and I will make it large enough for wagons and carriages to pass.' " These rabbinic teachers believe that God is not passive but active in encouraging us to recognize our transgressions and to correct our behavior. (*Midrash* on Psalms 120:7; *Numbers Rabbah* 2:10; *Song of Songs Rabbah* 5:2)

This emphasis by Moses, the prophets, and rabbinic interpreters that *teshuvah,* or "repentance," is possible raises significant questions. Does the opportunity for *teshuvah* mean a person can deliberately hurt or wrong others, say a few prayers, and be forgiven? Is returning to God accomplished by piously proclaiming on Yom Kippur, "*Avinu Malkenu,* inscribe us in the Book of Forgiveness," or by confessing our errors with *Al Chet,* "For the sin we have sinned against You . . ."?

Fourteenth-century Spanish philosopher Joseph Albo confronts these questions about *teshuvah,* explaining that the improvement of our behavior through the process of *teshuvah* is neither automatic nor easy. It requires a careful, painstaking process of "correcting thought, speech, and behavior." By "correcting thought," he means that a person "should feel regret for the wrongs he has done to others." By "correcting speech," he means that a person "should confess his wrongs." By "correcting behavior," he means that a person "pledges never to repeat the wrong again and takes on deeds meant to rectify any damages done, intentionally or unintentionally." For Albo, repentance is more than a pious expression of regret. It moves a person toward a change of heart, mind, and behavior. (*Sefer ha-Ikkarim* 4:26)

In his discussion of *teshuvah,* Moses Maimonides stresses the difficulty of achieving such personality transformation or "true repentance." He points out at least twenty-four different things that hinder human beings from dealing with their mistakes: (1) deliberately misleading others to sin; (2) enticing others to wrongdoing; (3) allowing your children to sin; (4) saying "I will sin and then repent"; (5) standing aloof from the community; (6) opposing the authority of community leaders; (7) making a mockery of the laws of Torah; (8) insulting one's teachers; (9) refusing to hear criticism; (10) cursing others; (11) sharing with a thief; (12) failing to return lost property; (13) robbing from the poor; (14) taking bribes and tampering with justice; (15) taking food from those in need; (16) making profit from a poor person's property; (17) looking lustfully at those of the opposite sex; (18) elevating oneself at the expense of others; (19) condemning others with suspicions, not proof; (20) gossiping; (21) slandering others; (22) acting out of anger; (23) nurturing designs for wrongdoing; and (24) keeping company with those who might influence you to evil ways.

Rambam (Maimonides)

All the above "hinder" but do not "prevent" us from achieving *teshuvah*. Maimonides points out that human beings can achieve repentance by "reviewing and confronting their evil traits" and by "seeking to get rid of them." He argues that none of us is "completely righteous." Every person sins, commits errors, and makes mistakes. "If a person is sincerely remorseful about them and repents, he can achieve full repentance."

Repentance, however, is important not only for individuals but also for society. "Human beings," says Maimonides, "should see themselves and the world as always balanced delicately on scales, hovering between half-guilty of evil and half-innocent of evil." If we think constantly in such terms and measure our every action on such scales, then each action will be seen as either tipping the scales of the world to evil or to good. Our choices of action may either do harm to society or improve the lot of all human beings. Quoting Proverbs 10:25, Maimonides con-

cludes: "A righteous person is the foundation of the world." *(Mishneh Torah, Teshuvah 4:1–6; 7:2–4, 8)*

Cheshbon ha-nefesh
In discussing the harm of sin and the power of repentance, modern philosopher Israel Knox calls attention to the rabbinic concept of cheshbon ha-nefesh, *"taking stock of one's soul, an inner accounting, a sitting-in-judgment upon oneself." He regards this as the essence of* teshuvah. *"As we make our* cheshbon ha-nefesh, *we confess our failure to span the gap between conscience and conduct, between the standards we profess and the actions we perform. . . . This chasm between* believing *and* living *may or may not always be surmountable, but the refusal to try to span it is* sin *and the will to bridge it, at least to narrow it, is* atonement [repentance]." *(The Jewish Spectator, vol. 27, no. 7, September 1963, pp. 7–9)*

Steinsaltz

Reaching out
Repentance does not bring a sense of serenity or of completion but stimulates a reaching out in further effort. Indeed, the power and the potential of repentance lie in increased incentive and enhanced capacity to follow the path even farther. The response is often no more than an assurance that one is in fact capable of repenting, and its efficacy lies in growing awareness, with time, that one is indeed progressing on the right path. In this manner the conditions are created in which repentance is no longer an isolated act but has become a permanent possibility, a constant process of going toward. It is a going that is both the rejection of what was once axiomatic and an acceptance of new goals. (Adin Steinsaltz, The Thirteen Petalled Rose, *Basic Books, New York, 1980, pp. 131–132)*

On the basis of these views of Moses Maimonides, modern interpreter and philosopher Rabbi Joseph B. Soloveichik elaborates on another important aspect of *teshuvah*. He claims that struggling with our failures and errors and seeking forgiveness for them leads us to *taharah*, or "purification." Through the process of admitting our sins, asking God and those we have hurt to forgive these sins, and correcting them, we "strive to convert them into a spiritual springboard for increased inspiration and evaluation."

This, Soloveichik points out, is the other benefit of *teshuvah*. It allows us to use our mistakes and selfish behavior as building blocks for human growth. The memory of our wrongdoings has the potential of transforming us into more generous, kind, and loving human beings. Our sins, observes Soloveichik with sharp psychological insight, "become part of our ego . . . awaking a creative force that shapes a new and loftier personality." In other words, confronting our sins forces us to improve ourselves, and remembering them helps us change our behavior for the good.

"When a person stumbles and falls . . . he should not despair . . . but should cultivate hope . . . 'gaining' by his experience new visions and vistas. Our ideal," Soloveichik concludes, "is not repetition but re-creation on a higher level. *Teshuvah* contains hope and purification." It motivates us to mature and develop positive aspects of our personalities. (*Gesher,* vol. 3, no. 1, June 1966, pp. 5–29)

Soloveichik's view is in harmony with another modern interpreter, Rabbi Mordecai M. Kaplan, who argues that *teshuvah* "stands for nothing less than the continual remaking of human nature." It is a form of "introspection," a means of achieving "progressive self-realization." Kaplan claims that repentance has the potential for repairing "three types of failure."

The first type is the failure "to integrate our impulses, habits, social activities, and institutions in harmony with those ethical ideals that make God present in the world." For example, we may busy ourselves with feeding strangers but be careless and hurtful in our family relationships. Through *teshuvah* we can examine honestly and critically what we are doing and close the gap between our "aspirations" and behavior.

The second type of failure is "fixation," ceasing to change and grow as human beings. Kaplan points out that at various stages in our lives we develop different responses and habits. They may work while we are children but are inadequate, even dangerous, in adulthood. As children we depend on our parents and teachers and what the community provides for us. As we mature, we realize we can no longer "depend on others." We must not only take care of ourselves but also contribute to the welfare of the entire community. Repentance, Kaplan claims, helps us "recognize the inadequacy of our acquired personality to do justice to the demands of a new situation." It spurs our ethical growth.

The third type of failure *teshuvah* helps us confront is the failure to realize "to the fullest degree the potentialities inherent in our natures and in the situations in which we find ourselves." Kaplan points out that "we all have latent powers for good, powers we do not summon to active use." For example, we will plunge into petty arguments with others or refuse to cooperate because of jealousy, rather than build friendship and enjoy the benefits of trust and mutual support. Through the introspection of *teshuvah*, we examine how we waste our potentials and discover how we should use them creatively and constructively, not only for ourselves, but for our society. The act of repentance, Kaplan concludes, is meant "for the reconstruction of our personalities in accordance with the highest ethical possibilities of human nature." (*The Meaning of God in Modern Jewish Religion,* Reconstructionist Press, New York, 1962, pp. 178–187)

Jewish tradition places great emphasis upon the importance of *teshuvah*. While various interpreters offer different points of view about its meaning, process, and potential, none doubts its power to transform human behavior. Rabbi Simeon ben Lakish summarizes the overwhelming agreement of our commentators. "Great is repentance," he writes, "for it turns sins into incentives for right conduct." It is through *teshuvah* that human beings find forgiveness for their mistakes and summon the strength to repair their faults and errors. Repentance leads to renewal and to new opportunities for ethical and personal growth. (*Yoma* 86b)

PEREK BET: *Moses Passes on Leadership to Joshua*

On two occasions the Torah speaks of Moses' retirement and of his responsibility to pass on his leadership to the next generation. In *Parashat Pinchas,* Moses is told he will not be allowed to enter the Land of Israel but, like Aaron, will die in the wilderness because of his excessive anger in striking the rock and damning the people at the Waters of Meribath-kadesh. (Numbers 27:12–14)

Moses responds by asking God to "appoint someone over the community who shall go out before them and come in before them, and who shall take them out and bring them in, so that *Adonai's* community may not be like sheep that have no shepherd." God answers Moses: "Single out Joshua son of Nun, an inspired man, and lay your hand upon him." Moses then confirms the appointment publicly before the priests and the entire people. (Numbers 27:15–19)

In *Parashat Vayelech,* Moses has reached the age of one hundred and twenty years and is about to die. He calls Joshua and "in the sight of all Israel," transfers the powers of leadership to him. Moses tells him, "Be strong and resolute, for it is you who shall go with this people into the land . . . and it is you who shall apportion it to them. . . . Fear not and be not dismayed." (Deuteronomy 31:1–8)

Interpreters ask several questions about the Torah's description of the passing of leadership by Moses to Joshua: Why doesn't Moses choose one of hi s sons to succeed him? What is special about Joshua? Why does Moses *publicly* confer his leadership powers upon Joshua?

Some of the first rabbinic commentators seek to explain why Moses' sons, Gershon and Eliezer, do not inherit the leadership from their father. Because the Torah does not contain any direct information about the decision, rabbinic interpreters use their imagination. They portray Moses as a concerned father, worried about the rights of inheritance of his sons. Arguing with God, Moses says, "Whoever keeps the fig tree should

have the right to eat its fruits. Let them succeed me." But Moses is told, say the rabbis, that Gershon and Eliezer are not worthy of leadership. "They idle away each day. They do not study Torah or put it into practice. Joshua does. Furthermore, Joshua honors you. He cleans and arranges the room where students gather to learn from you, and he has protected you from harm. For those reasons he is more worthy to succeed you than your own sons." (*Numbers Rabbah* 21:16)

In their imaginative reconstruction of a conversation between Moses and God about the succession, rabbinic commentators highlight the criteria for leadership of the Jewish community. The accident of birth, as in the case of Gershon and Eliezer, is insufficient; character is all important. Moses' sons are unworthy because they waste their energies and talents, and they are not dedicated to growing intellectually and spiritually through study. Nor are they committed to putting their knowledge into practice.

Joshua, on the other hand, is worthy of inheriting the leadership from Moses. Rabbinic commentators note not only his inquiring mind devoted to learning but his willingness to work hard and serve as an apprentice to Moses, honoring and protecting him. Joshua is chosen because of his demonstrated commitment to Moses and his loyalty to the Israelites.

 Rashi

Agreeing with this assessment, Rashi adds another reason for the choice of Joshua as successor to Moses. Rashi points out that Joshua's competition was neither Gershon nor Eliezer but Pinchas, Aaron's son. Pinchas had demonstrated loyalty to both Moses and God when he rushed forward to murder an Israelite who had, in violation of the law of Torah, taken a Midianite woman into his tent for sexual pleasure.

Pinchas's action, however, revealed his propensity for quick, careless, and violent action. Instead of consulting with Moses, Pinchas took matters into his own hands, acting rashly and self-righteously. Rashi reasons that Moses' successor could not be impulsive or tend to act in anger. The Israelites required a person who would understand their diverse nature and regard each individual with patience. Leadership demanded tolerance and a temperament of careful and cautious judgment.

Pinchas was not such a person. He acted before he questioned. He was a single-minded zealot and, therefore, unworthy of leadership. Joshua, on the other hand, is seen by Rashi as judicious, careful, slow to act, and sensitive to differences of opinion. While forming his own conclusions, Joshua is a person who listens and learns from others. Rashi implies that only a person with such characteristics deserves to succeed Moses and lead the people into the Promised Land. (Comments on Numbers 27:16)

Peli

Fair and firm
As the future leader, Joshua is described as "a man in whom there is spirit." Here Rashi comments: "A man who knows how to stand up against the spirit of each one of them" [and who knows how] to teach us that to be tolerant does not necessarily imply passivity or spinelessness. A good leader must know his own mind; he must be able to stand up for his views; and he also must be capable of changing his mind, of freeing himself from preconceived ideas. He must not be the type who declares: "My mind is made up—don't confuse me with facts." (Pinchas H. Peli, Torah Today, *p. 186)*

Leading
Leaders who truly lead their people will raise them to their own level. They have a chance to "lead them out" of corruption and to "bring them in" to holiness. Leaders who trail behind their people will finally be dragged down by them to their own low level. (Avnei Ezel, from A. Z. Friedman, Wellsprings of Torah, *p. 337)*

Modern interpreter Pinchas H. Peli points out that Joshua is chosen by Moses because of his bravery and courage. In his prayer for a successor, Moses asks God to "appoint someone over the community who shall go out before them and come in before them, and who shall take them out and bring them in." Joshua is chosen, says Peli, because Joshua is "not like leaders of other nations who send their troops into battle while they themselves stay behind." Instead, he is a person "who goes before his troops."

Moses, explains Peli, is concerned about the great task of leading the people in the many battles that will be necessary to conquer the land. "He knew well that it is one thing to take a people out to war and another to get them out of war and bring them back home. The second task is much harder. A true leader has to be capable of both." Joshua had collaborated with Moses for years. The old leader had confidence in his determination and courage. Joshua was a man who would "go before them," bravely shouting, "Follow me." (*Torah Today,* pp. 186–187)

Philosopher and commentator Martin Buber offers another perspective. He says Moses chooses Joshua as his successor because of Joshua's personal loyalty and for his "physical and instinctive interest in everything connected with fighting." Buber speculates that young Joshua proves himself to Moses by helping put down the many revolts against Moses by the Israelites. He silences the opposition against Moses and defends Moses against his critics. Moses entrusts him with guarding his tent against those who might come to do him harm; Joshua demonstrates his total commitment. When the spies return with their fearful report, doubting the Israelites' ability to conquer the Land of Israel, it is Joshua who contradicts them, boldly telling the people: "Have no fear . . . *Adonai* is with us." It is all this evidence of enthusiasm, determination, courage, and faith that leads Moses to choose Joshua as his successor. (*Moses,* pp. 197–198)

Aaron Wildavsky agrees with Buber. He points out that Moses at times is a guide for Joshua's enthusiasm and leadership skills. For example, when two men, Eldad and Medad, are overheard speaking in a prophetic manner in the camp,

Joshua immediately reports the matter to Moses. Believing they represent a dangerous challenge to Moses' authority, Joshua urges Moses to stop them. Instead of acting rashly against the men, Moses calms Joshua's fears, telling him: "Do not be concerned about me. Would that all of God's people were prophets." (Numbers 11:26–29)

Moses' lesson to Joshua is twofold. A leader must not make quick decisions. Taking counsel with others, a good leader can allow other voices, even dissenting ones, a place in the community. Leading is not silencing or repudiating the opinions of others. It is providing an atmosphere where all views flourish and where even diverse decisions are made, still maintaining the unity of the community. Moses, Wildavsky maintains, seeks to train Joshua with such wisdom. (*Moses as a Political Leader*, pp. 143–44)

Ramban (Nachmanides)

Nachmanides appears to agree when he stresses the educational role Moses played in preparing Joshua for succession. In his commentary, Nachmanides observes that Moses' instruction of Joshua was not private. It was not a closed-door tutorial with student and teacher sharing information and wisdom. Instead, says Nachmanides, it was, as the Torah indicates, "before the eyes of the community."

In other words, Nachmanides maintains that Moses taught Joshua before the entire community. Moses *publicly* "instructs him in his duties as a leader and judge." Moses emphasizes Joshua's role as the one who should go out before them, care for them, be concerned about bringing them back safely from battle, and be careful in all matters of judgment. Every direction and explanation of the law Moses gives to Joshua is open for all to hear and discuss.

The reason for such a public, open process of leadership education and transition, concludes Nachmanides, has to do with the morale of the people. Hearing all Moses' instructions to Joshua and witnessing everything being taught to him, the people are encouraged to trust him. They

come to believe he would treat them honestly and fairly. The prospect of change appears less traumatic. Moses wants a smooth shift in power and authority from him to Joshua. Building up the confidence of the people in Joshua is critical for that smooth transition. (Commentary on Numbers 27:19)

Although Moses prepares Joshua to succeed him, loving him as a disciple, the reality of retirement and death is difficult for Moses to accept. Leading the people for forty years, making all the decisions, interpreting the law, and fighting off detractors and enemies, Moses must have become accustomed to power and responsibility. Giving up such responsibilities and power must have resulted in personal pain.

The rabbis capture Moses' feelings in those transition moments between retirement and death. They call attention to the deal Moses seeks to make with God. "Please let me live," the rabbis imagine him saying. "Let Joshua take over my office, but allow me to live by his side." God grants Moses' wish, and the next day he goes with Joshua to the sanctuary. They enter, and a pillar of cloud separates them. When it departs, Moses asks Joshua, "What did God tell you?" Joshua, looking at the aged leader, responds, "When God spoke to you, did you tell me what was said?" Stunned, Moses realizes that authority has shifted to Joshua. The transition is complete, and Moses is deeply jealous. "Better to die than to experience such envy," he mutters to God. Now Moses is ready for death. (*Deuteronomy Rabbah* 9:9)

This rabbinic tale about Moses makes the point that retirement is not easy. Giving up authority, power, position, status, and office is difficult, even if you have trained your successor. Envy and jealousy, bewilderment and resentment are natural feelings surrounding the loss of one's position. So, too, is fear—especially fear about the unknown future, about the end of one's career, and possibly about impending death. Will others forget me? Will I die unnoticed, alone?

These fears must burden Moses as he prepares to pass on to Joshua the mantle of leadership. Nonetheless, Moses turns his concerns to the future of his people, rising above his envy and anxiety, urging Joshua to go forward and reconquer the Land of Israel. He inspires his successor with the promise, "God will be with you. God will not fail you or forsake you." Moses transforms his retirement and death into a legacy of courage and love.

QUESTIONS FOR STUDY AND DISCUSSION

1. How is *teshuvah,* or "repentance," a process for healing? Can it repair relationships? Can it bring inner peace? Can it bring world peace?

2. Are there some acts for which there can be no *teshuvah?* What about abandoning a friend in time of need? What about failure to speak out when injustice is being done?

3. According to the commentators, what character traits did Moses find in Joshua? Are these qualities still important for leadership today? How?

4. At the moment of passing on his authority to Joshua, Moses assembles all the people and says to Joshua, "Be strong and resolute, for it is you who shall go with this people into the land that *Adonai* swore to their ancestors . . . it is you who shall apportion it to them." Why does Moses choose to say those words "in the sight of all Israel"? Why did he not choose to voice them in a private ceremony?

PARASHAT HA'AZINU
Deuteronomy 32:1–52

Parashat Ha'azinu is a prayer-poem that Moses presents to the people of Israel just before he ascends Mount Nebo, where he will die. In these verses, Moses declares that God's "deeds are perfect . . . and just," and God is "never false" but always "true and upright." He warns against those who act dishonestly against God. He tells the Israelites to "remember" their history and their special relationship with God, who guided their ancestors and cared for them despite the many times they turned to idolatry. God, Moses declares, could have obliterated the Israelites many times for their disloyalty but decided against doing so lest their enemies assume Israel's destruction was their doing rather than God's punishment. Indeed, says Moses, it is God who constantly saves Israel from destruction. It is God "who deals death and gives life." God, Moses concludes, will bring vengeance upon Israel's enemies. Moses warns the people to "take to heart" all of the Torah and its laws and to teach the laws to their children. "The Torah is your very life," he tells them, and "through it you shall long endure. . . ." Moses is then told to climb Mount Nebo from which he will be able to see the Land of Israel. There he will die, without entering the land, punishment for his anger at the Waters of Meribath-kadesh.

OUR TARGUM

·1·

Moses prays that his words of poetry will be heard by all the Israelites. "Give glory to our God," he tells them, for "God's deeds are perfect . . . all God's ways are just. God is faithful, never false, always true and upright. . . . God creates and sustains" all human beings and the people of Israel.

·2·

He urges them to "remember your history" and advises them to ask their parents to inform them

about their past and their relationship as a nation to other peoples. He then recounts how God found the Israelites in a desert region, "guarded [them] as the pupil of God's eye," and cared for [them] as an eagle cares for its young.

God, Moses says, "set the Israelites on the highlands to feast on the yield of the earth, fed them honey and the milk and meat of the best herds." The people "grew fat" and spoiled, and they turned against God and worshiped idols.

God threatened to forsake them, to punish them by sending enemies against them. But God, explains Moses, did not do so lest their enemies conclude that "our own hand has prevailed; none of their defeat was brought about by God."

Moses declares that God alone will punish the people for turning away and bring them back so they understand "there is no God beside Me. I deal death and give life; I wounded and I will heal."

·3·

After reciting his poem, Moses declares: "Pay attention to all I have told you today. Teach it to your children that they may observe faithfully all the terms of the Torah . . . for it is your very life, the guarantee that you will endure on the land that you will occupy across the Jordan River."

Moses is then told to climb Mount Nebo from where he can view the Land of Israel. This is where he will die.

THEMES

Parashat Ha'azinu contains two important themes:

1. God and evil.
2. The importance of history.

PEREK ALEF: *If God's Ways Are Just, What about Evil?*

Moses stands before the people of Israel as an old man. He has led them for forty years; he has been their liberator and their teacher. Now, he is about to die. The people will follow Joshua, his successor, into the Land of Israel. One can imagine Moses' agony as he ponders the question: What shall be my final message to my people?

The Torah presents his answer in a powerful poem. It begins with a plea that his thoughts be heard.

> Give ear, O heavens, let me speak;
> Let the earth hear the words I utter!
> May my discourse come down as the rain,
> My speech distill as the dew,
> Like showers on young growth,
> Like droplets on the grass.
> For the name of *Adonai* I proclaim;
> Give glory to our God!
>
> (Deuteronomy 32:1–3)

Moses continues his poem, offering within it his understanding of God. His words are carefully chosen. They portray God in a number of significant ways. He tells the people:

> The Rock!—God's deeds are perfect,
> Yes, all God's ways are just;
> A faithful God, never false,
> True and upright is God.
>
> (Deuteronomy 32:4)

> God is the Source who created you,
> Fashioned you and made you endure!
>
> (Deuteronomy 32:6)

> . . . God wounds and heals. . . .
>
> (Deuteronomy 32:39)

> . . . Those who reject God will be punished.
>
> (Deuteronomy 32:41)

> Those who harm Israel will be punished.
>
> (Deuteronomy 32:43)

Moses' portrait of God is complex and raises a number of important questions: What does Moses mean when he calls God "perfect," "just," "faithful," "true," and "upright"? Can God be "just" and "faithful" and "wound and heal" at the same time? How can we understand God's justice?

Interpreters of Torah have constantly struggled with such questions. From ancient to modern times, human beings have asked in the midst of their pain and suffering, "Where is God? If God is 'perfect,' why is the world that God created so imperfect? Why do people hurt one another? Why does a God of justice allow hunger, war, and disease? Why does God permit loving and generous human beings to be tortured by disease or cruelty or innocent children to be abused, starved, or killed? Can we really say that 'God's deeds are perfect . . . just . . . never false, true and upright'?"

Despite the anguish they have experienced, many Jews like the prophet Isaiah maintain the faith expressed by Moses that *Adonai* is a God of justice. (Isaiah 5:16) In his time, the Psalmist articulates the same determination: "Your righteousness is like the mighty mountains; Your judgments are like the great deep. . . ." (Psalms 36:7) For centuries, even in the darkest times of persecution, many Jews have declared their faith in the ultimate justice of God.

Others go even further. For them, God's justice is tempered with the equally powerful claim of God's mercy and love. They, too, base their view on Moses' experience and testimony within the Torah. Just before receiving the Ten Commandments at Mount Sinai, Moses experiences and defines God as "compassionate and gracious, slow to anger, rich in kindness and faithfulness, extending kindness to the thousandth generation, forgiving iniquity, transgression, and sin." (Exodus 34:6–7) Reflecting this view of God, the Psalmist (Psalms 119:64) comments that "the earth, *Adonai,* is full of Your mercy," underscoring the conviction that while God may judge the world and all its creatures and even punish them for their sins, God also cares for them and loves them.

Rabbinic commentators teach that God's "power for justice" (*midat ha-din*) and "power for mercy" (*midat ha-rachamim*) are always combined. Without their interconnection, the rabbis argue, the world cannot endure. It will be out of balance and incomplete, resulting in destruction. Only by simultaneously exercising justice and mercy, say the rabbis, can God create and sustain the world. "Mercy or justice alone is insufficient."

Zugot

This idea that justice and mercy are blended is both suggested and extended by Hillel. He claims that when judging human beings or the world, "God weighs the scale of judgment toward the scale of mercy." God actually favors the "power for mercy" over the "power for justice."

Rab, a later sage, agrees, portraying God at a moment of judgment as saying, "Let My power of love overcome My power of anger." This view that God's powers of mercy and justice are blended with a tendency toward mercy allows rabbinic interpreters to accept Moses' claim that "God's deeds are perfect . . . God's ways are just." (*Genesis Rabbah* 12:15; *Tosefta, Sanhedrin* 13:3 and *Berachot* 7a)

How, then, can we account for the suffering of the innocent, of good people? How does this blending of justice and mercy apply to their situations? How can one maintain that "God's ways are just . . ." when, at times, they appear to be cruel?

Early rabbinic commentators commonly answered these questions by claiming that while righteous human beings may suffer in this world, they will be rewarded by God in the *olam ha-ba,* or the "world to come." Pain in this world is temporary and brief. The righteous may suffer at

the hands of cruel human beings or, in the case of illness or disease, because of the inability of human beings to find a cure. Such pain is identified by the rabbis as *yisurim shel ahavah,* or the "sufferings of love," and God, the *Dayan ha-emet,* or the "Judge of truth," rewards those who endure these sufferings with mercy forever in the *olam ha-ba.* (*Ta'anit* 11a)

This concept of God as *Dayan ha-emet,* balancing justice and mercy in this world and in the *olam ha-ba,* became a standard explanation for the reason bad things happen to good people. For rabbinic commentators it justified Moses' claim that "God's deeds are perfect, and all God's ways are just. God is faithful, never false, true and upright." For them, God's justice and mercy might not be apparent in the lives of victims of pain and evil in this world, but—in the *olam ha-ba*—God's justice and mercy eventually will prevail.

With this belief in mind, the rabbis prescribe that, at the death of a loved one, a person should recite the words: "Be praised, O *Adonai* our God, Ruler of the universe, *Dayan ha-emet,*" affirming that God, the "Judge of truth," will consider each life according to its deeds and dispense the appropriate reward in the *olam ha-ba.*

It is this faith in God's ultimate justice and mercy that strengthened Jews throughout the centuries when they were faced with persecution, torment, and death. It is said that when Rabbi Hananiah ben Teradyon, his wife, and daughter were taken by the Romans to be put to death after the Bar Kochba revolt in 135 C.E., they publicly declared God's justice in the words of Moses: He boldly told his tormenters, "God's deeds are perfect"; she said, "God is faithful, never false!" Their belief that God had not forsaken them, even in the midst of their torture and death, but would reward them in the *olam ha-ba* provided the courage and faith they required to face their enemies with strength and pride. (*Avodah Zarah* 18a)

> **No good without evil**
> *The Koretzer Rabbi taught that human beings cannot be consciously good unless they know evil. They cannot appreciate pleasure unless they*

have tasted bitterness. Good is only the reverse of evil, and pleasure is merely the opposite of anxiety. Without the evil impulse human beings do no evil, but neither can they do good. (Louis I. Newman, The Hasidic Anthology: Tales and Teachings of the Hasidim, *Schocken Books, New York, 1963, p. 97)*

Rambam (Maimonides)

In his book *The Guide for the Perplexed* (3:22–23), Moses Maimonides raises a serious objection to the view that trials and suffering are sent "as an opportunity for achieving great reward" in the *olam ha-ba*. He argues that this is not what Moses had in mind when he declared that "God's ways are just. . . ." Using Job and his loss of wealth, property, and children as an example, Maimonides argues that there are no explanations for the suffering of innocent people. We cannot understand the mysterious and miraculous ways in which God brings the universe to life. "We should not fall into the error of imagining God's knowledge to be similar to ours or God's intention, power, and management comparable to ours."

According to Maimonides, if we appreciate, as Job finally did, that God's ways are not our ways and God's knowledge is not our knowledge, we will find suffering more bearable. "We will not be filled with doubts about God. Instead, our faith will increase our love of God."

Maimonides' view that God's powers of justice and mercy are beyond human understanding is not shared by Jewish mystics. They believe that evil enters the world at creation. Rabbi Isaac Luria teaches that God created the world out of a clash between the powers of mercy and judgment. In that collision, sparks of light and love were lodged into dark shells that make up all the substance of the world. We suffer, Luria maintains, because so much is still locked in such shells. The human responsibility is to liberate the light, to free goodness and healing. God's will is

for justice, truth, and mercy. God, dependent upon human beings, is waiting for them to break the dark shells and release God's power for mercy and love.

Modern philosopher Martin Buber amplifies this mystic insight about evil. He writes: "What we call 'evil' is not merely in human beings; it is in the world . . .; it is the uncleanness of creation. . . . We know what has been proclaimed by the anonymous prophet whose words stand in the second part of the Book of Isaiah: like light and darkness, good and evil have been created by God . . . the abyss of the absence of light and the struggle for light . . . [have been created by God]."

For Buber and for Jewish mystics, evil is real. It is embedded in the "dark shells," the material of the universe. Since God could not create the universe without such "material" or "potentials," human beings, like all other forms of life, must be subjected to evil and its awful consequences. Nevertheless, Buber adds that we have the power to liberate the good and diminish the evil. "Everything wants to be hallowed, to be brought into the holy . . . everything wants to come to God through us. . . . God wills . . . man for the work of completing creation. . . . God waits for us." The task of humanity is to reduce evil and its suffering in the world. God, whose ways are just, true, and merciful, depends upon us. (*The Way of Response: Selections from His Writings,* Nahum N. Glatzer, editor, Schocken Books, New York, 1971, pp. 134, 148, and 151)

Controlling the yetzer ha-ra, or the "evil inclination"
The rabbis tell the story of the people who capture the yetzer ha-ra, *or the "source of evil." They are about to destroy it when they are warned that if they do, they will also destroy the world. Instead, they put it in prison. Three days later, they notice that the world about them is changing in dangerous ways. No eggs are being hatched anywhere. Fearful that the world and they will not survive, they decide to liberate the* yetzer ha-ra *and seek ways to control it. (Yoma 69b)*

God's power against evil

I believe . . . the only intellectually satisfying answer that has been given to the Holocaust: God "allowed" it because God didn't have the power to stop it. God was not strong enough yet to prevent this torment, and we did not use our moral capacity to compensate for God's weakness.

The same may be said of other evils we face. God is doing all the good [that] God now can do. We cannot blame our suffering on a God who, like ourselves, does not have all power. (Eugene B. Borowitz, Liberal Judaism, *UAHC Press, New York, 1984, p. 203)*

Evil is chaos

Evil is chaos still uninvaded by the creative energy; [it is] sheer chance unconquered by will and intelligence. . . . In the measure that human beings learn to release their potentialities for good, they transform and transcend evil and associate themselves with the divine energies that inhere in the universe. . . . (Mordecai M. Kaplan, The Meaning of God, *pp. 72–79)*

Rabbi Robert Gordis rejects the views of both Jewish mystics and Martin Buber. "The suffering of the innocent in painful disease, the death of a child, the cutting off of genius or talent before its fulfillment—all these categories of evil are too agonizing to yield to such views." Like Maimonides, Gordis argues that there are some forms of suffering and evil we can understand, but many others are "beyond all the resources of the human intellect.

"The universe is a work of art, the pattern of which cannot be discerned if the spectator stands too close to the painting. Only as one moves back a distance, do the scales and blotches dissolve and does the design of the artist emerge in all its fullness. In the world that is our home, we are too close to the pattern of existence, too deeply involved in it, to be able to achieve the perspective that is God's alone. . . . Perhaps the truest word was spoken by a third-century sage, Yannai: 'It is not in our power fully to explain either the well-being of the wicked or the suffer-

ing of the righteous.' " (*A Faith for Moderns,* Bloch Publishing Co., New York, 1960, pp. 187–189)

Not so, says Rabbi Abraham Joshua Heschel. Rescued from Europe when Nazism began to rise, Heschel draws a distinction between the evil of natural catastrophes or diseases and the evil perpetrated by human beings. God, he argues, gives us commandments for justice, truth, goodness, and love. Human beings are unfaithful to them and unfaithful to God. They bring the evil upon themselves, and then they bitterly turn on God like selfish children looking for someone to blame, crying out: "Where are You?"

Quoting the chasidic teacher Ba'al Shem Tov, Heschel observes: "If people behold evil, they may know it was shown to them in order that they learn their own guilt and repent; for what is shown to them is also within them." Continuing, Heschel declares: "We have profaned the word of God, and we have given the wealth of our land, the ingenuity of our minds, and the dear lives of our youths to tragedy and perdition. . . . We have failed to fight for right, for justice, for goodness; as a result we must fight against wrong, against injustice, against evil. We have failed to offer sacrifices on the altar of peace; thus we offered sacrifices on the altar of war." Such evil is done by human beings.

Heschel agrees with Moses' declaration of faith that "God's deeds are perfect . . . all God's ways are just. . . . God is faithful, true, and upright." God, says Heschel, abhors evil and, therefore, demands of us deeds that are *perfect, just, faithful, true,* and *upright.* God "has not created the universe that we may have opportunities to satisfy our greed, envy, and ambition. We have not survived that we may waste our years in vulgar vanities." Our task, concludes Heschel, is to use our energies and gifts to banish all evil from the world. "God will return to us when we shall be willing to let God in. . . . God is waiting constantly and keenly for our effort and devotion." (*Man's Quest for God: Studies in Prayer and Symbolism,* Scribner, New York, 1954, pp. 147–151)

Rabbi Eugene Borowitz offers a philosophy about God and evil slightly different from that of Heschel. "I believe . . . the only intellectually satisfying answer that has been given to the

Holocaust [is] God 'allowed' it because God didn't have the power to stop it. God was not strong enough yet to prevent this torment, and we did not use our moral capacity to compensate for God's weakness."

Borowitz here breaks with traditional Jewish theology, which sees both good and evil as flowing from God. For him, evil emerges because God is limited in power and cannot do anything to stop it. God's will is for goodness, mercy, justice, and peace, but God requires our help and, at times even with our help, may not prevail.

"The same," argues Borowitz, "may be said of other evils we face. God is doing all the good [that] God now can do. We cannot blame our suffering on a God who, like ourselves, does not have all power." God may want a world without anguish and injustice, but, like that of a human being, God's will is limited by the harsh realities of available resources, by the unexpected flurry of opposing forces, and by the failure of human beings to cooperate. Evil happens because God cannot yet prevent it, not because God plans it. (*Liberal Judaism*, p. 203)

Why is there evil in this world created by a God of justice, mercy, and love? Why do some people suffer and others live long lives of happiness and peace? What does Moses mean by his claim that "God's deeds are perfect . . . are just . . . true and upright"?

Jewish commentators offer a variety of views in response to these difficult questions. They challenge us to formulate our own answers and integrate them into our lives. Perhaps the very process of struggling to understand the meaning of evil is the means through which God triumphs over evil. Some debates, say the rabbis, are truly for the sake of God. Confronting the power and temptations of evil in God's world may be one of them.

PEREK BET: *"Remember the Days of Old": The Importance of History*

In his poetic declaration to the people of Israel, Moses tells them: *Zechor yemot olam*, "Remember the days of old,"/*Binu shenot dor va-dor*, "Consider the years of ages past. . . ." Are these the words of an old man fearful of being forgotten by his people, or is this statement an important piece of wisdom?

Modern historian Yosef Hayim Yerushalmi notes that while "memory is always problematic, usually deceptive, sometimes treacherous," the Torah has "no hesitations" in commanding it. He points out that "the verb *zachar* [remember] appears in its various forms in the Bible no less than one hundred and sixty-nine times." The people of Israel are commanded to remember and are warned not to forget.

Yerushalmi explains that, within the Torah, "remembering" functions within "two channels: ritual and recital." Each of the festivals celebrates a historical event. Pesach and Sukot tell the tale of the people's liberation from Egypt and their wandering through the Sinai desert. Shavuot, during the time of the Temple in Jerusalem, becomes a celebration of the giving of the Torah on Mount Sinai. The recital of history, the encounter with memory, takes place with each ritual. Every Shabbat *Kiddush* over the wine includes the phrase *zecher li-tziat Mitzrayim*, or "a remembrance of the Exodus from Egypt."

Calling the creation of Israel's history "an astonishing achievement," Yerushalmi concludes that while "biblical history has, at its core, a recital of the acts of God, its accounts are filled predominantly with the actions of men and women and the deeds of Israel and the nations. . . . The result was . . . history on an unprecedented scale." (*Zakhor: Jewish History and Jewish Memory*, University of Washington Press, Seattle, 1982, pp. 1–26)

Why recall or study the past? Why recite it at festival times?

Rashi

Rashi suggests that one should "remember" and "consider" history "in order to be conscious of what may happen in the future." He explains that understanding how God created the heavens and earth, spread human beings throughout the world, made a covenant with Abraham, divided peoples into lands, and gave the Torah with its laws to the people of Israel helps to promote an appreciation of God's power and presence in human life. The knowledge of what God has done encourages faith in what God will continue to do. Knowing about the past, says Rashi, promotes the truth that "God has the power to bring good into human life and will one day bring the world to a messianic time of justice and peace." (Comments on Deuteronomy 32:7)

 Peli

Modern commentator Pinchas Peli sees another value in "remembering." He quotes a statement by the great chasidic master Nachman of Bratzlav, which is inscribed in huge stone letters at the entrance to the Yad va-Shem Holocaust Memorial in Jerusalem: "In remembering is the secret of redemption." Peli argues that "recalling the past and understanding it help us put events into their proper focus." Retrieving the past, he says, enriches us. "Even though we may think of ourselves as wise, resourceful, and technologically advanced, we are brought to realize that there is still much we can learn from our parents, and even our grandparents have much that is worth sharing with us."

Peli also believes that knowing about our past provides an important source of "constructive pride." Jews emphasize the "pride to be derived from getting to know their roots. This pride was not aimed at inflating one's sense of importance. . . . On the contrary, it was reason for imposing more obligations and restrictions. There is a short but very meaningful Yiddish expression that is invoked on such occasions: *s'pa'ast nisht*. It does not suit a person of distinguished lineage. . . . Being proud and getting to know the roots of one's culture is not just a hobby or pastime," Peli concludes, "but a delicate and sophisticated business." It is the means through which we adopt and absorb ethical values and standards into our behavior. Considering and understanding our past provides a proud set of models, guidelines, and goals. (*Torah Today,* pp. 239–241)

Studying and recalling history, however, can sometimes be very painful, teaching lessons that are often difficult to accept. Holocaust survivor and Nobel Prize-winning author Elie Wiesel points out that people often are resistent to dealing with what the past teaches. After years of writing about the Nazi attempt to destroy the Jewish people, Wiesel feels "discouragement and shame." Society, he says, "has changed so little."

Hatred, prejudice, and anti-Semitism continue. "So many strategists are preparing the explosion of the planet and so many people willingly submit . . . so many still live under oppression and so many others in indifference, only one conclusion is possible: namely, the failure of the black years has begotten yet another failure. Nothing has been learned. Auschwitz has not even served as warning. For more detailed information, consult your daily newspaper."

Why follow Moses' advice: "Remember the days of old,/Consider the years of ages past"?

Wiesel argues that we must study history because we owe it to those who perished and to new generations who will need to know "where they come from, and what their heritage is." Remembering the past is critical in forming the future. "We need to face the dead, again and again, in order to appease them, perhaps even to seek among them, beyond all contradiction and absurdity, a symbol, a beginning of promise."

To demonstrate the importance of passing memories from one generation to another, Wiesel relates how the famed Jewish historian Simon Dubnow encouraged those about him as they walked to their death, telling them: "Open your eyes and ears, remember every detail, every name, every sigh! The color of the clouds, the hissing of the wind in the trees, the executioner's every gesture: the one who survives must forget nothing!"

As a result Jews wrote plays and poems describing the agony, torture, and degradation of those who perished in the death camps. "Jews," says Wiesel, "went without sleep, bartered their food for pencils and paper. They gambled with their fate. They risked their lives. . . . They did not write them for me, for us, but for the others, those on the outside and those yet unborn. There was then a veritable passion to testify for the future, against death and oblivion, a passion conveyed by every possible means of expression."

As Wiesel notes, those writing history under such circumstances recorded it for those in the future. It was their last gift, a testimony of pride and faith, of courage and determination. Those about to die in gas chambers or be shot at the edge of mass graves or be beaten to death sealed their memories in documents so they would live again in those who read about their experiences. This "historic consciousness," writes Wiesel, provides Jews with a solidarity with other Jews "and those who survive within you."

Studying Jewish history, therefore, bonds Jews to a "collective memory," a legacy reaching back to Abraham and Sarah, Isaac and Rebekah, Jacob, Leah, and Rachel, through Moses and all the prophets, poets, philosophers, and Torah commentators. It means, concludes Wiesel, "choosing to be a link between past and future, between remorse and consolation, between the primary silence of creation and the silence that weighed on Treblinka. . . . To be a Jew today means to bear witness to what is and to what is no longer." (*One Generation After*, pp. 9, 11, 38–39, 168–174)

Modern philosopher Emil L. Fackenheim also addresses the importance of memory and history. For him, Moses' command to "remember . . . and consider the years of ages past" is not a suggestion that Jews have the right to accept or reject. Fackenheim points out that, before the Holocaust, Jews sought to live by the 613 commandments (mitzvot) of the Torah. Following the Holocaust, an additional commandment has been added to Jewish practice.

Jews, Fackenheim writes, must "remember" their history. They must study it carefully, know all its details, celebrate their traditions, teach them to their children, and do everything possible to assure their regeneration and growth as a people. That is the only way they will triumph over Hitler whose policy of extermination was designed to put an end to Jewish memory and existence. *The authentic Jew of today,*" explains Fackenheim, *"is forbidden to hand Hitler yet another, posthumous victory."* (*The Jewish Return into History: Reflections on the Age of Auschwitz and a New Jerusalem*, Schocken Books, New York, 1978, pp. 19–24)

Jewish history and purpose
A robust sense of identity has not prevented this people from sending the repercussions of its influence far and wide into the oceans of universal history. It is when historic Israel is most persistently distinctive that its universal vocation is enlarged. The lesson of history is plain. There is no salvation or significance for the Jew except when he aims high and stands straight within his own authentic frame of values. (Abba Eban, My People, p. 522)

Making history
Human beings make their own history, but they do not make it just as they please; they do not make it under circumstances chosen by themselves but under circumstances directly found, given, and transmitted from the past. (Karl Marx)

Ignoring history
Those who ignore the past are doomed to repeat it. (George Santayana)

The choice of confronting and embracing Jewish history in very personal terms does not apply only to being, in Wiesel's terms, "a witness" or, in Fackenheim's formulation, an instrument in the "triumph over Hitler." For many Jews, "remembering" and "considering" the Jewish legacy is a means of recapturing Jewish identity.

Modern writer Paul Cowan grew up without a Jewish education, without Jewish celebrations, and with almost no experience with his Jewish relatives. He recalls suffering bitter moments of anti-Semitism, while attending a private school where he hid his Jewish identity. "I never told anyone. I felt guilty about it, as if I were personally responsible for my plight."

In his thirties, Cowan began a writing project about Jewish socialism as it had flourished on the Lower East Side of New York. The research led him to questions about his own family, where they had come from, why some bore the name Cohen and others Cowan. Soon he was enmeshed in reclaiming his Jewish heritage. Explaining his motivation, Cowan writes, "For my part, I am reacting to the rootlessness I felt as a child—to the fact that, for all the Cowan family's warmth, for all its intellectual vigor, for all its loyalty toward one another, our pasts had been amputated. We were orphans in history."

Cowan explains that when he met people who made Judaism attractive, "I was faced with a clear choice—a choice, indeed, about history, though I never knew how to articulate it until my sister Holly furnished the words. Should I explore Judaism, the real, living link with my ancestors and the six million? Or should I reject it and be another conscious participant in the obliteration of five thousand years of history? Put that way, of course, it wasn't really a choice." For Paul Cowan, carrying out Moses' commandment to "remember the days of old,/Consider the years of ages past" was the means through which he retrieved his legacy as a Jew. (*An Orphan in History: Retrieving a Jewish Legacy,* Doubleday, New York, 1983, pp. 3–21)

What about a convert to Judaism? Is Moses' command also applicable to Jews-by-choice? If one has not been born a Jew and is, therefore, not related to generations of Jews by birth, how can one feel a part of the Jewish past?

Lydia Kukoff, herself a convert, offers some important insights into such questions. She comments: "When I became a Jew, my husband and I lived far away from our extended Jewish family. Fortunately, however, I found some friends who were quite Jewishly literate. We started a study group and met regularly to learn, to cook together for holidays, and just to be together. These friends gave me a great deal of support. I had a comfortable environment in which to learn and ask questions, while gradually becoming part of a Jewish community. By doing and learning I began to build my own Jewish past."

Creating a "Jewish past" takes time and discipline. Kukoff underscores the importance of Shabbat and festival celebrations in the home and synagogue, constant study, reading cookbooks, history, literature, Jewish religious thought, placing a *mezuzah* on the door, using a Jewish calendar, learning Hebrew, and acquiring synagogue skills. She advises, "Don't be impatient. You won't get it all right away. Nobody does. . . . What you are learning and doing will slowly

become internalized. You will make Judaism your own, and you will feel authentic." Studying, accumulating knowledge about Jewish history, and celebrating the traditions of Jewish life provide a convert with a Jewish memory. It is the means through which a sacred heritage is transfused into the soul. (*Choosing Judaism*, pp. 23–29)

Jewish history carries with it a distinct task, which we encounter in Moses' demand to "remember the days of old,/Consider the years of ages past." The great lawgiver and leader does not stop there. He also declares that "God's portion is the people of Israel." What does such a claim mean? How can it be understood within the context of Jewish history?

Modern interpreter Rabbi Leo Baeck sees in the study of Jewish history an extraordinary explanation for the purpose of the Jewish people. "According to an old saying," he writes, "Israel was called into existence for the sake of the Torah; but the Torah can live only through its people. . . . The Jewish right to existence was dependent upon the Jews retaining their peculiarity. All education was directed to this end: To be different was the law of existence. According to an ancient interpretation, the Jews were exhorted: 'You shall be different, for I *Adonai* your God am different. . . .' The Jew was the great nonconformist, the great dissenter of history. That was the purpose of Jewish existence."

Baeck underscores his view by observing that "often it seems that the special task of Judaism is to express the idea of the community standing alone, the ethical principle of the minority. Judaism bears witness to the power of the idea as against the power of mere numbers and worldly success; it stands for the enduring protest of those who seek to be true to their own selves, who assert their right to be different against the crushing pressure of the vicious and the leveling. . . . If Judaism did not exist," argues Baeck, "we should have to invent it. Without minorities there can be no world historic goal."

For Rabbi Baeck, Israel is "God's portion" because of its unique role in history as a community "standing alone," questioning the power of the multitude, and representing the sanctity of each human being as a child of God. Knowing and understanding that history are crucial for every Jew and for the world. "So long as Judaism exists," Baeck concludes, "nobody will be able to say that the soul of humanity has surrendered." (*The Essence of Judaism,* pp. 260–273)

Is this what Moses has in mind when he emphasizes, "Remember the days of old,/Consider the years of ages past"? Undoubtedly, Moses was concerned with several of the considerations expressed by our interpreters on the significance of Jewish history. He must have sensed the power in reviewing history, realizing that acquiring and confronting one's past is a source of pride and identity that builds a commitment for future survival. The past leads through the present into tomorrow.

QUESTIONS FOR STUDY AND DISCUSSION

1. At the death of a loved one, a Jew says a blessing: "Be praised, O *Adonai, Dayan ha-emet,* Judge of truth." What does this blessing acknowledge about God and human life? How does it relate to Moses' statement that God's "deeds are perfect . . . all God's ways are just"?

2. Some Torah interpreters claim that evil is a necessary part of human existence. What do they mean by this argument? How would you apply their claim to the evils of sickness, dishonesty, murder, child abuse, war, and famine? Which explanation of the relationship between evil and God presented by the Torah interpreters makes most sense to you? Why?

3. In her book *Generation without Memory* (Linton Press/Simon and Schuster, New York, 1981, pp. 99–100), writer Anne Roiphe quotes a friend: "We Jews are molded together like a family; because of our incredible and unique history we have developed our own intellectual modes, the modes of logic and humor that we share with other Jews. We are a single family that traces its history back to before the Flood. Being Jewish is one of the major ingredients of my psyche. I could not live suspended in air. I need my roots, my feelings of belonging." How does a study of Jewish history create a sense of belonging to "a family"? How does such study prevent one from feeling "suspended in air"?

4. For Jews, as Torah interpreters point out, memories of the past, a shared history, are very important in the formation of a proud identity. Today, however, there are many converts to Judaism and many born-Jews who have not accumulated a "memory bank" of Jewish experiences or knowledge. If you were shaping a program meant to help them acquire such a "memory bank," what would you include?

PARASHAT VEZOT HA-BERACHAH
Deuteronomy 33:1–34:12

Parashat Vezot ha-Berachah, meaning "This is the blessing . . .," begins with Moses' blessing of and his farewell to the people of Israel. He blesses each of the twelve tribes, noting that the Torah is "the heritage of the congregation of Jacob." He concludes with the pronouncement: "O happy Israel! Who is like you,/A people delivered by *Adonai,*/Your protecting Shield, your Sword triumphant!" Then Moses climbs Mount Nebo, located in Moab just across from Jericho and the Dead Sea, from whose peak he sees the Land of Israel. He dies there at the age of one hundred and twenty years and is buried in Moab. No one knows the location of his grave. At the end of a thirty-day mourning period, Joshua assumes leadership of the people. "Never again," declares the Torah, "did there arise in Israel a prophet like Moses— whom *Adonai* singled out, face to face. . . ."

OUR TARGUM

· 1 ·

Moses speaks words of poetry and blessing in his last statement to the people of Israel. He recalls how God "came from Sinai . . ./Lightning flashing" at the people, and how they accepted the Torah as their heritage.

· 2 ·

Moses blesses each of the tribes. He prays that "Reuben may live and not die"; that Judah be restored and aided against his enemies; that all the undertakings of Levi be blessed; that Benjamin continue to be protected; that Joseph and his sons, Ephraim and Manasseh, be blessed "with the bounty of earth and its fullness"; that Zebulun and Issachar enjoy the bounty of sand and sea; that Gad be enlarged and rewarded for his leadership and courage in battle; that Dan "leap forth" to victory; that Naphtali be "sated with favor"; that the tribe of Asher "be the favorite of his brothers," dipping "its foot in oil" and enjoying security.

·3·

Concluding his blessing, Moses declares that "there is none like God,/ Riding through the heavens to help you,/ . . . God is a refuge,/ A support . . ./O happy Israel! Who is like you,/ A people delivered by *Adonai,*/ Your protecting Shield, your Sword triumphant!/ Your enemies shall come cringing before you,/ And you shall tread on their backs."

·4·

Moses climbs to the peak of Mount Nebo in Moab just opposite the city of Jericho near the Dead Sea. From there he can see the Land of Israel that is promised by God to the people. Moses, who is forbidden to enter the land, dies in Moab at the age of one hundred and twenty. No one knows the place of his burial.

The Israelites mourn his passing for thirty days. Afterwards, Joshua son of Nun succeeds him as leader of the Israelites.

The Torah concludes by citing Moses' unique-

ness. "Never again did there arise in Israel a prophet like Moses—whom *Adonai* singled out, face to face, for the various signs and portents that *Adonai* sent him to display in the land of Egypt, against Pharaoh and all his courtiers and his whole country, and for all the great might and awesome power that Moses displayed before all Israel."

THEMES

Parashat Vezot ha-Berachah contains two important themes:

1. The significance of Torah to the Jewish people.
2. The role of Moses as prophet and leader.

PEREK ALEF: *Torah: "The Heritage of the Congregation of Jacob"*

In his farewell message to the Israelites, Moses again recites a poem. He recalls the spiritual experience of the people at Mount Sinai, declaring:

> *Adonai* came from Sinai;
> God shone upon them from Seir;

Lightning flashing at them from the right.
Lover, indeed, of the people,
Their holy ones are all in Your hand.
They followed in Your footsteps,
Accepting Your pronouncements,
When Moses commanded us with the Torah
As the heritage of the congregation of Jacob.

About to die, the aged leader impresses upon the people their historic relationship to the Torah.

It originates in the "lightning flashing at them" at Mount Sinai. It is proof of God's love for the people of Israel; following the commandments of the Torah is proof of the people's loyalty to God. Torah is the unique "heritage of the congregation of Jacob," of the Jewish people.

Rashi

In commenting on the meaning of Moses' observation on the relationship of the Jewish people to the Torah, Rashi writes: "We have taken the Torah and will not abandon it." For Rashi, the people have chosen to accept the Torah, and they are defined by their attachment and devotion to it. Torah forms the basis of Jewish tradition. There can be no Jewish people without it. Adherence to its wisdom, ethics, and rituals is essential for preserving the people. (Comment on Deuteronomy 33:4)

Rashi's emphasis on defining the Jewish people by its relationship to Torah may be based on earlier comments by Rabbi Eleazar. In a rhetorical question, Eleazar asks, "What was the blessing Moses made before reading the Torah?" He answers his question with the claim that Moses said: "Be praised, O God, who has chosen the Torah and made it sacred and finds pleasure in those who fulfill it."

"Moses," Rabbi Eleazar stresses, "does not say 'those who study it or meditate upon it.' He claims that God 'finds pleasure in those who fulfill it,' who practice it by carrying out its commandments. It is the 'practice' of Torah that transforms it into 'a heritage of the congregation of Jacob.' " (*Deuteronomy Rabbah* 11:6)

Ramban (Nachmanides)

Nachmanides widens Rabbi Eleazar's claim to include both those who are born-Jews and those who convert to Judaism. He points out that Moses does not speak of the Torah as belonging to the "house of Jacob" or to the "seed of Jacob," which could have led to the assumption that Torah is "the heritage" only of those born to Jewish parents. Instead, he emphasizes that the Torah is "the heritage of *kehilat Ya'akov*, or the 'congregation of Jacob.' " It is not an exclusive birthright but a legacy that can be adopted or chosen by any person. (Comment on Deuteronomy 33:4)

Hertz

On the meaning of Torah
The real Torah is not merely the written text of the Five Books of Moses; the real Torah is the meaning enshrined in the text, as expounded . . . and unfolded . . . by successive generations of sages and teachers in Israel. (Rabbi Joseph H. Hertz, Authorized Daily Prayer Book, *p. 35*)

The purpose of the whole Torah is that each person should become a Torah. (Ba'al Shem Tov)

If not for Torah, the people of Israel would not at all differ from the nations of the world. (Sifre Deuteronomy 32:29)

Blessing before reading the Torah
Blessed is the Eternal, our God, Ruler of the universe, who hallows us with mitzvot and commands us to engage in the study of Torah. Eternal our God, make the words of Your Torah sweet to us, and to the house of Israel, Your people, that we and our children may be lovers of Your name and students of Your Torah. Blessed is the Eternal, the Teacher of Torah to the people Israel. (Gates of Prayer, *p. 52*)

When two people meet to study Torah, God is present. (Hananiah ben Teradyon, Avot 3:6)

Rambam (Maimonides)

 Steinsaltz

In his discussion of the importance of Torah to the Jewish people, Moses Maimonides observes that as soon as children begin to talk, parents must teach them the words: "Moses commanded us with the Torah as a heritage of the congregation of Jacob," and "*Shema Yisrael*, 'Hear, O Israel,' *Adonai* is our God, *Adonai* is One." Children must be taught the importance and the lessons of the Torah as soon as they can speak. Teachers, says Maimonides, are to be employed if parents cannot provide education. "Every person is commanded to study Torah, whether poor or rich, in sound health or sick, young or old . . . one must study until the day of death."

Maimonides even suggests how the time for studying Torah should be divided. One-third of the time should be spent on the Torah; one-third on commentaries and the Talmud; and one-third in "thinking and reflecting" upon what has been covered. One subject should be compared to another; questions should be asked; ethical rules should be inferred from the standards found within the Torah. Furthermore, the study of Torah may not be postponed with the excuse that one has no leisure time. "Should such a thought enter your mind," writes Maimonides, "you will never win the crown of Torah. Instead," he concludes, quoting *Avot* 1:5, "make the study of Torah a fixed obligation."

For Maimonides, no commandment "is equal in importance to the study of Torah. Indeed, the study of Torah is equal to all the commandments because it leads to the practice of Torah." He concludes, "Thus the study of Torah takes precedence over practice." In Maimonides' view, the Torah constitutes God's truth, given to the people of Israel. Deciphering that truth and understanding the commandments motivate one not only to fulfill God's will for justice, mercy, and peace but to make the Torah "the heritage of the congregation of Jacob." (*Mishneh Torah, Sefer ha-Madah* 1–5)

Modern commentator Rabbi Adin Steinsaltz builds on Maimonides' emphasis on the importance of Torah study as a means of knowing what God wants from us. Defining Torah as not only the Five Books of Moses but also as all the works of the Talmud and subsequent commentaries, Steinsaltz claims that "the Torah of the Jews is the essence of divine revelation; it is not only a basis for social, political, and religious life but is in itself something of supreme value . . . it is the spiritual map of the universe . . . for the Torah expresses the divine will and wisdom . . . the intellectual study of Torah and the emotional involvement in its contents are a form of identification with the divine will, with what may be called God's dream of the existence of the world and the existence of human beings."

Knowing Torah is more for Steinsaltz than understanding what God wants for the world and its human beings. Torah is not just an "intellectual" document for study. It is also "Law." Torah compels people "to behave in certain ways." It "is a way of life, showing both how to relate inwardly and how to conduct oneself outwardly, practically. . . . One finds the Torah significant in every aspect of community, commerce, agriculture, and industry, in the life of feeling and love, in relations between the sexes—down to the most minute aspects of living, like buttoning one's shoes or lying down to sleep. . . ." Steinsaltz's view of the Torah as a "divine map of the world" and as God's Law, which "directs the conduct of one's daily business from waking to sleeping," represents a widely held view within Jewish tradition. (*The Thirteen Petalled Rose*, pp. 87–98)

The evolving Torah
Torah results from the relationship between God and the Jewish people. The records of our earliest confrontations are uniquely important

to us. Lawgivers and prophets, historians and poets gave us a heritage whose study is a religious imperative and whose practice is our chief means to holiness. Rabbis and teachers, philosophers and mystics, gifted Jews in every age amplified the Torah tradition. For millennia the creation of Torah has not ceased, and Jewish creativity in our time is adding to the chain of tradition. (From Reform Judaism: A Centenary Perspective, *CCAR, New York, 1976)*

Differing with Steinsaltz and others who believe that the Torah is the product of a single revelation to Moses at Mount Sinai, Rabbi Mordecai M. Kaplan maintains that the Torah is a sacred document that evolved through many centuries. He argues that "all the basic elements of human culture are represented" in the written Torah and in the later Talmud. As such, the Torah "contains folklore and a world perspective; it outlines a national policy; it prescribes ethical and religious conduct; it lays the foundation of a system of jurisprudence. . . . The Torah, especially as developed in life and interpretation, can, therefore, without exaggeration be regarded as the full equivalent of what we understand by a national civilization."

Kaplan, in terms of this evolving "national civilization," sees the Torah as "the embodiment of Israel's quest through the ages for the moral law that expresses the will of God." The Torah, therefore, "is not infallible." It contains errors and deals with matters that are no longer relevant, such as the dress of the priests or the sacrifices offered on ancient altars. At times, as in the case of capital punishment or the treatment of women, it presents ideas that are questionable. However, Kaplan maintains that, as the Jewish people quest for an understanding of what is morally right, the Torah, even with its errors, "when submitted to study and analysis, may prove instructive and enlightening. We learn the moral law, as we learn natural law, by trial and error."

Kaplan adds an important element to his view of Torah as an evolving, imperfect record of the Jewish people's search for what is morally right. He believes that while God did not present the whole Torah to Moses on Mount Sinai, God is the power continuing to urge the Jewish people in an ethical quest for love, justice, purity, and peace. For him, the Torah is a record of God's continuing influence upon them. "The Torah reveals the working of God in the life of our people, in that it articulates the earliest striving of our people to live up to the highest potentialities of human nature." (*The Meaning of God*, pp. 311–318; also *Questions Jews Ask*, pp. 167–168)

As the "heritage of the congregation of Jacob," the Torah holds the secret of Jewish survival. The people's devotion to and study of Torah guarantee the Jewish future. It has never become a static "literature" or "tradition." Commentators have constantly applied its ethics to the challenging realities of their times. Mystics and philosophers have explored its views of God, history, and the nature of human life. The rituals and festivals first described in its chapters have nurtured the flowering of Jewish celebrations. The Torah has evolved with the Jewish people and has remained its main source of historical identification and moral teachings. Jews are the people of an ever-expanding Torah.

Rabbi Leo Baeck captures the meaning and challenge of the Torah "as the heritage of the congregation of Jacob." He observes that "Judaism did not affix itself to any particular period so as to finish up with it; never did it become complete. The task abides but not its solution. The old revelation becomes a new revelation: Judaism experiences a *continuous renaissance*." The ancient Torah of Moses continues to unfold.

PEREK BET: *Moses "Whom Adonai Singled Out, Face to Face"*

Parashat Vezot ha-Berachah refers to Moses as *ish ha-Elohim*, or a "man of God" (Deuteronomy 33:1), and as *eved Adonai*, or a "servant of God." (Deuteronomy 34:5) We are told also that, unlike all other prophets, Moses knew God with a special intimacy that is described as "face to face." Within rabbinic tradition, Moses is called *Moshe rabbenu*, or "Moses, our teacher." These various descriptions and names for the leader whose life fills the books of Exodus, Leviticus, Numbers, and Deuteronomy and who is known in Jewish tradition as the bearer of *Torat Moshe*, the "Torah of Moses," dramatize his central place in both Jewish and world history. Today, his religious teachings and powerful political image continue to influence millions. Yet, this great man, who dies alone on Mount Nebo, outside the Promised Land of Israel, and whose burial place "no one knows to this day," remains an enigma.

Commentators throughout the centuries have sought to uncover his motives, unmask his personality, and reveal the secrets of his greatness. Piecing together the fragments of his life collected from the Torah or using their imagination, interpreters have speculated about his origins, family relationships, complex association with the people of Israel, emotional stability, instincts for leadership, moral sensibilities, and his mysterious connection with God.

Each spark disclosed about this "man of God" brings us nearer to understanding what constitutes a "great" human being, a "servant of God." Taken together, the critical elements become a powerful inspiration and model—a goal for the cultivation of character.

Who, according to our commentators, is Moses? What are the elements of his greatness?

In analyzing Moses within the context of great biblical personalities, early rabbinic commentators assert that he is superior to Adam, Noah, Abraham, Isaac, and Jacob. Adam, they say, is created in God's image but, failing to follow God's command, is banished from the Garden of Eden. Moses' loyalty to God is never diminished. Noah saves himself, but Moses saves himself and his generation. Abraham provides hospitality to passersby, but Moses feeds all Israel in the desert. Isaac glimpses God at the time Abraham is about to slaughter him on the altar, but Moses sees God face to face with eyes that never dim. Jacob wrestles with an angel on earth, but Moses takes on all the angels of heaven!

Moses' greatness, however, is not only a matter of comparing his "powers" with those of others. He is also superior in deeds. Rabbi Isaac speaks for many rabbinic interpreters in underscoring the Torah's portrayal of Moses as honest, pure of motive, selfless, scrupulous about never taking advantage of others or of representing his own needs, and always acting out of justice, in defense of the people of Israel.

Other rabbinic commentators point out that Moses constantly seeks to bring peace between the people of Israel and God. When the time comes for Israel to receive the Torah, Moses willingly climbs Mount Sinai, enduring forty days and nights of hunger, cold, and frightening thunder and lightning. Later, each time God is about to destroy the people because of their complaining and disloyalty, Moses intervenes to save them. When he learns that he is about to die, he immediately selects Joshua to succeed him so there will be no lapse in the leadership of the Israelites. It is this character profile, says Rabbi Tanchuma, that "makes Moses worthy of transmitting blessings to others." (*Deuteronomy Rabbah* 11:2, 3; *Mechilta, Beshalach* 6; *Sifre Deuteronomy, Haʾazinu* 306; and *Sifre Numbers, Pinchas* 138; *Tanchuma, Chukat* 63b)

This rabbinic composite of Moses presents an ideal portrait. It is a Moses without faults, a larger than life "perfect" hero. Rabbinic commentators, however, are well aware that Moses had his faults. He was human and flawed like all people.

According to the Torah, he is forbidden to enter the Land of Israel because of his sins at the Waters of Meribath-kadesh in the wilderness of Zin. There, instead of speaking to the rock and bringing forth water as God requests, he loses his temper at the complaining people, insults them by calling them "rebels," and strikes the rock with his staff. As punishment for his rage and his public demonstration of unfaithfulness to God, he is not allowed to enter the Promised Land. (See discussion in *A Torah Commentary for Our Times, Parashat Chukat, "Perek Bet."*)

While Moses is portrayed by rabbinic commentators as a flawed but great hero, Nachmanides believes that the real clue to his unique place in history has nothing to do with his personality. What defines Moses' uniqueness, says Nachmanides, is his relationship to God. Moses, as the last lines of Deuteronomy testify, was "singled out by God" who knew him "face to face."

Nachmanides explains that "when two people

see each other face to face, they become acquainted with each other through that meeting." That, however, was not the kind of acquaintance shared by Moses and God. The Torah says that "God knew Moses face to face"; it does not say that "Moses knew God face to face." In other words, continues Nachmanides, "Moses knew God to the extent that such knowledge is possible." Unlike other prophets or the people of Israel who knew God's power, felt God's hand upon them, sensed God's Presence in the midst of the fire and thunder at Mount Sinai or in the cloud they followed day and night across the desert, Moses was "singled out" for special meetings of intimacy with God. Because of these moments of sharing, the Torah was given to Israel. This constitutes the greatness of Moses. "Never again," concludes Nachmanides, quoting the Torah, "did there arise in Israel a prophet like Moses." (Commentary on Deuteronomy 34:10)

Hirsch

Nachmanides' view is repeated by many interpreters and finds clear expression in the writings of Rabbi Samson Raphael Hirsch. "Moses," explains Hirsch, "stands unique for all time. The direct contact in which God's will is manifest to Moses in raising him out of the rest of humanity for the mission he is to carry out was not attained by any later prophet. . . . Moses alone receives every word of his mission face to face, and no word not received in a similar direct manner can ever shake in the tiniest degree that which is given so directly to Moses." (Commentary on Deuteronomy 34:10–12)

Hirsch's argument is meant not only to etch out the extraordinary quality of Moses but also to "prove" the superiority of his prophetic career over that of all other religious prophets and traditions. Such arguments and claims are common, but they are dangerous because they often lead to unwarranted assumptions about who possesses the authentic truth or word of God. Instead of accepting that God speaks to many prophets and peoples, that all human beings and nations are precious to God, and that there are many equally sacred and wise ways for fulfilling God's will, human beings have often gone to war to establish the preeminence of their faith.

Hirsch's intimation of the exclusivity and superiority of God's relationship to Moses misses a very important point that the Torah text itself corrects. The Torah does not say "never again did there arise a prophet like Moses," but it says "never again did there arise *in Israel* a prophet like Moses." With that special emphasis, the Torah avoids a dangerous arrogance and remains open to God's revelation to other prophets and other peoples.

Psychologist and biblical interpreter Erich Fromm sees Moses as a person "who, in spite of his extraordinary talents and genius, is aware of his inadequacy for the task he is supposed to accomplish." Nonetheless, because of his experience with the suffering of his own people, Moses acquires "the necessary impulse for liberation." As the first of the prophets, writes Fromm, Moses fulfills a fourfold function: (1) He announces that there is a God and that our human goal "is to become fully human; and that means to become like God"; (2) he demonstrates the alternatives that human beings can choose and the consequences of these alternatives; (3) he expresses his dissent and protest when Israel chooses the wrong road but never abandons the people; and (4) he does not "think in terms of individual salvation only but believes that individual salvation is bound up with the salvation of society."

It is this unique role of first prophet that makes Moses so important a figure in history. He sets the standard for future Jewish prophets. It is Moses, Fromm emphasizes, who articulates the common themes of the prophetic tradition, especially "the establishment of a society governed by love, justice, and truth"; it is Moses who insists "that politics must be judged by moral values and that the function of political life is the realization of these values." (*You Shall Be as Gods,* Holt, Rinehart and Winston, New York, 1966, pp. 94–95, 117–118)

Sarna

Nahum M. Sarna perceives other dimensions of Moses' greatness. Noting that "the advent of Moses marks a radically new development in the religion of Israel," Sarna underscores and defines his innovations. They include: "the concept of a national covenant between God and an entire people, the insistence on the exclusive worship of one God, the thoroughgoing ban on representing God in any material or corporeal form, and the emergence as a national institution of the messenger-prophet." Taken together, says Sarna, these innovations constitute nothing less than "a revolutionary religious phenomenon, a sudden and new monotheistic creation the like of which had not hitherto existed. . . ."

Sarna maintains that this revolution is the work of the outstanding creative genius of Moses. He is the powerful personality transforming his people. "Moses must be seen as the towering figure behind the . . . religious developments that took place in Israel . . . his role as the first and greatest leader of Israel, as the spiritual titan, the dominating personality that powerfully informed for all time the collective mind and self-consciousness of the community, is unassailable." (*Exploring Exodus: The Heritage of Biblical Israel*, Schocken Books, New York, 1986, pp. 61–62, 148–157)

Loyalty to Israel
Author Elie Wiesel singles out Moses' loyalty to the people of Israel as a sign of Moses' greatness. While he occasionally became enraged with them, he constantly rose to rescue them. "If others spoke ill of Israel, he was quick to come to its defense, passionately, fiercely. . . . Moses defended them not only against their enemies but, at times, even against God. . . . In spite of his disappointments, in spite of his ordeals and the lack of gratitude he encountered, Moses never lost his faith in his people. Somehow he found both the strength and the courage to

---

remain on Israel's side and proclaim its honor and its right to live." (Messengers of God: Biblical Portraits and Legends, translated by Marion Wiesel, Summit Books, New York, 1976, pp. 199–201)

Peli

A mentsh
Many were the epithets and titles given to Moses in the course of his long career. Now, close to his death, he is referred to as ish ha-Elohim, "man of God." I believe that he was called this not to emphasize his relationship to God but rather to underscore his remaining a "man" even now. Being closer to God than ever before and about to leave this mundane world to embrace eternity, Moses was not concentrating only on himself, pondering his life in preparation to meet his Maker. His attention, even at this moment, was given to blessing the children of Israel. Intoxicated with godliness, he remains, to his very last breath, a man among men, a human being preserving that precious quality represented by the untranslatable Yiddish expression—to be a mentsh. (Pinchas Peli, Torah Today, *p. 243)*

Welding Israel together
I believe there was a Moses, that he played a central role in the life of the tribes that escaped from Egypt, and that his major achievement was not so much getting them out but the far more difficult task of welding a disparate group of tribes, a motley riffraff by the Torah's own account, into a community over the course of a long, punishing wilderness trek. . . . (Rabbi Daniel Jeremy Silver, Images of Moses, *Basic Books, Inc., New York, 1982, p. 16)*

Yeshayahu Leibowitz agrees with Sarna's evaluation of Moses. He goes on to point out, however, that "the greatest deed that Moses accomplished was not the deliverance from Egypt nor transmitting the Torah but that he shatters the tablets that had been engraved by God, when the people worshiped idolatry, and the holy words given on these tablets might have been desecrated."

Leibowitz refers to the moment when Moses, on Mount Sinai, is receiving the tablets with the Ten Commandments. Below, the people, led by Moses' brother Aaron, build and then worship a golden calf. Hearing their shouts and wild enthusiasm for the idol they have molded out of gold, Moses throws the tablets against the jagged rocks of the mountain. He refuses to tolerate idolatry. His demonstration of faith in that crisis, argues Leibowitz, is the true mark of his greatness. For him, not even the tablets on which the Ten Commandments are inscribed are sacred. They are to be broken if the situation demands such radical behavior.

"To break idolatry, not to sanctify values that stem from human drives and interests—that is faith. The main thing in faith in God is not to believe in anything that is not divine, not to sanctify things that stem from the drives and interests and plans and ideals and visions of man, even if, in human terms, they are the most lofty of matters." Moses teaches us that "when things are made into something holy, they are to be smashed."

Applying the lesson to our times, Leibowitz warns against setting up false gods; of worshiping nation, land, leaders or cult, any thing or any object. Idolatry of any kind is forbidden, including the idolatry of stones containing the words of God! "The holiness of God alone—that is the content of faith. If one adds to it the holiness of the nation and the holiness of the land, in one breath and in the same context, the holiness turns into its opposite. And this great thing was shown to us by Moses when he smashed this counterfeit and distorted holiness." (*Weekly Parashah,* pp. 206–208)

Rabbi Abba Hillel Silver singles out this same strength and genius of Moses. "With Moses," he reflects, "religion entered the nonrepresentational world, the inner world of thought, will, quest, and motivated conduct. It was one of the few radical shifts in the religious history of humanity—a new enlightenment that opened up roads to new horizons. Religion became boundless and dynamic, a progressive revolution in humanity's quest for security in God. Moses, in his radical monotheism, and his uncompromising opposition to any form of material embodiment of the idea of God, not only spiritualized the concept of the divine for all time, but negated all forms of worship known to the heathen world of his day."

Moses' contributions, however, go beyond his smashing of the idols of his time and his giving birth to a pure spiritual understanding of God. Silver also points out that it is Moses who transforms the tribes of Israel into the people of Israel. Though centuries elapse before they "would become a *people* in the true sense of the word . . . the events of liberation and escape into a new life had transformed them into a community of shared interests and a single purpose." Moses, Silver insists, gives the people a soul; binds them together; and endows them with a pioneering spirit, task, and goal. Under his leadership, they become a "whole community" fused "to a spiritual and ethical purpose."

And it is to that "whole community" that Moses devotes his life. Despite all the disappointments and rebellions, Moses never abandons his people. He battles for them, constantly arguing their case before God. As Silver points out, he endures unflinchingly . . . "ingratitude, rebellion, vilification, feuds, and rivalries. . . . He felt the gibes and stings to which all leaders come to be subjected. . . . Yet, compact of firmness and compassion, his heart was always full of concern for the people that so often failed him. It was the people that was at all times uppermost in his mind." (*Moses and the Original Torah,* Macmillan, New York, 1961, pp. 16–38)

Aaron Wildavsky also emphasizes Moses' loyalty to his people, but his perspective is different from that of Rabbi Abba Hillel Silver. He maintains that Moses' unique leadership of Israel marks his greatness. "The genius of Moses lies in joining revolution with evolution. He leads the people out of Egypt, introduces them to new values, creates new institutions, yet he does so gently and with patience. He urges them to accept the commandments, but when they fail to do so, or fall into complaining about conditions on the desert, he supports them, even defends them when God is ready to destroy them.

Moses the leader, Wildavsky points out, understands that change does not come easily to society. It requires patience, the willingness to risk new ideas and to fail. He stresses in his leadership "the ongoing necessity of learning from error" and the wisdom of "discovering new coalitions of interests" that can bring about desired ends. In Moses we see a leader using strength when the people require judgment, mercy when they fall into despair, and anger when they need to be punished for their selfishness and lack of patience. He demonstrates an ability to be both critical and constructive, to uplift and inspire with visions of a Promised Land, even to accept his death and the need to transfer leadership to another. Moses, concludes Wildavsky, "is politically productive. . . ." It is as a model of leadership that he achieves his extraordinary place in history. (*Moses as a Political Leader*, pp. 211–212)

The character of Moses continues to fascinate those who search for the secrets defining human greatness. Was it his humility, compassion, moral sensibility, defense of his people, organizing skills, ability to accept criticism, anger, articulation of law, formulation of monotheism, belligerence under attack, vindictive punishment of enemies, political leadership, or some special combination of all these traits?

No one answer or theory seems to satisfy our curiosity. Perhaps that alone is a clue to his greatness. There is a mystery residing in the human soul. It is beyond our understanding. We barely sense it or comprehend its power. We encounter and know its presence in the lives and unique contributions of human beings who, like Moses, are said to have known God "face to face."

QUESTIONS FOR STUDY AND DISCUSSION

1. Rabbi Meir teaches that every Jew should take time from business to study Torah. Moses Maimonides writes that every Jew, rich or poor, healthy or sick, young or old, is obligated to study Torah. Given the variety of meanings associated with Torah in Jewish tradition, why is the study of Torah considered critical to the survival of the Jewish people and its traditions of celebration and ethics?

2. Which view on what constitutes Moses' greatness makes the most sense to you? Why?

3. Rabbi Nachman ben Jacob teaches that "a leader must always show respect for the community." In what ways does Moses fulfill this qualification for leadership? In what ways does he fail?

4. Select four modern leaders, two of whom you respect for their successes and two of whom you judge as failures. How do their strengths and weaknesses compare with those of Moses?

Glossary of Commentaries
and Interpreters

(For further information on those entries followed by an asterisk, see Introduction II in A Torah Commentary for Our Times, Volume One: Genesis.)

Abravanel, Don Isaac.*

Adani, David ben Amram (13th century). (See *Midrash ha-Gadol*.)

Akedat Yitzhak. A commentary to the Torah by Isaac ben Moses Arama. (See Arama, Isaac ben Moses.)

Alshekh, Moshe ben Chaim (1507–1600). Lived and taught in Safed in the Land of Israel. His commentary to the Torah contains his Sabbath sermons.

Arama, Isaac ben Moses (1420–1494). Author of the Torah commentary *Akedat Yitzhak*. Spanish rabbi. Known for his sermons and allegorical interpretations of Torah. Defended Judaism in many public disputes with Christians and settled in Italy after the expulsion of Jews from Spain in 1492.

Ashkenazi, Eliezer ben Elijah (1513–1586). Lived in Egypt, Cyprus, Venice, Prague, and Posen. Died in Cracow. Emphasized the gift of reason and in his commentary, *Ma'aseh ha-Shem*, urged students to approach the Torah with care and independence. Worked as a rabbi, Torah interpreter, and physician. (See *Ma'aseh ha-Shem*.)

Ashkenazi, Shimon (12th century). (See *Yalkut Shimoni*.)

Ashkenazi of Yanof, Jacob ben Isaac (13th century). Author of *Tze'enah u-Re'enah*. (See *Tze'enah u-Re'enah*.)

Astruc, Anselm Solomon. (See *Midrashei Torah*.)

Attar, Chaim ibn (1696–1743). Born in Morocco and settled in Jerusalem, where he opened a school. His Torah commentary, *Or ha-Chaim*, combines talmudic and mystical interpretations. (See *Or ha-Chaim*.)

Avot or *Pirke Avot*, "Sayings of the Fathers." A book of the *Mishnah*, comprising a collection of statements by famous rabbis.

Avot de-Rabbi Natan (2nd century). Compiled by Rabbi Nathan, sometimes called "Nathan the Babylonian." Based on *Pirke Avot*.

Ba'al Ha-Turim, Ya'akov (1275–1340). Born in Germany. Fled persecutions there in 1303 and settled in Spain. Author of the very important collection of Jewish law *Arba'ah Turim*, "Four Rows," the basis for the later *Shulchan Aruch*, "Set Table," by Joseph Karo. His Torah commentary known as *Ba'al ha-Turim* often includes interpretations based on the mathematical meanings of Hebrew words.

Bachya ben Asher (14th century). Lived in Saragossa and Aragon. Known for his Torah commentary.

Bachya ben Joseph ibn Pakuda (11th century). Lived in Spain as poet and author of the classic study of Jewish ethics *Hovot ha-Levavot*, "Duties of the Heart." (See *Hovot ha-Levavot*.)

Bamberger, Bernard J.*

Berlin, Naphtali Zvi Judah (1817–1893). Head of the famous yeshivah at Volozhin. Supporter of early

Zionism. His Torah commentary, *Ha-Emek Davar,* is a record of his lectures on the weekly portions. (See *Ha-Emek Davar.*)

Bin Gorion, Micha Joseph (Berdyczewski) (1865–1921). Though a Russian citizen, spent most of his years in Germany. A Hebrew writer, his collection of Jewish folktales, *Mimekor Yisrael,* is considered a classic. (See *Mimekor Yisrael.*)

Biur. *

Buber, Martin Mordecai (1878–1965). Born in Vienna. Became renowned as a twentieth-century philosopher. With Franz Rosenzweig, translated the Bible into German. His *Moses* is a commentary on Exodus.

Caspi, Joseph ben Abba Mari (1280–1340). A philosopher and commentator who lived in France. His commentary seeks to blend reason with religious faith.

Cassuto, Umberto. An Italian historian and biblical scholar. Accepted chair of Bible Studies at Hebrew University, Jerusalem, in 1939, when Italian racial laws made continuation of his work impossible. Wrote famous commentaries on Genesis and Exodus.

Da'at Zekenim mi-Ba'alei ha-Tosafot. A thirteenth-century collection of Torah commentaries by students of Rashi who sought to resolve contradictions found within the talmudic discussions of the rabbis.

De Leon, Moses. (See *Zohar.*) *

Deuteronomy Rabbah. One of the early collections of *midrashim.* *

Dubno, Solomon. (See *Biur.*) *

Ecclesiastes Rabbah. One of the early collections of *midrashim.* *

Edels, Shemuel Eliezer ben Yehudah Halevi (1555–1631). One of the best-known and respected interpreters of Talmud. Born in Cracow. Also known as the *Maharsha.*

Epstein, Baruch (1860–1942). Murdered by the Nazis in the Pinsk ghetto. (See *Torah Temimah.*)

Exodus Rabbah. One of the early collections of *midrashim.* *

Genesis Rabbah. One of the early collections of *midrashim.* *

Gittin. A tractate of Talmud that discusses the laws of divorce.

Guide for the Perplexed. A philosophical discussion of the meanings of Jewish belief written by Moses Maimonides. (See Maimonides, Moses.)

Ha-Cohen, Meir Simcha (1845–1926). (See *Meshekh Hochmah.*)

Ha-Emek Davar. A Torah commentary written by Naphtali Zvi Judah Berlin. (See Berlin, Naphtali Zvi Judah.)

Ha-Ketav ve-ha-Kabbalah. A Torah commentary written by Jacob Zvi Meklenburg. *

Halevi, Aharon (1230–1300). Born in Gerona, Spain. Served as rabbi and judge in Barcelona, Saragossa, and Toledo. Lecturer in Montpellier, Provençe, France, where he died. While *Sefer ha-Hinuch* is said to have been written by him, many doubt the claim. (See *Sefer ha-Hinuch.*)

Halevi, Isaac ben Yehudah (13th century). (See *Paneah Raza.*)

Halevi, Yehudah (1080–1142?). Born in Spain. Poet, philosopher, and physician. His book *The Kuzari* contains his philosophy of Judaism. It is a dialogue between the king of the Kazars and a rabbi who convinces the king of the superiority of Judaism.

Hallo, William W. *

Ha-Midrash ve-ha-Ma'aseh. A commentary to Genesis and Exodus by Yehezkel ben Hillel Aryeh Leib Lipschuetz. (See Lipschuetz, Yehezkel ben Hillel Aryeh Leib.)

Heinemann, Yitzhak (1876–1957). Born in Germany. Israeli scholar and philosopher. His *Ta'amei ha-Mitzvot,* "Reasons for the Commandments," is a study of the meaning of the commandments of Jewish tradition.

Hertz, Joseph Herman. *

Hirsch, Samson Raphael. *

Hirschensohn, Chaim (1857–1935). Born in Safed. Lived most of his life in Jerusalem. Supported the work of Eliezer ben Yehuda's revival of Hebrew. (See *Nimmukei Rashi.*)

Hizkuni. A Torah commentary by Hizkiyahu (Hezekiah) ben Manoah (13th century) of France.

Hoffman, David Zvi (1843–1921). A leading German rabbi. His commentary on Leviticus and Deuteronomy is based on lectures given in the 1870s, seeking to refute biblical critics who argued that the Christian New Testament was superior to the Hebrew Bible.

Hovot ha-Levavot, "Duties of the Heart." A classic study of Jewish ethics by Bachya ben Joseph ibn Pakuda. Concerned with the emphasis on ritual among the Jews of his times, Bachya argues that a Jew's highest responsibility is to carry out the ethical commandments of Torah. (See Bachya ben Joseph ibn Pakuda.)

Hullin. A tractate of Talmud that discusses laws dealing with killing animals for food.

Ibn Ezra, Abraham.*

Jacob, Benno.*

Kasher, Menachem. (See *Torah Shelemah.*)

Kelei Yakar. A Torah commentary written by Solomon Ephraim ben Chaim Lunchitz (1550–1619) of Lvov (Lemberg), Poland.

Kiddushin. A tractate of Talmud that discusses laws of marriage.

Kimchi, David (RaDaK).*

Leibowitz, Nehama.*

Lekach Tov. A collection of *midrashim* on the Torah and the Five Scrolls (Song of Songs, Ruth, Lamentations, Ecclesiastes, and Esther) by Tobias ben Eliezer (11th century C.E.).

Lipschuetz, Yehezkel ben Hillel Aryeh Lieb (1862–1932). Lithuanian interpreter of Torah and author of *Ha-Midrash ve-ha-Ma'aseh.* (See *Ha-Midrash ve-ha-Ma'aseh.*)

Luzzato, Moshe Chaim (1707–1746). Known also as *Ramhal.* Italian dramatist and mystic whose commentaries were popular among chasidic Jews. His textbook on how to become a righteous person, *Mesillat Yesharim,* became one of the most popular books on the subject of Jewish ethics. (See *Mesillat Yesharim.*)

Luzzato, Samuel David.*

Ma'aseh ha-Shem. A commentary by Eliezer ben Elijah Ashkenazi, published in 1583. (See Ashkenazi, Eliezer ben Elijah.)

Maimonides, Moses, Rabbi Moses ben Maimon (1135–1204). Known by the initials RaMBaM. Born in Cordova, Spain. Physician and philosopher. Wrote the *Mishneh Torah,* a code of Jewish law; *Guide for the Perplexed,* a philosophy of Judaism; *Sefer ha-Mitzvot,* an outline of the 613 commandments of Torah; and many other interpretations of Jewish tradition. Famous as a physician. Served the leaders in the court of Egypt.

MaLBIM, Meir Lev ben Yechiel Michael.*

Mechilta.

Megillah. A tractate of Talmud that discusses the biblical Book of Esther.

Meklenburg, Jacob Zvi. (See *Ha-Ketav ve-ha-Kabbalah.*) *

Mendelssohn, Moses.*

Meshekh Hochmah. A Torah commentary published in 1927. Written by Meir Simcha Ha-Cohen, rabbi of Dvinsk. Combines insights from the Talmud with a discussion of the philosophy of Judaism. (See Ha-Cohen, Meir Simcha.)

Mesillat Yesharim, "Pathway of the Righteous." A discussion of how one should pursue an ethical life. Written by Moshe Chaim Luzzatto. (See above.)

Messengers of God. A study of several important biblical personalities by Elie Wiesel. (See Wiesel, Elie; also Bibliography in this book.)

Midrash Agadah. A collection of rabbinic interpretations. (See discussion of *midrashim.*)*

Midrash ha-Gadol. A collection of rabbinic interpretations dating to the first and second centuries by David ben Amram Adani, a scholar living in Yemen. (See Adani, David ben Amram.)

Midrash Sechel Tov. Compiled by Menachem ben Solomon in 1139. Combines selections of *midrash* and *halachah* on every Torah portion.

Midrash Tanchuma. Known also as *Tanchuma Midrash Yelamedenu.* A collection said to have been collected by Rabbi Tanchuma (427–465 C.E.). Many of the *midrashim* begin with the words *Yelamedenu rabbenu,* "Let our teacher instruct us. . . ."*

Midrashei Torah. A Torah commentary by Anselm Solomon Astruc, who was murdered in an attack on the Jewish community of Barcelona in 1391.

Mimekor Yisrael. A collection of folktales from Jewish tradition by Micha Joseph Bin Gorion (Berdyczewski). (See Bin Gorion.)

Mishnah.

Mizrachi, Eliyahu (1440–1525). A Chief Rabbi of Turkey during the expulsion of Jews from Spain. Helped many immigrants. Wrote a commentary to Rashi's Torah interpretation.

Morgenstern, Julian.*

Nachmanides.* (See RaMBaN.)

Nedarim. A tractate of Talmud that discusses vows or promises.

Nimmukei Rashi. A commentary on Rashi's Torah interpretation by Chaim Hirschensohn. (See Hirschensohn, Chaim.)

Numbers Rabbah. An early collection of *midrashim.**

Or ha-Chaim. A Torah commentary by Chaim ibn Attar. Combines talmudic observations with mystical interpretations. (See Attar, Chaim ibn.)

Paneah Raza. A Torah commentary by Isaac ben Yehudah Halevi, who lived in Sens. (See Halevi, Isaac ben Yehudah.)

Peli, Pinchas Hacohen (20th century). Jerusalem-born scholar, poet, and rabbi. His "Torah Today" column in the *Jerusalem Post* seeks to present a contemporary view of the meaning of Torah.

*Pesikta de-Rav Kahana.** A collection of *midrashim* or early rabbinic sermons based on Torah portions for holidays of the Jewish year. *Pesikta Rabbati* is similar in both content and organization.

*Pesikta Rabbati.** (See *Pesikta de-Rav Kahana.*)

*Pirke de-Rabbi Eliezer.** A collection of *midrashim* said to have been written by the first-century C.E. teacher Rabbi Eliezer ben Hyrkanos. Contents include mystic interpretations of creation, early human life, the giving of the Torah at Mount Sinai, comments about the Book of Esther, and the Israelite experience in the Sinai.

Plaut, W. Gunther.*

RaDaK, Rabbi David Kimchi.*

RaMBaM, Rabbi Moses ben Maimon. (See Maimonides.)

RaMBaN, Rabbi Moses ben Nachman.* (See Nachmanides.)

RaSHBaM, Rabbi Shemuel (Samuel) ben Meir.*

RaSHI, Rabbi Shelomoh (Solomon) Itzhaki.*

Reggio, Yitzhak Shemuel (1784–1855). Known also as YaSHaR. Lived in Italy. Translated the Bible into Italian. Created a Hebrew commentary that sought to harmonize science and religion.

Rosenzweig, Franz (1886–1929). German philosopher. Worked with Martin Buber in translating the Bible into German. Best known for book *The Star of Redemption,* which seeks to explore the meanings of Jewish tradition.

Sa'adia ben Joseph Ha-Gaon.* (See Introductions I and II of *A Torah Commentary for Our Times, Volume One: Genesis.*)

Sanhedrin. A tractate of Talmud that discusses laws regulating the courts.

Sarna, Nahum M.*

Sefer ha-Hinuch. Presents the 613 *mitzvot,* "commandments," found within the Torah. Divided according to weekly Torah portions. Said by some to have been written by Aharon Halevi of Barcelona. (See Halevi, Aharon.)

Sforno, Obadiah.*

Shabbat. A tractate of Talmud that discusses the laws of the Sabbath.

*Sifra.** A *midrash* on Leviticus. Believed by scholars to have been written during the fourth century C.E.

*Sifre.** A *midrash* on Numbers and Deuteronomy. Believed to have been composed during the fifth century C.E.

Simeon (Shimon) ben Yochai.* (See *Zohar.*) *

Solomon, Menachem ben. (See *Midrash Sechel Tov.*)

Sotah. A tractate of Talmud that discusses laws concerning a woman suspected of adultery.

Speiser, Ephraim Avigdor.*

Steinsaltz, Adin (20th century). An Israeli Talmud scholar. His book *Biblical Images* contains studies of various biblical characters.

Ta'amei ha-Mitzvot. (See Heinemann, Yitzhak.)

Ta'anit. A tractate of Talmud that deals with the laws concerning fast days.

*Talmud.** Combines the *Mishnah* and *Gemara.* Appears in two versions: the more extensive *Talmud Bavli,* "Babylonian Talmud," a collection of discussions by the rabbis of Babylonia from the second to the fifth centuries C.E., and *Talmud Yerushalmi,* "Jerusalem Talmud," a smaller collection of discussions from the second to the fourth centuries C.E.

Tanna Debe Eliyahu. A *midrash* and book of Jewish philosophy and commentary believed by scholars to have been composed during the third to tenth centuries. Author unknown.

*Targum Onkelos.**

*Targum Yerushalmi.**

Toledot Yitzhak.

Torah Shelemah. A study of each Torah portion, which includes a collection of early rabbinic interpretations along with a commentary by Rabbi Menachem Kasher of Jerusalem, Israel.

Torah Temimah. A Torah commentary by Baruch Epstein. Includes a collection of teachings from the Talmud on each Torah portion. (See Epstein, Baruch.)

Tosafot. "Supplementary Discussions" of the Talmud. Collected during the twelfth and thirteenth centuries in France and Germany and added to nearly every printing of the Talmud since.

Tzedeh Laderech. An interpretation of Rashi's Torah commentary by Issachar Ber ben Israel-Lazar Parnas Eilenberg (1550–1623), who lived in Italy.

Tze'enah u-Re'enah. A well-known Yiddish paraphrase and interpretation of the Torah. First published in 1618. Written for women by Jacob ben Isaac Ashkenazi of Yanof. Divided by weekly Torah portions. One of the first texts developed to educate women. (See Ashkenazi of Yanof, Jacob ben Isaac.)

Wessely, Naftali Herz. (See *Biur*.)*

Wiesel, Elie (1928–   ). Nobel Prize-winning novelist. Author of *Messengers of God,* among other books. (See *Messengers of God*.)

Yalkut Shimoni. A collection of *midrashim*. Believed to be the work of Shimon Ashkenazi. (See Ashkenazi, Shimon.)

Yevamot. A tractate of Talmud that deals with laws concerning sisters-in-law.

Yoma. A tractate of Talmud that deals with laws concerning Yom Kippur.

Zohar.*

Bibliography

Abbott, Walter M.; Gilbert, Arthur; Hunt, Rolfe Lanier; and Swain, J. Carter. *The Bible Reader: An Interfaith Interpretation*. New York: Bruce Publishing Co., 1969.

Adar, Zvi. *Humanistic Values in the Bible*. New York: Reconstructionist Press, 1967.

Adler, Morris, *The Voice Still Speaks*. New York: Bloch Publishing Co., 1969.

Aharoni, Yohanan, and Avi-Yonah, Michael. *The Macmillan Bible Atlas*. New York: Macmillan, 1976.

Alshekh, Moshe ben Chaim. *Torat Moshe*, Vols. I and II, Eliyahu Munk, trans. Jerusalem: Rubin Mass Ltd. Publishers, 1988.

Alter, Robert. *The Art of Biblical Narrative*. New York: Basic Books, 1981.

Asimov, Isaac. *Animals of the Bible*. Garden City, New York: Doubleday, 1978.

Avi-Yonah, Michael, and Malamat, Abraham, eds. *Views of the Biblical World*. Chicago and New York: Jordan Publications, Inc., 1959.

Bachya ben Asher. *Kad ha-Kemach*. Charles B. Chavel, trans. New York: Shilo Publishing House, Inc., 1980.

Baron, Joseph L., ed. *A Treasury of Jewish Quotations*. New York: Crown Publishers, Inc., 1956.

Ben-Gurion, David. *Israel, a Personal History*. New York: Funk and Wagnalls, Inc., and Sabra Books, 1971.

Blumenthal, David R. *God at the Center*. San Francisco: Harper and Row Publishers, Inc., 1987.

Borowitz, Eugene B. *Liberal Judaism*. New York: UAHC Press, 1984.

———. *Renewing the Covenant*. Philadelphia: Jewish Publication Society, 1991.

Braude, William G., and Kapstein, Israel J., trans. Author unknown. *Tanna Debe Eliyahu*. Philadelphia: Jewish Publication Society, 1981.

Buber, Martin. *Moses: The Revelation and the Covenant*. New York: Harper and Row Publishers, Inc., 1958.

Bulka, Reuven P. *Torah Therapy: Reflections on the Weekly Sedra and Special Occasions*. New York: Ktav, 1983.

Cassuto, Umberto. *A Commentary on the Book of Exodus*. Jerusalem: Magnes Press, 1951.

Chavel, Charles B., trans. *Ramban (Nachmanides) Commentary on the Torah*. New York: Shilo Publishing House, Inc., 1974.

Chiel, Arthur. *Guide to Sidrot and Haftarot*. New York: Ktav, 1971.

Chill, Abraham. *The Minhagim: The Customs and Ceremonies of Judaism, Their Origins and Rationale*. New York: Sepher-Hermon Press, 1979.

Cohen, Philip. *Rambam on the Torah*. Jerusalem: Rubin Mass Ltd. Publishers, 1985.

Culi, Ya'akov. *The Torah Anthology, Yalkut Me'am Lo'ez*. Aryeh Kaplan, trans. New York and Jerusalem: Maznaim Publishing Corp., 1977.

Danby, Herbert, trans. *The Mishnah*. London: Oxford University Press, 1933.

Deen, Edith. *All of the Women of the Bible*. New York: Harper and Brothers, 1965.

Doria, Charles, and Lenowitz, Harris, trans. and eds. *Origins, Creation Texts from the Ancient Mediterranean*. New York: Anchor Press, 1976.

Dresner, Samuel H., and Siegel, Seymour. *The Jewish Dietary Laws*. New York: Burning Bush Press, 1959.

Efron, Benjamin. *The Message of the Torah*. New York: Ktav, 1963.

Epstein, Baruch Halevi. *The Essential Torah Teminah*. Shraga Silverstein, trans. Jerusalem: Feldheim Publishers, 1989.

Epstein, I., trans. and ed. *The Babylonian Talmud*. London: Soncino Press, 1952.

Fields, Harvey J. *Bechol Levavcha: With All Your Heart*. New York: UAHC Press, 1976.

Freedman, H., and Simon, Maurice, trans. *Midrash Rabbah: Genesis,* Vols. I and II. London: Soncino Press, 1961.

Friedman, Alexander Zusia. *Wellsprings of Torah*. Compiled and edited by Nison Alpert. Gertrude Hirschler, trans. New York: Judaica Press, 1986.

Friedman, Richard Elliott. *Who Wrote the Bible?* New York: Summit Books, 1987.

Fromm, Erich. *You Shall Be as Gods*. New York: Holt, Rinehart and Winston, 1966.

Frye, Northrop. *The Great Code: The Bible and Literature*. New York: Harcourt Brace Jovanovich Publishers, 1981.

Gaster, Theodor H. *Festivals of the Jewish Year*. New York: William Morrow and Co., Inc., 1953.

Gilbert, Martin. *Jewish History Atlas*. New York: Macmillan, 1976.

Ginzberg, Louis. *Legends of the Jews*. Philadelphia: Jewish Publication Society, 1968.

Gittelsohn, Roland B. *Man's Best Hope*. New York: Random House, 1961.

Glatzer, Nahum N., ed. *Hammer on the Rock: A Midrash Reader*. New York: Schocken Books, 1962.

———. *On the Bible: 18 Studies*. New York: Schocken Books, 1968.

Goldman, Solomon. *In the Beginning*. Philadelphia: Jewish Publication Society of America, 1949.

Gordis, Robert. *A Faith for Moderns*. New York: Bloch Publishing Co., 1960.

Graves, Robert, and Patai, Raphael. *Hebrew Myths: The Book of Genesis*. New York: Greenwich House, 1983.

Greenberg, Moshe. *Understanding Exodus*. New York: Behrman House, 1969.

Hartman, David. *A Living Covenant*. New York: The Free Press, 1985.

Herford, R. Travers. *Pirke Aboth, The Ethics of the Talmud: Sayings of the Fathers*. New York: Schocken Books, 1971.

Hertz, J.H., ed. *The Pentateuch and Haftorahs*. London: Soncino Press, 1966.

Heschel, Abraham J. *The Prophets*. Philadelphia: Jewish Publication Society, 1962.

———. *God in Search of Man: A Philosophy of Judaism*. New York: Farrar, Straus and Cudahy, 1955.

Hirsch, Samson Raphael, trans. *The Pentateuch*. London, England: L. Honig and Sons Ltd., 1959.

———. *Horeb: A Philosophy of Jewish Laws and Observances*. I. Grunfeld, trans. 4th ed. New York: Soncino Press, 1981.

The Interpreter's Bible. 12 vols. Nashville: Abingdon, 1951–1957.

Jacobson, B.S. *Meditations on the Torah*. Tel Aviv: Sinai Publishing, 1956.

Kahana, S.Z. *Heaven on Your Head*. Morris Silverman, ed. Hartford: Hartmore House, 1964.

Kaplan, Mordecai M. *Questions Jews Ask: Reconstructionist Answers*. New York: Reconstructionist Press, 1956.

———. *The Meaning of God in Modern Jewish Religion*. New York: Reconstructionist Press, 1962.

Katz, Mordechai. *Lilmod Ul'lamade: From the Teachings of Our Sages*. New York: Jewish Education Program Publications, 1978.

Korn, Lester. *The Success Profile*. New York: Fireside, 1988.

Kushner, Harold S. *When Bad Things Happen to Good People*. New York: Schocken Books, 1981.

Lamm, Maurice. *The Jewish Way in Death and Mourning*. New York: Jonathan David Publishers, 1975.

Leibowitz, Nehama. *Studies in Bereshit*. Jerusalem: World Zionist Organization, 1980.

———. *Studies in Shemot*. Jerusalem: World Zionist Organization, 1980.

———. *Studies in Vayikra*. Jerusalem: World Zionist Organization, 1980.

———. *Studies in Bemidbar*. Jerusalem: World Zionist Organization, 1980.

———. *Studies in Devarim*. Jerusalem: World Zionist Organization, 1980.

Leibowitz, Yeshayahu. *Weekly Parashah*. Shmuel Himelstein, trans. Brooklyn, New York: Chemed Books, 1990.

Levin, Meyer. *Beginnings in Jewish Philosophy*. New York: Behrman House, 1971.

Levine, Baruch A., ed. *JPS Torah Commentary: Leviticus*. Philadelphia: Jewish Publication Society, 1989.

Levine, Moshe. *The Tabernacle: Its Structure and Utensils*. London: Soncino Press, 1969.

Maimonides, Moses. *The Book of Knowledge: Mishneh Torah*. Moses Hyamson, trans. Jerusalem and New York: Feldheim Publishers, 1974.

Matek, Ord. *The Bible through Stamps*. New York: Hebrew Publishing Company, 1967.

Milgrom, Jacob, ed. *JPS Torah Commentary: Numbers*. Philadelphia: Jewish Publication Society, 1990.

Miller, Madeline S., and Lane, J. *Harper's Encyclopedia of Bible Life*. New York: Harper and Row Publishers, Inc., 1978.

Morgenstern, Julian. *The Book of Genesis*. New York: Schocken Books, 1965.

Munk, Eli. *The Call of the Torah*, Vols. I and II. Jerusalem and New York: Feldheim Publishers, 1980.

Neusner, Jacob. *Meet Our Sages*. New York: Behrman House, 1980.

———. *Tzedakah*. Chappaqua, New York: Rossel, 1982.

Orlinsky, Harry M., ed. *The Torah: The Five Books of Moses*. A New Translation. Philadelphia: Jewish Publication Society, 1962.

———. *Understanding the Bible through History and Archaeology*. New York: Ktav, 1972.

Peli, Pinchas H. *Torah Today*. Washington, D.C.: B'nai B'rith Books, 1987.

———. *Shabbat Shalom*. Washington, D.C.: B'nai B'rith Books, 1988.

Peters, Thomas J., and Waterman, Jr., Robert H. *In Search of Excellence*. New York: Harper and Row Publishers, Inc., 1982.

Pfeiffer, Robert H. *Introduction to the Old Testament*. New York: Harper and Brothers, 1941.

Phillips, Anthony. Exodus Commentary. *The Cambridge Bible Commentary: New English Bible*. Cambridge, England: Cambridge University Press, 1972.

Plaut, W. Gunther, ed. *The Torah: A Modern Commentary*. Commentaries by W. Gunther Plaut and Bernard J. Bamberger. Essays by William W. Hallo. New York: Union of American Hebrew Congregations, 1981.

———. *The Case for the Chosen People*. New York: Doubleday, 1965.

Pritchard, James B., ed. *Ancient Near Eastern Texts Relating to the Old Testament*. Princeton, New Jersey: Princeton University Press, 1955.

Quick, James C., and Jonathan D. *Organizational Stress and Preventive Management*. New York: McGraw-Hill, 1984.

Rabbinowitz, J., trans. *Midrash Rabbah* (Genesis, Exodus, Leviticus, Numbers, Deuteronomy). London: Soncino Press, 1961.

Rabinowitz, Louis I. *Torah and Flora*. New York: Sanhedrin Press, 1977.

Rad, Gerhard von. *Deuteronomy*. Commentary and translation by Dorothea Barton. Philadelphia: Westminster Press, 1966.

Reed, Allison. *The Story of Creation*. New York: Schocken Books, 1981.

Rosenbaum, M., and Silbermann, A.M., trans. *Pentateuch with Targum Onkelos, Haphtaroth and Rashi's Commentary*. Jerusalem: Silbermann Family Publishers, 1973.

Rosenberg, David, ed. *Congregation: Contemporary Writers Read the Jewish Bible*. New York: Harcourt Brace Jovanovich Publishers, 1987.

Samuel, Maurice. *Certain People of the Book*. New York: Alfred A. Knopf, Inc., 1955.

Sandmel, Samuel. *Alone Atop the Mountain: A Novel about Moses and the Exodus*. New York: Doubleday, 1973.

Sarna, Nahum M. *Understanding Genesis*. New York: Schocken Books, 1966.

Schneerson, Menachem M. *Torah Studies*. London: Lubavitch Foundation, 1986.

———. *Likutei Sichot*. London: Lubavitch Foundation, 1975–1985.

Sheehy, Gail. *Pathfinders*. New York: William Morrow, 1981.

Silbermann, A.M., ed. *Pentateuch with Rashi Commentary*. Jerusalem: Silbermann Family Publishers, 1933.

Silver, Abba Hillel. *Moses and the Original Torah*. New York: Macmillan, 1961.

———. *The World Crisis and Jewish Survival*. New York: Richard R. Smith, Inc., 1931.

Silver, Daniel Jeremy. *Images of Moses*. New York: Basic Books, Inc., 1982.

Silverman, Hillel E. *From Week to Week*. New York: Hartmore House, 1975.

Simon, Solomon, and Morrison, David Bial. *The Rabbis' Bible*. New York: Behrman House, 1966.

Speiser, E.A., trans. *The Anchor Bible: Genesis*. New York: Doubleday, 1964.

Steinberg, Milton. *Basic Judaism*. New York: Harcourt Brace, 1947.

Steinsaltz, Adin. *The Thirteen Petalled Rose*. New York: Basic Books, Inc., 1980.

Van Doren, Mark, and Samuel, Maurice. *In the Beginning . . . Love*. Edith Samuel, ed. New York: John Day Company, 1973.

Weinstein, Jacob J. *The Place of Understanding*. New York: Bloch Publishing Co., 1959.

Wiesel, Elie. *Messengers of God*. New York: Random House, 1976.

Zakon, Miriam Stark, trans. *Tze'enah u-Re'enah: The Classic Anthology of Torah Lore and Midrashic Commentary*. Brooklyn, New York: Mesorah Publications Ltd./Hillel Press, 1983.

Zeligs, Dorothy F. *Psychoanalysis and the Bible*. New York: Bloch Publishing Co., 1974.

Zlotowitz, Meir, trans. *Bereishis*. Art Scroll Tanach Series. New York: Mesorah Publications Ltd., 1977–1981.

A
TORAH
COMMENTARY
FOR OUR
TIMES

VOLUME II : EXODUS AND LEVITICUS

HARVEY J. FIELDS

Illustrations by
GIORA CARMI

UAHC PRESS • New York, New York

For
the members of
WILSHIRE BOULEVARD TEMPLE
Los Angeles, California

Library of Congress Cataloging-in-Publication Data
(Revised for volume 2)
Fields, Harvey J.
A Torah commentary for our times.
Includes bibliographical references.
Contents: v. 1. Genesis—v. 2. Exodus and Leviticus.
1. Bible. O.T. Pentateuch—Commentaries. 2. Bible.
O.T. Pentateuch. I. Karmi, Giyora, ill. II. Title.
BS1225.3.F46 1990   222′.1077   89–28478
ISBN 0–8074–0308–3 (v. 1)
ISBN 0–8074–0334–2 (v. 2)

This book is printed on acid free paper
Copyright © 1991 by Harvey J. Fields
Manufactured in the United States of America
10 9 8

Feldman Library

THE FELDMAN LIBRARY FUND was created in 1974 through a gift from the Milton and Sally Feldman Foundation. The Feldman Library Fund, which provides for the publication by the UAHC of selected outstanding Jewish books and texts, memorializes Sally Feldman, who in her lifetime devoted herself to Jewish youth and Jewish learning. Herself an orphan and brought up in an orphanage, she dedicated her efforts to helping Jewish young people get the educational opportunities she had not enjoyed.

In loving memory of my beloved wife Sally
"She was my life, and she is gone;
She was my riches, and I am a pauper."

"Many daughters have done valiantly,
but thou excellest them all."

Milton E. Feldman

Contents

Acknowledgments

As with Volume I of *A Torah Commentary for Our Times* , Volume II has been enriched through the constant wise advice of teachers, students, and editors. I am particularly grateful to Aron Hirt-Manheimer for his continuing enthusiasm and direction; to Rabbi Howard I. Bogot, Rabbi Shelton Donnell, and Rabbi Steven Z. Leder for carefully reacting to the text. Annette Abramson's meticulous editing and interest in this project are deeply appreciated, as are the understanding and production care of Stuart L. Benick.

I am grateful to the leadership and membership of Wilshire Boulevard Temple who have encouraged my conviction, borrowed from Hillel, that "the more Torah, the more life; the more Torah, the more freedom; the more Torah, the more peace." (*Avot* 2:8) I dedicate this volume to them.

Finally, my wife, Sybil, continues to read and critique my work with devotion; her support and love are a source of inspiration.

Harvey J. Fields

EXPLORING TORAH
Questions and Meanings

Nobel Laureate Isaac Bashevis Singer observes that, whenever he takes the Bible from his bookcase, he cannot put it down. "I always find new apsects, new facts, new tensions, new information in it. I sometimes imagine that, while I sleep or walk, some hidden scribe invades my house and puts new passages, new names, new events into this wonderful book." (David Rosenberg, editor, *Congregation: Contemporary Writers Read the Jewish Bible,* Harcourt Brace Jovanovich Publishers, New York, 1987, pp. 7–8)

Singer's view of the Hebrew Bible grows out of a deep knowledge of its contents and an appreciation of its literary power and beauty. *A Torah Commentary for Our Times,* Volume I: Genesis, introduces the reader to a vast array of ancient legends about creation, early human life on our planet, and the origins of the Jewish people. The stories of Adam and Eve; Abraham and Sarah; Isaac and Rebekah; Jacob, Leah, and Rachel; and Joseph and his brothers are all more than ordinary narratives. They present distant memories and moral lessons passed on from one generation to the next as tribal pride and history.

For centuries Jews have read the Torah not only like a map, charting the adventures of the Jewish people, but like a guide, revealing the ethical and spiritual purposes for human life. The tales of treachery and jealousy between Cain and Abel, Sarah and Hagar, Jacob and Esau were read, not only because they were "good stories," but also because the readers found themselves inside the confusion, turmoil, and ambitions of their biblical ancestors.

Noah deciding whether to save himself or to protest against the evil of his time, Abraham rising above his pain to welcome visitors into his home, Rebekah deliberately favoring Jacob over Esau, or Joseph declaring his dreams of superiority over his brothers—all these are examples of choices facing each of us. The characters of Genesis, as we have noted in Volume I of *A Torah Commentary for Our Times,* mirror us. The ancient stories are amazingly contemporary. They seem always fresh, novel, and pertinent to our lives.

Mining the treasures of Torah

Little wonder that Jewish interpreters throughout the centuries have felt so challenged by the Torah text. According to the Jerusalem Talmud there are forty-nine different ways to decipher the Torah's meanings. (*Sanhedrin* 4:2) With so many diverse approaches to the text promoted, it should not surprise us to find within Jewish tradition a wide variety of points of view among commentators. In our discussions of Genesis we have seen how Rashi may present a differing view from the early rabbis, or how Nachmanides will sharply criticize Rashi or take issue with Maimonides. We have also noted the way in which mystic commentators will find insights into words or phrases of the Torah text; or how modern biblical critics, using new knowledge taken from the study of ancient languages or from recent archeological findings, will introduce explanations unavailable to earlier interpreters. Mining the treasures of Torah is unending.

Clearly, the Torah and our tradition of commenting upon its stories and characters, conflicts and commandments deal with every aspect of human life. Out of the tales of Genesis we extract wisdom about such diverse topics as settling disagreements; hospitality; defining beauty, love, justice, and leadership; dealing with "power"; reconciliation between enemies; and achieving peace. Genesis is largely about individual human beings and their personal struggles to find purpose and fulfillment in life. It is the drama of their relationships with one another and with God that captures our interest and imagination.

In this volume, *A Torah Commentary for Our Times,* Volume II, we turn to the second and third books of the Torah: Exodus and Leviticus. Here we encounter a very different kind of narrative and literature. Where Genesis is about individuals, Exodus is about the Jewish people. While Genesis unlocks private stories, Exodus moves us onto the huge stage of history, where nations battle for existence and where the Jewish people, beaten and oppressed, seek their liberation from Egypt and their way back to the Promised Land.

In Genesis, the human relationship with God is portrayed as personal and private. Adam, Noah, Abraham, Isaac, Jacob—all meet God alone. In Exodus and in Leviticus, God speaks not only to Moses but constantly to the Jewish people. They stand at Sinai and are given "the Torah." Laws and commandments are formulated for "the people of Israel." They are told to build a sanctuary for worship and are provided, not only with all the architectural details, but also specific directions for offering sacrifices to God.

We will discover inside these pages that Jewish interpreters relish the drama on the larger stage of Israel's history just as they did in exploring the lives of the patriarchs and matriarchs. Moses is portrayed as a young revolutionary defending his people, as a humble shepherd, as a reluctant leader, as a brave spokesman before the powerful Pharaoh, and as a liberator, lawgiver, and short-tempered manager of a complaining and confused people. The first chapters of Exodus are filled with high drama, the "stuff" from which movies are made. For Jewish commentators these first chapters are rich with opportunities for discussing themes of liberation, civil disobedience, stubbornness, leadership, treatment of strangers, and the obligation of *tzedakah,* or "charity."

Problems, challenges
Yet they also present unusual problems. While the first chapters of Exodus contain the exciting tale of Israel's liberation from Egypt and experience at Mount Sinai, where they receive the Ten Commandments, the last sections of Exodus and most of the Book of Leviticus contain long chapters filled with details for building the ancient sanctuary. Instructions are given to the priests on how they are to preside over the variety of sacrifices offered by the Israelites to God. Several chapters describe how those with skin infections are to be treated.

At times these chapters read like an architect's plan, sometimes like an interior decorator's notepad, at times like a clothing designer's sketches, occasionally like the grizzly directions in a slaughter-house, and at other times like the prescriptions of a specialist in infectious diseases.

Seeking to understand the significance of these chapters of Exodus and Leviticus, Jewish commentators throughout the ages have asked: "What lessons can you derive from such remote subjects and seemingly irrelevant material?"

The following example illustrates the point: If a person suddenly notices a rash and swelling or discoloration on the skin, the Torah instructs that person to seek out the advice of a priest and to observe seven days of isolation. If the rash is cured, the person is to offer sacrifices on the altars of the sanctuary.

The questions growing out of this example of what may have been leprosy are important: Is this a description of an outdated medical procedure, or does it contain ideas and values of continuing importance? If we no longer diagnose skin diseases the way the ancient priests once did and do not offer sacrifices in the Temple, then why should we continue to read and study such chapters of

Torah? Why not skip them? Indeed, if we take the Torah text seriously, how should patients with infectious diseases be treated? Should they be isolated? What care should be provided?

What emerges from the various discussions by commentators of such subjects as skin disease, construction of the sanctuary, the details of priestly dress, the collection of donations for the sanctuary, and many others is a serious and fascinating confrontation with major questions about our own human motives and ethical behavior. Attention to the construction details of the sanctuary leads commentators to a discussion of the importance of dealing with the seemingly small details of our lives. The subject of collecting donations for the sanctuary provides an opportunity for asking important questions about the accountability of public officials for public funds.

The ritual of spilling blood at the altar allows the opportunity for dealing with the sacredness of life. Dietary rules advanced within Leviticus become a forum for examining the art of eating as a function of holiness, not just a response to hunger.

Join the adventure

The adventure of Torah study offered by Exodus and Leviticus is often surprising and always challenging. Little wonder that students of Torah have constantly been enriched by exploring the themes encountered in these sacred books of Jewish tradition. In the pages ahead you will join the debate and adventure and, perhaps, discover why Rabbi Meir taught that those who study Torah not only make the world a more caring place but are called lovers of human beings and of God. (*Avot* 6:1)

THE
TORAH
PORTIONS
OF
EXODUS

PARASHAT SHEMOT
Exodus 1:1–6:1

Parashat Shemot begins by mentioning the *shemot*, or "names," of Jacob's sons and telling us that after they died a new pharaoh, who did not know Joseph, comes to power. Fearing the Jewish people, the new ruler orders taskmasters to enslave them and drown their male children in the Nile River. Defying that order, one mother places her son in a basket and casts the basket into the river. Pharaoh's daughter who was bathing nearby rescues the child and adopts him as her own. She names him Moses. Some time after Moses has grown up, he sees an Egyptian beating a Jew. Defending the Jew, Moses strikes the Egyptian and kills him. When Pharaoh hears what has happened, he orders Moses put to death. So Moses flees from Egypt. When he arrives in Midian, he is welcomed by Jethro, a local priest, whose daughter, Zipporah, he later marries. While Moses is shepherding Jethro's flock, God speaks to him out of a burning bush, promising that Aaron, his brother, will help him liberate the Israelites from oppression. Moses then returns to Egypt where he and Aaron go to Pharaoh to demand freedom for their people. Pharaoh refuses and imposes hard labor upon the people, who blame Moses for making their situation worse. When Moses complains to God, he is told, "You shall soon see what I will do to Pharaoh: he shall let them go because of a greater might."

OUR TARGUM

· 1 ·

The second book of the Torah is called *Shemot*, or "names," since it begins with a list of the names of Jacob's sons. It is also known as Exodus because it relates the history of the Jewish people's liberation from Egyptian slavery.

We are told that, after Joseph's death, the Jewish population in Egypt increases, and a new pharaoh, who does not know Joseph, comes to power. Suspecting the loyalty of the Jewish people, the new pharaoh fears that, if Egypt is attacked, the Jews

will side with his enemy. So he orders the Israelites enslaved and puts them to work building the cities of Pithom and Raamses. Yet, the more the Israelites are oppressed, the more they increase in numbers.

Pharaoh speaks to Shiphrah and Puah, the Jewish midwives, and orders them to kill all male Jewish babies, but they refuse. Pharaoh then orders that all Jewish male babies be drowned in the Nile.

Hoping to save her son, one Jewish mother places him in a basket and floats it in the Nile near the place where Pharaoh's daughter is bathing. When Pharaoh's daughter rescues the child, the woman's daughter rushes forward and asks if she might find a mother to nurse him. Pharaoh's daughter agrees. She treats the child like a son

and names him Moses, which means "drew" him out of the water.

· 2 ·

As a young man, Moses sees an Egyptian beating a Jew. When he notices that no one is looking, Moses strikes the Egyptian and kills him. Afterwards, he buries him. The next day he comes upon two Jews fighting. When he tries to stop them, one of them says to him, "Do you mean to kill me as you killed the Egyptian?" Moses realizes that others know what he has done and that he is in danger. When Pharaoh learns that Moses has killed an Egyptian, he orders him put to death.

So Moses flees Egypt. He travels to Midian, which is located in the southern part of the Negev desert. In Midian, Moses is taken in by Jethro, a local priest and shepherd. He marries Jethro's daughter, Zipporah, and they have a son whom Moses names Gershom, meaning "I have been a stranger in a foreign land."

· 3 ·

One day, while caring for Jethro's flock, Moses sees a strange sight: a bush that burns but is not consumed. When Moses approaches the bush, God speaks to him from the flames, telling him to return to Egypt to free the Israelites from bondage. Moses wonders how he will be able to prove to the Israelites that God has sent him.

"When they ask me, 'Who sent you?' what shall I say?" he says to God.

And God tells him, "Say that *Ehyeh-Asher-Ehyeh* [which means 'I will be what I will be'] sent you. The Lord, the God of your people, the God of Abraham, the God of Isaac, and the God of Jacob, has sent me to you."

Because Moses still has his doubts, he asks God, "What if they do not believe me or insist on proof that God has spoken to me?" God then turns Moses' staff into a snake and makes his skin white with leprosy. God tells Moses that, if the Israelites do not believe him after seeing both these signs,

he is to take water from the Nile and pour it on the ground, where it will turn to blood.

Moses still hesitates about taking on the task of freeing the Israelites. He tells God that he is "slow of speech and tongue," meaning that he is no public speaker. God tells him that his brother, Aaron, will be appointed to speak to Pharaoh and to the Israelites.

· 4 ·

Moses returns to Egypt and is met by Aaron. Together, they go to Pharaoh to request that he allow the Israelites to celebrate a festival. Pharaoh refuses and accuses them of troublemaking. He orders the taskmasters to increase the work of the slaves and to beat those who fail to produce. Finding themselves in trouble, the Israelites complain to Moses and Aaron.

Their complaints stir up new doubts in Moses. He turns to God and asks, "Why did You send me? Ever since I came to Pharaoh to speak in Your name, he has dealt worse with this people; and still You have not freed Your people at all."

God promises Moses that the people will be liberated.

THEMES

Parashat Shemot contains three important themes:

1. Pharaoh's war against the Jews.
2. Civil disobedience.
3. Moses' self-doubt and humility.

PEREK ALEF: *Pharaoh's War against the Jews*

The Book of *Shemot,* or Exodus, continues the history of the Jewish people. Jacob and his family follow Joseph to Egypt, settle in Goshen, and increase in numbers. A new pharaoh comes to power. He has forgotten Joseph's role in saving Egypt and decides to enslave the Israelites.

Why? What brings the Egyptian ruler to such a decision? Does he worry that the loss of slave labor will ruin Egypt's economy and his plans for building great cities and monuments to himself? Does he calculate that if he liberates the Israelites

others will demand their freedom? Or is it possible that the Jews themselves bring on their own persecution and enslavement?

Sarna

Biblical scholar Nahum M. Sarna speculates that the new pharaoh feared an invasion of foreigners from the East. Like many Egyptian leaders, he knew of his country's national humiliation and defeat by the invading Hyksos during an earlier period (1700–1680 B.C.E.) and was determined that no such shame would happen during his rule. Sarna explains that the Israelites were living in the Delta region, where an invasion from the East would begin. Pharaoh's "anxiety," he writes, was "quite understandable." He feared that the Jews would join Egypt's enemies. For that reason he decided to enslave the Israelites and to reduce their numbers and power.

Sarna also provides another reason for Pharaoh's decision. He wished to build his capital in the midst of Goshen, or in the Delta region because it was a very fertile land, closer to the critical borders of Syria and Canaan. Enslaving the Jews produced a double benefit. It forced them to give up their lands and provided Pharaoh with an abundance of cheap labor for the construction of his capital cities. (*Exploring Exodus: The Heritage of Biblical Israel*, Schocken Books, New York, 1986, pp. 15–17)

Under the Hyksos

Under the Hyksos domination, Egyptian culture had sunk so low that the period has been described as the "Great Humiliation." But the successful war of liberation against the Hyksos led to an Egyptian revival on such a grand scale that the period of the New Kingdom which followed, especially during the eighteenth and nineteenth dynasties (about 1570–1200 B.C.E.), has been called the Golden Age. . . . (Harry M. Orlinsky, Understanding the Bible through History and Archaeology, *Ktav, New York, 1972, p. 54)*

Ramban (Nachmanides)

Nachmanides also believes that Pharaoh began his campaign against the Israelites for both strategic and economic reasons. Pharaoh, he says, was afraid that the Israelites would join an invading enemy and escape with a considerable portion of Egypt's wealth. Instead of killing off the Israelites, Nachmanides explains, Pharaoh cleverly developed a plan for taxing their property and for put-

ting them to work on his projects. He chose Egyptian officers to command them and then allowed the Egyptians to enslave the Jews for their own projects and homes. In this way all of Egypt profited from Jewish slave labor. (On Exodus 1:10)

Hirsch

Rabbi Samson Raphael Hirsch believes that Pharaoh's war against the Jews had to do with the weakness of his government. He had just come to power and was seeking a way of rallying the people behind his rule. So he encouraged the masses to oppress the Jews, hoping that his popularity would increase because he had allowed his people to engage in violence and to enrich themselves through theft against strangers living in their midst. (On Exodus 1:8–10)

Hirsch's view is not far from an interpretation offered by a group of ancient rabbinic commentators. Based on the Torah's observation that "a new king arose who did not know Joseph," these commentators taught that the people had come to Pharaoh demanding the right to attack the Israelites. At first he refused, telling them that it would be wrong to harm them since Joseph had saved all the people from ruin. But the people did not listen. They threatened to remove Pharaoh from power. Finally, he was persuaded to go along with their plan to enslave the Jews. The Torah calls him "a new king" because he ceased his protest and accepted the "new" view of those who plotted to destroy the Jewish people. (*Exodus Rabbah* 1:8)

The cause for the oppression
The root and beginning of this indescribable maltreatment was the supposed lack of rights of a foreigner, as such. . . . In Egypt, the cleverly calculated lowering of the rights of the Jews on the score of their being aliens (foreigners) came first, the harshness and cruelty followed by itself, as it always does and will, when the basic idea of Right has first been given a wrong conception. (S.R. Hirsch, translator, The Pentateuch, L. Honig and Sons Ltd., London, England, 1959, on Exodus 1:14)

In contrast with those who believe that Pharaoh's persecution and enslavement of the Israelites may be blamed on the Egyptian leader's political, economic, or strategic considerations, others argue that Jewish suffering was the fault of the Jews themselves.

For instance, some interpreters believe that after Joseph died the Israelites of Egypt stopped practicing the ritual of circumcision. They said to one another, "Let's be like all the other Egyptians." Other rabbis say that they began to attend sports events at amphitheaters and to visit circuses for entertainment. Their attraction to such events became more important to them than their own traditions and faith. They also moved into homes in Egyptian neighborhoods rather than remaining together in their own "Jewish communities."

Because Jews chose to abandon their traditions and to assimilate, they were oppressed by Pharaoh. He became suspicious of their motives. So did the Egyptian people, who did not want Israelites invading their neighborhoods or competing with them for business opportunities. These commentators maintain that, had the Jews remained loyal to their people and not tried to act like Egyptians, they might not have become targets for Pharaoh's oppression. (*Exodus Rabbah* 1:8–9, *Yalkut Shimoni, Ha-Emek Davar*, as in Nehama Leibowitz, *Studies in Shemot*, World Zionist Organization, Jerusalem, 1980, pp. 2–3)

Causes of anti-Semitism
Historian Barbara Tuchman identifies three "principles" regarding anti-Jewish sentiment: (1) "It is vain to expect logic—that is to say, a reasoned appreciation of enlightened self-interest"—when it comes to anti-Semitism. (2) Appeasement is futile. "The rule of human behavior here is that yielding to an enemy's demands does not satisfy them but, by exhibiting a position of weakness, augments them. It does not terminate hostility but excites it." (3) "Anti-Semitism is independent of its object. What Jews do or fail to do is not the determinant. The impetus comes out of the needs of the persecutors and a particular political climate." (Newsweek, February 3, 1975)

Leibowitz

Nehama Leibowitz blames the Israelites for not protesting against Pharaoh's decision to enslave them. She says that the Jews were without heros, without those who were brave enough to stand before Pharaoh and say no to his oppression. There was no resistance, no battle for their rights. As a result, Pharaoh easily did away with their freedoms and enslaved them. (*Studies in Shemot* pp. 15–17)

As we can see, a number of theories have been

developed by interpreters to explain the causes for Pharaoh's oppression of the Jewish people. In many ways the ancient story of Israel's enslavement in Egypt is a parallel to the treatment of Jews and other minorities by host nations. Oppression is often the tragic result of suspicions, jealousies, inferiority complexes, together with economic and social rivalries. Only when these are overcome can mutual trust and respect lead to peaceful and productive coexistence.

PEREK BET: *When Is Civil Disobedience Justified?*

The power of Pharaoh in Egypt was absolute. No one dared defy his rule or his whim. He was honored, not only as the king of Egypt, but as a god. His command was the law of the land. Those who disobeyed him were subject to death.

That is what makes the story of the Hebrew midwives, Shiphrah and Puah, so unusual. Pharaoh commands them to kill every male child born to a Jewish woman. It is an easy order to follow. After all a new mother is weak and defenseless at the birth of her child. Yet, according to the Torah, both Shiphrah and Puah refused to carry out Pharaoh's command.

Why? What moved them to say no to Pharaoh, endangering their own lives by disobedience to his rule?

Many commentators believe that the answer is quite clear. The midwives were Jewish. As Jews they had no choice. No Jewish midwife could kill a Jewish baby. Jewish tradition forbids murder.

Rashi   *Ibn Ezra*   *Ramban (Nachmanides)*

This line of reasoning is followed by Rashi, ibn Ezra, and Nachmanides. They base their opinions on the earlier observation of the famous talmudic teachers, Rav and Samuel. Rav taught that Shiphrah was another name for Yocheved, Moses' mother, and that Puah was actually Miriam, the sister of Moses and Aaron. Samuel disagreed, holding that Puah was not Miriam but rather Elisheva, Aaron's wife. (*Sotah* 11b, *Exodus Rabbah* 1:13)

Other rabbinic interpreters praise Shiphrah and Puah as brave Jewish heroines. These interpreters point out that the two midwives revived babies that were close to death because of difficult deliveries, and, when Pharaoh summoned them to his court and asked, "Why are you not obeying my orders?" they refused to answer. Instead, they defiantly offered him simple excuses: "The Hebrew women are vigorous. They have their babies before we arrive to help them."

Rabbi Isaac argues that Puah, who he believes was Miriam, not only defied Pharaoh, but also bravely criticized her own father, Amram. He maintains that Amram became so depressed about Pharaoh's order to kill all Jewish male babies that he stopped having sexual intercourse with his wife for fear that she would become pregnant. Then he divorced her. When other Hebrew slaves saw what he had done, they also decided to divorce their wives.

According to Rabbi Isaac, Puah confronted Amram and told him that he was acting more cruelly than Pharaoh. "The king ordered the death of all Jewish male children, but you are preventing the conception and birth of all children. Furthermore, because you are a leader, others are following you." Hearing her criticism, Amram immediately remarried his wife, and the other Israelite men followed his example. (*Exodus Rabbah* 1:13)

What the midwives did
The rabbis whose comments are included in the Midrash praise the midwives for many acts of kindness during the oppression of Pharaoh: (1) They took food and drink from the rich and brought it to the houses of the poor and hungry. (2) They prayed that each child would be born in good health and not crippled in any way. (3) They prayed that no child or mother would die at childbirth. (4) They made Abraham's hospitality a model for themselves by opening their homes to all who required food and shelter. (Exodus Rabbah 1:15)

Rabbi Akiba agrees with those who argue that Shiphrah and Puah were brave Jewish women. He even goes so far as to state that "God liberated the Jewish people from Egypt because of the heroic and righteous deeds of the women." Akiba justifies his observation by pointing out that, when they saw their husbands suffering as slaves—overworked, starved, and beaten—they did not think selfishly of themselves, but they went out to comfort them in the fields. They took food. They brought them water and bathed them. They even insisted on having sexual intercourse, telling their husbands that they had to preserve the Jewish people. They did not allow their husbands to become physically weak or to lose faith in the future. For all of their disobedience to Pharaoh's orders, Akiba says, these women are credited with the liberation from Egypt. (*Exodus Rabbah* 1:12)

Not all interpreters, however, agree that Shiphrah and Puah were Jewish. Nor is there any proof within the Torah text that the midwives were Yocheved, Miriam, or Elisheva. The meaning of the Hebrew of the Torah is unclear. While *meyaldot ha-Ivriyot* could mean "Hebrew midwives," it could also mean "midwives of the Hebrews" and be understood as Egyptian midwives of the Hebrews.

Both the commentator-philosopher Philo, who lived in Alexandria, Egypt (20 B.C.E.–40 C.E.), and the historian-general Flavius Josephus (37 B.C.E.–105 C.E.) maintain that Shiphrah and Puah were Egyptian. Others agree.

Abravanel   *Luzzatto*

Both Don Isaac Abravanel and Samuel (Shemuel) David Luzzatto, known also as Shadal, argue that the midwives must have been Egyptian. "How," they ask, "would Pharaoh order Jewish women to put to death children of their own people and not expect that they would make such a plan public?" It is only logical, they conclude, to assume that the Egyptian king gave his orders to Egyptians, whom he thought he could trust to carry them out.

> **They were converts**
> *Some interpreters, noting that the Torah says that Shiphrah and Puah "feared God," believe that they were Egyptians converted to Judaism. Out of reverence and loyalty to God, Jews are commanded to die rather than commit idolatry, incest, or murder. Therefore, the Egyptian midwives must have converted to the Jewish faith.* (Imrei Noam, *as in N. Leibowitz*, Studies in Shemot, *p. 34*)

If Shiphrah and Puah were Jewish or converts to Judaism, then their defiance of Pharaoh's order was a heroic act against the oppression of their people. By demanding that they murder every Jewish male newborn, Pharaoh had declared war on the Jewish people. Once Pharaoh began to oppress them, their loyalty was to their people and to God, not to the ruler or to the laws of Egypt. As Jews, they were victims. Their disobedience of Pharaoh's orders was justified by their obedience to the law of God and to the survival of their people.

But, if Shiphrah and Puah were Egyptian, what justification might they offer for their "civil disobedience" to Pharaoh?

Modern biblical scholar Nahum M. Sarna observes that the Torah provides us with an explanation of their motivation. We are told that Shiphrah and Puah refused to follow Pharaoh's order out of "fear of God." They believed in the sanctity of human life. For them each human being was sacred and filled with possibilities for creativity and good. They acted out of a conviction that there is a "Higher Power" than Pharaoh "who makes moral demands on human beings" for the preservation of life. Their belief, Sarna explains, led them to reject the Egyptian ruler's command to murder the newborn babies of the Hebrews. "Here we have history's first recorded case of civil disobedience in defence of a moral cause." (*Exploring Exodus*, pp. 24–26)

> **Questions for civil disobedience**
> *Civil rights leader Bayard Rustin once suggested these questions as a guide for civil disobedience:*

"(1) Have I exhausted the available constitutional methods of bringing about the desired change? (2) Do the people I urge to join me sincerely seek to improve the society or do they wish to excite passions that would destroy society itself? (3) What is likely to be the effect of the resistance on me, on others, and on the community? (4) Are my own motives and objectives clear to myself and to others; is my aim genuine social change or mere self-gratification? (5) Given that I oppose specific laws, am I prepared, out of my deep respect for law itself, to suffer the consequences of my disobedience." (New York Times Magazine, *November 26, 1967*)

Peli

Civil disobedience and liberation

We may understand how Hebrew women would muster the courage to disobey the king's orders and refuse to kill Hebrew children. But consider the significance of their deed if Shiphrah and Puah were valiant Egyptian women who rebuffed the great pharaoh. They did not say, "My country, right or wrong. . . ." The case of the Hebrew midwives is proof that dissenting individuals can resist evil and thus start a whole process of liberation. (Pinchas Peli, Torah Today, B'nai B'rith Books, Washington, D.C., 1987, p. 58)

The midwives bravely said no to Pharaoh's command that they kill every male Jewish baby. They refused to follow their national leader because they considered his order to be immoral. Instead of making excuses that they were "only following orders" or that "good citizens uphold the law even if they believe it is unjust," Shiphrah and Puah refused to carry out Pharaoh's demand. Forced into making a difficult decision, one that risked their safety, they chose the higher principle of saving life over carrying out Pharaoh's command. Their conviction that each human being is created

"in the image of God" led them to disobey Pharaoh's order to murder Jewish babies.

PEREK GIMEL: *Moses: Fear, Courage, Self-Doubt, or Humility?*

When Moses is called by God to return to Egypt to lead the Jewish people to freedom, his first response is a question: "Who am I that I should go to Pharaoh and free the Israelites from Egypt?" When God tells him, "I will be with you," Moses is unsatisfied and asks for proof. After God tells him what to say to the Israelites, Moses still has his doubts. "What if they do not believe me and do not listen to me?" he asks. Even after God shows him signs and gives him a staff with which to perform magical wonders, Moses continues to hesitate. He offers excuses. "I have never been a man of words," he says, hoping that God will choose someone else to lead the Israelites to freedom.

Why didn't Moses happily and quickly accept God's call to leadership? Why does he offer excuses? Is he afraid? Has he no courage? Is it his way of showing humility?

Zugot

What should a person do?

Rabbi Hillel taught: "If I am not for myself, who will be for me? But, if I am only for myself, what am I? And, if not now, when?" (Avot *1:14*)

Rabbi Judah taught: "Which is the right path to choose? One that is honorable in itself and also wins honor from others." (Avot *2:1*)

Rabbi Hillel said: "In a place where people are without courage, act bravely!" (Avot *2:6*)

Interpreters throughout the ages have wondered about Moses' reaction and response to God. For example, the rabbis who wrote the Midrash speculate that it took God an entire week to convince Moses to return to Egypt to work for the liberation of his people. Some of the rabbis explain that he hesitated because he did not want to hurt or anger his older brother, Aaron. Aaron had led the people in Egypt for eighty years. Moses felt that he could not suddenly return and announce that he was replacing him.

Others argue that Moses was truly humble. He feared that he did not possess the political or spiritual skills to liberate his people, especially the talent of public speaking. So he pleaded with God to choose someone else for the task. (*Exodus Rabbah* 3:14,15)

Rabbi Nehori, who lived in Israel during the second century C.E., claimed that Moses weighed the situation and decided that what God was asking him to do was impossible. The rabbi imagines Moses arguing with God: "How do You expect me to take care of this whole community? How shall I shelter them from the heat of the summer sun or the cold of winter? Where shall I find food and drink for them once I have taken them out of Egypt? Who will care for the newborn babies and all the pregnant women?" For Rabbi Nehori, Moses was a realist asking hard questions and concluding that he was being asked to take on an impossible mission. (*Exodus Rabbah* 3:4)

Rashbam, the grandson of Rashi, also believes that Moses hesitated to accept God's call to liberate the Jewish people because he was a realist and saw no chance for success. Seeking to understand Moses' logic, Rashbam explains that Moses must have asked himself: "Is Pharaoh such a fool as to listen to me and send his slaves away to freedom?" Filled with such doubts, Moses, says Rashbam, concluded that his mission to free the Israelites would end in failure. (On Exodus 3:11)

Shadal provides another excuse for Moses' hesitation. He says that by the time God called Moses to return to liberate his people, Moses was an old man. He was weak and felt infirm from many years of shepherding from early in the morning until late at night. Since he had spent most of his time in silence, he could not imagine himself standing before Pharaoh and arguing for the freedom of his people. So, argues Shadal, Moses made excuses to God and asked that someone else be sent to free the Jewish people. (On Exodus 4:10)

Modern writer Elie Wiesel speculates that Moses had another reason for refusing God's request that he return to Egypt. Wiesel writes that "Moses was disappointed in his Jews." When he had defended a Jew being beaten by an Egyptian, no Israelite came forward to help him. Instead, two Jews criticized him the next day for what he had done. Nor had any Israelites offered help to him when Pharaoh put out a warrant for his arrest. "Clearly," Wiesel comments, "Moses had no wish to return to his brothers, no wish to reopen a wound that had still not healed." (*Messengers of God*, Random House, New York, 1976, pp. 188–190)

> **Jewish tradition and humility**
> *No crown carries such royalty as that of humility.* (*Rabbi Eleazar ben Judah*)
>
> *The summit of intelligence is humility.* (*Ibn Gabirol*)
>
> *The test of humility is your attitude to those who are working for you.* (Orhot Tzadikim *12c, ch. 2*)
>
> *Humility for the sake of approval is the worst arrogance.* (*Nachman of Bratzlav*)

In contrast to Wiesel's explanation of Moses' reluctance to return to Egypt, Rabbi Daniel Silver suggests that Moses' response to God was very typical of Middle Eastern behavior at the time. It was a matter of good manners to plead that you were unworthy of taking on major responsibilities. To say "I am not capable" or "I do not possess the right talents" or "let others more able than I do the job" was considered not only correct behavior but also a demonstration of strength of character. Bragging about yourself or singing your own praises was unacceptable. It was a sign of weakness and false pride. So Moses demonstrated his fitness for leadership through his hesitation to accept God's command to free his people. His humility was proof that he was truly the right person for the job.

Prophetic reluctance

When Amos was questioned about being a prophet, he told Amaziah, the priest of Bethel: "I am not a prophet, and I am not the son of a prophet. I am a cattle breeder and a tender of sycamore figs. But the Lord took me away from following the flock. . . ." (Amos 7:14–15)

It is reported that, when Isaiah was chosen by God to become a prophet, he responded by saying: "Woe is me; I am lost! For I am a man of unclean lips and I live among a people of unclean lips. . . ." His lips were then touched with burning coals, and he was sent on his way to speak to the people of Israel. (Isaiah 6:5–6,9)

After Jeremiah was appointed by God to become a prophet he responded: "Ah, Lord God! I don't know how to speak, for I am still a boy." And God answered him: "I will put My words into your mouth." (Jeremiah 1:6,9)

Moses' hesitation to take on the task of leading his people is very similar to the reluctance later expressed by the great prophets Amos, Isaiah, and Jeremiah. They also doubted their abilities and asked God to find other messengers. Like Moses, they feared that they were incapable of doing what God wanted of them. Their hesitation arose out of genuine modesty, a feeling that they were unworthy of the burden of leadership. Judging from their accomplishments, however, their humility was proof of their real strengths and of their loyalty to God.

Moses, too, has serious doubts about his ability to rescue his people. He knows that the challenge is enormous and that the dangers are great. Pharaoh is the most powerful ruler in the world. The Israelites are weakened by years of slavery, beaten into submission. Moses' fears and hesitations are understandable. There is realism and wisdom in his modesty. He knows that the liberation of his people depends upon his ability to inspire their confidence, courage, and hope. He wonders if he will ever be able to convince them that God is calling them to march out of Egypt into freedom.

Great leaders are not blind to the difficulties they face. They realize the difficulties of the challenges before them. At times they feel unworthy and filled with doubts about themselves and those they lead. Sometimes they want to run away and hide rather than face the hard decisions that need to be made.

Perhaps that is how Moses felt when God called him to return to Egypt. He may have hesitated out of fear that he was incapable of doing what God asked or out of a sense that he could do nothing about a hopeless situation. In the end, however, he had the strength and faith to take on the task. He returned to Egypt and worked for liberation of his people.

QUESTIONS FOR STUDY AND DISCUSSION

1. Author Israel Zangwill has commented: "If there were not Jews, they would have to be invented [as a] guaranteed cause for all evils." Did Pharaoh need a scapegoat, or was it out of fear that he oppressed the Israelites? Would you agree that those who assimilate or abandon Jewish tradition may cause anti-Semitism?
2. Shiphrah and Puah refused to carry out Pharaoh's orders to kill Jewish babies. Under what other conditions is civil disobedience necessary and justified?
3. Moses expresses doubts about his ability to lead his people out of Egyptian oppression. How do you interpret his motives? Was his "humility" a demonstration of weakness or strength, of fear or leadership?

PARASHAT VA'ERA
Exodus 6:2–9:35

Parashat Va'era begins with God saying to Moses: "*Va'era* . . . 'And I appeared to Abraham, Isaac, and Jacob.' " We are told of the relationship between God and the Jewish people and of the promise to give the Land of Israel to the people. God tells Moses that the time has come to free the Israelites from Egyptian bondage. Moses is told that he should go before Pharaoh to ask that the Egyptian ruler allow the Israelites to depart. Twice Moses responds by saying that Pharaoh will not listen and apologetically explains that, because of a speech impediment, he is not the right person to represent the Jewish people. God answers by declaring that Moses' brother, Aaron, will accompany him as the spokesman.

The two brothers appear before Pharaoh to request the freedom of their people, but Pharaoh refuses to liberate them. As a consequence, terrible plagues are set upon Egypt. The waters of the Nile are bloodied; then the land is filled with frogs and swarms of insects; then there is the death of Egyptian livestock; and later there is destructive hail. These plagues are sent to punish Pharaoh and to force him to free the Israelites.

OUR TARGUM

· 1 ·

Moses returns to Egypt and speaks to the Israelites. He tells them that God, who was called *El Shaddai,* meaning "God Almighty," by Abraham, Isaac, and Jacob, appeared to him by the name *Yahveh* and instructed him to return to Egypt and say to the Israelites:

"I will free you from the burdens of the Egyptians and deliver you from their bondage. . . . I will take you to be My people, and I will be your God. . . . I will bring you into the land which I swore to give to Abraham, Isaac, and Jacob, and I will give it to you for a possession."

When Moses shares God's promise with the people, they reject it. Their spirits have been crushed by slavery.

God then tells Moses: "Go to Pharaoh and tell him to free the Israelites." Moses refuses, arguing that, if the Israelites would not listen to him, Pharaoh will also reject his request. He also reminds God of his speech impediment. God answers Moses by declaring that his brother, Aaron, would be his spokesman.

· 2 ·

God also warns Moses that Pharaoh will not easily be convinced that he should free the Israelites. "I will harden Pharaoh's heart," God tells Moses. "I will lay My hand upon Egypt and deliver My ranks, My people, the Israelites, from the land of Egypt with heavy punishments. And the Egyptians shall know that I am the Lord. . . ."

· 3 ·

The first time Moses and Aaron approach Pharaoh they follow God's direction, and Aaron magically turns his staff into a serpent. Pharaoh's magicians respond by turning their staffs into serpents, but Aaron's serpent swallows theirs. Pharaoh's heart, however, is hard; he will not listen to their plea for the freedom of the Israelites.

So Aaron and Moses appear before Pharaoh a second time as he is finishing his morning swim in the Nile River. Speaking for God, Moses says to him: "Let My people go. Today I will turn the waters of the Nile into blood. All the fish will die. The stink will fill Egypt, and no one will be able to drink the water." Aaron waves his staff over the river, and everything God has predicted comes to pass. But, when Pharaoh's magicians perform the same act, Pharaoh's heart hardens once again.

Seven days later, God tells Moses to return to Pharaoh and threaten him with a plague of frogs unless he frees the Israelites. When Aaron waves his staff and brings the frogs, the Egyptian magicians also perform the same act. This time, however, Pharaoh tells Moses that, if God will remove the frogs, he will allow the Israelites to depart and worship God. But, when Moses removes the frogs, Pharaoh's heart once again hardens, and he refuses to free the Israelites.

God then instructs Moses to have Aaron strike the earth with his rod. When he does, Egypt is suddenly filled with lice. Afterwards, the Egyptian magicians try to produce lice, but they cannot. They say to Pharaoh, "This is the power of God," but Pharaoh's heart remains hard.

During the next days, Moses pleads with Pharaoh on behalf of God, but each time Pharaoh refuses to listen. God sends swarms of insects; then God kills off Egypt's livestock (horses, asses, camels, cattle, sheep). Afterwards, boils appear on the bodies of all Egyptians; then hail storms are sent. After each terrible event, Pharaoh seems to weaken. He promises to free the people, but then, quite suddenly, his heart hardens, and he refuses.

Speaking for God, Moses warns the Egyptian ruler: "Let My people go to worship Me. For this time I will send all My plagues upon your person, and your courtiers, and your people, in order that you may know that there is none like Me in all the world."

THEMES

Parashat Va'era contains two important themes:

1. Different "names" for God.
2. The "hardening" of Pharaoh's heart.

PEREK ALEF: *Why So Many Names for One God?*

This Torah portion begins with a surprising statement. Using the name *Yahveh,* God speaks to Moses, telling him that Abraham, Isaac, and Jacob all called God by the name *El Shaddai* ("God Almighty"), but they did not know God by the name *Yahveh.* Why does the Torah use two names for *one* God?

While the question is logical, the fact is that the Torah uses many different names for God. For instance, earlier, as Moses speaks with God at the burning bush (Exodus 3), Moses inquires: "When I come to the Israelites and say to them, 'The God of your fathers [Abraham, Isaac, and Jacob] has sent me to you,' and they ask me, 'What is God's name?' what shall I say to them?" God tells him to say *"Ehyeh-Asher-Ehyeh.* Tell them *'Ehyeh* sent me to you.' "

> **Ehyeh: another view**
> *Philosopher Hugo Bergmann writes that "Eh-yeh is an imperfect tense (I will be)," and it teaches us that God is the "yet to be perfected 'I.' "*

Commentators and Jewish philosophers have tried to unravel the meaning of the phrase *Ehyeh-Asher-Ehyeh,* just as they have sought to understand the meaning of *Yahveh* and all the other names for God found in the Torah. Since the Hebrew of *Ehyeh* translates into "I will be," many accept the translation "I will be what I will be" as the name for God. By comparison, the most likely Hebrew root for *Yahveh* is *hayah,* meaning "to be." Both *Yahveh* and *Ehyeh-Asher-Ehyeh* suggest that God is not a fixed thing, or person, or object of any kind known to human beings; God is rather an evolving, mysterious, dynamic power that is always in the process of becoming more than what it was or is.

Jews believe that God can never be fully defined. All we can know are traces of God's wonder. We perceive hints of God in the beauty and order of nature, in the triumphs of justice and freedom in history, in the advance of human knowledge, or in the quest for love and peace by human beings. Nonetheless, Jewish tradition counsels great caution when it comes to speaking or writing about God.

For example, through the centuries, Jews were forbidden to say the word *Yahveh.* Instead, it was pronounced *Adonai,* which means "my Lord." Only once a year, on Yom Kippur, was the name used and then only by the High Priest at the Temple in Jerusalem. (*Yoma* 39b) Later, among some Jews, it became the custom to refer to God as *ha-Shem,* "the Name," and to write the word "God" with a hyphen, "G-d." In this way, referring to God was separated from the ordinary use of language and uplifted to the highest realm of honor.

Throughout the ages, many names for God other than *Yahveh, El Shaddai,* and *Ehyeh-Asher-Ehyeh* emerged within Jewish tradition. Within the Torah the oldest is *El,* which some scholars speculate means "the Most Powerful." Other names for God within the Torah include *El Elyon,* "the Highest God"; *El Olam,* "the Everlasting God"; *El Ro'i,* "God who sees me"; and *Eloha,* or its plural, *Elohim,* which are used over two thousand times in the Hebrew Bible and mean "God" or "gods."

The rabbis of the Talmud also developed a number of names for God. Among them were *ha-Kadosh Baruch Hu,* "the Holy One, praised be He"; *Ribono shel Olam,* "Sovereign of the universe"; *ha-Rachaman,* "the Merciful One"; *ha-Makom,* "the Place"; *Shamayim,* "Heaven"; *Shechinah,* "Presence"; and *Avinu sheba-Shamayim,* "our Father in heaven." During the Middle Ages,

Jewish mystics who believed that no person could understand the dimensions of God's power called God the *Ein Sof,* "Without End."

What is clear is that, throughout Jewish history, various designations for God have emerged. Why? Why so many different names for *one* God?

Some modern commentators believe that the names used within the Torah actually identify various traditions within early biblical religion. For instance, all the stories that use the name *Yahveh,* or *Jehovah,* are grouped together and called the J documents; those using *Elohim* are called the E documents. Biblical scholar Richard Elliot Friedman suggests that the J documents were created by people living in the kingdom of ancient Judah while the E documents originated in the kingdom of Israel.

Friedman also points out that "E has much less than J about the world before Moses. E has no creation story, no Flood story, and relatively less on the patriarchs. But E has more than J on Moses." The emphasis in E on Moses, Friedman argues, has to do with those authors who traced their history to the liberation from Egypt. For them, the Exodus was the most important event in the history of the Jewish people. So they worked to combine the past as reported by the J tradition with that event. As a result, says Friedman, they were the first to combine the two names for God, *Yahveh* and *Elohim,* and to link them in the story of Moses asking God, "What is Your name?" (*Who Wrote the Bible?* Summit Books, New York, 1987, p. 83)

For other biblical interpreters the names for God are more than a means of identifying the origins of different Torah stories.

Sarna

The modern commentator Nahum Sarna explains that names for God in the Torah reveal the "character and nature"—the "makeup of the whole personality"—of God. As for the variety of names for God found in the Torah, Sarna reports that it was a common custom in the ancient Middle East for gods to have many names. Each name provides another valuable insight into how biblical Jews thought about God. (*Exploring Exodus,* pp. 42–45, 50–52)

Sarna's view is close to the one advanced by Rabbi Abba Hillel Silver. Silver says that "it was a common practice among ancient peoples to change the names of their deity or to add an additional one to indicate that the deity had assumed a new or an additional role." Since God was about to liberate the Israelites from Egyptian bondage, a new name, *Yahveh,* was announced to Moses. The new name, Silver speculates, means "accomplisher," or the "God who performs what is promised." God's new name would not only inspire confidence and hope in the hearts of the enslaved Israelites but would be a reminder to all Jews, after their liberation, that God had freed them from oppression. God's name foreshadowed what God was about to do.

The idea that names for God reveal what God does or will do was also held by Rabbi Abba ben Mammel, who lived in Tiberias during the third century. He claimed that God is called *Elohim* when making judgments about people and nations; *Tzevaot,* "Hosts," when making war against evildoers; *El Shaddai,* "God Almighty," when forgiving human beings for harming themselves and others; and *Adonai* when increasing compassion and love in the world. "God's names reveal God's deeds." In other words, just as the names we sometimes give to people identify their most important traits, so also with the names Jewish tradition has given to God. They identify God as a doer of justice, righteousness, compassion, and love. (*Midrash Rabbah* 3:6)

Peli

Modern commentator Pinchas Peli argues that the names for God serve a very valuable function. "Human beings are not capable of grasping the essence of God. All they are able to perceive is God's name, to wit, that side of God's being revealed to them through God's acts." For that reason, Peli says, the rabbis claim there are seventy names for God within the Hebrew Bible. God's powers are so great, awesome, and mysterious that even seventy names are not enough to exhaust the number of ways we encounter God in our lives. Peli, however, concludes with a note of warning: "Even after we call God by all the names—the mystery of God's being is not lifted." ("Torah Today," *Va'era,* in the *Jerusalem Post,* January 18, 1985, p. 16)

Psychologist and philosopher Erich Fromm also believes that the mystery of God is beyond human comprehension, but he offers a very different view of names for God in the Torah. Fromm believes that all names for God are forms of idolatry. God, he writes, "cannot be represented by any kind of image, neither by an image of sound— that is, a name—nor by an image of stone or wood." He suggests that the best translation of the answer God gives to Moses after he has asked "What is Your name?" is "My name is *Nameless.*" In other words, names can be misleading, even dangerous if people assume that they are representations of the whole truth. God cannot be grasped or defined by a name. God is beyond all names, all designations, and definitions. (*You Shall Be as Gods,* Holt, Rinehart and Winston, New York, 1966, pp. 29–32)

As we can see, the issue of giving God names is a controversial one among Jewish commentators. Names help us express our understanding of God, our reverence for God. Yet all are agreed that no "name," however clever or beautiful, lofty or wise, can completely describe God's power or the mystery of God's presence in our lives. Names are merely human language, the tools we use to capture and express concepts, ideas, and meanings. God is beyond our "names," beyond the bounds of our wonder. No human being can depict in words or any other forms of expression the essence of God.

PEREK BET: The *"Hardening" of Pharaoh's Heart*

Our Torah portion presents us with a difficult question. Moses and Aaron come before Pharaoh. They ask that he allow the Israelites to leave Egypt. Pharaoh listens to their request but refuses to let the people go. Then a terrible plague is sent to punish Egypt and to force Pharaoh into changing

his mind. The same cycle is repeated ten times. Each time the Egyptian ruler seems to indicate that he is ready to say yes to the demand for freedom put forth by Aaron and Moses. Then, mysteriously, his "heart hardens," and he says no.

The difficult question is what the Torah means by "hardening of the heart." What happened to Pharaoh each time he was about to say yes and instead said no? Was God overriding the Egyptian ruler or playing with him like a puppet on strings? Or was Pharaoh freely making his own decisions?

Interpreters point out that the Torah mentions the "hardening" of Pharaoh's heart a total of twenty times. The first ten have to do with the first five plauges, and in each case we are told that "Pharaoh hardened his heart." Clearly, it would seem that whatever is happening is being caused by Pharaoh. Yet the next ten references to the "hardened heart" are different. They occur with the last five plagues, and in each case we are told that "God hardened Pharaoh's heart." Here it would seem that God, not Pharaoh, is in control and is bringing about the change in Pharaoh's heart. (Sarna, *Exploring Exodus,* p. 64)

Ten plagues
The ten plagues are (1) blood in the Nile River; (2) frogs; (3) swarms of insects; (4) flies; (5) cattle disease; (6) boils; (7) hail; (8) locusts; (9) darkness; and (10) death of the firstborn.

Hirsch

One reading of our Torah text might be that God "hardened" Pharaoh's heart in order to demonstrate divine power over all creatures. Rabbi Samson Raphael Hirsch points out that the Torah uses three different Hebrew words to describe the "hardening" of Pharaoh's heart. The first is *kashah,* meaning "to be hard altogether, to let everything pass over one without making any impression." The second is *kaved,* meaning "heavy." One can receive impressions, but there can be a big gap between the impression and the moment one lets oneself be guided by this impression. Finally, the

Torah uses the word *chazak*, meaning "firm," consciously opposing any pliancy, any submission.

Hirsch argues that "Pharaoh's coldness, his apathetic insensibility" was used by God so that "all subsequent ages could derive a knowledge and conviction of the Almightiness, the Presence, and the Direction of God in human history." Never again, Hirsch says, would there be a "necessity for miracles." In other words, God pulled the strings and directed the choices for the Egyptian ruler. God made his heart *kashah*, *kaved*, and *chazak* in order to demonstrate where the power and control really is!

Zugot

Centuries ago Rabbi Yochanan was troubled by an explanation similar to the one offered by Rabbi Hirsch. In contrast, he reasoned that if God is pulling all the strings, and Pharaoh has no free choice, then the Egyptian ruler could not be held responsible for his choices. That would mean that none of us is really free and that our choices between acts of love or hatred, caring or selfishness, justice or indifference are an illusion. "Is that what the Torah teaches us when it speaks of God hardening Pharaoh's heart?" Rabbi Yochanan asked his brother-in-law who was his close friend and study companion, Rabbi Simeon ben Lakish.

Resh Lakish, as he was known, responded by explaining that God gave Pharaoh several opportunities to change his mind and allow the Israelites to leave Egypt. The plagues were warnings. God hoped that Pharaoh would repent and free the slaves. "Since God warned him five times and Pharaoh refused to pay any attention and continued to stiffen his heart, God told him, 'I will now add more trouble to what you have made for yourself.' " That is what the Torah means when it says that "God hardened Pharaoh's heart." Pharaoh brought on the condition by his own stubbornness. (*Exodus Rabbah* 13:3)

Making choices
Resh Lakish taught: "If a person seeks to do evil, that person will find a way. If one seeks to do good, to improve oneself, and to better one's society, God will help." (Shabbat 104a)

God does not predetermine whether a person shall be righteous or wicked; that is left to the free choice of each person. (Tanchuma, Pikude, 3)

Every time we disobey the voice of conscience, it becomes fainter and feebler, and the human heart becomes harder to reach and move. Judaism affirms the principle of free will. We are each the master of our own spirit. "One evil deed leads to another." (Pirke Avot 4:2) And, conversely, "One good deed leads to another," and we are that much more liberated from bondage. (Rabbi Hillel E. Silverman, From Week to Week, Hartmore House, New York, 1975, p. 57)

Rambam (Maimonides)

Moses Maimonides agrees with Resh Lakish emphasizing "that it was not God who forced Pharaoh to do evil to Israel"; the decision was his alone. Free will "is a fundamental principle of Judaism," says Maimonides. "No one forces, preordains, or impels a person to act. People do as they wish to do. Each is absolutely free to perform any deed, be it bad or good." Pharaoh made his choices, one after the other; as he made them, it became more difficult for him to reverse them. One bad choice led to the next and then to the next until his range of choices narrowed, and he could no longer turn back.

Modern psychologist Erich Fromm amplifies Maimonides' view about the hardening of Pharaoh's heart. Fromm writes that the Torah's description presents "one of the most fundamental laws of human behavior. Every evil act tends to harden man's heart, that is, to deaden it. Every good act tends to soften it, to make it more alive. The more man's heart hardens, the less freedom he has to change; the more is he determined already by previous action. But there comes a point of no return, when man's heart has become so hardened and so deadened that he has lost the possibility of freedom, when he is forced to go on and on until the unavoidable end which is, in the last analysis, his own physical or spiritual destruction." (*You Shall Be as Gods*, p. 101)

So Pharaoh's first choices to continue persecuting and oppressing the Israelites ultimately led him to "a point of no return." He must have thought that "if I give in to their demands and do not stiffen my heart and rule them harshly, then both the Jews and the Egyptians will conclude that I am weak and will rebel." Trapped by fear of failure and unable to develop creative solutions to his problems, Pharaoh fell victim to his own bad decisions. In a tragic way, he chose the steep path and, once he was plunging down it, could not stop or save himself from crashing at the bottom.

One other view about this story of Pharaoh's hardening heart deserves consideration. A comment in the Midrash explains that "Pharaoh used to boast that he was a god." Certainly he had more power at his disposal than any other human being alive in his time. He ruled great armies equipped with weapons to slaughter and trample anyone who might rise against him. Through his taskmasters, he dictated the life or death of thousands of slaves building his cities, Pithom and Raamses. The author of the Midrash imagined that, because Pharaoh possessed the power of life and death over so many, the Egyptian ruler concluded that he was invincible. Nothing could defeat him or ruin his plans. (*Exodus Rabbah 8:2*)

The plagues against Pharaoh
Pharaoh was destroyed by ten plagues because he claimed to be a god. What did he say? "My Nile is my own, I made it for myself." (Ezekiel 29:3) As a consequence of Pharaoh's claim, God punished him with plagues. (Exodus Rabbah 8:2)

Leibowitz

The purpose of the plagues was educational—to instill acknowledgment of God in those who had refused to recognize God's power. . . .

The purpose of our Torah portion is to "describe the relentless attempt to break Pharaoh's arrogant heart and teach him to "know the Lord." (Nehama Leibowitz, Studies in Shemot, *pp. 170–177)*

Finally, it must be remembered that the entire story of the plagues is about a contest between the will of the Pharaoh and the will of the God whom only the Israelites recognized. . . . Consequently, the plagues, the ignoble defeat, and the ignominious end of the god-king constitute a saga that breathes contempt for Egyptian paganism. (Nahum M. Sarna, Exploring Exodus, *p. 80)*

Yet Pharaoh was defeated. All his armies and weapons were not enough to snuff out the will of freedom God had placed in the hearts of the Israelites. The more Pharaoh brutalized them, the stronger became their determination to be free. Each time he had a chance to stop the plagues and let them go, he hardened his heart. He thought he was battling with weak, beaten slaves. He could not understand that within them God had planted a yearning for liberation against which he was powerless.

Finally, according to those who related this *midrash*, God decided to teach Pharaoh, and all who would hear of him, a lesson. Now God would harden his heart. The Egyptian ruler, who had claimed to be a god and who had brought suffering to thousands, would be destroyed. God would reveal Pharaoh's weakness to all his people and demonstrate that the God of liberation ultimately wins every battle against oppression.

According to this version, the story of God and Pharaoh is not about whether human beings are free or not free to make good or bad choices. Rather, it is about the confrontation between those who claim to be god and God, between those who claim to rule the world and the liberating God of the world. It is the victory of the spiritual God, who wills freedom, justice, and the sacred equality of each human being, over the godlike Pharaoh, who must enslave and crush others to rule them.

The hardening of Pharaoh's heart and the miraculous plagues that are sent to destroy him are all meant to dramatize the power of the God of freedom. Nothing, the Torah claims, neither hard-hearted Pharaoh nor any other ruler or institution, can stop God's will for human liberation. It is always triumphant. God wants us to be free!

QUESTIONS FOR STUDY AND DISCUSSION

1. How might the various names for God in Jewish tradition help us to understand what Jews believe and do not believe about God and the origins of Torah? If you were creating new names for God today, what might some of them be? Make a list and explain each name you suggest.

2. Erich Fromm claims that "every evil act tends to harden man's heart, that is, to deaden it." Would you agree? Do we bring on our own stubbornness or do other people and stressful situations cause us to become insensitive and incapable of making balanced and just decisions? How was Pharaoh's heart "hardened" each time he changed his mind and refused to free the Israelites?

PARASHAT BO
Exodus 10:1–13:16

Parashat Bo takes its name from the first word of God's command to Moses, "Go (*Bo*) to Pharaoh." Moses and Aaron continue to plead with Pharaoh to let the Israelites go free. Because he refuses, the Egyptians are punished with plagues of locusts, darkness, and, finally, the death of their firstborn. Pharaoh tells Moses, "Be gone from me!" God then tells Moses that, after the last plague, Pharaoh will let the Israelites leave. That midnight Moses leads the Israelites out of Egypt and proclaims that each year on the evening of the fourteenth day of the first month a festival lasting seven days will be celebrated in order to recall their liberation from Egypt. *Matzah,* or "unleavened bread," shall be eaten during the seven days, and on the first night of the festival the children will be told how God freed their people from the house of bondage.

OUR TARGUM

·1·

After sending seven plagues upon Egypt (blood in the Nile River, frogs, swarms of insects, flies, cattle disease, hail, and boils), God, once again, sends Moses and his brother, Aaron, to Pharaoh. Standing before the Egyptian ruler, they ask him, "How long will you refuse to humble yourself before God?" They warn him that, if he does not free their people, God will bring a plague of locusts upon Egypt.

Pharaoh's advisors counsel him: "Let the men go to worship the Lord their God! Are you not yet aware that Egypt is lost?" So the ruler invites Moses and Aaron back to his palace. "Whom do you wish to take with you?" he asks them. Moses tells him: "We will all go, young and old: we will go with our sons and daughters, our flocks and herds; for we must observe the Lord's festival." Pharaoh denies the request and expels Moses and Aaron from the palace.

God then brings a plague of locusts upon Egypt. The whole land is covered with them. When Pharaoh sees what has happened, he calls for Moses. "Forgive me," he cries. Moses pleads for him, and God ends the plague, but Pharaoh's heart hardens once again.

This time God punishes Egypt with a plague of darkness. For three days there is blackness in the land except in the locations where the Israelites are living. Again, Pharaoh calls Moses. He offers him a deal. "Go, worship the Lord! Only your flocks and your herds shall be left behind; even your children may go with you." Moses refuses, and Pharaoh's heart stiffens again. "Be gone from me!" he tells Moses.

God informs Moses that one more plague will be sent upon Egypt. God also instructs Moses to tell the Israelites to borrow objects of silver and gold from their Egyptian neighbors. The Egyptians willingly give the Israelites the objects they request.

God sends the tenth plague upon Egypt. Every firstborn son and every firstborn of the cattle dies. Having lost his own son, and seeing the disaster that has come upon his people and land, Pharaoh summons Moses and Aaron. Broken by God's power, he tells them, "Go, worship the Lord . . . and may you bring a blessing upon me also!"

The other Egyptians urge the Israelites to leave in haste. So they take their dough before it has leavened and the gold and silver that they had requested from their Egyptian neighbors. At midnight, on the fourteenth day of the first month of the year, after living in Eygpt for 430 years, Moses leads the people out of Egypt.

· 2 ·

On that evening of the Exodus from Egypt, Moses declares that God has commanded the people to recall their liberation each year with a special commemoration ceremony. Every household is to take a lamb on the tenth day of the month and slaughter it at twilight on the fourteenth day of the month. Its blood is to be painted on the doorposts of each family house, and its meat is to be roasted and eaten with unleavened bread (*matzah*) and bitter herbs during the night so that it is consumed by morning. Anything left by morning is to be burned.

As the meal is eaten, Israelite men are to dress

with a belt around their waists and sandals on their feet. Each is to hold a staff in his hand and to eat the lamb quickly. When the children see this strange ritual and ask "What do you mean by this ceremony?" they are to answer: "It is the passover sacrifice to the Lord, because God passed over the houses of the Israelites in Egypt when God killed the Egyptians, but saved our houses."

Moses also informs the Israelites that God has commanded them to recall their liberation from Egypt each year by eating only unleavened bread for seven days. All leaven is to be removed from their homes; none is to be found in all their lands during the seven days of the festival. Furthermore, the first day and the seventh day are to be set aside for a solemn gathering of the community. As with the Sabbath, no work is to be done on them.

THEMES

Parashat Bo contains two important themes:

1. Taking the gold and silver from the Egyptians.
2. The creation of the Pesach celebration.

PEREK ALEF: *Were the Israelites Justified in Taking Gold and Silver from the Egyptians?*

Just before the tenth and final plague is brought upon Pharaoh and the Egyptians, Moses is commanded by God to tell the Israelites "to borrow, each man from his neighbor and each woman from hers, objects of silver and gold." The Torah informs us that the Egyptians willingly gave the Israelites what they requested and that "thus they stripped the Egyptians."

The description raises many troubling questions. Does the Torah justify robbery from the Egyptians? Why were the Egyptians willing to hand over their wealth to the Israelites? Did the Israelites take advantage of the Egyptians when they "stripped" them of their gold and silver?

The Hebrew word for "borrow" is *sha'al*. It can also mean "ask" or "demand." Which is the most accurate translation for this incident? Did the Israelites "borrow," "ask for," or "demand" riches from the Egyptians? Were the gold and silver gifts, or were they the "spoils" of victory?

Among all Jewish interpreters of this significant Torah story, none suggests that the Israelites deliberately set out to rob the Egyptians of their wealth. Nearly all are agreed that the Egyptians willingly presented their gold and silver to the departing Israelites.

Rabbi Ishmael says that the response on the part of the Egyptians was immediate and without qualification.

Zugot

Rabbi Jose agrees, explaining that there was a high level of trust and respect between the Egyptian people and the Israelites. For three days the Egyptians were living in a plague of "black darkness" while the Israelites had light in their dwellings. The Israelites could have taken advantage of them and robbed them, but they did not. For that reason, Rabbi Jose maintains, the Egyptians trusted the Israelites and graciously rewarded them with silver and gold. (*Mechilta* on Exodus 12:36)

Hirsch

Jewish honesty
Rabbi Samson Raphael Hirsch comments that the Israelites "proved their sterling moral quality" during the three days of darkness. "For three

days long their oppressors . . . were completely helpless in their power; for three days long all their treasures lay open in their houses, and no Jew took the opportunity to take the slightest advantage either against their persons or their possessions." (Comment on Exodus 11:2–3, The Pentateuch, p. 119)

Josephus agrees. He claims that the Israelites did not steal anything. Instead, the Egyptians offered them gifts, insisting on honoring them out of friendship and neighborliness.

Rashbam also believes that the Egyptians willingly turned over their wealth to the departing Israelites. "They merely asked for it, and the Egyptians responded by giving them gifts." Rashbam implies that there was no force, no persuasion.

Sarna

Modern commentator Nahum Sarna disagrees. He explains that the silver and gold were not just neighborly gifts but rather spoils of a justified Jewish victory over the Egyptians. For years the Egyptians had treated the Israelites cruelly, insulting their dignity and intelligence as human beings. Taking "gifts" from the Egyptians was a means of restoring Jewish pride. It proved that Jews were equal in every way to their oppressors. The Israelites, Sarna writes, "escaped from Egypt with their dignity intact."

Sarna's explanation, however, differs from early Egyptian interpretations of the story. During the time that Alexander the Great ruled over Egypt (332–323 B.C.E.), many Egyptians complained to him that the Israelites had stolen riches from their ancestors. As proof they cited the Torah report of Jews taking silver and gold from the Egyptians. Hearing what some Egyptians were claiming, Ga-

viha ben Pasisa, a well-known Jewish leader, asked for a public debate. Alexander agreed.

After listening to the Egyptian argument from the Torah, Gaviha answered: "I will also use a proof from the Torah. We are told that Israel 'lived in Egypt four hundred and thirty-six years.' Do you Egyptians not owe the Israelites payment for all their years of slavery?" After hearing Gaviha's argument, Alexander gave the Egyptians three days to formulate an answer. They considered the matter but could not find one. (*Sanhedrin* 91a)

Gaviha's argument that what the Israelites had taken was neither a gift nor stolen property but rather "reparations" or repayment for years of slave labor is also one that other commentators have raised. For instance, the philosopher Philo Judaeus, who lived in Alexandria during the first century, believed that the silver and gold taken from the Egyptians was a just payment to the Israelites for all their suffering and for the wages they had never been paid. The gifts were owed to the Israelites by the Egyptians.

> *A just payment*
> *The Hebrew slaves had worked for their masters . . . they were entitled to their freedom and, therefore, at the same time, to a just farewell payment. Justice demanded it. (Umberto Cassuto on Deuteronomy 23:8)*

In 1951 the government of Israel debated the question of whether or not to seek "reparations" from Germany. Six million Jews had been killed by the Nazis. Jewish-owned businesses and properties worth millions of dollars had been confiscated or destroyed. Careers were ruined; hundreds of thousands were left sick, homeless, and orphaned. David Ben-Gurion, then prime minister of Israel, argued that, while the losses could never be fully calculated, the State of Israel was justified in seeking $1.5 billion from Germany as "material reparations." The money would be used "to secure compensation (indemnification) for the heirs of the victims and rehabilitation of the survivors."

By January 1952, Jews throughout the world, but especially in Israel, were locked in heated debate as to whether such reparations should be either requested or accepted. Ben-Gurion explained that the amount of $1.5 billion had been chosen because it was "the minimal sum required for the absorption and rehabilitation of half a million immigrants from the countries subjected to the Nazi regime." Menachem Begin, then head of the opposition Herut party, objected, claiming that the acceptance of reparations would mean "a surrender of political independence" and would represent "the ultimate abomination" of those who had been murdered by the Nazis. After a month of protests against the government proposal, the Knesset voted (61–50) to accept reparations. The payments were spread over a twelve-year period. (David Ben-Gurion, *Israel, a Personal History,* Funk and Wagnalls, Inc., and Sabra Books, New York, 1971 pp. 399–400)

Were these "reparations" from Germany to the Jewish people after the Holocaust a parallel to the gifts of silver and gold that the Israelites took from the Egyptians? Should victims, or their children, accept "payment" for such cruelty? Can a price be placed on a human life—or on six million human lives?

Ramban (Nachmanides)

Nachmanides suggests that the gold and silver that the Egyptians gave to the Israelites represented "atonement," a payment of regret, for the damages they had inflicted upon the Jewish people. The Egyptians sought forgiveness with their gifts. It is as if the Egyptians were saying, "We are the wicked ones. There is violence in our hands, and you merit God's mercy." Their gifts were an admission of guilt, a confession of all the wrongs they had done, and a request for pardon. (Comment on Exodus 11:3)

On forgiving others
Each night, before retiring, forgive those who offended you during the day. (Asher ben Yehiel, 14th century)

Since I myself stand in need of God's pity, I have granted an amnesty to all my enemies. (Heinrich Heine, 1797–1856)

In requesting and accepting Egyptian "gifts," perhaps the Israelites were also expressing their readiness to forgive their oppressors. They were liberating themselves from all the suffering of the past. Reparations would help build a foundation for a strong future. Forgiving their enemies did not mean forgetting the past; it meant rising above it to create new opportunities. Instead of becoming fixed in anger and resentment against those who had caused them so much pain and had reduced them to poverty and slavery, the Israelites accepted the Egyptian gifts and left Egypt to fashion their future as a proud and independent people.

PEREK BET: *Origins of the Pesach Celebration*

Pesach is one of the most popular celebrations of the Jewish year. On the evening of the fourteenth day of Nisan, families and friends gather for the *seder*. The table is festively decorated with holiday symbols including the *pesach* (*zeroah*), a roasted shankbone or chicken neck; the *matzah*, unleavened bread; the *maror*, bitter herb; the *charoset*, a mixture of apples, nuts, honey, cinnamon, and wine; the *chagigah* (*betzah*) roasted egg; the *kar-*

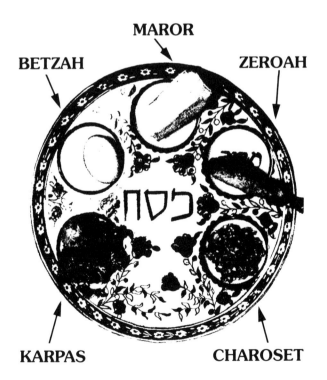

pas, parsley; the cups of wine; and one cup of wine set aside for Elijah. At each place is a *haggadah,* a book containing the *seder,* or "order," of the evening's service and the story of the Jewish people's liberation from Egypt.

Those celebrating the *seder* will drink four cups of wine, invite a child to recite four questions, and read about four different children representing four attitudes to the Pesach festival. Near the beginning of the banquet, a *matzah* will be broken, and half of it will be set aside as the *afikoman,* or "dessert." Holding a piece of *matzah,* sometimes at an open door, the leader of the *seder* will say, "Let all who are hungry come and eat. . . ."

The retelling of the Exodus from Egypt will include songs and discussion and a reminder from the rabbis of the *Mishnah* who said, "In every generation a Jew is to see himself or herself as though he or she were escaping from Egypt." The *haggadah* also contains the story of five famous rabbis who extended their celebration from early evening until the break of dawn the next morning. The festive meal concludes with the words, *Le-shanah ha-ba'ah bi-Yerushalayim,* "Next year in Jerusalem!"

What modern Jews celebrate as a *seder* actually evolved over thousands of years. Each generation added important elements to the ceremony while abandoning others. Within our Torah portion we find important descriptions of the first Pesach rituals observed by the people of Israel.

At springtime in ancient times, before the enslavement of Hebrews in Egypt, shepherds set aside a year-old lamb for each household. At twilight on the fourteenth day of the month of Nisan, when the moon was full and bright, the lamb was slaughtered. Its blood was smeared on the doorposts of the houses where it would be eaten, and it was then roasted for the festival feast. When the meat was ready, it was eaten with *matzah* and *maror.*

Early Hebrew farmers also observed a spring festival. Their custom included removing all leavened products from their houses and eating only *matzah* for seven days, from the fourteenth day until the twenty-first day of the month of Nisan.

No one knows when the two traditions of the shepherds and the farmers were combined. That may have occurred at the time Moses liberated the Jewish people from Egyptian bondage—or later. All accounts of the festival within the Torah link it to the historic moment of the Exodus. For instance, we are told that the lamb is to be called "the Pesach sacrifice, because God passed over the houses of the Israelites in Egypt when the Egyptians were killed." (Exodus 12:27) The Torah also contains instructions about eating the lamb. It is to be eaten quickly while each male stands with a staff in his hand, sandals on his feet, and a girdle around his waist. The dress and dramatic posture are of those escaping danger, fleeing for their lives.

All these strange customs were meant to capture the attention of young people. When they saw the lamb killed; its blood painted on the doorposts; their fathers dressed as if they were about to leave on a journey, standing with a staff in their hands and quickly eating the roasted meat, it was hoped that they would ask, "What are you doing? What is the meaning of this strange ceremony?" In answer, fathers were to tell their children how God liberated them from Egyptian slavery.

This early ceremony was known as *Seder Mitzrayim,* or "the *Seder* of Egypt" because it records the early history and rituals of Pesach. The rabbis named the celebration that evolved over the centuries *Seder Dorot,* or "the *Seder* of the Generations." *Seder Dorot* includes many of the old traditions, though they have been changed to meet new circumstances.

For instance, emphasis is still placed upon the festive family meal and upon the importance of eating *matzah* for seven days. *Maror* is still eaten as a reminder of the bitterness of slavery. All that is left of the *pesach* lamb, however, is a roasted shankbone, placed on the *seder* plate and, at the appropriate moment in the ceremony, held up by the leader who explains that it is a reminder of God's saving the Israelite firstborn on the night when all of the Egyptian firstborn were killed.

Each according to his or her ability
The rabbis point out that four times the Torah mentions the questions that children will ask on the evening of Pesach. Three of the questions are found in the Torah portion Bo, *Exodus 12:26–27; 13:8,14, and one is found in Deuteronomy 2:20–21.*

One explanation of the four different questions is that they represent four different kinds of human abilities to listen and to learn. "When God spoke to Israel," the rabbis teach, "each person heard according to his or her ability. The elders, the children, the babies, the young, even Moses—each understood what God was saying according to his or her capacity to listen." (Tanchuma on Exodus 19:19)

The difference between the "wicked" child and the "wise" child

The "wise" child asks, "What do the laws and traditions that God has commanded you mean?" The "wicked" child asks, "What does this ritual service mean to you?"

What is the difference between them? It has been suggested that the "wise" children ask the reason for the various types of rituals while the "wicked" children do not care about the meanings of the ceremony. For them the festival is merely a burden God has imposed upon the Jewish people year after year.

Leibowitz

Nehama Leibowitz points out that the real difference between the "wise" and "wicked" children is not in their words but in the introductions to their questions within the haggadah. *We are told that "the 'wise child' will ask you" and that "the 'wicked child' will say to you." It is the attitude of each that makes the difference. "So long as a child asks, no matter how difficult the questions are, it is a sign that he expects an answer. . . . He is far from being malicious but is a student thirsty for knowledge. The wicked one, however, does not ask and desires no reply. . . . His attitude is fixed and predetermined. He is not interested in your answers but only in*

what he "will say to you." (Studies in Shemot, pp. 207–208)

At the *seder*, Jewish fathers no longer dress as if they were about to leave on a long journey, but the *haggadah* created by the rabbis does include four questions to be asked by children at the festive meal. There is also a section about four types of children, each representing different attitudes and learning abilities. The emphasis of the *seder* remains the same as it was in ancient times. It is a unique banquet in which Jews are to relive the historic experience of being liberated from Egyptian oppression and are to pass on that story from generation to generation.

QUESTIONS FOR STUDY AND DISCUSSION

1. Many commentators argue that the Hebrews were justified in taking gold and silver from the Egyptians when they escaped from bondage because they had been exploited for so many years. Do you agree? Is there a parallel here to the "reparations" paid by Germany to Israel and to Jews who suffered during the Holocaust? What about the payment to Japanese-Americans who were placed in concentration camps in the United States during the Second World War? How should the amounts for such reparations be determined? What about affirmative action that guarantees a percentage of student and job opportunities for those minorities that may have been exploited in the past and whose levels of education and employment may not provide them with openings enjoyed by others within society?

2. Using a *haggadah*, make an outline of the *seder*. Compare it with Exodus 12:1–27, 43–49. What has been added since biblical times by the rabbis who created the *haggadah*? In what dramatic ways is the history of the Exodus from Egypt passed on from generation to generation at the *seder* meal?

PARASHAT BESHALACH
Exodus 13:17–17:16

Parashat Beshalach takes its name from the second word of the Torah portion. *Beshalach* means "when he sent forth" and refers to Pharaoh's decision to free the Israelites. Led by Moses, they depart from Egypt, but Pharaoh changes his mind and decides to pursue them. When the Israelites see Pharaoh and his army approaching, they complain to Moses that he has brought them into the wilderness to die. He assures them that God will save them and leads them through the Sea of Reeds. From the other side they watch as the pursuing Egyptians are drowned. In celebration, Moses and the Israelites sing a song of praise to God. Afterwards they begin their journey through the Sinai desert. Despite their victory over the Egyptians and their liberation, however, the Israelites continue to complain to Moses. They cry out that they have no water to drink, no bread to eat. God grants them water and provides them with "manna," a food substance resembling flour. While the Israelites are camped at Rephidim, they are attacked by the Amalekites. Joshua, who has been appointed by Moses, successfully destroys the Amalekite forces.

OUR TARGUM

· 1 ·

Upon departing from Egypt, Moses does not lead the people directly to the Land of Israel. Wishing to avoid a war with the Philistines, which might frighten the people and make them want to return to Egypt, Moses takes them south from Goshen towards the Sea of Reeds [Red Sea]. God leads them with a pillar of fire by night and a pillar of cloud by day.

Pharaoh, who has finally agreed to free them, suddenly regrets his decision. He sends his whole army to bring the Israelites back to Egypt. When the Israelites see Pharaoh and all his chariots approaching, they cry out to Moses: "What have you done to us, taking us out of Eygpt? . . . Let us be, and we will serve the Egyptians, for it is better for us to serve the Egyptians than to die in the wilderness." Moses responds by assuring them that God will save them. God then says to Moses, "Tell the Israelites to go forward."

As Moses holds out his hands, the Israelites enter the Sea of Reeds. The waters split and form a corridor through which they pass safely. When the pursuing Egyptian army led by Pharaoh enters the corridor, the waters crash in upon them. The Egyptians panic, their chariot wheels lock, and the whole army is drowned in the sea.

Victoriously, Moses and the Israelites sing a song of praise to God: . . . "Pharaoh's chariots and his army/God has cast into the sea;/And the pick of his officers/Are drowned in the Sea of Reeds./. . . Who is like You, O Lord, among the mighty;/Who is like You, majestic in holiness,/Awesome in splendor, working wonders!/. . . The Lord will reign for ever and ever!" Miriam,

the sister of Moses and Aaron, leads all the women in a festive dance.

· 2 ·

From the Sea of Reeds, the people travel to Marah, or "bitter," so named because of its bitter waters. When the people complain about the taste of the water, God tells Moses to throw a piece of wood into it. He does, and the waters sweeten.

Later, the people journey to the wilderness of Sin. There they turn on Moses again. "If only we had died by the hand of the Lord in the land of Egypt, when we sat by the fleshpots, when we ate our fill of bread! For you have brought us out into this wilderness to starve this whole congregation to death!" Hearing their complaint, Moses and Aaron answer the people: "By evening you shall know it was the Lord who brought you out from the land of Egypt."

That evening, the camp is covered with quail to eat; in the morning, manna, a flaky substance like coriander seed, white in color and tasting like honeyed wafers, rains down upon the people. Moses orders the people to collect an *omer*'s measure, approximately a hand full, for each person and a double amount on the sixth day for the Sabbath.

Nonetheless, some people go out to gather manna on the Sabbath. They find nothing, and God declares to Moses: "How long will this people refuse to obey My commandments and My Teachings? . . . Let the people remain where they are and observe the Sabbath."

· 3 ·

From the wilderness of Sin, Moses leads the Israelites to Rephidim. Finding no water to drink, the people complain once again. "Why did you bring us from Egypt to die of thirst?" Frustrated,

Moses cries out to God, "What shall I do with this people?" God tells Moses: "I will be standing before you on the rock at Horeb. Strike the rock [with your rod] and water will come forth from it." Moses does this, and the people are given enough to drink. The place is named Massah, which means "trial," and Meribah, which means "quarrel."

· 4 ·

While camping at Rephidim, the Israelites are attacked by the forces of Amalek, a group of tribes that live in the Sinai desert. Moses orders Joshua to organize a response to the attack. Joshua successfully overwhelms the enemy, and Moses builds an altar and names it Adonai-nissi, meaning "God is my banner." He declares that "God will be at war with Amalek throughout the generations."

THEMES

Parashat Beshalach contains three important themes:

1. The "miracle" of the Israelites' escape from Egypt.
2. The Israelites' "complaints" in the desert.
3. Amalek's attack upon the Israelites.

PEREK ALEF: *Was Israel's Escape from Egypt a "Miracle"?*

The Torah's report of Israel's departure from Egypt makes it clear that the liberation was not only a human effort. We are told that the people were led by an angel of God and by a pillar of fire by night and a pillar of cloud by day. When they arrived at the Sea of Reeds and saw the Egyptian army advancing upon them, God split the waters of the sea so that they could walk safely on dry land to the other side. Then, God rolled back the waters upon the Egyptians, drowning all of them together with their horses and chariots. Upon seeing the "miracle" that God had performed for them, the Israelites sang out: "I will sing to the Lord, for God has triumphed gloriously;/Horse and driver God has hurled into the sea./ . . . You made Your wind blow, the sea covered them;/They sank like lead in the majestic waters." (Exodus 15:1,10)

Is that really what happened? Can we believe that God sent angels to lead the Israelites, split the sea for them, and destroyed the Egyptians by drowning them? Did Moses play any role in the victory? Did the Israelites do anything to save themselves? Is the Torah story an exaggeration beyond belief?

> *If I told you what the teacher told us . . .*
> *We are told about the ten-year-old whose father was driving him home from religious school. "What did you learn about today?" his father asked. The child responded: "The teacher told us about the Israelites' escape from Egypt. They came to the Sea of Reeds and built pontoons and drove across the water. As soon as the Egyptians and their tanks were on the pontoons, the Israelites sent in their air force and bombed them."*
> *The father looked with surprise at his child. "Is that really what the teacher told you?" "Not*

really," answered the child, *"but, if I told you what the teacher told us, you would never believe it!"*

It was a miracle

There are always those who will deny the existence of miracles. They claim that the works of ha-Shem (God) are simply natural phenomena. This was the attitude that many nonbelievers assumed in regard to the splitting of the Red Sea. It was caused by an earthquake, they might claim; it was just a freak accident of nature.

To forestall any such beliefs, ha-Shem magnified the miracle of the Red Sea. He split not only the Red Sea but also all the waters in the world. Even water that was in a cup gravitated to two separate sides! Because of this no one could deny that the splitting of the Red Sea was a true miracle. . . . (*Rabbi Mordechai Katz,* Lilmod Ul'lamade: From the Teachings of Our Sages, *Jewish Education Program Publications, New York, 1978, p. 75*)

According to the author of the *Zohar,* God created one miracle after another to liberate the Israelites. Plagues were sent to convince Pharaoh to free the people. When they reached the Red Sea, God caused the waters to split and harden so that the Israelites could walk safely from one shore to the other on dry land. As soon as Pharaoh and his army entered the sea, God allowed the waters to crash in upon them, destroying the entire army.

Many commentators ask: How can God allow such miracles? Would the world not be destroyed if the laws of nature, like gravity that causes the Red Sea to flow, were suspended even for a second?

The *Zohar* provides an answer. Quoting Rabbi Isaac (perhaps second century C.E.), we are told that, when the Israelites approached the Red Sea, God called upon the great angel who had been appointed to rule over it. "At the time I created the world," God said to the angel, "I appointed you angel over this sea, and I made an agreement with you that, later when the Israelites would need to pass through your waters, you would divide them. Now they have arrived at the sea; open it and allow them to pass through safely." (*Zohar, Beshalach,* 48a–49a)

Clearly, the early rabbis were troubled by the Torah's claim that God had made a miracle at the Red Sea. Rabbi Isaac's explanation seems to overcome the problem by saying that the splitting of the sea had already been fixed or preordained at the time God created the world. In other words, God anticipated the need for dividing the Red Sea and "programmed" the event. Therefore, according to Rabbi Isaac, it was not a matter of a miraculous suspension of the laws of nature. Instead, the splitting of the Red Sea occurred exactly as God had preplanned it!

Other interpreters agree, but their explanations of what happened at the Red Sea are different. Some say that the splitting of the sea occurred in a natural way.

Hertz

Rabbi J. H. Hertz speculates that "a strong east wind, blowing all night and acting with the ebbing tide, may have laid bare the neck of the water joining the Bitter Lakes to the Red Sea, allowing the Israelites to cross in safety." Rabbi Hertz also explains that "a sudden cessation of the wind . . . would . . . convert the low flat sandbanks first into a quicksand and then into a mass of waters" which would have drowned the pursuing Egyptians. (*The Pentateuch and Haftorahs,* Soncino Press, London, 1966, pp. 268–269)

Rambam (Maimonides)

Use of miracles

A miracle cannot prove what is impossible; it is useful only to confirm what is possible. (*Moses Maimonides,* Guide for the Perplexed *3:24*)

Believing in miracles

In short, I do not believe in miracles. Not if the word be interpreted in its usual sense as exceptions to the laws of nature. I believe in miracles only as occurrences and events that are far too marvelous for me fully to comprehend but that are entirely consistent with nature's accustomed patterns. . . . Do you know any word more descriptive than miracle for the fact that within the tiny, submicroscopic cell each of us was at the moment of conception were already contained the seeds of all the physical traits, all the mental characteristics, all the emotional proclivities, all the creative possibilities of the adults we are today? Compared to that, a sea splitting in two . . . is simple child's play. There are more miracles without magic in this universe than the wisest of us could ever identify. The trouble is that most of the time we're looking for them in the wrong places. (Roland B. Gittelsohn, Man's Best Hope, *Random House, New York, 1961, pp. 114–118*)

Modern Bible scholar Umberto Cassuto claims that what happened at the Red Sea "is a common occurrence in the region of the Suez." He explains that "at high tide, the waters of the Red Sea penetrate the sand, from under the surface, and suddenly the water begins to ooze up out of the sand, which has been dry. Within a short time the sand turns to mud, but the water continues to rise and ultimately a deep layer of water is formed above the sand, the whole area becoming flooded. . . . Against this natural background the biblical account can easily be understood."

Cassuto, however, does not reject the notion that a "miracle" occurred at the Red Sea. "The miracle," he says, "consisted in the fact that at the very moment when it was necessary, in just the manner conducive to the achievement of the desired goal, and on a scale that was abnormal, there occurred, in accordance with the Lord's will, phenomena that brought about Israel's salvation." (*A Commentary on the Book of Exodus,* Magnes Press, Jerusalem, 1951, pp. 167–168)

Philosopher Martin Buber seems to agree with Cassuto, but from a different point of view. Buber argues that the details of what happened at the Red Sea are not important. "What is decisive . . . ," he writes, "is that the children of Israel understood this as an act of their God, as a 'miracle.'" Buber explains that from a historical point of view a miracle is "an abiding astonish-

ment," a feeling of surprise and awe that people sense in especially significant moments. That is what happened at the Red Sea—and afterwards. The Israelites saw Pharaoh's advancing army drowned and destroyed. They were astonished by the events that saved them. At that moment, as Buber comments, "the people saw in whatever it was they saw 'the great hand of God.'" Afterwards, generations of Jews who retold the story continued to find in it traces of wonder that they identified as the miraculous work of God. (*Moses: The Revelation and the Covenant,* Harper and Row Publishers, Inc., New York, 1958, pp. 75, 77)

Whatever happened at the Red Sea, it is clear that the Egyptians were defeated and the Israelites went forth to freedom. The victory was surprising, a critical turning point in Jewish history. For those who were there, and for those who would tell the tale afterwards, something momentous and "astonishing" happened. God split the sea, saved the Israelites, and assured their liberation. All of this seemed more than the work of ordinary people. Something wonderful occurred, something awesome beyond human comprehension. So they called their victory "a miracle."

PEREK BET: *Why All the Complaints against Moses and God?*

As astonishing as their victory over Pharaoh's army and their Exodus from Egypt, the Israelites are not portrayed as particularly grateful to God or to Moses. Our Torah portion, in fact, is filled with their complaints, angry questions, and discontent. On four occasions the people turn on Moses and attack him with harsh accusations.

The first time occurs just as they are escaping from Egypt. When the people see Pharaoh's army pursuing them, they ask Moses, "Was it for want of graves in Egypt that you brought us to die in the wilderness? What have you done to us, taking us out of Egypt? Is this not the very thing we told you in Egypt, saying, 'Let us be, and we will serve the Egyptians, for it is better for us to serve the Egyptians than to die in the wilderness'?" (14:10–12)

The second time occurs just after their "miraculous" victory at the Red Sea. They travel for three days and camp at Marah, meaning "bitter," located in the desert region of Shur. Because the water there tastes bitter, the people grumble against Moses and ask him, "What shall we drink?" (15:22–24)

Two and a half months later, they express their displeasure with Moses for a third time. Having just arrived in the wilderness of Sin, they are hungry, hot, and frustrated. So they tell Moses: "If only we had died by the hand of the Lord in the land of Egypt, when we sat by the fleshpots, when we ate our fill of bread! For you have brought us out into this wilderness to starve this whole congregation to death!" (16:1–3)

On the fourth occasion, the people are camped at Rephidim in the wilderness of Sin. Again, they complain about not having sufficient water. Angrily, they ask Moses, "Why did you bring us up from Eygpt, to kill us and our children and livestock with thirst?" (17:1–3)

What accounts for all of these complaints and accusations? Several theories are advanced.

Rashi

Rashi explains that the people see "the guardian angel of Egypt marching after them," and they are seized by fear. The guardian angel represents the military power of Egypt. It is advancing quickly upon the Israelites who are unarmed and unable to defend themselves. They are frightened that they will be overtaken and destroyed. Out of fear and disappointment they turn upon Moses, accusing him of leading them to their deaths at the brutal hands of the Egyptians. The terror of death, Rashi believes, generates their complaints.

Handling our disappointments
The Israelites were disappointed and angry when they saw the Egyptians pursuing them. They felt tricked and used by Moses when they found themselves in the wilderness without food and water. Given the steps for handling anger suggested below by psychologist Haim G. Ginott, how did the Israelites do when they were "pushed to the brink"?

Describe what you see.
Describe what you feel.
Describe what needs to be done.
Do not attack the person.
(Between Parent and Teenager, *Macmillan, New York, 1969, p. 100*)

Ibn Ezra

Ibn Ezra disagrees with Rashi. He points out that there were six hundred thousand Israelites, and they could have easily taken on Pharaoh's army and defeated it. However, they were psychologically incapable. They still saw themselves as slaves, not free people. They thought that they were weak, still subservient and inferior to the Egyptians who had enslaved them. "How would it be possible," they asked themselves, "to go to war and win against those who ruled us?"

According to ibn Ezra it was not fear that brought on the Israelites' complaints. It was their perception of themselves as "weaklings" before their former Egyptian masters. Even though they outnumbered Pharaoh's army, their morale was so low and their self-esteem so shaken that they could not imagine themselves successfully battling the Egyptians. Instead, they turn upon Moses, make him a scapegoat for their frustrations, and blame him for bringing them out to the desert to die. (14:13)

Rabbi Eleazar of Modi'im explains their behavior from a different point of view. As soon as the Israelites left Egypt, he says, they began to experience the difficulties of thirst and hunger in the desert. They were uncomfortable, anxious, and irritable. As a result they began to look back upon their slave experience with nostalgia. They forgot about the beatings and humiliation; they remembered the abundance of food on their tables.

From where did such recollections come? Rabbi Eleazar points out they were based on their experience in Egypt. The people had been slaves to rulers and had been permitted "to go out to the markets and fields to help themselves to grapes, figs, and pomegranates, and no one would stand in their way."

Facing the hardships of the desert, the people began to idealize their situation in Egypt, to look at it through "rose-colored glasses." Rabbi Eleazar says it was out of that twisted point of view about the conditions of their slavery in Egypt that the Israelites complained to Moses. (*Mechilta, Vayasa,* on Exodus 15:27–16:3)

Zugot

They were testing God
Rabbi Joshua said: The Israelites argued that if God is truly the Power over all things, then we shall serve the Lord. If not, then we shall not serve God. Rabbi Eleazer claimed that they argued that if God fulfills our needs for food, water, and shelter, then we shall serve the Lord. If not, we shall not serve God. This is what the people meant when they said, "Is the Lord among us or not?" (Mechilta, Vayasa, *on Exodus 17:7*)

Leibowitz

Nehama Leibowitz, quoting an observation found in the commentary *Hemdat ha-Yamim,* observes that the Israelites may have lied to one another about their slave existence in Egypt. They recalled all the positive aspects of slavery, not the negative ones. "There was not an ounce of truth in their words" to one another, Leibowitz writes. Like all slaves they were free "from responsibility for their own destiny, their own economic and social ordering. They were in the charge of a taskmaster who forced them to work, beat them, urged them to finish their tasks but also fed them that they might have strength for their labor. Now they were free, no longer dependent upon taskmasters who beat and fed them! The whole burden of taking care of themselves was theirs. This was

the source of their discontent." In other words, the Israelites grumbled at Moses because they now had to make their own decisions, find their own food and shelter. They resented the burdens of freedom. (*Studies in Shemot,* p. 265)

Ramban (Nachmanides)

Ramban sees the situation of the Israelites in a different way. They had left Egypt bravely and were now in the desert. They had thought that Moses would lead them to a city or safe place where they would find food, drink, and shelter; they believed it would not be long before they entered the Promised Land of Israel. However, after a month of wandering in the desert, their provisions were nearly gone. They were thirsty and hungry. Their essential needs were not being met, and they feared for the safety of their children. So they said to Moses, "What shall we eat? With what will this great wilderness into which we have come supply us?" Their complaints were not only understandable but both realistic and justified. (Comment on Exodus 16:2)

They were disloyal to God
God performed marvels . . . split the sea and took them through it . . . split rocks in the wilderness and gave them drink as if from the great deep. . . .
But they went on sinning against God, defying the Most High in the parched land . . . because they did not put their trust in God, did not rely on God's deliverance. (Psalms 78:12–13, 15, 17, 22)

Sarna

Nahum Sarna rejects the notion that the people were justified in their complaints. Instead, he argues that they were like spoiled children. Moses had led them out of slavery. God had freed them from bondage. Even after they had been given sweet water at Marah and manna to eat, they still found reasons to murmur against Moses and God. They remained skeptical, doubtful of God's goodness and of Moses' intentions.

When the Israelites should have been grateful to both God and Moses for their liberation, they appear selfish and unfaithful. "The extreme language of the complaints betrays profound lack of faith in God and base ingratitude," Sarna argues. He points to Psalm 78 as an indication that Jerusalem poets living during the time of the Temple (second century B.C.E.) also saw in all the grumbling of the Israelites an example of their ingratitude, faithlessness, and disloyalty to God.

One other explanation may provide a significant understanding of their behavior. In his *Guide for the Perplexed,* Moses Maimonides makes the observation that God deliberately tested the Israelites with difficulties and challenges. When the time came to leave Egypt, God instructed Moses to take the Israelites the long way through the desert to the Promised Land rather than the direct route across the northern border of the Sinai peninsula, which would have taken only ten days. In the wilderness, God tested the people with thirst and hunger. All these tests, Maimonides explains, were meant to toughen the people and to prepare them for conquering the Land of Israel.

"It is a fact," Maimonides argues, "that the Israelites would not have been able to conquer the land and fight with its inhabitants if they had not previously undergone the trouble and hardship of the wilderness. . . . Ease destroys bravery while trouble and concern about food create strength. This strength that the Israelites gained was the ultimate good that came out of their wanderings in the wilderness." (3:24)

Maimonides viewed the complaints as natural. The people were tried by unpleasant conditions. One would expect them to grumble about their troubles and difficult circumstances. What was important, however, was not their complaints but the lessons they were learning. In coping with all the hardships of the wilderness, they were preparing themselves to conquer the Promised Land.

In the variety of explanations for the people's many complaints against Moses and God, we encounter not only different approaches to our Torah text but also a rich array of opinions about motives for human behavior. The Talmud teaches that "a person is to be judged by his anger." Might it also be correct to say that a person and a community are also judged by their "complaints"?

PEREK GIMEL: *Amalek's Attack upon the Israelites*

Near the end of our Torah portion and again in Deuteronomy 25, we are told about the Amalekites' attack on the people of Israel. The version in Exodus 17:8–16 informs us that Amalek declares war upon Israel while the newly liberated people are camping at Rephidim. In response, Moses appoints Joshua to take troops and to engage the enemy in battle. While the war wages, Moses climbs to the top of a hill known as Hur and holds up his staff in prayer to God. After Joshua's victory, God instructs Moses to write out the following promise and reminder: "I will utterly blot out the memory of Amalek from under heaven."

The other version of the war with Amalek, as reported in Deuteronomy 25:17–19, adds some interesting details to the story. We are informed that the Amalekites attack the Israelites by surprise when they are "famished and weary," and they deliberately target the weak "stragglers," who are at the end of their lines. As in Exodus, after their victory, the Israelites are commanded: "You shall blot out the memory of Amalek from under heaven. Do not forget!"

Why this unforgiving command concerning the Amalekites?

Within Jewish tradition the Amalekites are identified as a nomadic people, who lived in the Sinai peninsula and were the descendants of Edom. (Genesis 36:12) In two major wars, the Amalekites were defeated by the Israelites, first under the leadership of King Saul and then under the leadership of King David. (I Samuel 15:5 ff. and 27:8 ff.) In the Book of Esther (3:1), Haman, who schemed to destroy the Jewish people, is described as a descendant of Agag, king of Amalek.

According to Jewish tradition, the Sabbath before the festival of Purim, when the Book of Esther is read, is called *Zachor* ("Remember"), and the Torah passage designated for that Sabbath day is from Deuteronomy 25:17–19, containing the commandment not to forget Amalek. In this way, the tradition preserves the connection between the Amalekites and wicked Haman.

Why remember Amalek?

Possibly the fact that the Amalekites were the first foes Israel met after its liberation stamped them in the people's mind as the archenemy, the prototype of all whom they would and did meet subsequently. This sentiment is reflected in an old midrash: Moses was to write the judgment on Amalek in a document to let all men know that those who harm Israel will in the end come themselves to harm. (W. Gunther Plaut, editor, The Torah: A Modern Commentary, *Union of American Hebrew Congregations, New York, 1981, p. 511*)

There can be no doubt that the attack of the Amalekites upon the newly liberated Israelites left bitter memories. Yet, there were many other battles and wars in Jewish history; other peoples sought to destroy Israel and to prevent it from occupying its national homeland. Why then does the Torah single out Amalek for special condemnation, calling for the end of its existence upon earth? Why are we commanded to "remember Amalek" rather than to "forgive Amalek"?

These questions obviously bothered those who studied Torah and sought to understand its meanings. As a result, several commentators provide us with their explanations.

Rabbi Joshua and Rabbi Eleazar Hisma both agree that Amalek's attack was brought about by Israel's behavior and lack of faith in God. From their viewpoint, the people of Israel had not "occupied themselves with the study of Torah." Therefore, they deserved the assault upon them. The command to "remember Amalek" was meant to remind Jews of the consequences of disloyalty to God's commandments. If Jews refuse to study Torah and observe its laws, then God will send enemies like Amalek to persecute and even destroy the people of Israel.

This explanation by Rabbi Joshua and Rabbi Eleazar Hisma, however, represents a minority point of view. By contrast, Rabbi Eleazar of Modi'im, who was put to death by his nephew, Bar Kochba, when he refused to cooperate with the plans for rebellion against Rome in 135 C.E., believed that the Amalekites were condemned because of the tactics they used in their war against Israel. "Amalek," Rabbi Eleazar of Modi'im explains, "would sneak under the wings of the cloud at the rear of the Israelite lines, steal people away, and kill them." In other words, the Amalekites are to be remembered for their trickery and treachery. They deliberately ambushed the weak, exhausted, and hungry. They surprised their victims from behind and then brutally murdered them. Because of their shocking and deplorable tactics, the Amalekites are never to be forgotten.

Another teacher, Rabbi Eliezer, presents the very opposite argument. He argues that the Amalekites did not attack the Israelites secretly, but "defiantly." They did not hide in the darkness of night or use the cover of the cloud at the rear of the Israelite lines. Instead, they maimed and murdered the poor, innocent, and weak during the day, publicly so that everyone could see what they were doing. Amalek stands for random killing and torture without cause—or just for the "sport" of it. The Amalekites are remembered for their public brutality in defiance of respect for the sanctity of human life.

Rabbi Jose ben Halafta offers another view. For him, the evil done by the Amalekites was not a matter of their tactics but of their efforts to solicit and organize other nations to aid them in their effort to destroy the people of Israel.

Rabbi Judah agrees with Rabbi Jose and points out that, in order to attack Israel, the Amalekites had to travel through five other nations. From each nation they sought allies for their plans to exterminate the Israelites. Rabbi Judah warns that we dare not forget their deliberate, cool, and calculated design to end Jewish existence. Remembering Amalek, he says, reminds us to be careful and always on guard about the safety and survival of the Jewish people. (*Mechilta, Amalek,* I)

Modern commentator Nehama Leibowitz presents a different observation. She points out that the Torah's report about Amalek makes it clear that the killing of the weak and feeble was because "they did not fear God." Leibowitz says that "we were commanded to blot out the memory of Amalek since they came and fell upon the defenseless and weary without any pretext whatsoever. The children of Israel were not entering their territory, and it was purely a wanton attack." In other words, had the Amalekites honored the worth of each human life as created in the image of God, it would have been impossible for them to kill without any cause. "Where the fear of God is lacking," Leibowitz points out, "the stranger who is homeless in a foreign land is liable to be murdered." We are urged to recall Amalek so that we guard against those who have no fear of God and, consequently, do not believe that each human being is created in God's sacred image. (*Studies in Devarim,* World Zionist Organization, Jerusalem, 1980, p. 253)

Hirsch

Rabbi Samson Raphael Hirsch finds another reason for not forgetting the Amalekites' war against the Israelites. Hirsch claims the Amalekites were seeking fame. Because they wanted to demonstrate their bravery and strength, they took up arms against those who had just defeated Pharaoh. "This seeking renown by the force of arms is the first and last enemy of the happiness of mankind," Hirsch writes. Human beings need to be reminded of the danger of seeking fame through the power of arms and military might. For that reason, the memory of Amalek must never be forgotten.

Peli

Pinchas Peli believes that Amalek's war against the Jewish people was not only calculated to take their lives but was also intended to rob them of their enthusiasm for freedom. "Amalek rushed to pour cold water on the fire of enthusiasm and faith generated by Israel and its miraculous deliverance from Egypt." Recalling the observation of Jewish mystics that the numerical value of the name "Amalek" in Hebrew adds up to 240, which equals the word *safek* (meaning "doubt"), Peli concludes that the Amalekites represent doubters and cynics, who see their roles as "undermining, defaming, delegitimatizing, cutting off in its bud, any sign of hope wherever it appears." In remembering Amalek, Peli observes, we make certain that the cynics and doubters, those who tear down dreams with their contempt and defeatism, are not allowed to triumph. (*Jerusalem Post,* September 13, 1986, p. 22)

To have forgiven the Amalekites and forgotten their attack might have robbed the Jewish people and the world of valuable lessons. The Amalekites have emerged through the ages as a prototype for aggressive, dangerous human behavior. Understanding the consequences of such evil, and battling against it, may be critical for human survival. Remembering Amalek is a first significant step.

QUESTIONS FOR STUDY AND DISCUSSION

1. Which explanation for the "miracle" of Israel's Exodus from Egypt makes the most sense?
2. Martin Buber defines a miracle as an "abiding astonishment." Of other human experiences that can be recalled, which are so wonderful that people refer to them as "miracles"? What do they have in common with the Exodus of Israel from Egypt?
3. Why do the Israelites offer so many complaints against God and Moses? Do the reasons given by the various commentators also explain why so many people complain about their lives today? What lessons might we learn from the way the early Israelites handled their gripes and grievances?
4. Why does Jewish tradition insist on encouraging people to "remember Amalek"? Wouldn't it be better for people "to forgive and forget"? Why make a mitzvah out of remembering the past—especially if that past is filled with unhappiness, horror, and fear?

PARASHAT YITRO
Exodus 18:1–20:23

Parashat Yitro continues the journey of the Israelites across the Sinai desert. Before returning to Egypt, Moses had left his wife, Zipporah, and his two sons, Gershom and Eliezer, with his father-in-law, Jethro. Hearing that Moses has freed the Israelites from Egypt, Jethro brings Zipporah and her children to the Israelite camp. Moses tells his father-in-law about the Israelite liberation, and they offer sacrifices of thanksgiving to God. The next day Jethro observes that the people are bringing all their problems to Moses. He suggests that the burden is too great for one person to bear and advises Moses to choose trustworthy people to share leadership with him. Moses takes his advice. Three months after entering the Sinai desert, Moses and the Israelites camp at Mount Sinai. Moses goes up to the top of the mountain, and God speaks to him, giving him the Ten Commandments. Below, the people hear thunder and see lightning. They remain at a distance while Moses communes with God.

OUR TARGUM

· 1 ·

Jethro, Moses' father-in-law, hears that the Israelites have escaped from Egypt. He takes Zipporah, Moses' wife, and his grandsons, Gershom and Eliezer, to where Moses and the Israelites are camping in the Sinai desert. Moses tells Jethro about the wondrous liberation from Egypt. Jethro is delighted and says: "Blessed be the Lord who delivered you from the Egyptians and from Pharaoh. . . . Now I know that the Lord is greater than all gods."

During the next day Jethro sees large numbers of people bringing their disputes to Moses. "Why do you act alone?" he asks him. Moses explains that the people need a judge to deal with their disagreements and a teacher to instruct them in God's laws.

"What you are doing is wrong," Jethro tells him. "The task should not be done by one person." Jethro urges Moses to find "trustworthy people who will not take bribes" and appoint them as "chiefs of thousands, hundreds, fifties, and tens. Let them . . . decide every minor dispute themselves. Make it easier for yourself, and let them share the burden with you."

Moses follows Jethro's advice. Later Jethro returns to Midian.

·2·

Three months after departing from Egypt, Moses leads the people to the wilderness of Sinai. They camp before Mount Sinai, and God tells Moses to say to the people: "You have seen what I did to the Egyptians, how I bore you on eagles' wings and brought you to Me. Now then, if you will obey Me faithfully and keep My covenant, you shall be My treasured possession among all the peoples. . . . You shall be to Me a kingdom of priests and a holy nation."

Hearing God's words, the Israelites respond: "All that God has spoken we will do!"

·3·

Three days later Moses leads the people to Mount Sinai. The mountain appears to be on fire. Smoke rises from its peaks. The people hear the loud blasts of a horn and are frightened. Moses leaves them and goes to the top of the mountain. There he receives the Ten Commandments.

1. I the Lord am your God who brought you out of the land of Egypt, the house of bondage.

2. You shall have no other gods beside Me. You shall not make for yourself a sculptured image, or any likeness of what is in the heavens above, or on the earth below, or in the waters under the earth. You shall not bow down to them or serve them. . . .

3. You shall not swear falsely by the name of the Lord your God. . . .

4. Remember the Sabbath day and keep it holy.

5. Honor your father and mother. . . .

6. You shall not murder.

7. You shall not commit adultery.

8. You shall not steal.

9. You shall not bear false witness against your neighbor.

10. You shall not covet your neighbor's house; you shall not covet your neighbor's wife, or his male or female slave, or his ox or his ass, or anything that is your neighbor's.

THEMES

Parashat Yitro contains two important themes:

1. Sharing leadership of the community.
2. Appreciating what happened at Mount Sinai.

PEREK ALEF: *The Burden of Leadership*

During Jethro's visit to the Israelite camp, he notices long lines of people waiting to bring their disputes before Moses. Sitting alone from morning until evening, Moses listens to each argument, hears each problem, and states his judgment on each situation brought before him. Jethro is astounded. "What is this thing that you are doing for the people?" he asks Moses. "Why do you act alone, while all the people stand about you from morning until evening?"

Noting that Jethro was deeply upset with Moses, an ancient sage suggests that what disturbed Jethro was not that Moses appeared overworked but that Moses had become full of self-importance. Moses, he says, was "behaving like a king who sits on his throne while all the people stand."

Rabbi Judah of the village of Akko also detected a dangerous element of conceit in Moses. Why, he asks, did Moses tell Jethro that "the people are coming to *me*" instead of saying that "the people are coming to *God*"? Rabbi Judah's question raises other questions about Moses. Did he believe that he was superior to his people or even to God in helping them solve their problems? Was he beginning to assume that he alone had the wisdom to advise them?

Rabbi Judah's questions seem to imply that Jethro was upset with Moses because he saw him losing his humility, becoming a pompous leader who believed only he could make decisions for his people. For that reason, Rabbi Judah argues, Jethro criticized Moses and told him to find others with whom to share the responsibilities of leadership. (*Mechilta, Amalek,* IV)

While most interpreters do not criticize Moses for holding himself above his people or for playing the role of "king of the Israelites," many cite the dangerous consequences of his decision to judge the people by himself.

Zugot

For instance, Rabbi Joshua comments that Jethro's warning to Moses was a practical one. Jethro saw that Moses had taken on too much. The work was overwhelming. Fearful that Moses would collapse from exhaustion, Jethro told him, "They will tire you out and cause you to fail in your leadership of them."

Rabbi Eleazar of Modi'im agrees that the danger to Moses was "exhaustion," but he offers a different perspective. He claims Jethro also believed that Moses was exhausting the people. By insisting that he was the only one who could hear their problems and disputes, he forced them to stand in long lines for many hours in the hot desert sun. As a result they became irritable. They turned to one another with complaints. "Moses is taking too long to hear these cases. By the time he hears us he will be too tired to make a fair decision." Rabbi Eleazar says that Jethro heard their dissatisfaction and warned Moses: "The people will despise and reject you with their criticisms." Jethro saw that Moses' desire to do everything himself was wasteful and inefficient. Instead of helping the people, it was creating frustration and dissatisfaction among them. (*Mechilta, Amalek,* IV)

Ramban (Nachmanides)

Nachmanides observes that the trouble with Moses' decision to hear all the disputes and make all the judgments by himself was not simply the frustration of the people but the danger of increasing violence and injustice among them. Jethro, Nachmanides says, told Moses that the people "will tolerate the violence committed against them because they have no opportunity to tell it to you. They do not want to abandon their work and affairs to wait for a free moment when they will be able to approach you." In other words, Jethro saw that, as the people lost faith in Moses' ability to hear their cases, they began to take the law into their own hands. Because they refused to waste their time waiting for him to make judgments, violence and injustice increased among them.

Essentially, in Jethro's critique of Moses, Nachmanides sees a very important criticism of courts not equipped to handle the large number of cases brought to them. The results are long delays, mounting frustration, a loss of faith in the system's capacity to deliver justice, and, often, the decision of some people to take the law into their own hands. Because, at first, Moses insisted on doing everything himself, he increased the dangers of violence and injustice, rather than providing for efficient and fair judgment. (Commentary on Exodus 19:22)

Excellence in management

The excellent companies have a deeply ingrained philosophy that says, in effect, "respect the individual," "make people winners," "let them stand out," "treat people as adults." (Thomas J. Peters and Robert H. Waterman, Jr., In Search of Excellence, *Harper and Row Publishers, Inc., New York, 1982, p. 277*)

Participating in management

(Decentralization) . . . increases the amount of discretion and autonomy that individuals have at work by decentralizing decision-making and increasing participation in decision-making processes as much as possible. . . .

The benefits of decentralization in terms of reduced distress and strain are illustrated in the experience of an officer of a hospital equipment corporation. Over a ten-year period, this officer had worked for two different corporations. One company was very centralized; the other used a very decentralized decision-making approach. During his ten years in the centralized corporation, he had insomnia, depression, and nightmares about going to jail and about running afoul of corporate policies and procedures. . . . After a year of this distress, he left the centralized corporation and subsequently joined the decentralized corporation. Following the move to the new corporation, his insomnia and depression cleared. . . . His family reported that he was much easier to be around, and he was more the man they used to know. (James C. Quick and Jonathan D. Quick, Organizational Stress and Preventive Management, *McGraw-Hill, New York, 1984, pp. 163–171*)

Sarna

Modern interpreter Nahum Sarna agrees with Nachmanides' observation. "Jethro," he says, "is appalled at the inefficiency of the system of justice, with its inevitably debilitating effects on Moses himself and the hardships it imposes on the public." It is for that reason that he suggests a new system to Moses. He recommends that he appoint judges for thousands, hundreds, fifties, and tens, allowing them to hear disputes and make judgments. "Make it easier for yourself," he counsels Moses, "and let them share the burden with you." (*Exploring Exodus*, pp. 126–127)

The benefits of sharing the burden of leadership, of "decentralizing" seem clear in this situation. Justice will be dispensed more quickly. The people will be less frustrated and less likely to take the law into their own violent hands. Trust will be established and strengthened by confidence in a system of justice that works. Leadership will be more rested, more alert, and more accessible. Jethro's suggestion to Moses about dividing up the burdens of leadership is both functually wise and socially just.

Jethro, however, not only recommends the sharing of leadership but offers a critique for choosing leaders. He tells Moses: "You shall seek out from among all the people those who are capable and fear God, those who are trustworthy and spurn ill-gotten gain." Not surprisingly, interpreters from all ages have explored the meaning of this remarkable definition of leadership.

Rashi

One ancient sage suggests that "capable" means "wealthy, people of means." Rashi agrees, saying that people of "wealth will not need to flatter others or show them favor."

Nachmanides disagrees. "A capable person," he argues, is "wise, alert, and fair" in the administration of justice and is "strong and alert" when it comes to "organizing troops for battle." (*Mechilta, Amalek,* IV; Rashi on Exodus 18:21; Nachmanides on Exodus 18:21)

Ibn Ezra

Ibn Ezra offers another point of view. He writes that the phrase "capable people" means "people who have the strength to tolerate without fear the hardship of those who criticize their decisions." For ibn Ezra leadership means independence, confidence in one's opinions, and the strength to stand behind them. (Comment on Exodus 18:21)

Sforno believes that when the Torah uses the words "capable people" it has in mind individuals "who possess the talent to lead Jews out of a fight, and a sufficient enough knowledge of an enemy's strategies and resources to guarantee victory." "Capable people" are those who understand how to compromise and resolve differences between angry parties. But they are not naive. According to Sforno, they also realize that not all disagreements can be settled. Often there are anger, hard feelings, and threats of violence between parties. In such a situation a "capable person" will know how to judge the weaknesses and strengths of the opponent, and how to make efficient and effective use of all resources available for victory. (Comment on Exodus 18:21)

The commentators also ask the question: What can the description "trustworthy people who spurn ill-gotten gain" mean?

Rabbi Joshua suggests that the phrase describes those "who would never accept money while they were sitting in judgment." Clearly, Joshua has in mind people who refuse to accept bribes or judges who, while hearing a case, refuse to accept any money from anyone for fear that it might appear as though they were accepting bribes.

Rabbi Hanina ben Dosa and his friends argue that the phrase "spurn ill-gotten gain" describes "those who do not put great importance on their own money." According to Rabbi Hanina and his friends, such people are to be respected and revered. They are to be trusted because "if they do not put great importance on their own wealth, then they are not likely to place much importance upon taking the money of others to increase what they possess." (*Mechilta, Amalek,* IV)

> **Rules for judges**
> *Any judge who takes money from the judgments he makes is no longer qualified to be a judge.* (Baba Batra *58b*)
>
> *Any judge who is in the habit of borrowing things from his neighbors is forbidden to act as a judge in a lawsuit involving them.* (Ketubot *105b*)

Nachmanides explains that people who do not place much importance upon their own wealth are likely to be trustworthy because they will not be intimidated by those who offer bribes or threaten their property. Instead, they will say, "Even if this person will burn my property, or destroy it, I will render a just decision." Such people, Nachmanides argues, "love the truth and hate oppression. When they see oppression and violence, they cannot tolerate them. Therefore, they put all their efforts into 'rescuing those who are robbed from those who defraud them.'" (Comment on Exodus 18:21 with quote from Jeremiah 21:12)

Commenting on Jethro's suggestion to Moses that he share the leadership of the community with others, the ancient sage Rabbi Nehemiah taught that "as soon as a person is appointed to leadership, he or she must no longer say: 'I live for my own benefit. I do not care about the community.' For now the whole burden of the community is on his or her shoulders. If a person is seen causing harm to another, or breaking the law, the leader must act to prevent the wrongdoing or be punished." (*Shemot Rabbah* 27:9)

Leadership has always been a serious responsibility. Caring for the safety of a community and preserving its culture and traditions are complex tasks. Jethro appreciated the need to share the burden, and the interpreters of his advice to Moses creatively define for us the qualities of leadership required by Jewish tradition. It is a high ethical standard, which continues to be useful as a measure for excellence in leadership today.

PEREK BET: *What Happened at Mount Sinai?*

The giving of the Ten Commandments at Mount Sinai is one of the most important events in Jewish history. It is also a moment filled with mystery. The Torah reports that, while the people of Israel stood at the bottom of the mountain, they not only saw flames and smoke rising from it but also heard the blare of horns and felt "the whole mountain tremble violently." According to the report, the people were so frightened that they remained below while Aaron and Moses climbed to the top. Afterwards, Moses descended and presented the Ten Commandments to the Israelites.

From that moment until today, Jews have asked the question: "What happened at Mount Sinai?" Is the Torah report an accurate recording of history or a legend in which some kernels of truth are hidden?

How the Torah was given

The Torah was given portion by portion. (Gittin 60a)

The Torah was not given to angels. (Berachot 25a)

When the Torah was given, God showed Moses all the details of Torah and all the innovations that would later be introduced by the rabbis. (Megillah 19b)

Moses received the Torah at Mount Sinai and handed it on to Joshua. Joshua handed it to the elders, and the elders handed it to the prophets. The prophets handed it on to the people of the Great Assembly. (Avot 1:1)

There are many differing views about what happened at Mount Sinai. For instance, Rabbi Yochanan claims that God's voice was divided into seven voices, and the seven voices were further divided into the seventy languages spoken by all the peoples of the world at that time. Other rabbis of Yochanan's time disagree. They claim that God spoke with a single voice.

Rabbi Isaac taught that "the message of all the prophets who were to arise in later generations—people like Isaiah, Jeremiah, Ezekiel, Amos, Micah, and Hosea—was given to Moses with the Torah." Rabbi Simeon ben Lakish agrees. (*Exodus Rabbah, Yitro,* 38:6)

Extending this idea that all the books of the Hebrew Bible were given to Moses at Mount Sinai, some of the ancient rabbis claim that God gave two Torahs to Moses. One they call *Torah Shebichetav,* "Written Torah," comprising the Five Books of Moses: Genesis, Exodus, Leviticus, Numbers, and Deuteronomy. The other they call *Torah Shebealpeh,* "Oral Torah," made up of all the books of the Prophets, the *Midrash Agadah,* the Talmud, and all decisions and explanations of Jewish law by rabbinic scholars through the ages.

Agreeing that two Torahs were given by God to Moses and the Jewish people, other sages explain that God said to Moses: "Write down everything I tell you, for I have made a covenant with Israel." God then dictated the Torah, the Talmud (*Mishnah* and *Gemara*), the Midrash, and even answers to all the questions that leading rabbis in the future would require when they were asked "What did God say to Moses on Mount Sinai?" (*Tanchuma, Ki Tisa,* 58b; *Pesikta Rabbati* 7b)

Clearly, the ancient rabbis have added their own versions of what actually happened between God, Moses, and the people of Israel at Mount Sinai. Their belief that two Torahs were given, including answers to all questions that might arise throughout all time, not only adds to the mystery of whatever occurred at Mount Sinai, but also grants special authority to all subsequent interpreters. This is an important point that should not be overlooked. As a result of their theory of "two Torahs," rabbis now have the right to say that their own interpretations or decisions are "the law according to Moses at Mount Sinai!"

Rambam (Maimonides)

The whole Torah
I believe with perfect faith that the whole Torah, now in our possession, is the same that was given to Moses our teacher. (Moses Maimonides, Principles of Faith, #8)

This view of what happened at Sinai became the most dominant interpretation among Jews from early rabbinic times until the beginning of the nineteenth century. Philosopher Yehudah Halevi, for example, writes that "the people believed that Moses held direct communication with God, that his words were not creations of his own mind. . . . They did not believe Moses had seen a vision in sleep, or that someone had spoken with him between sleeping and waking so that he only heard the words in his imagination but not with his ears, that he saw a phantom and afterwards pretended that God had spoken with him." Halevi concludes by citing proof of God's speaking to Moses at Mount Sinai. He says there was no "trickery" there. "For God's speaking was followed by God's writing. For God wrote the Ten Commandments on two tablets of precious stone and handed them to Moses." (*The Kuzari*, New York, Schocken Books, 1964, pp. 60–61)

Orthodox Jews continue to claim that God gave the Torah, both the Written Law and the Oral Law, to Moses on Mount Sinai. It was a onetime gift or revelation. A complete Torah with everything that Jews would ever need to know was presented to Moses and passed on afterwards from generation to generation as *Torah mi-Sinai*, "Torah from Sinai." As proof for this claim today's Orthodox authorities, like Halevi in his time, cite the Torah text itself. It says, they argue, that "God spoke all these words." Therefore, they conclude that is obviously what happened.

A few Orthodox thinkers, however, disagree. Like Rabbi David Hartman of Jerusalem, they do not believe that the Torah given at Mount Sinai

was "a complete, finished system." Hartman explains that "belief in the giving of the Torah at Sinai does not necessarily imply that the full truth has already been given and that our task is only to unfold what was already present in the fullness of the founding moment of revelation." What happened at Mount Sinai, he says, "gave the community a direction, an arrow pointing toward a future filled with many surprises. . . . The Sinai moment of revelation . . . invites one and all to acquire the competence to explore the terrain and extend the road. It does not require passive obedience and submission to the wisdom of the past." (*A Living Covenant*, The Free Press, New York, 1985, p. 8)

Torah for Reform Jews
Torah results from the relationship between God and the Jewish people. The records of our earliest confrontations are uniquely important to us. Lawgivers and prophets, historians and poets gave us a heritage whose study is a religious imperative and whose practice is our chief means to holiness. Rabbis and teachers, philosophers and mystics, gifted Jews in every age amplified the Torah tradition. For millennia, the creation of Torah has not ceased and Jewish creativity in our time is adding to the chain of tradition. (From "A CCAR Centenary Perspective: New Platform for Reform Judaism," Reform Judaism, November 1976, p. 4)

What the Torah reveals
There is little reason to question that Moses, who led our people in the wilderness and organized them into a nation, also gave them laws. Those laws formed the basis of the various decisions and practices by which the Israelites lived after they entered the Land [of Israel]. In the course of time, those decisions and practices were recorded, compiled, and edited, a process which continued down to the time of Ezra (420 B.C.E.), some centuries after the sojourn in the wilderness. . . . The Torah reveals the working of God in the life of our people in that it articulates the earliest striving of our people to live up to the highest potentialities of human nature. (Mordecai M.

Kaplan, Questions Jews Ask: Reconstructionist Answers, *Reconstructionist Press, New York, 1956, pp. 167–168)*

Hartman's view—what happened at Mount Sinai was an unforgettable "founding moment" in Jewish history but not the conclusion of God's gift of Torah to the people of Israel—is close to the view held by Rabbi Jakob J. Petuchowski, a leading Reform Jewish scholar. In explaining what occurred, Rabbi Petuchowski comments: "The thunders and lightnings at Sinai, as they appear in the biblical narrative, are an echo sounding through the ages of what had happened there. They testify to the fact of Revelation, to the impact it had on the people. But it is only the man of a prosaic mind, the man lacking in imagination, who would read this biblical account as if it were a news bulletin reporting in every detail what has actually happened."

For Petuchowski, the giving of Torah at Sinai was a momentous event in the history of the Jewish people, but it is not to be seen as the moment in which the entire Torah was given to Moses. Quite the contrary. "The laws and commandments of the Torah," Petuchowski writes, "do not all go back to that moment—at any rate, not in the form in which we read them today. They have evolved in the course of the centuries. Different circumstances called forth different responses. Life in the days of the Hebrew monarchy was different from life in the days of the Judges. And the generations engaged in the task of settling in Palestine faced different problems from those that beset the wanderers in the desert. Yet all the different responses to all the different challenges were made from the perspective of the initial commitment at Sinai. . . . The 'giving of the Torah,' therefore, is not confined to the occasion at Sinai. . . . What parts of the Torah really and truly took on their present form already at Sinai we shall probably never know. . . ." (*Ever Since Sinai,* Milwaukee, Wisconsin, Arbit, 1979, pp. 67–80)

Petuchowski's view of an evolving Torah of commandments and their interpretations is shared by Rabbi W. Gunther Plaut who, in considering what happened at Mount Sinai, asks the question: "What precisely was revealed?" Plaut argues that "the traditional answer that the Written and Oral Laws in their entirety were entrusted to Moses at Sinai is unacceptable to me. Only the Written Law then? I rebel equally against this thought." Plaut bases his conviction that the entire Torah tradition evolved over the long course of history on the basis of archeological and historical research.

So what does Plaut believe happened at Mount Sinai? In answering the question, he recalls the explanation of modern philosopher Franz Rosenzweig, who believed that the people did not hear words spoken at Mount Sinai at all. What happened there and what left a lasting impression, Rosenzweig speculates, is that the people encountered God. It was at Sinai that the people began the process of searching out what God wanted of them. From that moment on, the Jewish people has been engaged in a covenant, a partnership with God. "A Jew," Plaut comments, "by the very condition of his Jewishness, pays the continuing price of Sinai. If Jewishness remains his fate, Judaism remains the framework of his native spiritual existence, and God his partner. . . . Each generation should regard itself as standing at Sinai." (*The Case for the Chosen People,* Doubleday, New York, 1965, pp. 90–95)

This conviction that something wonderful and awesome took place between God and the people of Israel at Mount Sinai is also central in the philosophy of Rabbi Abraham Joshua Heschel. He comments that "a cosmic fear enveloped all those who stood at Sinai, a moment more staggering than the heart could feel." Heschel explains: "*What* we see may be an illusion; *that* we see can never be questioned. The thunder and lightning at Sinai may have been merely an impression; but to have suddenly been endowed with the power of seeing the whole world struck with an overwhelming awe of God was a new sort of perception. . . . Only in moments when we are able to share in the spirit of awe that fills the world are we able to understand what happened to Israel at Sinai."

Heschel's conception of the wonder-filled event at Mount Sinai maintains that something extraordinary took place between God, Moses, and the Jewish people. He does not, however, identify what of the Torah might have been revealed at that time. What is significant about the moment at Mount Sinai is that God spoke and the people of Israel responded. "It was both an event in the life of God and an event in the life of humanity. . . . The wonder of Israel's acceptance was as decisive as the wonder of God's expression. . . . Without that power to respond, without the fact that there was a people willing to accept, to hear, the divine command, Sinai would have been impossible." (*God in Search of Man: A Philosophy of Judaism,* Farrar, Straus and Cudahy, New York, 1955, pp. 195–197, 259–260)

So what did happen at Mount Sinai? According to Heschel, God spoke, and the people of Israel listened. They heard the commandments and responded that they would live according to them. The moment was one of the most important in Jewish history because in it God chose and challenged the Jewish people to live according to Torah, and the Jewish people answered, "All that God has spoken we will do!"

We have discovered many theories about what actually happened at Mount Sinai between God, Moses, and the Jewish people. Perhaps two complete Torahs were given by God in that wonder-filled moment. More likely, a God-inspired Moses delivered the Ten Commandments, and later generations, also inspired, wrote down the other commandments that were compiled and edited into what we know today as the Torah. No one can be sure.

All that can be said with certainty is that, whatever happened at Mount Sinai, the people of Israel never forgot the wonder of it. They recalled it as momentous, mysterious, and awesome. They believed that God had spoken and that they had been chosen to become a "treasured people . . .

a holy nation." At Sinai, God and the Jewish people entered into a sacred covenant filled with mitzvot—ethical and ritual responsibilities that not only continue to evolve but give meaning to Jewish lives and justification for the existence of the Jewish people.

QUESTIONS FOR STUDY AND DISCUSSION

1. What problems do the commentators believe Moses created for the Israelites by setting himself up as their only judge? Do these same problems exist today? How might Jethro's advice to Moses help solve contemporary problems?

2. Is "decentralization" really necessary for good management and effective institutions? What are some of the negative aspects of "sharing leadership" rather than relying upon one strong personality? How might some of these problems be overcome? How did Jethro anticipate such problems?

3. Orthodox Rabbi J. David Bleich writes: "The text of the Bible as we have it today—that of the Torah scroll read in the synagogue—is identical in every significant detail with the original scroll of the Torah written by Moses in the wilderness." How do the interpreters in our chapter agree or disagree with Bleich?

4. How has the Oral Torah tradition of evolving new interpretations of Jewish law and practice actually guaranteed the survival of the Written Torah? Is there a parallel between the Constitution of the United States and its interpretation by the courts and the Torah with its long history of rabbinic interpretations?

PARASHAT MISHPATIM
Exodus 21:1–24:18

Parashat Mishpatim presents the *mishpatim*, "rules" or "laws," that govern the ancient Jewish community. The code of law deals with the treatment of slaves; crimes of murder and kidnapping; personal injuries; damages through neglect or theft; offenses against others through lying, witchcraft, idolatry, oppression, unfair business practices; and unjust treatment by judges. This Torah portion also includes a warning against following others to do evil, along with directives to care for the distressed animals of your enemy and to show impartiality in making judgments. Israelites are reminded to demonstrate sensitivity to the stranger because they were strangers in the land of Egypt. Finally, the portion presents rules for the Sabbath, sabbatical year, Pesach, Shavuot, and Sukot. Upon hearing all these laws, Moses gathers the people at Mount Sinai to offer sacrifices and declares, "All the things that God has commanded we will do!"

OUR TARGUM

· 1 ·

While still at Mount Sinai, Moses presents the people with the laws that will govern their community.

About slavery, which was common among all peoples at that time, Moses declares that a slave will be free after seven years and clarifies the rights of slaves and their children in cases of marriage.

Those who deliberately murder are to be put to death. Those who accidentally kill another person are provided a safe place where they can seek judgment. Kidnappers or those who curse their parents are to be put to death.

If a person injures another in a quarrel, payment is to be made for both the cure and loss of work time. If the injured party is a pregnant woman who happens to miscarry, then the one responsible will pay damages agreed to by her husband. If, however, the injury is to the body, the penalty will be "life for life, eye for eye, tooth for tooth, hand for hand, foot for foot, burn for burn, wound for wound, bruise for bruise."

If an ox gores a man or woman, the ox will be stoned or put to death; but, if the ox is known

to be dangerous and its owner has not taken steps to guard it, both the ox and the owner shall be put to death. When a person's ox kills another ox, the owners are to sell the live ox and split the money received for both the live and dead animals. However, if it was known as a dangerous ox and the owner did not guard it, he must restore it with a live ox and keep the dead animal.

If a person digs a pit and neglects to cover it, he is responsible to pay for whatever falls into it and is harmed.

Fines shall be paid for stealing, for allowing one's animals to graze on another's property, for damages related to starting a fire, for misappropriation of property, for animals that are borrowed and die of injuries, and for seducing a virgin.

Witchcraft is forbidden; also forbidden is having sex with an animal or offering sacrifices to other gods.

Jews are forbidden to wrong or oppress the stranger. They are to remember that they were strangers in Egypt.

Widows and orphans must be treated with care. The poor are to be given interest-free loans. If a person gives a garment as guarantee for a loan, that garment must be returned by sunset so the person will be safe from the chill of night.

Spreading rumors, cursing leaders, joining with others to give false testimony, siding with others to do wrong, showing favoritism to rich or poor in courts of law, making false charges, or taking bribes are all forbidden.

Returning an enemy's lost animal or caring for it if it is in distress is considered the right thing to do.

· 2 ·

Serving God includes not only the ethical conduct commanded above but also the celebration of special rituals. The firstborn of the flocks are to be sacrificed to God as thanksgiving offerings. Eating the flesh of beasts killed by other animals is forbidden. The Sabbath is to be observed each week, and a sabbatical year in which the fields are allowed to rest from planting is to be practiced every seventh year. A kid is not to be boiled in its mother's milk.

Three times a year, on Pesach, Shavuot, and Sukot, the people are to celebrate before God.

· 3 ·

God promises the Israelites that, if they will be faithful to these laws and not follow the idolatrous practices of other peoples, God's angel will lead them victoriously into their land.

Moses is instructed to climb Mount Sinai along with Aaron, Nadab and Abihu, and seventy of the elders of Israel. On Sinai, Moses repeats all the laws, and the people answer, "All the things that God has commanded we will do!" Moses offers a sacrifice to mark their commitment to God's laws. Afterwards, he ascends Mount Sinai to receive the stone tablets of the law. He disappears from sight inside a cloud at the top of the mountain, where he remains for forty days and nights.

THEMES

Parashat Mishpatim contains two important themes:

1. The importance of the *mitzvot,* or "commandments."
2. Care for the *ger,* or "stranger."

PEREK ALEF: *Ethical and Ritual Mitzvot*

Parashat Mishpatim begins with the words of God to Moses, "These are the rules that you shall set before them." It then continues with a detailed list of the mitzvot or commandments that the people are to follow. It is a long list containing a wide variety of rules. There are commandments having to do with the treatment of slaves; the consequences of murder, kidnapping, or cursing one's parents; the responsibilities of one person to another in cases of damage or neglect; concern for the stranger and the poor; warnings to judges and witnesses about honesty and fairness in court. There are also mitzvot dealing with the observance of the Sabbath, the sabbatical year, the festivals of Pesach, Shavuot, and Sukot, along with those prohibiting the boiling of a kid in its mother's milk, of worshiping idols, or even mentioning the names of other gods.

While this Torah portion is called *mishpatim,* or "laws," it is not the only portion containing such a list of commandments. Throughout the five books of the Torah we find hundreds of commandments or mitzvot that begin with the words

"You shall . . ." or "You shall not. . . ." Many of these are repetitious. The Ten Commandments, for example, mentioned in Exodus 20:2–14 are repeated in Deuteronomy 5:6–18, and many of the rules recorded in *Mishpatim* are also found scattered throughout Leviticus and Deuteronomy.

Perhaps the first commentator to ask the question "How many mitzvot did God give to the Jewish people at Sinai?" was Rabbi Simlai. Simlai, who taught in both the Land of Israel and Babylonia during the fourth century C.E., declared that Moses received 613 commandments at Sinai. Simlai divided these into two categories: 248 were *mitzvat aseh,* "positive commandments," which begin with the words "You shall . . ." and correspond to the 248 parts of the human body; 365 were *mitzvat lo ta'aseh,* or "negative commandments," which begin with the words "You shall not . . ." and correspond to the number of days in the solar year. The commandments, Simlai emphasized, were meant to guide human beings in the use of all their physical powers during each day of the year. (*Makot* 23b)

Other commentators divide the mitzvot of the Torah into two different categories. Those commandments dealing with the observance of the Sabbath, holidays, diet, and other religious practices are called *mitzvot bein adam le-Makom,* "commandments between the human being and God." Those commandments dealing with the ethical and moral relationships between human beings are labeled *mitzvot bein adam le-chavero,* "commandments between the individual and other human beings. (*Yoma* 85b)

This division of the mitzvot into ritual and ethical categories, however, does not mean that the interpreters of Jewish tradition considered one set of commandments more important than the other. Both were of equal significance, and often commentators point out that the ritual mitzvot lead a person to ethical action. For instance, a part of fulfilling the mitzvah of making a Pesach seder is to invite "all who are hungry to eat."

Despite the fact that early commentators had created two categories of mitzvot and that Rabbi Simlai uses the figure of 613 mitzvot, it is not until the eighth century that the Babylonian teacher Simeon Kairo actually tried to identify which of the hundreds of commandments mentioned in the Torah were to be counted among them. Kairo offers an explanation for each mitzvah, but he also differs with Rabbi Simlai in his count of the positive and negative commandments. Kairo lists 265 positive mitzvot and 348 negative mitzvot. Following Kairo, many other scholars offer their own explanations and lists of what has become known as the *Taryag Mitzvot* (made up of the letters *tav,* representing the numerical value of 400, *resh,* representing the value of 200, *yod,* representing the Ten Commandments, and *gimel,* representing the value of 3).

While most commentators agree with Rabbi Simlai and Kairo that *Taryag Mitzvot,* 613 commandments, were given by God to Moses, there is no agreement about which of the commandments were to be included on the list. Great scholars like Sa'adia Gaon, poets like Solomon ibn Gabirol and Elijah the Elder, as well as philosophers like Hafetz ben Yatzliah—all differ with one another. Each offers a different point of view, underscoring the fact that Jewish tradition was never static and unchanging but always made room for the evolution of new insights and interpretations

of how Jews should practice their faith.

Rambam (Maimonides)

It was the great teacher Moses Maimonides, however, who formulated the most authoritative list of the *Taryag Mitzvot.* Writing in Egypt, in 1168 C.E., at the age of thirty-five, Maimonides created his *Sefer ha-Mitzvot.* Using as his basis both Rabbi Simlai's division of the 613 commandments and the two categories of *mitzvot bein adam le-Makom* and *mitzvot bein adam le-chavero,* Maimonides offers an explanation for each mitzvah and arguments for living one's life according to the discipline of each one. He argues that the commandments are "meant to suppress the human being's natural tendency . . . to correct our moral qualities and to keep straight all our doings." (*Mishneh Torah,* bk. 9, chap. 4)

But Maimonides also realizes that there are many commandments that do not seem to improve human behavior. Such commandments as not eating pork or crab meat or those having to do with sacrifices during Temple times do not seem to have any meaning at all. How shall we explain them? How can we even justify continuing their observance? In response, Maimonides writes: "It is fitting for a person to meditate upon the laws of the holy Torah and to comprehend their full meaning to the extent of his ability. However, a law for which a person finds no reason and understands no cause should not be considered trivial. . . . One should be on guard not to rebel against a commandment decreed for us by God only because the reason for it is not understood. . . ." (Ibid., chap. 8)

Like Maimonides, many other commentators have tried to understand the reasons for the mitzvot of Jewish tradition. While some agree with Maimonides that it is difficult and often impossible to find meanings for all the commandments, most believe that the mitzvot have special purpose and significance.

Reasons for doing mitzvot

Ibn Ezra

The essential reason for the commandments is to make the human heart upright. (Abraham ibn Ezra, *Commentary on Deuteronomy 5:18*)

Each commandment adds holiness to the people of Israel. (Issi ben Akabia, Mechilta, *Exodus 22:30*)

The purpose of the mitzvot is . . . to promote compassion, loving-kindness, and peace in the world.
(*Maimonides,* Yad, Shabbat, *1180, 2, 3*)

The talmudic teacher Rab holds that the commandments were given by God to the Jewish people in order to discipline them. Through their observance they will be refined and strengthened in character and behavior. Another ancient interpreter claimed that it made no difference to God how animals were slaughtered. All the mitzvot having to do with ritual slaughter, and others as well, were meant "to purify the people of Israel." In other words, the commandments were considered exercises, a means of training people to be more sensitive to one another and to the world in which they live.

Another teacher suggests that the commandments are meant to make us more righteous. Each of us has the potential of adding kindness and justice to the world, or of adding to the pain and suffering of others. We should see ourselves as half-good and half-evil. By observing mitzvot we become more just and loving and add to the good in our lives and in the world. (*Genesis Rabbah* 44:1; *Tanchuma, Shemini,* 5; *Pesachim* 50b)

For Rabbi Abahu the commandments were not necessarily just a way of improving human behavior but also a means of preserving the survival of the world! He argues that God created the world as a gardener creates a beautiful orchard. The commandments given to Israel are like instructions given to those chosen to tend the garden. If they are followed, the orchard would survive, flower, and feed all who require its food. (*Exodus Rabbah* 30:9)

Other interpreters believe that the purpose of the mitzvot is only partially connected to improving human behavior or to promoting the survival of the world. The commandments, they maintain, are meant to guarantee entrance into the *olam ha-ba,* "the world to come," or "heaven." "All the mitzvot that the people of Israel do in this world will come and testify in their favor in heaven," says one teacher. Another poetically declares that "each commandment a person does in this world forms a thread of light in heaven, and all of the threads are spun together to form a garment for that person to wear when he dies and goes to heaven." For these commentators, the mitzvot are the means through which one insures a place and "a garment" in the world to come. (*Avodah Zarah* 2a; *Zohar* III:113a)

Sarna

In his study of Exodus, contemporary interpreter Nahum Sarna makes an observation about the unique nature of the ethical and ritual laws found within the Torah and, especially, within *Parashat Mishpatim.* While the laws of other ancient people are divided between secular and religious matters, the Torah presents an "indiscriminate commingling and interweaving . . . of cultic topics and moral imperatives" for which there is "absolutely no analogy." Within the Torah there is no attempt to separate ethical and ritual concerns. They are combined. Ritual commandments and celebrations often lead to ethical action. "The Torah," Sarna writes, "treats life holistically"; everything a person does, secular or religious, is seen as a potential mitzvah meant to serve God and uplift life with meaning. (*Exploring Exodus,* p. 174)

Sarna's view is shared by Rabbi Abraham Joshua Heschel. For Heschel, Judaism is "a science of deeds" or mitzvot that are meant to add the "taste or flavor" of holiness to human life. Being a Jew, Heschel explains, is not just a matter of performing rituals and moral deeds. It is realizing that in the doing of the mitzvah one is seeking to do what God wants of us. It is lighting a lamp before God. It is changing or transforming ourselves by that light so that we "absorb the holiness of deeds." The purpose of the mitzvot, Heschel says, "is to refine man. They were given for the benefit of man: to protect and to ennoble him, to discipline and to inspire him." (*God in Search of Man*, chap. 34)

While for Heschel the doing of mitzvot is meant to elevate us to new levels of holiness, to deepen our sensitivities and our awareness of what God requires of us, for Rabbi Herman E. Schaalman, we are to do the mitzvot "because we are the descendants of those ancestors, the children of those parents who said at Sinai: *Na'aseh ve-nishma*, 'We shall do and we shall hear.' " The commandments, in other words, are our historical inheritance. They are the way in which God continues to speak to us.

Rabbi David Polish agrees. "Mitzvot," he says, "are 'signs' of the covenant, affirmed and reaffirmed through the ages at various turning points in which Jewish existence stood in the balance. . . . Thus the mitzvot around birth, *milah* (circumcision), naming, education, marriage, and death take on added meaning because in each case the individual is made conscious of his own role in Jewish history." For these thinkers, the doing of each commandment is a way of identifying as a Jew. It is a means of linking oneself to the historical covenant of the people of Israel with God. (Simeon J. Maslin, editor, *Gates of Mitzvah*, Central Conference of American Rabbis, New York, 1979, pp. 100–107)

The 613 commandments form the essential core of Jewish practice and tradition. Their blend of both the ethical and ritual is unique. Perhaps that explains why Jews in every age sought to understand the purpose and meaning of the mitzvot and felt compelled to shape their lives and the quality of their community by practicing them.

In ancient times Rabbi Ishmael taught that the commandments were given to the people of Israel so they might "*live* by them." In other words, the mitzvot are for enhancing life, for celebrating it with special meanings, for filling it with deeds of justice, kindness, and peace. Today the challenge of living a mitzvah-filled life continues as the central goal of Jewish tradition.

PEREK BET: *Caring for the Stranger*

Twice in the midst of *Parashat Mishpatim* we find a commandment dealing with care for the *ger*, or "stranger." (Exodus 22:20; 23:9) This emphasis upon the treatment of aliens or foreigners—those who are new to a community or society—is not unusual within the Torah. Early Jewish tradition emphasizes the pain of the outsider and seeks solutions to it. Commandments calling for sensitivity and justice for the *ger* are found in thirty-six different places within the Torah, more than the mention of any other mitzvah.

Even the language of the commandments dealing with the *ger* is special. At times we are given a positive formulation such as "you shall love the stranger . . ."; in other places, a negative formulation such as "you shall not oppress the stranger. . . ." Treatment of the stranger is one of those rare rules that is listed not only among the 248 *mitzvat aseh* but also among the 365 *mitzvat lo ta'aseh*. Frequently, the mitzvah also includes the reminder that "you were strangers in the land of Egypt."

Many commentators note this unique emphasis of the Torah upon justice for the stranger and ask: "Why all these warnings? Why all this attention to the *ger*?"

Early rabbinic interpreters offer a variety of opinions. Many understand that the word *ger* does not mean only "stranger." They point out that it also translates as "convert." For instance, we are told that "God so loves *gerim*, or 'converts,' that God postponed Abraham's circumcision until he was ninety so future converts would know one can become a Jew at any age." Another sage suggests that Jews are commanded to love converts because the Torah uses similar descriptions for both Jews and *gerim*. Both are called "servants," "ministers at the altar," "friends of God." Even the notion of a covenant with God is mentioned in connection with both.

Concern for the convert
Should a convert come to study Torah, one may not say to him or her, "How can one who has eaten forbidden foods have the presumption to study God's Torah?" (Baba Metzia 58b)

Those who bring others near to Judaism by warmly welcoming them as converts are considered by God as if they have given birth to them. (Bereshit Rabbah)

The treatment of converts is a sensitive matter. Entering a new group, whether religious or secular, is always frightening. One is not sure of what to expect and, therefore, is uncertain and uncomfortable. The welcome given by a family or group to a newcomer can make the difference between feeling accepted or rejected. Perhaps that is why Jewish tradition emphasizes reaching out with friendship to the *ger* to make certain that he or she is "at home" within the Jewish community.

For many early rabbinic interpreters, all this concern for the feelings of the *ger* meant that Jews had a special obligation to treat converts fairly, never to take advantage of them, insult them about their past, or find fault with them. "Converts," the rabbis declare, "are beloved by God." (*Mechilta, Nezikin,* 18, on Exodus 22:20)

Later commentators not only note that Jews must welcome and appreciate converts but also treat any *ger* justly. They point out that the Torah cautions us not to oppress the *ger* because "you know the feelings of the stranger, having yourselves been strangers in the land of Egypt." This warning, say these teachers, raises significant questions: Do memories of the past, especially a painful past, teach us to be more sensitive to the feelings of others? Can those who recall being abused or oppressed prevent themselves from abusing or oppressing others?

Rashi

In answer to these questions, there is a serious division of opinion among interpreters. For example, Rashi's view is that for many people memories of cruel treatment do not teach sensitivity and that what the Torah really meant by its warning was that, if you oppressed the *ger,* he or she might answer by reminding you of your own lowly origins. You might be told, "Don't try to elevate yourself by demeaning me. After all, you also come from strangers. Your people were *gerim* in Egypt!"

On the other hand, Rashi does allow for those who might be more enlightened and made aware of the suffering of the stranger through their study of Jewish history and their understanding of how their people were persecuted in Egypt. Commenting on the Torah's observation, "you know the feelings of the stranger," Rashi suggests that because you have been in pain "you know how painful it is for him when you oppress him." (Comment on Exodus 22:20; 23:9)

Sixteenth-century commentator Moshe ben Alshekh, who spent most of his life in Safed, amplifies Rashi's view with his own. He maintains that the Torah's linkage of the warning about "knowing the feelings of the stranger" with the reminder that "you were strangers in Egypt" is deliberate. The Torah, Alshekh claims, teaches us not to oppress the stranger by noting our own treatment by God. "When you lived in Egypt," Alshekh explains, "you worshiped idols. Afterwards you accepted the Torah. Just as God did not look down on you for having worshiped idols and [thus] decide not to give you the Torah, so you must not look down upon the stranger." Clearly, it is Alshekh's conviction that Jews who recall their origins before being given the Torah will be more sensitive to the feelings of strangers and will treat them with more understanding and fairness. (Comment on Exodus 22:20)

Ramban (Nachmanides)

Nachmanides presents a differing point of view. For him the linkage between the commandment not to oppress the stranger and the observation "for you know the feelings of the stranger, having yourselves been strangers in the land of Egypt" is not simply a reminder about "common origins."

It is a warning about how God works in history on behalf of the oppressed.

Nachmanides argues that God speaks through the words of Torah, saying to the people: "You should not think that the stranger has no one to save him from the violence or oppression of your hands. On the contrary, you should know that, when you were strangers in Egypt, I saw the oppression with which the Egyptians were persecuting you and I brought punishment upon them. For I see the sufferings that are inflicted by evildoers on people and the tears of the oppressed who have none to comfort them. And I free every person from hands of violence. Therefore, do not afflict the stranger, thinking there is no one to save him. For he will be helped more than any other person!" (Comment on Exodus 22:20 and 23:9)

Nachmanides' view is that the Torah's reminder to the Jewish people that "you were strangers in the land of Egypt" is not just for the purpose of recollecting their painful status as persecuted people. It is also a lesson about whose side God takes in situations of oppression. God, Nachmanides teaches, stands by the persecuted. God comforts and heals the wounds of the abused, and God refuses to rest until, like the enslaved Israelites, they are free. The recollection of what God did for the Israelites in Egypt is meant to encourage Jews, who are God's partners, to help the oppressed.

Leibowitz

Differing with Nachmanides, modern commentator Nehama Leibowitz looks carefully at the Torah text and questions whether the memory of persecution really prevents one from becoming a persecutor. For the enlightened, she argues, such a recollection of history may be sufficient. It may lead to sensitivity and to a genuine concern for the strangers. For others, however, this is not the case. "The hate, persecution, and shame the individual or community experiences in the past do not act as a deterrent, preventing them from adopting the same attitude to those entrusted to their power, later on."

> **On abuse and oppression**
> *Enlarging upon her observation, Leibowitz writes, "The fact that 'you were strangers in the land of Egypt' is certainly no adequate motivation for not oppressing or troubling the stranger. On the contrary, how often do we find that the slave or exile who gains power and freedom, or anyone who harbors the memory of suffering to himself or his family, finds compensation for his former sufferings by giving free rein to his tyrannical instincts when he has the opportunity to seize power over others?"* (Studies in Shemot, p. 384)

Contemporary studies of abuse in marriage, or by parents or teachers, demonstrate the correctness of Leibowitz's observation. Tragically, patterns of battering and harassment often repeat from generation to generation. Those who are victimized and oppressed often turn their frustration and anger upon others and become brutal oppressors themselves.

What is true about physical abuse is also the case with "substance" abuse. Alcoholics, smokers, and drug addicts have often inherited their "habit" from parents or other adults in their environment. Having suffered from the results of neglect and even violence by substance abusers or having seen the illness and destructive results of narcotics, drinking, and smoking does not necessarily lead to a rejection of them. More often than not the cycle of violence to oneself and others continues. Victims take up the "habit," and the tragedy becomes a bitter cycle.

The answer to these cycles of abuse, whether of "substances" or of strangers, requires two different kinds of education, according to Leibowitz. The first is to appeal to the intellect and to teach people sensitivity by allowing them to learn the harmful effects of violence through a study of history. However, many people, Leibowitz maintains, are incapable of learning such a lesson. They require a second form of education. Memories of their own suffering do not act as a deterrent to their oppression of others. The only way to break the cycle of violence, argues Leibowitz, is by shocking such people with the realization that they will pay a high price for taking advantage of the stranger or for abusing substances. Only then will they change their patterns of behavior.

As we have seen, many interpreters understand that the Torah identifies the *ger,* or "stranger," as a *convert* to Judaism. Yet not all commentators adopt this rather narrow reading of the Torah text. For many Jewish teachers through the ages, the word *ger* meant any stranger, anyone new to the community, whether Jew or non-Jew.

Protecting the ger

Ger *was the term applied to the resident non-Israelite who could no longer count on the protection of his erstwhile tribe or society. . . . The ger was to be given every consideration, and care must be taken that not only his rights but his feelings as well were safeguarded. He must never be shamed. . . .* (Plaut, editor, The Torah: A Modern Commentary, *p. 582*)

It is forbidden to wrong or oppress the stranger . . . the reason given is purely ethical: you yourselves suffered as sojourners in a strange land, and you know the soul of the sojourner; therefore, take heed not to embitter the life of the sojourner living in your midst just as you did not wish the Egyptians to embitter your lives when you dwelt among them. (Umberto Cassuto, comment on Exodus 22:20 and 23:9)

Hirsch

Protecting the stranger, as Leibowitz notes, is a matter of high ethical priority within Jewish tradition. More is at stake, however, than the feelings or rights of the alien. Rabbi Samson Raphael Hirsch makes this clear in his comment that "the treatment given to strangers is always the surest standard by which to measure the respect for human rights and the humanitarianism that prevails in any state." For that reason, Hirsch argues, the Torah places great emphasis upon assuring justice and charity for the alien and protection from oppression and harassment. "The granting of un-restricted rights of living, working, and earning a livelihood to aliens is demanded from the community or nation."

For Hirsch, however, the treatment of the stranger is also a special test of living ethically as a Jew. Because of their history of persecution, Jews should be more sensitive to the suffering of foreigners or strangers. "Though others may discriminate against the Jew," Hirsch says, "you must not fail to recognize every stranger as a human being! . . . show that you are a Jew—hold the stranger sacred." (Comment on Exodus 23:9; also in *Horeb: A Philosophy of Jewish Laws and Observances,* translated by I. Grunfeld, Soncino Press, New York, Fourth edition, 1981, pp. 254–256)

Rabbi Leo Baeck agrees with Hirsch. For him, as well, treatment of the stranger is a test of the creative power of Jewish teachings in the lives of Jews. Baeck points out that within the Torah the word *ger* takes on a special meaning because all human beings are called "strangers," "pilgrims," or "aliens." We are told that God says, ". . . the land is Mine; for you are strangers and settlers with Me." (Leviticus 25:23) That statement, Baeck argues, reminds us that no people is superior to any other, no person is more sacred than any other. We are all strangers and must care for one another. (*The Essence of Judaism,* Schocken Books, New York, 1948, pp. 197–198)

As we have noted, Jewish tradition emphasizes just treatment for the *ger,* or "stranger." For some commentators that meant special concern and sensitivity for converts to Judaism. Many others understood that the term *"ger"* meant any stranger. Jews were commanded by God to protect the rights and feelings of the alien, not only because such treatment was just, but also because they themselves had been persecuted strangers in Egypt and throughout their history. The Torah's attitude toward the *ger* is perhaps best summed up in the commandment "You shall love the stranger as yourself." (Leviticus 19:34)

QUESTIONS FOR STUDY AND DISCUSSION

1. How do the commentators see the relationship between ethical and ritual mitzvot? How

would you describe the purpose of mitzvot in Jewish life?

2. In the *Centenary Perspective* of Reform Judaism, adopted in 1976 by the Central Conference of American Rabbis, it is stated that "the past century has taught us that the claims made upon us may begin with our ethical obligations but they extend to many other aspects of Jewish living, including: creating a Jewish home centered on family devotion; lifelong study; private prayer and public worship; daily religious observance; keeping the Sabbath and the holy days; celebrating the major events of life; involvement with the synagogue and community; and other activities that promote the survival of the Jewish people and enhance its existence." Is it true that the doing of mitzvot guarantees the survival of Jews and Judaism?

3. What have "strangers" and "converts" in common, justifying that, in Hebrew, both are called *gerim*?

4. Do you agree or disagree that the repetition of the reminder that Jews were strangers in Egypt has tended to teach greater sensitivity for the plight of the stranger and the alienated? How do you create conditions of just treatment for strangers?

PARASHAT TERUMAH
Exodus 25:1–27:19

Parashat Terumah is about building the first sanctuary, or the Tabernacle. The Israelites are still wandering through the Sinai desert. Moses instructs each person to bring a *terumah,* or "donation," "gift," for the building of the sanctuary. The contributions may be of gold, silver, and copper; of blue, purple, and crimson yarns, fine linen, goats' hair; tanned ram skins, dolphin skins, and acacia wood; oil for lighting, spices for the anointing oil and for the aromatic incense; lapis lazuli and other precious stones for the *ephod* and breastplate. Concerning the Tabernacle, God says to Moses, "And let them make Me a sanctuary that I may dwell among them." Instructions for the architecture of the sanctuary are detailed. The ark and poles for carrying it shall be made of acacia wood overlaid with gold. Two gold cherubim with large wings are to be placed above the ark, facing each other. A table of acacia wood overlaid with gold is to be made, along with special bowls and jars for offering sacrifices. Moses is also instructed to build a *menorah,* or "lampstand," of pure hammered gold to hold seven lamps. As for the sanctuary itself, Moses is given details of its size, the material to be used in its construction, and instructions on how to assemble it.

OUR TARGUM

· 1 ·

While still on Mount Sinai after receiving the Ten Commandments, Moses is also given instructions for building the sanctuary in which the people will worship God during their wanderings through the desert. God tells him to ask each Israelite to bring a *terumah,* or "gift," "contribution," for the construction. God says to Moses, "And let them make Me a *mikdash* ["sanctuary"] that I may dwell among them."

· 2 ·

Details for the creation of each aspect of the sanctuary are given to Moses.

The ark and two poles for carrying it are to be of acacia wood overlaid with gold. A cover of gold is also to be made for it, along with two winged gold cherubim who are to be placed facing each other above the ark. "There I will meet with you, and I will speak to you . . . and I will command you concerning the Israelite people," God tells Moses.

· 3 ·

Moses also receives instructions about making a table and poles to carry it. They are to be made of acacia wood overlaid with gold. Special bowls, ladles, jars, and jugs are to be fashioned to hold the liquids for offerings to God.

Along with the table and its poles, other furnishings for inside the sanctuary include a seven-branched lampstand, or *menorah*. There are to be three branches on each side of its center. Each branch will contain three cups shaped like almond-blossoms with calyx and petals. The center lampstand is to contain four cups shaped like almond-blossoms. Moses is told, "Note well, and follow the patterns. . . ."

· 4 ·

Moses is also given an architectural plan and instructions for the materials to be used in creating the Tabernacle. Included are the sizes for the acacia wood planks for the walls, the number of cloths of goats' hair for coverings, and the number of sockets for attaching the planks and cloths. A curtain of blue, purple, and crimson yarns and fine twisted linen with the design of cherubim worked into it is to cover the ark.

· 5 ·

The plan of the altar, which will be made of acacia wood, calls for a horn overlaid with copper on each of its four corners. Pails, scrapers, basins, flesh hooks, and fire pans—all for use when sacrifices are offered—are also to be made of copper. Poles of acacia wood overlaid with copper are to be used in carrying the altar when it is moved.

A description of the Tabernacle's inside furnishings includes hangings of fine twisted linen, silver-banded posts, copper pegs, and sockets.

THEMES

Parashat Terumah contains two important themes:

1. The function of the *mikdash,* or "sanctuary," in Jewish tradition.
2. The Torah's emphasis upon the "details" of the sanctuary.

PEREK ALEF: *The Sanctuary in Jewish Tradition*

Before the creation of the first *mikdash,* or "sanctuary," the Hebrews worshiped God on hilltops, beside streams, or wherever they felt moved to pray. Abraham and Isaac traveled to Mount Moriah; Jacob encountered God in a lonely place on the desert and near the river Jabbok; Moses met God through an ordinary bush and at the top of Mount Sinai. Now, after their liberation from Egypt and the acceptance of the laws given to them at Mount Sinai, the people are commanded to build a sanctuary.

The sanctuary is to contain the Ark of the Covenant with its sacred stones on which the Ten Commandments are inscribed. It is to be placed in the Holy of Holies chamber inside the inner tabernacle. The opening of the Holy of Holies chamber is to be covered by a curtain. Outside the curtain is a special altar for incense, a table for the shew bread, and a golden *menorah,* or "lampstand." In front of the inner tabernacle is another curtain, outside of which are the laver and an altar for burnt offerings. Clearly, the sanctuary is designed for offering sacrifices and prayers to God.

Some scholars believe that the description of the *mikdash* did not belong to the original Torah but was added to the story of the Exodus by later priests who wanted to justify the existence of the

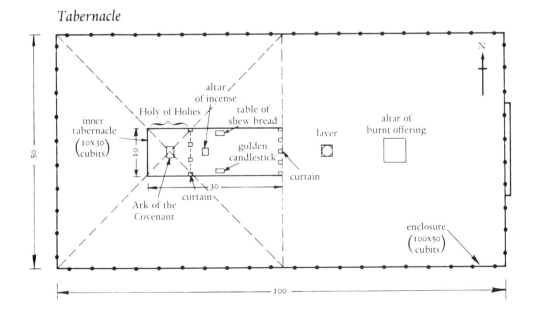

Tabernacle

Temple and priesthood in Jerusalem. To prove their point, these critics argue that many of the materials mentioned in the Torah's description of the *mikdash* were not available to the ancient Israelites in the Sinai desert.

Other scholars disagree, maintaining that the *mikdash* was one of the earliest of all Jewish institutions, though later authors of the Torah may have exaggerated about how it was built or about the materials used in its construction. H. M. Orlinsky explains: "Acacia wood—cedar, cyprus, or olive was later used in Canaan—ramskins, lambskins, cloths of goats' hair, and the like are all manifestations of nomadic existence." (Plaut, *The Torah: A Modern Commentary,* p. 599)

While we may never be able to prove when the *mikdash,* or the first Jewish sanctuary, came into existence, the Torah does seek to clarify its purpose. Moses is instructed by God to tell the people, "And let them make Me a sanctuary that I may dwell among them."

What do these words really mean? Is it possible God was telling the people that, without a sanctuary, a building, a place for the Ark of the Covenant, or altars for sacrifice, they would not sense the presence of God in their lives? Are sanctuaries necessary for worship, for finding God? Does God require a building in order to "dwell" among human beings?

Where does God dwell?
O God, where shall I find You?
All hidden and exalted is Your place;
And where shall I not find You?
Full of Your glory is the infinite space. (*Yehudah Halevi*)

There is no place without God. (*Sa'adia ben Joseph Ha-Gaon*)

Wherever you find a human footprint, there God is before you. (Mechilta *to Exodus 17:6*)

The Kobriner Rabbi turned to his Chasidim and said: "Do you know where God is?" Then he took a piece of bread, showed it to them, and continued: "God is in this piece of bread. With- *out God's nurturing power in all nature, this piece of bread would have no existence."*

"Where is the dwelling of God?" This was the question with which Rabbi Mendel of Kotzk surprised a number of learned people who happened to be visiting him. They laughed at him: "What a thing to ask! Is not the whole world full of God's glory!" Then he answered his own question: "God dwells wherever we let God in." (Martin Buber, Tales of the Hasidim: The Later Masters, *Schocken Books, New York, 1961, p. 277*)

Jewish tradition teaches that we experience God in many ways. God is to be found in the beauty and mystery of nature, in the love and friendship we share with others, in the spiritual impact of a ritual or celebration, and in the work done to promote justice, generosity, and peace. There is no exclusive "place" for God. There are many places where God dwells. King Solomon, who built the first Temple in Jerusalem, admitted that God, who could not be contained by all the heavens, could certainly not be limited to "this house that I have built!" (I Kings 8:27)

If that is so, if no *mikdash,* or "sanctuary," can be the exclusive place of God, then what can the Torah mean when it reports that God said to Moses, "Make Me a sanctuary that I may dwell among them"? What is the purpose or the function of the sanctuary in Jewish tradition?

The early rabbis offer an answer through an imaginary conversation between God and the people of Israel. They picture the people explaining to God that all human rulers have beautiful palaces, rooms where offerings are brought to them and where the people can demonstrate their loyalty and love. The people say to God, "Shouldn't You, our Ruler, have such a palace?" And, according to the rabbis, God responds, "My children, I have no need for such a place. After all, I do not eat or drink. Obviously, however, you have a need for such a place. It will help you experience Me. For that reason, build a sanctuary and I will dwell in your midst."

What the early rabbis sensed was our human need for a place of worship, a special space set aside for meditation and prayer. It is the nature of human beings to uplift the importance of ordinary buildings by assigning them unique functions and names. Out of bricks and mortar, steel and poured concrete, we create and decorate structures we call "capitals," "museums," "concert halls," theaters," and "courts." Sometimes we add to their importance by linking to them the names of popular personalities or donors.

Like capitals, museums, or concert halls, religious sanctuaries serve a significant function. They are the unique spaces we set aside for our "meetings" with God through prayer, study, and sharing with others. Does that mean that they are the only places where "God dwells"? Of course not. Just as we enjoy music and art in a variety of places outside of concert halls and museums, we can pray and encounter God in many different places as well.

We create religious sanctuaries, however, out of our need for beautiful and inspiring environments where we can find moments for reflection, comfort, and hope in difficult times, direction and wisdom when we face moral choices, and beautiful rituals with which to celebrate the most important moments of our lives. Our sanctuaries provide us with spaces where we can share with others and sense the support and enthusiasm of a community. As the early rabbis taught, our sanctuaries answer our human and spiritual needs.

Commentator Umberto Cassuto sees another purpose in the creation of the sanctuary. He points out that the people of Israel experienced God in a powerful way at Mount Sinai. They heard the Ten Commandments and felt themselves connected to God in a unique covenant. "But once they set out on their journey [away from Mount Sinai]," says Cassuto, "it seemed to them as though the link had been broken, unless there was in their midst a tangible symbol of God's presence among them."

In other words, the *mishkan* was a tangible, visible assurance of the bond that God had forged with the people of Israel at Mount Sinai. While they would journey to distant places from that wonderful mountain where God addressed them, their sanctuaries with their arks and eternal lights would be a constant reminder that "God dwelled among them." Every synagogue sanctuary is an extension of Mount Sinai. (*A Commentary on the Book of Exodus*, p. 319)

Why a "sanctuary"?

Peli

The mikdash *was not a dwelling place for God but a place set aside for people to come and experience more intensely the in-dwelling presence of God in the world at large. It represented a way of re-creating the universe in the center of which is God. (Pinchas H. Peli, "Torah Today,"* in the Jerusalem Post, *February 20, 1988)*

Our sages believed that the building of holy palaces, the exercise of piety, prepares the heart for godliness. People who build sanctuaries are more likely to feel the spirit of holiness, the mood of sanctity. (Jacob J. Weinstein, The Place of Understanding, *Bloch Publishing Company, New York, 1959, p. 58)*

If you would know the mystic source from where
Your persecuted people facing slaughter drew
In evil days the strength and fortitude
To meet grim death with joy, and bare the neck
To every sharpened blade and lifted ax . . .
If you would know the bosom where streamed
Your people's tears, its heart and soul and gall . . .
If you would know the fortress where
Your ancestors carried to a safe haven
Their Torah scrolls,
The sacred treasure of their yearning souls . . .
If you would know the shelter which preserved
Immaculate, your people's spirit . . .
Then go to the house of prayer. . . . (Chaim Nachman Bialik)

Hirsch

Rabbi Samson Raphael Hirsch offers another view of the Torah's command "And let them make Me a sanctuary that I may dwell among them." For Hirsch, the *mikdash* symbolizes the unique relationship between the Jewish people and God. The people create the sanctuary when they seek to shape their lives with the commandments of Torah. And the direct result of fulfilling all the commandments is that God's "protecting and blessing-giving presence" is experienced in their "private and national lives." The sanctuary is much more than a building. It is a symbol reminding Jews of their covenant relationship to God. If they observe the mitzvot of their contract with God, then their "reward" will be the joy of knowing that God dwells among them. (Commentary to Exodus 25:8)

Rabbi Morris Adler differs from Samson Raphael Hirsch in his discussion of the sanctuary. Rather than seeing it as a symbol, Adler emphasizes its important functions. He identifies four "tasks" for the ancient *mikdash* and for the modern synagogue.

The first is "to conserve, to guard against oblivion the great insights and concepts that have been developed" by human beings through the ages. Adler points out that new generations often destroy their past, and it is the role of religion to preserve "the accumulation of insights" of human wisdom. Our religious sanctuaries proclaim, "Do not destroy the ancient landmarks."

The second task of the sanctuary "is to scrutinize, to criticize, to evaluate." Religious sanctuaries, Adler argues, must constantly present "an ethical code that does not surrender to expediency, that does not give way to hysteria, that sees the problems of our time from the perspective of a great background of experience and faith."

The third function of the sanctuary is "to enlarge the lives of people." Religion seeks to tell people, "Do not starve yourself by limiting yourself only to the struggle for a livelihood. Do not become the prisoner of your own ego."

Finally, Adler says that "the Jewish sanctuary seeks to remind the Jewish community that what keeps Jews together is not a common sorrow . . . is not charity, not defense, but common history, common culture, and common hope." (*The Voice Still Speaks,* Bloch Publishing Company, New York, 1969, pp. 175–178)

Throughout the ages, the *mikdash,* or "temple," "synagogue," has functioned as a *bet tefilah,* "a house of prayer," a *bet midrash,* "a house of study," and a *bet knesset,* a "house of meeting." It has been the sacred space where Jews have worshiped and celebrated together, educated themselves and new generations, and met to face new challenges. It is the meeting place between God and the Jewish people. Today, the synagogue, like the ancient *mikdash,* remains the most significant institution of Jewish life; it is the guarantor of Jewish tradition and survival.

PEREK BET: *"Exactly as I Show You . . . So Shall You Make It"*

Following the commandment to construct the *mikdash,* the Torah presents several chapters containing hundreds of detailed descriptions of every object and material to be used in the building of the ancient sanctuary. The text reads like a combination architect's blue print and decorator's design.

For example, we read that the sanctuary planks should be made of acacia wood, each plank ten cubits in length and a cubit and a half in width. We are informed that there should be twenty planks on both the north and south sides and six on the front and rear sides. Each plank is to have two silver sockets and two tenons overlaid with gold.

The same attention to details is given to the creation of the curtain, the ark, the altar, and all other aspects of the sanctuary. With each description we are given specific measurements, colors, instructions about the various materials to be used, and how the ancient tent is to be fastened together.

Why? Why all this attention to details? Why does the Torah present God as concerned about every single item used in the creation of the sanctuary?

Sarna

Bible scholar Nahum Sarna explains that the Torah's detailed description of the sanctuary "belongs to a common Near Eastern genre of temple building reports." In other words, such descriptions were common among ancient peoples, who believed that God ordered every feature and design of their sacred shrines. So what we have here is not surprising or even special. It is similar to other temple plans passed on within the religions and cultures of the Middle East.

Abravanel

Many other commentators disagree. Through the ages, various rabbinic scholars saw in the details of the sanctuary many different meanings. Don Isaac Abravanel, for example, maintains that the entire sanctuary and each of its parts have "allegorical meaning." When the Torah speaks about the *mikdash*, it is not only describing a sacred building in which worship takes place but it also has in mind the body of each human being. That is to say, each human being is a sacred sanctuary. Each detail, Abravanel explains, teaches an ethical lesson meant to guide people in their relationships with one another and with God.

As an example of his allegorical explanation, Abravanel points out that the *menorah* is made of "pure gold," teaching the truth that one must be careful of impure ideas. He also suggests that the *menorah* is to be placed so that it faces the Holy of Holies. The placement reminds us that true wisdom is always in harmony with the teachings of Torah.

Agreeing with Abravanel's allegorical approach, other commentators provide a number of fascinating insights about the meanings of the various sanctuary details.

Moshe ben Adrianopolis Alshekh compares the *menorah* to the "human soul," which also provides light. Just as the *menorah* is made of "beaten gold,"

so human beings "can only become a lamp of pure gold through the cleansing and refining effect of suffering." When one learns humility—not to answer back with anger and insults but rather with kind, pure, caring words—then one becomes like the *menorah*, full of light for others.

Describing the ark, the Torah informs us that it was to be overlaid with gold on the outside and inside. Why, some teachers ask, should gold, which would not be seen, be used inside? Is that not a waste of precious metal?

In answer, early Jewish teachers suggest the principle *tocho kevaro*, "the outside must match the inside." As Rabbi Hillel Silverman comments: "This is the true meaning of integrity. A person's exterior—words and deeds—must reflect his inner being and character. We must mean what we say, and say what we mean." (*From Week to Week*, p. 74)

Basing his own comments on those of both Rashi and Nachmanides, Joseph of Piavinitz seeks to explain why the description for the cherubim, the two angel-like creatures placed above the ark, includes the command "They shall face each other. . . ." Again, his interpretation is allegorical. The cherubim are symbols for how God wants human beings to care about one another. They are to make an effort to see one another, to understand what brings pain or joy into one another's lives. It is forbidden to turn away, to avoid others, to practice indifference. Like the cherubim, human beings are meant to serve God by keeping their eyes upon the needs of others.

Samson Raphael Hirsch offers another view. He observes that the description of the ark includes details about the poles used to carry it from one place to another. The Torah says, "The poles shall not be removed." "Why not?" asks Hirsch. After all, nothing is said about removing the carrying poles for the table and lampstand of the sanctuary. Why are the poles of the ark singled out for such prohibition?

"The poles of the ark symbolize . . . the mission of the ark and what it housed," says Hirsch. The message is that "the Torah is not parochial, not restricted to the particular country where the Temple is situated." It is always ready to move with the people, to be their guide, their source of wisdom and faith. Since no one knows when it will be necessary to move, or where the Torah's teachings will be required, the poles of the ark must always be in place so that it can be carried to where it is needed. (Commentary on Exodus 27:7)

Clearly, Jewish commentators found many significant lessons in the Torah's detailed descriptions of the *mikdash*. For many of them, the Torah offered more than quaint architectural plans or decorative descriptions. Each detail had hidden meaning, and like creative detectives they sought to uncover and reveal them. Sometimes they focused attention on the entire sanctuary, at other times on a small feature.

More often, however, they combined approaches, pointing out that the sanctuary symbolizes all our human achievements. In its details are all the small, seemingly unimportant, efforts we make on the road to our successes. No real achievement is possible without attention to detail. The musician must practice note after note, day after day, to play with excellence. The athlete must stretch, run, and lift weights to compete successfully. Students must gather facts one by one, detail after detail, to master a subject. Genuine accomplishments, like magnificent sanctuaries, are the products of hard work, deed after deed, and careful attention to every detail.

So why does the Torah spend so many chapters describing the building of the *mikdash*? Modern biblical scholars see nothing special about the details of these chapters in Exodus. They say they are very much like other descriptions of temples found in ancient Middle Eastern literature. Rabbinic commentators, however, look upon the Torah's portrait of the *mikdash* as a sacred work of art. Multiple meanings and messages are present in each detail. The challenge to the student of Torah, like to the student of great art, is to appreciate the beauty and mystery of the object.

QUESTIONS FOR STUDY AND DISCUSSION

1. Some historians believe that the synagogue was the most important institution in the survival of the Jewish people. What other institutions helped to preserve Jewish life? What important place does today's synagogue play in guaranteeing the survival of Jewish tradition and culture?

2. Given our discussion of the sanctuary, what can we mean when we say that "God dwells in this place"?

3. As we have seen, many commentators interpret the description of the sanctuary and its details in a symbolic way. Review "Our Targum." What "symbolic" interpretations and lessons come to mind?

PARASHAT TETZAVEH
Exodus 27:20–30:10

Parashat Tetzaveh continues the description of the *mikdash,* begun in the previous Torah portion. It includes commandments to create a *ner tamid,* "a constantly burning light," above the sanctuary ark and to appoint Aaron and his sons as priests to manage the sacrifices offered in the sanctuary. Also included are detailed instructions about clothing for Aaron. He is to wear an *ephod,* a breastpiece, a robe, a fringed tunic, a headdress, and a sash. Aaron's ceremony of ordination as priest is described, along with instructions for the slaughtering of the offerings. The portion concludes with directions for building an altar for burning incense before the ark.

OUR TARGUM

·1·

The Israelites are commanded by God to bring clear oil of beaten olives to the sanctuary and to use it for the *ner tamid,* or "continually burning light." Aaron and his sons are to keep the light over the ark burning continually from evening to morning.

·2·

Aaron and his sons, Nadab and Abihu, Eleazar and Ithamar, are appointed priests with the responsibility for managing all the sacrifices and offerings of the community at the *mikdash.* Aaron is to wear eight specially decorated garments crafted by skilled artists: (1) the *ephod,* an apron of gold, of blue, purple, and scarlet yarns, and fine linen, with a belt around the middle and two shoulder straps, each containing a lazuli stone inscribed with six names of the twelve sons of Jacob; (2) the breastplate of judgment, a square-shaped container decorated on the front with four rows of precious stones, each framed and mounted in gold, and each bearing a name of the twelve sons of Jacob. The breastplate is attached by gold chains to the shoulder straps of the *ephod;* (3) the Urim and Thummim, a small box through which it was believed God spoke; it was worn by the priest inside the breastplate of judgment; (4) the blue robe embroidered with a hem of pomegranates of blue, purple, and crimson yarns with bells of

gold; (5) the gold plate engraved with the words "Holy to the Lord" and attached to Aaron's headdress so that it hung on his forehead; (6) a fringed linen tunic; (7) a linen headdress; and (8) an embroidered sash.

Aaron's sons are to wear tunics, pants, sashes, and turbans for dignity and beauty.

· 3 ·

The ceremony of consecrating Aaron as priest includes leading him to the *mikdash*, bathing him and dressing him in his special garments, and pouring anointing oil over his head. His sons are also brought forward and dressed in their priestly garments.

A bull is brought forward for slaughtering. Aaron and his sons lay their hands upon its head. After it is slaughtered, some of its blood is painted on the horns of the altar; the rest is poured at the base. The fat of its entrails, the lobe above the liver, and the two kidneys are burnt on the altar; the rest of its flesh is put into a fire outside the borders of the camp. Following the sacrifice of the bull, rams are slaughtered; Aaron and his sons are sprinkled with anointing oil and the blood of a ram. At one point in the ceremony, Aaron and his sons hold pieces of the sacrificed ram in one hand, and flat loaves of bread, cakes of oil bread, and wafers in the other hand. They wave them before God as an offering. The ram's flesh is then boiled and eaten by Aaron and his sons.

The ceremony of ordination lasts seven days. On each day the sacrifices are repeated in order to purify the priests and the altar. At the end of Aaron's life, his priestly garments and duties are to pass on to his sons.

The priests and sacrifices in the *mikdash* remind the people that God is in their midst and that God brought them out of the land of Egypt to abide among them as their God.

·4·

An acacia altar, overlaid with gold, decorated with horns, and carried by acacia wood poles also overlaid with gold, is to be placed in front of the curtain before the ark. Aaron is commanded to burn incense on this altar every morning and evening at the time he extinguishes and kindles the lights. Once a year, he is to consecrate the altar by painting the horns with the blood of a sin offering.

THEMES

Parashat Tetzaveh contains two important themes:

1. The meaning of the *ner tamid,* or "continually burning light."
2. The significance of the priestly dress of Aaron and his sons.

PEREK ALEF: *What Is the Ner Tamid?*

For centuries, the light hanging just above the ark where the Torahs are kept on the eastern wall of a synagogue has been called the *ner tamid,* or "eternal light." It is part of the architecture and religious symbolism of every Jewish sanctuary. Sometimes it is an electric light; at other times it may be a flame fueled with oil. Often it is artfully crafted out of precious metal or glass.

Many commentators believe that the origin of the *ner tamid* is found in the opening lines of our Torah portion, Exodus 27:20–21. There is disagreement, however, over how the original Hebrew of those lines is to be translated and understood. Compare the following versions.

- *From* The Torah, *Jewish Publication Society of America:*
  You shall further instruct the Israelites to bring you clear oil of beaten olives for lighting, for kindling lamps regularly.

- *From* The Jerusalem Bible, *Doubleday and Company:*
  You are to order the sons of Israel to bring you pure olive oil for the light and to keep a flame *burning there perpetually.*

- *From* The Living Torah, *Aryeh Kaplan, translator:*
  You [Moses] must command the Israelites to bring you clear illuminating oil, made from hand-crushed olives, to keep the lamp *constantly burning.*

It is clear from these three different translations that there is disagreement as to whether one light or many lights are to be kept burning. In one version, the words *ner tamid* are translated "lamps regularly." In the other two versions, the translation refers to one "flame," or one "lamp." So which is the correct translation of *ner tamid?* Is it one light or many lights? Did it always burn or was there a specially designated time when it was kindled?

If one reads the original Hebrew sentence in context with the sentence that follows it, the meaning of the *ner tamid* becomes clear. We are told: "You shall command the Israelites to bring you clear oil of beaten olives for lighting, for kindling the *ner tamid* [continually burning lamp]. Aaron and his sons shall set *them* up in the Tent of Meeting, outside the curtain which is over the Pact [ark], [to burn] from evening to morning before the Lord."

In context, it becomes clear that the *ner tamid* of the *mikdash* was a lamp with several flames. How else can we explain the word *"them"* appearing in the sentence after the command? The lamp with its multiple flames stood in front of the ark curtain and was lit every evening at sundown and kept burning through the night until dawn. In the only other reference within the Torah to the *ner tamid,* we are informed that this lamp with many flames had its own seven-branched lampstand (*menorah*). (Leviticus 24:2–4)

Later, during the time of the Jerusalem Temple, the *ner tamid* was also called *ner ma'aravi,* or "western light," because it lit up the Holy of Holies (containing the Ark of the Covenant), which was on the western end of the Temple. It became the custom to light six wicks of the *menorah* from sunset to sunrise and to keep one of its wicks burning *tamid*, "continually," twenty-four hours a day. When the Temple was destroyed by the Romans, they carried the *menorah* off as booty to Rome. Perhaps as a reminder of the Temple's *ner tamid*, a light was kept burning in each synagogue. At times it was placed near the western wall facing the ark, which was on the eastern wall; sometimes it was placed in a container on the eastern wall near the ark. Eventually it became the custom to hang it just above the ark.

For the early rabbinic commentators, the *ner tamid* and its fuel, "the clear oil of beaten olives," were powerful symbols representing the Jewish people. For example, they point out that the prophet Jeremiah (11:16) says that God calls the Jewish people a "verdant olive tree, fair, with choice fruit." What, the rabbis ask, does Israel have in common with an olive tree, or with the clear oil of beaten olives?

The answer is not a happy comparison. The life of the olive, the rabbis explain, is a hard one. It dries and shrivels while still on the tree. Then it is cut down, crushed, ground, and pressed until it yields oil.

So it is, the rabbis claim, with the history of the people of Israel. They have been beaten, chained, imprisoned, and surrounded by those threatening to crush them. Enemies constantly endanger them. Yet they have survived because they were loyal to God, asked God's forgiveness for their errors, and repented their wrongdoings. In this interpretation, the *ner tamid* with its beaten olive oil symbolizes the cruel oppression Jews have endured and their constant faith in God. Like the *ner tamid* that burns forever, the Jewish people will survive forever despite their persecutors.

Does suffering make Jews better?
The people of Israel is likened to an olive, which yields up its oil only when it is crushed, for the people of Israel reveals its true virtues only when it is made to suffer. (Ya'akov Shmuel Khaquiz, 1672–1761)

Israel's suffering—a barometer
And just because it was always a minority, Judaism has become a standard of measurement of the level of morality. How the Jewish community was treated by the nations among which it lived has always been a measure of the extent to which right and justice prevailed; for the measure of justice is always its application to the few. (Leo Baeck, The Essence of Judaism, pp. 273–274)

Pride in Jewish suffering?
The story of the Jews since the Dispersion is one of the epics of European history. Driven from their natural home . . . scattered by flight . . . persecuted and decimated . . . shut up within congested ghettos . . . mobbed by the people and robbed by the kings . . . outcast and excommunicated, insulted and injured . . . this wonderful people has maintained itself in body and soul, has preserved its racial and cultural integrity, has guarded with jealous love its oldest rituals and traditions . . . has emerged . . . renown in every field for the contributions of its geniuses, and triumphantly restored, after two thousand years of wandering, to its ancient and unforgotten home. What drama could rival the grandeur of these sufferings, the variety of these scenes, and the glory and justice of this fulfillment? (Will Durant, The Story of Philosophy, Simon and Schuster, New York, revised edition, 1961)

In another interpretation, some early rabbis suggest that the people of Israel and the olive oil of the *ner tamid* react in similar ways when mixed with foreign matter. When other liquids are mixed together, they form one substance. Not so with olive oil. When mixed with another liquid, it remains separate; it always floats to the top, above all the other substances.

So it is, say these rabbis, with the people of Israel. Their survival depends on their remaining separate, on Jews marrying Jews and creating Jewish homes in which children experience the celebration of Shabbat and Jewish holidays. Jewish survival also requires that Jews know their language, Hebrew; appreciate their history; visit or live in the Land of Israel; and support the educational, religious, charitable, and social institutions of the Jewish community. Those maintaining this point of view argue that, when Jews demonstrate such loyalty, they are like pure olive oil, which separates above all other liquids. In other words, they rise above all other peoples of the world. Their talents grow into greatness, and they guarantee their own survival. (*Genesis Rabbah* 36:1)

"Light to the nations"

The Jews regarded themselves as the chosen people, not because of their racial qualities, but because of having been selected to be the servants of God to carry His moral law to the world. They looked upon themselves as a covenanted people, a kingdom, not of supermen but of priests. . . . Admission into this covenant was open to all people of all races at all times, also as a matter of choice. . . . The mission was not conquest or racial mastery or territorial Lebensraum, *but to be a "light unto the nations." . . . Israel's sole prerogative lay in carrying on an arduous and self-sacrificing moral and religious leadership. (Abba Hillel Silver,* The World Crisis and Jewish Survival, *Richard R. Smith, Inc., New York, 1931)*

Other rabbis see the comparison of the olive oil and *ner tamid* to the people of Israel differently. God, they argue, needs Israel as a source of light in the world. It is like two people walking together at night along a rocky path. One is blind; the other can see. Without a light they will stumble and injure themselves. So the one who can see says to the one who is blind, "Hold this light that I may see the path."

So it is with God, explain some of the rabbis. God commands the people of Israel to keep the *ner tamid* burning. Its brightness and pure olive oil are to remind the people that they are responsible for God's light in the world. Just as they need God to show them the way, God needs them to bring the light of justice and the hope for peace into the world. That is the unique purpose of the Jewish people. God has chosen Israel, as the prophet Isaiah said, to be "a light to all the nations." (*Genesis Rabbah* 36:2)

Still other early rabbis argue that the *ner tamid* is not a symbol for the people of Israel but for the Torah, which provides the light of wisdom and faith to all who study it. These teachers make the comparison to those who foolishly try to walk in a dark place without the help of light. Such people take the chance of falling against stones or injuring their heads against the ground. So it is with those who try to live without the knowledge of Torah.

On the other hand, those who study Torah accumulate wisdom and learn to discipline their desires by its ethical teachings. They are constantly enriched by the cultural and spiritual views accumulated through thousands of years of human experience. Such individuals provide light for themselves and for others. The *ner tamid* in the sanctuary reminds the Jew of that important lesson.

Not so, say other interpreters. The *ner tamid* is really a symbol meant to remind the Jew of all the mitzvot, all the ethical and ritual commandments one should observe in order to brighten the world. Basing their argument on Proverbs 6:23, which says that "the mitzvah is a lamp; the teaching is a light," they point out that every good deed "brightens" the world. Each mitzvah is an opportunity to serve God, to make the world a more just and kind place for all human beings. When, for example, a person gives to charity, supports a friend in time of trouble, visits the sick, cares for the homeless, or feeds the hungry, the world is brightened with God's light. The *ner tamid* symbolizes all the love, kindness, and generosity brought into the world by those who carry out the commandments and teachings of Torah. (*Genesis Rabbah* 36:3)

From the time the ancient Israelites installed the "continually burning lights" in their sanctuary to the creation of the *ner tamid,* or "eternal light," of the synagogue, interpreters have found in the flickering flames a variety of messages. Symbols often evoke different meanings. They reflect the sad and joyous moments of human life, and they function like signals calling people to take on new challenges. Throughout Jewish history, the *ner tamid* has represented a variety of meanings for the people of Israel. Today those meanings continue to challenge the faith and ethical commitment of Jews everywhere.

PEREK BET: *Priestly Clothing: Fashionable Style or Significant Symbol?*

According to the Torah, Aaron and his sons were not only appointed as priests to carry out all of the special animal sacrifices and rituals inside the *mikdash*, but he as the High Priest and his sons as assistants were to dress in uniquely designed and decorated clothing—or costumes. Aaron is commanded to wear eight different garments: the *ephod*, breastplate of judgment, Urim and Thummim, blue robe, fringed tunic, embroidered sash, linen headdress, and gold plate worn over the headdress. Each garment is to be made by artists out of the finest materials.

Many commentators questioned all this attention to the dress of the priests. Why is the Torah so concerned with costume and style?

Sarna

One answer may have to do with the role of priests in early Jewish society. Nahum Sarna suggests that "the priests are set apart from the rest of the people by dedication to the service of God, by their consecration to a distinctive way of life that gives expression to this intimate involvement with the Divine through special duties and restrictions, and by the obligation to serve the people." (*Exploring Exodus*, p. 131)

Because they are set apart from the rest of the people by special duties, it seems logical that their priestly clothing should also call attention to their unique work and role in their society. Throughout human history, uniforms have been used to signify status, membership in a group, special skills, or privileges. Uniforms are symbols of identity. Whether they are the colorful jerseys of a football team, the blue shirts of the police, or the black robes of a judge, special attire signals not only

what those who wear it do but also whom they represent. Costumes are often badges of identity.

The garments worn by Aaron, however, appear to have a function beyond identifying him as the High Priest. Modern commentator Umberto Cassuto suggests that Aaron's special costume was "a symbol of his consecration" to God. It was a reminder to him that he played a unique role as God's servant. Wearing the *ephod*, the Urim and Thummim, his blue robe, and the gold plate over his linen headdress made him conscious of his sacred responsibilities. (*A Commentary on the Book of Exodus*, p. 371)

Hertz

Rabbi J.H. Hertz agrees with Cassuto. He comments that "these garments distinguished the priest from the lay Israelite and reminded him that even more than the layman he must make the ideal of holiness the constant guide of his life." In other words, the heavy weight of all his priestly garments were a constant signal to Aaron that his duties, and how he carried them out, were a matter of great importance to God and to the people. (*The Pentateuch and Haftorahs*, p. 339)

Most interpreters agree that Aaron's priestly garb distinguishes him from others and reminds him of his sacred duties. However, some suggest that each of the garments may have had special symbolic meaning. These meanings, they maintain, are rich with significant lessons.

Peli

Writing about the *ephod* and breastplate of judgment, Pinchas Peli points out that the Torah not only describes the *ephod* with its two precious stones on which are written the names of the twelve tribes of Israel, but it also tells us that Aaron is to wear them over his heart when entering the sanctuary for prayer. (See Exodus 28:29.)

Peli argues that much more than style and decoration are intended in the Torah's description. "It seems that the design of the *ephod* and the breastplate is meant to teach us an important lesson about responsible leadership. There are many leaders who, after they are elected or chosen for high office, swiftly forget the people whom they are supposed to represent. The names of the twelve tribes of Israel were to be carried on the 'shoulders' of Aaron, so that he should never forget the burden of their needs." Furthermore, Peli explains that the symbols were to be "carried on *his* shoulders," so that he would remember "to be a loyal spokesman for them . . ." filling "his heart with love and compassion for each and every one of his people." (*Torah Today,* p. 88)

Leibowitz

Nehama Leibowitz sees the symbolism of the breastplate with its twelve gemstones, each engraved with the name of a tribe of Israel, not as a reminder to Aaron of his responsibilities, but as a sign of the people's holiness. Aaron, wearing his linen headdress and gold plate with "Holy to the Lord" inscribed upon it, represented the entire people when he stood before God in prayer. He and his garments, writes Leibowitz, "were not an end in themselves, but both he and the task undertaken by him in the sacred vestments constituted a means of stimulating the awareness and consciousness that Israel is holy to the Lord."

For Leibowitz, the priestly costume is meant to encourage the people to be holy—distinct in their moral standards and performance, as well as loyal to their ritual traditions. The challenge to Aaron was to fulfill all the responsibilities of the High Priest, and the challenge to the people was to be known as "priests of God." Aaron's colorful garments symbolized their mutual mission. (Comment on *Tetzaveh;* also Isaiah 60:6)

Several commentators notice that the Torah calls for Aaron to wear a blue robe underneath the *ephod.* It is to be embroidered with a decorative hem of alternating golden bells and pomegranates. As U. Cassuto points out, the pomegranate was a "common ornamental device" among ancient Middle Eastern peoples. The bells, however, are given a special significance within the Torah's description of them. We are told that "Aaron shall wear it while officiating, so that the sound of it is heard when he comes into the sanctuary before the Lord and when he goes out—that he may not die." (Exodus 28:35)

Were the bells really meant to save Aaron's life? What was the danger of entering the sanctuary that made it necessary for a "noise maker" to protect Aaron?

Cassuto suggests that the ancients saw the sanctuary as the royal palace of God. Just as one would never enter the king's place without a proper announcement, so one is not allowed to enter God's "palace-sanctuary" without ringing the bell. Cassuto puts it this way: "It is unseemly to enter the royal palace suddenly; propriety demands that the entry should be preceded by an announcement, and the priest should be careful not to go into the sanctuary irreverently." Among Hindus and Buddhists, bells are often used to announce the presence of worshipers in the sanctuary and the beginning of sections of prayer. The bells on the Torah crowns are also meant to signal honor for the Torah and the joy of its study. Chimes in a church often announce the beginning or conclusion of prayer. The use of sound in religious ritual is universal.

Meklenburg

Jacob Zvi Meklenburg believes that the bells on Aaron's robe represented more than an announcement of his coming and going into the sanctuary. He writes that, unlike the rest of the Israelites, the High Priest had many additional responsibilities relating to the rituals and sacrifices of the people. The bells, Meklenburg explains, functioned as symbols, warning Aaron with each step that he must discharge his sacred duties with care and diligence. They were auditory reminders. With each ring, the High Priest knew that he was an instrument of God, serving not himself but his people. (Comment on Exodus 28:35)

Was all of this attention to the beauty of the priestly garments or the expenditure of community resources for the creation of a magnificent sanctuary necessary? It is clear that the builders of the first *mikdash,* and of the Jerusalem Temples after it, used the finest materials and employed the most skilled artisans. Their standard was one of excellence. They demanded of themselves that their sanctuaries and services be beautiful.

Their motive, however, seems to have been more than the outward appearance of beauty. Perhaps they demanded that their *mikdash* symbolize the kind of world they believed they were commanded to create—one of beauty, harmony, and riches shared by all. They may have insisted also on what later Jewish tradition called *hiddur mitzvah,* a standard that calls upon every Jew to enhance each mitzvah with special enthusiasm, additional effort, and, where appropriate, the highest quality of product affordable. For example, one performs *hiddur mitzvah* when one gives charity, not only generously but in a way that protects the feelings of the recipient. The use of a beautiful silver cup rather than an ordinary goblet for Shabbat *Kiddush* is another example of *hiddur mitzvah.* For the ancients, beautifying the sanctuary was a means of uplifting it to a place of honor.

Additionally, all the attention given to the quality of the material from which the priestly garments were made, including every detail of their decoration, carries the message that valuable creations—whether a sanctuary, a worship service, a sacred garment, or a holy object—are all the result of careful, patient, disciplined hours of artistic skill and work. They do not arise magically; they do not result from indifference, laziness, or neglect. Achieving excellence and beauty requires discipline, time, devotion, and much effort.

QUESTIONS FOR STUDY AND DISCUSSION

1. Which of the various interpretations of the *ner tamid* is most appealing to you? How would you apply the interpretation today?
2. Would you agree that suffering improves human beings or has made Jews more sensitive to the pain of others?
3. Do you believe that "mixing" with other peoples has weakened or strengthened Jewish survival? Why?
4. The priestly garments with their colors and sounds added beauty to the sanctuary. What can we do today to add "beauty" to the ethical and ritual mitzvot we perform?
5. Which interpretation of the dress and symbols worn by Aaron and his sons has the greatest appeal to you?

PARASHAT KI TISA
Exodus 30:11–34:35

God instructs Moses to collect a half-shekel from every person over the age of twenty when he takes a census of the community. He is told to make a copper container, fill it with water, and place it in the sanctuary that the priests might wash themselves before approaching the altar; he is also to create a special anointing oil for consecrating the furniture of the *mikdash*. Moses is told that the sanctuary furnishings, including the priestly garments, are to be made under the supervision of Bezalel, a skilled artisan. Moses is commanded to remind the people that in observing the Sabbath they celebrate the covenant between themselves and God. The Torah text now shifts back to the time of Moses standing on Mount Sinai. He is given the two tablets containing God's commandments. Forty days have passed, and below the people of Israel approach Aaron, requesting that he create a golden calf for them to worship. Aaron agrees. God tells Moses what has happened, threatening to destroy the Israelites, but Moses pleads for the people and saves them from God's anger. When Moses sees the idol they have built, however, he shatters the tablets God has given him. Entering the camp, Moses also destroys the golden idol and punishes those who have not shown loyalty to God. Fearful that God will abandon the people, Moses asks for proof that God will continue to lead them. God's Presence is shown to Moses as assurance that neither he nor the Israelites will be abandoned. Afterwards, God directs Moses to carve two new tablets and return to Mount Sinai. God commands the Israelites to observe Pesach, Shavuot, and the Sabbath. When, after the second forty days and nights, Moses returns to the people, his face is bright red, radiant from speaking with God; so he covers it with a veil.

OUR TARGUM

·1·

God explains to Moses that, when a census is taken, each person over the age of twenty shall pay a half-shekel. The donation will assure the forgiveness of all sins for the person enrolled in the census.

·2·

God commands Moses to make a copper water container that the priests can wash themselves when they enter the sanctuary to perform their rituals. Moses is also told to create anointing oil out of choice spices and to consecrate the sanctuary furnishings and priestly garments with the oil.

·3·

Bezalel, son of Uri son of Hur, of the tribe of Judah, is appointed as the artisan in charge of making all the furniture and priestly garments to be used in the sanctuary. Oholiab, son of Ahisa-mach, of the tribe of Dan, is designated as his assistant.

·4·

God commands the people of Israel to observe the Sabbath, calling it "a sign for all time" of the covenant between the people and their God.

·5·

While Moses remains on Mount Sinai, the Israelites protest to Aaron, telling him to make them a golden calf, an idol, to worship, for they did not know what had happened to Moses. Aaron tells them to bring their gold to him. He creates a golden calf, and the people shout, "This is your god, O Israel, who brought you out of the land of Egypt!" The next day they offer sacrifices before the golden calf and sit down to eat, drink, and make merry.

God tells Moses what the people have done and threatens to destroy them. Instead of accepting God's judgment, Moses argues with God on behalf of his people. He tells God, "Let not Your anger . . . blaze forth against Your people . . ." so the Egyptians will not be able to say that "the God of Israel liberated this people,

only to . . . annihilate them from the face of the earth." Moses pleads with God to recall the promises made to Abraham, Isaac, and Jacob that the Israelites would one day be as numerous as the stars of heaven, secure in their own land. His argument convinces God not to punish the people.

Holding the tablets, Moses comes down the mountain. From a distance Moses, accompanied by Joshua, sees the Israelites dancing before the golden calf. In a rage, he shatters the tablets on the ground and burns the calf. He grinds the calf into powder, sprinkles it into water, and forces the people to drink it.

"What did this people do to you that you have brought such great sin upon them?" Moses asks Aaron.

Aaron immediately blames the people, explaining that they requested an idol and that they are "bent on evil." Aaron explains to Moses that he told them to give him their gold, which he threw "into the fire and out came this calf!"

Judging that the people are out of control, Moses calls upon all who are loyal to God to join him. All the Levites come forward and, following his direction, they kill those who have demonstrated disloyalty to God. In addition, a plague is sent among the people as punishment for the sin of creating the golden calf.

God promises to give the Land of Israel to the people—after driving out the Canaanites, Amorites, Hittites, Perizzites, Hivites, and Jebusites—but not to dwell in their midst because they are "stiff-necked." The people react with fear, take off their fine clothing and jewels, and begin to mourn. God instructs them to leave off their fine clothing and jewels, pledging to decide their destiny.

·6·

Moses appeals to God, "Unless You go in the lead, do not make us leave this place." God responds by assuring Moses that he has gained God's favor and that the people will be led by God's Presence. "Let me see Your Presence," Moses challenges. God answers, "You cannot see My face, for no person may see Me and live." Moses is told to hide in the cleft of a rock to await God's Presence.

Afterwards, as instructed by God, Moses carves two new stone tablets and carries them to the top of Mount Sinai. There God's Presence passes before him, declaring: "The Lord! the Lord! a God compassionate and gracious, slow to anger, rich in kindness and faithfulness, extending kindness to the thousandth generation, forgiving iniquity, transgression, and sin."

Moses asks God to forgive the people, and God makes a covenant with them. God will drive out the inhabitants of the land against which the Israelites are advancing. The Israelites are commanded by God to tear down all altars of idol worship, not to marry from among the inhabitants of the land, and to observe Pesach, Shavuot, and Shabbat. In addition, God orders them to bring choice first fruits to the sanctuary for an offering and to refrain from ever boiling a kid in its mother's milk.

Moses writes down all these commandements. After forty days and nights of fasting, Moses returns to the people. The skin of his face is bright red, radiant from speaking with God. When he finishes teaching the people all that God had said, he covers his face with a veil. From that time on, whenever he concludes speaking to the people, he replaces the veil over his face.

THEMES

Parashat Ki Tisa contains two important themes:

1. The sin of the golden calf.
2. Protesting on behalf of others.

PEREK ALEF: *Why Did They Build the Golden Calf?*

Consider the following facts: Moses returns to Egypt in order to free the Israelites fron bondage.

He and his brother, Aaron, risk their lives in persuading Pharaoh to liberate the Israelites. The people achieve freedom and are saved from pursuing Egyptian troops. They arrive safely at Sinai, hear the words of God spoken to them through

Moses, and are commanded to build a sanctuary for the worship of God. Finally, Moses climbs to the top of Mount Sinai where he stays for forty days and nights in order to bring back the sacred tablets of the Ten Commandments.

Everything seems to point to success for the people of Israel. They have known the bitterness of slavery, the pain of oppression, but now they are tasting the pleasures of victory and liberation. Each day they are fed with manna and, through Moses, are receiving instruction and commandments from God.

With all of these benefits, why do they suddenly lose faith in Moses? Why do they gather before Aaron demanding that he build them a golden calf? Why are they willing to donate their gold for such an idol? Why, after hearing the first of the Ten Commandments, "I am the Lord your God who brought you out of the land of Egypt," and the second, "You shall not make for yourself a sculptured image. . . ," does Aaron deliberately mold a golden calf, saying nothing when the people proclaim, "This is your god, O Israel, who brought you out of the land of Egypt"? What prompts the people to abandon the teachings of both Moses and God?

The answer given by many interpreters is "fear." Forty days and nights have passed since Moses left them and climbed to Mount Sinai. Perhaps he is dead; perhaps he has abandoned them. Their anxiety mounts. What are they to do? Where are they to turn? Who will lead them now? Terrified, filled with uncertainty, they say to Aaron, "Come, make us a god who shall go before us, for that man Moses, who brought us from the land of Egypt—we do not know what has happened to him."

Peli

The masses must have a leader
Moses is but a few hours late, and they, without much hesitation, with little reservation, un-

ashamedly rewrite history; this calf is your god that brought you out of the land of Egypt. . . . Moses, the teacher and lawgiver, is all but forgotten. . . . How swift and how shocking! And how typical of mass psychology! They, the masses, must have a leader. What a gap between Moses and a handmade calf! But to them this gap does not matter. "Make us a god who shall go before us!" They are ready to follow blindly any leader, be he a Moses or a golden calf. (Pinchas Peli, Torah Today, pp. 91–92)

What the people might have said
Philosopher Martin Buber suggests that the people were in a state of panic and said to one another: Moses "has vanished completely. He said that he is going aloft to the God up there, when we need the God down here just where we are; but he has not come back, and it must be supposed that that God of his has made away with him, since something or other between them was clearly not as it should have been. What are we to do now? We have to take matters into our own hands. An image has to be made, and then the power of God will enter the image and there will be proper guidance." (Moses: The Revelation and the Covenant, *Harper and Row Publishers, Inc., New York, 1958, p. 151*)

Philosopher Yehudah Halevi agrees with this assessment of their situation and claims that only 3,000 of the 600,000 people liberated actually requested that Aaron build the golden calf. These people were not really idolaters, Halevi explains. In the absence of Moses, they were simply desperate to have "a tangible object of worship like the other nations without repudiating God who had brought them out of Egypt." Having waited so long for Moses to return, they were overcome with frustration, confusion, and dissension. As a result, they divided into angry parties, differing with one another over what they should do. No longer able to control their fears, a vocal minority pressured Aaron into taking their gold and casting it into a golden calf.

Furthermore, argues Halevi, the creation of the golden calf was not such a serious sin. After all, he explains, making images or using them for worship was accepted religious practice during ancient times. God had commanded the people to create the cherubim and place them above the ark. If the people made a mistake, Halevi says, it was not in refusing to worship God, but in their impatience. Instead of waiting for the return of Moses or for a message from God, they took matters into their own hands and acted as if they had been commanded to replace their leader with a golden idol. It was for their impatience, not for creating an idol, that they were punished. (*The Kuzari* 1:97)

Yehudah Halevi's carefully reasoned excuse for the behavior of the Israelites is very different in tone from the criticism of them offered by the author of Psalm 106. Speaking of their liberation, the Psalmist writes, "God delivered them from the foe, redeemed them from the enemy. . . . But they soon forgot God's deeds. . . . There was envy of Moses in the camp, and of Aaron. . . . They made a calf at Horeb and bowed down to a molten image. They exchanged their glory for the image of a bull that feeds on grass. They forgot God who saved them, who performed great deeds in Egypt. . . ." In other words, the creation and worship of the golden calf by the Israelites was a brazen act of disloyalty to the God who had freed them from Egyptian bondage.

Many of the early rabbinic interpreters of Torah agree with the author of Psalm 106. Building the golden calf was an act of idolatry, and the people's worship of it was nothing less than a signal that they accepted idolatry and were defying the second of the Ten Commandments: "You shall have no other gods beside Me. You shall not make for yourself a sculptured image. . . . You shall not bow down to them or serve them. . . ." (Exodus 20:3–5; *Avodah Zarah* 53b)

As to why the Israelites chose idolatry, some of the early rabbis suggest that they found the worship of a God without form, shape, and color very difficult. They wanted a god like the Egyptians— one that was carried from place to place; one of glistening gold; a bull symbolizing power that would march before them and, they believed, protect them. So they came to Aaron and said, "Come, make us a god. . . ." Because the Israelites sought to imitate the Egyptians and practice idolatry, say the rabbis, they were punished for their sin. (*Pirke de-Rabbi Eliezer* 45)

Some interpreters put forward the observation that it was the men, not the women, who were guilty of creating the idol and worshiping it. They point out that Aaron cleverly looked for a way to divert the men from their desire for an idol. Because Aaron knew that the women would refuse to donate their gold rings to such a project, he deliberately told the men: "Take off the gold rings that are on the ears of your wives. . . ." As Aaron had hoped, the women were unwilling to donate their rings. "We will not give our rings to create an idol!" they told the men. So the men removed the rings from their own ears and built the golden calf. (*Pirke de-Rabbi Eliezer* 45)

Other interpreters blame Aaron, not the Israelites, for the sin of creating the golden calf. They maintain that, when the people began to speak critically of Moses and his failure to return after forty days, Aaron failed to provide an explanation to calm their fears.

These same interpreters also embellish the Torah's report. They say that, when Hur, one of Moses' loyal assistants, accused those who were speaking against Moses of being "brainless fools," Aaron said nothing. As a result, the mob murdered Hur. Then they approached Aaron, warning that they would do the same to him. Fearing for his life, Aaron gave into their demands, took their gold, and created the calf. Instead of taking the risk, speaking out, and providing strong guidance in the absence of his brother, Aaron capitulated to the demands of the mob. His lack of courage and leadership, these interpreters believe, brought about his people's shocking sin of idolatry. (*Exodus Rabbah* 41:7)

Aaron refuses to take responsibility
When Moses asks Aaron why he allowed the people to create an idol, he protests "that he never intended to fashion a golden calf. It was all a tragic accident. He simply threw the gold into the fire to be melted down, and 'there came out this calf.' He could not foresee the consequences of his acquiescence to the demands of a rebellious people." (Silverman, From Week to Week, *p. 79)*

Steinsaltz

Modern commentator Adin Steinsaltz agrees with this assessment of Aaron. He labels the episode of the golden calf "the worst failure of his career." Yet, just as Yehudah Halevi sought to excuse the behavior of the Israelites, Steinsaltz offers an apology for Aaron. "When he agreed to cooperate in the casting of the golden calf, he was undoubtedly proceeding along his own mode of leadership—given to compromise and acquiescence—with the accompanying perils of 'distorting the truth for the sake of peace.'" Aaron is willing to indulge in idolatry in order to pacify the people. (*Biblical Images,* Basic Books, New York, 1984, pp. 75–79)

As Steinsaltz portrays him, Aaron leads by testing the wind, by sensing where the pressure is likely to be, and then rushing to carry out the expectations of others. His guiding principle is peace at any price, compromise to avoid confrontation. For that reason, he offers no argument when the people tell him to create an idol. He desperately wants to be loved and to be popular. If the price others demand is a golden calf, that's what he will give them.

Leibowitz

Nehama Leibowitz sees in the story of the golden calf not just Aaron's failure, or the sin of the Israelites, but a deliberate warning that human beings are capable of acting nobly at one moment and ugly at the next. Leibowitz observes that "we should not be astonished at the fact that the generation that had heard the voice of the living God and had received the commandment 'You shall not make other gods besides Me' descended to the making of the golden calf forty days later. One single religious experience, however profound, was not capable of changing the people from idol worshipers into monotheists. Only a prolonged disciplining in the laws of Torah directing every moment of their existence could accomplish that." (*Studies in Shemot,* pp. 554–556)

From Nehama Leibowitz's point of view, the story of the golden calf is not just about what happened on the Sinai desert centuries ago. It is about human beings in every age. The Torah relates the tale of the Israelites' sin to teach that yesterday's charity may be followed tomorrow by selfishness and insensitivity. Each day is filled with new choices. The role of constant Torah study is to keep an individual asking, "What is the next mitzvah I must do?"

Why does the Torah include this incident about the golden calf? No one can be sure. It may have been placed in this section of Torah because those who experienced it could not forget it. The shock of the incident remained, and they related it from generation to generation as a story they could neither understand nor give up. Perhaps it is included in the Torah because, as some interpreters suggest, it captures the fear and confusion of the people and Aaron when Moses failed to return from Mount Sinai. Still other commentators may be correct in viewing this incident as an indication of Aaron's lack of leadership or as a significant insight into the way people fall from their good intentions when they are confronted with the glitter of gold.

What can be said is that the story of the golden calf has stimulated the genius of Jewish interpreters throughout the ages. They have found within it a wide variety of meanings and lessons. Today, however, the riddle remains. What is the meaning of this curious tale? Why was it included in the Torah text?

PEREK BET: *Moses Protests on Behalf of His People*

Imagine Moses carefully making his way down Mount Sinai, holding the heavy carved tablets of the Ten Commandments. Among the words inscribed on them are "You shall have no other gods beside Me. You shall not make for yourself a sculptured image. . . ." For forty days and nights he has been alone at the top of the mountain. Now, as he is descending, God informs him that the Israelites have not only made a golden calf but are worshiping it as their god.

Before Moses has a chance to answer, God tells him that, because the Israelites are a stubborn people, God will destroy them and create another people for Moses to lead.

Moses, of course, could have accepted the offer. He had already experienced many unpleasant moments with the Israelites. They had complained about his leadership and about the lack of food and water on the desert. They had even accused him of liberating them from Egypt in order to let them die in the wilderness. Why not exchange the Israelites for another people?

Despite the arguments in favor of abandoning them, Moses surprisingly seeks to protect the Israelites from God's decision to destroy them. For centuries, Jewish interpreters of this Torah portion have been questioning the reason. Why does Moses choose to intervene and plead for the survival of those who are worshiping a golden calf?

Among the early rabbis, there were those who believed that Moses defended his people because he was convinced that God's judgment was unfair. It was God, they explained, who had brought the Israelites to Egypt where they had learned about idolatry. "How," they imagined Moses asking, "could God now blame them for worshiping a golden calf?"

Rabbi Huna compared the situation to a father who opened a business for his son on a street filled with evildoers. When his son began acting unethically, the father became angry and threatened to punish him. A friend intervened and told the father: "You are as guilty as your son. Did you not place him on a street of evildoers, in a place where he could pick up bad habits? Did you not expect that the environment would have an influence upon him?" (*Exodus Rabbah* 42:10)

Abravanel

The blame for bad habits
Don Isaac Abravanel believes that Moses said to God: "You know very well that You brought

them forth out of the land of Egypt, a land filled with idolatry. . . . Why do You become angry when they fall back on their old practices? For habit has become second nature to them, and that was what led them to build and worship the golden calf."

In other words, Rabbi Huna believes that Moses intervened on Israel's behalf because he was convinced that their worshiping the golden calf was actually God's fault. The people had not chosen to live among idolaters in Egypt. God had placed them in an evil environment where they had learned bad habits. They were incapable of overcoming the conditions in which they had been reared as children and had survived as adults. Moses understood their burden and, according to Rabbi Huna, intervened to save the Israelites to prevent God from doing a great injustice.

Modern author Elie Wiesel agrees with Rabbi Huna. He sees Moses as a brave defender of his people who argued: "Whose fault is it, God, theirs or Yours? You let them live in exile, among idol worshipers, so long that they have been poisoned; is it their fault that they are still addicted?"

Wiesel also observes: "In spite of his disappointments, in spite of his ordeals and the lack of gratitude he encountered, Moses never lost his faith in his people. Somehow he found both the strength and the courage to remain on Israel's side and proclaim its honor and its right to live." (*Messengers of God*, pp. 200–201)

Excusing the idolatry of the people of Israel because of their exposure to an evil environment, however, is not the only reason given for Moses' intervention on their behalf. The early rabbinic interpreters also point out that Moses was upset by the language God used when talking about the people of Israel. At other times, God had always referred to Israel as "*My* people." Now, in announcing their punishment to Moses for making the golden calf, God called them "*your* people," as if to imply that their evildoing was Moses' fault—when they were "good," they belonged to God, but, when they were "bad," they were Moses' responsibility.

Rabbi Berechiah, quoting Rabbi Levi, compared the situation to a king who had a vineyard that he rented out to a grower. When the wine produced by the grapes of the vineyard was excellent, the king would proudly proclaim, "What fine wine *my* vineyard produces!" When the wine was inferior, the king would blame the grower. "What terrible wine *you* produce!" Upon hearing the criticism, the grower confronted the king and told him, "The vineyard is yours whether it produces superior or inferior wine!"

Moses spoke out, explains Berechiah, because he felt that he was being blamed unfairly for the evil behavior of the people. Berechiah imagines Moses complaining to God: "Ruler of the universe, You can't have it both ways. It cannot be that, when they are good and follow all Your commandments, they are *Your* people, and, when they are unfaithful and do not carry out Your commandments, they are *my* people. They belong to both of us, and neither of us can abandon them." (*Pesikta de-Rav Kahana* 16)

As Rabbi Berechiah sees it, Moses is upset, not only with God's failure to take responsibility for Israel's building and worshiping an idol, but also for blaming him for their evildoing. Such blame is unjust. It is even a sign of disloyalty. How can you abandon that which you love? So Moses intervenes, protesting to God.

Reasons for protest

U. Cassuto imagines that Moses told God: "Don't let other people conclude that all Your work in liberating this people was done in vain!" And Moses also argued: "These Israelites are Your people. Don't allow the Egyptians to come along and say that You intended to destroy them from the very beginning of their liberation." Furthermore, Cassuto says that Moses reminded God that, if the Israelites were annihilated, God would be known as a liar. Had not God promised Abraham, Isaac, and Jacob, the patriarchs of the people, that their descendants would live forever? It was these arguments, Cassuto explains, that convinced God to forgive the people. (A Commentary on the Book of Exodus, *pp. 415–416*)

Nehama Leibowitz points to another reason Moses chose to plead for the survival of the people

of Israel rather than allow God to destroy them. It was a matter of God's reputation!

Leibowitz reminds us that Moses challenged God with a warning. "Let not the Egyptians say, 'It was with evil intent that God delivered them, only to kill them off in the mountains and annihilate them from the face of the earth.'" (Exodus 32:12)

According to Leibowitz, Moses feared that God's punishment of Israel, no matter how just, would be misinterpreted by the Egyptians and other peoples. They would conclude that their idols were more loyal and generous than the unseen power of God and that it was dangerous to follow the God of Israel. "Far from educating and promoting the cause of justice," Leibowitz comments, God's destruction of Israel "would bring the divine reputation into disgrace . . . the cause of falsehood would be promoted and that of truth set back." For these reasons, Leibowitz explains, Moses decided to plead with God to forgive Israel rather than to punish the people for making and worshiping the golden calf. (*Studies in Shemot*, pp. 575–576)

Why does Moses intervene to save the people from God's intention to destroy them for creating the golden calf? Interpreters provide a variety of reasons that may have moved the great liberator and leader of the Israelites. He was motivated by sensitivity to their past and to the habits and customs they had learned through long years of living in a corrupt environment of slavery and idolatry. Perhaps he felt pity for them, sensing that the Israelites were frightened and uncertain of where he and God were leading them. It is also possible Moses concluded that destroying the Israelites was a bad strategy for God. It would ruin God's reputation. No one would have faith in a God who liberated in order to destroy and whose promises were lies!

Did Moses really think all these thoughts? No one really knows. Yet the biblical story of his protest to God on behalf of the Israelites captures our attention, just as it appealed to the imagination of commentators. For them, Moses became a model from whom to learn. Just as he intervened to save his people from what he believed was God's unjust punishment, so too were human beings to intervene and save the innocent whenever they were threatened.

Protecting others from harsh judgments by pleading their case, by urging an understanding of those pressures and conditions over which they may have little or no control, is judged within Judaism as a high moral obligation.

Zugot

Rabbi Hillel taught: "Judge not another until you are standing in his place." (*Avot* 2:5) Philosopher Hasdai Crescas observed that "true justice is tempered with mercy." (*Or Adonai*)

Moses' intervention on behalf of his people is an ethical model worthy of imitation. Undoubtedly, that is why the *Zohar* praises him above all the heroes of the Torah as the "faithful shepherd" of Israel. (Commentary on Exodus 32:32)

QUESTIONS FOR STUDY AND DISCUSSION

1. How do fear and frustration cause a people to abandon democracy or freedom? Can you give other examples when, out of confusion or fear, people have given up their liberties and accepted the tyranny of dictatorships?

2. What role did Aaron play in the building of the golden calf? Could he have intervened and stopped the people from creating the idol, from breaking the law? Did he demonstrate weak or clever leadership? Was he a failure or success? Why?

3. Does society today worship idols? What are our "golden calfs"?

4. What do the commentators identify as the reasons for Moses' protest to God on behalf of the Israelites? How would you compare Aaron's agreement to build the golden calf with Moses' defense of the people when God announces that they are about to be destroyed? What arguments does he use to convince God not to punish the people for building the golden calf?

PARASHAT VAYAKHEL-PEKUDE
Exodus 35:1–40:38

Vayakhel-Pekude is one of seven designated Torah portions that, depending upon the number of Sabbaths in a year, is either read as two separate portions or combined to assure the reading of the entire Torah. While this volume will combine them, it will present an interpretation on each of their most important themes.

Parashat Vayakhel repeats the commandment to observe the Sabbath, emphasizing that no work is to be done on that day. It continues with Moses asking the Israelites to donate gifts of gold, silver, copper, precious stones, fine linen, wood, oil, or spices to be used for building the *mishkan,* or "sanctuary." Moses appoints Bezalel and Oholiab, skilled craftsmen, to oversee the construction of the sanctuary, and they report to Moses that the people are giving more gifts than are needed. So Moses tells the people to stop bringing their donations. Under the direction of Bezalel and Oholiab, skilled craftsmen work on the cloths, planks, bars, curtains, screens, lampstands, altars, and priestly garments of the sanctuary.

Parashat Pekude describes the records kept of all the work and materials used in the construction of the *mishkan,* as well as of all the donations given by the Israelites. When the *mishkan* is completed, Moses and the Israelites celebrate by anointing it. God's Presence fills the sanctuary and leads the people throughout their journeys.

OUR TARGUM

·1·

Moses gathers the community together, reminding them that, on the Sabbath, they are to do no work or light any fires. It is to be a day of complete rest.

·2·

He also asks them to bring donations of gold, silver, copper, fine yarns, linen, goats' hair, skins, acacia wood, oil, spices, and precious stones for the construction of the *mishkan,* or "sanctuary." "Let the Israelites contribute whatever their hearts move them to give," Moses tells the people.

He invites all skilled artisans to donate their efforts in building and decorating the sanctuary. Both men and women come forward to help. Bezalel and Oholiab are appointed to receive all gifts from the Israelites and to organize the construction. Shortly afterwards, they inform Moses that the people are bringing more than is required. In response, Moses issues a proclamation: "Let no man or woman make further effort toward gifts for the sanctuary!"

· 3 ·

The Israelites construct the *mishkan,* working on curtains and decorations, planks, sockets, bars and rings, the screens, ark, table, utensils, lampstand (seven-branched *menorah*), and altars.

Records of each object are kept, noting how much gold, silver, copper, and half-shekels are offered. Details of the materials and how they are used in making the priestly clothing, including the breastplate of the High Priest, his robe, and *ephod,* are all described.

After the building of the sanctuary is complete, Moses is told to arrange for its dedication on the first day of the first month of the year, Nisan. The ark, table, and *menorah,* along with all the other furniture and special utensils for the sacrifices, are placed within the *mishkan.* Aaron and his sons are anointed as priests. Moses lights the *menorah* and offers special sacrifices to God.

A cloud hovers over the sanctuary, indicating that God now dwells inside. When the cloud lifts, the Israelites follow it as a sign that God is with them throughout their journeys in the wilderness.

So ends the second book of the Torah, Exodus.

THEMES

Parashat Vayakhel-Pekude contains three important themes:

1. The Sabbath as a day of *no work*.
2. The obligation of giving charity, *tzedakah*.
3. Accountability of public officials.

PEREK ALEF: *The Sabbath Is for Celebration, for Rest, Not Work!*

The commandment to celebrate the Sabbath is mentioned several times in the Torah. We are told that, after laboring for six days to create the heavens and earth, God rests on the seventh day and calls it *Shabbat*, "day of rest." (Genesis 2:1–3) The Ten Commandments include the directive "Remember the Sabbath day and keep it holy," along with the statement "Six days you shall labor and do all your work, but the seventh day is the Sabbath of the Lord your God: you shall not do any work. . . ." (Exodus 20:8–9) Once again, the commandment is repeated at the beginning of the Torah portion *Vayakhel*. (See Exodus 35:1–3.)

Moses calls the people together in order to speak with them about building the sanctuary. He is about to ask them for donations of gold, silver, and copper and for their time and talents in the construction of their holy place. First, however, he reminds them that they are to work for six days and then observe a day "of complete rest." Nothing is to supersede celebrating the Sabbath, neither their work nor even the construction of the sanctuary. Working on the Sabbath carries a harsh penalty. Moses warns them that "whoever does any work on it shall be put to death." (Exodus 35:1–2)

Several centuries after Moses, the prophet Isaiah calls the Sabbath "a delight," and Rabbi Hiyya ben Abba, who taught in the third century, tells his followers that the Sabbath is a day "given only for pleasure." Most students of Jewish tradition agree with the evaluation of Rabbi Leo Baeck that "there is no Judaism without the Sabbath." (Isaiah 58:13; *Pesikta Rabbati* 23)

Yet, if the Sabbath is meant to be such a "delight" and "pleasure" and of such importance to the Jewish people, why does the Torah specifically forbid "work"? Furthermore, how does Jewish tradition define "work"? Might there not be certain activities that one person calls "work" and another calls "pleasure"?

The Torah repeats the commandment not to work on the Sabbath twelve times and, specifically, forbids making a fire, baking and cooking, gathering wood, moving from one boundary to another, plowing and harvesting, carrying objects, engaging in business, and buying and selling. (Exodus 35:3; 16:23,29; 34:29; Numbers 15:32–36)

Despite the mention of such activities forbidden on the Sabbath, the Torah contains no definition of "work." It is the early rabbis who created such a definition. They identify thirty-nine different categories of work from their study of our Torah portion and its description of the construction of the sanctuary. Since the people were forbidden to work on the Sabbath, it was assumed by the rabbis that every kind of labor associated with building the sanctuary, or supporting the builders, was prohibited.

Rabbi Judah Ha-Nasi, editor of the *Mishnah*, provides us with the thirty-nine categories. They include: sowing, plowing, reaping, sheaving, threshing, winnowing, cleansing crops, grinding, sifting, kneading, baking, shearing, blanching, carding, dyeing, spinning, weaving, making a minimum of two loops, weaving two threads, separating two threads, tying, untying, sewing a minimum of two stitches, ripping out stiches in order to replace them, hunting a gazelle, slaughtering it, flaying it, salting it, curing, scraping its hide, slicing its hide, writing a minimum of two characters, erasing in order to write them, building, wrecking, extinguishing, kindling, hammering, transporting. (*Shabbat* 7:2)

As one can see, Jewish tradition took seriously the prohibition of any labor on the Sabbath. Why? Why set aside the Sabbath as a day of *no work*? Several answers are suggested.

One suggestion is found within an imaginative dialogue, invented by the rabbis, between God and the Torah. The rabbis say that, after God created the heavens and earth and placed the people of Israel in their land, the Torah came to God with a complaint. "O God," said the Torah, "what will become of me when the Israelites are busy every day of the week with their occupations?" God answered, "I am giving them the Sabbath, and they will devote themselves on that day of rest to studying Torah." (*Exodus Rabbah*)

In other words, for the ancient rabbis, the Sabbath is meant as a time for reviewing and examining important lessons of Torah. Studying each week's Torah portion exposes a person to questions of history, ethical challenges, and to the varying perspectives of great thinkers on some of the most perplexing issues facing human beings. Sabbath Torah study provides food for thought, time-tested insights, and experiences meant to enrich our understanding of ourselves, others, and the world in which we live. One refrains from work on the Sabbath to benefit from the wisdom of Torah tradition.

Rabbi Mordecai M. Kaplan, however, suggests that the Sabbath is more than a time for Torah study. He calls it "a pause in our brush-work" of life and compares its importance to the critical rest moments of an artist. "An artist," he observes, "cannot be continually wielding his brush. He must stop at times in his painting to freshen his vision of the object, the meaning of which he wishes to express on his canvas."

For Kaplan, the Sabbath is a time for pausing, for taking a fresh look at what we are trying to do with our lives. It is a weekly opportunity to scrutinize our goals, hopes, successes, and failures. Getting away from "work" allows us a chance to assess its worth and the value of what we are doing with our energies and talents. After celebrating the Sabbath, we are ready, Kaplan says, "to take ourselves to our painting with clarified vision and renewed energy." (*The Meaning of God in Modern Jewish Religion,* Reconstructionist Press, New York, 1962)

We are not machines
The Sabbath . . . prevents us from reducing our life to the level of a machine. The gathered experience of humanity that the break in the routine of work one day in seven will heighten the value of the very work itself is not lightly to be put aside. The Sabbath is one of the glories of our humanity. (Claude G. Montefiore, 1858–1938)

Not working on the Sabbath, however, is not only connected with gaining a fresh perspective on life. Jewish tradition also celebrates the Sabbath as a "day of liberation." Each Sabbath is welcomed with the singing of the *Kiddush,* the blessing over the wine, which makes reference to the Sabbath as a "remembrance of the Exodus from Egypt."

This connection of the Sabbath with the theme of freedom is also captured in the comments of modern psychologist and biblical commentator Erich Fromm. Fromm claims that "it is no exaggeration to say that the spiritual and moral survival of the Jews during two thousand years of persecution and humiliation would hardly have been possible without the one day in the week when even the poorest and most wretched Jew was transformed into a man of dignity and pride. . . ."

The power of the Sabbath, Fromm argues, "is the expression of the central idea of Judaism: the idea of freedom; the idea of complete harmony between humanity and nature. . . . By not working—that is to say, by not participating in the process of natural and social change—man is free from the chains of time, although only for one day a week." (*You Shall Be as Gods,* pp. 193–197)

For Fromm, the Sabbath celebrates the liberation of human beings from "the chains of time." It frees us from the obligations of meeting a schedule, of producing by a certain hour in the day, of dealing with all the stress and pressures that derive from imposed, and necessary, timetables, agendas, and calendars. The Sabbath liberates us from "slavery" to the clock.

Rabbi Abraham Joshua Heschel agrees with Fromm. "We have fallen victims," he comments, "to the work of our hands; it is as if the forces we had conquered have conquered us. . . . The Sabbath is the day on which we learn the act of surpassing civilization. . . . On the Sabbath we live, as it were independent of technical civilization."

Not working on the Sabbath allows a person

to enter what Heschel defines as a "realm of time where the goal is not to have but to be, not to own but to give, not to control but to share, not to subdue but to be in accord." Resting on the Sabbath, using it as a day for prayer and study and for sharing friendships and the love of family, is a way of ruling time rather than allowing time to rule us. By setting aside the Sabbath, argues Heschel, we seize control of the time of our lives. It becomes ours, and we become liberated. Celebrating the Sabbath is a declaration of our freedom. (*The Sabbath: Its Meaning for Modern Man*, Farrar, Straus and Giroux, New York, 1951, pp. 1–10)

Peli

Pinchas Peli extends Heschel's views by pointing out that the purpose of the Sabbath is to remind us of what is really important in human life. For six days we work. We compete. We struggle to shape the world to fit our needs, desires, and expectations. Celebrating the Sabbath as a day of no work reminds us that "the real purpose of life is not to conquer nature but to conquer the self; not to fashion a city out of a forest but to fashion a soul out of a human being; not to build bridges but to build human kindness; not to learn to fly like a bird or swim like a fish but to walk on the earth like a human being; not to erect skyscrapers but to establish mercy and justice; not to manufacture an ingenious technical civilization but . . . to bend our will to God's will."

Yet, not working on the Sabbath, Peli points out, is a discipline. Celebrating the Sabbath is not a matter of occasionally rescuing oneself from exhaustion or of taking "time off" when it is convenient. In order for the Sabbath to make a difference, it must be set aside and welcomed each week. Rest must also be "scheduled" or "created." (*Shabbat Shalom*, B'nai B'rith Books, Washington, D.C., 1988, pp. 59–67)

By uplifting the Sabbath as a special day of no work, Jews reserve time for achieving a fresh perspective on life, for studying the wisdom of Torah, and for celebrating their freedom. Observing the Sabbath each week heightens sensitivity to the essential questions and meanings of human existence.

PEREK BET: *The Obligation of Giving Charity, Tzedakah*

This Torah portion contains a remarkable story about giving charity, or *tzedakah*.

Moses gathers the people of Israel together and invites them to contribute to the building of their sanctuary. "Let all of those whose hearts move them bring forward their gifts of gold, silver and copper, precious linens, yarns, and goats' hair, along with spices, valuable skins, and precious stones." Apparently Moses was a persuasive fundraiser because, not long after he had invited the people to give, Bezalel and Oholiab, whom he had appointed to oversee the building of the sanctuary, came to him and told him: "The people are bringing more than is needed."

So Moses stops the building campaign! He tells the people, "You are giving more charity than can be used!" It's an amazing and surprising report.

In the process of interpreting its meaning, many commentators draw a very subtle distinction between support for public institutions and *tzedakah* for the needy. While the first biblical sanctuary seems to have been constructed from the generosity of those whose "hearts moved them," we are also informed that the sanctuary and later the Jerusalem Temple were maintained by a system of tithes, or obligatory taxes of 10 percent of one's property. These tithes were not a matter of freewill giving. Like our contemporary taxes, they were collected by community or government representatives and were distributed by the king or those in authority.

During the medieval period such communal taxes were allocated, not only to support local synagogues, but to maintain all other Jewish communal institutions, including schools, libraries, courts, jails, health facilities, ritual baths or *mikvaot*, shelters for the poor and hungry, cemeteries, and the supervision of *kashrut*, or "standards of food preparation for the community."

Giving charity beyond the "taxes" collected by the community to support the needy and maintain institutions, including synagogues, was always considered a mitzvah, an obligation and responsibility of every Jew. The Torah instructs Jews to leave the corners of their fields for the strangers, the poor, the widows, and the orphans. Later the rabbis emphasize that providing for the poor brings one into the Presence of God and those who use their energies for helping others less fortunate than themselves shall be rewarded with "long life, prosperity, and honor." Indeed, giving aid to the poor was considered so important a commandment that Zutra, a leader of the Babylonian Jewish community at the beginning of the fifth century, teaches that "even a poor person must give to charity!" (*Baba Batra* 10a; Proverbs 21:21; *Gittin* 7b)

How much should one give?
How much should one give to the poor? Whatever it is that the person might need. How is this to be understood? If he is hungry, he should be fed. If he needs clothes, he should be provided with clothes. If he has no household furniture or utensils, furniture and utensils should be provided. . . . If he needs to be spoon fed, then we must spoon feed him. (Shulchan Aruch, Yoreh Deah *250:1*)

With the rise of contemporary Jewish communities, where Jews pay taxes to their governments and support such Jewish communal agencies as synagogues, schools, special family and childrens' services, and various Jewish civil rights organizations, all charitable giving by Jews has become voluntary. As with the first sanctuary, Jews give as their "hearts move them." No longer are they "taxed" by a Jewish authority unless they are living in Israel and paying taxes to the government.

Given this new circumstance, what are the obligations of *tzedakah* in Jewish tradition? Is giving charity simply a matter of making a donation when you are "moved by the cause," or does Jewish tradition "demand" *tzedakah* from each Jew?

The consensus of Jewish teachings through the ages makes giving charity to the needy and maintaining all the institutions of Jewish life a mitzvah, a required duty. Rabbi Assi of the third century teaches: "*Tzedakah* is equal to all the mitzvot, all the commandments!"

Joseph Karo, author of the *Shulchan Aruch*, one of the most important collections of Jewish law in the Middle Ages, writes: "Each person must contribute to charity according to his or her means." Regarding those who might themselves be considered needy, Karo comments: "Even if one can give only very little, yet he or she should not abstain from giving, for the little is equally worthy to the large contribution of the rich." (*Baba Batra* 8–9; *Kitzur Shulchan Aruch* 34:2)

But how much is considered "a little," and what is a "large contribution"? How much is one obligated to give to charity? Does Jewish tradition suggest standards for giving?

The rabbis warn that, while a person should be generous in giving, one "should not give away all that he or she possesses." Others say that "one should not go beyond a fifth of one's property."

Joseph Karo draws a distinction between "the acceptable and meritorious" ways of fulfilling the mitzvah of charity. It is acceptable to give a tithe, or 10 percent of annual profits over and above household expenses. It is meritorious to give a fifth, or 20 percent of one's annual profits over and above household expenses. He also adds to this standard that at the time of death it is appropriate to give as much as a third of one's estate to charity. (*Arachin* 28a; *Ketubot* 50a; *Kitzur Shulchan Aruch* 34:4)

Considering tzedakah
To the person who has the means and refuses the needy, God says, "Bear in mind that fortune is a wheel." (*Nachman*, Tanchuma, Mishpatim, 8)

Zugot

The more charity, the more peace. (*Hillel*, Avot 2:7)

Boasting about the charity you give another cancels the goodness of your deed. (*Samuel Ha-Nagid*, Ben Mishle *11c,8*)

What about deciding which cause is more important? Does Jewish tradition suggest any priorities for the obligation of *tzedakah?*

Feeding the hungry, sheltering the homeless, clothing the naked are all considered priorities of Jewish charity. So, too, are providing a funeral and burial for the poor, clothing for a needy bride, care for those who are sick, scholarships for poor students, and ransoming those who are held captive.

There is some disagreement about whether funds used to feed the poor may be diminished to pay ransom for a captive or marriage expenses for poor brides. All Jewish authorities are agreed, however, that, when it comes to providing relief for needy men and women, needy women take precedence over men. They also teach that no distinction is to be made between Jews and non-Jews.

Joseph Karo argues that, when it comes to aiding the poor, one must give preference to immediate family members, then to other relatives. After one's relatives, one is obligated to care for the poor servants of one's home, then the poor of one's town, then the needy of another town, then the needy of one's own land, and then beyond. In other words, the needs of the hungry, homeless, and poor who live closest to us have first claim on our charitable giving. (*Sotah* 14a; *Eruvin* 18a; *Shabbat* 127a–b; *Peah* 4:16; *Baba Batra* 8–9; *Tosefta Ketubot* 6,8; *Shulchan Aruch* 34:3,6)

Supporting the needy and maintaining the institutions of the Jewish community have always been considered a mitzvah, a religious responsibility for every Jew. The Torah's report about the Israelites' generous response to Moses' request concerning the building of the sanctuary is pointed to with pride. Their standard of giving immediately and unselfishly became a measure for all *tzedakah*. No excuses for *not* giving charity were acceptable. The rabbis taught that "whether we are rich or poor, we must take from what God has given us and share it with others." (*Tze'enah u-Re'enah, Vayakhel*)

PEREK GIMEL: *Accountability of Public Officials*

The Torah portions *Vayakhel-Pekude* repeat descriptions of the sanctuary construction, including long, detailed lists of items donated by the Israelites.

Abravanel

Biblical interpreter Don Isaac Abravanel counts five repetitions of building plans and donation lists within the Torah. The matter is "puzzling," says Abravanel. "Why keep on recapitulating such details?"

Ramban (Nachmanides)

Commentator Ramban answers Abravanel by claiming that all the repetition "reflects the love with which the sanctuary was viewed by God. Such repetition is designed to underscore its importance in the hearts of the Israelites." On the other hand, modern commentator Umberto Cassuto suggests that all the duplication is merely a matter of "style." Ancient Middle Eastern documents, he claims, all contain repetitions of details, especially plans describing sacred places of worship.

Early rabbinic commentators disagree with Cassuto. They believe that the details and lists serve a very important function. Moses, they say, carefully records each charitable gift. Afterwards he reviews the contribution and checks his list against others made by Bezalel and Oholiab. Then he rechecks each entry, making sure that none has been overlooked or misplaced. All this repetition, attention to detail and recapitulation of what was given and how it was used, is a matter of "accountability." For Moses, the rabbis observe, accountability by public officials of what they collect and how they use it is a moral responsibility. Public officials must be beyond reproach.

Furthermore, rabbinic commentators teach that

at least two people are to be appointed to look after the finances of a community. They point out that, in the case of Moses, he was acting alone, and for this reason he insisted on having all the accounts he supervised publicly audited by the people. The repetition of the long lists of donations and how they were used, the rabbis maintain, was the actual public examination of Moses' records. (*Exodus Rabbah, Pekude,* 1–3)

Why did Moses insist on such accountability? Was he not the trusted leader of his people? Could anyone have thought that he was misusing public charity?

Apparently that is the impression the rabbis believe Moses wanted to avoid. There are gossips in every community, those who spread false rumors or question the integrity of public servants. Moses realized, say the rabbis, that there were those who pointed at him and said, "Look how well he is eating and drinking. He is living off our money. He is getting rich from our donations." In order to answer such false rumors and gossip, Moses insisted that his accounting books be public and open to all the Israelites. (*Tanchuma, Pekude,* 7)

The rabbis also claim that, when Moses realized the people were giving more than Bezalel and Oholiab required for the building of the sanctuary, he asked God, "What shall be done with the surplus gifts?" God instructed him to build a special chapel inside the sanctuary. When it was complete, Moses reported to the people: "We spent this amount on the sanctuary, and with the additional funds we built the chapel." Because he accounted for *all* the gifts, even the additional ones, Moses placed himself above suspicion. (*Exodus Rabbah, Pekude,* 1–3)

Stealing

It is better to eat a poor person's meal and be respected as honest than to eat the richest meal and be hated for swindling and cheating others. Stealing is the worst of all sins. (Tze'enah u-Re'enah, Pekude)

Collecting and distributing charity

Collecting charity for the poor must be done by at least two people jointly. It is to be distributed by a committee of three to assure just criteria and fairness. (Peah 8:7)

If collectors of charity must make change or invest surplus funds, they must do so with others present so that no one may suspect them of deriving personal benefit from their transactions. (Baba Batra 8b)

Using Moses as an example, the teachers of the Talmud held that public officials should always be above suspicion. Their actions, and those of their families, should prove their honesty and integrity. The rabbis point out that, as models of behavior, those who prepared the special fine bread offering for the Temple never allowed their children to enjoy any of it. In this way no one could accuse them of profiting from their office. The same rule applied to members of the house of Avtinas, who were experts in preparing spices for the Temple incense. They never allowed their daughters to wear perfume, even as brides, because they did not want anyone to suspect that they prospered or took advantage of their service to the Temple. (*Yoma* 38)

For the teachers of Jewish tradition, the appearance of honesty was a critical factor in assuring public trust. They ruled, for instance, that officials of the Temple treasury, when taking an offering, were not permitted to wear clothing with pockets. Also they were not permitted to wear shoes or sandals. Why? "Because, if such officials become rich, others will assume that they have taken money from the Temple treasury for themselves." (*Shekalim* 3:2)

Jewish tradition maintains that public officials must be above suspicion. The community must have full confidence in the integrity and honesty of those chosen to serve. Handling the funds of others demands open and careful scrutiny. Just as Moses makes a detailed public accounting of his collection and expenditure of funds, so all public officials are to be held to such high ethical standards.

QUESTIONS FOR STUDY AND DISCUSSION

1. Review Rabbi Judah Ha-Nasi's categories of work. How, in our present society, would you define "work" that should not be done on the Sabbath? What are the benefits of *no work* on the Sabbath? Why, in Jewish tradition, can Sunday not serve as a substitute for the Sabbath?

2. How does Sabbath observance continue to benefit Jews?

3. The Talmud suggests that we give a minimum of 10 percent of our earnings above household expenses to charity and up to 20 percent if we are able. What would you suggest as appropriate standards for *tzedakah* today? Are some charities more deserving of our support than others?

4. Would you agree that standards of accountability for public officials ought to be higher than the standards of those they serve? Why?

THE
TORAH
PORTIONS
OF
LEVITICUS

PARASHAT VAYIKRA
Leviticus 1:1–5:26

Parashat Vayikra describes five different kinds of sacrifices to be offered in the sanctuary. They are the *olah*, or "burnt offering"; the *minchah*, or "meal offering"; the *zevach shelamim*, or "sacrifice of well-being"; the *chatat*, or "sin offering"; and the *asham*, or "guilt offering." The manner in which each offering is made is described in detail.

OUR TARGUM

·1·

God speaks to Moses concerning the way in which the *olah*, or "burnt offering," should be made by the people of Israel. It is to be a sheep, goat, or bull without a blemish, or a turtledove or pigeon. The person offering the sacrifice is to place a hand upon its head. The animal is then to be slaughtered, and the priests are to pour its blood against the sides of the altar. In the case of a sheep, goat, or bull, the animal is then to be cut up into sections and burned on the altar. If the sacrifice is a turtledove or pigeon, its head is to be removed and the blood is to be poured against the sides of the altar; it is to be torn open by its wings and placed upon the altar to be consumed by the fire.

·2·

Concerning the *minchah*, or "meal offering," Moses is told it shall consist of choice flour, and oil should be poured upon it, along with frankincense. When it is presented to Aaron and his sons, they are to scoop out a handful of it and place it upon the altar for burning. Afterwards they are to eat the remainder of the offering.

All of the *minchah* offerings are to be of unleavened flour or grain of the finest quality. If the offering is brought on a griddle or pan, it is to be mixed with oil and seasoned with salt. Then a piece of it is to be burned on the altar.

·3·

The *zevach shelamim*, or "sacrifice of well-being," is to be taken from the herd or flock. The animal offering should be without blemish, and the

priests are to cut it up and offer the entrails and all the fat upon the altar.

· 4 ·

When a person accidentally fails to fulfill God's commandments, a *chatat*, or "sin offering," is to be made. If the person is a priest, the offering is to be an unblemished bull of the herd. It is to be brought to the entrance of the Tabernacle, where the priest is to lay his hands upon its head. Afterwards it is to be slaughtered, and the priest is to sprinkle its blood seven times inside the Tabernacle before the Ark of the Covenant. All the fat and entrails are to be offered on the altar; the rest of the sacrifice is to be taken outside the camp and burned.

If the community accidentally fails to fulfill God's commandments, the elders of the community are to lay their hands upon the head of a bull. After the bull is slaughtered, the priest is to sprinkle some of its blood seven times in front of the curtain. Some of the blood is to be put on the horns of the altar in the Tabernacle, and some is to be poured at the altar base. The fat is to be burned on the altar, and the rest of the bull is to be burned outside the camp.

If the head of a tribe accidentally sins, that person is to offer a male goat without blemish. If an ordinary person sins, that person must bring a female goat without blemish. After the person's hands have been laid upon the head of the animal being sacrificed, it is to be slaughtered by the priests, and its fat is to be burned on the altar. In this way sins are forgiven.

·5·

If a person is guilty of a wrongdoing, an *asham*, or "guilt offering," shall be made. For example, if a person withholds reporting on a matter seen or heard, touches an unclean carcass or an unclean person, or makes an oath and does not fulfill it, that person offers a "guilt offering." If the person cannot afford a sheep for the offering, a turtledove or two pigeons may be offered. If the person cannot afford the turtledove or two pigeons, a tenth of an *ephah* of choice flour will do for the "guilt offering."

Furthermore, if one deals dishonestly with another in the matter of a loan or a pledge, through robbery or fraud, by finding something lost and lying about it, or by swearing falsely, one must first restore or repay that which has been wrongly taken, along with a fifth of its value. Afterwards one may offer a ram without blemish as a "guilt offering." The priest is to sacrifice it, and the person's wrongdoing shall be forgiven.

THEMES

Parashat Vayikra contains two important themes:

1. Sacrifice and prayer.
2. Sin and guilt.

PEREK ALEF: *The Meanings of Sacrifice and Prayer*

The third book of the Torah is named in Hebrew by its first word, *Vayikra*, "And [God] called." In Latin the book is called Leviticus because the priests whose duties it describes were of the tribe of Levi. By the first century C.E., it was known among the early rabbis as *Torat Kohanim*, "Instruction of the Priests."

Most of the book describes in detail how the *korbanot*, or "sacrifices," of the people of Israel were to be offered in the ancient sanctuary. While the descriptions seem to be applicable to the time when Moses and the people were still wandering through the desert, many modern scholars believe this book was written by priests for the priests who presided over the sacrifices offered at the Jerusalem Temple.

In our modern society, the idea of sacrificing animals—of extracting their blood and spilling it on the side of an altar, of cutting out various organs and arranging them for burning—is both foreign and unpleasant. Some would describe it as disgusting and repugnant; others would call it "cruelty to animals," protesting it as morally offensive.

> **Beauty of the sacrifice**
> *The author of* Sirach, *a book of the* Apocrypha, *provides the following description of the sacrifice service in the Jerusalem Temple:*
>
> *How glorious he (Simon the High Priest) was when the people gathered round him as he came out of the inner sanctuary!*
> *. . . When he put on his glorious robe and clothed himself with superb perfection and went up to the holy altar . . . when he received the portions from the hands of the priests, as he stood by the hearth of the altar with a garland of brethren around him . . . with the Lord's offering in their hands, before the whole congregation of Israel. Finishing the service at the altars, and arranging the offering to the Most High, the Almighty, he reached out his hand to the cup and poured a libation of the blood of the grape; he poured it out at the foot of the altar, a pleasing odor to the Most High, the King of all. (50: 1–15)*

In ancient society, however, sacrifices and offerings to God were considered not only appropriate but necessary expressions of faith. The word *korban*, or "sacrifice," literally means "draw near" and reveals the purpose of the Temple offerings. They were meant to unite the worshiper with God. By offering sacrifices, a person said thanks to God or sought forgiveness for sins. The drama and beauty of the sacrificial service, along with the music, prayers, and strong odors of incense, created an atmosphere of awe. In presenting a sacrifice, one was giving something important of oneself to God. For the ancients, the smoke of a burning sacrifice on the altar was proof of a person's love and reverence for God and for God's commandments.

Those who misused the ritual sacrifices, however, were severely criticized. When the prophet Isaiah, for example, saw people ignore the poor and sick, cheat, and deal dishonestly with one another but take their offerings to the Jerusalem Temple, he scorned and denounced them. He told them that God did not want their sacrifices because their "hands were stained with crime." (Isaiah 1:11,15) Among ancient Jews, hypocrisy was ridiculed. Sacrifices were not considered a means of removing guilt for wrongdoing.

Acceptable sacrifices

Let no person say, "I will go and do ugly and immoral things. Then I will bring a bull with much meat and offer it as a sacrifice on the altar, and God will forgive me." God will not have mercy on such a person. (Leviticus Rabbah 2:12)

Let a person do good deeds, study Torah, and bring an offering. Then God will have mercy and extend repentance. (Eliyahu Rabbah, Friedman, editor, p. 36)

After the destruction of the Jerusalem Temple by the Romans in 70 C.E., Jews faced the question: "What shall be done with the institution of sacrifices?" The rabbis determined that, since sacrifices were to be offered only at the Jerusalem Temple, Jews would need to wait until the Temple was rebuilt before reintroducing them. Thus the reintroduction of animal sacrifices and offerings is unlikely.

Even before the last sacrifices were being offered in the Temple, *prayer* was already on the way to replacing sacrifice as the most acceptable means of worship for Jews. With the introduction of the synagogue in the third century B.C.E., words of prayer by both individuals and congregations often replaced journeying to Jerusalem. By the time the Temple was destroyed, there were many thousands of synagogues throughout the Land of Israel, with 480 in Jerusalem alone. Many of the prayers that form the basis of Jewish prayer books today were created long before the offering of sacrifices at the Temple ceased.

After the Temple was destroyed, the rabbis included prayers for its revival in the ritual of the synagogue. For example, the traditional version of the *Avodah* prayer of the *Amidah* includes: "Restore the worship [sacrificial] service of Your Temple, and receive in love and favor [the offerings and] the prayers of Israel. . . ." Recalling the "additional sacrifices" offered on Sabbaths and festivals, the rabbis added a special service called *Musaf*, meaning "Additional Service," to the Sabbath and festival celebrations of the synagogue as a way of praying for the day when the Temple would be rebuilt and the sacrifices of animals reintroduced.

In his time, poet-philosopher Yehudah Halevi dreamed of the day when he would awaken in Jerusalem and experience "the Levites' song and sacrificial service." Later, Zionist Rabbi Tzvi Hirsch Kalisher predicted that the Jewish people would be gathered from the four corners of the earth to the Land of Israel, rebuild the Temple, and "offer sacrifices upon the altar of God. . . ."

Leibowitz

In her commentary, modern interpreter Nehama Leibowitz explains that the sacrifices are a "positive means of promoting communion with the Divine" and "a symbol and expression of a person's desire to purify himself and become reconciled with God." (B. S. Jacobson, *Meditations on the Torah*, Sinai Publishing, Tel Aviv, 1956, pp. 137–142; Nehama Leibowitz, *Studies in Va-*

yikra, World Zionist Organization, Jerusalem, 1980, pp. 18, 22)

Despite the fact that rabbis and Jewish interpreters honored the tradition of Temple sacrifices, even praying for their reintroduction, many believed prayer was superior to sacrifice as a form of worship. They argued that, while the Temple offerings depended upon a particular place and altar, prayer could be offered anywhere and anytime. Prayer consisted of the quiet meditations of the heart or words of the mouth expressed in a whisper, a song, or simply spoken. "Prayer," the rabbis say, "is greater than all the sacrifices." (*Tanchuma, Vayera,* 31b)

It is reported that the leader of the Jewish people at the time of the destruction of the Temple actually counseled his students by telling them not to mourn the fact that they could no longer offer sacrifices. Standing in the ruins of the Temple, Rabbi Yochanan ben Zakkai told his students, "Do not grieve. We have a means of atonement that is equal to sacrifice. It is the doing of kind deeds. For God teaches us, 'I desire mercy, not sacrifices. . . .'" (*Avot de-Rabbi Nathan* 4; Hosea 6:6)

Citing the virtues of prayer as opposed to sacrifices, other rabbis also claimed that prayer was superior. "If the people of Israel say, 'We are poor and have no sacrifices to bring for offering,' God tells them, 'I need only words.'" Furthermore, say the rabbis, "even if they complain that they have no synagogue in their city, God tells them to pray in their fields and, if not there, on their beds and, if not on their beds, then in their hearts." The point is clear. Unlike sacrifices, which depend on an altar, an animal, or a gift, prayer is dependent only upon the hopes and honesty of one's heart. (*Exodus Rabbah, Tetzaveh,* 38:4; *Pesikta de-Rav Kahana* 158a)

What is prayer?
Prayer is the heart . . . of significant living. . . .
Prayer is a step on which we rise from the self we are to the self we wish to be.
Prayer affirms the hope that no reality can crush, the aspiration that can never acknowledge defeat. . . .

Prayer seeks the power to do wisely, to act generously, to live helpfully. . . .
Prayer is the search for silence amidst noise. . . .
Prayer takes us beyond the self . . . our prayers are answered . . . when we are challenged to be what we can be. (*Rabbi Morris Adler*)

 Rambam (Maimonides)

In his famous book *Guide for the Perplexed,* Moses Maimonides argues that sacrifices were an early form of worship given to the Jewish people so that they could learn how to serve God without feeling different from all other peoples surrounding them. Slowly, Maimonides says, the people learned that "the sacrificial service is not the primary objective of the commandments but that prayer is a better means of obtaining nearness to God." Agreeing with the early rabbis, Maimonides emphasizes that the superiority of prayer is that "it can be offered everywhere and by every person."

In his study of prayer, Rabbi Abraham Joshua Heschel suggests that "prayer is not a substitute for sacrifice. Prayer *is* sacrifice." By that observation, Heschel means that in true prayer "we try to surrender our vanities, to burn our insolence, to abandon bias, dishonesty, envy." Prayer is the means through which we sacrifice our selfishness and greed and get in touch with our powers for truth, mercy, and love. (*Man's Quest for God: Studies in Prayer and Symbolism,* Scribner, New York, 1954, pp. 70–71)

PEREK BET: *Defining "Sin" in Jewish Tradition*

Parashat Vayikra not only speaks of five different kinds of sacrifices to be offered by the people and their leaders, but it also identifies the reasons for offering sacrifices. Many were presented as gifts to bring the worshiper closer to God and to express thanks for harvests, festivals, personal celebrations, good fortune, healing in time of sickness, or the achievement of peaceful relations between individuals and nations.

Among the many different kinds of sacrifices are those having to do with the "sins" of the people of Israel or of individuals. *Parashat Vayikra* speaks of the *olah* offering and the *chatat* and *asham* sacrifices as means of achieving relief from guilty feelings and forgiveness from God for wrongdoing. In identifying forms of behavior that require offerings at the Temple, the Torah and those who interpret it present us with a unique definition of "sin."

For example, the *olah,* or "burnt offering," the first sacrifice mentioned in our Torah portion, is to be given by all people. The Torah, however, does not provide a reason for the offering. It is Rabbi Simeon ben Yochai, a student of the famous Rabbi Akiba and a leader of the Jewish community in the Land of Israel just after the destruction of the Temple, who teaches that the *olah* offering is given for sinful thoughts and intentions even if they are not carried out. (*Leviticus Rabbah* 7:3)

Ramban (Nachmanides)

Nachmanides agrees, explaining that it is natural for human beings to have all kinds of evil thoughts. We think of cheating our neighbors, of twisting the truth to suit our selfish purposes, of secretly taking that which does not belong to us, of committing sexual offenses. Many different thoughts and intentions rise in our minds. For Nachmanides, these "secret thoughts," known only to God, are the first level of "sin." They are the first inclinations that lead to wrongdoing. For that reason, one offers the *olah* as a means of removing any guilt for such reflections or intentions. (Comment on Leviticus 1:4)

> **Sinful thoughts**
> *Rabbi Bachya ben Asher, author of* Kad ha-Kemach, *commenting on the rabbinic observation that "sinful thoughts are more injurious than the sin itself," says: "It is more difficult to withdraw from sinful thoughts, for habitually*

thinking about a sin will ultimately lead to its commission." He also notes the opinion of others that "when one plans to commit a sin, one actually prepares oneself to do more than one sin. For example, if one thinks of stealing or robbing, one prepares oneself even to kill in order to accomplish one's desire. . . ." (Charles B. Chavel, translator, Shilo Publishing House, Inc., New York, 1980, p. 276)

A second kind of "sin" defined in this Torah portion occurs when a person unintentionally breaks the law. Examples of this kind of "sin": one may harvest but forget to leave a portion for the poor and needy; one may neglect paying a worker at the end of the day; or one may accidentally eat a food prohibited by the Torah.

Hirsch

Commenting on the seriousness of "unintentional sin," Rabbi Samson Raphael Hirsch writes: "The sinner through error is one who sins from carelessness. In other words, at the moment of omission, that person did not take full care, with whole heart and soul, that the act be in keeping with the Torah and commandments, because the person was not, in the words of the prophet Isaiah [66:2], 'concerned about My word.'" Because one has not been careful and thoughtful, but lackadaisical in carrying out God's commandments, one's actions are considered sinful, and one is required to bring a sacrifice and to offer it in order to gain forgiveness.

Agreeing with Hirsch, Nehama Leibowitz states that "it is no excuse that the sinner had no *evil intention* and that it was *merely* forgetfulness, *just* carelessness and irresponsibility. . . ." She also notes that the Torah clearly includes priests and other leaders in its concern for unintentional sins. Leibowitz argues that "the greater the person, the greater the responsibility. Each negligence, each slip of the mind, each indiscretion, each error borders on deliberate wrongdoing." (*Studies in Vayikra*, pp. 28–29)

Sins of a leader

An acknowledged leader must be even more careful than ordinary people not to fall into the trap of wrongdoing. Even sins committed unintentionally may lead others to do evil, for others are eager to point to such a person as their example when they sin. (Jacob ben Jacob Moses of Lissa)

In other words, wrongdoings, even those committed in error or by accident, have serious consequences. They are not to be whitewashed or treated lightly as if they had no impact on others. Jewish tradition does not permit one to run away from the responsibility for one's actions. The Torah commands those who unintentionally sin to bring a *chatat*, or "sin offering," to God.

In addition to defining sins committed in thought or by error, the Torah also specifies other wrongdoings for which one must present an *asham*, or "guilt offering." These sins include: (1) withholding evidence from a court by refusing to be a witness; (2) promising to do something, or making an oath, and then failing to keep it; (3) dealing falsely with another person in matters having to do with deposits, pledges, theft, unfair treatment, or lost articles. All of these are considered serious violations of Torah.

Commenting on the sin of withholding evidence from a court, Abraham Chill observes that "since justice is the foundation of society, anyone who deliberately impedes justice is thereby guilty of perpetrating an act of injustice. If one could give testimony that would help a court of justice come to a decision but fails to do so, that person has committed a sin." (*The Mitzvot: The Commandments and Their Rationale*, Bloch Publishing, New York, 1974, p.150)

Rabbi Hisda asks the question: "What does the Torah mean when it uses the terms unfair treatment and theft?" He answers by pointing out that a person must not say to a neighbor, "I have something belonging to you, but I will wait until tomorrow to return it." Hisda defines such behavior as the sin of "unfair treatment." And, if a person says to another, "I have something belonging to you, but I will not return it,"—that, says Hisda, is the sin of "theft." (*Baba Metzia* 111a)

For such wrongdoings, it is not enough for the sinner to bring a sacrifice to the Temple. The Torah clearly states that the guilty person shall "repay the principal amount and add a fifth part to it" so the injured party will be fully compensated for any losses. Jewish tradition insists on appropriate repayment of stolen property *before* any offerings are acceptable to God.

This first Torah portion of Leviticus offers a significant definition of "sin" in Jewish tradition. It includes wrongdoings that result from thoughtlessness and careless error, from accidentally misleading others, from deliberately withholding evidence, lying, robbing, or treating others unfairly. This definition is important because it demonstrates the high ethical principles that form the basis of Jewish tradition.

QUESTIONS FOR STUDY AND DISCUSSION

1. Review *Perek Alef.* List the reasons Jewish tradition favors prayer over sacrifice. What other reasons would you add to that list? Why?

2. Maimonides and Rabbi Bachya ben Asher argue that sinful thoughts can lead to sinful deeds. Do you agree? Should a person feel guilty for such thoughts? How can prayer lead a person away from such sin?

3. The rabbis raise a significant question of who is responsible in society for sin? Is it the thief or the one who knowingly purchases stolen property? They say that a governor once put to death all those who knowingly had purchased stolen goods from thieves. When the people heard what the governor had done, they protested. "You have not acted justly," they told him. So he took them to a field and put out food for animals. The animals came and took the food to their holes in the ground. The next day he took the people to the field and again put out plates of food for the animals. This time, however, while the animals rushed to the food, the governor had his guards cover their holes. When the animals discovered they could not enter their holes, they returned the food to the plates. The governor did this to demonstrate that troubles are due to those who knowingly purchase stolen property (*Leviticus Rabbah* 6:2) Would you agree or disagree with the governor?

PARASHAT TZAV
Leviticus 6:1–8:36

Parashat Tzav repeats and enlarges upon the descriptions of the sacrifices already discussed in *Parashat Vayikra*. Included in this portion are details about how the ancient offerings of the *olah*, *minchah*, *chatat*, *asham*, and *zevach shelamim* were performed. We are also given a description of the ordination of Aaron and his sons as priests in the sanctuary and of the dedication of the first sanctuary.

OUR TARGUM

·1·

Moses, as commanded by God, instructs Aaron and his sons concerning the presentation in the sanctuary of the *olah*, or "burnt offering." The ashes from the offering are to be removed from the altar every morning, and the priests are to keep the fire of the altar burning continually.

·2·

Aaron and his sons are told to bring a *minchah*, or "meal offering," to present on the altar. Once the offering is presented, the priests spread a handful of the fine flour, together with the oil and frankincense, upon the altar and set it afire. The remains of the offering are to be eaten by the priests.

·3·

The *chatat*, or "sin offering," for unintentional wrongs is to be slaughtered by the priests. If it is cooked in an earthen pot, the pot is to be broken. If it is cooked in a copper pot, the pot is to be scrubbed clean and rinsed with water. The priests may eat of this sacrifice.

The *asham*, or "guilt offering," is slaughtered, and its blood is poured on all sides of the altar. The priest is to burn all of the animal's fat together with its entrails, kidneys, and parts of its liver. Only the sons of priests may eat of this sacrifice.

·4·

The *zevach shelamim*, or "sacrifice of well-being or peace," is offered as a gift of thanksgiving. It includes the sacrificial animal, along with unleavened cakes mixed with oil, unleavened wafers spread with oil, and cakes of fine flour with oil

from an ox, sheep, goat, or animals killed by other animals. He also forbids the eating of any blood, warning that a person who eats blood shall be cut off from the people of Israel.

The *zevach shelamim* is offered by individuals for themselves. One part of the sacrifice is to be burned on the altar, another eaten by the priest who offers it, and a third part eaten by the person bringing it.

·5·

In a solemn ceremony before all the people of Israel, Moses ordains Aaron and his sons as priests. They are dressed in beautiful garments and sprinkled with oil. Aaron is given a robe, and the *ephod,* "breastpiece," Urim and Thummim, along with a special headdress are placed upon him.

Afterwards Moses sprinkles oil throughout the sanctuary, upon the altar and all the utensils used for sacrifices, and upon Aaron's head. Sacrifices are then offered by Moses, Aaron, and Aaron's sons. Moses touches the right ears, thumbs, and toes of each priest with some of the sacrificial blood. He then takes parts of the sacrificial animal, along with cakes of unleavened bread, and waves them as an offering to God.

Concluding the ceremony of consecrating Aaron and his sons as priests, Moses commands them to boil the sacrificial animal and eat it at the entrance of the sanctuary. Whatever is left over is to be consumed by fire. They are also told to remain at the entrance of the sanctuary for seven days and nights as a part of their celebration.

mixed in and well soaked. After it is presented to the priest, blood from the sacrificial animal is sprinkled around the altar. The offering is to be eaten the day it is brought to the priest.

If the sacrifice offered is a freewill offering, it may be eaten on either the same day or the day after it is given to the priest. Such an offering may not be eaten by any priest who has been made ritually unclean by touching a dead human body.

Moses commands the people not to eat any fat

THEMES

Parashat Tzav contains two important themes:

1. Finding meaning in obsolete traditions.
2. The holiness of blood.

PEREK ALEF: *Finding Meaning in Obsolete Traditions*

Parashat Tzav presents a detailed description of the sacrifices offered in the first sanctuary of the Jewish people as they wandered through the Sinai desert. Most scholars believe that the description applies also to the sacrifices that were brought to the Jerusalem Temple after it was built by King Solomon in the tenth century B.C.E.

During the period when thousands of people journeyed to Jerusalem to offer their sacrifices, the Torah's instructions on how the priests were to prepare and receive these sacrifices must have been extremely important. If they were not prepared correctly or offered properly, they were unacceptable. Therefore, knowing and following the directions of the Torah concerning sacrifices was a high priority for both the people and the priests. Studying the details for the presentation of each sacrifice had great importance.

After the Temple was destroyed by the Romans in 70 C.E. and the offering of sacrifices was replaced by prayer, many must have asked: "Do these descriptions and commandments concerning the offering of sacrifices still have any meaning for us? Are they now obsolete? Is there anything for us to learn from these details about the *olah, minchah, chatat, asham,* and *zevach shelamim* offerings?"

For Torah interpreters since the destruction of the Temple, such questions have constantly been asked and imaginatively answered. Sometimes a commentator will find a word or phrase describing a ritual of the sacrifice that calls to mind a significant moral lesson or symbolizes an important truth about human life. At other times, a command about an offering will remind a commentator of another statement or description in the biblical tradition, and, in exploring the meaning of both, new insights are born.

Several examples of finding, or even inventing, meanings from what seems like obsolete and irrelevant descriptions of ancient rituals are presented below.

Example One: Rabbi Levi, who lived during the third century, pointed out that the word *olah,* meaning "burnt offering," can also be read and translated as *alah,* meaning "behave boastfully." Therefore, he argued, the Torah's statements "This is the law concerning the *olah.* It shall go up upon its burning place on the altar . . ." can be understood to mean "This is the law concerning the *alah,* the boastful person. He shall be destroyed by fire."

To prove his point, Rabbi Levi cites several examples of insolence or pretentious behavior that were punished by fire. For instance, Noah's generation suffered the Flood; for their injustice and selfishness, however, they were also punished by fire. The people of Sodom and Gomorrah suffered destruction by fire for their cruel treatment of strangers and their snobbish and arrogant behavior toward one another. (Genesis 19:24) Pharaoh was punished by fire because he boastfully questioned God's power, saying: "Who is the God

that I should heed and let Israel go [from Egypt]?" (Exodus 5:2)

By reading the word *alah* for *olah,* Rabbi Levi avoids dealing with a discussion of the "burnt offering" and focuses instead upon the dangers of acting in a boastful, self-centered, and prideful way. The haughty or arrogant person, he declares, will ultimately end up as a burnt sacrifice on his or her own altar. (*Leviticus Rabbah* 7:6)

Example Two: Rabbi Menachem M. Schneerson, known as the "Lubavitcher Rebbe" (b.1902), teaches that the sanctuary built by the Jewish people in the desert symbolizes the sanctuary that is inside every Jew. Just as the sanctuary has an inner and outer altar, so each Jew, Schneerson writes, possesses a "surface personality" and an "essential core."

When the Torah says "The fire on the altar shall be kept burning, not to go out . . ." it is referring, not only to the duty of the priest to keep the altar of the sanctuary burning, but also to the way in which one practices Jewish tradition. "It is not a private possession to be cherished subconsciously," argues Rabbi Schneerson. "It must show in the face a person sets towards the world."

Using the symbol of the continually burning fire on the altar, Schneerson stresses that a Jew must be "involved," bringing life and fire to the three aspects of Jewish existence: (1) to the learning of Torah, (2) to prayer, and (3) to the practice of charity.

"Words of Torah," he comments, "should be spoken with fire. . . . They should penetrate every facet of a person's being." In other words, learning must not be dull exercise but a way of filling each person with a desire to practice the wisdom, ethics, and traditions of Torah. One's prayer must be done not as a routine but as an expression of love for God and appreciation of the world created by God. In practicing the mitzvah of *tzadakah,* or "charity," it is not enough to provide money and services for the poor and sick. One must do it "with an inner warmth that manifests itself outwardly," providing an example for others. In all these ways, "the fire on the altar will be kept burning." (*Likutei Sichot,* Vol. I, Lubavitch Foundation, London, 1975–1985, pp. 217–219)

Example Three: The Yiddish commentator Jacob ben Isaac Ashkenazi, author of *Tze'enah u-Re'enah*, notes that the Torah commands that the *olah*, or "burnt offering," and the *chatat*, or "sin offering," be sacrificed on the same altar. "Why," he asks, "are these two sacrifices to be made at the same place?"

He answers his own question by declaring that "the Torah teaches us not to embarrass people."

The "burnt offering" is brought by one who is guilty of sinful thoughts. Perhaps that person coveted something belonging to someone else or thought about cheating or stealing from another person. A "sin offering" is a sacrifice brought by someone who has actually committed a wrongdoing.

The Torah, says Jacob ben Isaac Ashkenazi, commands that both should offer their sacrifices in the same place so no one will know the difference between the person who has sinned in thought and the person who has sinned in deed. In this way, embarrassment is avoided. No one can point an accusing finger and say, "There is a thief."

By calling attention to the detail of how the two sacrifices were to be offered, Jacob ben Isaac Ashkenazi emphasizes a significant ethical lesson. It is forbidden to humiliate or shame another person. (*Tze'enah u-Re'enah: The Classic Anthology of Torah Lore and Midrashic Commentary, Tzav,* Miriam Stark Zakon, translator, Mesorah Publications Ltd. in conjunction with Hillel Press, Brooklyn, N.Y., 1983, p. 573)

Example Four: Rabbi Meir, a leading teacher in the Land of Israel during the second century, studied the Torah's command about offering sacrifices: "These are the rituals of the burnt offering, the meal offering, the sin offering, the guilt offering, the offering of ordination, and the peace offering." He pointed out that the peace offering is mentioned last and concluded that this was not by accident. By mentioning the *zevach shelamim*, or "peace offering," last, Rabbi Meir taught, the Torah emphasizes the importance of *shalom*, or "peace."

"Great is peace," he told his students. "For the sake [of peace] a person may suffer humiliation."

The story is told of a woman who was fond of listening to Rabbi Meir teach his students. Once, when the rabbi's lesson lasted a long time, she was late in returning to her home. Angrily her husband asked, "Where have you been?" When she told him she had been listening to Rabbi Meir's lesson, he refused to believe her, saying: "I will not allow you into this house until you have spit in Rabbi Meir's face!"

Friends of the couple, who learned what had happened, suggested they go with her for counsel to Rabbi Meir.

When Rabbi Meir heard what happened, he said to the wife, "I have a favor to ask. Since the time you left my lesson, I have developed a serious eye infection that can be cured only with the spital of your mouth. Therefore, please spit in my eye seven times." After the woman had done as Rabbi Meir requested, he told her, "Now go and be reconciled with your husband. Say to him, 'I have spit in Rabbi Meir's eye.'"

After the woman left, Rabbi Meir said to his students, "Great is peace. You may suffer shame to make peace between friends, between a wife and husband." (*Leviticus Rabbah* 9:9)

Rabbi Meir, and other rabbis of his time, taught that "peace is the culmination of all blessings," the most important pursuit for human beings. For the rabbis, the fact that the Torah mentioned the *zevach shelamim*, or "peace-offering," after all the other sacrifices was proof of their claim.

Parashat Tzav, with all of its details of the sacrifices offered in the ancient sanctuary and in the Jerusalem Temple, presents Jewish teachers with a crucial challenge. How do you find meaning or relevant messages in obsolete ritual practices?

The challenge is a serious one. And, as we have seen from the examples above, it was answered with creative imagination and innovation. Sometimes in their study of the details of the sacrifices, the commentators suggest a new meaning by altering a word like *olah* to *alah* or by making an analogy between the altars of the sanctuary and those within each human being. Other interpreters suggest lessons by noting the coincidence of two offerings made in the identical place or by calling attention to the order in which the Torah lists the sacrifices.

All of these creative devices of interpretation were used to uncover significant ethical messages to be passed on from generation to generation. No part of the Torah was ever considered obsolete. Through imagination and inventiveness it would yield important lessons. The challenge to commentators was to seek out the meanings of Torah and to reveal its gems.

PEREK BET: *The Holiness of Blood*

Jewish tradition forbids the eating of blood. *Parashat Tzav* contains the commandment: "And you must not consume any blood, either of bird or of animal, in any of your settlements." (Leviticus 7:26) This prohibition against eating blood also appears in Leviticus 3:17, in 17:14, and later in Deuteronomy 12:23.

> ### Do not eat the blood
> And if any Israelite or any stranger who resides among them hunts down an animal or a bird that may be eaten, he shall pour out its blood and cover it with earth. For the life [soul] of all flesh—its blood is its life. Therefore, I say to the Israelite people: You shall not eat of the blood of any flesh, for the life [soul] of all flesh is its blood. (Leviticus 17:13–14)

The early rabbis who interpreted the Torah's prohibition against eating blood developed a number of methods for slaughtering and removing the blood of animals: The knife used is to be razor sharp and perfectly smooth without any nicks or dents so as to cause as little suffering to the animal as possible. The blood spilled at the moment of slaughter is to be poured on a bed of dust and to be covered with the dust and buried. After the slaughter, the blood is to be removed from the meat by soaking it for a half hour and by salting it for one hour. Then the meat is rinsed and ready for cooking. One may also remove the blood by broiling the meat. (Abraham Chill, *The Mitzvot*, pp. 168–169)

Why this unusual attention to blood? Why does Jewish tradition forbid the eating of blood?

Most commentators agree there are two reasons for the Torah's prohibitions against eating blood. The first has to do with the common use of blood by pagan cults. In pagan ceremonies the blood of animals was eaten in the belief that it would provide strength or healing from sickness. At times such ceremonies also included the offering of human blood in hope that it would satisfy thirsty demons who, it was believed, might cause harm. Early Jewish tradition rejected such ritual practices as dangerous and misleading.

 Rambam (Maimonides)

Philosopher and commentator Moses Maimonides discusses the Torah's prohibition against eating blood in his *Guide for the Perplexed*. He explains that pagans believed that, by collecting the blood of animals and placing it in pots and bowls, the spirits would come and dine with them. These spirits would even appear to them in dreams revealing the future or reward them with good luck.

Maimonides argues that the Torah "seeks to cure humanity of such idolatry . . . and to do away with such misconceptions." For that reason, it forbids the eating of blood.

 *Ramban (Nachmanides)*

Nachmanides disagrees with Maimonides and offers a second reason for the rule against eating blood. Pointing to the Torah's statement that "the soul of all life is its blood," Nachmanides argues that, while God permits human beings to eat the flesh of other creatures for nourishment and to use the blood of specified creatures for atonement, all blood is forbidden for eating because "all souls belong to God." In other words, one must consider blood as sacred because it contains the soul given by God to all creatures.

Having made the point that human beings are forbidden to eat blood because it is a "sacred container of the soul," Nachmanides adds a curious observation out of the medieval medicine of his times. "It is well known," he writes, "that the food that one takes into the body becomes a part of the flesh." Therefore, if one eats the blood of a lower animal, "the result would be a thickening and coarseness of the human soul . . . thus combining the human soul with the animal soul." (Comments on Leviticus 17:11)

Nachmanides' belief that eating the blood of animals might have the effect of making a person more "animallike," of decreasing human sensitivity, intellect, and powers of understanding, was common in his day. While modern science rejects such a view, there are many vegetarians who maintain that the eating of blood does have psychological significance. They refuse to eat meat, not only because they are opposed to slaughtering animals, but also because they believe that such "slaughter" has a brutalizing effect upon human beings.

A vegetarian speaks
Early in my life I came to the conclusion that there was no basic difference between man and animals. If a man has the heart to cut the throat of a chicken or a calf, there's no reason he should not be willing to cut the throat of a man. (Isaac Bashevis Singer)

Leibowitz

According to Nehama Leibowitz, Rabbi Abraham Isaac Kook, the famed Chief Rabbi of the Land of Israel just before the establishment of the Jewish state, held such a view. He taught that the eating of meat was "a temporary dispensation given to humanity, which has not yet reached the stage of overcoming its murderous instincts." For Rabbi Kook, eating meat or blood was a sign of human cruelty, proof that human beings were still primitive. Commenting on Kook's view, Leibowitz writes that the rabbi believed "human beings must slowly be trained to show mercy to their own kind and ultimately to the rest of the animal creation." Refusing to eat blood or meat was a means of furthering such an education in sensitivity and reverence for life. (*Studies in Vayikra,* p.55)

Rabbi Kook's view as presented by Nehama Leibowitz is close to the opinions of Rabbis Samuel H. Dresner and Seymour Siegel in their discussion in *The Jewish Dietary Laws* (Burning Bush Press, New York, 1959). Commenting on the prohibition against eating blood, they write: "There is no clearer visible symbol of life than blood. To spill blood is to bring death. To inject blood is often to save life. The removal of blood . . . *kashrut* (the laws of slaughtering animals for food) teaches is one of the most powerful means of making us constantly aware of the concession and compromise that the whole act of eating meat, in reality, is. Again, it teaches us reverence for life." (p. 29)

The Torah's rule against eating blood because it contains the sacred essence of life—the soul—demonstrates the high value Jewish tradition places upon each human and animal life. When blood is spilled, either at the altar as part of the ritual of atonement or in the process of slaughtering for food, the blood is gathered and buried. It is treated with respect. Through such practices, human beings were to learn that blood is synonymous with life, and life, like blood, is sacred.

QUESTIONS FOR STUDY AND DISCUSSION

1. Interpreters of Torah sought to find new meanings in ancient and obsolete rituals and even in the language used by the Torah. For example, Rashi notes that the words "And God spoke to Moses, saying, 'Command Aaron and his sons . . .'" (Leviticus 6:1,2) might also be understood as *"Urge* Aaron and his sons. . . ." What is the distinction between "command" and "urge"? Which word do you believe is the more effective in getting something accomplished? Why?

2. Many interpreters of Torah notice that the duties of the priests are very ordinary and menial. The priests clean the altar every morning. They carry the ashes to a special place outside the camp. Some commentators have asked if there is an important lesson here. Could it be that the most important religious deeds are to be found in the most ordinary and even menial tasks? What are some other examples?

3. Author Isaac Bashevis Singer was once asked why he was a vegetarian. He answered, "Because it's good for the animals." Is it also *good* for human beings? For the global environment?

4. Rabbi Joseph H. Hertz stresses that the rule against consuming blood teaches human beings to curb their violent instincts and tames their tendency toward bloodshed. Do you agree? Why?

PARASHAT SHEMINI
Leviticus 9:1–11:47

Parashat Shemini opens with Moses' instructions to Aaron and his sons for bringing offerings to the sanctuary as atonement for any sins that they or the people may have committed. Aaron follows Moses' instructions carefully and places the offerings on the sanctuary altar. Afterwards two of Aaron's sons, Nadab and Abihu, decide to bring fire offerings of their own. Because they have brought offerings not commanded by God, they are punished by death. Moses tells Aaron and his other sons, Eleazar and Ithamar, not to mourn for them. Later God tells Moses and Aaron which foods are permitted for eating and which are forbidden to the people of Israel.

OUR TARGUM

·1·

Moses tells his brother, Aaron, and Aaron's sons to bring a calf, a ram, a he-goat, and a lamb to the sanctuary for sacrifices. They are to be sin and burnt offerings and an offering of well-being. In offering them, Aaron, his sons, and the entire people are to be forgiven by God for any wrongs they may have done.

Aaron and his sons carefully follow the instructions for offering sacrifices. They slaughter the animals, burn the fat of the sacrifice on the altar, and spill the blood at the base of the altar. Then Aaron lifts his hands toward the people and blesses them. Afterwards God sends a fire to burn everything they have placed on the altars. When the people see the fire, they fall to the ground in prayer.

·2·

Acting independently, without a command from God, two of Aaron's sons, Nadab and Abihu, take pans, place fire and incense upon them, and offer them upon the altar. God sends a fire and destroys Nadab and Abihu, telling Aaron, "Through those near to Me I show Myself holy, and assert My authority before all the people." Hearing God's judgment, Aaron is silent.

Moses commands Aaron and his other sons, Eleazar and Ithamar, neither to bare their heads

nor tear their clothing as signs of mourning for Nadab and Abihu. "The people of Israel will mourn their deaths," he counsels. He also tells them they must drink neither wine nor any other intoxicant when entering the sanctuary. Their task is to distinguish between the sacred and the profane, the clean and the unclean and to teach the people all the laws that have been given by God to Moses.

Later Moses criticizes Eleazar and Ithamar for not eating the sin offering inside the sanctuary as they had been commanded. Aaron answers his brother by pointing out that the sin offering had been presented as he commanded, and the result had been the death of his two sons, Nadab and Abihu. "Would it have been different today? Would such things have happened?" Aaron asks Moses. Hearing Aaron's painful words and rec-

ognizing the truth of his argument, Moses approves what had been done.

·3·

Moses and Aaron are told by God to instruct the Israelites about which foods they are permitted to eat and which foods are forbidden to them.

They present the following list of permitted foods: all animals with split hoofs that chew their cud; all that live in water that have fins and scales; all locusts, bald locusts, crickets, and grasshoppers.

The following are forbidden foods: camel, daman, hare, and swine; the eagle, vulture, black vulture, kite, falcon, raven, ostrich, nighthawk, sea gull, hawk, little owl, cormorant, great owl, white owl, pelican, bustard, stork, heron, hoopoe, and bat; all animals that walk on their paws; the mole, mouse, great lizards of every variety, the gecko, land crocodile, lizard, sand lizard, and chameleon; anything that crawls on its belly or has many legs.

One may not eat or touch the body of an animal that has died of natural causes. If one has such contact, all clothing shall be washed, and the person shall be considered unclean until sundown. If a dead carcass touches any article of wood, cloth, or skin, sack, or any implement, it shall be dipped in water and remain there until sundown. If the implement is made of pottery, it shall be broken.

Any water or food in such an implement is unfit for eating or drinking. Should the carcass be found near a spring or cistern, the water there shall be considered fit for drinking; if it is found on seed grain, the seed is considered fit for planting.

Moses tells the people that all these rules concerning permitted and forbidden foods and what is clean and unclean have been given to them that they might be holy before God.

THEMES

Parashat Shemini contains two important themes:

1. The dangers of excess.
2. Eating as a function of "holiness" in Jewish tradition.

PEREK ALEF: *What Did Nadab and Abihu Do Wrong?*

According to the Torah, Nadab and Abihu, sons of Aaron, each took a fire pan, placed incense upon it, and brought it to the sanctuary altar for an offering. The fire they offered had not been authorized by God nor had they been commanded to bring it to the sanctuary. As a result, they were both put to death.

What did they do to deserve such severe punishment? Were they put to death for offering the wrong kind of fire on the sanctuary altar?

The story of Nadab and Abihu raises issues with which interpreters have struggled for many centuries. Early rabbinical commentators, for example, claim that the two brothers were not punished for offering the wrong kinds of incense or fire. They were condemned for the evil intent that motivated them. Nadab and Abihu, say the rabbis, were ruthlessly ambitious.

Supporting their interpretation, the rabbis creatively invent an imaginary conversation between Nadab and Abihu as they stand with Moses and Aaron at Mount Sinai. "Look at those two old men," they say to each other. "Soon, they will be gone, and we will be the leaders of this community."

According to the rabbis, God warns Nadab and Abihu about the consequences of such ambitions by asking them: "Who will bury whom? Will it be you who will outlive them, or will they outlive you?" The two young men are stunned. After a moment of silence, God tells them: "Your fathers will bury you and go on to lead My people." (*Sifra* on Leviticus 10:1; also *Leviticus Rabbah* 20:10)

From the point of view of the early rabbis, Nadab and Abihu were punished because they plotted to remove Moses and Aaron from their positions of leadership. They appeared at the sanctuary with their own offerings, hoping that the people would be impressed and bring pressure upon Moses and Aaron to transfer their authority to them. Envy and impatience fueled their scheme, say the rabbis, and, in the end, they were punished because of their lust for position and power.

By contrast, Rabbi Levi argues that it was not ambition but arrogance that motivated Nadab and Abihu. Again employing creative imagination, he claims that the two set themselves off from all their peers and bragged that no woman was good enough for them to marry. In fact, says Rabbi Levi, they insensitively took advantage of women's feelings, raising their expectations and hopes for a serious relationship when they had no intention of marriage.

Rabbi Levi claims that they publicly declared: "Our father's brother is king, our mother's brother is a prince, our father is High Priest, and we are both deputy High Priests. What woman is good enough for us?" Because they arrogantly demeaned others, they were punished. (*Leviticus Rabbah* 20:10)

Rashi

Rashi agrees but cites other evidence. Basing his interpretation of the behavior of Nadab and Abihu upon a discussion of it in the Talmud, Rashi points out that, rather than following the carefully detailed directions for offering a sacrifice or bringing fire to the sanctuary, they took upon themselves the power of deciding what to offer, how to bring the offering, and when. For disregarding the process and failing to consult with Aaron and Moses about what they planned to do, Nadab and Abihu were punished. Rashi argues that their arrogance led them to believe that they were accountable to no one.

They failed to consult . . .
Not only did Nadab and Abihu fail to consult Moses and Aaron about their plan to bring a "foreign fire" into the sanctuary, they also failed to communicate with each other. Instead of discussing the matter in a way that might have led them to speak with the fathers, or others in authority, they acted quickly, without carefully subjecting their ideas to criticism. For not consulting, they suffered serious consequences. (Leviticus Rabbah 20:8)

Rashbam, Rashi's grandson, bases his view of what Nadab and Abihu did wrong upon the Torah text. He points out that the Torah states "each took his fire pan, put fire in it . . . and they offered before God alien fire, *which God had not commanded them.*" Their sin, Rashbam explains, is that they offered a kind of fire that had not been commanded. That is why the Torah calls it *esh zarah,*

or "alien or foreign fire." In other words, Nadab and Abihu took the law into their own hands.

Rashbam also speculates on why they did so. He explains that Nadab and Abihu were deeply impressed when God appeared in the midst of the fire on the altar after Moses and Aaron offered their sacrifices. Afterwards, he concludes, they assumed that, if they offered "fire," God would once again appear, and they would be given credit by the people for their special powers—powers equal to those of even Moses and Aaron. They, therefore, were willing to take the law into their own hands to improve their reputations and their chances for deposing Moses and Aaron.

Rabbi Morris Adler believes that the story of Nadab and Abihu is filled with symbolism. The "fire" that they brought, says Adler, "burned within them." It was the "fire of ambition," and their death was "the kind of death people bring upon themselves."

Adler writes: "It was a fire of willfulness and hostility. It was a fire of impulse and desire. As they ministered at the altar, they were the victims of their own appetites and greed, whims and ambitions. No fire came from on high to consume them; they were consumed by their own fierce and false ambitions." (*The Voice Still Speaks,* Bloch Publishing Co., New York, 1969, p. 218)

On ambition
Ambition is bondage. (Solomon ibn Gabirol)

Look for cake, and you lose your bread. (Yiddish proverb)

Ambition destroys its possessor. (Yoma 86b)

Do not seek greatness for yourself . . . do not crave a seat at royal tables. (Avot 6:4)

Requirement for success
This is the indispensable requirement for success: you have to want it and want it badly. "You have to have a will to accomplish whatever it is you're setting out to accomplish," says Rita Hauser, who had to overcome formidable barriers of sex discrimination to become one of the leading female attorneys of her generation. "I believe in

will. I think the will to succeed, the will to win, the will to overcome adversity is an absolute major force in the success of anybody." (Lester Korn, The Success Profile, *Fireside, New York, 1988, p. 39*)

In his reflections on Nadab and Abihu, Naphtali Hertz Wessely is much less critical than other commentators. Wessely calls Nadab and Abihu "religious personalities of the highest order," who did not act out of selfish ambition or any other mean purpose. Quite the opposite, says Wessely. The two sons of Aaron were deeply moved by the beauty and meaning of the ritual sacrifices offered by Moses and Aaron. In their enthusiasm and joy "they lost their heads and entered the Holy of Holies to burn incense, something that they had not been commanded to do by Moses."

Their wrongdoing, Wessely argues, was not the deliberate breaking of the law but rather their failure to control their religious enthusiasms. They should not have gone beyond what Moses had commanded. They should have been more humble instead of blindly assuming that whatever they did in the sanctuary would be acceptable. They were punished, says Wessely, because they occupied positions of importance, which they misused in their misguided excitement and zeal. (*Biur*, comment on Leviticus 10)

Hirsch

Rabbi Samson R. Hirsch criticizes Nadab and Abihu for similar reasons. He explains that Judaism is a tradition of laws and commandments given to bond the community together as a sacred people. When individuals act out of their own zeal to change or break the law, they end up disrupting community expectations and unity. Nadab and Abihu may have been dedicated priests, as Wessely argues, but they endangered community discipline and trust with their new and "alien" fire.

Hirsch goes on to identify the actions of Nadab and Abihu with modern Reform and Conservative rabbis who make changes in Jewish tradition. He comments: "We can understand that the death of the priestly youths . . . is the most solemn warning for all future priests (rabbis) . . . against . . . every expression of caprice and every subjective idea of what is right and becoming! Not by fresh inventions, even of God-serving novices (students), but by carrying out that which is ordained by God has the Jewish priest (rabbi) to establish the authenticity of his activities." (Commentary on Leviticus 10:1)

Disturbed by the rising tide of Reform leaders, who called for more flexibility in interpreting the meaning of Torah and Jewish law and for changes in the law to make it more relevant to modern Jewish experience, Hirsch condemns "reformers" for bringing "alien fire" into the sanctuary. He identifies them as the Nadabs and Abihus of his time.

Most Reform and Conservative Jewish leaders would defend themselves by pointing out that Jewish law has never been static, inflexible, or resistant to change. In every generation, Jews have sought to shape the laws of Torah to meet contemporary needs. Jewish practice is dynamic, always evolving to meet new circumstances and situations. Instead of being Nadabs and Abihus, "reformers" view themselves as carrying on the Torah traditions of Akiba, Hillel, Maimonides, and Rashi by reverently reinterpreting and expanding the meanings and relevance of Torah.

Having surveyed a variety of observations, we are left to decide why Nadab and Abihu were punished. Was it ruthless ambition, arrogance, insensitivity, or the failure to consult others and to honor elders? Was it youthful zeal, blind faith, or the failure to realize the dangers in changing rituals and practices of a community? As we have seen, Jewish commentators see in this sad tale significant ethical and social lessons that continue to challenge Torah interpreters today.

PEREK BET: *Different Views on Kashrut—the Jewish Art of Eating*

As we have already noted in our discussion of the Torah's laws against the eating of blood (see *Parashat Tzav, Perek Bet*), Jewish tradition links "holiness" with "diet." *Parashat Shemini* presents a list of foods that are permitted for eating and a list of foods that are forbidden. These lists, together with the prohibition against eating blood, form the basis for *kashrut,* or "laws relating to approved Jewish diet."

When we refer to a food as *kosher* (from the Hebrew *kasher,* meaning "proper" or "fit"), we mean any food fit for eating according to Jewish law. The term *terefah* (from the Hebrew *toraf,* meaning "torn to pieces") describes any food unfit for consumption or any utensil that may have become contaminated and is, therefore, unfit for use in the preparation or eating of food.

The Torah permits the eating of all animals with cloven hoofs that chew the cud. The pig is not permitted because it does not chew the cud. All fish with fins and scales may be eaten. Shark and shrimp are not permitted because they have no scales. Some rabbinic authorities permit the eating of sturgeon and swordfish while others do not. There are twenty-four kinds of fowl permitted for eating. They are not birds of prey; all of them have one toe larger than the others; they have a crop and a gizzard with an inner lining that can easily be removed. The Torah also permits the eating of locusts as long as they have four wings, feet, and jointed legs.

All "creeping things," including the weasel, mouse, "great lizard," gecko, land crocodile, lizard, sand lizard, and chameleon, are forbidden foods. So are snakes, scorpions, worms, and insects. The Torah also forbids the eating of any foods that have been contaminated by contact with prohibited animals, carcasses, or decomposed foods. (See Abraham Chill, *The Mitzvot,* pp. 173–180.)

Kashrut also includes the separation of all milk and meat products as well as utensils used in their preparation or serving. The Torah forbids "boiling a kid in its mother's milk." (See Exodus 23:19; 34:26; and Deuteronomy 14:21.) To make certain that this prohibition was observed, the rabbis of the *Mishnah* forbade the mixing of all milk and meat. They also designated a waiting period of six hours between eating meat and milk and a waiting period of three hours between milk and meat. (Some authorities say that one hour between milk and meat is permissible.) (See Abraham Chill, *The Mitzvot,* pp. 113–115.)

> **Kosher terms**
> *What is referred to as* milchik *in Yiddish,* de'lehe *in Ladino, and* chalavi *in Hebrew is any food containing a dairy product.* Fleishik *in Yiddish,* de'carne *in Ladino, and* besari *in Hebrew is any food product derived from a meat substance.* Pareve *is a neutral food, containing neither meat nor milk products, which can be eaten with either meat or milk foods.*

What explanation is given for this emphasis upon diet in Jewish tradition? Why does the Torah, and subsequent Jewish law, place such importance upon *kashrut* or the art of eating?

Rabbi Bernard J. Bamberger notes in his commentary to Leviticus that "most peoples have some food taboos." Americans, for example, do not eat horse meat. Buddhists avoid all animal food. Hindus look upon the cow as sacred and do not eat beef. Studies of ancient cultures in Syria and Mesopotamia also reveal dietary codes reflecting an understanding of what might be considered "unhealthy" and "healthy" foods. (See *The Torah: A Modern Commentary,* Union of American Hebrew Congregations, New York, 1981, pp. 808–813.)

Rambam (Maimonides)

Physician and commentator Moses Maimonides believed that "food that is forbidden by the laws of Torah is unfit for human consumption." Quoting the rabbis of the Talmud, he writes, "The mouth of the pig is as dirty as dung itself." Regarding the prohibited fat of the intestine, Maimonides comments that "it makes us full, interrupts the digestion, and produces cold and thick blood." As for mixing meat and milk, he says that the result "is undoubtedly gross food and makes the person overfull." (*Guide for the Perplexed* 3:48)

The author of *Sefer ha-Hinuch* (possibly Aharon Halevi) agrees with Maimonides' medical approach. He argues that "our perfect Torah separated us from harmful factors. This is the common-sense reason for the Torah's dietary prohibitions. If the harmful character of some of these forbidden foods is unknown to us or to medical science, do not be puzzled since the True Physician (God) who warned us regarding them is wiser than us about them." (#73)

Many interpreters of Torah disagree with Maimonides and the author of *Sefer ha-Hinuch*. Speaking for them, Isaac Arama strongly denounces any hygienic justifications of the Torah's laws. "We would do well," he warns, "to bear in mind that the dietary laws are not, as some have asserted, motivated by medical considerations. God forbid! Were that so, the Torah would be denigrated to the status of a minor medical study and worse than that."

Arama feared that, if the Torah's laws about forbidden foods were reduced to medical suggestions, with the discovery of a medical cure for the harm caused by a particular food, there would be no further reason for the Torah prohibition to be observed. The effect would make the Torah "superfluous." Afraid of such a conclusion, Arama argues that the Torah is not a medical text. Its purpose, he says, is to teach us how to live a life of "holiness."

Most interpreters would agree with Arama, pointing out that a medical or dietary justification for the laws of *kashrut* is indefensible. While some laws make sense in terms of hygiene, the Torah also forbids the eating of many foods that present no danger at all to human beings. (Crab, scallops, shrimp, catfish, shark, swordfish, pork, to mention a few.) Furthermore, the separation of milk and meat products does not seem to be justified by any dietary or medical consideration.

Abravanel

For these reasons, Abravanel, agreeing with Arama, concludes that "the Torah did not come to take the place of a medical handbook but to protect our spiritual health." He declares that foods forbidden by the Torah and by the rabbis who developed the dietary laws of Jewish tradition "poison the pure and intellectual soul, clogging the human temperament, demoralizing the character, promoting an unclean spirit, defiling in thought and deed, driving out the pure and holy spirit. . . ." In other words, they bring spiritual trouble—disaster—to those who consume them!

Unfortunately, Abravanel never explains how the forbidden foods of the Torah lead to such moral and intellectual corruption. However, other interpreters make a connection between the dietary laws and "spiritual health."

The philosopher Philo explains that the dietary laws teach human beings to control their bodily appetites. For instance, the law permitting the eating only of animals that have divided hoofs and chew their cud contains a special message: It teaches that a person will reach true wisdom only by learning to divide and distinguish various ideas from one another and by "chewing over" the facts and concepts that may have been gained through study. (*The Special Laws,* IV, 97f.)

A chasidic teacher, Levi Isaac of Berdichev, also offers an interpretation for the laws of *kashrut* that pertains to "spiritual health." He points out that the laws concerning permitted and forbidden foods have to do with what one allows to enter the mouth. If there is no discipline concerning what one eats, if one is careless about consuming forbidden foods, it is likely that one may also be insensitive and careless about what one says, about slandering and lying, about what comes out of the mouth. *Kashrut,* for Levi Isaac, is not only about food; it is also meant to help us keep our mouths clean and pure from harmful talk.

David Blumenthal elaborates on Levi Isaac's observation. "Keeping kosher is a way of preparing oneself to receive the word of God. It is a way of cultivating the bodily habits that will make one a fit receptacle for the Divine Presence." In other words, observing the dietary laws sensitizes one to all the other laws of Torah. It leads to the observance of them, and [it] leads one to be more open to the spiritual message of Judaism. (*God at the Center,* Harper and Row Publishers, Inc., San Francisco, 1987, pp. 60–82)

Steinsaltz

Rabbi Adin Steinsaltz makes a similar observation. He argues that all the laws pertaining to *kashrut* "are based on the principle that a man cannot live a higher, nobler life of the spirit without having the body undergo some suitable preparation for it." For Steinsaltz body and soul are connected. What a person eats influences feelings, responses, and readiness to unite with influences of good or evil in the world. Observing the dietary laws, says Steinsaltz, makes one more sensitive to holiness and to the tasks of bringing "all things in the world to the state of *Tikkun* or perfection. . . ." (*The Thirteen Petalled Rose*, Basic Books, New York, 1980, pp. 163–165)

Luzzatto

In contrast to those who argue that the laws of *kashrut* protect and promote "spiritual health," other commentators argue that they are a means of separating Jews from non-Jews. Samuel David Luzzatto observes that "every Jew must be set apart in laws and ways of life from other nations so as not to imitate their behavior . . . the laws we observe make us remember at every moment the God who commanded them. . . . The numerous mitzvot and laws of our Torah accustom human beings to exercise self-control. . . ." Luzzatto's point is clear. The dietary laws are a way of preventing Jews from abandoning their faith by falling into the imitation of non-Jewish customs. Since eating is a constant activity, a natural process, observing *kashrut* will become a constant reminder of the unique values, traditions, and obligations of Jewish living.

Mordecai M. Kaplan agrees with Luzzatto but extends his conclusions about the power of the dietary laws to the preservation of the Jewish people. Kaplan explains that the purpose of *kashrut* is to make "the people of Israel aware of its dedication to God as a priestly or holy people." However, argues Kaplan, that purpose has expanded over the centuries. "*Kashrut* has contributed to the perpetuation of the Jewish people and the retention of its way of life."

In other words, the dietary laws regulating what a Jew shall and shall not eat are a means of preserving Jewish identity and Jewish loyalty. *Kashrut*, Kaplan concludes, "is particularly effective in lending Jewish atmosphere to the home, which, in the Diaspora, is our last-ditch defense against the inroads of assimilation." In Kaplan's view, the benefit of *kashrut* is neither medical nor symbolic. *Kashrut* is an effective means of guaranteeing Jewish survival.

Milton Steinberg expands Kaplan's argument. The dietary laws, he says, have "high survival-value for the Jewish group, serving as a reminder to Jews of their identity and as a deterrent to their being swallowed up by the non-Jewish world. Judaism, like all minority faiths, stands constantly in the peril of being absorbed into oblivion. Only on a foundation of preservative group practices can it persevere in its higher aims." The dietary laws of Judaism are, therefore, a means to an end. Observance of them preserves the Jewish people against assimilation so that it can pursue its task of enriching the world through its ethical and spiritual values. (*Basic Judaism*, Harcourt Brace, New York, 1947, pp. 117–118)

As we have seen, the Jewish view of diet differs from that of other cultures. While the Torah forbids some foods and allows others, the dietary laws are not based upon hygienic or medical considerations. Many of the foods that are considered "abominable," or *terefah*, in the Jewish diet are not only considered safe for eating but are even considered staples in other peoples' diets. The laws of *kashrut*, according to most of our commentators, excepting Maimonides, are meant not to guard Jews from poisonous foods but to serve as a means through which the Jewish people attains *kedushah*, or "holiness," "separation," and "uniqueness."

QUESTIONS FOR STUDY AND DISCUSSION

1. Aaron's reaction to the death of his sons, Nadab and Abihu, is silence. What do you sup-

pose he was thinking? Which of the interpretations we have noted would be closest to his? Why?

2. Rashi and other commentators fault Nadab and Abihu for not consulting before bringing their offering to the sanctuary. Why are they so harsh on the sons of Aaron for not seeking the approval of Moses? What is so wrong about acting independently, spontaneously, and enthusiastically?

3. Author Gail Sheehy observes: "The new young men do not want to work hard. They demand more time for personal growth than for any other purpose in life. They dream of achieving the perfectly balanced life in which there is time for love and leisure and children and personal expression and playing lots of tennis. Their new happiness formula is expressed in a startling shift of values. Highest on the list of personal qualities these young men consider important is 'being loving.' Dismissed to the bottom of the list of qualities they care to cultivate are 'being ambitious' and 'being able to lead effectively.' " (*Pathfinders,* William Morrow, New York, 1981, p. 42) How would you describe yourself and your parents in terms of such a "happiness formula"?

4. A question is raised about whether or not garfish is considered *kosher.* It has microscopic scales and a split tail, which would argue for its acceptance. Modern rabbinic scholars have rejected the garfish as *kosher,* however, because its scales are not "visible to the naked eye." Given the various reasons for the dietary laws by the commentators, why should it matter whether or not one eats garfish?

5. In discussing reasons for observing *kashrut,* the following reasons have been presented: (a) uplifting ("sanctifying") and imposing discipline on eating; (b) identification and solidarity with the worldwide Jewish community; (c) the ethical discipline of avoiding certain foods . . . because of scarcity of food in parts of the world; (d) living by the authority of Jewish law; (e) desire to have all Jews able to eat in your home. (Simeon J. Maslin, editor, *Gates of Mitzvah,* Central Conference of American Rabbis, 1979, p. 132) Which of these reasons makes the best sense to you? Why?

PARASHAT TAZRIA-METZORA
Leviticus 12:1–15:33

Parashat Tazria-Metzora is one of seven designated Torah portions that, depending upon the number of Sabbaths in a year, is either read as two separate portions or combined to assure the reading of the entire Torah. While this volume will combine them, it will present an interpretation on each of their most important themes.

Parashat Tazria presents the rituals of purification for a woman after childbirth and the methods for diagnosing and treating a variety of skin diseases.

Parashat Metzora continues the discussion of skin diseases and the purification rituals for a person cured of them. Attention is given also to the appearance and treatment of fungus or mildew in the home and to the ritual impurity resulting from contact with the discharge of sexual organs.

OUR TARGUM

·1·

Moses tells the people that after the birth of a son a woman will remain in a state of impurity for thirty-three days, and if she bears a daughter for a period of sixty-six days. Afterwards she will bring a lamb for a burnt offering and a pigeon or turtledove for a sin offering. If, however, she cannot afford a lamb, she shall give the priest of the sanctuary two turtledoves for the offering.

·2·

When a person notices a swelling, rash, or discoloration that develops into a scaly infection, it must be reported to the priests, who also function as physicians. If, in examining the infected area, the priests notice that the hair within it has turned white and the infection is deeper than the skin, they are to declare the person *tzara'at,* meaning "infected with a serious skin disease." *Tzara'at* may refer to such skin ailments as eczema, psoriasis, impetigo, or leprosy. Such an infected person is considered *tamei,* or "impure."

However, if the infection does not appear

public, that person was to call out, "Unclean! Unclean!" so that others might be protected from infection and impurity.

·3·

The same examination and rules applied to the discovery of an infection, or mold, on garments. After a seven-day period, if the garment was still infected, it was to be either washed or burned.

·4·

Moses also describes the ceremonies for welcoming the cured *tzara'at* back into the community after healing was confirmed by the priests. The cured *tzara'at* is to bathe, shave all the body hair, and wash his or her garments. Special offerings of lambs and birds are then to be presented at the sanctuary. Afterwards the *tzara'at* is pronounced cured and able to reenter the community and participate in all its sacred rituals.

If, however, the person is poor and cannot afford the required offerings, a reduced number is acceptable. The principle followed here is that a person will offer "depending upon his or her means—whichever he or she can afford."

·5·

Moses also instructs the people about what to do if mold or fungus is discovered in the home. In that case, the priests are to quarantine the house for seven days. If the mold remains, they will order either the walls removed or the entire structure destroyed. After seven days, if the mold is gone, repairs are to be made on the home and offerings brought to the sanctuary.

·6·

Regulations concerning the infection of sexual organs are also given to the people. Such infections, like *tzara'at,* make a person unclean. Bedding, clothing, or objects touched by an infected person are to be washed. Anyone who has touched the infected person, or who has used an object touched by that person, shall wash his or her body and clothes. He or she will remain unclean until evening. As with *tzara'at,* the people are told to wait seven days to make sure that the person infected is cured. Similar regulations are followed in the case of the emission of semen by men or

deeper than the skin and the hair of the area has not turned white, the priests are to isolate the person for seven days. At the end of seven days, the person is to undergo another examination. If the discoloration is fading, the priests will pronounce that person cured and clean. Should the area remain infected, the person is to be quarantined for another seven days. Afterwards he or she is to be reexamined and pronounced either impure or clean.

Similar examinations were to be performed for scaly infections, for the appearance of a white discoloration of skin streaked with red, for an infection resulting from a burn by fire, or for an infection on the head or beard. In all these cases, priests were to isolate those infected for seven days and then reexamine them. If the infection had healed, the person was considered clean. If not, the person was pronounced *tzara'at,* or "infected," and, therefore, unclean.

A person declared *tzara'at* and unclean was to wear torn clothes similar to those worn by a person in mourning and was not to wear a head covering. Whenever such an infected person appeared in the discharge of menstrual blood by women, which, in ancient times, were signs of impurity.

Offerings at the sanctuary are to be made to celebrate the end of the impurity.

THEMES

Parashat Tazria-Metzora contains two important themes:

1. Medical-ritual practices and ethics.
2. The sin of slander.

PEREK ALEF: *Biblical Medicine, Ritual, and Ethics*

Parashat Tazria-Metzora presents us with what seems like a discussion of skin diseases and bodily infections. We are told that, upon finding a swelling, rash, or discoloration on the skin that results in a scaly infection, a person is to report the problem to the priest. This is also to be done if a person notices loss of hair, fungus on clothing, or mold on the walls of a home.

All these are signs of *tzara'at*, a variety of skin diseases, and of being considered *tamei*, "unclean" or "impure." The same applies to a person whose sexual organs are infected. In all these situations, waiting periods of healing are prescribed, as are ritual offerings at the sanctuary after one has been cured and pronounced "clean."

In these chapters of Leviticus we have an important view of ancient medicine and ritual. The priest functions not only in his religious role but also as a kind of diagnostician. As modern biblical scholar Baruch A. Levine notes, the priest "combined medical and ritual procedures in safeguarding the purity of the sanctuary and of the Israelite community, which was threatened by the incidence of disease. He instructed the populace and was responsible for enforcing the prescribed procedures." (Baruch A. Levine, editor, *JPS Torah Commentary: Leviticus,* Jewish Publication Society, Philadelphia, 1989, p. 75)

Most Torah interpreters throughout the ages, however, have not considered these chapters about skin infection to be a collection of "medical instructions." Priests prescribe rituals; they do not dispense treatments or medication. Even the use of quarantine regulations shows very little regard for guaranteeing public health. They are more a form of ritual than a means of isolating sick people. For instance, there is no mention of preventing healthy people from contact with the contents of a house where disease has been discovered.

If, as most interpreters suggest, these commandments having to do with infections are not strictly "medical instructions," then what significance did they have to the people of Israel?

The ancients were undoubtedly baffled by skin diseases. Swellings, rashes, boils, and skin discolorations must have frightened and bewildered them. So did molds and fungi on the walls of homes or infections associated with sexual organs. Often they watched these symptoms progress into terminal diseases. Knowing little about the cause or treatment of such infections, they concluded that they must be the result of God's displeasure and that they endangered both the individual infected and the community.

That may explain why those diagnosed with such infections, or those whose homes were discovered with a threatening fungus, were labeled "unclean" and isolated from the rest of the community. In ancient times such people were considered "cursed" by God and "impure." Touching them, or anything that they may have touched, could spread the "curse" to others.

The important matter here, however, was not only looking for signs that the infected person had been cured but guaranteeing the community that the "curse" would not doom everyone. For that reason, priests not only examined the infected person or home, but they also conducted special rituals in the sanctuary celebrating the end of the infection. Their medical-ritual procedures were meant not only to provide some elementary sanitary safety for the community but, more significantly, to save the community from spreading among them what they understood as God's curse.

Because the diagnosis of such infections and the rituals celebrating their conclusion affected everyone in the community, the services of priests had to be accessible and the costs of sanctuary offerings had to be affordable to everyone. Essentially, public need necessitated ethical and economic fairness. If the offerings required by the infected person could not be brought to the sanctuary because they were not affordable, the entire community might suffer a continuing curse.

For that reason, the Torah commands that, if a person is poor and cannot afford to bring birds, lambs, hyssop, cedar wood, crimson stuff, choice flour and oil as offerings for the altar of the sanctuary, "one lamb, one-tenth of a measure of choice flour with oil mixed in, and two turtledoves or pigeons—within his means—" may be acceptably substituted. In this way, the poor were made equal to those who could afford the medical-ritual procedures required. This reduction in the cost of offerings for the poor is mentioned several times in the Torah. (Leviticus 5:7–10; 14:21; 27:8)

The Torah identifies six categories of wrongdoing for which individuals were to bring offerings to the sanctuary: (1) a person who swears he has testimony to give but does not; (2) a person who promises to do a certain thing but does not; (3) a ritually unclean person who takes something forbidden or (4) who enters the sanctuary; (5) a woman in labor who swears that she will never again have intercourse with her husband; and (6) a person who suffers from a skin disease because of slandering others.

For such wrongdoing special offerings were required. Yet, in each situation, the Torah provides against financial discrimination. If the person who sinned is poor and cannot afford the offerings required, special provisions are made. Other less expensive sacrifices are substituted and are acceptable. The guiding principle of Jewish ethics, whether in the area of ritual or medicine, is equal treatment for the poor and rich. Each human being is created in God's image. The offerings of each person, rich or poor, are of equal value to God.

The poor belong to God
The poor are called the people of God, as the sages expounded: "If you lend money to any of My people . . ." Who are "My people"? They are the poor, as it is said, "For the Eternal has comforted the people and has compassion upon the

poor among them." At times a person who is rich does not pay attention to poor relatives. . . . However, this is not so with God. . . . God cares for the poor. The proof of this is what Isaiah has said: "The Eternal has founded the city of Zion, and in her the poor of God's people take refuge." (*Bachya ben Asher,* Kad ha-Kemach, *Charles B. Chavel, translator, pp. 533–534*)

 Hirsch

In his commentary on Leviticus, Rabbi Samson Raphael Hirsch explains the reason for making these offerings of the poor affordable. The "poverty-stricken and suffering people," he writes, "often presume that they have been forsaken by God's care, abandoned by God." As a result, "they abandon themselves, give themselves up to despair . . . lose their self-respect. . . . They fall because they have given up all thoughts of betterment." In commanding that the offerings be made affordable to the poor, the Torah demonstrates that the poor are as important to God as the rich. They and their offerings are equally sacred and acceptable. God has not forsaken them. (See comments on Leviticus 5:13ff.)

Commenting on charitable gifts of the poor, Rabbi Hillel Silverman draws a parallel to the offerings once given in the sanctuary. "Every Jew is enjoined to contribute offerings according to his or her individual means. The wealthy bring more; the poor bring what they can. In the words of the Talmud: 'But one and the same are the generous and the meager offering, provided that a person's intention and sincerity are directed to God.' [*Berachot* 5b] . . . We should understand that the small gift of the less affluent person may be a far greater sacrifice than the large gift of the wealthy donor. A contribution of time and service given with *kavanah* [enthusiasm] is even more valuable than material gifts." (*From Week to Week,* p. 105)

Jewish tradition seeks to heighten sensitivity to the plight of the poor without ever robbing them of their dignity. Perhaps that explains why the Torah insists on affordable sacrifices for those who must bring sin offerings to the sanctuary but who are impoverished. There was to be no discrimination, no special access by the rich to the priests of the sanctuary who examined for skin diseases and conducted the rituals for declaring a person cured and ready for reentry into the community. Rich and poor were to be treated alike. Their gifts were of equal importance to God.

PEREK BET: *The Sin of Slandering Others*

As we have already noted, the Torah and its interpreters present neither a medical diagnosis nor treatment for the skin disorders of their times. While the ancient priests examined infections on the body or fungi in the home, they did not prescribe any medicine or therapy for healing. They did determine a period for quarantine, which may have been unrelated to the fear of passing the infection from one person to another. Instead, the isolation of the infected person seems to grow out of a concern for guarding the community against people who were "unclean" or "impure" because of some wrongdoing.

It is for that reason that the offering brought by a person who has been cured of a skin disease, or whose home has been infected, is called a "sin" offering. The rituals of the offerings in the sanctuary are meant to celebrate "purification," the end of being considered unclean. All such wrongdoings that cause infections are forgiven through the sacrifices and offerings brought to the priest at the sanctuary.

Many commentators ask: "What was the wrongdoing or the sin that brought on such serious infections and prompted the emergency procedure of quarantine?"

In answering that question, interpreters focus attention upon the record of major biblical personalities who are said to have been afflicted with *tzara'at,* or "skin disorders."

Rashi

Rashi, for example, points out that Moses suffered from a serious skin disease after he complained to God that the people of Israel would not listen to him. Because he implied that the people refused to follow God's commandments, Moses was punished. The Torah says that "his hand became infected, as white as snow." (See comment on Exodus 4:1–6.)

Earlier rabbinic tradition argues that Miriam, the sister of Moses and Aaron, was stricken with a skin disease because she slandered her brothers by gossiping about their relationships with their wives. "They are busy leading the people and make no time to spend at home," the rabbis accuse her of saying. They also point out that she embarrassed Moses publicly by questioning his marriage to a Cushite woman and by implying that she was as important a prophet as he was. For her gossip, slander, and public accusations, say the rabbis, Miriam was punished with a serious skin infection. (See Numbers 12:1–13; also *Leviticus Rabbah* 16:1.)

Zugot

Rabbi Yochanan, quoting Rabbi Yosi ben Zimra, warns that "spreading *leshon ha-rah*—slander, lies, or misinformation—is identical to denying the power of God." God commands honesty and the truth. If a person is dishonest, God's desire is undermined. Such a person, says Rabbi Yochanan, will be punished with skin infections.

The talebearer is a cannibal
Teaching the power of gossip to do harm, the Talmud comments that "the gossiper stands in Syria and kills in Rome." (Jerusalem Talmud, Peah *1:1)*

Have you heard something about someone? Let it die with you. Be of good courage, it will not harm you if it ends with you. (Ben Sira 19:10)

Your friend has a friend, and your friend's friend has a friend, so be careful of what you say. (Ketubot 109b)

> *Where there is no wood, a fire goes out;*
> *Where there is no whisper, a quarrel dies down.*
> *(Proverbs 26:20)*

At another time, Rabbi Samuel bar Nachmeni, quoting Rabbi Yochanan, argues that "the serious skin infections mentioned by the Torah are the result of seven kinds of wrongdoing: slander, bloodshed, perjury, adultery, arrogance, misappropriation, and meanness." Several examples are given: Joab is punished with skin disease because he murders Abner. (IISamuel 3:29) Gehazi is inflicted because he lies to Na'aman. (IIKings 5:23) Pharaoh is penalized because he takes Sarah away from her husband, Abraham. (Genesis 12:17) King Azariah is inflicted with skin disease because he seeks to appropriate the priesthood under his power. (IIChronicles 26:16) For the rabbis, all these examples prove that *tzara'at* is the result of wrongdoing. (*Arachin* 15b–16a)

 Rambam (Maimonides)

It should not surprise us that Moses Maimonides agrees. The great physician and Torah interpreter maintains that "*tzara'at* [skin disease] is not a natural phenomenon but rather a sign and wonder for the people of Israel to warn them against *leshon ha-ra*—evil talk."

Obadiah Sforno enlarges upon Maimonides' observation, arguing that the quarantine ordered by the priest is meant to prompt a person to ask God's forgiveness for his or her sins. The quarantine is a time to reconsider one's actions, both the intentional and the unintentional ones. In confronting one's shortcomings, honestly scrutinizing one's treatment of others, there is chance for personal improvement and repentance. In this way the affliction of *tzara'at* leads to isolation, which leads to repentance, which brings about God's forgiveness for wrongdoing and the rehabilitation of each sinful human being. (See comments on Leviticus 14:21.)

 Leibowitz

Nehama Leibowitz extends Sforno's logic in a different way. She quotes the Talmud's observation that "the house affected by *tzara'at* . . . exists for the purpose of education." In other words, she says that "the plague teaches us that society should take notice of the first sign of misconduct, however small. Just the same as a disease begins with hardly noticeable symptoms and can be stopped if detected in time, so a moral disease in society can be prevented from spreading if immediate steps are taken. Otherwise it will spread throughout the community." (*Studies in Vayikra*, pp. 137–138)

 Peli

Pinchas Peli also links the sin of *leshon ha-ra* to the skin infections and fungus mentioned in our Torah portion. He defines *leshon ha-ra* as "slander, gossip, talebearing, and all the other forms of damage to the individual and society that may be caused by words." The result of such wrongdoing, says Peli, is a "justly deserved punishment—leprosy, an illness that cannot be hidden."

> **Dangers of the tongue**
> *The Book of Proverbs (18:21) teaches: "Death and life are in the hands of the tongue. . . ." One who loves the tongue and uses it to speak words of Torah and commandments will be justly rewarded, but one who speaks slander brings upon himself much sorrow. (Tze'enah u-Re'enah, comment on Leviticus 14:1–2)*
>
> *A person may think, "Of what importance are my words? A word has no substance, neither can it be seen or touched. . . ." It is true that words have no substance and cannot be seen, but, like the wind, they can cause entire worlds to crash. (A.Z. Friedman, Wellsprings of Torah, 2 vols., Judaica Press, New York, 1969, p. 234)*

> *Eleazar Ha-Kappar taught: "If you slander others, you will also commit other such wrongdoing."* (Derech Eretz, *chap. 7*)

Why is the punishment so harsh? Peli explains: "Jewish tradition sees a lethal weapon in the evil tongue and minces no words in its condemnation. The Talmud equates speaking *leshon ha-ra* with flagrant atheism, with adultery, and with murder. In fact, it is worse than murder since it simultaneously destroys three people: the one who relates the gossip, the one who listens to it, and the one it concerns." (*Torah Today*, B'nai B'rith Books, Washington, D.C., 1987, pp. 127–131)

As we have discovered, most commentators connect the skin infections and the outbreak of fungus on clothing or in homes with the sins of an evil tongue. While today we may reject the connection, seeing no medical evidence between such afflictions and what people say or do, Torah interpreters still leave us with much to consider.

The spread of lies, gossip, slander, character assassination, derogatory statements, and fraudulent stories can infect society and destroy human lives. Drawing a parallel to the spread of contagious and dangerous disease, the commentators warn about the damage such evil talk can bring to individuals and society. Learning to quarantine such evil and to cure ourselves from the temptations of *leshon ha-ra* are still significant challenges today.

QUESTIONS FOR STUDY AND DISCUSSION

1. The Torah teaches that there must be no financial discrimination between rich and poor when it comes to the purchase of offerings for sacrifice in the Temple. The offerings must be affordable to all for the dignity of every human soul is precious to God. How would you extend this ethical principle to synagogue membership and to the cost of health care, hospital insurance, and education?

2. The *Zohar Hadash* teaches that "if a person be in debt to God because of his or her sins, God does not consider it a debt because poverty often misleads a person's powers for reasoning." (Comment on Leviticus 49) Is this so? How may such an argument justify accepting less from the poor by way of an offering for wrongdoing?

3. Rabbi Yannai told of a peddler who went from town to town crying out: "Who wants to purchase the secret of guaranteeing a long and happy life?" When he challenged the peddler to prove that he possessed such a secret, the peddler opened a Hebrew Bible to the Book of Psalms. He then pointed to the words: "Guard your tongue from evil, your lips from deceitful speech. . . ." (34:14; *Leviticus Rabbah* 16:2) Compare Rabbi Yannai's lesson to the dangers of slander emphasized by other Jewish commentators.

4. The Talmud asks the question: "Why does the sin offering of those with skin diseases consist of birds?" In answer, we are told: "Because the sin of such persons is gossip. They are chirping all the time. Therefore, their offering must remind them of their wrongdoing—warn them of how dangerous it is to engage in gossip." (*Arachin* 16a) Why do the teachers of Jewish ethics consider gossip and slander such serious offenses?

PARASHAT ACHARE MOT-KEDOSHIM
Leviticus 16:1–20:27

Parashat Achare Mot-Kedoshim is one of seven designated Torah portions that, depending upon the number of Sabbaths in a year, is either read as two separate portions or combined to assure the reading of the entire Torah. While this volume will combine them, it will present an interpretation on each of their most important themes.

Parashat Achare Mot, which means "after the death of," recalls the death of Nadab and Abihu, Aaron's sons. It describes the rituals for the sin offerings that Aaron is to present in the sanctuary for himself and the people. Mention is made of Yom Kippur, or "Day of Atonement." Laws regarding forbidden sexual relations are also presented.

Parashat Kedoshim, which means "holiness," lists those ritual and ethical laws that, if followed, will make the Jewish people a "holy" people.

OUR TARGUM

· 1 ·

Parashat *Achare Mot* begins by referring briefly to the death of Aaron's sons, Nadab and Abihu, who had entered the sanctuary without permission and with foreign fire for the altar. God instructs Moses to tell Aaron that he alone is permitted to enter the inner sanctuary, the Holy of Holies. When he enters, he is to dress with special linen garments and to bring a sin offering for himself, his household, and for all the people of Israel.

For himself, he is to bring a bull; for the people, two he-goats. Standing at the entrance of the sanctuary, he is to mark one of the goats "for God," and the other "for Azazel," as the "scapegoat" for the failings, mistakes, and errors of the people.

Afterwards Aaron slaughters the bull and the he-goat marked "for God," offering them upon the altar and sprinkling their blood around the altar as a means of asking God to forgive the people for their sins. When that ritual is concluded, the he-goat marked "for Azazel" is brought to Aaron. He places his hands upon it and confesses all the wrongdoing of the people. The goat is then sent off into the wilderness, where it is set free to wan-

der and to die, thereby bringing forgiveness for the people's sins.

· 2 ·

The people are commanded to observe Yom Kippur, a "Day of Atonement." It is to be a day of fasting and complete rest, where no work is done and where the people seek forgiveness for all their sins.

· 3 ·

Chapters 17–26 of Leviticus are known as the "Holiness Code." They contain the ritual and ethical practices that one must carry out to live a sacred or holy Jewish life.

Moses warns the people against offering any sacrifices outside the sanctuary or to any other gods. They are told that they may neither drink the blood of animals nor eat the flesh of animals killed by other animals.

· 4 ·

Moses condemns the sexual practices of surrounding peoples and tells the Israelites they must follow God's commandments regarding family purity. These commandments include rules against debasing and shaming oneself or others by removing one's clothing or by having sexual intercourse outside of marriage or with animals. Such acts are abhorrent and defile the people of Israel.

· 5 ·

Parashat Kedoshim continues the "Holiness Code" with God's commandment to the people of Israel. They are told: "You shall be holy, for I, the Lord your God, am holy." Echoing the laws given at Mount Sinai, the people are told to (1) honor their parents, (2) observe the Sabbaths and festivals, (3) refrain from worshiping idols, (4) offer sacrifices acceptably, and (5) leave corners of the field and parts of the vineyard for the poor.

They are also commanded *not to* (6) steal, (7) deal deceitfully, (8) swear falsely in God's name, (9) defraud others, (10) commit robbery, (11) keep the wages of laborers overnight, (12) insult the deaf, (13) place a stumbling block before the blind, (14) render unfair decisions in court, (15) favor the poor or rich in court decisions, (16) pass on rumors or stories about others, (17) profit from the difficulties of others, (18) hate others, (19) suffer guilt for truthfully warning others about the consequences of otheir actions, (20) take vengeance, and (21) bear a grudge.

In conclusion Moses tells them: (22) "Love your neighbor as yourself."

·6·

To these commandments are added others: people must not allow their animals to mate with different kinds of animals; they must not plant a field with two different kinds of seed; they must not wear garments made of two different kinds of material.

The people are presented with regulations for planting fruit trees. They are told they may eat the fruits of these trees only after five years. The people are also forbidden to eat blood, to practice magic or soothsaying, to shave off the side-growth of the beard, to cut the flesh as a way of mourning the dead, or to turn to ghosts, spirits, or to the cult of Moloch, which practiced child sacrifice. In addition, a man who has sexual relations with a slave is to pay damages to her.

The people are also instructed to show honor to the aging and love to the stranger, "for you were strangers in the land of Egypt." They are also warned against using false weights and measures and insulting parents.

·7·

Several laws are given regarding family relationships. Adultery, homosexuality, sexual relations with animals, and marriage to siblings, half-sisters and brothers, or former in-laws are prohibited, as are sexual relations with aunts or uncles.

The Israelites are promised that, if they observe all these commandments, they will be set apart from all nations as "holy." They will be God's people.

THEMES

Parashat Achare Mot-Kedoshim contains three important themes:

1. Yom Kippur and the "scapegoat."

2. "Holiness" in Jewish tradition.

3. "Loving" others.

PEREK ALEF: *Seeking Meaning for the Strange Ritual of the Scapegoat*

Yom Kippur, or "Day of Atonement," has been called "the climax and crown of the Jewish religious year." Through twenty-four hours of fasting and prayer, Jews are challenged to review the ethical and spiritual standards by which they live and to reaffirm their commitment to carry out the mitzvot, or "commandments," of their faith. In defining the message of Yom Kippur, Rabbi Bernard B. Bamberger writes that "it speaks to each human being and seeks to bring each person into harmony with others and with God."

The origins of Yom Kippur are shrouded in mystery. There are, however, some fascinating traditions associated with the sacred day that help us understand its popularity among the ancient Israelites. One of the most significant and baffling of these is the ceremony of the "scapegoat."

Defining "scapegoat":
The term "scapegoat" was apparently coined by William Tyndale, the first great English Bible translator. Thereafter, it came to be used for a person, animal, or object to which the impurity or guilt of a community was formally transferred and then removed . . . in common usage today, a scapegoat is someone whom people blame for

their own misfortunes, and even for their faults and sins. . . ." (Bernard J. Bamberger, The Torah: A Modern Commentary, p. 860)

As described in the Torah, Aaron is to take two he-goats from the Israelite community as a sin offering. After he has slaughtered a bull as a sin offering for himself and his household, he is to bring the two he-goats to the entrance of the sanctuary. There he is to cast lots upon the two he-goats, designating one "for God" and the other "for Azazel." The one "for God" is to be slaughtered as a sin offering on the altar of the sanctuary. Aaron is then to place his hands upon the head of the other marked "for Azazel" and to confess all the transgressions of the Israelites upon it. Afterwards the goat is to be sent off to wander and die in the wilderness. (See Leviticus 16.)

According to the *Mishnah*, the ritual of taking the scapegoat from the Jerusalem Temple into the wilderness began as a very important ceremony, but later it became a cause for great commotion, even embarrassment. People would stand along the path and ridicule the ceremony. Some would point a finger at the goat marked "for Azazel," upon which the High Priest had confessed Israel's sins, and mockingly remark: "Such a tiny scapegoat for such a huge load of sins!" (*Yoma* 6:4)

As we may imagine, many interpreters have asked: What is the meaning of this strange ceremony? How does it relate to the religious significance of Yom Kippur?

Ibn Ezra

Commentator ibn Ezra refers to the ritual of the scapegoat marked "for Azazel" as a "mystery." He suggests that it may be connected with a pagan religious practice of offerings to "goat-demons," which were prohibited by the Torah. Such sacrifices may have been gifts to a god many believed ruled the wilderness and was a power for bringing evil into the world. (See Leviticus 17:7.) The scapegoat was offered to protect people from evil influences.

If ibn Ezra is correct, why would Jews have used a ritual that seems to mimic pagan practices forbidden by the laws of Torah? Modern interpreter Baruch A. Levine explains that the ritual of the he-goat "for Azazel" was not considered a gift to a pagan god. Nor was it seen as a pagan rite. Instead, the scapegoat marked "for Azazel" was a dramatic means through which the Jewish people rejected the influences and temptations of evil symbolized by Azazel.

Levine argues that the sanctuary ceremony was "based on an awareness that, even in a world ruled by God, evil forces were at work—forces that had to be destroyed if God's earthly home . . . was not to be defiled."

In transferring all the sins of the people to the scapegoat and then sending it out into the wilderness marked "for Azazel," ancient Jews believed they were forcing "the iniquities of the people back on Azazel." In a way, Levine concludes, they created a "boomerang effect," returning evil influence "back to its point of departure, to the wilderness!" In doing so, they demonstrated that only God had power in their lives and that they had defeated the symbol of evil—Azazel. (*JPS Torah Commentary: Leviticus*, pp. 250–253)

Levine admits that "this entire complex of rituals seems to be predicated on magical perceptions" and that his interpretation is "unacceptable to many modern students of the Bible, as it was to certain traditional schools."

Rambam (Maimonides)

One of those commentators is Moses Maimonides, who rejects any identification of the scapegoat with powers or angels of evil. He declares, "It is not a sacrifice to Azazel, God forbid." Instead of being a ritual with magical powers, says Maimonides, the scapegoat ceremony is an "active allegory" meant "to impress the mind of the sinner that his sins must lead him to a wasteland." When those who have broken the laws of Torah see that their sins are placed upon the he-goat and sent out into the wilderness, it is hoped that they will "break with their sins . . . distance themselves from them, and turn back to God in sincere repentance." (*Guide for the Perplexed* 3:46)

Function of the scapegoat

The function of the scapegoat . . . serves as an expression of the educational message of Yom Kippur. Every year one is afforded the opportunity to determine one's own life for better, to purify the heart for service according to the will of God. This holy day teaches us our greatest gift: "Freedom of choice is given." (Avot 3:19; B.S. Jacobson, *Meditations on the Torah, p. 173*)

Abravanel

Abravanel also suggests a symbolic interpretation for the ritual of the scapegoat. He believes that the two he-goats, one marked "for God," the other marked "for Azazel," are to remind Jews of the twin brothers Esau and Jacob. Esau, like the he-goat marked "for Azazel," wandered into the wilderness away from his people, its laws, and its traditions. Jacob, like the he-goat marked "for God," lived a life devoted to God's service. According to Abravanel, when Aaron, and the High Priests after him, cast lots to decide which of the two he-goats would be marked "for God" or "for Azazel," Jews were to be reminded that they had a significant free choice to make. They could live like Jacob or Esau, "for God" or "for Azazel." (See commentary on Leviticus 16.)

Hirsch

The meaning of casting lots

Rabbi Samson Raphael Hirsch sees in the ceremony of deciding which goat will be "for God" and which "for Azazel" a symbol of the choice each Jew makes on Yom Kippur. "We can decide for God, *gathering together all the powers of resistance we have been given to resist everything that would tear us away from our vocation to be near to God. . . . Or we can decide* for Azazel *and uphold, unmastered, our selfish life of desires, and . . . give ourselves over to the uncontrolled might of sensuality. . . ."* (Comment on Leviticus 16:10)

Rabbi Hillel Silverman calls attention to the fact that, according to the Talmud, the two he-goats "must be identical in size, appearance, and value." In this, he contends, is an important lesson. The two goats symbolize what we are willing to give for our own pleasure and enjoyment (for Azazel) and what we are willing to give for the welfare and security of others (for God).

The Talmud insists, says Silverman, that the two goats be identical in size, appearance, and value in order to teach the lesson that "all we devote to personal pleasure and self-aggrandizement (for Azazel) goes 'into the wilderness,' unless we also sacrifice for the Lord and 'make atonement.'" (*From Week to Week*, pp. 108–109)

In other words, the ancient ritual is not just about the "scapegoat," but it is about what is done to both he-goats. One of them ends up as a sacred sacrifice "for God," symbolizing our generosity to others and loyalty to God; the other, "for Azazel," is sent off to wander and die in the wilderness, a sign that serving only our selfish pleasures and pride is a waste of our precious potentials. It is like wasting them in the wilderness. The ritual for both he-goats on Yom Kippur is a reminder of the delicate balance, between caring about oneself and about others, that each person is challenged to achieve.

While its origins are clouded in mystery, the ceremony of the two he-goats continued until the destruction of the Temple in 70 C.E. Interest in uncovering its meaning and connection to Yom Kippur, however, has not ceased. Was it a magical way of ridding the people of Israel of its sins? Was the scapegoat, marked "for Azazel," actually sent out into the wilderness as a sacrifice to a demon or god of evil? Is the scapegoat ceremony a symbol of the various spiritual and ethical choices Jews must make on each Yom Kippur?

Perhaps, in the case of this ancient tradition of the scapegoat, we have an example where all the interpretations provided through the centuries may be correct!

PEREK BET: *Defining "Holiness" in Jewish Tradition*

Parashat Kedoshim begins with God's command to the Jewish people: "You shall be holy (*kedoshim*), for I, the Lord your God, am holy (*kadosh*)." (Leviticus 19:2)

Many Torah interpreters ask what such a commandment means. Does it have to do with a special state of ritual purity? Since it is stated in the midst of a description of rituals associated with the ancient sanctuary, can it have to do with being qualified to enter the sanctuary? Is the commandment to "be holy" possible or practical? Is it realistic to expect a human being to "be holy" as God is "holy"?

Three of the oldest interpretations of the commandment to "be holy" provide some valuable answers to such questions. Rabbi Hiyya, who lived in Israel during the third century, stresses that Moses was told to present the commandment, "You shall be holy, for I, the Lord your God, am holy," to *the whole Israelite community.*" The commandment was given not to a few pious priests or individuals but rather to the entire community. Achieving the state of holiness, therefore, is not something done by one person or a small group of persons but rather by the whole people.

Rabbi Levi, who taught with Rabbi Hiyya, emphasizes that the commandment to "be holy" and the section of Torah following it were presented directly to the people because "the Ten Commandments are contained in it." Rabbi Levi may be hinting that the way to holiness is through observance of all the commandments listed in this section of Torah. Seeing a parallel between the contents of the Ten Commandments given to Moses on Mount Sinai and the mitzvot presented in these chapters of Leviticus, Levi concludes that God not only commanded the people to "be holy" but stressed the particular moral way of life that would demonstrate that they were a distinct people. (*Leviticus Rabbah* 24)

The *Sifra*, a fourth-century commentary on Leviticus, echos Rabbi Levi's view. It interprets the words *kedoshim tiheyu* ("you shall be holy") as *perushim tiheyu* ("you shall be separate"). Some scholars say this is a reference to the Pharisees, who were known by the Hebrew name *Perushim* and who taught that Jews achieved "holiness," or a special status of honor by God, if they carefully observed all the commandments.

Other interpreters argue that the authors of the *Sifra* meant to emphasize the unique responsibility of Jews to become a "kingdom of priests and a *goy kodesh*, or 'holy nation.'" They believed that, by living a Jewish life through carrying out the commandments of Torah, Jews were to be different from other nations, religions, and peoples. By interpreting the word *kedoshim* as *perushim*, the *Sifra*'s authors contend that the words "be holy" mean "be different, unique, separate from the ways of others. Be distinct in your moral and ritual way of life."

Does this mean that Jews are to withdraw from the societies in which they live or from contact with people of other religions and national origins? Modern philosopher Martin Buber says no. He writes: "Israel must, in imitating God by being a holy nation, similarly not withdraw from the world of the nations but rather radiate a positive influence on them through every aspect of Jewish living." For Buber being *kadosh*, or "different, unique," does not mean retreating from contact with other religious and national groups. Instead, it is a special goal and responsibility. It means that the Jewish people must achieve an ethical and spiritual excellence that can enrich and "influence" all other peoples. (*Darko shel Mikra*, p. 96)

Yet what is the source of that positive "influence"? What may Buber mean by "every aspect of Jewish living"?

Surveying the commandments clustered around the words "Be holy, for I, the Lord your God, am holy" provides a significant answer. Taken together they add up to a definition of "holiness" in Jewish tradition. Nearly "every aspect of Jewish living" is noted. Chapters 17–26 of Leviticus, which have become known to biblical scholars as the "Holiness Code," contain commandments that deal not only with the Sabbath, the festivals, and the different sacrifices to be offered at the sanctuary but also include commandments regulating the moral life of the Jewish community.

The list of ethical commandments encompasses nearly every aspect of human relationships. According to these commandments, Jewish morality forbids: exposure of nakedness, incest, infidelity by husband or wife, idolatry or the worship of other gods, declaring false oaths, stealing, dealing deceitfully or falsely, defrauding another, retaining a worker's wage overnight, insulting the deaf, misleading the blind, rendering unfair decisions, favoring the poor in a dispute, showing partiality to the rich in a dispute, dealing dishonestly in business, profiting by taking advantage of others' misfortune, carrying grudges, spreading hated, taking vengeance, practicing divination, soothsaying, or turning to ghosts and spirits. On the positive side, Jewish ethics command: reverence for parents, leaving the corners of the field and some of the fruit of the vineyard for the poor and stranger, judging all people fairly, warning others who are about to commit a wrong doing, and loving others as you love yourself.

What emerges in this Torah definition of "holiness" is a unique combination of both ethical and ritual demands. When the people are commanded "Be holy," they are actually being challenged with a unique combination of moral and spiritual obligations. God demands that they live by these practices and shape their relationships and community with them. In so doing, they will become a "kingdom of priests and a holy nation." As a model of holiness, they will also inspire or, to use Martin Buber's phrase, "radiate a positive influence on them."

To be holy
Rabbi Chaim Sofer comments that "to be holy" . . . means "not merely in the privacy of your home and ashamed of your faith in public. Be not, as the assimilationists put it, 'A Jew at home and a man outside.' Be holy 'in the community,' in public, out in the open, in society. Among your own people or in the midst of strangers, wherever you may find yourself, never be ashamed of your character and sanctity as a Jew." (Divre Sha'are Chaim)

Rabbi Aha explained the meaning of "be holy" by quoting the opinion of Rabbi Tanhum, the son of Rabbi Hiyyah: "If a person can protest a wrongdoing of another and does not, or if he can help support students of Torah and does not, such a person is not considered holy. But, if a person

does protest the wrongdoing of others and does support students of Torah, that person attains to holiness." (Leviticus Rabbah 15:1)

The idea of holiness implies that what we do and what we make of our lives matters not only to us as individuals, not only to society, but to the entire cosmos. A divine purpose runs through all existence. We can ally ourselves to it or oppose it—or, perhaps, worse, we can ignore it. (Bernard J. Bamberger, The Torah: A Modern Commentary, *pp. 891–892)*

The rabbis of the Talmud emphasize that each Jew has the power to add to the achievement of holiness by the people of Israel. They speak of the "influence" of those who study Torah, calling attention to two types of students. One type studies Torah, generously supports scholars, speaks kindly to others, and is honest and honorable in all business dealings. Of such a person, people say: "Such and such studies Torah. His father and his teacher deserve to be proud of him, for his deeds reflect honor upon his tradition." The other type of person studies Torah but is dishonest, unkind, and selfish. So others say: "He learns Torah, but his deeds are corrupt and objectionable. He brings dishonor to his people, to the Torah, and to God." (*Yoma* 86a)

Clearly, the rabbis of the Talmud are concerned with the reputation of the Torah and of the Jewish people. If one lives by the commandment "Be holy" and carries out the laws that define "holiness," then the people of Israel are strengthened in their responsibility to be a model of moral decency and an influence for good among all peoples. For the rabbis of the Talmud, to "be holy" means that every Jew must ask: "What are the consequences of my decisions, choices, words, and promises? Will they improve the world in which I live? Will they reflect credit upon my people, upon the Torah, and upon God?"

Achieving holiness
To say that God is "holy" is similar to saying that He is great, powerful, merciful, just, wise. . . . In order to achieve a holiness of the kind associated with God . . . Israel would have to

observe His laws and commandments. The way to holiness, in other words, was for Israelites, individually and collectively, to emulate God's attributes. . . . God shows the way and Israel follows. (Baruch A. Levine, JPS Torah Commentary: Leviticus, p. 256)

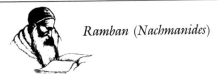

Ramban (Nachmanides)

Such questions may have been on the mind of Nachmanides as he thought about the meaning of the words "You shall be holy, for I, the Lord your God, am holy." In his discussion of the commandment he raises a significant point. He argues that one can carry out the commandments but also be a selfish, mean, and corrupt human being. "A person," he comments, "can be a scoundrel with the full permission of the Torah."

Proving his point, Nachmanides says a person can follow all the sexual laws mentioned in the Torah but take advantage of his own wife in satisfying his uncontrolled passions. Or a person can drink too much, eat excessively, carelessly use obscenities, or speak derisively about others. In business dealings a person can uphold the law of not wronging another but still cheat others by being unwilling to reach fair compromises.

Nachmanides believes that, because one can always find loopholes in the Torah law, people will take advantage of it. That is why the Torah not only provides a long list of commandments dealing with every aspect of ethical and ritual life but also contains the "general command" to "be holy," reminding us "to separate ourselves from those things that are permitted but that we can do without . . . from unnecessary and ugly things." To "be holy," as Nachmanides interprets it, is to refuse to take advantage of legal loopholes or overindulge in matters permitted by the Torah. (See commentary on Leviticus 19:2.)

While interpreted in a variety of ways, the words "You shall be holy, for I, the Lord your God, am holy" have been a constant challenge to the Jewish people. In some ages they influenced Jews to separate themselves from other cultures and peoples. At other times they were understood as a reminder that the highest aim of Jewish living is to reach

a "holiness" that reflects honor upon God, Torah, and the Jewish people. Today the ancient words continue to demand new interpretations and new standards for defining what is *kadosh*, or "holy," in Jewish tradition.

PEREK GIMEL: *Can We Love Others as Ourselves?*

Parashat Kedoshim contains one of the most quoted of all commandments within the Torah: "Love your neighbor as yourself." (Leviticus 19:18)

What does this statement mean? Can "love" be *commanded*? Is it possible for human beings to love others, especially outside their families, with the same level of interest and commitment that they have for themselves? What about those who come to harm us or who treat us unjustly? Can we be expected to love them as we love ourselves?

Zugot

One of the earliest explanations of the Torah's commandment comes in the form of a story told about Rabbi Hillel, a popular teacher of the first century B.C.E. Once a non-Jew challenged him with the promise: "I will convert to Judaism if you can teach me the whole Torah while I stand on one foot." Rabbi Hillel's response was immediate. "What is hateful to you do not do to your neighbor. That is the whole Torah. The rest is commentary. Now go and learn it." (*Shabbat* 31a)

It is obvious that Hillel preferred stating the Torah's positive commandment to "love your neighbor as yourself" in a negative way. On other occasions, Hillel also deliberately chose a negative formulation instead of a positive one. For example, he taught: "If I am not for myself, who will be for me? If I care only for myself, what am I? And, if not now, when?" (*Avot* 1:14) He also taught: "Do not separate yourself from the community. Do not be certain of yourself until the day of your death. Do not judge your neighbor until you have stood in his place. Do not say:

'When I have leisure time, I will study.' You may never have leisure time." (*Avot* 2:5)

From Hillel's statements we might conclude that he transposed the positive commandment about loving one's neighbor into a negative formulation because he was convinced that it was easier to understand. We can identify what hurts and harms us. We can say what brings us pain. Hillel's statement counsels that "loving our neighbors as ourselves" means asking, "If my neighbor did to me what I am thinking of saying or doing to him, would it hurt or harm me?" If the answer is "it would bring pain or harm," then it must be avoided.

But what if my tastes are different from my neighbor's? What if my neighbor is hurt by matters or statements that simply do not affect me at all? Is it fair to make judgments about what is hurtful or enjoyable to others from my own narrow perspective? Is it not true that "one person's meat is another person's poison"?

We are told that, when Rabbi Akiba, who considered himself a student of Rabbi Hillel, suggested that the commandment "Love your neighbor as yourself" was "the greatest principle of the Torah," his colleague ben Azzai disagreed. Ben Azzai argued that the teaching "God created man in the likeness of God" (Genesis 5:1) was a more important principle.

Ben Azzai's view is that people cannot use their own feelings or attitudes as a basis for deciding how to treat others. Preferences, tastes, and perceptions of what brings happiness and what brings pain are very different. Some people are careless about their property; others are not. Because a person may not consider a remark insulting does not mean that another will agree. "You should not say," ben Azzai explains, " 'Since I am hated, let my neighbor be similarly hated or, since I am in trouble, let my neighbor be similarly in trouble.' You should remember that both you and your neighbor were created in the likeness of God." In other words, we are to treat others with respect and love, not because we are commanded to do so, nor because we understand their feelings, tastes, or reactions to be like our own. We are to respect the rights, dignity, and feelings of others because, like us, they were created in God's likeness. (*Genesis Rabbah* 24)

Why should we love our neighbor?
Commenting on the commandment "Love your neighbor as yourself: I am the Lord," ibn Ezra explains that one is responsible to love other human beings because the one God has created all of them. (See Leviticus 19:18.)

Moses Maimonides also seeks to clarify what the Torah means when it commands "Love your neighbor as yourself." What is meant, says Maimonides, is that "you should love your neighbor with all the qualities and modes of love with which you love yourself." In other words, "the quality and nature of our love must be of the highest category—parallel to that which we employ in promoting our own welfare."

Maimonides, however, realizes the difficulty of the challenge of loving others. Therefore, he suggests it may not always be possible for human beings to provide an equal quantity of concern for the welfare of others. Love and concern, he counsels, are expressed in varying intensities "depending upon the circumstances." There are times when promoting the welfare of others may clash with what we believe is in our own best interest and welfare. In such cases, Maimonides suggests that the intensity and quantity of our love may be compromised. "The Torah," Maimonides concludes, "does not command the extent of our love but rather the genuine character of it."

As to the character of our love, Maimonides is quite specific. Loving your neighbor as you love yourself means visiting the sick, comforting mourners, joining a funeral procession, celebrating the marriage ceremony with bride and groom, offering hospitality, caring for the dead, or delivering a eulogy. Concluding his list of examples, Maimonides writes: "All the things that you would want others to do for you—do for your brothers and sisters." (*Mishneh Torah, Hilchot Evel 14:1*)

Like Maimonides, Nachmanides also senses that "loving" another person with the same intensity and quantity of concern that one has for oneself is not possible. He bluntly declares that "human beings cannot be expected to love their neighbors as they love their own souls." What the

Torah means by the command to "love your neighbor as you love yourself," Nachmanides argues, is that people should "wish their neighbors well in all things, just as they wish success for themselves."

Nachmanides maintains that "even if a person wishes another well in everything, in wealth, honor, learning, and wisdom, he will not want him to be absolutely equal with him. He will want to be superior to him in some ways." The Torah recognizes this truth about human beings. That is why, says Nachmanides, "the Torah condemns this form of selfishness." We are commanded "to love your neighbor as yourself" so that "we will learn to wish others success in all things, just as we wish well for ourselves—and to do so without reservations." (See discussion on Leviticus 19:18.)

Malbim

Rabbi Meir Lev ben Yechiel Michael, known as Malbim, disagrees with both Maimonides and Nachmanides. He argues that the matter of loving one's neighbor is not an expression of feelings or wishing others "success in all things." Instead, the commandment has to do with how one behaves toward others, with actions and not with thoughts.

Drawing upon Hillel's negative teaching and upon the philosophical writings of a contemporary, German philosopher Immanuel Kant (1724–1804), Malbim says that a person should not just wish for his neighbor what he wants for himself, namely, "advantage and protection from harm. He should endeavor to do everything that is to the advantage of his neighbor, whether in terms of bodily health or success in business . . . and it goes without saying that he should not be responsible for doing anything to his neighbor that he would not wish to be done to him. . . . For instance, if a person is prepared to harm his neighbor for the sake of his own advantage, he should ask himself whether he would wish this kind of conduct to become a universal rule." A person would say to himself: "Do I want to live

in a world where everyone is free to do what I am about to do?" (See discussion on Leviticus 19:18.)

Peli

Loving is also forgiving
Basing his observation on one first created by the Ba'al Shem Tov, Pinchas Peli writes: "It does not take much effort to love good people, nice people. The test of the fulfillment of the commandment is in loving those who are not as good and lovable in one's eyes. 'Love your fellow human—as yourself,' as you accept yourself with all your faults and shortcomings, accept others the same way." (Torah Today, p. 141)

Loving without qualifications
Simcha Zissel Ziv, a teacher of the Musar, or "Ethical," movement of Judaism, writes: "The Torah demands that we promote the best interests of others. This cannot be accomplished by repressing our hatred or our rejection of them, nor by summoning up our love as a duty. Such endeavors will never bring genuine love. We simply have to love human beings as we love ourselves. We do not love ourselves because we are human beings, but our self-love comes to us naturally, without calculations, without qualifications and reservations, without any aims and ends. We never hear anybody say: 'I have already fulfilled my obligation towards myself!'—We must love others the same way, naturally and spontaneously, joyously and creatively, without set limits, purposes, or rationalizations." (As found in B.S. Jacobson, Meditations on the Torah, pp. 180–181)

This idea that love for oneself and love for others are mutually connected forms the basis of modern psychologist Erich Fromm's classic work *The Art of Loving* (Harper and Row, New York, 1974). Stressing the importance of "self-love," Fromm writes, "The idea expressed in the biblical 'Love your neighbor as yourself!' implies that respect for one's own integrity and uniqueness, love for and understanding of one's own self, cannot be separated from respect and love and understanding for another individual. The love for my own self is inseparably connected with the love for any other being."

Fromm explains that "love is an activity . . . it is primarily *giving*, not receiving." In the act of giving, we do not lose, sacrifice, or "give up" that which is precious to us. Instead, giving allows us to experience our power, our vitality. "In giving," Fromm observes, "I experience my strength, my wealth, my power. This experience of heightened vitality and potency fills me with joy. I experience myself as overflowing, spending, alive. . . . Giving is more joyous than receiving . . . because in the act of giving lies the expression of my aliveness."

In defining "genuine love" as "giving," Fromm stresses that one must learn to give to oneself even before giving to others. "Love of others and love of ourselves are not alternatives. . . . Love, in principle, *is indivisible as far as the connection between 'objects' and one's own self is concerned*. Genuine love," Fromm writes, "is an expression of productiveness and implies care, respect, responsibility, and knowledge (of one's self and others). . . . It is an active striving for the growth and happiness of the loved person, rooted in one's own capacity to love. . . . If," Fromm warns, "an individual is able to love productively, he loves himself too; if he can love *only* others, he cannot love at all."

The Torah's command to "love your neighbor as yourself" continues to provoke significant questions about the meaning of love. Despite the various opinions and definitions, however, it is clear that Jewish tradition challenges us to love ourselves by striving for self-understanding, respect, and a sense of our powers for giving and to transform our love of self into a generous love for others. (pp. 18–19, 48–53)

QUESTIONS FOR STUDY AND DISCUSSION

1. Compare the various interpretations given for the "scapegoat." Which makes the most sense? Why?

2. Jews have often been the target for hatred, the "scapegoat" for the frustrations, anger, and disappointments of others. Rabbi Milton Steinberg suggests that only Jews who are knowledgeable and proud of the "positive healthful values" of their tradition will not be "invaded by self-contempt." Such Jews would not be affected by the hatred of those who would try to make them scapegoats. Do you agree? Why?

3. How would you define "holiness" in Jewish tradition? What are its elements? What must the individual Jew do to achieve "holiness"? What must the Jewish people do?

4. Is it realistic to expect that human beings can really fulfill the commandment "Love your neighbor as yourself"? Do you agree or disagree with Erich Fromm that, unless you love yourself, you cannot really love your neighbor?

5. Rabbi Leo Baeck notes the talmudic teaching that "the person who withholds love from another is like one who rejects the service of God." Baeck comments: "To place oneself in the position of our neighbor, to understand his hope and his yearning, to grasp the needs of his heart is the presupposition of all neighborly love, the outcome of our 'knowledge' of his soul." (*The Essence of Judaism*, Schocken Books, New York, 1948, pp. 211–212) How would you compare Baeck's observations with those of Hillel, Maimonides, Nachmanides, and Malbim?

PARASHAT EMOR
Leviticus 21:1–24:23

Parashat Emor presents the laws regulating the lives of priests, who presided over the sanctuary and its sacrifices. Mention is made of the donations and offerings that are acceptable for the sanctuary. This portion also includes a calendar of celebration, including the Sabbath, Pesach, Shavuot, Rosh Hashanah, Yom Kippur, and Sukot. It concludes with the laws dealing with profanity, murder, and the maiming of others.

OUR TARGUM

· 1 ·

Rules concerning the holiness of priests are presented to Aaron and his sons. They are not to touch a dead body except that of an immediate relative. They are not to shave their heads or the side-growth of their beards, or deliberately cut their skin to leave marks upon it. Neither are they allowed to marry divorced women. Only one without any physical impediment can become a priest.

A priest who has a skin disease, has touched a dead body, or has had a sexual emission is considered unclean and may not officiate in the sanctuary, nor may he take donations or offerings from the people. After sunset he is to be declared clean, and he can eat once again from the donations and offerings. Lay people, except those belonging to the priests, may not eat from the donations or offerings.

All offerings, whether donated by Israelites or non-Israelites, are acceptable in the sanctuary. However, any blemished or contaminated offering is to be rejected by the priests.

Moses reminds the people that the purpose of "faithfully" observing all these commandments is to "sanctify God," to demonstrate their love and loyalty to God.

· 2 ·

Moses continues by presenting the people with the *moadei Adonai*, the "sacred times or occasions [festivals] of God" that they are to observe.

The Sabbath is to be celebrated every seventh day as a time of complete rest—a day of no work.

On the evening of the fourteenth day of the first month (Nisan) and for the next seven days,

Pesach is to be celebrated. The first and last days are to be treated as sacred occasions during which work is prohibited.

Seven weeks are to be counted from the first day of Pesach until the festival of Shavuot, or "Weeks." Special offerings of grain, two bread loaves, choice flour, one bull, two rams, and seven unblemished lambs are to be brought to the priests for offerings on the fiftieth day. It is to be observed as a sacred occasion, a day of no work.

In the midst of presenting the sacred calendar of celebration, Moses reminds the people that, when they reap their harvests, they must leave the edges of the field and the gleanings of the harvest for the poor and the stranger.

He then tells the people that the first day of the seventh month (Tishri) is to be celebrated with loud blasts of a horn and is to be a sacred day of no work.

Ten days later they are to observe Yom Kippur, a sacred day of no work, of "self-denial" and fasting. It is to be a day of complete rest from evening to evening.

For seven days from the fifteenth day of the seventh month (Tishri), the festival of Sukot, or "Booths," is to be celebrated. The people are to build booths and, during the festival, reside in them as a reminder that the Israelites lived in booths when they were freed from Egyptian slavery. On the first day of the festival the people are to bring the fruit of the hadar tree, the *etrog*, or "citron"; branches of palm trees, the *lulav;* boughs of leafy trees, myrtle; and branches of willow to the sanctuary. The first and eighth days of the celebration are rest days of no work. Burnt offerings, meal offerings, sacrifices, and libations are to be brought to the sanctuary.

· 3 ·

The Israelites are also told, as they were in Exodus 27:20–21 (see *Parashat Tetzaveh*), to bring clear oil of beaten olives to fuel continually the lamps of the sanctuary.

They are also instructed to bake twelve loaves and place them in the sanctuary along with pure frankincense as a token offering for the bread. Afterwards the priests are to eat the loaves.

· 4 ·

Moses reports an argument between an Israelite man and another man whose mother was an Israelite and whose father was Egyptian. The man, whose Israelite mother was a woman named Shelomith daughter of Dibri of the tribe of Dan, profaned God's name and was placed in custody.

Moses orders him to be taken outside the camp and to be stoned to death, declaring that whoever profanes God's name shall be punished with death.

He also declares that, if one person murders another, he shall be put to death. If one causes bodily harm to another, then the same will be done to him or her as punishment. In other words, declares Moses, "fracture for fracture, eye for eye, tooth for tooth." Furthermore, whoever takes the life of an animal shall make restitution for it. In all these matters, Moses tells the people, Israelites and non-Israelites shall be treated with the same standard of justice.

THEMES

Parashat Emor contains two important themes:

1. The evolution and meaning of the three festivals: Pesach, Shavuot, and Sukot.
2. Eye for eye: Retribution or compensation?

PEREK ALEF: *The Jewish Festivals: Pesach, Shavuot, and Sukot*

Rabbi Abraham Joshua Heschel observed that "Judaism is a *religion of time* aiming at *the sanctification of time.* Unlike the space-minded man to whom time is unvaried . . . homogeneous, to whom all hours are alike . . . the Bible senses the diversified character of time . . . Judaism teaches us . . . to be attached to sacred events, to learn how to consecrate sanctuaries that emerge from the magnificent stream of a year." (*The Sabbath: Its Meaning for Modern Man,* Farrar, Straus and Giroux, New York, 1951, p. 8)

Parashat Emor contains the calendar of sacred celebrations through which Jews have sanctified time, setting aside days for uplifting, enjoying, and sharing the meanings of human existence. Chapter 23 of Leviticus describes the weekly Sabbath, Rosh Hashanah (known within the Torah as "the first day of the seventh month" and "the day of blowing of the horn"), and Yom Kippur, as well as the three festivals of Pesach, Shavuot, and Sukot.

Both Pesach and Sukot begin on the evening of the fourteenth day of the month, at the time of the full moon, and both festivals are seven days in length. According to the Torah, the first and last days of these festivals are observed like the Sabbath: from sundown to sundown, with no work. Shavuot is also a no-work day but is celebrated on the fiftieth day after the beginning of Pesach.

The Jewish calendar
The Jewish calendar consists of 12 months with a little more than 29½ days in each month. It is a lunar calendar with each month beginning at the time of a new moon. An entire year consists of about 354⅓ days, 11 days less than the 365¼ days of the solar calendar year. As a result, every few years, an extra month is added to the Jewish calendar to make a leap year and to keep accurate the adjustment of the months to the season. This extra month is known as Adar Sheni, *or* Adar II.

Months and celebrations
The Jewish calendar begins in the spring. The first month of the year is Nisan.

Nisan	15–22	—Pesach
	2	—Yom ha-Shoah
Iyar	5	—Yom ha-Atzmaut
	18	—Lag ba-Omer
Sivan	6–7	—Shavuot
Tamuz	17	—Fast Day
Av	9	—Fast Day
Elul		

Tishri	1	—Rosh Hashanah
	3	—Fast Day
	10	—Yom Kippur
	15–21	—Sukot
	22	—Shemini Atzeret
	23	—Simchat Torah
Cheshvan		
Kislev 25—Tevet 2		
		—Chanukah
Tevet		
Shevat	15	—Tu Bishvat
Adar	13	—Fast Day
	14	—Purim

Just as Jewish commentators have seriously questioned the motives of biblical personalities and the reasons for the Torah's laws and commandments, they have also focused upon the meanings and evolution of Jewish holy days. What makes them "holy"? How are they unique? What do they contribute to our human quest for purpose and fulfillment?

Probing the meaning of Pesach

There are several descriptions of Pesach within the Torah. The one found in *Parashat Emor* indicates that the celebration begins on the evening of the fourteenth day of the first month of the year and is to last seven days. The first and last days are to be celebrated, like the Sabbath, as rest days. No work is to be done on them. At the evening celebration on the fourteenth of the month, a *Pesach offering to God* is to be presented. On the fifteenth, the people are to celebrate *Chag ha-Matzot,* or "Festival of Unleavened Bread." In addition, Chapter 23 of Leviticus informs us that *matzah,* or "unleavened bread," is to be eaten by the people for the seven days of the celebration, and offerings are to be brought to the sanctuary.

Other sections of the Torah offer more information about the early Pesach festival. For example, just before the tenth and last plague is sent upon the Egyptians, Moses and Aaron are told that "this month" (the spring month of Nisan) will mark the beginning of the calendar year, in other words, the "new year." On the tenth day of the month, the head of the household will pick a lamb to be set aside until the evening of the four-teenth day. At twilight, the lamb will be slaughtered, its blood painted on the doorpost of each Israelite house, and its flesh roasted and eaten together with *matzah* and *merorim,* or "bitter herbs." Everything not eaten is to be destroyed by fire before dawn.

We are also informed that the head of each family is to wear a cloth around his loins and sandals on his feet, and he is to hold a staff in his hand. His special costume will make him look as if he were leaving on a journey. All these observances will stimulate children to ask: "What is the meaning of this ritual?" According to the Torah, he is to explain his strange costume to them by saying: "It is the *pesach* sacrifice to the Lord, because God passed over the houses of the Israelites in Egypt when God smote [killed] the Egyptian [firstborn], but saved our houses." (Exodus 12:1–27; also Deuteronomy 16)

This early description of ceremonies on the first night of Pesach contains some of the elements that are today part of the festival's *seder* ceremony. They include the *matzah, maror,* special meal, gathering of family, and the questions asked by the young people. While the *seder* ceremony did not evolve until the second century C.E., it is clear from the beginning that Pesach commemorates the liberation of the Jewish people from Egyptian slavery. It is a reminder of how God saved their "houses" and their firstborn and rescued them from oppression. The significance of freedom was to be dramatized at the beginning of each year, and it was to be taught to all the children.

Many centuries later, Jews in the Land of Israel journeyed, at Pesach time, to Jerusalem. The heads of each household would slaughter the *pesach* sacrifice, prepare it for roasting, and then take it to a place where the family group would eat it. By the time of Hillel and Shammai (first century B.C.E.), the Pesach meal had evolved into an elaborate banquet with a special *seder,* or "order," to it. The festivities included four cups of wine; the blessings for the wine; the eating of *matzah, maror, charoset* (a mixture of chopped nuts, apples, wine, and honey); the asking of questions by the children; mention of the *afikoman* (entertainment after dessert); the retelling of the liberation from Egypt; and the singing of Psalms 113–118. (*Mishnah, Pesachim* 5, 10)

The importance of the Pesach celebration is, however, not lost in the festivities of the banquet. The leader reminds the family group of its origins. He tells the group, "My father was a fugitive Aramean . . ." and he concludes the reflection upon its history with "the Lord freed us from Egypt. . . ." After explaining the symbols of the *pesach*, *matzah* and *maror*, he quotes the words of Rabban Gamaliel: "In every generation a person is obligated to see himself [herself] as if he [she] went forth from Egypt."

While the first *haggadah*, or "narration" of the Exodus, does not emerge until the ninth century in Babylonia, nearly all elements of the *seder* ceremony were already known. Rav Amram, who edited the first *haggadah*, however, adds some important innovations of his own. Building upon discussions and decisions of teachers in the great Babylonian academies, he introduces the *Kiddush*, or "ceremonial blessing for the wine," at the Pesach meal, organizes the Four Questions asked by the children at the *seder*, and includes a section describing four different kinds of participants at the *seder* meal.

In Rav Amram's *Haggadah*, the *seder* has become a "family learn-in," a time for recalling and discussing Jewish history and the miracle of freedom from Egyptian oppression. Referring to an all-night Pesach discussion in the town of Lod among Rabbi Eliezer, Rabbi Joshua, Rabbi Eleazar ben Azariah, Rabbi Akiba, and Rabbi Tarfon, Rav Amram's *Haggadah*, and all others after it, suggests a model for celebration. The Pesach *seder* is for bringing family and friends together. It is for bonding Jews to their history and to one another. Its discussion emphasizes all the difficult questions we ask about freedom, and its prayers offer thanks to God for liberating the Jewish people from Egyptian slavery.

In the gradual evolution of Pesach one sees how Jewish rituals and ceremonies have changed to meet new circumstances, needs, and tastes throughout the centuries. From sharing an all-night sacrifice and meal to the development of an elaborate banquet with a carefully written script, Pesach has become one of the most popular festivals of the Jewish year. Yet its powerful message and pupose have not been lost. Pesach remains the Jewish people's great celebration of freedom.

Probing the meaning of Shavuot

Just as the rituals of Pesach changed through the centuries, so did the celebration of the festival of Shavuot. What began as a harvest festival of rest and sacrifices on the fiftieth day after the first day of Pesach evolved through the centuries into *Zeman Matan Toratenu*, or "Season [Festival] of the Giving of Our Torah."

How and why did such a transformation take place?

Within the Torah, Shavuot is also known as *Chag ha-Katzir*, or "Harvest Festival" (Exodus 23:16), and as *Yom ha-Bikkurim*, or "Day of the First Fruits of the Harvest" (Numbers 28:26). *Shavuot* means "weeks" and refers to the span of seven weeks stretching from Pesach at the beginning of the barley harvest in the Land of Israel to the beginning of the wheat harvest. For the ancients, the fifty-day countdown was a journey from one harvest to the next.

On the fiftieth day the Israelites celebrated by bringing two loaves of bread, seven yearling lambs, one bull, and two rams with their meal offerings and libations to the sanctuary. These, along with one he-goat as a sin offering and two yearling lambs as a sacrifice of well-being, were presented to the priests. The festival was observed as a Sabbath and as a day of thanksgiving for a bountiful harvest. All forms of work were prohibited.

The *Mishnah* contains a description of how offerings were made at the Jerusalem sanctuary. When the Israelite entered, he would stand before a priest and declare: "My father was a fugitive Aramean. He went down to Egypt with meager numbers and sojourned there; but there he became a great and very populous nation. The Egyptians dealt harshly with us and oppressed us; they imposed heavy labor upon us. We cried to the Lord, the God of our ancestors, and the Lord heard our plea and saw our plight, our misery, and our oppression. The Lord freed us from Egypt by a mighty hand, by an outstretched arm and awesome power, and by signs and portents. God brought us to this place and gave us this land, a land flowing with milk and honey. Wherefore I now bring the first fruits of the soil that You, O Lord, have given me." (*Mishnah, Bikkurim* 3:2–5; also Deuteronomy 26:5–10)

As we have already noted, the words "My father was a fugitive Aramean . . ." are also used at the beginning of the Pesach *haggadah*'s narration about Jewish history. Here again on Shavuot the prayer expresses the individual's relationship to the slavery and liberation of the Jewish people. When reciting the story of oppression and freedom, one relives it, becomes part of it. By connecting thanksgiving for the harvest with gratefulness to God for liberty, the ancient Jew celebrated the fruits of the past and hope for the future.

Shavuot merged Jewish identity into a sacred partnership with the God of freedom and the harvest. The same God who liberates the seed from the darkness of earth to bloom in the bright sun and yield its fruit also liberates the Jewish people from oppression. For the ancients, Shavuot, like Pesach, was a time of rebirth, harvest, awakening, and liberation.

So how did this festival later emerge as *Zeman Matan Toratenu,* or "Festival of the Giving of Our Torah"?

No one can be sure. There are, as we may imagine, many theories. For instance, the rabbis of the Talmud point out that the Israelites arrived at Mount Sinai "on the third new moon" after their Exodus from Egypt. There they camped for three days and spent another three days creating boundaries around the mountain. That brought the date to the sixth of Sivan, fifty days after the beginning of Pesach. All of which, for the rabbis of the Talmud, proves that Shavuot is also the day on which the Israelites received the Torah at Mount Sinai. (*Shabbat* 86a)

Others, among them many modern scholars, believe that the attachment of the giving of the Torah at Mount Sinai to Shavuot coincides with the emergence of the synagogue and perhaps came after the destruction of the Jerusalem Temple in 70 C.E. With that destruction, pilgrimages to Jerusalem ceased, and the focus of the festival shifted from giving thanks for the harvest to giving thanks for God's revelation, the "harvest" of Torah.

This theory complements the view held by many teachers whose observations were included in the Midrash. For them the journey of the Jewish people from the fleshpots of Egypt led to the glorious moment at Mount Sinai when Moses received the Torah and the people accepted it with the pledge "We will do and we will hear." (Exodus 24:7) Within the newly emerging synagogue with its emphasis on Torah study, the drama of giving thanks for the first fruits was superceded on Shavuot by the drama of giving thanks for God's gift of Torah.

However—and whenever—the decision was made by the rabbis to recast Shavuot as *Zeman Matan Toratenu,* or the "Festival of the Giving of Our Torah," they made their intentions clear when they selected the Torah portion to be read on the festival. Rather than choosing a selection of Torah that describes the celebration of first fruits at the sanctuary, they designated Exodus 19:1–8 and 20:1–14, describing the arrival of the Israelites at Mount Sinai and containing the Ten Commandments. Clearly for them, the journey of liberation from bondage led to accepting the ethical and ritual laws of Torah and to the challenge of creating a just and caring society. For the rabbis whose views are recorded in the Midrash, it was the acceptance of the mitzvot, the commandments of Torah, that gave purpose to the Jewish people and justified their existence.

Rabbi Abdimi ben Hama ben Hasa playfully makes this point in his version of what happened at Mount Sinai: He describes God as picking up the mountain and holding it over the heads of the people. They look up at the danger, and God says to them, "If you accept the Torah, you will live. If not, I will bury you under Mount Sinai." Seeing their situation, the people respond with the words of Proverbs 3:18, "It is a tree of life to those who hold on to it. . . ."

Rabbi Abdimi's humor is meant to emphasize the choice for the Jewish people: life, if they choose to embrace the Torah; death, if they do not. In other words, the Torah is the lifeline of the Jew, the reason for Jewish survival. Fulfilling its mitzvot, living by its ethical and ritual standards, is the purpose of Jewish existence.

Shavuot, as *Zeman Matan Toratenu,* celebrates that sacred moment at Mount Sinai when the Jewish people committed themselves and all the generations afterwards to making the Torah a "tree of life." From its early origins as an agricultural thanksgiving day, known as *Chag ha-Katzir,* "Harvest Festival," and *Yom ha-Bikkurim,* "Day of the First Fruits of the Harvest," Shavuot emerges into a festival marking the central role of Torah in Jewish life. On Shavuot, Jews return to Mount Sinai, hear the Ten Commandments, and are reminded that they are partners with God in applying the teachings of Torah to every corner of society and to their personal lives.

Probing the meaning of Sukot

What we have already discovered about the evolution of Pesach and Shavuot is also true of the seven-day festival of Sukot. Named *Sukot,* from the plural of the Hebrew word *sukah,* or "booth," the week of celebration began as a harvest festival, but its rituals and meanings, like those of Shavuot, have changed and enlarged throughout Jewish history.

Like Pesach, Sukot begins in the middle of a month (Tishri) at a full moon. Its first and last days are sacred no-work Sabbaths. The sacrifices prescribed by the Torah for offering at the sanctuary include a fire offering, burnt and meal offerings, and libations. In addition, on the first day of the festival, the Israelites were to bring a special bouquet consisting of an *etrog,* or "citron," together with palm, myrtle, and willow branches.

Special accommodations were also commanded. The Israelites are to construct *sukot,* or "booths," and they are to eat and sleep in them during the seven days of celebration. Our Torah portion makes clear the purpose of dwelling outside the comforts of one's home. The Israelites are to live in booths for the same reason they are to celebrate Pesach: The Israelites are to celebrate in booths for seven days "in order that future generations may know that I made the Israelite people live in booths when I brought them out of the land of Egypt." (Exodus 23:37–43) The booths are a reminder of their liberation from oppression.

Furthermore, Sukot is also known in the Torah by the terms *he-Chag,* or "the Festival," and *Chag ha-Asif,* or "Festival of Ingathering." As the fall harvest celebration, it was a time of thanksgiving for all the earth's bounty. Yet the festival also focused on the future. Farmers living in ancient times, like those of today, were concerned with adequate rains to guarantee a plentiful harvest in the next season. The uncertainty haunted them. Would the skies fill with rain clouds or would their crops wither and their flocks and herds die beside dry water holes?

Such concerns explain the ancient ceremony of bringing to the sanctuary the Sukot bouquet of the *etrog* and myrtle, willow, and palm branches. During Temple times, we are told that on each day of the holiday a procession would carry water from the Pool of Shiloach in Jerusalem to the Temple sanctuary. There the priests would pour the water onto the altar. The people would then wave their Sukot bouquets and beat them on the ground around the altar. Commenting on this ceremony, the rabbis make it clear that its purpose is to ask God for rains in the coming year. (*Rosh Hashanah* 16:1)

Today such rituals are defined as forms of "sympathetic magic." They imitate the wishes of those who employ them and remind God to fulfill them. In combining the rituals of pouring water on the altar and waving a palm branch, or *lulav* (which makes the sound of cracking thunder and falling rain), together with the myrtle and willow branches (which grow near water), it was hoped that these sounds of water would cause God to give plentiful rain for the next growing season.

If that was the meaning of Sukot rituals to the ancients, what may these rituals mean today? Can the *sukah,* or "booth," be more than a reminder of the booths used by the wandering Israelites? Is the Sukot bouquet more than a quaint form of sympathetic magic or a rite for rain?

In seeking answers for such questions, Torah interpreters have suggested many significant insights. For instance, Rabbi Akiba and a majority of his contemporaries declared that the *sukah* "must have the character of a nonpermanent residence." While one is to enjoy it with family and friends and eat and sleep in it, the roof of the *sukah* must be open to the stars. It is to be decorated with the fruits of the harvest and with *shach,* palm or tree branches, all of which will decay. (*Sukot* 23a; *Yoma* 10b; *Betzah* 30b; *Kitzur Shulchan Aruch* 134–135)

Rambam (Maimonides)

According to Maimonides, while beautifying the *sukah* with tapestries, streamers, and the use of special holiday dishes is praiseworthy, one must never make of it a permanent dwelling. (*Mishneh Torah, Sukot* 6)

The temporary nature of the *sukah* may be the key to its deeper meaning. Beyond reminding those celebrating the festival of the booths used by the Israelites after their liberation from Egypt, the *sukah* may also symbolize the nature of human life. This is the meaning Jewish philosopher Philo of Alexandria (20 B.C.E.–40 C.E.) suggests in his discussion of Sukot. He writes that the purpose of the *sukah* is to remind you "in wealth to remember your poverty. When you are popular and highly regarded . . . remember your insignificance. When you are in high office . . . remember that you are a humble citizen. When you enjoy peace . . . recall war. When you are on land . . . remember the storms at sea. When you are surrounded by friends in the city . . . remember those who are lonely and desperate for company." (*The Special Laws* 204, 206–211)

This association of the *sukah* with the fragile and constantly changing nature of human life was quite obviously in the thoughts of the rabbis who chose the Book of Ecclesiastes for reading and study on the Sabbath of Sukot. The message of Ecclesiastes, like the message of the *sukah*, is that life is fragile, constantly changing. There are moments for joy, then sadness; followed by times for laughter, then tears; succeeded by seasons for gathering, then losing; for love, then hatred; for war, then peace. (See Ecclesiastes 3.) Sitting in the temporary *sukah*, which has been built and made beautiful by harvest decorations, one not only senses gratefulness for the bounty of nature but also realizes all the varying seasons of human existence—of how quickly human beings journey from birth to death.

It was the custom of Levi Isaac of Berdichev to invite to his sukah *simple, unlearned people. Once his students asked him: "Master, why do you ask these people to be here with us each year?" Levi Isaac replied: "In the world to come, when the righteous are sitting at the holy feast in the heavenly* sukah, *I shall come there and seek to be admitted. But they will refuse me. For who am I that I should sit among the great, righteous ones? Then I shall present my case. I will tell them how I invited simple and unlearned persons into my* sukah. *And they will allow me to enter."*

According to the mystical text known as the *Zohar*, it is not enough to construct, decorate, and enjoy a *sukah* by eating, sleeping, and studying in it. One must also share it with guests of two different kinds. First, there are seven illustrious Jewish heroes, Abraham, Isaac, Jacob, Joseph, Moses, Aaron, and David, one for each day. However, according to the *Zohar* (*Emor* 23), they will not automatically visit the *sukah*. They will arrive only if those who have built the *sukah* first invite the other category of guests, the poor and needy. In other words, the meaning of the *sukah* is to remind us to share our good fortune with others. It is to be shared with guests—friends, great Jewish leaders of the past, and, above all, with the hungry and homeless.

Regarding the Sukot banquet of the *etrog*, *lulav*, myrtle, and willow, interpreters suggest a variety of meanings.

Many of the rabbis teaching after the destruction of the Jerusalem Temple explain that the *Arba'ah Minim*, or the "Four Species," symbolize the Jewish people. In one commentary, the *etrog*, which has both taste and odor, is compared to Jews who know Torah and practice good deeds; the *lulav*, which has taste but no odor, is equated with Jews who know Torah but fail to practice good deeds; the myrtle, which has odor but no taste, is likened to those who practice good deeds but know nothing of Torah; the willow, which has neither odor nor taste, is compared to the person who knows no Torah and fails to practice any good deeds. Since they are all Jews, God, the rabbis say, binds them together in a bouquet and says: "Let them atone for one another's failings." (*Leviticus Rabbah* 30)

This use of the Sukot bouquet as a means of teaching God's tolerance and concern for all Jews is also found in another commentary. The author points out that both the *etrog* and *lulav* produce fruit while the myrtle and willow do not. For the Sukot bouquet to be brought into the sanctuary, however, all four kinds must be bound and held together. "Just as the four kinds must be brought together," says the interpreter, "so the people of Israel will not be allowed to return to their land unless they are united." (*Yalkut Shemoni, Emor,* 188a)

What is particularly significant about these interpretations of the Sukot bouquet is not only their concern for Jewish unity but their acceptance of pluralism, of differences, within Jewish life. Each segment of the Jewish people, like each of the Four Species in the Sukot bouquet, has something special to contribute. They depend upon one another. Without respect for differences, people will never reach the Promised Land—the fulfillment of all their hopes and aspirations.

Twentieth-century teacher Rabbi Ya'akov Israel in his book *Knesset Israel* puts the argument for pluralism this way: "When Jewish groups stand apart, each in its place, and each claiming that it alone has justice on its side, and they refuse to listen to one another, then no cure will ever come to the Jewish situation. . . . The Four Species symbolize peace and unity. For just as they differ in taste, odor, and form but are united together, so, too, the different parties of our people must form one alliance and work together for the good of the people."

Underlying this interpretation of the Sukot bouquet is a concern for the future survival of the Jewish people. The insistence of binding all the various segments of the community together, of accepting differences and promoting unity, is seen as the only way of guaranteeing the vitality and future of the community. The bouquet of four kinds held together as an ancient prayer for rain to assure new harvests and survival is transformed into a symbol for holding the people together. Its purpose is to remind all segments of the Jewish community that their future depends upon mutual appreciation, cooperation, and unity.

A concluding comment about Pesach, Shavuot, and Sukot

Each of the festivals mentioned in *Parashat Emor* continues to play a central role in the celebration of the Jewish people. As we have seen, their ritual expressions have changed and evolved through the centuries. As the people adjusted to new circumstances—from the desert sanctuary to a Temple in Jerusalem; from the destruction of the Temple with its sacrifices to the creation and exclusive use of the synagogue; from living in the Land of Israel to exile and dispersion throughout the world; from pogrom and persecution to lands of safety; from the Holocaust to the birth of the State of Israel—Jewish rituals have taken on new forms, meanings, and significance.

Whether it is the addition of a *haggadah,* or the transformation of Shavuot from a harvest day to a celebration of the giving of the Torah, or the reinterpretation of the Sukot bouquet, each emerging ritual contains traces of its origins. While Jewish tradition has altered its rituals, even abandoned some, it has consistently retained and developed the original themes of the festivals. Pesach has remained the Festival of Freedom, Shavuot a harvest of thanksgiving for the fruits of nature and of Torah, and Sukot a celebration of thanksgiving and concern for the future. The relevance of these ancient themes underscores the continuing importance of these three Jewish festivals.

PEREK BET: *Eye for an Eye, Tooth for a Tooth: About Lex Talionis*

Three times within the Torah we find a formulation that deals with compensation for physical harm inflicted by one person upon another.

In *Parashat Emor* we are told: "If a man kills any human being, he shall be put to death. One who kills a beast shall make restitution for it: life for life. If anyone maims his fellow, as he has done so shall it be done to him: fracture for fracture, eye for eye, tooth for tooth. The injury he inflicted on another shall be inflicted on him. . . . You shall have one standard for stranger and citizen alike: for I the Lord am your God." (Leviticus 24:17–22)

In Exodus 21:22–25 we are told that, if one is involved in a fight and pushes a pregnant woman causing a miscarriage, the husband of the woman may ask for compensation for the loss of life. However, "if other damage ensues, the penalty shall be life for life, eye for eye, tooth for tooth, hand for hand, foot for foot, burn for burn, wound for wound, bruise for bruise."

A third example of this principle occurs in Deuteronomy 19:18–19, 21. Here the dispute between the two parties is not of a physical nature. It relates to one person's intention to harm another by deliberate falsification of testimony in court. In this situation, the Torah commands the judges to "do to him as he schemed to do to his fellow. . . . Nor must you show pity: life for life, eye for eye, tooth for tooth, hand for hand, foot for foot."

Many interpreters through the centuries have sought to explain what the Torah meant by such a penalty. For example, Robert H. Pfeiffer, a modern biblical critic, suggests that "eye for eye and tooth for tooth . . ." is "the old law of the desert" practiced "among the Israelites who never forgot their desert origin." He explains that " 'life for life' in its absolute form is the principle of the desert law of blood revenge. . . ." In other words, the practice sanctioned by the Torah was physical mutilation as recompense for any physical injury inflicted by others. If an eye was put out, the person responsible for the injury was to lose an eye. This was so with a foot, a tooth, a burn, a fracture, a hand. According to Pfeiffer, blood revenge is what the Torah sanctions. (*Introduction to the Old Testament,* Harper and Brothers, New York, 1941, pp. 219–220)

Sarna

Most commentators disagree with Pfeiffer's conclusion. Contemporary scholar Nahum Sarna points out that *lex talionis,* or the "law of retaliation," as it is called in Roman law, is based upon the principle that "the punishment must fit the crime." This concept, which had been a part of Israelite practice even before the people were enslaved in Egypt, was introduced by them into Mesopotamia. It represented a revolutionary idea. Rather than calling for the deliberate physical injury to others as blood revenge, the principle actually created "a law of equivalence." It allowed the injured party to be paid for damages. If an eye was lost, one paid the worth of an eye; if a tooth, the equivalent of a tooth.

Furthermore, not only in this way was the To-rah revolutionary. Sarna points out that other cultures surrounding the Israelites introduced monetary compensation for physical damages along class lines. In the *Code of Hammurabi* we are told that "if a seignior has knocked out the tooth of a seignior of his own rank, he shall knock out his tooth. If he has knocked out a commoner's tooth, he shall pay one-third mina of silver." (200–201) In other words, within the *Code of Hammurabi,* compensation is dictated by class rank, by one's position in society. Within the Torah, however, the person's class does not apply. No one person's eye or tooth is worth more than that of another. Equal and fair compensation for damages is the right of every person within the society.

Those, like Pfeiffer, who argue that the Torah actually calls for bodily mutilation in retaliation for physical injury miss the point, says Sarna. There is no way of assessing an equivalent mutilation. What if a person only loses part of his sight or partial use of a limb? How would it be possible to enforce the law, to punish with exactly the same injury? Sarna, therefore, concludes that the Torah passages, in reality, refer to "pecuniary compensation." If one injures someone's eye, or foot, or tooth, one must pay the designated worth of that injury.

Most Jewish commentators agree with Sarna. One of the earliest discussions of the matter in the Talmud stresses the importance of financial compensation for physical injuries. Rabbi Simeon ben Yochai teaches that "eye for eye" means "money." He then clarifies his conclusion with a question: "If a blind man maims another by blinding him, how is this considered just or sufficient compensation?" In asking the question, Rabbi Simeon means to reduce to nonsense the notion of physically injuring another as a form of compensation. (*Baba Kamma* 84a) Rabbi Simeon ben Yochai's interpretation of "eye for eye" as fair monetary compensation became the standard interpretation of Jewish tradition.

Ibn Ezra

In his commentary on the subject, Abraham ibn Ezra quotes the leader of Babylonian Jewry,

Sa'adia Gaon. Objecting to those who argued that "eye for eye" should be understood literally as justifiable retaliation for physical mutilation, Sa'adia asks: "If a person deprived his fellow of a third of his normal sight by his blow, how can a retaliatory blow be so calculated as to have the same precise results, neither more nor less. . . ?"

Answering his own question, Sa'adia declares that "such an exact reproduction of the effects is even more difficult in the case of a wound or bruise that, if in a dangerous spot, might result in death." It is clear that from Sa'adia's point of view, and from the view of ibn Ezra who quotes him, the Torah's intention was never physical retaliation by mutilation of another but rather some form of equal financial reimbursement. (See discussion of Leviticus 24:17–22.)

Maimonides makes a similar point. "When the Torah uses the words 'as he has maimed a person, so shall it be done to him,' it does not mean the literal inflicting of the identical maiming on the guilty person but merely that, though the latter deserves such maiming, the person who has inflicted the damage pays the monetary equivalent." (*Yad Hazakah, Hilchot Havel u-Mazik* 1, 3–6)

Leibowitz

In commenting on Maimonides' argument, Nehama Leibowitz goes one step further in explaining why monetary compensation instead of physical retaliation was preferred by the Torah. She suggests that the body is not an ordinary machine that can be used and discarded. It is sacred because it is the house of the human soul and a gift from God. In other words, says Leibowitz, "a person cannot dispose of his limbs in the same way he can dispose of his goods since his limbs, his entire body, are not under his authority. A person is not master of his body, but God to whom belongs both soul and body is master of them." Thus no person has the right to inflict harm on another person's body or upon his own. When justice demands compensation for damages to another's body, only financial compensation will do. Honoring the body is honoring God. (*Studies in Vayikra*, pp. 245–257)

If Jewish tradition rejects the notion of physical mutilation as retaliation for injury, then how does it assess a "monetary equivalent" for damages that have been done?

Five categories of consideration are used to calculate fair compensation:

First is *nezek*, an assessment of how the permanent physical disability will affect one's future earnings. Here the task is to establish the financial difference between what one could have earned and what one will now earn as a result of the injury. The amount lost must be compensated.

The second category is *tza'ar*, or "pain." One is to be paid the difference between the amount he would have requested for amputating the limb with anaesthesia and the amount he would have asked for without anaesthesia.

Third is *rippui*, or "medical treatment." It is the total amount of medical bills from the time of the injury to the time of a complete recovery.

Fourth is *shevet*, or "loss of earnings." It is calculated on the basis of the injury. If one must remain away from work while healing, then compensation must be given for each day lost. If, however, one's injury will be permanent, compensation is calculated by determining how much a person with such a disability would be paid if employed in his original field of work.

Finally, a person injured is compensated for *boshet*, or the "indignity" suffered. This is calculated by determining the status of the person who caused the damage. If it was a child who brought harm, compensation will be different from damages brought about by an adult. If one was injured by a leader or important person whose anger caused humiliation or embarrassment, compensation must be calculated to take mental anguish into consideration. (A. Chill, *The Mitzvot*, pp. 71–74)

In addition to these five conditions, Jewish tradition also demands that the person who has physically damaged another must ask forgiveness from the injured party. Maimonides puts it this way: "No compensation is complete, no wrong is forgiven until the person who has inflicted the injury requests the victim's forgiveness and has been forgiven."

Maimonides, however, does not leave the matter there. Knowing that the victim may be hurt, angry, and unforgiving, he warns: "It is forbidden for the injured party to be cruel and unforgiving. This is not the Jewish way . . . as soon as the guilty party has sought forgiveness, once or twice, and is sincere and regrets his action, then he must be forgiven. The quicker, the better." (*Yad Ha-zakah, Hilchot Hovevi u-Mazik* 5, 9)

While other ancient Middle Eastern cultures surrounding the early Israelites allowed physical mutilation as a form of retaliation, Jewish tradition introduces the practice of monetary compensation and reconciliation. When the Torah uses the formula "fracture for fracture, eye for eye, tooth for tooth . . ." it means payment for damages. As we have seen, rabbinic tradition refines this principle of equivalent compensation by ruling that payment must take into consideration disability, pain, cost of medical care, loss of earnings, and shame. Not only must the injured party be paid damages, but the person inflicting injury must seek forgiveness.

Regard for the human body as the sacred container of the human soul is at the heart of Jewish ethics. So, too, are guaranteeing equal treatment for damages and good relations between all members of society. Realizing that injury to the body, or the loss of a limb, can never be fully compensated and could spark bloody revenge, Jewish tradition mandates a just form of compensation and reconciliation. In doing so, it advances the cause of justice and the pursuit of peace.

QUESTIONS FOR STUDY AND DISCUSSION

1. List and discuss the rituals and benefits of the Pesach *seder* ceremony. Which ones are ancient in origin? Which are new, modern? Which are the most important and the least important to you? Why?

2. Some early rabbis suggest that the people of Israel should have received the Torah immediately after their Exodus from Egyptian slavery. Others argue that the people were not ready for its responsibilities. It was only after wandering for seven weeks in the desert that they were prepared to accept the teachings of Torah—and, even then, they abandoned God and built the golden calf. With which of these two views do you agree? Why?

3. Modern Jewish philosopher Abraham Joshua Heschel has written that "the Jewish people without Torah is obsolete." Given the celebration of Shavuot, what may Heschel mean by his bold declaration?

4. Given the differences among Jews on the interpretation of Torah and the practice of Jewish tradition, what lessons may modern Jews learn from the meanings of the Sukot bouquet and festival?

5. A mayor of a city, X, strikes a vocal and critical constituent, Y. Y's arm is broken, and he is unable to work for five months in his profession as a computer expert earning $5,000 a month. According to Jewish tradition, how would you assess the damages? What would you have X pay Y by way of compensation? What would you have X do by way of reconciliation? Consult with insurance experts. What do modern insurance companies cover? What don't they cover? How does this compare with Jewish tradition?

PARASHAT BEHAR-BECHUKOTAI
Leviticus 25:1–27:34

Parashat Behar-Bechukotai is one of seven designated Torah portions that, depending upon the number of Sabbaths in a year, is either read as two separate portions or combined to assure the reading of the entire Torah. While this volume will combine them, it will present an interpretation on each of their most important themes.

Parashat Behar presents laws regulating the sabbatical year and the jubilee year. The people are told that for six years they are to sow their fields and prune their vineyards, but, during the seventh year, the land is to be given a complete rest, a Sabbath. Every fiftieth year is to be a jubilee year in which land and vineyards must not be worked and in which liberty will be granted to all Israelites enslaved during the previous forty-nine years. The jubilee year also marks a return of any properties purchased during the previous forty-nine years to the original owner-families who had been given the land at the time the Israelites entered it.

Parashat Bechukotai is filled with God's promises to the people if they are loyal and faithfully follow all the commandments and with God's warnings if they disobey. Peace, security, and abundant crops are promised if they are faithful. Misery, suffering, and ruin will come if they spurn God's commandments. The portion also includes brief discussions of the payment of vows and gifts made to the sanctuary.

OUR TARGUM

· 1 ·

Parashat Behar begins with the commandment prohibiting the sowing or harvesting of lands or the pruning of vineyards during the sabbatical year. The Israelites are forbidden to use the aftergrowth of the harvest or to gather grapes from untrimmed vines during the year of rest. It is permissible, however, to eat whatever the uncultivated land happens to produce during the year of rest.

· 2 ·

After every forty-nine years a jubilee year is to be celebrated. It is to begin with the sounding of a *shofar* on Yom Kippur and with a proclamation of liberty, or release, throughout the land for all its inhabitants.

"Liberty," or "release," meant that all Israelites were to take possession of the original lands given to their ancestors at the time Joshua and the people conquered Canaan.

Given the rule about returning the land to its original owners, the people are told that, when they sell or buy property, they are to deduct for the years since the Jubilee and to charge for only the remaining potential years of productivity. The more years of use, the higher the price; the fewer the years of ownership, the lower the price. The people are taught: "When you sell property to your neighbor, or buy any from your neighbor, you shall not wrong one another." They are also instructed that the land belongs to God, and they are warned, "You are but strangers resident with Me."

· 3 ·

If an Israelite is in trouble and must sell part of his holding, a relative is to help him. If, for financial reasons, one must sell a house in a walled city, one has the right of repurchase for a year. Once the year has passed, the house belongs to the purchaser forever. Houses in villages, however, are classified as "open country" and are to be returned to their original owners at the Jubilee.

The people are instructed that, if brother or sister Israelites are in trouble, they are to be treated as resident aliens. They are not to be charged interest on loans or food. Nor are they to be treated as slaves. While they may work as hired laborers, they must be freed at the Jubilee. The people are told: "For they are My servants, whom I freed from the land of Egypt; they may not give themselves over in servitude. You shall not rule over them ruthlessly; you shall fear your God."

If an Israelite, having had financial troubles, comes under the authority of a resident alien or his family, who have prospered, he may be redeemed by a member of his own family. His price will be computed on the basis of the work years remaining until the Jubilee. Should no family member come along to pay for his release, he and his family will be liberated at the Jubilee.

·4·

Parashat Bechukotai opens with a promise by God to the Israelites. If they follow all the commandments, they will be rewarded with abundant rains and harvests. They will be secure in their land and enjoy peace. When attacked by enemies, they will be victorious. Parents will enjoy many children, and none of them will know hunger. God will care for them, and they will always walk proudly as free people.

However, if they refuse to follow God's commandments, they will suffer terrible illnesses, lack of harvests, and defeat by their enemies. The skies will be as iron and copper [unproductive]; no fruit trees will yield produce; and wild beasts will destroy them.

Should the people turn away from God and refuse to follow God's commandments, pursuing idolatry and cults, their cities will be laid waste, and they will be scattered among the nations. The land will be given a long Sabbath time with no harvests. Fear of enemies will be so great that the sound of a fluttering leaf will set the people fleeing. Those who survive this desolation will wish they had perished.

When the people have suffered exile and punishment because they failed to observe God's commandments, God will remember the covenant made with them, with Abraham, Isaac, and Jacob. They will not be rejected forever. God will not annul the covenant with them, for it is God who freed them from Egypt to be their God.

·5·

This Torah portion and the Book of Leviticus conclude with laws concerning vows, gifts, and payments to the sanctuary.

If a person vows, or promises, to donate the equivalent worth of a human being, he is to use the following scale: for a male from twenty to sixty years of age, fifty shekels of silver, and thirty for a female; for a male from five to twenty years of age, twenty shekels, and ten for a female; for a male from one month to five years of age, five shekels, and three for a female. If the person promising a donation cannot afford it, the priest will make an assessment according to what the person can afford.

For promises of donations of animals, houses, or land, the priest shall make the proper assessment. In the case of land given to the priest, it can be bought back at the time of the Jubilee for an additional twenty percent of the sum. If it is not redeemed, it belongs to the priest. If the land is not actually owned by the person giving it to the sanctuary, it is to be returned to the original owner at the Jubilee.

All tithes, or payments of ten percent of seed, fruit, or the herd, are to be given to the sanctuary. However, one can pay the equivalent value plus one-fifth more and retrieve them for his own use.

THEMES

Parashat Behar-Bechukotai contains three important themes:

1. The sabbatical and jubilee years.
2. Caring for the poor.
3. God's rewards and punishments.

PEREK ALEF: *Lessons from the Sabbatical and Jubilee Years*

Just as the Torah calls for a Sabbath day of rest for people after every six days of work, it also commands a Sabbath year of rest for the land after every six years of cultivation; it also calls for a *Yovel,* or "Jubilee," a fiftieth year, completing a cycle of seven sabbatical years.

Mention is made of the sabbatical year in Exodus 23:10–11, where the Israelites are instructed not to cultivate their lands, vineyards, or olive groves. During the sabbatical year they are to leave whatever grows for the needy and wild beasts.

Within our Torah portion, the Israelites are told that, while they may not work the land or prune their vineyards or orchards, it is permissible to eat whatever *happens* to grow during the sabbatical year. (Leviticus 25:1–7) In addition to the practice of resting the land, the Torah also commands that all debts are to be cancelled during the seventh year. (Deuteronomy 15:1–3)

During the year of the Jubilee, which is announced by sounding the *shofar* on Yom Kippur, all laws of the sabbatical year are to be observed. In addition, all properties are to be returned to the families who inherited them at the time Joshua led the Israelites into the Land of Israel. To guarantee fairness in land values, all prices of land were calculated on potential usage before the sabbatical when they would revert to their original owners. The Jubilee was also a time when Israelites forced to sell themselves into slavery because of poverty were freed. (Leviticus 25:8–17)

These practices concerning both the sabbatical and jubilee years were adapted and extended by the rabbinic tradition. For example, owners of fields were not allowed to collect and store large amounts of food in their homes because such a practice would deprive the poor. Individuals or families were to take only the amount of fruits and vegetables required for their normal needs. If there was no longer any food available in the fields, owners were commanded to remove all food from their storage places and make it available to the entire community. It was forbidden to buy or sell produce from the field during the sabbatical or jubilee years.

With Alexander the Great's domination of the Middle East (330 B.C.E.), Jews moved from an agriculturally centered economy to an urban economy. Loans of currency were required for business dealings. However, the strict laws of Torah called for a release of all debts by creditors during the sabbatical year. This meant that potential creditors, fearing their loans would never be repaid, refused to make loans available, resulting in a desperate situation for the poor who were unable to secure necessary loans. To solve this unjust situation, Rabbi Hillel created a financial arrangement known as *prosbol*. It allowed for the transfer of debts to the courts, with a guarantee that, even during the sabbatical year, loans would be repaid.

(See Abraham Chill, *The Mitzvot*, pp. 108–111, 297–300, 413–415.)

It is clear from our Torah portion, and from later rabbinic considerations of the commandments having to do with the sabbatical and jubilee years, that much concern was given to easing the plight of those who might suffer during years of no-work, no-production, and the release of debts. The needs of the poor were a primary concern of Jewish tradition. Why, therefore, was the practice of a sabbatical or jubilee year established if it produced hardships for parts of society? What did such years mean to the Israelites and to later generations of Jews?

Rashi

The commentator Rashi suggests that the reason for the sabbatical year is to give the land time to rest, just as the weekly Sabbath allows a human being to seek renewal and revitalization through rest. It is doubtful Rashi understood the process of natural fertilization and regeneration that occurred when the land was fallow for a year. Yet he, like the ancients, must have realized that crops usually grew more plentifully after the land had "rested" during a sabbatical year. For Rashi, the sabbatical and jubilee years, like the Sabbath, provided the land with a required period of reinvigoration. (See commentary on Leviticus 25:2.)

Rambam (Maimonides)

Moses Maimonides clearly understands the relationship between "rest" for the land and its productivity. The sabbatical and jubilee years, he explains, are commanded because "by releasing the land it will become invigorated; by lying fallow and not being worked it will regain its strength."

Maimonides, however, also stresses a social and ethical benefit of the sabbatical and jubilee years. In his discussion of charity, he emphasizes that such sabbatical and jubilee laws as guaranteeing food for the needy, freeing slaves, canceling debts, and returning lands are all meant to teach "sympathy toward others and promote the well-being of all." A significant side of these special years is to encourage and instruct Jews to be generous with those in need, to share their profits and products, and to be just in their business practices. (*Guide for the Perplexed* 3:39)

Ibn Ezra

A parallel to creation
Abraham ibn Ezra suggests that the seven-year agricultural cycle parallels God's plan for creation. God completes the work of creation in six days, then rests. So, too, the Jew is asked to work the soil. Each year parallels a day of creation. The seasons of summer, fall, winter, and spring parallel the morning and evening hours of each day. And the seventh year is like the weekly Sabbath, a time of no work, a rest period for the fields. (See comment on Leviticus 25.)

Not like creation at all
Rejecting Moses ibn Ezra's argument, the author of Kelei Yakar, *Ephraim ben Aaron Solomon, says that the purpose of the sabbatical and jubilee years is "to teach us not to think that human beings control the yield of the soil . . . [and] to teach us to trust that God will provide us with adequate crops during the sixth year so that we will be able to subsist during the rest years." The sabbatical and jubilee years are meant as exercises in faith and self-discipline. (See Chill,* The Mitzvot, *p. 110.)*

Peli

Protecting society against evil
This Sabbath of the land and the jubilee year that comes in its wake are considered by many thinkers to be among the most advanced social reforms in history. They protect society against the evils of feudalism and totalitarianism, as-

suring an inherent "liberty to all the inhabitants in the land" and the right of each individual to "return to his home and to his family." (Pinchas Peli, Torah Today, *pp. 146–148)*

Aharon Halevi, author of *Sefer ha-Hinuch*, also emphasizes the moral significance of the sabbatical and jubilee years. God commands us not to work the land and not to use its fruits, except for the poor, to remind us that the earth does not yield by itself or even by human cultivation. "There is a God who commands it to produce." Furthermore, Halevi says, "There is no nobler generosity than giving without expecting returns." That is the goodness God displays for all human beings to see in the sabbatical and jubilee years. God generously provides food for all, and human beings are to copy God's goodness in their relationships with one another. Just as God grants food during the years of rest, human beings are commanded to leave produce for the needy and hungry, acting out of compassion and generosity.

Concerning the commandments relating to the forgiveness of debts, the freeing of slaves, and the return of all lands to their original owners, Halevi argues that these laws of the sabbatical and jubilee years "mold ethical character." Their purpose is to "impress upon human beings that everything belongs to God, and ultimately everything returns to God and to whomever God wishes to give it."

Such an understanding is meant "to prevent people from stealing their neighbor's land or coveting it in their hearts." If they comprehend that everything belongs to God and will return to God, people are less likely to cheat others or deal unfairly with them in business. Knowing that all lands will be returned to their original owners and all slaves will be released assures security, justice, and liberty in society. (See B.S. Jacobson, *Meditations on the Torah*, pp. 188–189; also Nehama Leibowitz, *Studies in Vayikra*, pp. 260–261.)

Measuring life by sabbatical years
Rabbi Morris Silverman suggests that a person's "span of life normally consists of ten sabbatical periods of seven years each. . . ." [After] you have lived twenty-one years, or three sabbatical periods, "instead of saying that you have forty-

nine years ahead of you, you should say that you have only seven more sabbatical periods to live. And so you see the days of your life are all too short. You will better appreciate how precious is time when you think of life in terms of sabbatical periods and not of one year at a time." This is what the commandment to observe the sabbatical year teaches us. (S.Z. Kahana, Heaven on Your Head, *Morris Silverman, editor, Hartmore House, Hartford, 1964, pp. 134–135*)

Modern commentator Baruch A. Levine explains the goal of the jubilee laws regarding the return of lands to the original owners as a means of insuring the Land of Israel for the Jewish people. It was not a matter of morality, theology, or agricultural renewal; it was a matter of politics.

Levine explains that this part of the Torah may have been composed after the Jewish people returned from Babylonian exile in about 420 B.C.E. They had been promised by the Babylonian ruler, Cyrus, that they could repossess the land. In returning after nearly eighty years of exile, they found their holdings in the hands of other Jews and many non-Jews. A crisis faced them. How could they settle the land when it now "belonged" to others?

The jubilee law of returning the land to the original families, who had been given it at the time of Joshua, seemed to settle the issue. God had given the land to the people of Israel, family by family. While it could be sold for use, it could not be sold forever. At each Jubilee it was to revert to the original family. When Jews returned to the Land of Israel from Babylonia, this meant that, at the Jubilee, all lands, whether owned by Jews or non-Jews, were to be returned to their original owners. As Levine says, "The goal was to regain control over the land." In this way rich and poor were equal. Both classes would regain their lands. (*JPS Commentary: Leviticus, pp. 270–274*)

Leibowitz

Nehama Leibowitz also provides a social-political meaning for the jubilee laws concerning the return of property to its original owners. However, quoting the arguments of nineteenth-century American thinker Henry George, Leibowitz points out that the Jubilee was "a measure designed to maintain an even distribution of wealth." Moses realized from his experience in Egypt that oppression of the masses came about as a result of a monopoly of land ownership and wealth in the hands of the rich. According to George's view, says Leibowitz, "the Torah . . . intended to prevent the evolving of a landless class and the concentration of power and property in the hands of the few." The guarantee that land would return to its original owners, every fifty years at the Jubilee, was seen as the best means of promoting "justice and equity." (*Studies in Vayikra, pp. 260–261*)

The interpreters of Jewish tradition offer a variety of explanations and meanings for the sabbatical and jubilee years. Yet they all have one thing in common. Each explanation finds within the traditions of resting the land, feeding the hungry, returning the land to its original owners, and liberating the slaves measures of great ethical, political, or spiritual significance. By contrast, the ethical concerns underlying these ancient agricultural and economic laws challenge many of the social, religious, and economic policies and priorities of our own era.

PEREK BET: *The Mitzvah of Caring for the Poor*

According to Rabbi Assi, who lived and taught during the third century C.E., in Babylonia, the mitzvah of *tzedakah,* or caring for those in need, "is more important than all the other commandments put together." (*Baba Batra* 9a)

What are the origins of such an observation? Where do we find the basis within the Torah for Assi's conclusion about Jewish ethics?

The answer may be found in *Parashat Behar.* Just after the discussion of the sabbatical and jubilee years, the Torah deals with the question of how the poor and needy are to be protected and cared for by the community. Four times the words *ve-chi yamuch achicha,* or "and if your brother [or sister] should be reduced to poverty," begin an explanation of how the poor are to be treated.

Several examples are offered. The Israelites are told that, when a kinsman must sell his property, another should raise funds for its repurchase. If a kinsman falls into debt, it is forbidden to charge interest on any money or food given to him. If his situation of poverty continues and becoming enslaved is his only solution, he is to be treated as a hired laborer, not as a slave. If a poor Israelite is purchased by a resident alien (a non-Israelite), it is the obligation of his family to raise funds for his release; if he is fortunate and prospers while enslaved, he may purchase his own release. (Leviticus 25:25, 35, 39, and 47)

These regulations concerning treatment of the impoverished evolved into important discussions among Jewish commentators about the obligations of *tzedakah*. Through the centuries, ethical standards dealing with care for the needy emerge into a unique pattern of Jewish social responsibility.

For example, in discussing the meaning of the words "and if your brother should be reduced to poverty," the rabbis emphasize that helping those who have lost their property, who are without food, shelter, or clothing, or who are sick, infirm, or helpless, not only benefits the needy, but also brings happiness to the generous. Those who do *tzedakah*, says Abba ben Jeremiah in the name of Rabbi Meir, have the knowledge that their Good Inclination is ruling over their Evil Inclination. Rabbi Isi claims that those who give even a *perutah*, or "a small amount," feel fulfilled.

Several of the rabbis claim that the Torah's comment "and if your brother should be reduced to poverty" has to do with the obligation of rescuing those held by pirates or oppressors. Rabbi Huna argues that it refers to the mitzvah of visiting the sick and even estimates that one-sixtieth of a person's illness is cured by such visits.

Zugot

Rabbi Johanan says that the Torah means to instruct us to carry out the commandment to bury the poor with dignity and honor.

In another interpretation of reaching out to those who have fallen into poverty, Rabbi Jonah suggests that the Torah is particularly concerned about the feelings of the needy. They should not be embarrassed about their plight. By way of example, he tells about a person who had lost his money and was ashamed to ask for help. "I went to him," says Rabbi Jonah, "and told him I had news that he had inherited a fortune from a distant relative living far away. Then I offered him help, telling him that he could repay me when the inheritance was delivered. After giving him the gift, I assured him that it was not necessary for him to repay me. In that way I reduced his humiliation."

Other rabbis warn against shaming the poor with embarrassing questions. God, they warn, will punish those who are comfortable and ask the needy, "Why don't you go out and find a job, make some money, and put your own bread on the table?" Or, who say: "Look at those hips, look at those legs, look at that fat body. Such a person can work. Let him do so and take care of himself!" Such people, the rabbis observe, will bring evil upon themselves because they do not honor others as images of God. (*Leviticus Rabbah, Behar, 36:1–16*)

The art of doing tzedakah

The greatest charity is to enable the needy to earn a living. (Shabbat 63a)

The person who gives charity in secret is greater than Moses. (Baba Batra 9b)

A torch is not diminished though it kindles a million candles. A person does not lose by giving to those in need. (Exodus Rabbah 30:3)

Charity knows no race or creed. (Gittin 61a)

If you wish to raise a person from poverty and trouble, do not think that it is enough to stand above and reach a helping hand down to him or her. It is not enough. You must go down to where the person is, down into the mud and filth. Then take hold of him or her with strong hands and pull until both of you rise up into the light. (Solomon ben Meir ha-Levi of Karlin, 1738–

1798, as quoted in Francine Klagsbrun, Voices of Wisdom: Jewish Ideals and Ethics for Everyday Living, *Pantheon Books, New York, 1980, p. 331*)

The third-century teacher Eleazar ben Eleazar Ha-Kappar, who was known as Bar Kappara, maintains that we "are duty bound to view a poor person's body as if it were our own." In other words, we are to clothe, feed, and shelter the needy as if they were extensions of our own flesh and blood. Our standard of care for them ought to be what we would wish for ourselves. It should be given with respect for their dignity and concern for their feelings.

Tzedakah is not a matter only for the rich; nor is it exclusively material help. The poor are also responsible for giving *tzedakah*. Rabbi Levi explains that, "if you have nothing to give, offer consolation. Comfort the needy with kind words. Say, 'My soul goes out to you. Even though I have nothing to give you, I understand how you feel.'" (*Leviticus Rabbah* 24:1–15; see also *Sotah* 14a; *Baba Batra* 10a)

These observations by the early rabbis on the Torah's statement, "and if your brother should be reduced to poverty," define the obligations of charity within Jewish tradition. Building upon them, Moses Maimonides in his *Mishneh Torah*, written during the latter part of the twelfth century, identifies *tzedakah* "as the most important positive commandment" given by God to the Jewish people.

Agreeing with the early rabbis, Maimonides encourages generosity and sensitivity to the "cries of the needy." He counsels that human beings must learn to listen to one another, to speak to one another with sympathy, and never to insult those whose lives are broken by poverty and sickness. While the people of Israel are to care for one another because "they are bound together in a single destiny," the obligation of *tzedakah* also extends to non-Jews. "It is forbidden," writes Maimonides, "to let a poor person who asks for help go empty-handed."

Furthermore, helping a person who has fallen into trouble is not a matter of whim or sympathy. It is a *mitzvah*, an obligation, a commandment of God. The word used for "charity" in Hebrew is *tzedakah* from the root *tz-d-k*, meaning "right," "just," "morally correct." Within Jewish tradition, *tzedakah* is a matter of doing the "right thing." That, undoubtedly, is why Maimonides emphasizes the law: "If a person has no clothing, it is your responsibility to provide clothing. If furnishings for a home are needed, give furniture. If a poor person requires help in affording a marriage celebration for a child, help with the marriage celebration. If the person is hungry, offer food. And do so without delay, without any further begging!" (*Mishneh Torah* 6–8; see also Jacob Neusner, *Tzedakah*, Rossel, Chappaqua, New York, 1982, pp. 81–106)

In summarizing the attitude of Jewish tradition toward *tzedakah*, the giving of charity, Maimonides offers a ladder of eight levels. It is now a classic expression of Jewish ethics.

Maimonides' eight levels of tzedakah

1. *The highest degree of all is one who supports another reduced to poverty by providing a loan, or entering into a partnership, or finding work for him, so that the poor person can become self-sufficient.*
2. *Below this is giving to another so that the donor does not know the recipient, and the recipient does not know the donor.*
3. *Below this is giving to another so that the donor knows the recipient, but the recipient does not know the donor.*
4. *Below this is giving to another so that the recipient knows the donor, but the donor does not know the recipient.*
5. *Below this is giving to the poor without being asked.*
6. *Below this is giving to the poor after being asked.*
7. *Below this is giving to the poor less than is proper, but in a friendly manner.*
8. *Below this is giving, but in a grudging and unfriendly way.* (Mishneh Torah *10:7–15, based on translation by Jacob Neusner*)

The single emphasis of all interpreters of the Torah's words "and if your brother should be reduced to poverty" is the obligation to offer help. If a person is in debt, you are to lend him money without interest. If it is clothing, food, or shelter that is required, you are to provide it. Commenting on the Torah's statement, Rashi notes that it is followed by the words "you shall strengthen him." These words, Rashi says, mean: "Don't let the poor fall and become impoverished so that it will be hard for them to recover. Instead, strengthen them the moment their strength and fortune fail." (See also *Torah Temimah* on Leviticus 25:35.)

Within the realm of Jewish ethics, charity is to be given immediately, generously, and always in a way that protects the dignity of those in need.

PEREK GIMEL: *Rewards and Punishments: The Consequences of Our Choices*

Modern interpreter Rabbi Bernard J. Bamberger points out that many ancient Middle Eastern nations developed legal systems that promised great rewards for those who observed them and cruel punishments for those who violated them. Both the Sumarian *Code of Lipit-Ishtar* and the Babylonian *Code of Hammurabi* announce blessings for those who live by the law and suffering and death for those who do not.

The Torah, Bamberger maintains, does not follow either of these codes. Instead, it offers another view of the consequences of choices made by individuals and nations. While there are blessings and curses brought on by choices, the Torah also holds open "a glimmering of hope" of new opportunities for reward and happiness. In other words, we may suffer the consequences of our choices, but we are never completely doomed by them. (*The Torah: A Modern Commentary*, pp. 953–954)

In setting out the list of blessings and curses facing the Israelites, *Parashat Bechukotai* raises serious questions. First it describes the blessings that God will bring upon the people *if they follow* the commandments of Torah. They are promised prosperity and peace, safety from wild beasts, and victory over their enemies. Their land will yield abundant crops, and their population will grow. On the other hand, *if they do not follow* the commandments of Torah, they will be punished with

diseases, crop failure, and the death of their flocks and children. Fear of enemies and starvation will overwhelm them. Their cities will be ruined. They will be defeated, ravaged by their enemies, and taken into exile. (Leviticus 26:3–38)

A parallel of this catalogue of blessings and curses is found in Deuteronomy 28–30.

After reading such a list of blessings and curses, one may ask: Does God actually punish those who do not observe all the laws of Torah? Is it possible to say that the people of Israel actually suffered exile, starvation, and fear because they did not all choose to live by every law in the Torah? Does Jewish tradition teach that nations and individuals are punished by God for their wrong choices, for not living according to the laws of Torah?

Contemporary commentator Baruch A. Levine notes that "two major principles of biblical religion find expression" in this section of the Torah. The first is the concept of *freewill*, that is to say, the conviction that each person has the liberty to determine whether to follow what the Torah commands or to reject it. The second concept concerns *reward and punishment*. It holds that "obedience to God's will brings reward; disobedience brings dire punishment." (*JPS Torah Commentary: Leviticus*, p. 182) These two principles not only function within the Torah, but they are also found in the writings of many of its interpreters.

In elaborating on these principles, Rabbi Hama ben Hanina maintains that all the commandments of Torah were given to human beings in order to safeguard them from their inclination to make evil choices. If one faithfully acts according to the commandments, rewards will follow. If not, one will suffer the consequences.

Rabbi Eleazar illustrates this view by claiming that God presented the Jewish people with a package from heaven, containing the Torah and a sword. "If you observe what is written in the Torah," God told the people, "then you will be saved from the sword. If you do not live according to the Torah, then you will be destroyed by the sword." (*Leviticus Rabbah* 25:5–6)

This view of reward for obedience to the commandments of Torah and punishment for disobedience is echoed in a story told by the early rabbis. It is about a man who falls from the deck of a ship into the sea. The captain throws him a line and tells him: "Grasp it tightly. Don't let go. If you do, you will lose your life." The Torah, say the rabbis, is the lifeline of the Jewish people. If they grasp it faithfully and practice its commandments, then they will live. If they let go of it, pay no attention to it, then they will perish. Their rewards and punishments have to do with the choices they make. (*Tanchuma Buber* to Numbers, p. 74)

This classic view of reward for loyalty to the Torah and punishment for disloyalty is reflected within the "Thirteen Principles of Faith" written by Moses Maimonides and included in most traditional prayer books for many centuries. The eleventh principle declares: "I believe with perfect faith that the Creator . . . rewards those who keep the commandments and punishes those who transgress them." According to Maimonides, everything depends upon the free choice of human beings. If they do good, they will be rewarded with good. If they choose evil, they will suffer painful consequences.

What about those, however, who are loyal to the Torah, who faithfully observe all commandments, but, rather than enjoying the rewards of peace of mind and material benefits, bear burdens of misery and pain? How do those who claim that God rewards all who keep the commandments and punishes all who do not explain the suffering of good people?

Some Jewish thinkers, like Rabbi Eleazar ben Simeon, who suffered persecution by the Romans, teach that human beings and nations should always see themselves as half-guilty and half-worthy, knowing that the next choice will tip the balance to either reward or punishment. Clearly, from Eleazar's point of view, those who suffer have made wrong choices—even though they fail to recognize where they have made their mistakes.

On the other hand, there are teachers who believe that the rewards and punishments are not given in this world but in heaven. Human beings are judged by God at the end of their lives. They reap the benefits of living a good life or suffer the consequences of evil decisions throughout all eternity. Because the mix of good deeds and sins is so complex, it is only God who can make an ultimate judgment. For this reason, as the medieval Jewish philosopher Joseph Albo suggests, God dispenses material and spiritual rewards and punishments not only during life on earth but also after death in heaven. (*Kiddushin* 40 a–b; *Sefer ha-Iggarim* 4:29ff.)

A guarantee for the future world
Rabbi Harold M. Schulweis points out that some of the ancient rabbis "repudiate the doctrine of reward and punishment as running counter to their sense of justice. . . . The suffering of the righteous is, in fact, a badge of honor, not a stigma of transgression." The Holy One brings suffering upon the righteous of the world in order that they may inherit the future world. (Kiddushin *40b; see "Suffering and Evil," in Abraham E. Millgram, editor,* Great Jewish Ideas, *B'nai B'rith/Bloch Publishing Company, 1964, pp. 206–207)*

Causes of human suffering
Rabbi Roland B. Gittelsohn does not believe in a God who sits in heaven and rewards those who live in accordance with the commandments of Torah and punishes those who do not. Instead, Rabbi Gittelsohn holds that there are four sources of suffering. "One: defiance of nature's physical laws. Two: ignorance of these physical laws. Three: defiance of nature's spiritual laws. Four: ignorance of these spiritual laws." (Man's Best Hope, Random House, New York, 1961, p. 127)*

Explanation of suffering
Suffering brings out and develops character. It supplies a field for all sorts of virtues, for resignation, faith, courage, resource, endurance. It stimulates; it purifies. (Claude G. Montefiore)*

For many moderns, neither the conclusion that the world and human life in it are too baffling to understand nor that God rewards and punishes in mysterious ways or in an afterlife in heaven is acceptable. How, it is asked, can we explain the suffering of innocent children who were put to their deaths in Nazi concentration camps, or the agony of "good" people who endure the torture of disease, or the cruelty and brutality of others?

Where are God's rewards and punishments in situations like these?

Rabbi Harold S. Kushner, in his book *When Bad Things Happen to Good People* (Shocken Books, New York, 1981), argues that one reason for the suffering of innocent, good people "is that our being human leaves us free to hurt each other, and God can't stop us without taking away the freedom that makes us human." In other words, human pain is not the result of God rewarding or punishing, but it is the result of human beings harming one another.

Kushner puts the matter this way: "Human beings can cheat each other, rob each other, hurt each other, and God can only look down in pity and compassion at how little we have learned over the ages about how human beings should behave. . . . When people ask 'Where was God in Auschwitz? How could He have permitted the Nazis to kill so many innocent men, women, and children?' my response is that it was not God who caused it. It was caused by human beings choosing to be cruel to their fellow men."

But what about the sickness of innocent people, the suffering of those afflicted with disease, crippled by illness? Are these God's punishments for not observing the Torah's commandments? Kushner, whose son Aaron died in his teens of a rare disease, writes: "I don't believe that God causes mental retardation in children or chooses who should suffer from muscular dystrophy. The God I believe in does not send us the problem; He gives us the strength to cope with the problem." (pp. 81–86, 127)

Reward, punishment, and conscience
The whole tradition of Judaism helps us in the understanding of right and wrong that is contained in our conscience. If we want personally to believe that by this means God punishes wrong and rewards goodness, we are fully within what Judaism teaches.

But is all wrong punished, all goodness rewarded? What of people of whom we feel, "They have no conscience"?

Perhaps they are part of the abundant evidence that God's world is as yet very far from reaching perfection and that God has given man the task of developing a universal conscience.

(*Meyer Levin*, Beginnings in Jewish Philosophy, *Behrman House, New York, 1971, pp. 78–85*)

Quoting the third-century teacher Yannai, contemporary Rabbi Robert Gordis writes: "It is not in our power fully to explain either the well-being of the wicked or the suffering of the righteous." Gordis sees the universe "as a work of art, the pattern of which cannot be discerned if the spectator stands too close to the painting." He claims it is only "as one moves back a distance" that the "blotches dissolve and the design of the artist emerges in all its fullness."

Gordis's point is that human beings "are too close to the pattern of existence, too deeply involved in it, to be able to achieve the perspective that is God's alone." As a result we cannot fully comprehend the meaning of God's rewards or punishments, nor the reasons for our joys and sufferings. In the end, after all our explorations and explanations, we are left face to face with the mystery of life and with the choice to mold whatever we are given into blessings or curses, rewards or punishments. (*A Faith for Moderns*, Bloch Publishing Company, New York, 1960, chap. X)

Throughout the centuries, Jews have struggled to understand God's relationship to human beings. The study and practice of Torah became the means through which they sought to master ethical discipline, celebrate the seasons of existence, and unravel the deeper mysteries of life. For the ancient authors of Torah, obedience to the commandments was rewarded with material and spiritual benefits, disobedience was punished by deprivation and destruction.

Some later Jewish thinkers accepted this view of reward and punishment; others strongly disagreed. Instead they argue it is not clear when God rewards or punishes. Perhaps it is here on earth, perhaps in heaven—maybe on both sides of existence.

Still other Jewish commentators believe that God gave the commandments to human beings for their benefit but does not sit in heaven deciding who will suffer and who will have good fortune, who will live and who will die. Instead, the Torah's commandments help us to find strength in times of trouble and faith for the confusions and pain we endure as human beings. Our reward is in the meaning and discipline that the commandments give to our lives. If there is punishment for not observing them, it derives from the loss of wisdom and potential meaning observance may provide.

> ### Obligations of Liberal Jews
> *At its June 1976 meeting, the Central Conference of American Rabbis adopted a policy statement:* Reform Judaism: A Centenary Perspective. *In describing the relationship of Reform Jews to the commandments of Jewish tradition, it notes that "Judaism emphasizes action rather than creed as the primary expression of a religious life." Jewish responsibilities for action, the statement continues, "begin with our ethical obligations but they extend to many other aspects of Jewish living, including creating a Jewish home centered on family devotion; lifelong study; private prayer and public worship; daily religious observance; keeping the Sabbath and the holy days; celebrating the major events of life; involvement with the synagogue and community; and other activities that promote the survival of the Jewish people and enhance its existence. Within each area of Jewish observance Reform Jews are called upon to confront the claims of Jewish tradition, however differently perceived, and to exercise their individual autonomy, choosing and creating on the basis of commitment and knowledge."*

One other issue concerning the choice of carrying out the commandments of Torah is also important. While the ancient rabbis identified 613 commandments in the Torah, they did not expect that Jews would observe all of them, or all of the rituals traced to them. Since many of the commandments have to do with the sacrifices offered at the Jerusalem Temple, Jewish teachers held that all Jews are exempt from such commandments until the Temple is rebuilt.

Furthermore, there are many cases today, as in the past, where Orthodox Jewish authorities differ in their interpretation and follow diverse practices. For example, some view the commandment "Be fruitful and multiply" as a prohibition against using contraceptives. Other Orthodox Jews disagree, believing that use of contraceptives is permitted once a husband and wife have a male and female child.

Liberal Jews, among them Reform, Conservative, and Reconstructionist Jews, freely choose on an individual basis which commandments they will observe. They are not bound by rabbinic authority, and they reject the idea that God punishes them because of their choices. Instead, liberal Judaism stresses the obligation of every Jew to examine the ethical teachings and ritual observances of Jewish tradition and to choose to put into practice those that will enrich the meaning of life, "promote the survival of the Jewish people, and enhance its existence." The personal fulfillment derived from carrying out a commandment is its own reward.

Perhaps from the time students of Torah began debating whether God actually rewards those who seek to fulfill all the commandments or punishes those who ignore them, there have been Jewish thinkers who believed that the subject was beyond human comprehension. Indeed, to this very day, the matter remains controversial. No one has the answer.

We do not know why the innocent suffer, why cruelty comes into the world, and why some who are selfish have great fortune while some who are generous endure horrors of pain. All we can do is accept the mystery of life and seek to give it meaning with our choices. It is regarding those choices that the Torah tradition can help us. By asking each time we are faced with a significant decision, "What would Jewish wisdom command us to do?" we may increase our options for "rewards" and for "blessings."

QUESTIONS FOR STUDY AND DISCUSSION

1. What are the ethical lessons we may learn from the Torah's description of the sabbatical and jubilee years? Which of these are most important? Which are least important?
2. Do you agree with Moses Maimonides' ranking of charitable giving?
3. How would you explain why the innocent suffer?
4. Do you agree that suffering and pain result from failing to observe the commandments of Torah or that suffering actually improves character?

Glossary of Commentaries and Interpreters

(For further information on those entries followed by an asterisk, see Introduction II in A Torah Commentary for Our Times, Volume One: Genesis.)

Abravanel, Don Isaac.*

Adani, David ben Amram (13th century). (See *Midrash ha-Gadol.*)

Akedat Yitzhak. A commentary to the Torah by Isaac ben Moses Arama. (See Arama, Isaac ben Moses.)

Alshikh, Moshe ben Adrianopolis (1508–1600). Lived and taught in Safed in the Land of Israel. His commentary to the Torah contains his Sabbath sermons.

Arama, Isaac ben Moses (1420–1494). Author of the Torah commentary *Akedat Yitzhak.* Spanish rabbi. Known for his sermons and allegorical interpretations of Torah. Defended Judaism in many public disputes with Christians and settled in Italy after the expulsion of Jews from Spain in 1492.

Ashkenazi, Eliezer ben Elijah (1513–1586). Lived in Egypt, Cyprus, Venice, Prague, and Posen. Died in Cracow. Emphasized the gift of reason and in his commentary, *Ma'aseh ha-Shem,* urged students to approach the Torah with care and independence. Worked as a rabbi, Torah interpreter, and physician. (See *Ma'aseh ha-Shem.*)

Ashkenazi, Shimon (12th century). (See *Yalkut Shimoni.*)

Ashkenazi of Yanof, Jacob ben Isaac (13th century). Author of *Tze'enah u-Re'enah.* (See *Tze'enah u-Re'enah.*)

Astruc, Anselm Solomon. (See *Midrashei Torah.*)

Attar, Chaim ibn (1696–1743). Born in Morocco and settled in Jerusalem where he opened a school. His Torah commentary, *Or ha-Chaim,* combines talmudic and mystical interpretations. (See *Or ha-Chaim.*)

Avot or *Pirke Avot,* "Sayings of the Fathers." A book of the *Mishnah,* comprising a collection of statements by famous rabbis.

Avot de-Rabbi Natan (2nd century). Compiled by Rabbi Nathan, sometimes called "Nathan the Babylonian." Based on *Pirke Avot.*

Ba'al Ha-Turim, Ya'akov (1275–1340). Born in Germany. Fled persecutions there in 1303 and settled in Spain. Author of the very important collection of Jewish law *Arba'ah Turim,* "Four Rows," the basis for the later *Shulchan Aruch,* "Set Table," by Joseph Karo. His Torah commentary known as *Ba'al ha-Turim* often includes interpretations based on the mathematical meanings of Hebrew words.

Bachya ben Asher (14th century). Lived in Saragossa and Aragon. Known for his Torah commentary.

Bachya ben Joseph ibn Pakuda (11th century). Lived in Spain as poet and author of the classic study of Jewish ethics *Hovot ha-Levavot,* "Duties of the Heart." (See *Hovot ha-Levavot.*)

Bamberger, Bernard J.*

Berlin, Naphtali Zvi Judah (1817–1893). Head of the famous yeshivah at Volozhin. Supporter of early Zionism, his Torah commentary, *Ha-Emek Davar,* is a record of his lectures on the weekly portions. (See *Ha-Emek Davar.*)

Bin Gorion, Micha Joseph (Berdyczewski) (1865–1921). Though a Russian citizen, spent most of his years in Germany. A Hebrew writer, his collection of Jewish folktales, *Mimekor Yisrael,* is considered a classic. (See *Mimekor Yisrael.*)

*Biur.**

Buber, Martin Mordecai (1878–1965). Born in Vienna. Became renowned as a twentieth-century philosopher. With Franz Rosenzweig, translated the Bible into German. His *Moses* is a commentary on Exodus.

Caspi, Joseph ben Abba Mari (1280–1340). A philosopher and commentator who lived in France. His commentary seeks to blend reason with religious faith.

Cassuto, Umberto. An Italian historian and biblical scholar. Accepted chair of Bible Studies at Hebrew University, Jerusalem, in 1939, when Italian racial laws made continuation of his work impossible. Wrote famous commentaries on Genesis and Exodus.

Da'at Zekenim mi-Ba'alei ha-Tosafot. A thirteenth-century collection of Torah commentaries by students of Rashi who sought to resolve contradictions found within the talmudic discussions of the rabbis.

De Leon, Moses. (See *Zohar.*)*

Deuteronomy Rabbah. One of the early collections of *midrashim.**

Dubno, Solomon. (See *Biur.*)*

Ecclesiastes Rabbah. One of the early collections of *midrashim.**

Edels, Shemuel Eliezer ben Yehudah Halevi (1555–1631). One of the best known and repsected interpreters of Talmud. Born in Cracow. Also known as the *Maharsha*.

Epstein, Baruch (1860–1942). Murdered by the Nazis in the Pinsk ghetto. (See *Torah Temimah*.)

Exodus Rabbah. One of the early collections of *midrashim*.*

Genesis Rabbah. One of the early collections of *midrashim*.*

Gittin. A tractate of Talmud that discusses the laws of divorce.

Guide for the Perplexed. A philosophical discussion of the meanings of Jewish belief written by Moses Maimonides. (See Maimonides, Moses.)

Ha-Cohen, Meir Simcha (1843–1926). (See *Meshekh Hochmah*.)

Ha-Emek Davar. A Torah commentary written by Naphtali Zvi Judah Berlin. (See Berlin, Naphtali Zvi Judah.)

Ha-Ketav ve-ha-Kabbalah. A Torah commentary written by Jacob Zvi Meklenburg.*

Halevi, Aharon (1230–1300). Born in Gerona, Spain. Served as rabbi and judge in Barcelona, Saragossa, and Toledo. Lecturer in Montpellier, Provençe, France, where he died. While *Sefer ha-Hinuch* is said to have been written by him, many doubt the claim. (See *Sefer ha-Hinuch*.)

Halevi, Isaac ben Yehudah (13th century). (See *Paneah Raza*.)

Halevi, Yehudah (1080–1142?). Born in Spain. Poet, philosopher, and physician. His book *The Kuzari* contains his philosophy of Judaism. It is a dialogue between the king of the Kazars and a rabbi who convinces the king of the superiority of Judaism.

Hallo, William W.*

Ha-Midrash ve-ha-Ma'aseh. A commentary to Genesis and Exodus by Yehezkel ben Hillel Aryeh Leib Lipschuetz. (See Lipschuetz, Yehezkel ben Hillel Aryeh Leib.)

Heinemann, Yitzhak (1876–1957). Born in Germany. Israeli scholar and philosopher. His *Ta'amei ha-Mitzvot*, "Reasons for the Commandments," is a study of the meaning of the commandments of Jewish tradition.

Hertz, Joseph Herman.*

Hirsch, Samson Raphael.*

Hirschensohn, Chaim (1857–1935). Born in Safed. Lived most of his life in Jerusalem. Supported the work of Eliezer ben Yehuda's revival of Hebrew.

(See *Nimmukei Rashi*.)

Hizkuni. A Torah commentary by Hizkiyahu (Hezekiah) ben Manoah (13th century) of France.

Hoffman, David Zvi (1843–1921). A leading German rabbi. His commentary on Leviticus and Deuteronomy is based on lectures given in the 1870s, seeking to refute biblical critics who argued that the Christian New Testament was superior to the Hebrew Bible.

Hovot ha-Levavot, "Duties of the Heart." A classic study of Jewish ethics by Bachya ben Joseph ibn Pakuda. Concerned with the emphasis on ritual among the Jews of his times, Bachya argues that a Jew's highest responsibility is to carry out the ethical commandments of Torah. (See Bachya ben Joseph ibn Pakuda.)

Hullin. A tractate of Talmud that discusses laws dealing with killing animals for food.

Ibn Ezra, Abraham.*

Jacob, Benno.*

Kasher, Menachem. (See *Torah Shelemah*.)

Kelei Yakar. A Torah commentary written by Solomon Ephraim ben Chaim Lunchitz (1550–1619) of Lvov (Lemberg) Poland.

Kiddushin. A tractate of Talmud that discusses laws of marriage.

Kimchi, David (RaDaK).*

Leibowitz, Nehama.*

Lekach Tov. A collection of *midrashim* on the Torah and the Five Scrolls (Song of Songs, Ruth, Lamentations, Ecclesiastes, and Esther), by Tobias ben Eliezer (11th century C.E.).

Lipschuetz, Yehezkel ben Hillel Aryeh Lieb (1862–1932). Lithuanian interpreter of Torah and author of *Ha-Midrash ve-ha-Ma'aseh*. (See *Ha-Midrash ve-ha-Ma'aseh*.)

Luzzato, Moshe Chaim (1707–1746). Known also as *Ramhal*. Italian dramatist and mystic whose commentaries were popular among chasidic Jews. His textbook on how to become a righteous person, *Mesillat Yesharim* became one of the most popular books on the subject of Jewish ethics. (See *Mesillat Yesharim*.)

Luzzato, Samuel David.*

Ma'aseh ha-Shem. A commentary by Eliezer ben Elijah Ashkenazi published in 1583. (See Ashkenazi, Eliezer ben Elijah.)

Maimonides, Moses, Rabbi Moses ben Maimon (1135–1204). Known by the initials RaMBaM. Born in Cordova, Spain. Physician and philosopher. Wrote the *Mishneh Torah*, a code of Jewish law;

Guide for the Perplexed, a philosophy of Judaism; *Sefer ha-Mitzvot,* an outline of the 613 commandments of Torah; and many other interpretations of Jewish tradition. Famous as a physician. Served the leaders in the court of Egypt.

MaLBIM, Meir Lev ben Yechiel Michael.*

Mechilta.

Megillah. A tractate of Talmud that discusses the biblical Book of Esther.

Meklenburg, Jacob Zvi. (See *Ha-Ketav ve-ha-Kabbalah.*)*

Mendelssohn, Moses.*

Meshekh Hochmah. A Torah commentary published in 1927. Written by Meir Simcha Ha-Cohen, rabbi of Dvinsk. Combines insights from the Talmud with a discussion of the philosophy of Judaism. (See Ha-Cohen, Meir Simcha.)

Mesillat Yesharim, "Pathway of the Righteous." A discussion of how one should pursue an ethical life. Written by Moshe Chaim Luzzatto (see above).

Messengers of God. A study of several important biblical personalities, by Elie Wiesel. (See Wiesel, Elie; also Bibliography in this book.)

Midrash Agadah. A collection of rabbinic interpretations. (See discussion of *midrashim.*)*

Midrash ha-Gadol. A collection of rabbinic interpretations dating to the first and second centuries, by David ben Amram Adani, a scholar living in Yemen. (See Adani, David ben Amram.)

Midrash Sechel Tov. Compiled by Menachem ben Solomon in 1139. Combines selections of *midrash* and *halachah* on every Torah portion.

Midrash Tanchuma. Known also as *Tanchuma Midrash Yelamedenu.* A collection said to have been collected by Rabbi Tanchuma (427–465 C.E.). Many of the *midrashim* begin with the words *Yelamedenu rabbenu,* "Let our teacher instruct us. . . ."*

Midrashei Torah. A Torah commentary by Anselm Solomon Astruc who was murdered in an attack on the Jewish community of Barcelona in 1391.

Mimekor Yisrael. A collection of folktales from Jewish tradition by Micha Joseph Bin Gorion (Berdyczewski). (See Bin Gorion.)

Mishnah.

Mizrachi, Eliyahu (1440–1525). A Chief Rabbi of Turkey during the expulsion of Jews from Spain. Helped many immigrants. Wrote a commentary to Rashi's Torah interpretation.

Morgenstern, Julian.*

Nachmanides.* (See RaMBaN.)

Nedarim. A tractate of Talmud that discusses vows or promises.

Nimmukei Rashi. A commentary on Rashi's Torah interpretation by Chaim Hirschensohn. (See Hirschensohn, Chaim.)

Numbers Rabbah. An early collection of *midrashim.*

Or ha-Chaim. A Torah commentary by Chaim ibn Attar. Combines talmudic observations with mystical interpretations. (See Attar, Chaim ibn.)

Paneah Raza. A Torah commentary by Isaac ben Yehudah Halevi who lived in Sens. (See Halevi, Isaac ben Yehudah.)

Peli, Pinchas Hacohen (20th century). Jerusalem-born scholar, poet, and rabbi. His "Torah Today" column in the *Jerusalem Post* seeks to present a contemporary view of the meaning of Torah.

Pesikta de-Rav Kahana. * A collection of *midrashim* or early rabbinic sermons based on Torah portions for holidays of the Jewish year. *Pesikta Rabbati* is similar in both content and organization.

Pesikta Rabbati. * (See *Pesikta de-Rav Kahana.*)

Pirke de-Rabbi Eliezer. * A collection of *midrashim* said to have been written by the first-century C.E. teacher Rabbi Eliezer ben Hyrkanos. Contents include mystic interpretations of creation, early human life, the giving of the Torah at Mount Sinai, comments about the Book of Esther, and the Israelite experience in the Sinai.

Plaut, W. Gunther.*

RaDaK, Rabbi David Kimchi.*

RaMBaM, Rabbi Moses ben Maimon. (See Maimonides.)

RaMBaN, Rabbi Moses ben Nachman.* (See Nachmanides.)

RaSHBaM, Rabbi Shemuel (Samuel) ben Meir.*

RaSHI, Rabbi Shelomoh (Solomon) Itzhaki.*

Reggio, Yitzhak Shemuel (1784–1855). Known also as YaSHaR. Lived in Italy. Translated the Bible into Italian. Created a Hebrew commentary that sought to harmonize science and religion.

Rosenzweig, Franz (1886–1929). German philosopher. Worked with Martin Buber in translating the Bible into German. Best known for book *The Star of Redemption,* which seeks to explore the meanings of Jewish tradition.

Sa'adia ben Joseph Ha-Gaon.* (See Introductions I and II of *A Torah Commentary for Our Times, Volume One: Genesis.*

Sanhedrin. A tractate of Talmud that discusses laws

regulating the courts.

Sarna, Nahum M.*

Sefer ha-Hinuch. Presents the 613 *mitzvot,* "commandments," found within the Torah. Divided according to weekly Torah portions. Said by some to have been written by Aharon Halevi of Barcelona. (See Halevi, Aharon.)

Sforno, Obadiah.*

Shabbat. A tractate of the Talmud that discusses the laws of the Sabbath.

*Sifra.** A *midrash* on Leviticus. Believed by scholars to have been written during the fourth century C.E.

*Sifre.** A *midrash* on Numbers and Deuteronomy. Believed to have been composed during the fifth century C.E.

Simeon (Shimon) ben Yochai.* (See *Zohar.*)*

Solomon, Menachem ben. (See *Midrash Sechel Tov.*)

Sotah. A tractate of the Talmud that discusses laws concerning a woman suspected of adultery.

Speiser, Ephraim Avigdor.*

Steinsaltz, Adin (20th century). An Israeli Talmud scholar. His book *Biblical Images* contains studies of various biblical characters.

Ta'amei ha-Mitzvot. (See Heinemann, Yitzhak.)

Ta'anit. A tractate of the Talmud that deals with the laws concerning fast days.

*Talmud.** Combines the *Mishnah* and *Gemara.* Appears in two versions: the more extensive *Talmud Bavli,* "Babylonian Talmud," a collection of discussions by the rabbis of Babylonia from the second to the fifth centuries C.E., and *Talmud Yerushalmi,* "Jerusalem Talmud," a smaller collection of discussions from the second to the fourth centuries C.E.

Tanna Debe Eliyahu. A *midrash* and book of Jewish philosophy and commentary believed by scholars to have been composed during the third to tenth centuries. Author unknown.

*Targum Onkelos.**

*Targum Yerushalmi.**

Toledot Yitzhak.

Torah Shelemah. A study of each Torah portion, which includes a collection of early rabbinic interpretations along with a commentary by Rabbi Menachem Kasher of Jerusalem, Israel.

Torah Temimah. A Torah commentary by Baruch Epstein. Includes a collection of teachings from the Talmud on each Torah portion. (See Epstein, Baruch.)

Tosafot. "Supplementary Discussions" of the Talmud. Collected during the twelfth and thirteenth centuries in France and Germany and added to nearly every printing of the Talmud since.

Tzedeh Laderech. An interpretation of Rashi's Torah commentary by Issachar Ber ben Israel-Lazar Parnas Eilenberg (1550–1623), who lived in Italy.

Tze'enah u-Re'enah. A well-known Yiddish paraphrase and interpretation of the Torah. First published in 1618. Written for women by Jacob ben Isaac Ashkenazi of Yanof. Divided by weekly Torah portions. One of the first texts developed to educate women. (See Ashkenazi of Yanof, Jacob ben Isaac.)

Wessely, Naftali Herz. (See *Biur.*)*

Wiesel, Elie (1928–   ). Nobel Prize-winning novelist. Author of *Messengers of God,* among other books. (See *Messengers of God.*)

Yalkut Shimoni. A collection of *midrashim.* Believed to be the work of Shimon Ashkenazi. (See Ashkenazi, Shimon.)

Yevamot. A tractate of Talmud that deals with laws concerning sisters-in-law.

Yoma. A tractate of Talmud that deals with laws concerning Yom Kippur.

*Zohar.**

Bibliography

Abbott, Walter M.; Gilbert, Arthur; Hunt, Rolfe Lanier; and Swain, J. Carter. *The Bible Reader: An Interfaith Interpretation.* New York: Bruce Publishing Co., 1969.

Adar, Zvi. *Humanistic Values in the Bible.* New York: Reconstructionist Press, 1967.

Adler, Morris, *The Voice Still Speaks.* New York: Bloch Publishing Co., 1969.

Aharoni, Yohanan, and Avi-Yonah, Michael. *The Macmillan Bible Atlas.* New York: Macmillan, 1976.

Alter, Robert. *The Art of Biblical Narrative.* New York: Basic Books, 1981.

Asimov, Isaac. *Animals of the Bible.* Garden City, New York: Doubleday, 1978.

Avi-Yonah, Michael, and Malamat, Abraham, eds. *Views of the Biblical World.* Chicago and New York: Jordan Publications, Inc., 1959.

Bachya ben Asher. *Kad ha-Kemach.* Charles B. Chavel, trans. New York: Shilo Publishing House, Inc., 1980.

Baron, Joseph L., ed. *A Treasury of Jewish Quotations*. New York: Crown Publishers, Inc., 1956.

Ben-Gurion, David. *Israel, a Personal History*. New York: Funk and Wagnalls, Inc., and Sabra Books, 1971.

Blumenthal, David R. *God at the Center*. San Francisco: Harper and Row, 1987.

Braude, William G., and Kapstein, Israel J., trans. Author unknown. *Tanna Debe Eliyahu*. Philadelphia: Jewish Publication Society, 1981.

Buber, Martin. *Moses*. New York: Harper and Row Publishers, Inc., 1958.

Bulka, Reuven P. *Torah Therapy: Reflections on the Weekly Sedra and Special Occasions*. New York: Ktav, 1983.

Cassuto, Umberto. *A Commentary on the Book of Exodus*. Jerusalem: Magnes Press, 1951.

Chavel, Charles B., trans. *Ramban (Nachmanides) Commentary on the Torah*. New York: Shilo Publishing House, Inc., 1974.

Chiel, Arthur. *Guide to Sidrot and Haftarot*. New York: Ktav, 1971.

Chill, Abraham. *The Minhagim: The Customs and Ceremonies of Judaism, Their Origins and Rationale*. New York: Sepher-Hermon Press, 1979.

Cohen, Philip. *Rambam on the Torah*. Jerusalem: Rubin Mass Ltd. Publishers, 1985.

Culi, Ya'akov. *The Torah Anthology, Yalkut Me'am Lo'ez*. Aryeh Kaplan, trans. New York and Jerusalem: Maznaim Publishing Corp., 1977.

Danby, Herbert, trans. *The Mishnah*. London: Oxford University Press, 1933.

Deen, Edith. *All of the Women of the Bible*. New York: Harper and Brothers, 1965.

Doria, Charles, and Lenowitz, Harris, trans. and eds. *Origins, Creation Texts from the Ancient Mediterranean*. New York: Anchor Press, 1976.

Dresner, Samuel H., and Siegel, Seymour. *The Jewish Dietary Laws*. New York: Burning Bush Press, 1959.

Efron, Benjamin. *The Message of the Torah*. New York: Ktav, 1963.

Epstein, I., trans. and ed. *The Babylonian Talmud*. London: Soncino Press, 1952.

Fields, Harvey J. *Bechol Levavcha: With All Your Heart*. New York: Union of American Hebrew Congregations, 1976.

Freedman, H., and Simon, Maurice, trans. *Midrash Rabbah: Genesis,* Vols. I and II. London: Soncino Press, 1961.

Friedman, Alexander Zusia. *Wellsprings of Torah*. Compiled and edited by Nison Alpert. Gertrude Hirschler, trans. New York: Judaica Press, 1986.

Friedman, Richard Elliott. *Who Wrote the Bible?* New York: Summit Books, 1987.

Fromm, Erich. *You Shall Be as Gods*. New York: Holt, Rinehart and Winston, 1966.

Frye, Northrop. *The Great Code: The Bible and Literature*. New York: Harcourt Brace Jovanovich Publishers, 1981.

Gaster, Theodor H. *Festivals of the Jewish Year*. New York: William Morrow and Co., Inc. 1953.

Gilbert, Martin. *Jewish History Atlas*. New York: Macmillan, 1976.

Ginzberg, Louis. *Legends of the Jews*. Philadelphia: Jewish Publication Society, 1968.

Gittelsohn, Roland B. *Man's Best Hope*. New York: Random House, 1961.

Glatzer, Nahum N., ed. *Hammer on the Rock: A Midrash Reader*. New York: Schocken Books, 1962.

_____. *On the Bible: 18 Studies*. New York: Schocken Books, 1968.

Goldman, Solomon. *In the Beginning*. Philadelphia: Jewish Publication Society of America, 1949.

Gordis, Robert. *A Faith for Moderns*. New York: Bloch Publishing Co., 1960.

Graves, Robert, and Patai, Raphael. *Hebrew Myths: The Book of Genesis*. New York: Greenwich House, 1983.

Greenberg, Moshe. *Understanding Exodus*. New York: Behrman House, 1969.

Hartman, David. *A Living Covenant*. New York: The Free Press, 1985.

Herford, R. Travers. *Pirke Aboth, The Ethics of the Talmud: Sayings of the Fathers*. New York: Schocken Books, 1971.

Hertz, J.H., ed. *The Pentateuch and Haftorahs*. London: Soncino Press, 1966.

Heschel, Abraham J. *The Prophets*. Philadelphia: Jewish Publication Society, 1962.

_____. *God in Search of Man: A Philosophy of Judaism*. New York: Farrar, Straus and Cudahy, 1955.

Hirsch, Samson Raphael, trans. *The Pentateuch*. London, England: L. Honig and Sons Ltd., 1959.

_____. *Horeb: A Philosophy of Jewish Laws and Observances*. I. Grunfeld, trans. 4th ed. New York: Soncino Press, 1981.

The Interpreter's Bible. 12 vols. Nashville: Abingdon, 1951–1957.

Jacobson, B.S. *Meditations on the Torah.* Tel Aviv: Sinai Publishing, 1956.

Kahana, S.Z. *Heaven on Your Head.* Morris Silverman, ed. Hartford: Hartmore House, 1964.

Kaplan, Mordecai M. *Questions Jews Ask: Reconstructionist Answers.* New York: Reconstructionist Press, 1956.

_____. *The Meaning of God in Modern Jewish Religion.* New York: Reconstructionist Press, 1962.

Katz, Mordechai. *Lilmod Ul'lamade: From the Teachings of Our Sages.* New York: Jewish Education Program Publications, 1978.

Korn, Lester. *The Success Profile.* New York: Fireside, 1988.

Kushner, Harold S. *When Bad Things Happen to Good People.* New York: Schocken Books, 1981.

Lamm, Maurice. *The Jewish Way in Death and Mourning.* New York: Jonathan David Publishers, 1975.

Leibowitz, Nehama. *Studies in Bereshit.* Jerusalem: World Zionist Organization, 1980.

_____. *Studies in Shemot.* Jerusalem: World Zionist Organization, 1980.

_____. *Studies in Vayikra.* Jerusalem: World Zionist Organization, 1980.

_____. *Studies in Bemidbar.* Jerusalem: World Zionist Organization, 1980.

_____. *Studies in Devarim.* Jerusalem: World Zionist Organization, 1980.

Levin, Meyer. *Beginnings in Jewish Philosophy.* New York: Behrman House, 1971.

Levine, Baruch A. ed. *JPS Torah Commentary: Leviticus.* Philadelphia: Jewish Publication Society, 1989.

Levine, Moshe. *The Tabernacle: Its Structure and Utensils.* London: Soncino Press, 1969.

Maimonides, Moses. *The Book of Knowledge: Mishneh Torah.* Moses Hyamson, trans. Jerusalem and New York: Feldheim Publishers, 1974.

Matek, Ord. *The Bible through Stamps.* New York: Hebrew Publishing Company, 1967.

Miller, Madeline S., and Lane, J. *Harper's Encyclopedia of Bible Life.* New York: Harper and Row Publishers, Inc., 1978.

Morgenstern, Julian. *The Book of Genesis.* New York: Schocken Books, 1965.

Munk, Eli. *The Call of the Torah,* Vols. I and II. Jerusalem and New York: Feldheim Publishers, 1980.

Neusner, Jacob. *Meet Our Sages.* New York: Behrman House, 1980.

_____. *Tzedakah.* Chappaqua, New York: Rossel, 1982.

Orlinsky, Harry M., ed. *The Torah: The Five Books of Moses.* A New Translation. Philadelphia: Jewish Publication Society, 1962.

_____. *Understanding the Bible through History and Archaeology.* New York: Ktav, 1972.

Peli, Pinchas H. *Torah Today.* Washington, D.C.: B'nai B'rith Books, 1987.

_____. *Shabbat Shalom.* Washington, D.C.: B'nai B'rith Books, 1988.

Peters, Thomas J., and Waterman, Jr., Robert H. *In Search of Excellence.* New York: Harper and Row Publishers, Inc., 1982.

Pfeiffer, Robert H. *Introduction to the Old Testament.* New York: Harper and Brothers, 1941.

Phillips, Anthony. Exodus Commentary. *The Cambridge Bible Commentary: New English Bible.* Cambridge, England: Cambridge University Press, 1972.

Plaut, W. Gunther, ed. *The Torah: A Modern Commentary.* Commentaries by W. Gunther Plaut and Bernard J. Bamberger. Essays by William W. Hallo. New York: Union of American Hebrew Congregations, 1981.

_____. *The Case for the Chosen People.* New York: Doubleday, 1965.

Pritchard, James B., ed. *Ancient Near Eastern Texts Relating to the Old Testament.* Princeton, New Jersey: Princeton University Press, 1955.

Quick, James C., and Jonathan D. *Organizational Stress and Preventive Management.* New York: McGraw-Hill, 1984.

Rabbinowitz, J., trans. *Midrash Rabbah* (Genesis, Exodus, Leviticus, Numbers, Deuteronomy). London: Soncino Press, 1961.

Rabinowitz, Louis I. *Torah and Flora.* New York: Sanhedrin Press, 1977.

Rad, Gerhard von. *Deuteronomy.* Commentary and translation by Dorothea Barton. Philadelphia: Westminster Press, 1966.

Reed, Allison. *The Story of Creation.* New York: Schocken Books, 1981.

Rosenbaum, M., and Silbermann, A.M., trans. *Pentateuch with Targum Onkelos, Haphtaroth and Rashi's Commentary.* Jerusalem: Silbermann Family Publishers, 1973.

Rosenberg, David, ed. *Congregation: Contemporary*

Writers Read the Jewish Bible. New York: Harcourt Brace Jovanovich Publishers, 1987.

Samuel, Maurice. *Certain People of the Book*. New York: Alfred A. Knopf, Inc., 1955.

Sandmel, Samuel. *Alone Atop the Mountain: A Novel about Moses and the Exodus*. New York: Doubleday, 1973.

Sarna, Nahum M. *Understanding Genesis*. New York: Schocken Books, 1966.

Schneerson, Menachem M. *Torah Studies*. London: Lubavitch Foundation, 1986.

_____. *Likutei Sichot*. London: Lubavitch Foundation, 1975–1985.

Sheehy, Gail. *Pathfinders*. New York: William Morrow, 1981.

Silbermann, A.M., ed. *Pentateuch with Rashi Commentary*. Jerusalem: Silbermann Family Publishers, 1933.

Silver, Abba Hillel. *Moses and the Original Torah*. New York: Macmillan, 1961.

_____. *The World Crisis and Jewish Survival*. New York: Richard R. Smith, Inc., 1931.

Silverman, Hillel E. *From Week to Week*. New York: Hartmore House, 1975.

Simon, Solomon, and Morrison, David Bial. *The Rabbis' Bible*. New York: Behrman House, 1966.

Speiser, E.A., trans. *The Anchor Bible: Genesis*. New York: Doubleday, 1964.

Steinberg, Milton. *Basic Judaism*. New York: Harcourt Brace, 1947.

Steinsaltz, Adin. *The Thirteen Petalled Rose*. New York: Basic Books, 1980.

Van Doren, Mark, and Samuel, Maurice. *In the Beginning . . . Love*. Edith Samuel, ed. New York: John Day Company, 1973.

Weinstein, Jacob J. *The Place of Understanding*. New York: Bloch Publishing Co., 1959.

Wiesel, Elie. *Messengers of God*. New York: Random House, 1976.

Zakon, Miriam Stark, trans. *Tze'enah u-Re'enah: The Classic Anthology of Torah Lore and Midrashic Commentary*. Brooklyn, New York: Mesorah Publications Ltd./Hillel Press, 1983.

Zeligs, Dorothy F. *Psychoanalysis and the Bible*. New York: Bloch Publishing Co., 1974.

Zlotowitz, Meir, trans. *Bereishis*. Art Scroll Tanach Series. New York: Mesorah Publications Ltd., 1977–1981.

A
TORAH
COMMENTARY
FOR OUR
TIMES

VOLUME I : GENESIS

HARVEY J. FIELDS

Illustrations by
GIORA CARMI

UAHC PRESS · New York, New York

For
Norman and Reva Fields
Joseph and Reva Sandler

They taught Torah diligently to their children

Library of Congress Cataloging-in-Publication Data
Fields, Harvey J.
A Torah commentary for our times / Harvey J. Fields ;
illustrations by Giora Carmi.
    p.   cm.
Includes bibliographical references.
Contents: v. 1. Genesis.
ISBN 0–8074–0308–3 (v. 1)
1. Bible. O.T. Pentateuch—Commentaries. [1. Bible. O.T.
Pentateuch.]   I. Karmi, Givora, ill.   II. Title.
BS1225.3.F46   1990
222′.1077—dc20   89–28478
                                              CIP
                                              AC

Copyright © 1990 by Harvey J. Fields
Manufactured in the United States of America
10   9

Feldman Library

THE FELDMAN LIBRARY FUND was created in 1974 through a gift from the Milton and Sally Feldman Foundation. The Feldman Library Fund, which provides for the publication by the UAHC of selected outstanding Jewish books and texts, memorializes Sally Feldman, who in her lifetime devoted herself to Jewish youth and Jewish learning. Herself an orphan and brought up in an orphanage, she dedicated her efforts to helping Jewish young people get the educational opportunities she had not enjoyed.

In loving memory of my beloved wife Sally
"She was my life, and she is gone;
She was my riches, and I am a pauper."

"Many daughters have done valiantly,
but thou excellest them all."

Milton E. Feldman

Contents

Acknowledgments

Just over thirty years ago, I journeyed to Jerusalem in search of teachers who might open the gates of Torah and its wisdom to an inquiring student. By that time I was convinced, as I remain to this day, that the Torah and its centuries of interpretation are a fabulous treasure of the human spirit.

Appreciating that "treasure," however, requires the creativity and partnership of teachers and students. My own journey has been enriched by many with whom I have shared the joy of Torah study.

Noteworthy among them are: Dov Bin Nun, Rabbi Zev W. Gotthold, Nehama Leibowitz, Rabbi Sheldon Blank, Rabbi Samuel Sandmel, Rabbi Jakob J. Petuchowski, and Rabbi Roland B. Gittelsohn.

A host of students of all ages from four congregations have challenged and searched the Torah text with me. I am grateful to all of them from Temple Israel, Boston, Massachusetts; Anshe Emeth Memorial Temple, New Brunswick, New Jersey; and Holy Blossom Temple, Toronto, Ontario, Canada. Special thanks are due to the several junior high school, high school, and adult education classes at Wilshire Boulevard Temple, Los Angeles, California, who tested many sections of this commentary with me.

It was Aron Hirt-Manheimer who first urged me to pursue this project. His support, wisdom, and enthusiasm have all helped to make it possible. I am also deeply appreciative to Rabbi Howard I. Bogot for his critical suggestions, and to Rabbi Shelton Donnell, Rabbi Steven Z. Leder, Rachel Fields, Steven Schnur, Annette Abramson, and Dorian Kreindler for their wise advice and editing assistance, and to Stuart L. Benick for his understanding and important role in producing these volumes for Torah study.

Finally, thanks to my wife, Sybil, for her devotion, rich knowledge of Jewish tradition, and always for the gift of her love.

Harvey J. Fields

INTRODUCTIONS

·I·

SPARKS, FRAGMENTS, MEANINGS
A Reader-Friendly Introduction

What is the "Torah"?
The Torah is more than the treasure of the Jewish people, more even than the sacred scroll that bonds Jews to one another and to all the generations who have praised it with the words: "It is a tree of life to all who grasp it, and whoever holds on to it is happy; its ways are ways of pleasantness, and all its paths are peace." (Proverbs 3:17–18)

The Torah is a vast and diverse library. It contains ancient stories, science, histories, ritual practices, philosophy, and ethical standards. Its pages are filled with powerful prose and poetry about the clash of individuals and nations. Within its five books, Genesis, Exodus, Leviticus, Numbers, and Deuteronomy, we encounter the unique way in which the Jewish people views the universe, humanity, and God. No subject is excluded: birth and death, rivalries between children and parents, battles for power, lust, cheating, charity, sexual discrimination, greed, community building, responsibility for the homeless and hungry, taxation, real estate, ecology, business and medical ethics, marriage and divorce. First-century C.E. teacher Ben Bag Bag captured the truth when he told his students: "Turn the Torah, and turn it again, for everything you want to know is found within it." (*Avot* 5:25)

How can we understand the Torah?
Ben Bag Bag may have been correct, but, for many of us, reading and understanding the Torah is not easy. Often we find the language confusing and the stories or flow from one subject to another puzzling. We want to "turn it" and be enriched, even inspired by it, but we end up frustrated and bewildered. "What," we ask, "can the ancient Torah teach us today? What meaning can it have in our lives?"

A Torah Commentary for Our Times has been written with the conviction that there is not only much that we can learn from the Torah but also that studying and sharing its insights can be both inspiring and enjoyable. Our purpose is to present each *parashah*, or "weekly Torah portion," so that it is easy to understand and so that its themes are relevant and accessible.

With each *parashah* we will ask two basic questions: "What is this Torah portion about?" and "What meaning can this Torah portion have for us?"

For clarification, we will identify the most important themes of each *parashah* and then present the varying, and often clashing, opinions of Jewish interpreters throughout the ages. At times we will advocate a particular point of view, but most often we will leave final conclusions to the reader.

The art of "interpreting" Torah
While the organization and presentation of our material may be new, the method we are employing has been tested by Jews over thousands of years. We are not the first to find the contents

of the Torah difficult, confusing, and challenging. As far back as the fifth century B.C.E., when Ezra and Nehemiah read the Torah in Jerusalem to Jews who had just returned from Babylonian exile, it was apparently necessary to explain its meanings. We are told that Ezra and Nehemiah gathered all the people into the city square and opened the scroll so that everyone could see it. Afterwards, they read from the Torah in Hebrew, translated it, and interpreted it so that everyone present might understand its contents. (Nehemiah 8: 4–8)

Ever since that time, and perhaps even before, Jews have found it necessary not only to "hear" the Torah in its original Hebrew but also to hear a *targum*, or "translation," and to analyze the text for its messages and wisdom. The rabbis, who were among the earliest interpreters of Torah, called that process of analysis *midrash*, which means "probing" or "searching."

Among Jews, deciphering the intent and meanings of Torah is a high form of art. For many, it is the means through which God's voice speaks to the heart and is decoded by the human mind and soul.

Times change, so do explanations

Throughout most of Jewish history, the Torah functioned as "the law" for Jews. Its commandments and the interpretation of them regulated all of Jewish personal and communal life. The calendar was set according to the festivals and sacred holy days prescribed by the Torah. Regulations concerning business transactions, public safety, diet, criminal behavior, marriage, divorce, and the rearing of children were all derived from the sacred text.

Society, however, changes and evolves. New situations, circumstances, and questions arise. For the Torah to remain "the law," it was necessary for it to be interpreted and applied to every culture, society, and age in which Jews lived.

For instance, observance of the Sabbath in Jerusalem during the time of Ezra and Nehemiah was very different from circumstances one encountered in Babylonia during the third century B.C.E. The application of commandments having to do with care for the poor while Jews were farmers in the Land of Israel during King David's time was very different from the function of such laws in the thirteenth-century C.E. city of Seville, Spain. An interpretation of laws concerning the determination of death that might have worked for Jews living in seventeenth-century Europe clearly requires updating for the high-tech civilization of today.

In order to accommodate such changing needs and circumstances, Jews created a process of interpreting Torah that continues to this day. Early rabbinic scholars initiated this tradition with two kinds of *midrash: Midrash Agadah,* or "literary/ moral explanations" often in the form of sermons, and *Midrash Halachah,* or "legal explanations." Eventually, many of these interpretations were collected, organized, and expanded into the *Mishnah* and *Gemara,* which together make up the Talmud. Special collections of *midrashim* as well as many *targumim,* or "translations" of Torah, were also preserved by the scholars of Jewish tradition.

After the completion of the Talmud in the sixth century C.E., rabbis continued to evolve new interpretations of Torah to meet the conditions of Jews living throughout the world. Sa'adia Gaon in Babylonia; Bachya ibn Pakuda and Yehudah Halevi in Spain; Moses Maimonides in Egypt, Spain, and Morocco; and later Rashi, Rashbam, and Radak in France and Abraham ibn Ezra, Ramban, and Don Isaac Abravanel in Spain—all contributed to the vast literature of evolving new meanings and applications of Torah.

No generation of Jews has been without its commentators. In every age they have "turned" the Torah and produced creative insights and applications of its wisdom. Sometimes they have agreed; at other times they have clashed over whose explanation was "correct." Like the generations of critics who have studied the great Greek playwrights or the works of Shakespeare or like Supreme Court justices who interpret the United States Constitution, Jewish commentators have left us a legacy of differing views to consider.

Today the adventure of exploring the meanings of Torah continues. So do the differences of opinion. There are those who settle for what past authors have said. Others apply the new sciences of psychology or literary criticism to the ancient text. Many view the text as sacred poetry and probe it for new spiritual understandings about God's relationship to earth and to human beings. Still others—using the revolutionary discoveries of archeology, comparative religion, linguistic analysis, and even computer technology—are decoding what they argue are the authentic intentions and wisdom of the Torah. Like a fabulous gem, the Torah continues to surprise, baffle, and enrich those who study, explore, and possess it.

What's our strategy for exploring the Torah?
Our adventure with each *parashah* will employ a set of six tactics.

1. We shall begin with a brief and clarifying overview of the Torah text. It is meant for a "quick" read, the equivalent of a city map with just the major roads and highways outlined, without all the details of streets and neighborhoods. In other words, the overview is meant to tell us where we are and where we are going in the Torah text.

2. The next section we call "Our *Targum,*" or our "translation." Like the ancient translations, it provides a more detailed presentation of the *parashah.* The purpose of the *targum* is to translate the Torah into our idiom, into the way we use language today. Our *targum* will be divided into numbered parts, making it easier to grasp the flow of the story. You may wish to compare our *targum* with the actual text of the Torah. If you do, you will note that sometimes the *targum* contains explanations about the names of places or people or creates connections between one part of the Torah and another. Note that the numbers of the parts of our *targum* do not refer to the numbers of the chapters and verses of the text in the Bible.

3. Each *parashah* is crammed with potential themes or subjects for discussion. No one book or set of books could possibly cover them all. Our "Themes" section will present those themes that have been chosen for exploration. Again, our purpose is clarity. We want the reader to understand where we are headed. Surprises are for the next section.

4. Our commentary on each Torah portion proceeds one *perek,* or "segment," at a time. Each segment will examine one theme, but it will present a variety of opinions by commentators from different times and places. Often the points of view will clash and remain unresolved. It is not our intention to harmonize them. Instead, we want to call attention to the rich diversity of approaches and explanations that coexist within the tradition of interpreting Torah. To that end, we have often placed side by side ancient and modern views, suspending judgment so that the readers-explorers can draw their own conclusions.

5. Within each *perek,* you will also find additional boxed comments. These are meant to enrich the reader with special insights or to amplify ideas discussed within each section.

6. Concluding each chapter are "Questions for Study and Discussion." Their purpose is to stimulate discussion about some of the significant ideas and themes raised by both the Torah text and its commentators. "What can the Torah and the insights of its interpreters teach us today?" is the guiding question of this section.

A warning and final strategy!
Jewish tradition holds that the study of Torah is of supreme importance. Yet we are warned about how that study and exploration ought to be carried out. Rabbi Joshua ben Perachyah, who was president of the Sanhedrin, the Supreme Court of seventy-one scholars, during the second century B.C.E., taught that one should study Torah with a teacher and with a friend. (*Avot* 1:6) Sharing Torah with others has two advantages. It provides us with a check on our assumptions and a means of challenging our conclusions. It also has the advantage of sharpening our understandings against other points of view.

Take Joshua ben Perachyah's advice. Find a teacher and some friends with whom to investigate the meanings of Torah.

Sparks and fragments, or studying Torah is always a surprise!
According to an ancient legend, when God gave the Torah to Moses on Mount Sinai, the people grew frightened and stood at a distance from the mountain. Thunder shook the ground. Lightning lit up the sky. Then, as each word and sentence of Torah burst forth, an ear-shattering crash was heard. Sparks and fragments flew in every direction as God spoke to the people: "As the hammer

splits the rocks into thousands of sparks and fragments, so My Torah will generate thousands of interpretations." (*Sanhedrin* 34a)

A legend, of course! But within its drama is a significant message. The teachings of Torah are splendid sparks—glowing particles providing light for the seeker of knowledge and illumination for our ethical choices. Yet the teachings of Torah are also multifaceted fragments revealing a multitude of angles, features, and surfaces. Within each face are new meanings to be explored and revealed.

Today, after thousands of years of studying and interpreting Torah, the adventure continues. It is an enterprise without end.

Go and learn!

·II·

TURN IT AND TURN IT!
Introducing the Torah Commentators

The Torah grew and evolved over many centuries out of the ancient thoughts and experiences of the Jewish people. Within it are views about the creation of the world and the first human beings, along with accounts of Abraham and Sarah, Isaac and Rebekah, Jacob, Leah, and Rachel—the founders of the people of Israel. Its pages are filled with stories about Moses liberating the people from Egypt, about their wandering for forty years in the desert. We are told how they received God's law at Mount Sinai and built their first sanctuary.

No one knows how or when the Torah, the Five Books of Moses, was written or given its final form. Perhaps it existed for many hundreds of years as a tradition, memorized by priests or teachers and passed on from one generation to the next. Perhaps some of its most important parts—the Ten Commandments, the laws concerning sacrifices, details about the festivals, and regulations having to do with property—were written down and placed in arks or other special containers where they would be preserved.

It is possible that during the period from 1200 B.C.E., when the Israelites conquered the Land of Israel, until 586 B.C.E., when they were defeated and exiled by the Babylonians, various fragments of the Torah existed, and *soferim*, or "scribes," rescued them and took them to Babylonia.

We know that when Ezra and Nehemiah, both of whom were known as priests and scribes, led Jews back from Babylonian exile between the years 465 and 359 B.C.E., they brought with them the Torah. Most scholars believe that it contained the Five Books of Moses and had been compiled and edited by *soferim* during the exile in Babylonia. It was to serve as the "constitution," the *law*, for the rebuilt Jewish nation.

When Ezra and Nehemiah gathered the people in Jerusalem to hear the Torah, they faced a difficult problem. While in Babylonia for nearly three generations, Jews had abandoned Hebrew and now spoke Aramaic, the prevailing language of Babylonian culture. How then would they understand the Torah, the sacred text and laws of their tradition? Ezra and Nehemiah responded to the challenge by adding both a *targum*, or "translation," and a commentary to the public reading of Torah. (See Nehemiah 8.)

Clearly, this early tradition of translating the Torah into the vernacular and of explaining its contents set the stage for the creative evolution of both Judaism and the Jewish people. As the Torah was read and translated, the people became familiar with its stories and laws. As it was interpreted and applied to the questions and issues facing them, it emerged as their supreme source of wisdom.

Which came first, the targum or the midrash?
As we have already noted, Ezra and Nehemiah offered both a *targum*, or "translation," and a *mid-*

rash, or "explanation," of Torah to the people. What is impossible to know is which of these two critical "tools" for understanding came first. In truth, they seem to have developed simultaneously. For that reason, we are dividing the next part of this Introduction II into two sections.

Section One: Targumim—"Translations"

During the period of the Second Temple in Jerusalem until its destruction in 70 C.E., many different Torah translations in Aramaic, Greek, Egyptian, Median, and Elamean appeared. Most of these are now lost to us, but we can assume that some of their language and views are reflected in the later Greek and Aramaic versions that have been preserved.

The most famous Greek *targum* is known as the **SEPTUAGINT.** According to one tradition, the Greek leader Ptolemy II Philadelphus (285–247 B.C.E.) invited seventy-two rabbis to Alexandria, Egypt, and ordered each to prepare a translation of Torah into Greek. When they compared notes, all of them had composed the same translation. Beyond the charming story, the Septuagint is written in the Koine, or colloquial Greek spoken during the third century B.C.E. Even more significantly, it contains elaborations of the Torah text that are meant to clarify it for the listener. As early Christianity emerged, Church leaders selected the Septuagint as their official text of Torah.

During the second century C.E., after the destruction of the Jerusalem Temple and the emergence of Christianity, leading rabbis invited a convert to Judaism, Aquila, to prepare a new Greek translation of Torah. While fragments of the text have survived, the **TARGUM AQUILA,** as it became known, combines translation with interpretation by incorporating many early rabbinic views into the text. Some scholars believe that Aquila, and those who urged him to write his translation, were anxious to create a text that differed from the Septuagint and answered early Christian challenges about the meaning of Torah.

While Aramaic translations existed during the time of Ezra and Nehemiah, the best-known and most complete text is the **TARGUM ONKELOS.** Dating from the third century C.E., it, like Targum Aquila, was the work of a convert to Judaism. Indeed, there are some scholars who believe that Aquila and Onkelos were the same person! Targum Onkelos became the most important translation within Jewish tradition and appears alongside the Torah text in nearly every "rabbinic Bible."

Onkelos presents a straightforward translation while avoiding phrases that leave the reader with the impression that God possesses human attributes or reacts with human feelings. Excuses are often cited for the faults of major biblical personalities, and often the intent of the text is clarified. For instance, Onkelos translates "You shall not boil a kid in its mother's milk" (Exodus 23:19, Exodus 34:26, and Deuteronomy 14:21) as "You shall not eat meat with milk." This combination of translation and interpretation helped to make Targum Onkelos one of the most valued texts among later Babylonian rabbis.

Two other Aramaic translations were popular in their times, but they have been lost to us. We have a few fragments of a **TARGUM OF JONATHAN BEN UZZIEL** and of another called **TARGUM YERUSHALMI.** The first of these draws heavily on the Targum Onkelos and the Yerushalmi, and some of it may date back to the second century B.C.E. during the time of the Maccabees. On the other hand, the origins of Targum Yerushalmi seem to date from the first century B.C.E. Scholars discovered pieces of the text in a Cairo, Egypt, *genizah* (a storage place above a synagogue) and also called it the "Galilean" or "Neofiti Targum." The text often provides geographical information about remote places mentioned in the Torah. Like the Targum Onkelos, it avoids describing God in human terms and contains many observations about both the stories and laws of Torah.

The best-known Arabic translation of Torah is the **TARGUM TAFSIR,** prepared by the tenth-century Babylonian philosopher and interpreter Sa'adia ben Joseph Ha-Gaon. *Tafsir* means "commentary," and Sa'adia seems to have had as his purpose the creation of a Torah text that could be read by the majority of Jews who knew no Hebrew and felt ignorant about their tradition. Born and reared in Egypt, Sa'adia moved first to the Land of Israel and then to Babylonia. There, as head of the rabbinic academy at Sura, he emerged as both a political and religious authority.

Sa'adia's *targum* reveals his deepest anxieties about the future of the Jewish people. On the one hand, they were being attacked by Moslems who wished to make converts by demonstrating the superiority of their faith and the Koran over Judaism and the Torah. On the other hand, the Jewish community was deeply divided between those, like Sa'adia, who followed the rabbinic tradition of interpreting Torah, and the Karaites who claimed that the Torah was to be read literally, without any interpretations by the rabbinic tradition.

Targum Tafsir clarifies the Torah text with rabbinic explanations, and Sa'adia's bias against portraying God as a human being is similar to the treatment Onkelos gives to his translation. The text is clear, and Sa'adia's later commentaries to the Torah remain a valuable resource for those seeking to understand the divisions between Jews living in Babylonia at his time.

From Sa'adia's era to the present, the process of translating Torah continues. Today, the Hebrew Bible has been translated into nearly every language spoken by human beings.

Section Two: Midrashim—"Explanations"

Parallel to the evolution of the many *targumim* is the development of a tradition of explaining the Torah text called *midrash*. As we have already mentioned in Introduction I, the early teachers of Jewish tradition divided their explanations into two categories: *Midrash Halachah* (legal interpretations) and *Midrash Agadah* (literary/moral interpretations). These two approaches to the Torah text were most likely used from the time of Ezra and Nehemiah as the means for understanding and justifying how the Torah should be applied to the changing circumstances of political, economic, and personal life.

During the second century B.C.E., early rabbinic scholars pioneered in creating both legal and literary (sermonic) *midrash*. They taught that God had given the people of Israel two Torahs at Mount Sinai. One was the *Torah Shebichetav*, or "Written Torah"; the other was the *Torah Shebealpeh*, or "Oral Torah," which contained all the interpretations to be uncovered by students of Torah throughout the ages.

Zugot

Among the most famous of the early rabbinic interpreters were five *zugot*, or "leadership-pairs," who also served as president and vice-president of the Sanhedrin, the Supreme Court of the Jewish people. They were Jose ben Yoezer and Yosi ben Yochanan (about 165 B.C.E.), Joshua ben Perachyah and Nittai of Arbela, Judah ben Tabbai and Simeon ben Shetach, Shemayah and Abtalyon, and Hillel and Shammai.

These early rabbis compared the Torah to a wonderful "garden," whose fruits might be extracted by using four different methods signified by the Hebrew letters of the word for "garden," *PaRDeS*. They called the first method *peshat*, the search for the straightforward, literal meaning of the text. The second was *remez*, uncovering hidden or implied meanings. The third was *derash*, finding the meaning through comparing one text with another or drawing parallels between the text and human experiences. The fourth was *sod*, investigating the text for secret, mystical, or allegorical meanings.

In his time, the famed but modest Rabbi Hillel, who taught his students "to love peace, love human beings, and bring others to the study of Torah," suggested seven principles or rules for interpreting Torah.

1. *Kal va-Chomer:* You can draw a conclusion from either a minor or major assumption.

2. *Gezerah Shavah:* You can draw a conclusion from the similarity of words or phrases in two separate biblical sentences.

3. *Binyan Av mi-Katuv Echad:* You can derive a general principle from a single biblical sentence.

4. *Binyan Av mi-Shene Ketuvim:* You can derive a general principle from two biblical sentences.

5. *Kelal u-Ferat:* All general rules that are followed by one or more particulars are then limited to those particulars.

6. *Ka-Yotze Bo be-Makom Acher:* You may draw a similar conclusion from another Torah text.

7. *Davar ha-Lamed me-Inyano:* You may uncover the meaning of obscure or ambiguous words and phrases from the context in which you find them.

Later, the first-century B.C.E. leader Ishmael, who defied the Romans by continuing to teach Torah after they had forbidden him to do so, elaborated Hillel's seven rules into thirteen. Ishmael was put to death by the Romans, but his student, Akiba, continued to derive new meanings from the Torah text. Akiba held that each word, every letter, even the crowns on the letters possessed potential messages and wisdom. Eliezer ben Yose Ha-Galili, one of Akiba's students, extended the rules for interpreting Torah from Hillel's seven and Ishmael's thirteen to thirty-two different means for extracting new ideas and legal formulations from the Torah. With each increase in the rules of interpretation, the adventure and art of finding new meanings in the ancient text became more flexible and creative.

The many rabbis who continued to evolve new understandings of Torah between the second century B.C.E. and the third century C.E. were known as *tannaim,* or "teachers." Those living between the third century C.E. and sixth century C.E. were called *amoraim,* or "speakers," "interpreters." Many of their explanations of Torah are reported in the *Mishnah* and *Gemara,* which were later combined into the Talmud. They were also collected into books of *midrash,* which include: *Genesis Rabbah, Exodus Rabbah, Leviticus Rabbah, Numbers Rabbah, Deuteronomy Rabbah, Pesikta, Tanchuma, Mechilta, Sifre,* and *Sifra.* In each case, these collections of early rabbinic explanations of Torah, like the *targumim,* were the means through which generations of Jews kept expanding Jewish knowledge and law to meet new circumstances.

Meet those who never stopped turning it

Rashi

The most famous of all commentators of Jewish history is Rabbi Shelomoh (Solomon) Itzhaki, known by his initials as **RaSHI** (1040–1105), who was born in the city of Troyes, France. As a young man Rashi studied the talmudic scholars in Mayence (Mainz) and Worms and then returned to the expanding industrial and business center of his birth. Earning his living from his vineyard, Rashi, like many Jews of his time, was caught up in defending his faith against Christians who claimed that God had replaced Judaism and the Jewish people with Christianity and the Church. After the slaughter and destruction of the First Crusade in 1096, he played a significant role in comforting and supporting suffering Jewish communities.

Rashi's commentaries often include selections from the *Midrash.* He also made use of current French words for clarification and, today, his writings are a major source for the study of Old French. Throughout the centuries Rashi's work has remained a model of simplicity and clarity for all commentators, and his reputation as *Parshandata,* "the interpreter of the Torah," is firmly established.

Rabbi Shemuel (Samuel) ben Meir, known also by his initials, **RaSHBaM** (1085–1174), was Rashi's grandson and earned his living as a sheep farmer. Known for his piety, he defended Jewish beliefs in public disputes that had been arranged by Church leaders to demonstrate the inferiority of Judaism. Fearful of those who twisted the biblical text to suit their conclusions, Rashbam argued that the only justified meaning of the Torah text was the *peshat,* or "plain meaning." He criticized those, including his grandfather, who employed the methods of *remez, derash,* or *sod,* calling them "crooked explanations" and "nonsense."

Ibn Ezra

While Rashbam was writing his commentary in France, **ABRAHAM IBN EZRA** (1092–1167) was gaining a significant reputation as a poet, physician, philosopher, and astrologer in

Spain and Italy. The first part of ibn Ezra's life was spent in his native Spain. From about 1140 he resided for brief periods in France, England, Egypt, Ethiopia, Italy, and finally again in Spain, where he died. Many believe that his wandering began in the bewildered disappointment of his only surviving son's conversion to Islam. Ibn Ezra's interests in both science and grammar, along with his experiences as a traveler, are expressed within his commentary to the Torah. He often includes discussions of mathematics, astrology, and linguistics within his explanations.

Rabbi David Kimchi, or **RaDaK** (1160–1235), of Narbonne, France, was a popular teacher. His town was a crossroads for trade and for visiting Jewish scholars from Spain and France. Kimchi was well known as a lecturer and was often called upon to defend Judaism and the Jewish people before hostile Church leaders. Like ibn Ezra, he stressed the scientific and grammatical approach in his commentary. Concerned with Christian claims and misinterpretations of Genesis, Kimchi often engages in sharp philosophical argument and attempts to reveal the authentic intention of the Torah. His commentary makes use of the *targumim* and frequently quotes early rabbinic explanations.

Ramban (Nachmanides)

Rabbi Moses ben Nachman, known as **NACHMANIDES,** or by his initials, **RaMBaN** (1194–1270), was born in Gerona, Spain, and given the Spanish name Bonastrug da Porta. He earned his living as a physician, but his talents in the areas of poetry, philosophy, Torah interpretation, and leadership all earned him a reputation as *ha-Rav ha-Neeman,* "the trustworthy rabbi." Throughout his lifetime, Nachmanides worked to bring peace among differing Jewish factions in his community. In 1263, he defended Judaism at a public debate held in the court of King James. Two years later,

Christian authorities requested that the pope force the king to penalize Nachmanides for what he had said during the disputation. Fleeing Spain, Nachmanides settled in the Land of Israel, where he spent the last years of his life writing his commentary to the Torah.

Unlike Rashi's terse interpretations on nearly every verse, Nachmanides deals in depth with various ideas and issues raised by the Torah text. At times he will quote Rashi, ibn Ezra, or one of the rabbis of the Midrash, agreeing or disagreeing with them. His explanations are filled with psychological insights into biblical characters and contain many of his own philosophical, political, and scientific observations.

One of the most curious and fascinating commentaries to appear in the thirteenth century is the *ZOHAR.* This mystical interpretation of Torah, which seeks to unveil the *sod* and *remez,* the "secret" and "hidden" meanings, is said to have been collected and written by **SIMEON BEN YOCHAI** (100–160 C.E.). Many scholars, however, believe that it was the work of **MOSES DE LEON** (13th century) of Granada, Spain. Whoever wrote or compiled the *Zohar* created more than a book. It is a library of differing views, fragments of interpretations, and intriguing speculations about the relationship between God and the world. In it we are given a variety of explanations about God's concern for humanity and for the people of Israel. Using mathematics, combinations of letters and words, mystical observations, and a rich imagination, the *Zohar* seeks to reveal the unseen and to surprise students with new insights into the mysteries of the universe and human life.

Abravanel

The man who pleaded with King Ferdinand and Queen Isabella of Spain to reverse their March 31, 1492 decree to expel all Jews from their land was **DON ISAAC ABRAVANEL** (1437–1508). Born in Lisbon, educated in both Jewish and classic sources, Abravanel not only served as treasurer of Portugal but as finance minister to the rulers of Spain and Italy.

Drawing upon his experience as a statesman and his knowledge of history and philosophy, Abravanel's Torah commentary is crammed with observations about politics, along with warnings against the concentration of power and authority. He questions the ethical behavior of biblical characters and defends Judaism against attacks by leaders of the Inquisition. Abravanel's study of Torah is divided into separate chapters, each beginning with a list of critical questions. For Abravanel, Torah is the ultimate source of wisdom, and the practice of its commandments strengthens the bond between the Jewish people and God.

OBADIAH SFORNO (1475–1550) lived most of his life in Bologna, Italy. In his youth he studied philosophy, mathematics, linguistics, and medicine. While practicing as a physician, he also managed a Hebrew printing business and a Jewish educational center and was an active leader of the Bologna Jewish community. As his reputation as a scholar of Jewish tradition spread, Jewish leaders from throughout Italy turned to him seeking advice. In his Torah commentary, Sforno seeks to explain the *peshat,* or "plain meaning," of the text. He employs his knowledge of contemporary science and medicine in his interpretations, but unlike Abravanel he does not provide historical observations. His outlook has been called "humanistic" by some scholars because he seldom emphasizes the difference between Jews and non-Jews, choosing instead to teach that all humanity is God's treasure. (Deuteronomy 33:3)

Mendelssohn

Between 1780 and 1783, **MOSES MENDELSSOHN** (1729–1786) published his *Biur,* or "explanation" of the Torah. Mendelssohn, who had been born in Dessau, the son of a *sofer,* or "Torah scribe," had already gained a reputation among Jews and non-Jews as a respected philosopher, literary critic, and defender of his faith.

Making his living as a merchant, Mendelssohn concluded that Jews needed to abandon Yiddish and to learn German in order to play an active role in German society.

Mendelssohn's *Biur* presents not only a commentary on the meaning of the Torah text but also a translation of the Torah into German using Hebrew characters. Actually, Mendelssohn invited his friend Solomon Dubno to write the commentary to Genesis and Naftali Herz Wessely to create the commentary to Leviticus. The *Biur* emphasizes the literary and moral beauty of the Torah. Nonetheless, it was met with a storm of protest from traditional Jewish circles objecting to Mendelssohn's bias for German. Today it is recognized as one of the significant building blocks of the *Haskalah,* or Jewish "Enlightenment" movement, which was to sweep Jews into the emerging nineteenth-century Western culture and to generate early Reform Judaism.

Meklenburg

Opposing early Reform Judaism was **JACOB ZVI MEKLENBURG** (1785–1865), author of the Torah commentary *Ha-Ketav ve-ha-Kabbalah.* Meklenburg worked as a businessman until 1831 when he became rabbi of Koenigsberg. His commentary attempts to explain the laws of Torah and to prove that the talmudic laws are based upon the authority of Torah. In part, his approach reflects his disagreements in his community with Reform Jews who were claiming that some laws of Torah were no longer applicable to society.

Malbim

Meir Lev ben Yechiel Michael, known also by his initials, **MaLBIM** (1809–1879), was born in Volochisk, Russia. He married at fourteen and divorced soon afterwards. His early life was filled with wanderings and study in many different centers of European Jewish learning. In 1858, he was appointed Chief Rabbi of Rumania, but his battles with Reform Jews ultimately led to his dismissal.

Malbim bases his Torah commentary upon the Midrash of the early rabbis. For him each word is important and filled with insights from God. While he prefers explaining the literal meaning of the text, he does not hesitate to add observations of his own. For instance, he cleverly invents discussions of Jewish law and then places them in the mouths of biblical characters.

Luzzatto

While Malbim was interpreting Torah in Eastern Europe, **SAMUEL DAVID LUZZATTO** (1800–1865) was creating his commentary in Padua, Italy. Luzzatto, also known by his initials as **ShaDal,** worked as a philosopher, historian, translator, and interpreter of Torah. His life was marked by the tragic death of his first wife and their two sons. In 1821–1822, after publishing a translation of the Jewish prayer book into Italian, Luzzatto was appointed a professor at the Padua Rabbinical College. His Torah commentary shows great respect for Rashi's views and highlights moral lessons and ethical values he believes are central to the Torah text. Luzzatto seeks to foster a love for Jewish tradition and knowledge and a loyalty to the Jewish people. His urging of young people to return to the Land of Israel marks him as an early Zionist.

Hirsch

One of the most important nineteenth-century European Jewish leaders was **SAMSON RAPHAEL HIRSCH** (1808–1888) whose Torah commentary remains a classic expression of Orthodox Jewish beliefs. Born in Hamburg, Hirsch studied Talmud with his grandfather and was deeply influenced by Rabbi Isaac Bernays, an opponent of early Reform Judaism. Hirsch worked for the emancipation of Austrian and Moravian Jewry, and in 1851 he began thirty-seven years of service as a rabbi in Frankfort. By that time his philosophical study, *Nineteen Letters on Judaism,*

published in 1836, had won him the admiration of many in the Orthodox community.

Hirsch's Torah commentary "seeks to derive the explanation of the text from the words themselves." He makes use of early rabbinic views along with those of other commentators to underscore his belief that Jewish tradition offers the highest form of human life. Hirsch vehemently opposes the notion of Reform Judaism that the Torah tradition has historically evolved through the ages. He asserts that the Torah was revealed by God at Mount Sinai, and, therefore, nothing in it can or will be changed.

Hertz

JOSEPH HERMAN HERTZ (1872–1946) follows Hirsch's philosophy and approach to the Torah, yet his Torah commentary, one of the first written in English, is more concise and offers brief essays on significant questions. While Hertz was born in Slovakia, he arrived in the United States at the age of twelve and was the first graduate of the Jewish Theological Seminary in 1894. He served as rabbi in South Africa but was deported because of his outspoken criticism of the government's policy of discrimination against aliens. In 1913 he was appointed Chief Rabbi of England. His Torah commentary, published between 1929 and 1936, takes issue with biblical critics of his day, who argued that the Torah as well as the rest of the Hebrew Bible was edited from many different documents and that it evolved into a sacred literature through many centuries. Hertz maintains the fundamental-traditional view that the whole Torah was given by God to Moses at Mount Sinai.

Benno Jacob

BENNO JACOB (1862–1941), a rabbi and biblical scholar, escaped from Germany in 1939 and settled in England. In his commentary, Jacob not only takes issue with many biblical scholars of his time but also with fundamentalists like

Hirsch and Hertz. Jacob believed that a study of the Torah text did not justify the notion that Moses had either received it at one time or that he had written all of it. The Torah, however, was to be respected as a reliable and whole document representing the early religious history of the Jewish people.

Speiser

One of the first to apply the science of archeology to Torah commentary was **EPHRAIM AVIGDOR SPEISER** (1902–1965). Trained as an archeologist in the United States, Speiser spent many years in Iraq directing surveys of ancient cities. From 1928 until his death he lectured at the University of Pennsylvania. In his commentary on Genesis, Speiser applies the knowledge accumulated by modern historians, archeologists, linguists, and students of comparative culture and religion to the stories and history of ancient Israel. He sees Judaism emerging out of both Mesopotamian and Egyptian cultures.

Morgenstern

Biblical scholar **JULIAN MORGENSTERN** (1881–1976), who served as president of the Hebrew Union College from 1922 to 1947, also believed that the Torah had evolved through the Jewish people's experience with ancient Middle Eastern cultures. Morgenstern also applied economic and social considerations to his analysis of emerging Jewish beliefs and traditions. For him, however, the chief meaning of Genesis was in its moral message.

Israeli scholar **NEHAMA LEIBOWITZ** (1905–   ) differs from Morgenstern and Speiser in her approach to explaining the mean-

ings of Torah. Rather than seeing the Torah as limited to the history, religion, and social realities of a particular era, Leibowitz seeks meanings out of the tradition of rabbinic interpretation. By comparing and contrasting varying insights of rabbis from different periods and places, Leibowitz challenges her students to reach new understandings about the intent and purpose of the Torah text.

As a professor of Bible at Tel Aviv University, Leibowitz developed a large following of students in Israel and throughout the world with her weekly "teach-yourself" Torah study packets. Her guiding principle is that the Torah is crammed with potential meanings, and its students are invited to discover all of them.

Sarna

Professor of Bible **NAHUM M. SARNA** (1923–   ), like E. A. Speiser, seeks to uncover the message of Torah by studying it within the context of its time and culture. He compares the religious practices, mythologies, and legal procedures of ancient Near Eastern peoples with those described within the Torah. His *Understanding Genesis* and *Exploring Exodus* were written "as an aid to enhancing the message of the Bible for the highly sophisticated youngsters of our generation."

In 1981, after years of research and writing, the Union of American Hebrew Congregations published *The Torah: A Modern Commentary*. This first "official" commentary by the Reform movement was written and edited by Rabbis **W. GUNTHER PLAUT** and **BERNARD J. BAMBERGER,** with critical essays by Professor **WILLIAM W. HALLO.** Like many traditional commentaries, the UAHC Torah commentary offers a line-by-line analysis of the text. However, it also employs the accumulated knowledge of historians, archeologists, linguists, and students of comparative religion. Essays at the conclusion of each section deal with important questions raised by the text and present varying conclusions based not only upon traditional rabbinic views but also upon modern biblical study.

The turning of Torah continues

Today, scholars and students of Torah continue the process of exploring the ancient text for new insights and meanings. There are many differing views. Some see the Torah primarily as a history of the ancient Israelites; others view it as a record of early Middle Eastern religion and myth. Some believe that its worth is in its literary power; others argue that the Torah represents the primary ethical guide of Western civilization. Still others hold that the Torah evolved out of the Jewish people's relationship with God, that its interpreters in every age have continued to enlarge its meanings, and that God continues to speak each time the message of Torah is celebrated in study or ritual or in the ethical behavior of those who shape their lives with its commandments and wisdom.

The roll of Torah interpreters whose views are presented in *A Torah Commentary for Our Times* is long and distinguished. For a complete listing, see the "Glossary of Commentaries and Interpreters" at the back of the book.

The Jewish people has never ceased to "turn the Torah" and to extract from it valuable treasures. *A Torah Commentary for Our Times* invites you to participate in this great expedition. We will encounter a diversity of views and opinions, and we will sharpen our wits and sensitivities with a variety of perspectives. Yet, Torah study is more than an intellectual adventure, more than knowing what this commentator said or this scholar argues. It is a serious spiritual challenge. Its purpose is to *turn us* until we have the courage to begin transforming our lives and communities with the sacred truths of Torah. Through the study of Torah, the rabbis taught, a person makes the world worthwhile . . . and promotes peace. (*Avot* 6:1; *Sanhedrin* 99b)

So let your "turning" begin!

THE
TORAH
PORTIONS
OF
GENESIS

PARASHAT BERESHIT
Genesis 1:1–6:8

Bereshit may be translated as "In the beginning" or "At first." The Torah begins by telling us how God created the heavens and earth, human beings, and the Sabbath. It continues with the stories of Adam and Eve in the Garden of Eden and of their sons, Cain and Abel, and it concludes with the report that God regretted having created human beings because of all their wickedness. For that reason, God decided to destroy everything on earth except for Noah and his family.

OUR TARGUM

· 1 ·

In the beginning the earth was unformed, and there was only darkness. Then God commanded, "Let there be light," and saw how good it was. Then God separated between the light, which was named "Day," and the darkness, which was called "Night." That was the first day of creation.

On the second day Sky was created.

On the third day Earth and Seas were formed, along with plants and trees of every kind. And God saw how good it was.

On the fourth day the sun, moon, and stars were set in the sky to separate between day and night. And God saw how it, too, was good.

On the fifth day God brought forth birds out of the waters to fly, and creeping creatures of every kind, and swarms of fish and sea animals to swim in the seas. And God saw how good it was, and ordered them to be "fruitful and increase."

On the sixth day God created all the beasts of the earth. Seeing it was good, God then decided to create human beings. God said: "I will make Adam in My image, after My likeness." God created male and female human beings and commanded them to "rule the fish of the sea, the birds of the sky, the cattle, the whole earth." God also blessed them and told them to "be fruitful and increase." And God saw that it was very good.

When heaven and earth were finished, God rested and declared that the seventh day of each week should be set aside as a Sabbath, a day of rest. God blessed the Sabbath and called it *kodesh*, which means "holy," or "unique."

· 2 ·

God then planted a beautiful garden from which four rivers flowed. The rivers were named Pishon, Gihon, Tigris, and Euphrates. The garden was called *Gan Eden*, the "Garden of Eden," and was located in what was once known as Babylonia and afterwards called Persia and Iran.

Within the garden were colorful and fruitful trees of every kind. One special tree called the *Etz ha-Chayim*, or "Tree of Life," grew at the center of the garden. Nearby was another called the *Etz ha-Daat Tov va-Ra*, or "Tree of the Knowledge of Good and Bad."

God placed Adam, the first human being, in *Gan Eden* and warned him: "You may eat from every tree in the garden except from the Tree of Knowledge of Good and Bad. If you eat from it, you will die."

Then God brought all the creatures of earth and sky before Adam so that he might name each of them.

Afterwards, God saw that Adam was lonely and needed a partner, so God created a wife for him. And Adam called her *Chavah*, or "Eve," which comes from the word *chai* ("life") and means "mother of all the living."

One day a serpent tempted Eve by telling her that neither she nor Adam would die if they ate from the Tree of Knowledge of Good and Bad. So she tasted its fruits and then gave some to her husband. When God questioned them about what they had done, Adam blamed Eve, and she blamed the serpent. All three were punished for having disobeyed God's command. The serpent was condemned to crawl and eat dirt, and Adam and Eve were banished from the Garden of Eden.

· 3 ·

Later, Eve gave birth to Cain and then to another son named Abel. After they were grown, Cain turned on his brother in anger and killed him. When God asked him, "Where is your brother, Abel?" he answered, "I do not know. Am I my brother's keeper?" For murdering his brother, God punished Cain by sending him off to become a lonely wanderer on earth.

After creating heaven and earth, and all living creatures, God saw that human beings were wicked and constantly doing evil. So God decided to destroy humanity and all living things—but a man by the name of Noah changed God's intention.

THEMES

Parashat Bereshit contains four important themes:

1. God's creation of the heavens, earth, all living creatures, and humanity is a blessing.

2. Human beings are responsible for the survival of all that was created by God.
3. The expulsion of Adam and Eve from the Garden of Eden.
4. Human beings are responsible for one another and for the survival of humanity.

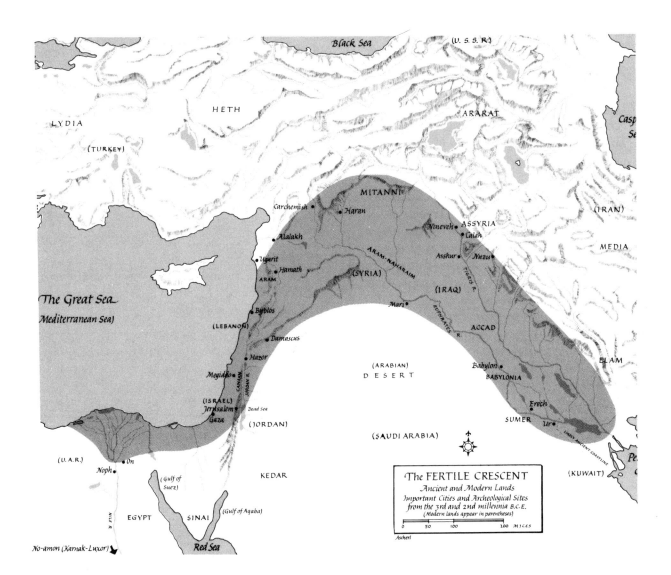

PEREK ALEF: *Is There a Jewish View about "Creation"?*

There are many different views about how our planet and galaxy of stars originated. Most scientists who study the stars (they are called astrophysicists and cosmologists) believe that, between ten and twenty billion years ago, all of the matter of the universe concentrated in a single place and then exploded in a "Big Bang." About a billion years later, clusters of galaxies, composed of gas, dust, and clumps of matter, began to take shape. There were over one hundred billion of them, each with an average of one hundred billion stars. Among these was our Milky Way galaxy containing a vast ocean of four hundred billion stars.

Scientists believe that many stars, such as our own, have planets revolving around them. When a star has revolving planets, this arrangement is called a solar system. Our planet, Earth, revolves around our star, Sol, the sun. Here on Earth, with all its shimmering blue skies, oceans, forests, deserts, and green valleys is the only place in the cosmos where, to our knowledge, intelligent life has evolved.

At the beginning . . .
Scientist and writer Carl Sagan describes the "awesome transformation" that the Torah calls "creation": "At the beginning of this universe, there were no galaxies, stars, or planets, no life or civilizations, merely a uniform radiant fireball filling all space. The passage from the Chaos of the Big Bang to the Cosmos that we are beginning to know is the most awesome transformation of matter and energy that we have been privileged to glimpse. And, until we find more intelligent beings elsewhere, we are ourselves the most spectacular of all the transformations—the remote descendants of the Big Bang, dedicated to understanding and further transforming the Cosmos from which we spring." (Cosmos, Ballantine Books, New York, 1980, p. 12)

One of the most famous of the "creation" stories is the Enuma Elish, *told by early Babylonians, Assyrians, Akkadians, and Sumerians:*

The holy house, the house of the gods, in a holy place had not yet been made;
No reed had sprung up, no tree had been created;
No brick had been laid, no building had been erected. . . .
The Deep had not been made. . . .
Then there was a movement in the midst of the sea. . . .
At that time Eridu was made. . . .
And the gods, the spirits of the earth,
Marduk made at the same time. . . .
Marduk laid a reed on the face of the waters,
He formed dust and poured it out beside the reed;
That he might cause the gods to dwell in the dwelling of their hearts' desire, He formed mankind. (Excerpt from Robert Graves and Raphael Patai, Hebrew Myths: The Book of Genesis, *Greenwich House, New York, 1983, p. 22)*

Throughout history people have gazed into the heavens—or observed life on earth—and wondered how it all began. Nearly every culture developed an explanation. Thousands of years ago in the Middle East the ancient Sumerians, Akkadians, Assyrians, Babylonians, and Egyptians all told "creation" stories.

Most of these, like the Babylonian epic *Enuma Elish,* put forward the belief that many gods had created the heavens, earth, and human life. In most of these versions of creation, everything depended upon the whim of the gods. It was believed that they could order rain or blow away the clouds, send plagues or wipe out whole populations with floods or famine. In these ancient stories human beings were helpless. Whether they suffered or were successful and happy did not depend upon their accomplishments but rather upon the arbitrary decisions of the gods.

The Jewish people introduced a revolutionary theory about the creation of the heavens, earth, and human life. Unlike the other ancient stories, which attribute all that was created in the heavens and on earth to numerous gods, the Torah begins by teaching that one God alone created everything. It puts forward the idea that creation is "good," that the world and the galaxy of stars in which it spins are not a random accident but have a unique design and purpose.

Furthermore, the Torah teaches that human life is a result of God's will, and human beings are not "toys" of the gods. Instead, human beings are created in God's image. They have choices and can exercise freedom. They are partners with God in shaping life and preserving the world.

Echoing the Torah's "creation" story, the Psalmist not only captures the mystery of God's creation but also elaborates the role and responsibility of human beings.

O God, our God,
How majestic is Your name throughout the earth,
You who have covered the heavens with Your
splendor! . . .
When I behold Your heavens, the work of Your
fingers,
the moon and stars that You set in place:
what are human beings that You have been
mindful of them,
mortals that You have taken note of them,
that You have made them little less than divine,
and adorned them with glory and majesty;
You have made them master over Your
handiwork,
laying the world at their feet. . . .

                                        (Psalms 8:1–7)

Jewish tradition holds that one God created the heavens and earth, but it also teaches that human beings are "masters" of the world. Their choices make a difference. The power of life or death, survival or destruction is in their hands.

But Jewish tradition goes a step further. While the first chapters of *Bereshit*, or Genesis, describe in detail what was created on each of the six days of creation, Jewish interpreters of Torah did not take that explanation as an exact report of what had happened. Instead, they offered many different opinions.

For example, some of the rabbis argued that God had created everything on the first day. Then, on each of the five following days, God introduced what had already been formed. Other rabbis disagreed. They believed that the creation of light came before everything else. Still others taught that God, like an unsatisfied artist looking for perfection, had created and destroyed many worlds before deciding that this one was acceptable. (*Genesis Rabbah* 1:15; 3:1,7; 9:2; and 12:14)

And do Jewish teachers say that the world was created in six twenty-four-hour days?

Rashi

The most famous interpreter of the Torah, Solomon ben Isaac, known best as Rashi, denied

this. He pointed out that the word *yom,* or "day," could mean "thousands of years." As proof for his argument he quoted the ancient Psalmist who had written: "For a day in Your sight is like a thousand years. . . . (Psalms 90:4) For Rashi, God's creation of the world did not happen within six twenty-four-hour days but rather over thousands of years. "The Torah," he explained to his eleventh-century students, "does not intend to teach us the order of creation." (Rashi on Genesis 1:1)

Most Torah interpreters agree with Rashi. The Torah does not offer us a "scientific" explanation of creation. It offers us something else of great importance.

Well before modern science, Jews realized that the purpose of Torah was not to tell us "how" the world was created but to help us understand "Who" created all the wonders of the heavens and earth. The "creation" story of *Bereshit* is not a lesson in evolution. It neither contradicts modern scientific theories nor requires proofs from the laboratory. The Torah's story of creation is meant to express our sense of wonder about the origins of the world in which we live. It affirms our faith that one God formed and sustains all of cosmic existence and that human beings are partners with God in preserving and advancing the precious gift of life.

PEREK BET: *We Must Care for Creation*

Modern scientists are fond of referring to our Earth as a "tiny fragile world . . . drifting in a great cosmic ocean." Certainly our contemporary studies about space confirm the vastness of the cosmos and the fact that our planet is a mere speck where, miraculously, all of the conditions that promote life happen to be present.

Scientists agree that there is a very delicate balance between all earthly life forms and the atmosphere surrounding our planet. They speak of a "cooperating system" between the five million separate species of animals and plants on Earth and its stone foundations, waters, and blue blanket of sky. Without the delicate interrelationship between all forms of life and the conditions of our atmosphere, Earth would be a lifeless planet.

As an example of our "cooperating system," British chemist and inventor James Lovelock describes how the Earth's atmosphere is amazingly shaped to fit life's needs. "With no oxygen, for instance, there would be no respiration. With just a little more oxygen, on the other hand—even 25 percent instead of 21—the whole living world would burst spontaneously into flames. . . . Similarly, without carbon dioxide, photosynthesis would fail, plants would die, and life would vanish from the Earth. With more carbon dioxide, however, so much heat would be trapped in air and sea by the greenhouse effect that the planet would descend into hell." (Jonathan Weiner, *Planet Earth,* Bantam Books, New York, 1986, p. 327)

Abravanel

Interpreters of the Torah's "creation" story also called attention to the fragile balance of conditions they observed in the heavens and on earth. For example, Don Isaac Abravanel, who lived and taught in late fifteenth-century Spain, speculated that, had the sun been larger, or placed closer to the earth, its heat would have destroyed our planet. Had it been placed a fraction farther away, our Earth would have been locked forever in a frozen winter. God, Abravanel taught, had wisely set each star in its precise position. (Abravanel on Genesis 1:1)

Other Jewish teachers went several steps beyond Abravanel. They likened the world to a "palace" brought into existence for the benefit of human beings. God, they explained, had not only created it but had furnished and filled it with opportunities for enjoyment. Then, God had presented it as a gift to human beings. From that point on, they maintained, human beings had been appointed as "caretakers" of the world. (*Sanhedrin* 38a)

> **It is up to human beings. . . .**
> *The heavens belong to God, but the earth God gave to humanity.* (Psalms 115:16)
>
> *In interpreting the phrase: "Let the earth sprout vegetation . . ."* Aderet Eliyahu *explains that God placed the potential for growth in the earth. It is up to human beings to sow the seeds.* (Genesis 1:11)

As "caretakers" of this "palace" called Earth, Jewish tradition teaches that human beings have important, even critical, choices to make, especially today.

The advance of industrial power and technology have brought us many blessings in this century, but they have also brought us serious "curses." For instance, we warm our homes from the cold of winter and cool them from the heat of summer by using huge quantities of energy drawn from critical resources. We are polluting the air we breathe, the water we drink, and our sources of food production. We are cutting down forests to build our homes, industrial centers, and cities and to make room for more farmlands on which to grow enough food to feed increasing numbers of human beings. One recent United Nations report warns that, because of overpopulation, by the end of the twentieth century "all accessible tropical forests will have disappeared."

And there is another frightening condition to add to our burden as "caretakers" of this "palace" we call Earth. It is the danger of nuclear destruction. Today, there are enough nuclear warheads to end all life on our planet. It is estimated that a full-scale nuclear war between the United States and the Soviet Union would not only bring death to hundreds of millions of human beings but would probably eliminate the civilizations of Europe, China, Japan, Russia, and the United States.

Jewish tradition teaches us that human beings are responsible for the earth. According to the rabbis, after Adam was created, God led him around the Garden of Eden, showing him all the beautiful flowers and trees. Then God told him: "See how beautiful everything is that I have created. It has all been made for you. Remember this, and do not corrupt or destroy My world. For, if you do, there will be no one left to save it." (*Ecclesiastes Rabbah 7:13*)

According to the Torah, God gave humanity the power to rule the world. We are its "caretakers." It is ours to enjoy, but it is also our responsibility to preserve. The choice is ours. The Torah challenges us with God's commandment: "I call heaven and earth to witness against you this day: I have put before you life and death, blessing and curse. Choose life. . . ." (Deuteronomy 30:19)

PEREK GIMEL: *Expelled from the Garden of Eden*

The Garden of Eden was a beautiful place in which to live. All of Adam's and Eve's needs were satisfied, but in the end they were expelled. What happened? What did they do to deserve such punishment?

One answer may be found in the differences between what God commanded them to do and how they reported it to each other and the serpent. Compare the following two versions found in the Torah:

God says to Adam: "Of every tree of the garden you are free to eat; but as for the Tree of Knowledge of Good and Bad, you must not eat of it; for as soon as you eat of it, you shall die." (Genesis 2:16–17)

Eve says to the serpent: "We may eat of the fruit of the other trees of the garden. It is only about fruit of the tree in the middle of the garden that God said: You shall not eat of it or touch it, lest you die." (Genesis 3:2–3)

It is clear that Adam was given one version of the commandment and that Eve reports another to the serpent. Adam is told that, if they eat from the Tree of Knowledge of Good and Bad, they will die. Eve reports that, if they either eat from the "tree in the middle of the garden" *or touch it,* they will die. She not only fails to report the name of the tree but clearly adds a new condition to

God's original statement. Later interpreters of Torah reached the conclusion that her alteration of God's commandment led to misunderstanding and, ultimately, to expulsion from the Garden of Eden.

For example, Rashi believed that the serpent took advantage of Eve's misrepresentation of God's commandment to Adam. He speculated that, when Eve told the serpent that God had warned her: "You shall not eat of it *or touch it,* lest you die," the serpent pushed her until she touched the tree. Then the serpent said to her: "You see, you have not died after touching it. Nothing has happened to you. And you will not die after you eat from its fruit."

Rashi's theory is that the serpent was very clever, using Eve's misrepresentation of what God had said to Adam as a way of tricking her into eating the fruit.

On the other hand, perhaps it was Adam who misrepresented the original commandment to Eve. The Torah does not tell us what he said to her. He might only have pointed to a tree in the middle of the garden without identifying it by name. And he may have even added the warning about *touching it* in order to frighten her.

We will never know what Adam did or did not tell Eve or who was to blame, but it is clear that the first small lie about what God had said led to much trouble and, ultimately, to the expulsion of Adam and Eve from the Garden of Eden. Perhaps that explains why Jewish teachers emphasize the importance of careful communication and accurate reporting.

Be careful of your words
We are warned: "Let your words be few," and "A fool multiplies words." (*Ecclesiastes 5:1 and 10:14; also Job 35:16 and 38:2*)

Zugot

The rabbinic teacher Abtalyon told his students: "You who are wise, be careful of your words. . . ." (Avot 1:11)

In the Book of Proverbs (30:6), we are taught: "Do not add to God's words, for you will be criticized and revealed as a liar." In other words, when we are given a message for someone else, we are expected to deliver it *exactly* as it was given. Adding to what we have been told, even if we believe that our interpretation will improve communication, may lead to distorting the truth.

That is the mistake that Eve, and perhaps Adam, made in the Garden of Eden. Then, after they had eaten the forbidden fruit and were about to be punished by God, they made things worse for themselves by blaming each other for what had happened. The Torah reports their conversation with God as follows:

> Then [God] asked . . . "Did you eat of the tree from which I had forbidden you to eat?"
> [Adam] said, "The woman You put at my side— she gave me of the tree, and I ate."
> And God said to Eve, "What is this you have done!"
> And Eve replied, "The serpent tricked me, and I ate."
>
> (Genesis 3:11–13)

Adam and Eve each offer an excuse for eating the forbidden fruit. Adam blames God for putting Eve at his side. Eve blames the serpent for tricking her. No one says: "It's my fault. I am sorry. Forgive me. I made a mistake." Neither Adam nor Eve is willing to take responsibility for what has happened.

Perhaps that is why they were expelled from the Garden of Eden. They changed the meaning of God's original commandment by not reporting it accurately. Then, after they had eaten from the fruit of the forbidden tree, they sought to place the blame on God, on the serpent, and on each other. For misrepresenting what they had been told and for refusing to accept responsibility for their actions, God expelled them from Eden.

PEREK DALET: *We Are Responsible for One Another*

The tenth-century Babylonian scholar and head of the Babylonian Academy at Sura, Sa'adia ben Joseph Ha-Gaon, commented that "the human being is the purpose of creation."

This understanding that human beings were created in "the image of God" and, therefore, represent the highest expression of God's power and love led Jewish teachers to the conclusion that every human life is sacred. And, because it is, human beings must not only care for the world in which they live but bear a special obligation to care about one another.

The life or death of the world
The Mishnah says that "Adam was created as a single person in order to teach that, if one murders another person, the Torah holds him responsible for the death of a whole world. And, if a person saves the life of one person, the Torah considers him as if he saved the whole world."
(Sanhedrin 4:5)

For Jewish tradition, each human life is a precious and sacred world of possibilities. Not only does each person possess special talents, thoughts, and abilities but from each person others are born and the chain of humanity continues. "Each person is a world," the rabbis commented. Therefore individuals contain within themselves future worlds.

That is what made the murder of Abel by Cain such a serious offense. When the rabbis discussed the murder, they pointed out an unusual phrasing of God's statement to Abel. God said to him: "Behold, your brother's blood cries out to Me from the ground!" (Genesis 4:10) In the Hebrew, the words *deme [achicha] tzoakim* are plural and may be translated, "[your brother's] *bloods* cry out."

According to the rabbis the phrase "*bloods* cry out" is an indication that Cain murdered more than just Abel. He also destroyed Abel's future generations. They tell us that God said to Cain: "Not only are you responsible for murdering your brother, but you have also murdered his unborn offspring. The voice of your brother's blood, and of all his would-be descendants whom you prevented from coming into the world, cries out to Me." (*Midrash Agadah* 4,9)

In killing Abel, Cain destroyed a whole line of humanity. The great tragedy was not only the death of Abel but the loss of all the thousands of future lives cut off with his murder.

Because Jewish tradition considers every human life sacred, it holds that each human being must care for others. We are guardians or caretakers of one another. Cain murdered his brother because he failed to understand that he was his brother's "keeper," or "guardian."

The Torah tells us that, when God saw what he had done, God asked, "Where is your brother Abel?" And Cain answered, "I do not know. Am I my brother's keeper?"

The word for "keeper" in Hebrew is *shomer,* which also means "guardian," or the one who is responsible to look out for the safety and security of others. Cain failed to see himself as the *keeper* or *guardian* of his brother. He did not believe that he was responsible for protecting or caring for him. As a result, when they quarreled and became angry with each other, he struck and killed him.

We are guardians

A famed chasidic teacher, Rabbi Mendel of Kotzk (1788–1859), once warned his students: "Be sure to take care of your own soul and of another person's body, not of your own body and of another person's soul."

From the Torah's report of Cain's murder of his brother, Abel, we are taught that each human life is sacred and that we are guardians of one another. Our duty is to protect one another both physically and spiritually. We are obligated to be concerned about one another's safety, health, and welfare. Human beings are responsible for one another.

QUESTIONS FOR STUDY AND DISCUSSION

1. Why have human beings throughout the centuries created explanations about the creation of the world and human beings?

2. The nineteenth-century philosopher Friedrich Nietzsche once commented: "The world is beautiful but has a disease called humanity." How would Jewish thinkers respond to such an observation?

3. In one day American miners dig up 625 acres of land, almost one square mile; they clean up and replant about 337 acres. In one day Americans produce 1.5 million pounds of hazardous waste. In what other ways are human beings not "caring" for the world we inhabit? Why? What, according to Jewish tradition, are our obligations?

4. There is a Yiddish proverb that states: "A half-truth is a whole lie." Would you agree? Are there times when the truth should not be spoken? Why do so many of us, like Eve, have difficulty telling the truth?

5. In light of our discussion of Cain and Abel, what can we say about the scope of human destruction during World War II when eleven million men, women, and children, including six million Jews, were killed?

PARASHAT NOACH
Genesis 6:9–11:32

Parashat Noach tells the story of God's decision to destroy the earth with a flood because of the corruption and wickedness found in the world. Only a righteous man by the name of Noah, his family, and pairs of every kind of creature were to survive. Noah was told to build a large boat, an ark, and to make a place on it for every creature he was to save. After the Flood, those aboard the ark started life on earth all over again, and God promised never to send another flood. Later, human beings decided to build a city and a huge tower that would reach from earth to heaven. Seeing what they were doing, God scattered them all over the earth and gave them different languages to speak.

OUR TARGUM

· 1 ·

God looked upon the earth and saw that it was a place of evildoing. Human beings were corrupt. They made laws and then refused to obey them. People were concerned only with their own personal gain. Selfishness, cruelty, and dishonesty prevailed.

So God decided to destroy all life on earth with a flood. Noah, who was considered a "righteous" person, was ordered to build a boat, or ark, which would hold his family and a male and female of every living thing upon the earth. Noah built the ark, and, when the Flood came, everything in the ark survived.

After one hundred and fifty days of flooding, the waters subsided, and the ark came to rest in the mountains of Ararat, located in Iran. Noah sent a raven out to search for dry land. Then he sent a dove, and, when it returned with an olive branch in its beak, he knew that the floodwaters were gone.

Noah, his family, and all the living creatures left the ark, and God promised that "never again" would the world be destroyed by a flood. As a sign of that promise, God put a rainbow in the sky.

other. The city in Shinar where all this took place was named *Babel*, which means "confusion."

·2·

After the Flood, human life increased on the earth. People spoke one language, and they built a city and a high tower in the land of Shinar. "Let's make a name for ourselves," they said to one another. "Let's build our tower so that it reaches high into the heavens!"

God saw what they were doing and was displeased. "If as one people with one language this is how they act, then they will be able to do anything they decide." Fearing their abuse of power, God scattered the people all over the earth and confused them so that they spoke many languages and were unable to understand one an-

·3·

Afterwards, Shem, Noah's son, had a son by the name of Arpachshad, whose son was Shelah, whose son was Eber, whose son was Peleg, whose son was Reu, whose son was Serug, whose son was Nahor, whose son was Terah. Terah had three sons, Abram, Nahor, and Haran. Abram was the founder of the Jewish people, and he married Sarai. Haran was the father of Lot.

Near the end of his life, Terah took Abram, Sarai, and his grandson, Lot, and they traveled from Ur of the Chaldeans, which is located on the Euphrates River in what is today Iraq, to Haran, which is located in Syria. They settled there, and Terah died.

THEMES

Parashat Noach contains three important themes:

1. One "righteous" human being can make a difference in saving the world.
2. Corruption, dishonesty, and selfishness can destroy the world.
3. When people create or build for fame or for power over others, they bring unhappiness and confusion into the world.

PEREK ALEF: *Was Noah Really a "Righteous" Person?*

At the very beginning of this Torah portion we are told three things about Noah: he "walked with God"; he was "blameless in his generation"; and he was "a righteous man." Later we read that God said to him: "You alone have I found righteous before Me in this generation."

There are those who maintain that the Torah's description of Noah is accurate. They point out that Noah followed what God commanded him to do. When God ordered him to build the ark, he did so. When he was told to round up pairs of all living creatures and to make a place for them in the ark, he did so. He did not doubt God's commandment but faithfully carried it out. As a result, life on earth was preserved after the Flood.

Ibn Ezra

Ramban (Nachmanides)

In addition, according to some commentators, Noah was a totally ethical person. Rabbi Abraham ibn Ezra taught that Noah was "righteous in his deeds." Nachmanides explained that Noah was "neither a person of violence, nor a person who cheated and lied as did the guilty people of his generation . . . he did not participate in the cults of astrology, enchantment, and soothsaying, nor did he worship idols. He walked with God."

But does the fact that Noah did what God commanded him to do make him a "righteous" person? Was it enough not to engage in violence or not to become involved in the cults of his day? Are we to consider Noah a "righteous" person because he followed God's orders without asking any questions? Was it sufficient for him to save himself, his family, and pairs of all living creatures from the destructive waters of the Flood?

Some teachers of Jewish tradition have compared Noah to Abraham. They point out that, when God was about to destroy the cities of Sodom and Gomorrah, Abraham argued on behalf of their citizens. Even though they were corrupt, dishonest, and violent, Abraham took their side and tried to save them and their cities.

By contrast, Noah said nothing on behalf of the people of his generation. He was indifferent to the suffering they were about to experience and expressed no regret over the pain of those who would drown in the waters of the Flood. He made no effort to defend them or to intercede with God on their behalf. Noah simply followed directions and built his ark.

Righteous but . . .
The Zohar *explains that Noah was out to save himself and his family. He did not intervene or speak up for the people of his generation when he was told that they would be destroyed.*

"His righteousness bore the stamp of mediocrity." (*Rabbi Mordechai Yaffe,* Levush ha-Ora)

Noah remained silent because he did not believe that God would really bring the Flood to destroy all life. He lacked faith. He thought that God was just going to frighten the wicked people of his generation into changing their evil and violent behavior. So he did not speak up and tell them to save themselves. (Toledot Yitzhak)

A great leader is not only a person of ideas, not only a person of personal integrity and devotion, but also a person of tenderness, a person of compassion. . . . If he is insensitive to the sorrows of people, all of his ideals and all of his personal qualities fail to confer greatness upon him. (*Rabbi Morris Adler,* The Voice Still Speaks, *Bloch, New York, 1969, p. 20*)

In the Talmud, Rabbi Berechia asks why Noah did not at least pray for his generation to repent and be saved. Apparently, Noah was a pious man who "walked with God," but his "piety" did not extend to a concern about the welfare of others. We have no report of his going out to warn the people around him that a terrible flood was about to destroy them. Nor are we told that he pleaded with them to change their evil ways and to save themselves. Noah, it appears, was more concerned with his own safety and survival than he was with the survival of his friends and neighbors.

The eighteenth-century chasidic master Rabbi Elimelech of Lizensk once observed that there are two kinds of "righteous" persons: one is genuinely "righteous"; the other dresses like a "righteous" person in a fur coat. Each of them faces a freezing winter in a different way: one will go out and collect wood for a fire; the other will wrap himself in his fur coat. The one who collects wood lights a fire and invites others to join him. He not only warms himself but others as well. The one who makes himself cozy in his own heavy coat is secure, but those around him will freeze. For Elimelech the genuinely "righteous" person was the one who shared warmth with others. In that sense, Noah was not truly "righteous."

The author of *Toledot Yitzhak* argues that Noah doubted what God had told him about a terrible flood that was going to destroy all life on earth. Noah couldn't believe that such a destruction would take place. Therefore, he kept the information to himself rather than sharing it with others. Instead of warning them—giving them a chance to appeal to God or to build their own arks—he said nothing.

Can we consider a person who hides such information a "righteous" person?

And what kind of leadership did Noah display? Nowhere are we told that he had any followers or any students. He built his ark all by himself. He seems to have been a loner, a "righteous" man whose influence extended only to the narrow circle of his family.

Interpreters even raise serious questions about Noah's family. Some argue that his children were saved only because of *his* "righteousness," not because of any good deeds of *their* own. Like their father, none of them spoke out on behalf of those about to be destroyed. Nor did they offer any

warnings or try to talk Noah into building some extra arks in which to save more people and other forms of life. Tragically, Noah failed to have a righteous influence even upon his sons, Shem, Ham, and Japheth.

Who is "righteous"?

". . . the righteous is generous and keeps giving." (Psalms 37:21)

"The righteous must be a lover of human beings." (Wisdom of Solomon 12:19; also Kiddushin 40a)

So there are questions to be asked about how "righteous" a person Noah really was. Was it enough for him to build an ark and save his family and all the living creatures God had commanded him to place inside? Should he have protested what God was about to do just as Abraham did when God told him that Sodom and Gomorrah were about to be destroyed? (See Genesis 18:16–33.) Can we call a person "righteous" if he does not inspire followers or if he refuses to share critical information with those whose lives may depend upon it? Was Noah really a "righteous" person?

PEREK BET: *Why Did God Send the Flood?*

When the Torah describes the creation of the world, we are told that it was "good." Yet a few chapters later in the story of Noah we are informed that God said: "I have decided to put an end to all flesh, for the earth is filled with lawlessness because of them: I am about to destroy them with the earth." (Genesis 6:13)

What had happened? How could the God who had called all that had been created "good," and even "very good," now plan to destroy everything?

The Torah uses two words to illustrate what was happening in Noah's generation and to explain why God decided to send the destructive waters of the Flood. They are *shichet*, meaning "corruption," and *chamas*, meaning "lawlessness."

What was the nature of that "corruption" and

"lawlessness"? Was it really so serious that it justified the destruction of all life?

What was their "corruption" and "lawlessness"?

The people of that generation said: "For what reason do we need God? . . . We have no need of rain. We get an abundant supply of water from other sources, from all the streams and wells of the earth." (Sanhedrin 108a)

A man would take two wives—one for childbearing, the other for pleasure. (Midrash ha-Gadol 10:5)

They exchanged wives. (Genesis Rabbah 23:3)

When a person brought a basket full of peas to the marketplace, he would be surrounded by a group of people. Each would steal an amount worth less than a pruta *(so small an amount that it was not considered a punishable offense). But soon the basket would be empty. The victim would be unable to present his case to a judge because each thief had cleverly taken less than the amount that was punishable by law.* (Genesis Rabbah 31:50)

They removed the landmarks of their neighbors in order to extend their borders. If someone saw an ox or a donkey in the hands of an orphan or widow, he took it away. (Midrash Tanchuma, Noach 26)

Those questions were also asked by the rabbis many centuries ago. They reasoned that Noah's generation had been blessed with "good times." Harvests were plentiful. People lived hundreds of years without sickness, pain, or fear. The weather was always pleasantly mild. No one lacked for anything.

As a result, the rabbis tell us, the people of Noah's generation began to take all the benefits of life for granted. They felt no need to give thanks to God for what they enjoyed. "Why shall we waste our time on prayers of praise to God?" they argued. "Don't we have everything we need? What more can God do for us?"

Many stopped worshiping God. Their self-interest led them to conclude that nothing was as important or "sacred" as taking care of themselves. The concerns of others were less important or of no importance at all. Since they no longer believed in God, they also no longer believed that each person was created in God's image or that every human life was sacred and must be protected.

As a result they became suspicious of one another. Trust between them broke down, and violence increased. No one cared about the poor, the sick, or the homeless. People took advantage of one another. They robbed, lied, and murdered. They bribed judges and found loopholes in the law, twisting it to suit their selfish purposes. In the end, cruelty, terror, fear, and hatred ruled their civilization.

The Torah informs us that God's decision to destroy life on earth was made because of *ra'at ha-adam*, "the evil of human beings." The people of Noah's generation, we are told, spent their days planning and devising "nothing but evil all the time." (Genesis 6:5)

Yet, was there no way to save them? If God is "good" and created such a "good" world, why was there no warning to the people of Noah's generation or any chance provided for them to change their evil ways? Perhaps they could have been rescued. Perhaps, like the people of Nineveh in Jonah's time, they might have repented and asked God to forgive their violence and cruelty. Perhaps the terrible Flood was unnecessary.

The rabbis who composed the *Midrash Tanchuma* explained that God wanted the people of Noah's generation to change their behavior. That is why God commanded Noah to build the ark. It was to serve as a warning to his generation. But no one paid attention. Here is how some of the rabbis described what happened:

God said: "If Noah starts to work on the ark, people will gather around him and say to him, 'What are you making?' He will answer, 'I am building an ark because God is about to bring a flood on the earth.'" God hoped that the ark would serve as a warning, but the people of Noah's generation paid no attention to what Noah was building.

In another version the rabbis tell us:

> Noah planted cedars, and the people of his day asked him, "What are you planting cedars for?" He told them, "God is about to bring a flood and has commanded me to build an ark for me and my family to escape in." When they heard his explanation, they all laughed and ridiculed him. Later, when he was cutting down the cedar trees and planing the wood, they asked, "What are you doing with that cedarwood?" At that point he warned them, again, about the Flood, but they paid no attention and refused to repent.
> (*Midrash Tanchuma, Noach*)

The rabbis make the point that God did not want to destroy all life on earth. Noah's generation was given every opportunity to prevent the Flood. But they would not change their "lawlessness" and "corrupt" ways. They continued their violence toward one another. Greed and distrust, cheating and dishonesty ruled their times.

God wanted to save them, to preserve all life, but they refused to cooperate. They could have changed the course of history, but they would not change themselves.

PEREK GIMEL: *What Went Wrong at the Tower of Babel?*

The Torah tells us that, after the Flood, people moved eastward and settled in the land of Shinar. They decided to build a city for themselves and a *migdal,* a "tower," that reached up into the heavens. "Let's make a name for ourselves," they said to one another, "or we will be scattered all over the earth."

Seeing the city and tower they were building, God decided to do what the people had feared. "If, as one people with one language for all, this is how they have begun to act," God reasoned, "then nothing that they may propose to do will be out of their reach." For that reason God scattered them throughout the world and made them speak different languages.

The city where this all took place was named *Babel,* which means "confused" or "mixed up." That seems an appropriate description of the entire episode, and it raises several questions. What was wrong with people building a *migdal,* a "tower"? Wouldn't we be better off if peoples everywhere spoke one language? Wouldn't that have improved communication and, perhaps, the chances for human cooperation and peace?"

Abravanel

Abravanel, a counselor to the kings and queens in Spain and Portugal, explained that, before they began building the tower, people had lived at peace with one another. They shared everything equally and generously. But, as soon as they began building, they started to argue bitterly with one another. They disagreed over who would bake the bricks, who would carry them, and who would place them on the tower. Each one wanted the credit for laying the first brick on a new level, for the design, for choosing the color, or for organizing the work. The project of building the tower made people jealous of one another. It caused them to hate one another. They became more interested in competing for fame than cooperating for the good of the whole human community. As a result, God destroyed the tower and scattered them throughout the world.

Benno Jacob

Rabbi Benno Jacob (1862–1945), a modern biblical scholar, suggests that those who built the tower failed because their goals were wrong. They had mastered the art of brick making, of molding and heating the clay. But, instead of using their new technology to improve living conditions in their city, to create housing for the poor, sick, and aging, they decided to use all their resources and efforts to build the highest tower in the world.

They reasoned that their high tower would bring them fame and glory. They wanted others to say, "Look what they have done!" Their terrible mistake was to use their technology for pride and vanity instead of using it to improve the quality of life in their society.

> ### No regard for a human life
>
> *The tower was built with seven steps on the east side and seven steps on the west side, and it was seven miles high. (Some versions of the story say that it was twenty-seven miles high!) It took a person one year to climb from the bottom to the top. The bricks were carried up from one side, and the line of workers went down on the other side. If a worker fell down and died, they paid no attention to him. But, if a brick fell, they would all sit and weep. "What a loss," they would say. "Look how long it will take until we can bring another brick to take its place." (Pirke de-Rabbi Eliezer 24)*

According to the ancient rabbis, the creation of the tower was a huge project. They report that, because there were no natural stones with which to construct the tower in the plain of Shinar, it was necessary to invent a special process of baking the bricks. Hundreds of people were required to run the furnaces where they were baked; hundreds of others were needed to prepare the material. Thousands were used to carry them from the location of the baking-furnaces to the base of the tower; thousands more were employed to carry them up the steep steps that reached high into the sky.

It did not take long before the "project" became more important than the health or safety of those who were involved in it. People were enslaved as laborers. Individual rights and liberties were taken away. The building of the tower and the achievement of fame for the community became justification for brutality and the end of individual freedom. Bricks became more important than individual liberties or lives.

The Italian Torah commentator, scientist, and philosopher Obadiah Sforno (1475–1550), who lived through the bitter times of the Inquisition when Jews suffered and were often put to death for their differing religious views, criticized the generation of tower builders for another reason. Their real crime, Sforno argued, was not simply the way in which they built the tower, but it was also in what they sought to accomplish by its creation. Their goal, Sforno explained, was *one* religion for everyone, *one* point of view on the world, *one* accepted political way of doing things.

The tower builders believed that differences of opinion, controversy, and diversity of belief were dangerous and unacceptable. They opposed freedom of thought or discussion. Those who questioned their views or authority were to be crushed. According to Sforno, when God saw that the tower builders were crushing freedom of thought and discussion, it became necessary to intervene and to scatter human beings throughout the world.

As we can see, the commentators found many important explanations for God's destruction of the Tower of Babel. The project produced jealousy and mean competition, a misuse of technology, and a cruel disregard for the worth of each individual life. It fostered a false patriotism and, ultimately, threatened the loss of freedom.

Could it be that God actually saved humanity from catastrophe by destroying the tower and dispersing us, with different languages and traditions, to all corners of the earth? Perhaps the real message of the Torah's story about the building of the Tower of Babel has to do with helping us understand that our differences in language, culture, and traditions all represent significant strengths and blessings for humanity.

QUESTIONS FOR STUDY AND DISCUSSION

1. One might defend or criticize Noah by claiming that he was "just following orders." Soldiers and bureaucrats have often used this excuse to justify their action or inaction. Is this a legitimate defense in Noah's case?

2. Would you have believed Noah if he had told you that God was about to destroy the whole world? Some scientists today are warning that we are in danger of "destroying our world." Why do people refuse to listen to the "bad-

news" predictions? Why do we disbelieve our experts?

3. What is so wrong with the tower builders' plan of *one* religion, *one* accepted political point of view, *one* point of view on the world?

4. In addition to buildings, what do human beings often value more than they should? Is there a difference between living as if you are "created in the image of God" or living as if you are a god?

PARASHAT LECH-LECHA
Genesis 12:1–17:27

Parashat Lech-Lecha begins with the story of Abram leaving his birthplace in Haran. God promises the land of Canaan to Abram and his descendants. Because of a famine in the land, Abram takes his family to Egypt. While there, the pharaoh orders Abram's wife, Sarai, to live in his palace. Plagues come upon Egypt as punishment for what Pharaoh has done, and Sarai is restored to Abram. Returning to Canaan, Abram and his brother's son, Lot, divide the land in order to prevent any disagreements between them. Later, Lot is attacked and taken hostage by enemy kings. Abram rescues him and his family. Because Abram and Sarai have trouble conceiving a child, Sarai, in the custom of ancient times, invites her maidservant, Hagar, to have a child with Abram. When Hagar becomes pregnant, she begins to abuse Sarai, who responds by chasing away Hagar. An angel tells Hagar to return, and she bears a son whom Abram names Ishmael. As this Torah portion concludes, Abram is instructed to circumcise himself and Ishmael. Abram is told that the circumcision of all males at eight days of age will be a sign of God's covenant with him and his people forever.

OUR TARGUM

·1·

God said to Abram, "*Lech-lecha*—go forth from your native land and from your father's house to the land that I will show you. I will make of you a great nation, and I will bless you." So Abram and his wife, Sarai, and his brother's son, Lot, set out for the land of Canaan, which today is the Land of Israel. When they reached the border of the land, God said to Abram, "I will give this land to your descendants."

·2·

Because of poor crops and a shortage of food in the land of Canaan, Abram and Sarai traveled to

Egypt. Abram feared that an Egyptian might admire Sarai and want to kill him in order to take her as a wife. He therefore instructed her to say that she was his sister.

His prediction proved correct. While in Egypt, the pharaoh saw Sarai and demanded that she come to live in his palace. Shortly after she had moved in, God sent plagues upon Egypt, and Pharaoh discovered Sarai's real identity. "Why did you not tell me that she was your wife?" Pharaoh asked Abram. Then, seeking forgiveness from God, he sent Abram and Sarai away with many gifts.

· 3 ·

From Egypt, Abram, Sarai, and Lot returned through the Negev desert to Bethel, which is located today about seventeen miles north of Jerusalem. When they reached Bethel, their herdsmen began to quarrel about where their cattle would graze. So Abram suggested that they divide the land between them. Lot chose the Plain of Jordan and settled near the city of Sodom. Abram remained in the land of Canaan, settling in Hebron.

· 4 ·

Later, four foreign kings raided the cities of Sodom and Gomorrah and took Lot as a captive. Hearing that Lot was in trouble, Abram gathered a troop of fighters and set out to rescue him. When they returned victoriously, the king of Sodom offered Abram a reward for having saved Lot and his city. Abram refused the reward. He told the king: "I will take nothing that is yours. I do not want you to say, 'It was I who made Abram rich.'"

· 5 ·

Now, God had promised that Abram's descendants would inherit that land, but Abram and Sarai had no children. So Sarai asked her maidservant, an Egyptian woman named Hagar, to have a child with Abram. That was a common custom in that time for childless parents. When Hagar became pregnant, she began treating Sarai disrespectfully. Sarai blamed Abram for Hagar's attitude. When Abram told Sarai: "Deal with her as you think right," Sarai forced Hagar to flee from her house.

An angel saw what had happened and told Hagar to return to Sarai's house. The angel also promised that she would bear a son whose name would be Ishmael. Abram was then eighty-six years old.

· 6 ·

Afterwards, God told Abram: "I will establish My covenant between Me and you, and I will make you exceedingly numerous." God changed Abram's name to "Abraham" (*Avraham*), meaning "father of a multitude," and promised the "land of Canaan, as an everlasting possession." As a sign of the covenant between God and Abraham's offspring, God commanded that every Jewish male be circumcised at the age of eight days. So Abraham circumcised himself and Ishmael.

God also changed Sarai's name to "Sarah," meaning "princess," and said to Abraham: "I will give you a son by her . . . rulers of peoples shall issue from her."

THEMES

Parashat Lech-Lecha contains five important themes:

1. The demands of leadership.
2. Honesty in our dealings with others.

3. Settling disagreements.
4. Rescuing captives.
5. The Jewish covenant of circumcision.

PEREK ALEF: *What Qualified Abram for Leadership of the Jewish People?*

The Torah tells us very little about Abram's early life. We are informed that he and Sarai, along with his nephew Lot, were brought by his father, Terah, from Ur of the Chaldeans to Haran. After Terah's death, Abram was commanded by God to leave Haran and promised that he would become "a great nation."

For thousands of years students of Torah have been asking: "Why was Abram chosen for such important leadership? What had he done to be named the founder of the Jewish people?"

The rabbis who studied this Torah portion suggested that, while the Torah might not tell us much about Abram's early life or why he might have been selected for leadership, there was much to learn from the legends collected and passed from generation to generation by Jews.

According to some of those reports, Abram rebelled against the worship of idols in his home and in the palace of Nimrod, who ruled at that time. At an early age he saw some people praying to different stars and planets and others making gods out of wood and stone. He said to himself: "How is it possible for this wonderful world to have been created by a star or a planet, or by an idol that is made by human hands? How is it possible for something manufactured of wood or stone to be considered responsible for the development of our human ethical sense of right and wrong or of our desire to improve the world?"

The more questions Abram asked, the more foolish idolatry seemed to him. So he began asking questions of his father and of others who worked in Nimrod's palace. They resented his questions because they could not answer them. They accused Abram of being a troublemaker and a "revolutionary." When he persisted with his questions and public rejection of idolatry, his father reported him to Nimrod, and he was persecuted for his ideas and put into prison.

Abram's rejection of idolatry
When Abram came to his father's home, he saw his father's gods, twelve in number. . . . He hurried from the room into his father's outer courtyard, where he found his father seated with all his servants; and he came and sat down before his father and asked him: "Father, tell me, where is the God who created the heavens and the earth and created all human beings on earth?" And Terah answered Abram his son, saying: "Why, those who created all these are with us in the house!"

. . . So Abram took dishes and brought them into the chamber before his father's gods . . . and saw that not one of them was stretching out a hand to eat. . . . So he took hammers and . . . smashed all the gods of his father.

. . . When Terah saw this, he grew very angry. . . . "What have you done to all my gods?" And Abram answered his father . . . "I only brought fine dishes of food before them. But, when I offered the dishes to them to eat, all of them put out their hands to begin before the biggest of them all had started eating. When the big one saw what they did without waiting for him, he grew very angry . . . and smashed them all."

When Terah heard this, he grew exceedingly angry. . . . "You are speaking falsehood to me! Have these gods any spirit or soul or strength to do all you have told me? Why, they are wood and stone, and I made them! How can you tell me such lies?"

. . . Then Abram answered his father: "Then how can you worship these idols, who do not have the strength to do anything? Are these idols in whom you trust going to deliver you? Can they really hear your prayers when you cry unto them?" (Micha Joseph Bin Gorion, Mimekor Yisrael, *Volume I, 15)*

God chose Abram as the founder of the Jewish people because of his wisdom and bravery. He was not afraid to ask hard questions or to stand up for what he believed. He was willing to risk ridicule, even suffering and persecution, for his convictions. He was willing to lead the minority of those who believed that idolatry was wrong and to devote his life to teaching that one God was the creative Source of all life. Those qualities made him a gifted leader.

Abram possessed other special qualities as well. The rabbis of the Midrash tell us that the prices he quoted in his business dealings were always fair, that people came to him for advice in times of trouble, and that when he was told that someone was sick he would not just offer a prayer but would visit and make the person feel better because of his concern and interest. (*Genesis Rabbah, Lech-Lecha,* 11)

Abram's priorities
Rabbi Levi explains that, when Abram was traveling through various lands, he saw people going to drunken parties. "May I not be a part of this country!" he would say. But, when he reached the location of Tyre, near the Land of Israel, and saw people working at weeding and hoeing in the proper seasons, he said: "May my portion be in this country." (Genesis Rabbah, Lech-Lecha, 8)

Abram valued creative work. He rejected the company of those who chose to waste their energies and time with drugs or drunkenness. He respected those who planned for the future and who were willing to work hard in order to transform their ideas and hopes into reality.

For all those reasons, our Torah interpreters tell us, Abram was selected as the founder and leader of the Jewish people.

PEREK BET: *Is It Ever Right to Lie?*

Abram and Sarai find themselves in a dangerous situation within our Torah portion. They have gone to Egypt in order to escape from famine in the Land of Israel. Fearing that some Egyptian will admire Sarai and kill him, Abram tells her not to reveal that she is his wife. When the pharaoh of Egypt asks her who she is, she tells him that she is Abram's "sister."

Later, after Pharaoh discovers the truth, he confronts Abram and asks: "Why didn't you tell me that she was your wife?" The Torah does not tell us what Abram answered. We are only informed that Pharaoh sent him away with Sarai and with all the riches he had acquired in Egypt.

Should Abram have lied? Was it permissible for him to say that his wife was his "sister" in order to save himself?

A half-truth
It was not a lie for Abram to call Sarai his "sister" since Sarai was his niece, and relatives may be termed brother and sister. (Midrash ha-Gadol 12:12)

On another occasion, Abram also told Sarai to say that she was his "sister." In his explanation of what he had done he said: ". . . she is in truth my sister, my father's daughter though not my mother's; and she became my wife." (Genesis 20:12)

Ramban (Nachmanides)

Faced with the fear that he might be killed by the Egyptians, Abram may have decided to tell a "half-truth." He would say that Sarai was his "sister" which, in fact, she was, but he would not reveal that she was his wife. The commentator Nachmanides condemns Abram for his behavior. He says that Abram "committed a great sin" by not telling the truth about his wife. "He should have trusted that God would save him and his wife and all his belongings. . . ." (Genesis 12:9)

Hirsch

Other commentators disagree. Rabbi Samson Raphael Hirsch, a leading scholar who lived in

Germany from 1808 to 1888, argued that Abram's actions were honorable. He knew that the Egyptians would not deal harshly with an unmarried woman traveling with her brother but that they would kill the husband of a beautiful woman and rape her. So he acted to protect both Sarai and himself. In fact, he was really telling the truth. She was the daughter of his father and actually his "sister."

The issue remains unresolved. Was Abram justified in lying? Is using a half-truth lying? And what about Sarai? Was it her responsibility to tell the truth rather than follow Abram's instructions?

PEREK GIMEL: *Dealing with Differences*

When Abram and Lot left Egypt, they took with them many flocks and herds. They had both become rich. When they reached Bethel, the Torah tells us that their herdsmen began to quarrel with one another.

What the Torah does not reveal are the reasons for their arguments. Those are suggested by the interpreters who commented on this section of our Torah portion.

One commentator explains that Lot's herdsmen paid no attention to posted borders or signs that read Private Property. They allowed their animals to graze wherever they happened to wander. Abram's herdsman saw what they were doing and accused them of robbery.

What they argued about:
Rabbi Berekiah said in Rabbi Judah's name: Abram's cattle would be muzzled and then taken out so that they could not graze in land that was not permitted. On the other hand, Lot's herdsmen refused to muzzle their cattle. As a result they grazed wherever they went.

When Abram's herdsmen asked, "Is what you are doing not robbery?" Lot's herdsmen replied, "Abram is a barren mule who cannot have children! Therefore Lot will inherit everything that belongs to him. If his cattle now graze on Abram's land, it is as if they were already grazing on what belongs to Lot!" (Genesis Rabbah 41:5)

Like many arguments, the one between Abram's and Lot's herdsmen began with a disagreement over what was considered the right thing to do and ended with Lot's people hurling public insults at Abram. "He's a barren mule who can't have children," they said. And Abram's herdsmen may have answered, "Lot has become an idolater, a dishonest unbeliever!" According to the rabbis, it was the insult that turned their disagreement into a bitter battle.

Yet there may have been another reason for the disagreement between Abram, Lot, and their herdsmen. The commentator Nachmanides explains that Abram and Lot had come back to Canaan with huge herds and that Abram opposed letting them graze together because he feared that the inhabitants of the land (the Canaanites and Perizzites), seeing how great they were, might decide to rise up and destroy them. So he ordered their herdsmen to graze their animals in different places.

Lot and his herdsmen paid no attention. They did not seem to care about making trouble with the other people of the land or about their security.

Seeing that there were considerable differences between them, Abram suggested that they go their separate ways. Furthermore, according to the Torah, he gave Lot his choice. He said to him, ". . . if you go north, I will go south; and, if you go south, I will go north." Lot agreed. He journeyed eastward, and Abram remained in the land of Canaan.

PEREK DALET: *Abram Rescues Lot*

It was not long after Lot had settled in the city of Sodom that it was attacked by Chedorlaomer, king of Elam; Tidal, king of Goiim; Amraphel, king of Shinar; and Arioch, king of Ellasar. They stormed the cities of Sodom and Gomorrah, seizing their wealth and taking Lot as a captive.

Hearing what had happened, Abram immediately organized an army to pursue them and to rescue his nephew. He defeated the kings and saved Lot. Upon Abram's victorious return, the king of Sodom praised him for his bravery and offered him a large reward. Abram refused to take anything.

Several questions come to mind: "Why, if

Abram and Lot had separated from each other, did Abram feel obligated to risk his life to rescue Lot? Why did he not take some of the spoils of the battle?"

Nachmanides suggests that, even though there had been disagreements between them, Abram remembered that Lot had been a faithful companion and friend. Another interpreter points out that Abram realized that, when a person is taken captive, others must see him as a "brother" and rush to rescue him. (*Akedat Yitzhak*)

Rescuing the captive
Pidyon shevuyin, *or "rescuing the captives," is one of the most important commandments of Judaism: Abram was ready to sacrifice his life in order to save Lot because he believed that saving a life by freeing a victim of oppression was one of the highest forms of serving God.* (Genesis Rabbah *43:2*)

Rambam (*Maimonides*)

Abram's rescue of Lot became an ethical model for Jews throughout the centuries. According to the great twelfth-century teacher Moses Maimonides, *pidyon shevuyim*, the "rescue of captives," is a more important mitzvah even than charity for the poor. The rabbis of the Talmud ordered that charity set aside for building a synagogue could be used to ransom Jews from their captors; they taught that whoever delays in rescuing a fellow Jew is regarded as if he had spilled his blood. During the Middle Ages, in many Jewish communities, associations were formed to collect funds for the ransoming of captive Jews. Thousands were saved from pirates, kidnapers, and hostile armies. (*Mishneh Torah, Aniyyim* 8:10, 12; *Baba Batra* 8b)

Abram's immediate and brave action to save his "brother," Lot, set the standard for fulfilling the mitzvah of *pidyon shevuyin*, the liberation of captives.

Yet, having fulfilled his obligation to rescue Lot, why did Abram refuse any reward?

The rabbis of the Midrash suggest that Abram was concerned that, if he took anything, people would say that he had gone to battle in order to increase his wealth and not to save his "brother." He wanted his purpose understood. His concern was with Lot's safety and welfare, not with acquiring more riches. (*Genesis Rabbah* 43:12)

Reward for a mitzvah
Concerning the doing of a mitzvah, Antigonos of Socho taught: "Be not like servants who work for their master only on condition that they receive payment, but be like servants who work for their master without looking for any reward; and be filled with reverence for God." And (Simeon) ben Azai commented that the "reward of doing one mitzvah is the opportunity of doing another." (Avot *1:3 and 4:2*)

While most interpreters praise Abram for his rescue of Lot and refusal to take any favors for it, Rabbi Yochanan, a famous third-century teacher in the Land of Israel, was very critical of Abram. He believed that Abram had missed an opportunity to convert Lot, and even the king of Sodom, to his new faith. Rabbi Yochanan argued that they were both in debt to him and that he should have taken advantage of them. (*Nedarim* 32b)

Most commentators disagree with Rabbi Yochanan's criticism of Abram. They praise Abram for refusing any reward for his rescue of Lot. Because he did so, his example of *pidyon shevuyin* and of doing a mitzvah without strings attached, without conditions or rewards, still stands as a powerful ethical model.

PEREK HEI: *Berit Milah—The Covenant of Circumcision*

The Torah informs us that, three years after Hagar gives birth to Ishmael, God promises to establish a *berit*, a "covenant" or "contract," with Abram. The symbol of that covenant was *berit milah*, or "circumcision." Circumcision is the removal of the foreskin from the penis of the male child. In our Torah portion God instructs Abram: "At the age of eight days, every male among you throughout the generations shall be circumcised. . . . Thus shall My *berit* be marked in your flesh as an everlasting covenant." (Genesis 17:12–13)

So Abram circumcised himself, his son Ishmael, and every other male who was a part of his community. As a part of the ritual, God changes Abram's name to *Avraham,* meaning "father of many nations," and Sarai's name to *Sarah,* meaning "princess."

The practice of circumcision was common among many ancient peoples in the Middle East. It was the custom of the Egyptians, Edomites, Ammonites, and Moabites, and later it became the practice of all Moslems. Among most ancient peoples, circumcision was performed just before marriage in hope that the "sacrifice" of the foreskin would make one a father of many children.

While the promise connected to Abraham's circumcision and change of name is that he will be the "father of many nations," the timing of the ceremony of *berit milah* was set at eight days after birth. Within the Jewish community, circumcision was not done to guarantee many children but, rather, as a way in which a male child became identified as a Jew. *Berit milah* became a ceremony of pride, an initiation of the newborn child into the faith and community of the Jewish people.

Perhaps that is why Jews have observed the *berit milah* ceremony with such care through the ages and why enemies of the Jewish people have tried to prevent its practice. Rulers who wished to destroy Jewish loyalties and put an end to Judaism very often prohibited Jews from practicing circumcision.

When, for instance, Antiochus Epiphanes (165 B.C.E.) declared war on the Jews by forbidding them to observe their Sabbaths and festivals or to practice the traditions of their Torah, he also made a special point of proclaiming that all Jewish sons should be left uncircumcised. He ordered any parent who arranged for a *berit milah* to be put to death. Those who attended such ceremonies were also threatened. The Maccabees, however, refused to follow the orders of Antiochus and declared a war of liberation against his oppressive rule.

For some Jewish teachers, circumcision represents more than a sacred sign of Jewish identity or a symbol of the covenant of the Jewish people with God. There are those interpreters who believe that circumcision is a way of teaching human beings that the world is imperfect and requires *tikun,* or "improvement." In the Midrash, the rabbis report the following:

> The Roman general Turnus Rufus once asked Rabbi Akiba: "If your God is so powerful, and wanted male children circumcised, then why isn't each child simply born with the circumcision already done?"
>
> Rabbi Akiba replied: "God gave all the commandments to the people of Israel so that they could perfect themselves by doing them. God wished that individuals would take on the responsibility of perfecting themselves and the world through the practice of the commandments. The commandment of circumcision reminds us that, just as we need to improve ourselves physically, so do we need to improve ourselves and our world spiritually.
>
> (*Midrash Tanchuma* and *Sefer ha-Hinuch* 57)

In other words, circumcision is a sacred lesson. It is a powerful symbol of Jewish identity. It serves as a reminder to Jews of their ethical tasks and responsibilities. It also teaches us that our talents and abilities require improvement. Our defects and deficiencies should be corrected and repaired. Just as the male baby requires the improvement of circumcision, so the world requires human beings to perfect it. *Berit milah* is the sign that Jews were "contracted" to God for the work of perfecting both themselves and the world.

QUESTIONS FOR STUDY AND DISCUSSION

1. What qualified Abram to become the founder of the Jewish people? How would you compare his qualities of leadership with leaders of our own times?

2. Did Abram do the right thing when he lied to Pharaoh about Sarai's identity? Is a half-truth or "white lie" permissible when it can save a life? Under what other conditions might half-truths be justified?

3. The commentators present Abram as a model for solving conflicts between competing factions. Which of his techniques, as described by the interpreters, might be applied today to international and personal disputes?

4. How can the mitzvah of *pidyon shevuyin* be carried out today? Is it still the obligation of individuals or are international matters so complex that we must leave liberation of the oppressed to the "experts"?

5. Since a Jewish male child is only eight days old when he is circumcised, the *berit milah* is hardly a demonstration of his commitment to Judaism or to the Jewish people. What, then, is the meaning of the ceremony? Might the same be asked about the naming of a baby girl?

PARASHAT VAYERA
Genesis 18:1–22:24

Parashat Vayera begins with the visit of three men to Abraham. He welcomes them with generous hospitality, and they promise that Sarah will soon bear a son. When the men depart for the city of Sodom, God appears to Abraham and tells him that the cities of Sodom and Gomorrah are about to be destroyed because of the sinful behavior of their residents. Abraham protests, asking God not to destroy innocent people along with the guilty ones. God promises that, if there are as few as even ten innocent people in the cities, they will not be destroyed. Afterwards, two men-angels arrive in Sodom and are offered hospitality by Lot. He protects them from the Sodomites, who threaten to harm them. The men-angels warn Lot to leave Sodom. He escapes the next morning as fire rains down upon the cities, but his wife looks back and is turned into a pillar of salt. Abraham travels to the Negev, where Abimelech, king of Gerar, sees Sarah and wants her for a wife. Fearing the king, Abraham claims that Sarah is his "sister." The king takes her as a wife, but God appears to him and reveals Sarah's real identity. Abimelech returns her to Abraham along with a great bounty. As the visitors to Abraham had predicted, Sarah bears a son whom they name Isaac. After a few years, Sarah persuades Abraham to send Hagar and Ishmael away, claiming that only Isaac should inherit Abraham's wealth and position. Abraham agrees when God tells him that "I will make a nation of him [Ishmael]." Several years later, God tests Abraham's faith by ordering him to sacrifice Isaac on Mount Moriah. Isaac is saved at the last moment when God praises Abraham's loyalty and tells him to sacrifice a ram in Isaac's place.

OUR TARGUM

· 1 ·

Abraham sees three men approaching his tent. He rises, runs out to greet them, and invites them to have some water and food with him. Sara prepares a meal for them. The men promise Abraham that Sarah will soon become pregnant with a son. Sarah hears what they say and laughs. She is convinced that she is too old to have children.

· 2 ·

The visitors depart and travel toward the city of Sodom, located in the Jordan Valley. God appears to Abraham and tells him that the cities of Sodom and Gomorrah will be destroyed because of the wicked behavior of their citizens. Abraham protests, arguing that, if God is just, innocent people cannot be destroyed along with evil ones. He asks: "What if there should be fifty innocent within the city; will You then wipe out the place and not forgive it for the sake of the innocent fifty who are in it?" God agrees to save the city if there are fifty innocent people. Abraham then begins to bargain. He asks God: "What if there are forty-five people?" Then, pursuing his argument, he asks about forty, then thirty, twenty, and, finally, if God will destroy the city if only ten innocent people are found. God tells him: "I will not destroy, for the sake of the ten."

· 3 ·

One evening two men-angels arrive in Sodom. Lot, who is sitting at the gate of the city, welcomes them and invites them to stay the night at his house. The wicked people of Sodom gather outside Lot's door, demanding that he turn over the visitors so that they might sexually abuse them. Fearing for the lives of his guests, Lot offers the Sodomites his daughters. The crowd becomes angry with Lot, threatening to break down the door. At that point the two visitors pull Lot into the house, and the people standing outside are struck with a blinding light.

The visitors tell Lot to gather his family and flee before Sodom is destroyed. Lot's sons-in-law refuse to believe the prediction or to follow him, and the rest of Lot's family delays. Finally, in the morning, the visitors take them by the hands and escort them outside the city. They tell them: "Flee for your life! Do not look behind you . . . lest you be swept away." As the cities are destroyed, Lot's wife looks back and is turned into a pillar of salt.

· 4 ·

Later, while Abraham and Sarah are traveling in the Negev, Abimelech, king of Gerar, sees her and wishes to have her for a wife. As he had done when Pharaoh desired Sarah (see *Parashat Lech-Lecha*), Abraham tells the king, "She is my sister." God appears to the king on the night he takes Sarah into his house and reveals that she is Abraham's wife. Fearing for his life, Abimelech returns Sarah to Abraham along with a huge treasure as payment for any wrong he might have done.

Soon Sarah conceives and gives birth to Isaac. After a few years, she demands that Abraham send away Hagar and her son, Ishmael, claiming that only Isaac is entitled to inherit Abraham's wealth and leadership. Abraham, greatly upset by Sarah's demand, agrees to do as she wishes after God

assures him that Ishmael will also become a great nation.

·5·

Some time later, God tests Abraham's loyalty by commanding him to sacrifice Isaac at the top of Mount Moriah. Abraham takes his son and travels to the place. There he builds an altar and, just as he is about to kill his son, an angel stops him, saying: "Do not raise your hand against the boy, or do anything to him. For now I know that you fear God." Abraham looks up and sees a ram caught by its horns in a bush. He takes the animal and offers it as a sacrifice in the place of Isaac. The angel tells him that he and all of his people after him will be blessed.

THEMES

Parashat Vayera contains three important themes:

1. The importance of hospitality.
2. The consequences of social injustice.
3. The meaning of "loyalty" to God.

PEREK ALEF: *The Hospitality of Abraham and Lot*

Twice in this Torah portion guests are welcomed in a home: once by Abraham at the beginning of the portion and the second time by Lot just before the cities of Sodom and Gomorrah are destroyed. In each situation, the "hospitality" offered is very different. And from each we learn something about the unique Jewish standards for welcoming people into our homes.

> **The importance of hospitality**
> "Hospitality," the Talmud says, is a "great mitzvah. It is considered more important to show hospitality than to attend classes or to greet God in prayer." (Shabbat 127a)
>
> "Why was the prophet Micah included among those who will live for eternity?" the rabbis asked.
> "Because he shared his bread with those who passed by his home." (Sanhedrin 103a)

The example of Abraham's special model of hospitality is clearly described by the Torah. Every gesture was important and recorded. We are told: "*Looking up, he saw* three men standing near him. *As soon* as he saw them, *he ran* from the entrance of the tent *to greet* them and, *bowing* to the ground, he said, 'My lords, if it please you, *do not go on past your servant. Let a little water be brought; bathe your feet and recline under the tree. And let me fetch a morsel of bread that you may refresh yourselves; then go on. . . .*'"

Abraham's hospitality is not passive. He is *looking* for guests. He is alert to those who might be passing by and in need of help. Nor does he wait until the strangers have approached his tent. Instead, *as soon* as he sees them, *he runs* toward them. He does not ask them all kinds of questions about their parents or people or where they are going, but, instead, he *greets* them and shows them respect by *bowing* before them. Abraham then pleads with them: "*Do not go on past your servant.*" He *comforts* them by bringing them water and then rushes to feed them.

Several commentators who have studied Abraham's welcoming of his guests point out that he was still recuperating from the pain of his circumcision. Even so, he was alert to the exhaustion and hunger of others and ran out to greet them and refresh them with food and drink. (*Akedat Yitzhak*)

Ramban (Nachmanides)

Furthermore, according to Nachmanides, Abraham thought only of the needs of his guests.

It was the middle of the day; they had been traveling and would want to rest and then continue their journey; their feet were sore; they were tired from the hot sun. So he gave them water with which to cool their feet and arranged for them to sit in the shade of a tree.

The angels can wait!

A young person once visited the famed teacher known as the Chofetz Chaim. The guest had arrived at the synagogue just as the Sabbath began, having been on the road for many hours. He was hungry and weak as they walked from the synagogue to the rabbi's home. To the surprise of the guest, the Chofetz Chaim skipped the singing of "Shalom Alechem" (a song that greets the Sabbath angels) and, after quickly reciting the Kiddush and the Motzi, began to eat. "Why did you skip the singing of 'Shalom Alechem,'" the young man asked his host.

The Chofetz Chaim replied: "You were hungry. A hungry person should be fed as soon as possible. The angels can wait to be greeted."

The Torah informs us that Abraham was not alone in offering hospitality to his guests. Sarah helped him. Many Torah interpreters explain that, as husband and wife, they shared the responsibility of preparing food for their guests. And they wasted no time. They *hurried* to care for the strangers. They also made an effort to serve their guests with bread made from *choice* flour and meat taken from a *choice* calf. Nor did they turn over the feeding of their guests to servants. Abraham and Sarah waited on the strangers, serving each an equal portion. They cared for each person according to that person's need. (See *Mesillat Yesharim* 7, *Numbers Rabbah* 10:5, and *Megillah* 12a.)

Furthermore, Abraham insisted on serving his guests at the entrance of his home.

Why?

Perhaps he wanted other strangers to know that they were welcome; perhaps he wanted to remind others that each human being is created in the "image of God" and that showing hospitality to strangers is a way of welcoming God into our lives.

And, when it came time for his guests to leave, the commentator Nachmanides comments that Abraham did not just bid them farewell at his gate, but he went with them until he saw that they were safely on their way.

Who is the stranger?

One day a group of strangers came to an inn. The innkeeper and his wife were known for their kindness and hospitality. They saw that the strangers were tired, and the innkeeper ran out to heat some water in the bathhouse. Among the strangers was a poor old man with ugly sores all over his back. The other guests refused to bathe with him or to help him wash himself. When the innkeeper's wife saw that the old man needed help, she took the brush and gently washed his back. "Thank you for your kindness," he said to her. "May all the children you bear be like me."

Some say that the poor old man was none other than Elijah the Prophet, who will someday bring an era of human understanding, kindness, and peace.

Abraham's treatment of the strangers who visited him is viewed by Jewish tradition as an outstanding model of hospitality. By contrast, Lot's reception of his guests raises troubling questions. According to the rabbis who explained our Torah portion, Lot brought visitors to his home only at night, never during the day. He also never led them directly to his house but chose a long way to get there and entered always through the back door. When they arrived, he would tell them, "Do not wash your feet. Should authorities from the city come checking on us, it must appear as though you just arrived and that I am not providing anything special for you." (*Pirke de-Rabbi Eliezer* and *Midrash ha-Gadol*; also Rashi and *Meam Loez*)

Why did Lot act in such an inhospitable manner?

Some explain that the officials of Sodom had decreed that it was against the law to show any kindness or hospitality to visitors. The punishment for anyone welcoming guests or caring for their needs was imprisonment and death. Strangers were to be taken advantage of, their possessions were to be stolen, and they were to be chased out of the town as quickly as possible. (Nachmanides and *Genesis Rabbah*)

Others point out that, unlike Sarah, Lot's wife opposed offering hospitality to strangers. She refused to cook for them or to help Lot make them comfortable. On many occasions she actually complained to her neighbors about "my husband's visitors" and even reported to the authorities when Lot was entertaining guests. (*Midrash Agadah* 19:4; *Genesis Rabbah* 50:8, 9)

While many commentators are critical of Lot, a few argue that his hospitality was heroic. They point out that, unlike Abraham, Lot lived in a city where one could be put to death for offering food, shelter, and friendship to guests. One interpreter suggests that Lot's daughter, Pelotit, had been put to death by the authorities of Sodom for giving bread to a stranger.

Others emphasize that, when the crowd gathered at his door, demanding that he turn over the strangers to them, he refused. Risking his life, he went outside, closed the door behind him, and tried to calm the mob. He bravely stood his ground and tried to convince them to leave. But they demanded that he open the door and send his visitors out to them. It was only then that Lot offered to give the mob his daughters as protection for the strangers. (*Sefer ha-Yashar* 10)

Should he have made such an offer? Was it a heroic gesture or a cruel decision? Given the circumstances, can we even compare Abraham's hospitality with Lot's?

Limits even to hospitality
Lot told the crowd: 'See, I have two daughters who have not known a man. Let me bring them out to you, and you may do to them as you please; but do not do anything to these men since they have come under the shelter of my roof." We have been taught that a person should sacrifice his own life for the sake of his wife and children. Lot was ready to hand over his daughters for abuse. Therefore, he brought shame to his life. (Midrash ha-Gadol *19:8*)

In some societies, the head of a household might be justified in turning over his wife or daughters to an angry mob in order to save innocent visitors. Jewish tradition, however, demands that a person give his own life rather than sacrifice the lives of his loved ones.

Zugot

Let your house be open
Rabbi Yosi ben Yochanan taught: "Let your house be open wide, and let the needy be treated as members of your home." (Avot *1:5*)

Judging others
Rabbi Hillel cautioned: "Do not judge another person until you have put yourself in that person's place." (Avot *2:5*)

Between Abraham and Lot we have two examples of hospitality. Yet the conditions faced by each of them were quite different. How then are we to judge between them?

PEREK BET: *Should Good People Suffer for the Evil That Bad People Do?*

The Torah informs us that, when God told Abraham that Sodom and Gomorrah were to be destroyed because of the terrible sins of their citizens, Abraham boldly asked: "Will You sweep away the innocent along with the guilty? What if there should be fifty innocent within the city; will You then wipe out the place and not forgive it for the sake of the innocent fifty who are in it? . . . Far be it from You! Shall not the Judge of all the earth deal justly?"

Abraham was concerned with justice. He did not believe that good people or innocent people should suffer for the evil actions of others. So he argued on behalf of the innocent people in Sodom. When God told him that the city would be saved for the sake of fifty people, Abraham went on to argue the case for forty-five, then for forty, then for thirty, then for twenty, and, finally, for ten.

Yet Sodom was destroyed. Why? The Torah text tells us only that "the outrage of Sodom and Gomorrah was great, and their sin was serious." That is all. We are given no details.

Later, the rabbis ask themselves the question: "What was so evil about the people of these cities that God decided to destroy them? They came up with several important reasons.

The first was the selfishness of the people of Sodom. Their land was rich with gold, silver, and precious stones. Their farmers produced an abundance of food. Every citizen had a comfortable home, a closet filled with clothing, and gardens of beautiful flowers and fruit trees.

Nothing for the stranger
Rabbi Nathaniel commented that the people of Sodom refused to give food to the stranger or traveler, and they even constructed fences above their gardens so that no bird flying by could eat from their trees. (Pirke de-Rabbi Eliezer 25)

Keep it all for ourselves
Because of their wealth, the people of Sodom became haughty. They said to one another: "Since gold and silver flow from our land, why should we allow strangers to visit in our borders, eat our food, use our resources, and share what is ours? They will only take what we have, and there will be less for us. Let's keep them from entering, and let's drive out those who get in as soon as possible—especially the poor or the sick ones." (Tosefta *to* Sotah 3; Sanhedrin *109a*)

Rather than being willing to share their wealth and good fortune with others, the people of Sodom wanted to keep it all for themselves. They expelled immigrants, strangers, or travelers. They chased away the poor and the sick and allowed no one in who would be a "burden" to their city. They felt no responsibility for others.

According to the rabbis, they went a step further in their selfishness. They developed clever ways of stealing from visitors without breaking the law. For example, when a stranger entered the gates of Sodom with grain, they would each steal only a few grains from his bags until the grain was gone. In that way no Sodomite could be taken to court for stealing. And, if the visitor took a Sodomite to court for taking his grain, the Sodomite would tell the judge, "I took nothing, just a few grains." (*Sanhedrin* 109a)

But that is not all. According to the rabbis, the Sodomites also created laws forbidding any citizen of Sodom from feeding the hungry, from offering help to the poor, or from healing the sick.

The proclamation of Sodom
Rabbi Yehudah said: The leaders of Sodom made a proclamation in which they declared: "Anyone who gives even a loaf of bread to the poor or the needy shall be put to death by fire." (Pirke de-Rabbi Eliezer 25)

In Sodom, "kindness to strangers" was against the law! If a citizen of Sodom happened to feel compassion for a needy person and offered him support, that citizen could be convicted of breaking the law and be put to death. According to the rabbis, that is what happened to Lot's daughter, Pelotit.

Lot's daughter is punished
Pelotit, the daughter of Lot, saw a poor person seeking bread on the streets. Her heart was filled with compassion. So what did she do? Each day she drew water for him and gave him bread and other food to eat. When the leaders of Sodom discovered that she was helping a poor man live, they put her to death. (Pirke de-Rabbi Eliezer 25)

The great evil of Sodom was that cruelty became public policy. The leaders made oppression and abuse of the needy the law of their city. Even the courts, the place where most societies look for justice, promoted injustice. Judges sided with the rich and treated the needy without pity or fairness.

> **Their evil courts and judges**
> *Rabbi Joshua ben Korchah commented that the leaders of Sodom appointed judges who were dishonest. They lied, they cheated, they oppressed strangers. They allowed wayfarers to enter Sodom, then convicted them of breaking the law. Afterwards, they robbed them of their possessions and expelled them from the city.* (Pirke de-Rabbi Eliezer 25)

Ibn Ezra

According to the Spanish Jewish interpreter Abraham ibn Ezra (1092–1167), not one citizen of Sodom protested the cruel treatment of strangers. Instead, they remained silent. They chose the safety of "not getting involved." They refused to serve in public office or try to change the evil laws that had been passed. Because these good people chose indifference rather than opposition to evil, they were destroyed with the rest of the city.

So why were the people of Sodom and Gomorrah destroyed? The commentators offer the following reasons:

1. They refused to share their wealth and abundant riches with others.

2. They made fun of those in need and deliberately made their lives more miserable.

3. They refused to care for the sick, aid the poor, help the needy, or offer hospitality to the immigrant or stranger in their midst.

4. Their leaders were so greedy and selfish that they made cruelty a public policy.

5. They went so far as to punish their own citizens who reached out to feed the hungry or provide shelter to the homeless.

6. Their judges practiced dishonesty and robbery, and their courts offered no fair treatment for victims of oppression or injustice.

For all these reasons, the rabbis inform us, Sodom and Gomorrah were destroyed.

But what about our original question? Even if there was one innocent, good person left in Sodom or Gomorrah, should that person have been destroyed with all the evil ones? Must good people suffer because of the bad things others do?

Unfortunately, they do.

Jewish tradition teaches us that we are free to choose between good and evil, between hurting others or helping them. That gift of freedom means that God does not interfere and cannot prevent us from doing things that not only harm us but others as well. God wants us to do the right thing, to be just, kind, loving, and generous, but God cannot force us to make the right choice. We must make our own choices, and we must live with the consequences—even the consequences of the choices that other people make.

God is like a parent who says to his children, "Go out into the world and make your own decisions, but remember that what you do will not only affect you but others as well." When the decisions are good and others benefit, the parent is happy and so is God. When the decisions are bad ones that bring pain and sorrow to innocent people, the parents weep and, perhaps, so does God. But God is not responsible for those bad decisions; human beings are. God cannot be blamed for our failings; we are responsible for them.

God did not plan the destruction of Sodom and Gomorrah. The people brought their end upon themselves and others.

> **Abusing human freedom**
> *. . . much evil is not God's fault but ours. The right to choose is a great good, but we often use it to be creatively malicious. We drive too fast and maim careful drivers and innocent pedestrians. We destroy reputations, squander resources, abuse power, and make the world the worse for our freedom. Some people even choose to be Nazis and engender a Holocaust. They were not compelled by God to do so. They did it freely. They faced their moral responsibility and rejected it, abusing human freedom worse than anything else we know in human history.* (Eugene B. Borowitz, Liberal Judaism, UAHC, New York, 1984, p. 198)

Sodom and Gomorrah were destroyed because, as we have seen, their people were guilty of "abusing human freedom." They brought on their own destruction—and the death of many innocent people—because they deliberately chose cruelty over charity, selfishness over caring, and greed over sharing.

PEREK GIMEL: *What Is Loyalty to God?*

The story of Abraham being called by God to sacrifice his son, Isaac, is a frightening one. It was also considered one of the most important events in the Torah. The rabbis, who divided and assigned portions of Torah to be read in the synagogue on Shabbat and on the holidays, titled it the *Akedah,* meaning "the binding for sacrifice," and chose it for reading on Rosh Hashanah. They believed that it was a "test" of Abraham's loyalty to God.

In the story, Abraham is told to bring Isaac to the land of Moriah and to offer him as a sacrifice on one of the high places there. Abraham follows God's orders but, just as he is about to kill his son, an angel of God stops him, telling him to sacrifice a ram instead. "For now I know," says the angel, "that you fear God, since you have not withheld your son, your favored one, from Me."

What is this strange story about?

Some say that, to test the strength of Abraham's loyalty, God ordered him to kill Isaac, his son. And, without hesitation, without asking any questions, without even consulting Sarah, Abraham followed God's orders. In doing so, he not only proved himself loyal to God, but he also showed the world what true faith is all about.

Rambam (Maimonides)

In his book *Guide for the Perplexed,* Moses Maimonides explained Abraham's test in the following way:

> The purpose of all tests mentioned in the Torah is to teach human beings how they are to act. . . . Abraham is commanded to sacrifice his son. . . . And, because he feared God and loved to do what God commanded, he thought little of his beloved child, and set aside all his hopes concerning him, and agreed to kill him. . . . Therefore, the angel said to him: "For now I know that you fear God," which means that from Abraham's action . . . we can learn how far we must go in the fear of God.

Many interpreters would criticize Maimonides' description of Abraham's test as an example of "blind faith." Abraham did as he was told; he did not protest. He did not say to God, "How can You do this to Sarah and me?" Nor did he take the side of his son and argue, "But he is a child. How can a just God who was willing to save Sodom if there were ten righteous people in the city now ask for the sacrifice of a child?" Instead, Abraham seems to follow "blindly" the command to take Isaac and offer him as a sacrifice on Mount Moriah.

Is that what Jewish tradition teaches us? Are we to follow the commandments of our faith without questioning them? Are we disloyal if we express doubts about what Jewish tradition says God "commands" us to do?

There is another interpretation of the *Akedah* that is also about "loyalty to God," but it is one that makes room for serious questions.

> *When God commanded Abraham, "Take your son . . ." Abraham did not set out immediately. He asked, "Which son?" God answered, "Your favored one . . ." Then Abraham said, "But I have two sons, Ishmael and Isaac. And one is favored by his mother, and the other is favored by his mother." So God answered: "Take the one whom you love . . ." And Abraham replied, "I love them both, so how can I choose?" Finally, God told him, "Take Isaac!"* (Pirke de-Rabbi Eliezer *31*)

According to some interpreters, Abraham had several questions and doubts about what God had commanded him to do. He did not march off immediately toward Mount Moriah. His was not a "blind faith"—but a questioning one. Because he wanted to be sure that he understood what he was being asked to do, he asked questions and evaluated the answers. He put to work his reasoning powers and examined what it was that God was asking him to do.

After hearing God's command, he waited until the next morning before setting out to fulfill it. He was not reckless or impetuous, but, instead, he gave himself time to think about it and to analyze the consequences of what he was being asked to do. Because it was one of the most important decisions of his life, he considered it carefully.

Furthermore, as Abraham was about to act on his decision and plunge his knife into Isaac, he was capable of reconsideration. His questions continued to the very end. He was constantly reexamining his understanding of what it was that God wanted of him. And, when the angel told him, "Do not raise your hand against the boy," Abraham was able to change what he had thought to do.

Abravanel

Abraham's example of faith
This story of Abraham's faith is an example, a banner for all the peoples of the world to follow. (Don Isaac Abravanel)

Loyalty to God does not mean "blind faith." Sometimes it means asking difficult questions about what it is that we should or should not be doing. Sometimes it means being willing to take risks for what we believe is just and right. Sometimes it means delaying action until the facts are analyzed carefully. Sometimes it means being willing to reconsider opinions and to make changes when presented with new evidence or a better perspective.

The *Akedah* is a story about Abraham's struggle to understand what it means to be loyal to God. He is an example of a person who tested his faith with questions and weighed his decisions carefully. He was not afraid to face doubts or to get all the facts. If necessary, he was ready to make sacrifices for what he believed, but he was also ready to rethink his convictions and commitments.

Perhaps for all those reasons this story of Abraham is considered one of the great examples of religious faith and loyalty to God.

QUESTIONS FOR STUDY AND DISCUSSION

1. Are we, as Jews, obligated to offer hospitality to strangers? Were non-Jews justified in not opening their homes to Jews during the Holocaust? Are there situations, when loved ones might be endangered, that require us to refuse giving others hospitality?

2. Read the story of Sheba, son of Bichri, in II Samuel 20:1–26. How does it compare to our story of Lot?

3. In what ways is the story of Sodom similar to the stories of Cain and Abel, Noah, and the building of the Tower of Babel?

4. Since other people and religions in Abraham's time believed in child sacrifice, perhaps the real message of the story of Abraham's willingness to sacrifice Isaac is to demonstrate that God does not require human sacrifice. If that is so, then what are the ways in which modern society "sacrifices" children? How can we protect our children from being victimized by the evil elements of the culture that surrounds us?

PARASHAT CHAYE SARAH
Genesis 23:1–25:18

While *Chaye Sarah* may be translated as "Sarah's lifetime," this Torah portion actually tells us about Sarah's death. Abraham seeks to purchase the cave of Machpelah, in Hebron, for her burial. Ephron, the son of Zohar, owns the land, and Abraham bargains with him for the purchase. After the burial, Abraham sends a trusted servant back to his native land to find a wife for Isaac. The servant chooses Rebekah and returns with her to the Land of Israel where Isaac takes her for his wife.

OUR TARGUM

· 1 ·

Sarah, Abraham's wife and the first Mother of the people of Israel, died at the age of one hundred and twenty-seven years. She died in the town of Kiriath-arba, known today as Hebron, located nineteen miles south of Jerusalem in the Judean Hills.

Abraham was filled with sadness at her death and wanted to find an appropriate burial place for her and for his family. So he spoke to the people of Heth who owned property around Hebron and said to them: "I am a foreigner living here with you. Sell me a burial place for my dead."

They replied: "You are a very special person among us. Simply choose the place you wish, and we will be happy to give it to you."

Abraham bowed, as was the custom in such negotiations, and told the people of Heth: "If you are so willing to be helpful, please go to Ephron the Hittite, the son of Zohar, and tell him that I would like to buy the cave of Machpelah, which is at the edge of his land. Also, inform him that I am willing to pay the total amount of its worth."

Now, Ephron happened to be among the people of Heth with whom Abraham was speaking. He stepped forward and told Abraham: "In the presence of my people, I present you, for no cost at all, with the cave of Machpelah and the field around it. Go bury your dead there."

Abraham thanked him but said: "Allow me to pay the full price."

Ephron replied: "My friend, what's a piece of land worth four hundred shekels of silver between us? Take it from me and bury your dead."

Instead of taking the land for no payment, Abraham gave Ephron the full price of four hundred shekels of silver before the people of Heth. The payment gave him all rights to the cave of Machpelah and to the field and trees around it. Having made the purchase, Abraham buried Sarah.

· 2 ·

After Sarah's death, Abraham called his trusted servant to his side and asked him to take an oath that he would not allow Isaac to marry a Canaanite woman but, rather, would return to Abraham's native land and find a wife for Isaac from among his people. The servant promised he would do so and set off for Aram-naharaim, which means "Aram of the two rivers," which was also called "Haran." It is located in northern Syria.

When the servant reached the place, he rested his camels near a well and prayed to God. "O God of my master Abraham, grant me good luck today. As I wait here and the women of the city are coming out to draw water from this well, let the woman You have chosen to be Isaac's future wife answer me when I say, 'Please lower your jar that I may drink from it.' Let her tell me, 'Drink, and I will water your camels.'"

As the servant finished his prayer, Rebekah the daughter of Bethuel, who was the son of Milcah the wife of Abraham's brother Nahor, came out with a jar on her shoulder. She was very beautiful, and, when she filled her jar, the servant ran to her side and said, "Please lower your jar that I may drink from it." And she replied, "Drink, and I will also water your camels."

After she had done so, Rebekah ran home and told her brother, Laban, about the man. He came out to welcome him and to invite him to be their guest. The servant accepted their hospitality, but, before he would take any food, he insisted on

telling them about his prayer and how Rebekah had answered it with generosity not only for him but for his animals. He then informed them that this was all a sign that Rebekah was the woman destined to be Isaac's wife.

Laban and Bethuel agreed and asked Rebekah if she would leave them to go with the servant back to the Land of Israel to marry Isaac. She was willing and so departed without delay.

As they reached the land, Isaac happened to be out walking in the field. Rebekah saw him and asked the servant, "Who is that man?"

"That is my master," he answered. Rebekah covered her face with her veil, which was the custom of modesty at the time.

After the servant told Isaac all that had happened to him in Aram-naharaim, Isaac took Rebekah home. They married, and he loved her and found comfort with her after the death of his mother, Sarah.

THEMES

Parashat Chaye Sarah contains four important themes:

1. Jewish attitudes and practices at the time of death.
2. Paying the full price for what we acquire.

3. Beauty.
4. The meaning of "love."

PEREK ALEF: *Mourning the Death of a Loved One*

When someone we love dies, we experience deep sorrow. We miss that person's presence and caring. We miss the support and all that we shared. At times we are angry and ask, "Why did that loved one have to die?" At other times we understand that death is something that happens to every living thing, but the pain is confusing. We find ourselves wishing to share just another day or a few hours so that we might say some things that we never found the time to say.

Death is so final. We can't turn back the clock.

That must have been the sadness Abraham felt when Sarah died. They had shared so much together. In his grief he must have remembered the close call with death they had both experienced with Abimelech or how upset Sarah had been when she could not become pregnant. He must have recalled how much she loved their son, Isaac, and how jealous she had become of Hagar and Ishmael. They had been partners for so many years. He would miss her. Little wonder that Abraham wept and mourned for Sarah.

Abraham must also have realized how helpful it was to share his grief with others who were there to comfort him. Talking and weeping with friends is healthy when we lose a loved one. Friends can support us and ease our loneliness and pain. So can the rituals and customs of Jewish tradition.

symbolizes the warmth, wisdom, and love that the dead person brought into the lives of the mourners.

Kaddish and Yizkor: *It is a mitzvah for the mourner to recite the* Kaddish *prayer in memory of the dead at services at home and in the synagogue and to attend* Yizkor *services in honor of those who have died.* Kaddish *and* Yizkor *are ways of giving thanks to God for the gift of life and the continuing influence upon us of those who have died.*

Jewish rituals and customs at the time of mourning are meant to help us face death realistically and to find comfort with friends. Jewish tradition helps us understand that "death is not the end" but that our loved ones continue to live in the memories and influences they leave behind.

This healthy-minded approach of Jewish teachers through the ages provided not only beautiful rituals for the expression of grief but also a warning that "if we dwell too long on our loss, we embitter our hearts and harm ourselves and those about us." In this regard, the Torah's description of Abraham's mourning for Sarah provides us with a very important model.

His grief was not endless. Abraham did not stop functioning or taking on responsibilities. While his heart was filled with sadness, he knew that he had to accept her death and get on with the task of her burial and the challenges of his life.

Jewish mourning customs
Keriah *is the symbolic cutting of one's garment or a black ribbon at the time of the funeral. It symbolizes the "tearing" that occurs when we lose a loved one.*
Comforting the mourners: *It is a mitzvah to visit a house of mourning to comfort those who have lost a loved one.*
Shivah candle: *After returning from the cemetery, mourners customarily light a special candle that burns for seven days. The* shivah *candle*

A time to mourn
A season is set for everything, a time for every experience under heaven:
A time for being born and a time for dying. . .
A time for weeping and a time for laughing,
A time for wailing and a time for dancing . . .
(Ecclesiastes 3:1–2, 4)

My child, let your tears fall for the dead, and as one who is deeply suffering begin your period of mourning. . . .

> *Let your weeping be bitter and your crying genuine; observe the period of mourning according to the merit of the one you have lost, for one day, or two, to avoid criticism; then be comforted for your sorrow. For too much sorrow results in death, and sorrow of heart saps one's strength. . . . (Ecclesiasticus 38:16–18)*

Like many people who suffer a loss, Abraham must have had moments when he felt cheated that Sarah would no longer be at his side. He must have missed her and been lonely. He may even have wondered if he could go on living without her sensitivity, love, and support. But his mourning and grieving helped overcome his loss. He was strengthened by those who cared for him and comforted by his traditions. He did not become embittered by his grief. Despite the pain of his loss, the Torah tells us that he "rose" from his sorrow and went on with his life.

PEREK BET: *Paying the Full Price*

After Sarah's death, Abraham seeks a burial place for her. He comes before the leaders of the Hittites, who then occupied the Land of Israel, and asks them if he might purchase a plot of land.

They bargain with him according to the traditions of the ancient Middle East. First they flatter him. "You're a great man," they tell him. "Please bury your dead in the best place in our burial grounds."

Abraham responds by thanking them for their offer. Then he requests that he be permitted to purchase the cave of Machpelah, owned by Ephron, son of Zohar. He says to them: "Let him sell it to me, at the full price, for a burial site in your midst."

Ephron hears his request and makes a big show by offering the cave for free to Abraham. In doing so, however, he cleverly announces to everyone listening the worth of the land. "A piece of land worth four hundred shekels of silver—what is that between you and me? Go and bury your dead."

Abraham refuses the gift. He does not want a free piece of land. Instead, he insists on paying the full price. And he does so, publicly—"in the hearing of the Hittites."

Ramban (Nachmanides)

"I will give it to you . . ."
Nachmanides points up the careful steps that Abraham took in order to establish his "legal" claim to the land. "First he paid the full price, then he took symbolic legal possession of the field and cave. In that way he established them as his possession in the presence of the people of the city, of all who sat on the council of his town, the merchants and the residents who happened to be there, and after that he buried her." (Genesis 23:11)

Malbim

In his commentary, Malbim writes: "Abraham said, 'Let me pay the price of the land; accept it from me. . . .' That, too, was wisely said. For after Ephron had given him the land . . . he might have changed his mind. . . . So Abraham said to him, 'If it were a gift, you could cancel it. For a gift is really not a legitimate possession. But, if it is purchased by an appropriate sum of money, the law is on our side. . . .'"

Most biblical scholars point out that four hundred shekels of silver was a very high price and that Ephron was taking advantage of Abraham's grief and need to find a burial place for Sarah. Despite the price, however, Abraham wanted official title to the land. He did not want a gift that might be taken back or one that might obligate him to Ephron sometime in the future.

So Abraham followed all the correct and formal

procedures of purchase. As a result, the field and cave "passed from the Hittites to Abraham"—and to the Jewish people—as the first purchased possession of the Land of Israel.

Paying for what we purchase

They tell the story of a pious Jew who entered a store to purchase some item he desired. When he asked the price, the merchant quoted a very low amount. The pious Jew understood that the merchant had recognized him and wanted to pay him special respect and honor. For that reason he had lowered the price of the item he wanted to purchase. So the pious Jew said to him, "I have come to you to buy at market value, not at a price set by the fear of God."

For the pious Jew, paying the "price set" was the just thing to do. He did not want to take advantage of the merchant's respect or to owe him any favors.

Abraham was not only willing to pay the full price, but he insisted upon it. Was he foolish? Should he have taken advantage of the Hittites' respect for him? Should he have tried to bargain with Ephron or even taken the burial place as a gift?

Most commentators argue that, by paying the full price even though Ephron's price was high, and by following the correct legal procedures of purchase, Abraham made certain that no one could later come along and raise questions about his rightful ownership of the land. Had he taken the land as a gift, or at a reduced price, he might have felt himself obligated to do favors for Ephron, or others might have questioned the right of his family to the land.

PEREK GIMEL: *Rebekah's Beauty*

The marriage of Isaac and Rebekah was arranged by Abraham's servant. After Sarah died, Abraham sent his servant back to his homeland to choose a bride for his son. The challenge for the servant was a difficult one. How do you find the most suitable marriage partner? What standards do you use? How do you judge that a person will be loving and loyal?

When the servant arrived in Aram-naharaim he met Rebekah at a well. The Torah describes her as *tovat mareh*, "very beautiful." By that description most readers would assume that the Torah is commenting on her appearance, emphasizing that Rebekah was a physically attractive woman.

That may be so. Then, again, the expression *tovat mareh* may mean much more than "good looks."

Defining Rebekah's real beauty

Rebekah deliberately planned her kindness to the servant. . . . First she provided him with water, then she ran to get water for his animals. In doing so she prevented the servant from feeling that he needed to help her. (Chaim ibn Attar, 1696–1748, Or ha-Chaim)

Meklenburg

Rebekah carefully thought about each word she spoke so as not to offend anyone. She did not repeat the same words used by the servant. She had said, "Drink, and I will also water your camels." She was sensitive about equating him with his animals, so she said, "Drink, my lord." Later on, after he had enjoyed his fill of water, she offered to give some to his animals. (Jacob Tsvi Meklenburg, 1785–1865, Ha-Ketav ve-ha-Kabbalah)

She stopped the servant from drinking too much because one must be careful not to have too much cold water after being in the heat and sun. But, in order to prevent him from thinking that she did not want him to have enough water to drink, she told him, "I will draw water for your camels until they finish drinking." In that way the servant knew that she was not selfishly holding back water from either him or his animals. (Rabbi Naphtali Zvi Judah Berlin, Ha-Emek Davar)

For the teachers of Torah, Rebekah is *tovat mareh*. She is not only physically beautiful, but she is a beautiful "person." She is kind and helpful to the servant even though he is a stranger. She is thoughtful of his feelings and careful of what she says to him. And her concern is not only about him but also about his animals.

Her beauty is not in what she is wearing. There is no description of her clothing. Nor are we told about her complexion—whether her skin was soft—or whether she was thin or plump, tall or short. The details we are given are about how she treats other people, how she speaks to them, how she offers hospitality, and how she reaches out to aid a stranger and a wanderer in her land.

Before Rebekah knows who the servant is, or that he represents Abraham and has come seeking a bride for Isaac, she demonstrates that she is a generous and giving person. That is what defines her as *tovat mareh* in the servant's eyes—and in the considered opinion of Jewish tradition.

PEREK DALET: *What Does the Torah Mean by "Love"?*

The Isaac-Rebekah romance seems to have begun with "love at first sight."

After a long journey from Aram-naharaim, Abraham's servant and Rebekah enter the Land of Israel and arrive in the area of Beer-lahai-roi in the Negev. It is near sunset and Isaac is out walking in the field. He is alone, still in sorrow over his mother's death.

Rebekah is riding on her camel and sees the lonely figure walking in the field. "Who is that man walking in the field toward us?" she asks the servant. He recognizes Isaac and tells her, "That is my master."

Rebekah and Isaac meet. The servant tells him about his journey and, afterwards, Isaac takes her to Sarah's tent. Then the Torah tells us "he took Rebekah as his wife, and Isaac loved her. . . ."

It's a strange twist for high romance. One would have thought that love came before marriage. Here, however, it seems to come afterwards.

Hirsch

Love is blind

A mere glance into the novels of true life teaches us the vast difference between love before marriage and after. . . . Such love [before] is blind, and therefore every step into the future leads to new disappointments. Jewish marriage, however, is described here as follows: He married Rebekah, and he loved her. The wedding is not the summit but only the seed of future love. (Samson Raphael Hirsch, 1808–1888, Timeless Torah, Phillip Feldheim, Inc., New York, 1957, on Genesis 24:67, pp. 53–54)

Another view about love

The meaning of the words, "he took Rebekah as his wife, and Isaac loved her . . ." are meant to indicate that he was deeply grieved by his mother's death and found no real comfort until he found love with Rebekah. It was that love that really comforted him.

In the Targum Onkelos, an early Aramaic translation of the Torah used in the synagogue, we read: "And Isaac brought her into the tent and, behold, she was like Sarah his mother." That is why the Torah mentions that Isaac "loved her." It is meant to teach us that, because of Rebekah's righteousness and the kindness of her deeds, Isaac loved her and was comforted by her. (Nachmanides on Genesis 24:67)

Those who comment on the Torah's description that Isaac first married Rebekah and then he loved her do not mean to deny that there is "love at first sight." What they are saying is that there is a significant difference between "infatuation" and the evolution of mature love.

In his book *Consecrated Unto Me*, Rabbi Roland B. Gittelsohn writes that there are four differences between *infatuation* and *love*. "The first is the test of time. . . . Except for the rare instance where infatuation leads to love, it begins more dramatically, develops far more rapidly, and expires while love may still be incubating." The second test "is to see whether the emphasis is on the self or the other person, on getting or on giving." The third test is whether the couple is "interested exclusively in themselves." Finally, "infatuation is a purely physical experience while love is both physical and spiritual."

> ### Defining love
>
> *Love is a consuming desire to share one's whole life both physically and spiritually with another person . . . to share that person's sorrows and pains no less than his/her pleasures and joys. In love one is at least as anxious to give as to receive. Love is a relationship in which each partner is able to develop his/her own abilities and fulfill his/her own hopes in far greater measure than either could have done alone. (Roland B. Gittelsohn,* Consecrated Unto Me, *UAHC, New York, 1965, p. 19.*

According to the biblical story, Isaac and Rebekah quite obviously began their relationship with "infatuation." They were attracted to each other. They wanted to spend time exclusively with each other. Yet, according to the commentators, their powerful attraction grew into a mature commitment and a readiness for marriage. Rebekah comforted Isaac about the loss of his mother, Sarah. He may have supported her in those moments when she longed for her family in distant Aramnaharaim. They learned how to reconcile their differences and to respect each other. Finally, through time and sharing, they came to love each other.

Jewish tradition teaches that, while our romantic meetings may be the miraculous work of God, and that we may be fortunate enough to "fall in love at first sight," the real success of our love relationships depends upon how we work at them. Love must be nurtured and negotiated each day. There are no instant and magic guarantees that love will grow and mature. It all rests on the quality of the commitment, honesty, trust, and openness both people build into their relationship.

In a time when the stress is on "romance" and immediate gratification, the Jewish wisdom that "the wedding is not the summit but only the seed of future love" is a significant warning and lesson.

QUESTIONS FOR STUDY AND DISCUSSION

1. What are some of the lessons this Torah portion teaches us about preparing for the death of a loved one and about dealing with our loss? How are the mourning customs of Jewish tradition helpful to us in times of sorrow?

2. We are all tempted "to buy at the best price." Should we take discounts and deals from friends? What are the benefits and the problems that come from accepting such bargains?

3. From what the commentators say about Rebekah, can we define a Jewish view of "beauty"? How do the views of "beauty" in Jewish tradition compare with those of our modern society?

4. Abraham's servant devised a test by which he could determine Rebekah's values and the values of her family. What are your most important values? How can you determine whether or not your partner in a possible long-term romantic relationship shares those values? What test or questions should be considered when choosing such a partner?

PARASHAT TOLEDOT
Genesis 25:19–28:9

Toledot may be translated as "generations," and "history." This Torah portion begins by describing the birth of Esau and Jacob, the twins born to Rebekah and Isaac. Esau is a rugged person of the outdoors; Jacob is a gentle person, preferring the quiet of his tent. Isaac favors Esau, and Rebekah loves Jacob. While still young, Esau sells his birthright to Jacob for a pot of stew. Later, at age forty, Esau brings pain to his parents by marrying two Hittite women. When Isaac is old and near death, Rebekah and Jacob trick him into giving Jacob the special blessing he had intended for Esau. Esau discovers what they have done and vows to kill his brother. Fearing for Jacob's life and desiring that he marry someone from her people in Paddan-aram, Rebekah persuades Isaac to send Jacob to her brother, Laban. Meanwhile, Esau took his first cousin, Mahalath the daughter of Ishmael, as his third wife.

OUR TARGUM

· 1 ·

For a time after their marriage, Isaac and Rebekah have difficulty conceiving. Finally, Rebekah becomes pregnant, but she suffers great pain. When she asks the reason for her discomfort, God tells her that she is carrying twins and that, from them, two battling nations will emerge.

When the children are born, the eldest is given the name Esau, meaning "hairy," because his body is covered with hair. The younger child is named Jacob, meaning "heel," because at birth his hand was holding onto Esau's heel.

As they grow, Esau becomes a skillful hunter while Jacob remains quietly within the camp. Isaac favors Esau because he brings him food from his hunting; Rebekah favors Jacob.

Once, while Jacob is cooking some stew, Esau returns from a hunt very hungry. "Give me some of that stuff you are cooking," he demands of Jacob. "Sell me your birthright," Jacob responds. "I'm starved. What do I care about a birthright!" Esau answers. So Jacob gives him some stew, and Esau gives up his birthright.

· 2 ·

Later, at a time of famine, Isaac visits Abimelech, king of the Philistines, in the Negev town of Gerar. As happened before with Abraham and Sarah, the men of Gerar admire Rebekah. Fearing that they will harm him, Isaac tells them that she is his "sister." When Abimelech discovers what has happened, he offers Isaac protection and, as a result, Isaac prospers greatly in the land of the Philistines.

As Isaac becomes richer, the Philistines envy him and stop up his wells. Seeing the trouble between them, Abimelech tells Isaac: "Leave our land, for you are becoming too powerful for us." Afterwards, Isaac travels to Beer-sheba, where Abimelech visits him in order to confirm a peace treaty between them.

· 3 ·

Near the time of his death, Isaac asks Esau to go out hunting and to bring him back a "tasty dish," promising that he will reward Esau with a special blessing.

Rebekah overhears their conversation and persuades Jacob to dress in Esau's clothing and to put on hairy skins so that he will fool Isaac into believing that he is Esau. "What if I appear to him as a trickster and he curses me?" Jacob asks his mother. Rebekah answers, "I will take your curse upon me."

Their disguise fools Isaac. He believes that Jacob is Esau, and he blesses him with the words: "Let peoples serve you, and nations bow to

you. . . . Cursed be they who curse you, blessed they who bless you."

When Esau returns from the field with a "tasty dish" as his father had requested, Isaac informs him that he has already given away his blessing. Esau is furious. Threatening to kill Jacob, he shouts: "First he took away my birthright, and now he has taken away my blessing!"

· 4 ·

At forty years of age, Esau married two Hittite women. The mixed marriage upset both his parents. Fearing that Jacob would also intermarry, Rebekah urged Isaac to send Jacob to her homeland in Paddan-aram where he might find a wife from the daughters of her brother, Laban. Isaac follows Rebekah's suggestion. In the meantime, Esau took his first cousin, Mahalath the daughter of Ishmael, as his third wife.

THEMES

Parashat Toledot contains three important themes:

1. Jealousy between brothers; the creation of stereotypes and prejudice.
2. Favoritism by parents.
3. Problems of intermarriage.

PEREK ALEF: *Esau and Jacob—The Bitter Struggle between Brothers*

The Torah tells us that, even before Esau and Jacob were born, Rebekah felt them battling with each other in her womb. It is natural for a pregnant mother to feel the fetus "kicking" and "punching" at the wall of her uterus. With twins the activity is doubled. Physicians identify such activity as "signs of life."

According to the Torah, however, what Rebekah felt was more than normal activity even from twins. She sensed that the babies she was carrying were to become two nations and that the older would eventually serve the younger.

The future struggle between the brothers was dramatized at their birth by the names they were given. The elder, Esau, was also called "Edom," from the Hebrew *adom* meaning "red," because he was born with a bloody red mat of hair covering his body and grew to crave reddish stew. Within the Torah, he is identified as the father of the people of Edom and of the Amalekites, who were bitter enemies of the Jews. Later, during the persecution of the Jewish people by the Romans, the rabbis often referred to the government of Rome as "Edom" or "Esau."

The second born was called Jacob, from the Hebrew *akev* meaning "heel," because, as the Torah indicates, he was holding onto Esau's heel as he emerged from Rebekah's womb. Later within our Torah story, Jacob's name is changed to Israel and becomes the historic name for the Jewish people.

From Esau to Amalek to Haman
Within the Torah we are informed: "This is the line of Esau—that is, Edom. . . . Timna was a concubine of Esau's son Eliphaz; she bore Amalek. . . ." (Genesis 36:1–12)

The Torah tells us that Amalek attacked the helpless people of Israel at Rephidim just after they had left Egypt. Because Amalek had taken advantage of the Israelites' weakness, Moses declared that God would "be at war with Amalek throughout the ages." (Exodus 17:8–16)

We are also told of a King Agag of Amalek who is connected by the author of the Book of Esther with Haman "son of Hamedatha the Agagite." Clearly, the intention here is to identify all the enemies of the Jewish people as the descendants of Esau-Edom. (I Samuel 15:8 and Esther 3:1)

Both before and after the destruction of the Temple by the Romans in 70 C.E., the rabbis used the name "Edom" as a code name for Rome. They believed that, one day, Esau-Edom-Rome would be defeated and that Jacob-Israel would be victorious. They predicted that "God will throw Edom-Rome out of heaven. . . . Edom-Rome will be slaughtered. . . . Edom-Rome will be destroyed by fire." (Pesikta de-Rav Kahana 4:9)

For many Jewish commentators, and perhaps for those who wrote the Torah, Esau and Jacob were more than just human beings. They were not only the sons of Rebekah and Isaac, but they were two different nations at war with each other. Their personalities were very different, and their descendants became enemies throughout all history. They were not only Esau and Jacob, but they became Israel and Edom, then Israel and Rome, then Israel and all who plotted the destruction of the Jewish people. Esau-Edom-Rome became a code name for all the opponents of the Jewish people.

How does it happen that names for two innocent children become labels for bitter enemies and memories? How do such stereotypes develop? Perhaps for three reasons:

1. *Historical experience:* Often our viewpoints or prejudices grow out of what history has taught us. In the case of the early Israelites, the descendants of Esau, who were Amalekites, attacked weak and helpless Jews just after their Exodus from Egypt. Later, in about 485 B.C.E., the Edomites led an alliance of nations seeking to end Jewish rule of Jerusalem. Writing at that time, the prophet Obadiah angrily declared:

Thus said my Lord God concerning Edom:
I will make you least among nations;
You shall be most despised. . . .
For the outrage to your brother Jacob,
Disgrace shall engulf you,
And you shall perish forever. . . .
And no survivor shall be left of the house of Esau.
(Obadiah 1:1, 2, 10, 18)

Obadiah's connection of Esau with Edom is similar to the link made by the biblical author of the Book of Esther between Haman and Esau-Edom and Amalek. Haman, who is identified as the son of Hamedatha the Agagite, is linked with King Agag the Amalekite.

Making the connection of Haman with the Amalekites or of Rome with Edom must have seemed very logical. After all, their goal was the same. They opposed Jewish survival. Their hands were bloody with the massacre, plunder, rape, and ruin of Jews and their communities.

For each generation it was as if the battle between the brothers, Jacob and Esau, never ended. Jews and non-Jews were still at war with one another. The old names still applied. Jacob was the persecuted Jew, and Esau-Edom the non-Jewish persecutor. Because the history of prejudice and brutality was so painful, it seemed to justify the continued use of "Esau-Edom-Rome-Haman-Hitler" as the stereotype name for all the enemies of the Jewish people.

2. *The need to depersonalize the enemy:* Bitter memories, however, are only one source of stereotypes. Special names, or labels, or numbers are invented and used because they are a way of categorizing those we fear or dislike. They make it easier to express our suspicion and hostility because they rob people of their individuality.

For example, by forcing Anne Frank to wear a yellow star, the Nazis, who took her off to be killed in a concentration camp, no longer had to deal with the fact that she was a teenager, a gifted writer, a person with hopes and dreams like many of their own children. By labeling her, they had removed her individuality and justified her death.

When Jews are called "kikes" or "sheenies," or Blacks are called "niggers," or Spanish-Americans are called "spics," or Italians are called "wops," the names are not simply insulting, but they are a means of confirming that those with different names are inferior as well. Having depersonalized people into categories, we can more easily dismiss their ideas or potential contributions. "Blacks are not fit to manage teams," a baseball executive told a news conference. "The Japanese have a talent for copying everything and creating nothing," a businessman announced to his computer company board. Labeling people allows us to turn them into objects of scorn—and sometimes into targets for violence.

3. *The need to organize against the enemy:* Slogans, stereotypes, and names also fuel our natural tendency to rally against real or perceived enemies. They not only define our opponents, but they fill us with a comfortable feeling of identity with others who share our views. They confirm our conviction that we are on the superior and correct side of the battle. We become the "good guys" while the targets of our hostility are, obviously, all the "bad guys" who are plotting against us. Having named our common adversary, we can organize for the war against "evil."

For example, by portraying Jews as "Christ-killers," non-Jews could easily organize and justify violence against them. By portraying Japanese-Americans as "dangerous aliens" during the Second World War, leaders of the United States justified placing thousands of them in concentration camps. By labeling political opponents as "enemies of the state," Joseph Stalin justified the exile and murder of millions of Soviet citizens.

Yet, prejudice also works the other way. Sometimes the victim becomes so battered and violated that he comes to see the rest of the world as "Esau-Edom," the enemy. That has been so for many Jews. Because so many suffered the bitterness of pogroms and exile—or in the twentieth century watched helplessly while the Nazis slaughtered their parents, husbands, wives, and children—many Jews still retain suspicions about the friendship of non-Jews. They still consider themselves endangered as Jacob-Israel against Esau-Edom. Such names, and the prejudices they contain, are abandoned very slowly.

Will there ever be a time when human beings will forgive and trust one another? Will Jews and non-Jews, the Jacobs and the Esaus, ever be brothers and sisters and not enemies? And what is our responsibility in creating such a time of understanding and goodwill?

In answer to our questions, the rabbis offer the following fascinating story based upon the Torah commandment "You shall not hate an Edomite, for an Edomite is your fellow human being." (Deuteronomy 23:8)

> Rabbi Elazar ben Shammua was once walking by the seashore when he noticed a boat sinking at sea. A moment later he watched as a man holding onto a plank of wood floated onto shore. Other Jews were walking by. Because the man was naked, he covered himself and pleaded: "I am a son of Esau, your brother. I have lost everything. Please give me a garment to cover myself." The Jews refused and said: "Your people have treated our people with cruelty. Therefore, may all your people be stripped bare as you are today." The man then turned to Rabbi Elazar and said, "You are an honorable man; please help me." Rabbi Elazar took off a garment and gave it to him. Then he brought him to his home, fed him, and gave him money with which to begin his life again.
>
> When the emperor died, the rescued man succeeded him. He ordered that all Jews in his state be killed. The Jews turned to Rabbi Elazar and asked him to plead for them. When the man, who was now the ruler, saw Rabbi Elazar standing before him, he said: "Does not your Torah teach 'You shall not hate an Edomite, for he is your brother'? I told your people that I was the son of Esau, and they treated me with hatred, not with kindness."
>
> Rabbi Elazar replied: "Though they are guilty of breaking the law of the Torah, forgive them."
>
> The king, recalling what Elazar had done for him, answered: "Because of what you did for me, I will forgive them."
>
> (*Ecclesiastes Rabbah* 11:1)

Rabbi Elazar ben Judah taught that "the most beautiful thing a person can do is to forgive." (*Rokeach* 13C) Bearing grudges only prolongs hostility. Forgiveness and understanding are the only genuine ways to reconciliation, cooperation, and peace. Perpetuating prejudices through slogans and names only increases human suffering. Perhaps that is why the Torah warns us: "You shall not hate an Edomite, for he is your brother.

You shall not hate an Egyptian, for you were a stranger in his land." (Deuteronomy 23:8)

PEREK BET: *Parental Favoritism*

Our Torah portion not only contains the story about the beginnings of the historic struggle between Esau-Edom and Jacob-Israel, but it also takes us into the biblical home of Rebekah and Isaac. We are told that the young brothers, Esau and Jacob, have very different personalities. Esau is a hunter; he prefers being outdoors. He is also impatient, demanding, and quick to lose his temper. Jacob is described as a "mild" person, quiet, patient, clever, and calculating.

The two brothers are portrayed as jealous of each other and in constant competition for their parents' interest and affection. To complicate family matters even further, we are told that each parent has chosen a favorite son. Isaac prefers Esau "because he also had a taste for freshly killed game." Rebekah "loved Jacob." Nor do Isaac and Rebekah hide their preferences. When Isaac decides to present his sons with his parental blessing, he tells Esau, not Jacob, to hunt him some fresh game and to prepare it for him. As a reward he promises to give him the gift of his "innermost blessing."

When Rebekah overhears what her husband has promised, she tells Jacob to bring her some game and she will prepare food for his father. Afterwards, she dresses him in animal skins so that Isaac might be tricked into blessing her favorite son, Jacob, instead of Esau. Her trick is successful. Isaac is fooled into blessing Jacob, but the results are tragic. The jealousy between the brothers hardens into hatred.

Did parental favoritism cause the hostility between Jacob and Esau or is such antagonism inevitable between brothers and sisters?

Some interpreters argue that the differences between Jacob and Esau made it impossible for them to get along as brothers. Jacob, they explain, was a quiet, timid, studious person while Esau spent his time trapping animals and associating with those who knew how to use a spear, a knife, and a sword. Jacob was calm and reasonable while

Esau demanded satisfaction immediately, losing his temper if he could not have his way.

A few commentators trace the differences between the brothers to their early childhood. Once, when Esau returned from hunting in the fields, he entered the house, smelled the sweet stew Jacob was cooking, and demanded a bowl of it. "I'm starving," he said. "I want it now."

Knowing that Esau would often make foolish mistakes when pressured or upset, Jacob took advantage of him. He wanted all the privileges of being the firstborn. So he said to Esau, "Sell me your birthright, and I'll give you some stew." Impulsively, Esau agreed.

The differences between them
Rabbi Pinchus said in Rabbi Levi's name that Esau and Jacob were like a myrtle and a wild rosebush growing side by side. When they had fully grown, one produced a sweet fragrance, and the other produced thorns. For thirteen years, both Esau and Jacob studied at school. Afterwards, Jacob continued to study, and Esau became an idolator. Jacob had learned that answers to questions came slowly and through hard work. Esau wanted immediate and easy answers.
(Genesis Rabbah *63:10*)

Rabbi S. Z. Kahana, a modern commentator living in Israel, claims that Esau and Jacob represented two different philosophies of living. "Esau accepts the world as it is: all is well. But Jacob is not satisfied with the world as it is. He recognizes that a great deal remains to be done."
(Heaven on Your Head, *Research Centre of Kabbalah, New York, 1986, p. 34.*)

While most commentators agree that Esau and Jacob had very different personalities, there are some who suggest that the jealousy, distrust, and hatred that developed between them was not their fault but the fault of their parents. Commenting on the relationship between Isaac and Esau, and Rebekah and Jacob, psychologist Haim G. Ginott points out that the competition and jealousy between them "was sparked" by parental favoritism and preferential treatment.

"Why did Isaac and Rebekah show such favoritism?" That is the question.

Abravanel

Don Isaac Abravanel argues that Isaac was simply blinded to Esau's faults. "Affection," Abravanel comments, "ruins judgment." Others suggest that Isaac was aloof, withdrawn, and out of touch with his sons. He spent no time with them. Therefore, he was not aware of their strengths or weaknesses.

Another explanation for Isaac's favoring of Esau is found in *Genesis Rabbah,* an ancient collection of interpretations by the rabbis. There it is suggested that Isaac never recovered from the terror he experienced when his father, Abraham, nearly offered him as a sacrifice on Mount Moriah. He remained fearful all his life and had trouble making decisions. He remained weak and frightened, always leaning on others who displayed strength. For that reason he favored Esau over Jacob.

David Kimchi disagrees. He holds that Isaac was neither weak nor incapable of making clear decisions. Isaac favored Esau because he realized that Esau was weak not strong and, therefore, required more support, more help, more direction, and care if he was to mature as a responsible adult. Isaac considered Esau the weaker son because he saw that Esau was "wild," irresponsible, undisciplined, and uncaring about others. Isaac believed that Esau would change if he gave him gifts and favored him with special attentions and blessings.

As for Rebekah, the commentators nearly all claim that she forced Jacob into dressing up like Esau and into lying about who he was in order to steal the blessing from his brother. One interpreter tells us that Jacob "acted out of duress"; another claims that he pleaded in tears with Rebekah that she not force him to deceive his father. (*Genesis Rabbah;* also *Ha-Ketav ve-ha-Kabbalah* on Genesis 18:2)

Why did Rebekah show such partiality to Jacob?

One view is that she, more than Isaac or anyone else, had a "mother's intuition" that Jacob was especially endowed with powers of wisdom to inherit the leadership of the Jewish people. Before the twins were born, God had told her: "Two nations are in your womb. . . . One people shall be mightier than the other, and the older shall serve the younger." She simply was following her inner voice, favoring the younger child she sensed was to be the "leader." (*Midrash ha-Gadol* 27:13)

Grandfather Abraham also favored Jacob
One tradition of interpretation claims that Abraham also favored Jacob over Esau. He praised his intellectual qualities and disapproved of Esau's wild behavior. Rebekah noted Grandfather Abraham's opinion and was influenced by it. (Louis Ginzberg, Legends of the Jews, *Vol. I, Jewish Publication Society, Philadelphia, 1968, p. 316*)

Esau was treated unjustly
Author Eli Wiesel writes the following about Rebekah's treatment of Esau. "His own mother seemed to resent him. She pushed him aside. Why didn't she love him? Because he preferred games to study? Because his hair was long and red? Because he always walked around armed? Because he was constantly hungry? She was hostile to him, that seems clear. And unjust." (Messengers of God, *Random House, New York, 1976, p. 117*)

Steinsaltz

Rabbi Adin Steinsaltz makes a different argument. He explains that, because Rebekah had

grown up in the "wheeling and dealing" corrupt world of her brother Laban, "she had learned the meaning of cheating, of hypocrisy." She was a realist where Isaac was an "easy victim of duplicity; he was neither suspicious nor afraid because there was no dishonesty in his own heart."

For those reasons, Isaac did not notice Esau's weaknesses but only that he seemed well behaved and did what his father requested of him. On the other hand, Steinsaltz explains that Rebekah "was an expert in such matters. She knew that someone like Esau could have another, less pleasant aspect, an aspect that reminded her of her own brother Laban. She recognized her own family in Esau, and she knew his shortcomings and his weak points." As a result of this understanding, "she manipulated Isaac into blessing Jacob instead of Esau out of her love for Isaac, in an attempt to shield and protect him from the emotional shock of his own error." (Adin Steinsaltz, *Biblical Images,* Basic Books, New York, 1984, pp. 46–47)

In other words, Rebekah favored Jacob, not only because she knew that Esau possessed shortcomings like her brother Laban, but also because she wished to protect her husband, Isaac, from making a mistake by giving Esau and not Jacob his blessing. Rebekah's favoritism was a form of saving Isaac from his own stupidity and foolish decisions.

Parents and sibling rivalry
Psychologist Haim G. Ginott comments about how parents handle jealousy between their children. "Some parents are so angered by sibling rivalry that they punish any overt sign of it. Other parents bend backward almost acrobatically to avoid giving cause for jealousy. They try to convince their children that all of them are loved equally and therefore have no reason to be jealous. . . .

Those who want to be superfair to each child often end up being furious with all their children. Nothing is so self-defeating as measured fairness. When a mother cannot give a bigger apple or a stronger hug to one child for fear of antagonizing the other, life becomes unbearable. . . .

Children do not yearn for equal shares of love: they need to be loved uniquely, not uniformly. The emphasis is on quality, not equality. We do not love all our children the same way, and there is no need to pretend that we do. We love each child uniquely, and we do not have to labor so hard to cover it up." (Between Parent and Child, *Macmillan, New York, 1965, pp. 127–132)*

Love them equally
Love equally all your children. Sometimes the favored disappoint, and the neglected make you happy. (Berekiah Ha-Nakdan, Mishle Shualim, *1260* C.E.*)*

No favoritism
Play no favoritism: Because Joseph got a multicolored coat, the brothers "hated him." (Rabbi Eleazar ben Azariah, Genesis Rabbah *84:8)*

Each child is unique
Each child carries its own blessing into the world. (Yiddish Proverb)

Interpreters of our Torah portion all seem to agree that the jealousy and bitterness between Jacob and Esau was not simply a matter of misunderstandings between them. Their troubled relationship grew, not only out of the differences in their personalities, but also from the way in which they were treated by their grandparents and parents. Isaac's and Rebekah's strengths and weaknesses, their backgrounds and judgments, the ways in which they rewarded and manipulated Esau and Jacob clearly contributed to the sibling rivalry between the brothers.

Tragically, that rivalry ultimately developed into a distrust and hatred that drove them apart. It poisoned their relationship forever. While later the brothers would meet and make peace, they would then go their separate ways without ever achieving genuine brotherly love.

PEREK GIMEL: *The Issue of Intermarriage*

The subject of marriage is raised twice in our Torah portion.

We are told that when Esau was forty years old he married two Hittite women and that the marriages were "a source of bitterness to Isaac and Rebekah." (Genesis 26:34)

Then, near the end of the Torah portion, it is reported that Rebekah tells Isaac that she is worried that Jacob, like Esau, will marry a woman from among the Canaanites rather than someone from their ancestral home in Paddan-aram. Isaac agrees with her. He sends for Jacob and instructs him to go to Paddan-aram to find a bride among the daughters of Laban, Rebekah's brother. He also blesses Jacob, telling him that God will give him and his children rights to the Land of Israel as was promised to Abraham, his grandfather.

When Esau hears that his father has instructed Jacob not to marry a Canaanite woman, has sent him off to Paddan-aram, and has given him an additional blessing, he is hurt and angry. Perhaps to find favor with his parents, he marries his first cousin Mahalath, the daughter of Ishmael. He does not, however, divorce his Hittite wives.

As the Torah portion indicates, the subject of intermarriage between Jews and non-Jews has been a concern since the beginnings of Jewish history. We are not told what it is that "displeases" Isaac and Rebekah about Esau's Hittite wives nor that they had forbidden him to marry them. Yet it is clear that they are troubled by what Esau has done and, therefore, warn Jacob not to marry from among the Canaanites. They tell him to find a wife from among his "tribal family."

Speiser

Most modern biblical scholars are agreed that the two mentions of intermarriage in our Torah portion were written by authors who believed that religion and nationality could only be preserved through marriages within the tribal group. For instance, E. A. Speiser comments that whoever wrote these two passages was interested in "purity of lineage." (*The Anchor Bible: Genesis*, p. 216)

> ### Separate for a holy purpose
> *But there was another factor in Israel that tended to lift what might have been only a fierce instinctive separatism to a higher level of emotion. That was the passionate conviction that Israel was meant to be not only a nation but a theocracy (rule of state by God, and by God's priests). To maintain its racial integrity therefore was to maintain the religious institution of covenant and law and holy faith.* (Interpreter's Bible, *Genesis, p. 678*)

The Christian scholarly commentary, *Interpreter's Bible,* agrees with E. A. Speiser that the authors of this part of our Torah portion were xenophobic. They feared strangers. They were concerned that strangers would marry their children and remove them from their community. As a result, they would not survive as a distinct people. For them, "to marry outside the clan was to mix its blood and to break its solidarity." Fear of others and their foreign ways and beliefs was the primary motivation for the opposition of Isaac and Rebekah to intermarriage. That is the reason they were grieved.

But that was not the only reason. It was not just fear but also a positive conviction of faith. The authors of the *Interpreter's Bible* also point out that those who created the story of the opposition of Isaac and Rebekah to intermarriage did so for a more important reason. They believed in the special covenant or *berit* between the Jewish people and God and that the best way to preserve it was to permit marriages only between Jews. Mixing with other peoples meant abandoning their relationship with God and their responsibility to live as a "holy" or "separate" people dedicated to God's service.

> ### The way to idolatry
> *Twice more the Torah warns about intermarriage. In Exodus 34:16 the Israelites are told:*

> *"And when you take wives from among their daughters for your sons, their daughters will lust after their gods and will cause your sons to lust after their gods."*
>
> *In Deuteronomy 7:3–4 the Israelites are commanded: "You shall not intermarry with them: do not give your daughters to their sons or take their daughters for your sons; for they will turn your children away from Me to worship other gods. . . ."*

Not only do we find other warnings against intermarriage in the Torah, but we are also told that, because King Solomon, in his old age, married non-Jewish wives who "turned away Solomon's heart after other gods," his sons were not eligible to inherit his throne. (I Kings 11:1–13) The opposition to intermarriage within the Torah seems to have been based on the belief that it led to idol worship and to disloyalty to the faith and covenant of the Jewish people with God.

Rashi

Rashi seems to agree with that argument. In commenting upon the "bitterness" of Isaac and Rebekah at Esau's marriage to the Hittite women, Rashi explains that it derived from the smell of the idolatrous offerings that the wives burned each day. He suggests that both Isaac and Rebekah realized that the wives' loyalty to their traditions would, eventually, influence Esau away from his faith and, ultimately, endanger the survival of Jewish tradition and the Jewish people.

> ### Opposition to intermarriage
> *"From the very beginning . . . Jewish opposition to mixed marriage was based not on any notion of racial superiority but rather on realistic recognition of the fact that such matches posed an ominous threat to the survival of the Jewish people and its faith."* (Roland B. Gittelsohn, Consecrated Unto Me, *p. 193*)

Group identity
"Jewish group identity is generally defined in terms of both religion and ethnic background. . . . Children of conversionary marriages were more than three times as likely to identify as Jews than were children of mixed marriages. The overwhelming majority of the children of conversionary marriages were identified as Jewish at birth, and virtually all continued to identify themselves as Jewish. . . ." (Egon Mayer, Love and Tradition: Marriage between Jews and Christians, *Plenum Publishing Corp., 1985, p. 253*)

Other commentators trace Isaac's blindness to the stress and unhappiness he suffered over Esau's intermarriages. They argue that God blinded him in order to relieve the pain he felt each time he saw his son or the smoke of idolatry rising from his home. (*Midrash Tanchuma, Toledot 7*)

Hirsch

Some Jewish interpreters, however, take the matter one step further. Rabbi Samson Raphael Hirsch argues that "with this marriage with two Hittite women Esau set the seal on his complete unfitness to be the one who was to carry on the mission of Abraham. In a home where even two daughters of Heth ruled, the Abrahamitic principle was just buried." By intermarrying, Hirsch contends, Esau became a house divided between Abraham's belief in one spiritual God and the many idol-gods of his wives. This disqualified him from inheriting the leadership of the Jewish people from Abraham. Hirsch reasons that a home where two religious traditions are practiced or where there is not a joint commitment to a single faith by both parents is often the cause of confusion, misunderstanding, and trouble between parents and children. Children may wonder which tradition they should follow. Sometimes, without being aware of it, a parent will signal that "if you love me, you will do it my way." Grandparents may reward children for showing a preference for their faith. Instead of providing them with a common tradition to practice and to share, religious tradition may become a source of arguments and bitter family division.

The role of religion
Ritual *"serves as a bridge from the past—across the present—to the future. It reminds us of the imponderables, the spiritual values by which our actions should be guided. We Jews are especially fortunate because our faith provides us with a rich treasury of beautiful ritual. The most important moments and emotions in life—birth, growth, adolescence, love, marriage, and death—are enhanced by rituals that grow out of our people's past and express our hopes for the future. The sharing of rituals—precisely because they are poetic symbols appealing to the emotions—can do more to bring husband and wife together than any intellectual sharing."* (Gittelsohn, Consecrated Unto Me, *p. 214*)

For the teachers of Jewish tradition, sharing a single religious tradition in the home is meant to unite husband, wife, and children. It is meant to provide a common identity and a rich resource of rituals and traditions for emotional and intellectual enrichment. Through sharing a historic faith, family members are bonded to one another and also to the Jewish community beyond their home. For all these reasons, Jews today continue to promote marriages where bride and groom strengthen their love and commitment to each other by sharing the joy and meaning of building a Jewish home.

QUESTIONS FOR STUDY AND DISCUSSION

1. How, according to the discussion of this Torah portion, do stereotypes and histories of hatred develop? Are there acts or words spoken by others for which there can be no forgiveness? Are there some strategies we might develop

for promoting forgiveness and the end to cycles of suspicion and hatred?

2. List the reasons given by the commentators for Rebekah's favoring of Jacob and for Isaac's favoring of Esau. Are these common factors in families you know? In your own? What can be done about such bias in relationships?

3. The Torah presents two statements critical of intermarriage: Exodus 34:16 and Deuteronomy 7:3–4. Compare these to what our commentators say about the subject in Perek Gimel. Are these observations still justified? Should we oppose interdating? How shall Jews preserve their tradition and their community in a free and open society?

PARASHAT VAYETZE
Genesis 28:10–32:3

Vayetze means "and he went out" and relates the story of Jacob's departure from Beer-sheba for distant Haran, Rebekah's birthplace. The first night of his journey, he dreams of a stairway reaching from earth to heaven and is told by God that his descendants will be blessed and that they will inherit the land already promised to Abraham and Isaac. After a long journey, Jacob arrives in Haran where he is welcomed by Rebekah's brother Laban and his two daughters, Leah and Rachel. Laban promises to allow Rachel to marry Jacob if he will work seven years for him. When it comes time for the marriage, Laban deceives Jacob by sending Leah to his tent. When Jacob protests, Laban tells him that, if he will serve another seven years, then he will also give him Rachel. Jacob agrees. With his two wives and their maidservants, Bilhah and Zilpah, he has twelve children: Reuben, Simeon, Levi, Judah, Issachar, Zebulun, and Dinah with Leah; Dan and Naphtali with Bilhah; Gad and Asher with Zilpah; and Joseph with Rachel. After working many years for Laban, Jacob decides to return to his homeland. He works out an agreement with Laban for payment of his wages. They will divide the herd. Jacob will be given all the spotted and speckled sheep and goats; Laban will keep the rest. Laban agrees, but, when Jacob's herd increases in numbers, Laban's sons accuse Jacob of cheating them. Fearing trouble, Jacob decides to leave secretly with all his family and cattle. Laban pursues him, but, when he overtakes him, they share their grievances and reconcile their differences. Afterwards, Jacob and his family continue on their way.

OUR TARGUM

· 1 ·

On the eve of his departure from Beer-sheba, Jacob makes a pillow with some stones and goes to sleep. He dreams of a stairway reaching from earth to heaven. On it, angels are going up and down, and God tells him that his descendants will be many, that they will spread out in all directions, that all peoples will be blessed by them, and that ultimately God will bring him back to his homeland. In the morning, Jacob names the place Bethel, meaning "House of God." He also promises that, if God will protect him on his long journey and return him to his homeland, he will worship God and set aside a tithe, ten percent, of his wealth for God.

· 2 ·

Jacob continues his journey and arrives in Haran. He asks some shepherds if they know his uncle, Laban, and they point to Rachel, Laban's daughter, who is bringing her flocks to a well. Jacob waters the flock and tells Rachel who he is. She runs to inform her father. Laban warmly greets Jacob as "my bone and flesh."

After a month, Laban says to Jacob, "You should not work for me without wages. How much shall I pay you?" Jacob, who has fallen in love with Rachel, answers, "I will serve you seven years if you will give me Rachel for a wife." Laban agrees, but after the seven years he tricks Jacob on the night of the wedding and sends his older daughter, Leah, into Jacob's tent.

The next morning Jacob complains to Laban. "Why have you deceived me?" Laban tells him that "it is not the practice in our land to marry off the younger before the older," but Laban promises to allow him to marry Rachel if he will serve him another seven years. Jacob agrees.

· 3 ·

Leah gives birth to Reuben, Simeon, Levi, and Judah. Rachel is jealous and upset that she cannot have children. So she sends her maidservant, Bilhah, to Jacob to have children for her. Bilhah bears Dan and Naphtali. Leah also instructs her maid-servant, Zilpah, to bear children with Jacob, and Zilpah gives birth to Gad and Asher. Afterwards, Leah bears Issachar, Zebulun, and a daughter, Dinah. Finally, Rachel conceives and bears Joseph.

· 4 ·

After Joseph's birth, Jacob approaches his father-in-law, Laban, and says, "Allow me and my family to leave and to return to my homeland."

Laban, knowing that his riches have increased greatly over the fourteen years of Jacob's service, tells him: "I have been blessed because of you. What shall I pay you?"

Jacob answers: "Pay me nothing, but do me a favor. Let me pass through your flocks and take all of those that are speckled and spotted, or dark-colored. They will be my wages." Laban agrees but secretly instructs his sons to remove all of the speckled and spotted or dark-colored sheep from the flock, taking them a distance of three days away from where Jacob is caring for his flock.

While pasturing Laban's flock, Jacob uses a form of magical rod, causing them to give birth, not only to speckled and spotted animals, but to stronger ones. As a result, Jacob becomes very prosperous. His household includes many maid-servants, menservants, camels, and asses.

Seeing Jacob's wealth, Laban's sons become

jealous. They accuse Jacob of stealing from their father. Even Laban's attitude toward Jacob changes to suspicion.

Jacob is told by God to return to his homeland. He discusses the matter with Leah and Rachel, and they agree. So he gathers his family and possessions and sets out for the land of Canaan. As they depart, Rachel enters Laban's tent and steals one of his idols.

When Laban learns that they have gone without informing him, he pursues them. Overtaking them, he asks Jacob: "Why did you flee in secrecy and mislead me and not tell me? I would have sent you off with festive music . . . [and] why did you steal my gods?"

Jacob answers that he was afraid to reveal his plans but that he has not taken anything belonging to Laban. After searching the tents of both Leah and Rachel, Laban finds nothing since Rachel has cleverly hidden the idol she had taken under the camel cushions on which she is sitting.

Jacob turns to Laban and asks, "What is my crime, what is my guilt that you should pursue me?" Laban responds by claiming that "the daughters are my daughters, the children are my children, and the flocks are my flocks," but then he suggests that he and Jacob make peace with each other. The Torah portion concludes with their setting up a pillar of stones between them, promising that they will not cross the mound against each other with hostile intent.

THEMES

Parashat Vayetze contains three important themes:

1. The meaning of angels in the Torah.
2. The difference between proper and improper prayer.
3. Dealing with dishonest people.

PEREK ALEF: *Who and What Are Angels?*

When Jacob flees from Beer-sheba, he camps the first night on the desert. Gathering some stones for a pillow, he goes to sleep and dreams of a stairway reaching from the ground to the sky. On it "angels of God were going up and down." Later in our Torah portion (Genesis 31:10–13), Jacob tells Leah and Rachel that he has dreamed of an angel who explained to him how the streaked and speckled flocks were increasing to his advantage and that he should return to his homeland.

Who and what are these angels appearing to Jacob?

Actually, the Torah contains many mentions of angels: When Hagar, Sarah's maidservant, flees to the desert, an angel comforts and counsels her. (Genesis 16:7–12) Two angels visit Lot in Sodom and urge him to escape from the city with his family. (Genesis 19) Just as Abraham is about to sacrifice Isaac, an angel appears and tells him, "Do not raise your hand against the boy. . . ." (Genesis 22:11) An angel speaks to Moses out of a burning bush and commands him to return to Egypt to free the Israelites from bondage. (Exodus 3:2–10)

Most scholars would define the angels mentioned in the Torah as "messengers of God." The Hebrew word for angel is *malach,* meaning "one who carries a message."

Belief in angels was quite common among peoples in the ancient Middle East. It was assumed that angels could fly, that they often had wings, that they could walk, talk, appear, and disappear, and that they were the designated agents of the gods. Within Jewish tradition, angels were believed to be slightly superior to human beings and to work as God's agents.

The Psalmist on angels
O God, our God,
How majestic is Your name throughout the earth!

*You who have covered the heavens with Your
splendor. . . .*

*When I behold Your heavens, the work of
Your fingers,*

*the moon and stars that You have set in
place:*

*What is man that You have been mindful of
him,*

*mortal man that You have taken note of
him,*

*that You have made him little lower than the
angels. . . .* (Psalms·8:2, 4–6)

Jews during the talmudic period also believed in
angels. Some rabbis taught that God had actually
consulted with angels before creating heaven,
earth, and human beings. Others point out that
angels have a life span of only one day. They are
created in the morning, praise God throughout
the day, and die in the evening. It was also believed
that angels accompany Jews at the beginning of
their observance of Shabbat and that they protect
those who are faithful in carrying out God's commandments.

Talmudic teachers on angels
*Rabbi Helbo taught that God creates a new choir
of angels each day. They sing God's praises and
then depart.* (Genesis Rabbah *78:1*)

*Great is peace, for God has given no more beau-
tiful gift to the righteous. When a righteous
person dies, angels accompany him to heaven and
say: "He shall enter in peace"; "He shall rest in
peace"; and "He walked uprightly."* (Numbers
Rabbah, Naso, *11:7*)

*If one does a mitzvah, a commandment, one is
given one angel. If one does two commandments,
one is given two, and, if one does all the commandments, one is given many angels. And who
are these angels? They guard people against bad
things happening . . . they make peace for them.*
(Tanchuma, Mishpatim, *19*)

Rambam (Maimonides)

For the medieval philosopher Moses Maimonides, angels were *forms* of intelligence through
which God "ruled the world." The human mind
was such a *form* or "angel." Maimonides taught
that, if God wished to send a message to a human
being, it was sent through the person's mind or
intelligence. For him, human minds were containers for God's signals or signs. That is why he
called them angels. Angels were a wonderful way
in which God spoke to human beings and inspired
them with new ideas and visions. (*Guide for the
Perplexed*, Part II, Chapters VI–VII)

Most modern Jewish philosophers and teachers
no longer believe in the existence of angels, special
nonhuman messengers of God. How, then, do
they interpret the mention of angels in our Torah
text?

Some simply explain that ancient authors accepted the existence of angels. They believed that,
like human beings, they could speak, think, and
see and that they could and did influence all aspects
of human life. For the ancients, who wrote and
edited the Torah text, angels were as real as people
are for us.

Other modern teachers argue that ancient authors used angels as a dramatic way of expressing
the inner thoughts of the characters they were
describing. In our Torah portion, the author may
have wished to portray Jacob's fear of leaving his
homeland for a distant unknown place. His dream
about the stairway stretching from earth to
heaven, with angels going up and down on it,
may depict his anxiety about his future. Would
his fortunes go up or down? Would he be a success
or failure? And would God help him and protect
him from evil?

In reading and interpreting the role of angels
in the Torah, both approaches prove helpful. At
times an angel will simply appear as a messenger;
at other times as a form of intelligence, a sign of
the future; and sometimes as an insight into the
fears and hopes of biblical characters. Clearly, angels add excitement, dimension, and color to the
Torah tradition.

PEREK BET: *Jacob's Prayer—Can You Bargain with God?*

The Torah tells us that, just after he awoke from his dream of the stairway reaching to the heavens, Jacob made a vow—a promise in the form of a prayer.

The word for vow in Hebrew is *neder.* On Yom Kippur evening, Jews recite the prayer *Kol Nidre,* "all these vows," requesting forgiveness from God for any promises made but not kept from one Yom Kippur to the next.

Within Jewish tradition a *neder,* or vow, is defined as a promise made to God to carry out some action ("God, I will give ten percent of what I earn to charity") or a commitment not to do something otherwise permitted ("God, I will not smoke").

Vows were considered so important within Jewish tradition that the rabbis devoted an entire section of the Talmud to the subject. They called the section *Nedarim,* "Vows," and it is one of the largest in the Talmud.

The Talmud on vows

The person who makes a vow places a burden around his neck. (Jerusalem Talmud, Nedarim 9:1)

It is better to do a good deed without making a vow to do it. (Nedarim *77b*)

A man came to Rabbi Judah ben Shalom, asking him to void a vow that he had made. The rabbi asked him: "What did you vow not to do?" The man answered, "I vowed to make no profit."

"How can a person in his right mind vow such a thing? asked the rabbi.

"What I meant," explained the man, "was that I would no longer make profits by gambling."

Rabbi Judah refused to void the man's vow. (Jerusalem Talmud, Nedarim 5)

Jacob's vow has raised serious questions for biblical commentators through the centuries. After

he had piled up stones to mark the place where he had slept and dreamed, he named it Bethel, "House of God." Then he made a vow: "If God remains with me, if God protects me on this journey that I am making and gives me bread to eat and clothing to wear, and if I return safe to my father's house—the Lord shall be my God . . . and of all that You give me, I will always set aside a tithe for You."

What has bothered interpreters is that Jacob seems to be bargaining with God. Rather than promising what he will or will not do, which is the accepted form for a vow, Jacob laces his commitment with conditions. Over and over again, he uses the qualifying *if* in his statement to God. He says: *"If* God remains with me . . . *if* God protects me . . . gives me bread . . . clothing . . . and *if* I return safe . . ." *then* "the Lord shall be my God" and "I will always set aside a tithe. . . ."

Abravanel

Don Isaac Abravanel, in his commentary on our Torah portion, asks: "How could Jacob act like those who serve upon the condition of receiving a reward? Is it possible that Jacob meant to say that, if God did not do all these things for him, Jacob would not believe in God and would not set aside charity?"

Clearly, Abravanel is bothered by the "deal" Jacob offers God in his vow. He considers it inappropriate to make a conditional promise. As a matter of fact, Abravanel's criticism of Jacob is stated quite bluntly. He compares Jacob with his grandfather, Abraham, and notes that "Abraham never made such vows, and he was tested many times."

Others have also questioned how Jacob could have made such a vow. Did he really mean to condition his devotion to God on whether or not God met his demands? Did he doubt God's power to bring him back to his homeland? Does the Torah mean to teach us that, if our prayers are not answered, God does not care about us?

Rabbi Jacob ben Isaac Ashkenazi, author and editor of the collection of Torah interpretation called *Tze'enah u-Re'enah,* was also bothered by such questions about Jacob's vow. Rather than criticizing Jacob, however, he suggests that Jacob did not mean to indicate that his belief in God was conditional at all. What Jacob meant when he used the conditional phrase ("if . . .") had to do with the place where he was making the vow, not with the vow itself.

In other words, we should understand what Jacob said in the following way: "If God helps and protects me, I will worship God on this very spot; if God does not, I will of course still worship God but not necessarily in this place." (Comment on Genesis 28:16)

Jacob, the deal maker
Rabbi Reuven Bulka explains that Jacob was not one of these "stock market" people who thank God when things are good and question or reject God when life turns sad and disappointing. Jacob's vow was a way of proving what God had promised. If God would return him to the place where he had experienced his dream of the ladder, then Jacob would know that God had chosen him "for special responsibility." (Torah Therapy, Ktav, New York, 1983, p. 20)

Some would label Rabbi Jacob ben Isaac's explanation a "clever excuse" for Jacob. Others, like the modern Israeli biblical commentator Nehama Leibowitz, would disagree. While she is also troubled by the appearance that Jacob was making a "commercial deal" with God through his vow, she writes that this is not what the Torah intended. Leibowitz explains that ". . . no deal is involved." What Jacob meant was that "if God would not grant him to return to his father's house, how would he be able to erect a temple on the spot? All that Jacob's vow implied was: 'Give me the possibility of serving you.'" (*Studies in Bereshit,* World Zionist Organization, Jerusalem, 1980, p. 307)

It is clear that most commentators were troubled by Jacob's vow. Either they criticize him for trying to "strike a deal" with God, or they try to find an excuse for all the conditions that he attached to his prayer. They consider a person's promises or vows as a sign of his integrity and character.

Perhaps that explains why Jewish teachers paid so much attention to the subject of vows and promises. Prayers that, like Jacob's, were filled with conditions ("God, if you will do this for me, I will take on responsibilities for you") were forbidden. The rabbis taught: "Be not like servants who work for their master only on condition that they receive payment, but be like servants who work for their master without looking for any reward—and be filled with reverence for God." (*Avot* 1:3)

Vows were to be made without any conditions attached. A promise was to stand without any excuses. One's integrity was measured by the fulfillment of one's vows. It was forbidden to mislead others or oneself. The teacher Ben Sirach warned that "before you make a vow or a promise, think well. Do not mislead yourself." (*Tanchuma, Vayishlach* 8)

Jewish tradition counsels us to make our promises and vows with care. Our prayers and actions in the service of God are to be made without conditions attached. God does not want our "deals" but our deeds of kindness, justice, charity, and love. "The joy of the mitzvah, of the good deed, is its own reward."

PEREK GIMEL: *Dealing with Dishonesty*

Twice in our Torah portion, Jacob must deal with the dishonesty of Laban, the father of Leah and Rachel. In the first incident, Laban promises to give Jacob his daughter Rachel as a wife. Instead, he deceives him and sends Leah in Rachel's place. In the second incident, Laban offers to pay Jacob for all his work by giving him his choice of animals from his herd. Then, he deliberately cheats him by sending away with his sons the animals that Jacob has chosen.

These two incidents point up Laban's dishonesty. He was willing to take advantage of Jacob when it came to marrying his daughters and also when it came to paying him fair wages for all his work. Laban did not hesitate to lie when it suited his purpose nor to steal when he believed he could get away with it.

The question many interpreters ask is how Jacob should have dealt with Laban. How should you treat a person who is dishonest and may even be stealing from you? How shall we handle deceit?

Defining deceit

What is deceit? It is creating a false impression. (Hullin *94a*)

A person who practices dishonesty shall not dwell in My house. (Psalms *101:2*)

It is forbidden to deceive anyone, Jew or non-Jew. (Hullin *94a*)

To deceive with words or abuse with the tongue is a greater offense than to cheat in matters of money. (Baba Metzia *58a*)

Jacob's first response to Laban's trickery was to confront him with a series of questions: "What is this that you have done to me? Was it not for Rachel that I have been in your service? Why did you deceive me?"

One impression we get from the questions Jacob asks is that he is conducting an investigation. He is trying to sort out Laban's motives and also seeking to test his own memory of their agreement. While his questions are clear and direct and reveal his disappointment, they are not asked in an angry or even hostile manner.

When Laban explains that "it is not the custom in our place to marry off the younger before the older," Jacob seems to accept the reasoning without protest. Could it be that Jacob, the younger son, felt guilty at that moment for the trick he had played on his own father in stealing the blessing from his older brother, Esau? Some commentators believe that is the reason why Jacob

agreed, without loud complaints, to Laban's explanation. (*Midrash Tanchuma*)

How is it possible that Jacob mistook Leah for Rachel?

A great chasidic rabbi, Levi Isaac of Berdichev (1740–1809), known for his defense of Jews and his forgiving attitude to all human beings, once explained that, when Rachel learned that Laban planned to trick Jacob by giving him Leah as a bride instead of herself, she decided to do all that she could to save her sister from shame. So she taught Leah all of the secret signs of love between herself and Jacob. In this way Rachel was sure that Jacob would take Leah as his wife and not reject her. Rachel was willing to sacrifice her own happiness for the sake of her sister. When Jacob learned of Rachel's sensitivity toward her sister and her concern about her being humiliated, his love for Rachel increased. In this case, deceit committed for a "righteous" not a selfish purpose brought reward.

Is a tzadik, a "righteous person," allowed to cheat?"

If the person with whom he is dealing is dishonest, one is permitted to outwit him. (Megillah *13b*)

Others point out that Jacob was naive and believed Laban because Laban was his mother's brother. He trusted him, but, after Laban broke his agreement and removed all the streaked and spotted animals from his flocks, Jacob was enraged. When Jacob finally confronted him, he angrily accused Laban of cheating him out of his wages and flocks. Torah interpreter Nehama Leibowitz writes that "the Torah here teaches us an instructive lesson in human conduct and self-control. Anger . . . should be deferred till the last possible moment, till there is no other alternative—only as a last resort." (*Studies in Bereshit*, p. 341)

Leibowitz also calls attention to the fact that Jacob's response to Laban's dishonesty was "controlled" anger. It was not a wild outburst. It was carefully constructed and thought out.

When Laban pursued Jacob after he had departed with his family and herds, Jacob did not go to war with him. Nor did he become belligerent when they met and Laban confronted him with the questions: "What did you mean by keeping me in the dark and carrying off my daughters like captives of the sword? Why did you flee in secrecy and mislead me and not tell me?" Rather than losing his temper at Laban, Jacob calmly reminded Laban that he had worked faithfully for him for twenty years, often suffering hardships while caring for his property. He pointed out that he had earned everything he had taken.

Leibowitz praises Jacob's cool management of his emotions in what might have been an angry confrontation. He kept his dignity. He neither attacked Laban nor lost control of his anger. Leibowitz claims that Jacob is a model for handling those who cheat us.

Dealing with dishonesty: advice to parents
Our policy toward lying is clear: On the one hand, we should not play District Attorney or ask for confessions or make a federal case out of a tall story. On the other hand, we should not hesitate to call a spade a spade. When we find that the child's library book is overdue, we should not ask, "Have you returned the book to the library? Are you sure? How come it's still on your desk?"

Instead, we state, "I see your library book is overdue. . . ."

In short, we do not provoke the child into defensive lying nor do we intentionally set up opportunities for lying. When a child does lie, our reaction should be not hysterical and moralistic but factual and realistic. We want our child to learn that there is no need to lie to us. (H. G. Ginott, Between Parent and Child, pp. 60–61)

One other way of handling cheaters and liars is to expose them publicly. Confrontation in front of an audience not only brings satisfaction to the party that has been harmed but also warns others about those who practice deceit.

It is clear from the Torah text that Jacob shares Laban's dishonesty with both Leah and Rachel. He tells them: "Your father has cheated me, changing my wages time and again." Yet his complaint is not a public one. It is kept within the family, and, while Leah and Rachel agree that their father has treated Jacob unjustly—and even cheated them—they do not expose him in the marketplace or to his friends.

In discussing what to do about a dishonest person, Rabbi Israel Meir Ha-Cohen, who lived for nearly a century (1838–1933) in Lithuania, and whose book, *Hafetz Chaim*, became one of the most popular treatments of Jewish ethics, suggested a very careful approach. He taught that exposing a cheating or deceitful person was permitted if it would help the injured party and might protect others. But, said the rabbi, seven conditions must be met: (1) You must have hard evidence not rumors. (2) You must be absolutely certain that it was deceit and must think it over before announcing it to others. (3) You must confront dishonest persons privately seeking to change their behavior. If those people will not change, then you can speak publicly. (4) You must not exaggerate the facts. (5) You must examine your motives, making sure that you are not exposing the person for your own selfish reasons. (6) You must try all other ways to solve the situation without using slander. (7) You must not bring more harm to the dishonest person than a court might bring if the person was found guilty.

Confronting the dishonesty of others is very difficult and distasteful. No one wants to be taken advantage of or cheated. Like Jacob, we want to be given honest wages and to enjoy trusting relationships with others. Unfortunately, we do not always have our way. Sometimes we find ourselves selfishly twisting the truth to our advantage; at other times we find ourselves face to face with those who are cheating us.

Our choices are similar to Jacob's with Laban. Shall we react in anger or rush to condemn publicly the person cheating us? Do we say nothing, wait, and give the person a second chance? Shall we see it as our fault or admit, "I once cheated X. Now it's my turn to be taken advantage of"? Do we make excuses for the liar? Do we act with calm and reasonable concern or with hostility?

The choice is ours. Our examination of how Jacob chose to react to Laban reveals the growth and development of his character. He enters Haran as a trickster and cheater, and as he departs he has matured into a man of strength, reason, and integrity.

QUESTIONS FOR STUDY AND DISCUSSION

1. We know from research done by scientists that dreams often reveal our subconscious fears and longings. In that sense, they are "messengers." Do you agree with the interpretations of Jacob's dream in our text? What other interpretations would you give to his dream?

2. According to the Torah and its commentaries, what special function and roles do angels play within Jewish tradition? Why do some modern authors continue to use mystical characters or angels in their fiction?

3. Why do the rabbis consider a vow a "burden around the neck"? Why were conditional vows forbidden in Jewish tradition?

4. Given what the commentators have to say about dealing with dishonesty, would you agree with H. G. Ginott's "policy toward lying"?

PARASHAT VAYISHLACH
Genesis 32:4–36:43

Vayishlach means "and he sent" and refers to Jacob sending messengers to his brother Esau before their meeting after twenty years of separation. We are told of Jacob's fears, of his division of his community into two camps, and of his wrestling with a man-angel who changes Jacob's name to Israel. Following that struggle, Jacob and Esau meet and part peacefully, each going his separate way. After Jacob and his community settle in Shechem, Dinah, the daughter of Leah and Jacob, is raped by Shechem son of Hamor the Hivite. Jacob's sons take revenge by murdering all the males of Shechem and plundering the city. Jacob is critical of his sons for what they have done. Rachel dies giving birth to Benjamin and is buried near Bethlehem. Isaac dies and is buried in Hebron near Abraham and Sarah. The Torah portion concludes with the genealogy of Jacob and Esau.

OUR TARGUM

· 1 ·

Having journeyed from Haran, Jacob now approaches Seir, the country of Edom, located in the green forested area in the mountains east of the Dead Sea. Jacob fears meeting Esau. Though twenty years have passed, he remembers that Esau had sworn to kill him.

So Jacob sends messengers ahead to Esau, hoping they will return with a message of peace from him. When the messengers return, they tell him that Esau is coming to meet Jacob with four hundred men. Jacob is terrified and immediately divides his community into two camps. He reasons that, if Esau attacks one camp, the other will escape.

Jacob spends the night in prayer, and in the morning he selects gifts of goats, rams, camels, cows, and asses for his servants to take to Esau. He hopes that Esau will like the gifts and, therefore, be kind and peaceful in his dealings with him. That night Jacob takes his family to a safe place across the river Jabbok, and then he wanders off alone.

Throughout that night a man-angel wrestles with Jacob. Near dawn, the man-angel says to him, "Let me go!" Jacob tells him that he will not let him go unless he gives him a blessing. The man-angel asks, "What is your name?" Jacob tells him his name, and the man-angel says: "Your name shall no longer be Jacob, but Israel, for you have wrestled with divine and human beings and have triumphed."

Jacob names the place "Peniel," which means "face of God," explaining, "I have seen a divine being face to face, yet my life has been preserved." At dawn, Jacob limps away from the place, injured by the man-angel who had wrenched his hip at the socket.

· 2 ·

That day Jacob sees Esau and his company of four hundred men approaching his camp. He lines up his wives and children and then goes out to greet Esau. Esau embraces and kisses him. "Who are these people?" he asks Jacob, pointing to Leah, Rachel, and the children. Jacob introduces his wives and children to his brother and offers Esau gifts. "To see your face," Jacob tells him, "is like seeing the face of God, and you have received me favorably."

Esau offers to accompany Jacob and his family to Canaan, but Jacob informs him that it is not necessary. Esau then returns to Seir, and Jacob travels to Succoth in the Jordan Valley, where he builds a home for his family. We are also told that he purchases a plot of land outside the city of Shechem, which is near the site of Nablus, thirty-two miles north of Jerusalem.

· 3 ·

While out visiting other young women, Dinah, the daughter of Jacob and Leah, is raped by Shechem, the son of Hamor the Hivite, chief of the country. Shechem declares his love for Dinah and asks his father to arrange their marriage.

Jacob hears that his daughter has been raped, but he takes no immediate action against Shechem because his sons are out in the field tending to the herds. When the brothers hear what has happened, they are enraged and return home.

Meanwhile, Shechem's father, Hamor, approaches Jacob and tells him that his son is in love with Dinah. "Please give her to him in marriage," he says. "Intermarry with us . . . and the land will be open before you." Shechem adds his own words to those of his father. "Ask of me a bride price ever so high, and I will pay what you tell me; only give me the maiden for a wife."

Angry over what has happened to Dinah, Jacob and his sons indicate that they cannot permit their women to marry uncircumcised men. "Circumcise yourselves," they tell them, "and we will give you our daughters, and we will become like one family."

Hamor and Shechem agree, and they go before all the people of their city and announce: "These people are our friends; let them settle in the land and move about in it, for the land is large enough for them; we will take their daughters to ourselves as wives and give our daughters to them. . . . Would not their cattle and substance and all their beasts be ours?" The people agree, and all the males circumcise themselves.

Three days afterwards, while all the males are in pain from their circumcision, two of Jacob's sons, Simeon and Levi, enter the city and murder all the males, including Hamor and Shechem. Their other brothers join them, and they plunder the city, taking flocks and herds as booty and children and wives as captives. When Jacob hears what they have done, he says to them: "You have brought trouble on me. Other peoples will not trust me. We are few in numbers, and we will be destroyed."

Simeon and Levi answered their father with a question: "Are we to allow our sister to be treated as a whore?"

· 4 ·

Afterwards God instructs Jacob to return to Bethel, where he had built an altar at the time he was fleeing from Esau. Jacob tells all in his household to give him their idols and earrings. He buries them near Shechem, and they set out for Bethel.

At Bethel, God says to Jacob: "I am El Shaddai [God Almighty]; be fertile and increase; a nation, many nations will descend from you. . . . The land that I gave to Abraham and Isaac I will give to you; and to your offspring to come will I give the land."

After leaving Bethel, Jacob and the community with him travel toward Ephrath, now called Bethlehem. On the way Rachel, who is pregnant, becomes ill and dies in childbirth. Jacob names his new son Benjamin and buries Rachel near the road. Over her grave he builds a pillar of stones.

Jacob returns to the area of Hebron where Isaac, his father, dwells. At one hundred and eighty years of age, Isaac dies, and Esau and Jacob bury him in the cave of Machpelah with Abraham, Sarah, and Rebekah.

THEMES

Parashat Vayishlach contains three important themes:

1. Dealing with powerful people and nations.
2. Wrestling with angels and ourselves.
3. The appropriate response to the violence of rape.

PEREK ALEF: *Jacob's Reunion with Esau—Dealing with Power*

Rabbi Yochanan, who lived in the second century during the bitter persecutions of Jews by Roman authorities, taught that "whoever wishes to deal with a king or powerful authority . . . should study this Torah portion about the reunion of Jacob and Esau." (*Genesis Rabbah 78:6*) Rabbi Yochanan was famous for his clearheaded thinking and good advice. Why did he believe our Torah portion contained such wisdom about the tactics of dealing with powerful people and governments?

Several details should be noted about the reunion of Jacob and Esau. Jacob sends messengers to his brother. He instructs them to demonstrate his humility by referring to Esau as "my lord Esau" and to himself as "your servant Jacob." Tell him, Jacob says to the messengers, that "I send this message to my lord in hope of gaining your favor."

When the messengers return and announce to Jacob that Esau is on his way to meet him and that he is bringing four hundred men with him, Jacob is frightened. But he does not panic. Instead, he divides his community into two camps, cal-

culating that, if Esau destroys one camp, the other will escape. Then he prays, asking God to save him from his brother. Afterwards, he selects choice animals from his herds of goats, rams, camels, cows, bulls, and asses and sends them as gifts to Esau. He reasons to himself, "If I appease his anger with presents in advance, and then face him, perhaps he will show me favor."

Jacob's strategy (sending a delegation to represent him, humility, practicality in dividing his community, prayer, and gifts to reduce the hostility of the enemy) was greatly praised by many biblical interpreters.

Compare the reed to the cedar
The rabbis of the Talmud commented that there is a lesson to be learned by comparing the reed to the cedar. "The reed, which is a humble plant, grows in the water, replenishing its roots which are many. No matter how hard the wind blows, or from which direction, the reed is not blown from its place. It simply bends away from the wind." By comparison, "the cedar, which is a high and prideful tree, stands tall against all

the winds of the world except for the south wind. When that wind blows, it can uproot the cedar and turn it upside down." (Ta'anit *20a*)

Zugot

Beware of those in power
Shemayah and Abtalyon, who lived in the Land of Israel during the first-century persecution of Jews by the Romans, taught: "Do not seek to be close with governmental authorities." (Avot 1:10)

Be careful in your relations with those in power, for they draw people near for their own interests. They appear as friends when it is to their advantage and will not defend a person in time of trouble. (Avot 2:3)

Rabbi Bechaye commented that, because Jacob remembered that Esau loved to hunt, he sent him a falcon, which noblemen carry when they go hunting in the woods. He hoped that his gift would make a friend instead of an enemy of Esau. Another interpreter writes that Jacob instructed the messengers to make sure that Esau understood that the animals Jacob was sending to him were a gift meant to ease any angry memories Esau might have of him. (*Tze'enah u-Re'enah, Vayishlach,* p. 165)

Obadiah Sforno, who lived in Italy (1475–1550), pointed out that Jacob's tactic of humility with Esau was successful. Jacob saved his life and possessions because he was ready to appease Esau. Realizing that Esau had the power to destroy him, Jacob humbled himself like a "reed bending against the wind," rather than standing tall like a "cedar" and taking the chance of being overturned and destroyed.

By comparison Sforno recalls the reaction of Jews to Roman persecution during the first cen-

tury. At that time Roman authorities heavily taxed the community, cruelly oppressed men, women, and children, and threatened to destroy places of Jewish learning. Sforno heaps criticism upon those Jews who refused to appease the Roman authorities. He quotes Rabbi Yochanan ben Zakkai, a leader during those troubled times, who argued that, had Jews cooperated and not followed the bad advice of those who organized protests and burned the marketplaces of Jerusalem, "our Temple would not have been destroyed." (*Gittin* 56b) They should have "bent like a reed," Sforno writes, instead of trying "to stand tall like a cedar."

Other interpreters disagree.

Rabbi Judah ben Simon, who lived in the Land of Israel during the fourth century, called the attention of his students to the lesson in the biblical Book of Proverbs that teaches: "A righteous person who humbles himself before a wicked person is like a muddied spring or a ruined fountain." (25:26) A righteous person like Jacob, Rabbi Judah argued, should not have humbled himself before Esau. It was the wrong thing to do.

In another comment, the rabbis point out that Jacob humbled himself eight times by calling himself Esau's "servant" or by referring to Esau as "my lord." God, the rabbis teach, was displeased with Jacob and told him that, because he had disgraced himself, God was appointing eight kings to rule over the Jewish people.

Clearly, the rabbis were critical of Jacob for his display of humility before the power of Esau. They also point out that his tactics were bad. Jacob should never have sent messengers to Esau. He should have moved his family through the land quietly, and Esau might not even have noticed them. It was like waking a robber or a bully who was sleeping, these commentators explain. Had Jacob moved quietly by, he would not have needed to confront Esau.

Rabbi Huna, who headed the great school of Jewish learning in Sura, Babylonia, during the third century, agrees with the criticism of Jacob. He should not have become involved with Esau or paid any attention to him, Huna explains, quoting the teaching from Proverbs 26:17: "A person who passes by and gets involved with other people's disagreements is like one who takes a dog by the ears."

Goats and wolves

The Talmud teaches: "A person who acts like a goat will be eaten up by the wolves."

"I'm just a servant"

Rabbi Judah Ha-Nasi ("the Prince"), who edited the Mishnah and lived during the Roman persecutions, once said to his secretary, Rabbi Aphes: "Write a letter to Emperor Antoninus." So Aphes wrote the letter, addressing it, "From Rabbi Judah Ha-Nasi to His Majesty the Emperor Antoninus." Rabbi Judah took the letter, read it, and tore it up. Afterwards he said to Aphes: "Address it as 'From your servant Judah to His Majesty the Emperor Antoninus." Aphes asked: "Why do you humiliate yourself?" Judah replied: "Am I better than my forefather Jacob? Did he not say to Esau, "Your servant, Jacob"? (Genesis Rabbah, Vayishlach, 78:6)

Peli

"Buttering up"

The rabbis chastise Jacob, not only for "buttering up" Esau by introducing himself as "your servant" and offering him lavish gifts, but also for the very fact of Jacob's seeking Esau's approval for resettling the land that he was forced to flee earlier. . . . (Pinchas Peli, Torah Today, B'nai B'rith Books, Washington, D.C., 1987, p. 34)

Ramban (Nachmanides)

Unlike the commentator Sforno, Nachmanides disapproves of Jacob's "buttering up" of Esau. He should have acted with strength not weakness. He should not have bent in the wind or appeased him. Nachmanides argues that, had the Jews during the Roman persecutions not given in to the Romans and not fooled themselves into believing that they could make allies out of their enemies,

the Temple and Jewish life in the Land of Israel would not have been destroyed.

Nehama Leibowitz agrees. In her commentary, she claims that the reason Jews have been persecuted and battered through the ages is that they acted with humility before power rather than meeting power with power and pride. "With our own hands we sealed our own fate by lowering ourselves, allowing others to lord it over us. As the prophet Jeremiah (13:21) words it: 'You have taught them to be captains and chief over you.' "

At least one interpreter suggests that Jacob did not humiliate himself before Esau but instead met him and said to him: "If you want peace, I am with you. If you want war, then I am ready for you. I have strong men for battle, and God answers my prayers." (*Genesis Rabbah, Vayishlach,* 75:11)

In other words, Jacob retained his pride and dignity. He took matters into his own hands. First he divided his camp so that, if Esau came for battle, half of his community might escape. Then he went out to meet Esau face to face. He did not appear afraid, nor did he seek mercy from him. He refused to bend before Esau. He met power with power. He let Esau know that he was ready to make peace or to engage in battle. From a position of strength he offered to negotiate peace between them.

Rabbi Yochanan once said that, if "one wants to know how to deal with powerful kings or governors, he should study closely the Torah portion about the meeting between Jacob and Esau." (*Genesis Rabbah, Vayishlach,* 78:6) The varieties of opinions about how to treat powerful people, groups, and nations, even their conflicting opinions, are still important considerations for us today.

PEREK BET: *Wrestling with Angels and Ourselves*

After being told that Esau is approaching with four hundred men, Jacob divides his community and his possessions into two camps on either side of the Jabbok stream. By evening they are settled, and he is left alone. That night, the Torah (Genesis 32:25) informs us, "And a man wrestled with him until the break of dawn." The man wrenches his hip and says to Jacob, "Let me go, for dawn is breaking." Jacob refuses, demanding that the man bless him. The man asks his name, and, when Jacob tells him what it is, the man says, "Your name shall no longer be Jacob, but Israel, for you have wrestled with beings divine and human, and have prevailed."

When Jacob, now Israel, asks the man to identify himself, the man answers, "You must not ask my name," and then disappears. Jacob names the place where this strange wrestling match occurred *Peniel,* meaning "face of God." At dawn he limps away, saying, "I have seen a divine being face to face, yet my life has been preserved."

What is this strange "wrestling match" all about? Who is this "man"—or "divine being"—Jacob encounters? What is the meaning of Jacob's change of name to Israel? And why does he walk away from this strange night experience injured, limping?

The first interpreters of this strange story were the ancient rabbis. Some of them believed that the "man" was an angel who appeared in the form of a robber. His intention was to frighten Jacob, but Jacob was strong and unafraid. "You cannot scare me," he told the angel-robber. And, because he was brave and refused to run away from his attacker, Jacob was victorious and blessed with a new name—Israel.

Religious persecution

Nachmanides suggests that the "man" Jacob wrestled with was Esau and that their battle "refers to the generation of religious persecution" during the time of Emperor Hadrian (117–138 C.E.) when Rome ruled in the Middle East. "What did the Romans do in that generation?" They would bring iron balls, heat them in fire, and then place them under the arms of Jewish leaders, causing their death. And there have been other generations when they have done such things to us and even worse, but in the end we have survived," just as Jacob prevailed over Esau.

The hollow of Jacob's thigh

We are told that the man wrestling with Jacob injured him by touching the hollow of his thigh. By "hollow of his thigh" is meant the place of his circumcision. Here, too, we have an indication of how the enemies of the Jewish people persecuted them and sought to destroy them. They would forbid Jews from practicing the ritual of circumcision through which a Jewish boy enters the covenant of Abraham. (Lekach Tov)

As we have already noted in our discussion of this Torah portion, the rabbis often portrayed Jacob and Esau as much more than competing brothers. They also thought of them as two competing national forces—as Israel and other nations, or as Israel and Rome. For some interpreters, the wrestling match between Jacob and the angel was a match between Jacob and Esau. Esau was the angel, and the battle between them symbolized the bitter war for survival between the Jewish people and those nations that sought to destroy them. Jacob's night battle, they taught, was a preview of the future. Jacob-Israel would be attacked by Esau-Rome. They would fight throughout a long night of terror in which Israel would suffer. But, at the end of the night, Israel would emerge secure, strong, and victorious against all its enemies.

Rashi

The commentator Rashi suggests a very different approach. He argues that the "man" with whom Jacob wrestled was "Esau's angel." Rashi points out that Jacob was worried because Esau was coming with four hundred men to kill him and to destroy his community, still bearing a grudge against him for stealing his blessing from their father, Isaac. Rashi explains that, when Jacob discovered that he was wrestling with Esau's angel, he realized that he might be able to force Esau into forgiving him for taking the blessing. If he succeeded, Jacob thought, then his community would be saved. So Jacob fought on, refusing to give up until Esau's angel cried out, "Let me go."

Rabbi Abraham Chill, a modern interpreter, agrees with Rashi that the "man" was "Esau's angel," but his explanation is different. Chill believes that the night battle between Jacob and Esau's angel was between two opposing views of how human beings ought to live. Jacob's view represented compassion, kindness, and mercy; Esau represents self-centeredness, crudeness, and destruction. What we have here, Chill argues, is "a combat of values." Because Jacob remained faithful to his high standards, the only thing Esau's angel could do was to injure him physically. In the end, however, Jacob and his principles prevailed.

Jacob wanted to run away

Actually, Jacob was frightened of meeting his brother. Fearing what Esau might do to him and his community, Jacob was about to flee. God saw this and sent the angel to prevent Jacob from running away. He injured the hollow of his thigh because he wanted Jacob to know that he should have shown greater faith and that no one can flee from God. (Rabbi Samuel ben Meir, Rashbam, 1085–1174)

Jacob's real enemies

". . . the greatest enemy of Jacob is not Esau; the greatest enemy of Jacob resides within himself. It is the enemy that makes him an idol worshiper, a pagan, serving false values and going after false ideas; it is the pride of learning, of knowledge that destroys the capacity of the mind to learn the truth. And, lastly, the enemy is the hostility, the hatred, the resentment that have become deeply embedded either in our conscious or our subconscious." (Rabbi Morris Adler, The Voice Still Speaks, *p. 92)*

Other commentators point out that the battle between Jacob and the angel took place inside Jacob's mind, and it represented a major turning point in his life. He could not meet his brother, Esau, without wrestling with the guilt that he felt about stealing both his birthright and blessing. All his successes were tarnished by his feelings of having taken what did not belong to him. He could not go on. He had to struggle with what he had done, and he had to repent. He needed to admit that Esau had been cheated. He had to become a different person, a person who cared about his brother. The battle was with himself. Jacob struggled to become a better, more honest, fair, and just human being. It was only after Jacob became Israel that he was ready to reconcile with his brother. (W. Gunther Plaut, editor, *The Torah: A Modern Commentary,* UAHC, New York, 1981, Genesis, p. 221)

The modern writer Elie Wiesel enlarges this view. Wiesel writes that "at Peniel . . . two Jacobs came together."

There was the Jacob who had doubts about himself, fears about his future, and regrets about how he had stolen the blessing from his brother. This side of him said: "I deserve nothing, I am less than nothing, I am unworthy of celestial blessing, unworthy of my ancestors as much as of my descendants, unworthy to transmit God's message. . . ."

And there was the other Jacob who was the "heroic dreamer," the brave, experienced, and future-looking Jacob. That voice reminded him of how he had worked to create his family and his fortune and how he had stood up to Laban and his sons when they had plotted against him. That voice reminded him that he was the son of Isaac and that through him the Jewish people was to survive.

That night, the two sides of Jacob fought with each other. He wrestled with the most serious questions of his life. Who was he? What was really important to him? What were his responsibilities to himself and to those he loved? As dawn broke, he knew that he would never be the same. He was a changed person. He would limp away from his night battle with himself, but he would have a new name. He would no longer be *Ya'akov,* "the one who holds on to his brother's heel" or "the one who steals his brother's blessing." Now he would be *Yisrael,* "the one who had wrestled with himself and was now ready to wrestle with the world."

Wiesel writes that "it was a turning point for Jacob. He had a choice: to die before dying or to take hold of himself and fight. And win. And win he did. . . . Such, then, is the prime meaning of this episode: Israel's history teaches us that man's true victory is the one he achieves over himself." (*Messengers of God*, pp. 122–129)

So who was this "man-angel" with whom Jacob wrestled? Perhaps a figment of his imagination. Perhaps it was Esau or Esau's angel in a dream. Perhaps it was meant to represent all the enemies who would arise to destroy the people of Jacob-Israel. Perhaps the man-angel was Jacob, and the battle was between two sides of Jacob's character.

At times the intent of the Torah is unclear. Great literature and art allow for many differing opinions and interpretations. Each person, and often each generation, uncovers new meanings. That, now, is our challenge with Jacob's mysterious night battle.

PEREK GIMEL: *The Rape of Dinah*

Hertz

In his commentary on the Torah, British rabbi and scholar Joseph H. Hertz (1872–1946) called the story of Dinah "a tale of dishonor, wild revenge, and indiscriminate slaughter." It is also a story that raises important ethical questions.

Dinah, who is the daughter of Leah and Jacob, goes out to socialize with other young women and is raped by Shechem, the son of Hamor who is the chief of the country. Afterwards, Shechem tells his father that he is in love with Dinah and wants to marry her. He asks his father to arrange the marriage with Jacob.

Jacob hears that Dinah has been raped, but he remains silent until his sons return home from the fields. When they hear what has happened they are furious.

When Hamor asks that Shechem be allowed to marry Dinah, her brothers refuse. Already plotting their revenge, they tell Shechem that only if all the males of his community are circumcised will they allow such a marriage. They also promise friendship. "We will marry one another," they say. "We will dwell among you and become as one kindred."

Shechem and Hamor convince their townsmen to circumcise themselves. "These people are our friends," they tell them. Pointing out the material gain, they declare, "Will not their cattle and substance and all their beasts be ours?" Convinced, all the males are circumcised.

Three days later, Dinah's brothers, Simeon and Levi, enter the town and murder all the males, including Hamor and Shechem. The other brothers follow and plunder the town. They seize all the wealth and take the women and children as captives.

When Jacob hears what they have done, he says to Simeon and Levi: "You have made trouble for me by giving me a bad reputation among the people of the land. I am few in number, and if attacked my house will be destroyed." The brothers respond: "Should our sister be treated like a whore?"

The question posed by Simeon and Levi takes us to the heart of the matter. What should they have done? Should they have allowed Shechem to rape Dinah, their sister, without taking some revenge? Given the fact that they were fewer and weaker than Hamor's powerful fighting men, were Simeon and Levi justified in tricking them into circumcising themselves so that Dinah's brothers could take advantage of their weakness, easily killing them and plundering their town? Finally, who was really responsible for this incident—Dinah, who went out socializing without a chaperon, or Shechem, who forced himself upon her?

Defining "rape"
Laws defining rape usually indicate that the crime must involve sexual intercourse by force and against the will of the woman.

The penalty for rape
Within the Torah the penalty for rape is compensation to the family for the disgrace and mar-

riage to the victim without the opportunity for divorce. (Deuteronomy 22:29) Later, the rabbis added the payment of compensation for "pain inflicted on the woman" during the rape.

Who was to blame?
A woman should not show herself in the street wearing conspicuous jewelry. Jewelry was given to the woman for the purpose of adorning herself in her own house for her husband. It would be wrong to set a stumbling block even before a righteous man and certainly before people who are on the lookout for an opportunity to sin. (Tanchuma, Vayishlach 5)

Rape is an act of violence whose cause has been debated over the centuries. Some interpreters of our Torah portion blame Dinah, not Shechem, for what happened to her. They point out that, had she stayed at home rather than putting on fancy jewelry, dressing in clothing that attracted attention, and running about to parties, she would not have fallen into trouble. Other commentators blame her mother, Leah. It was Leah's fault, they say, because she was constantly "running about and socializing." She set a bad example for her daughter, and that's why Dinah got into trouble. (*Genesis Rabbah, Vayishlach,* 80:1–5 and *Tze'enah u-Re'enah, Vayishlach,* 34:1)

Blaming the victim of rape, or her family, for the violence she has suffered happens frequently. "She must have done something to deserve such treatment," is a common statement. Yet, it is as logical and misleading a judgment as blaming the victims of Nazi brutality for the agony and death they suffered. In our Torah portion, Dinah was not at fault; she was the victim of Shechem's violent passions.

The question faced by Jacob and his sons was how to deal with such violence? Were they to sit by idly and do nothing? Were they to take revenge, answer the violence of Shechem's act with a massacre of his community?

Some interpreters argue that Simeon and Levi were justified in their revenge. Their sister had been treated "as public property." Shechem used her with no regard for her feelings, her rights, or

her dignity. He forced himself upon her, and she would live with the terrible memories throughout her life. (*Genesis Rabbah* 80:2)

Rabbi Bechaye comments that the people of Shechem were among the world's greatest thieves and liars. No one could trust them. Although they promised to live at peace with Jacob and his sons, actually, as soon as they healed from their circumcisions, they planned to kill all of them. What Simeon and Levi did, Rabbi Bechaye says, was an act of self-defense, not of revenge. (*Tze'enah u-Re'enah, Vayishlach,* p. 171)

Rabbi Moshe Weissman, in his commentary *The Midrash Says,* writes that "Simeon and Levi acted in accordance with *halachah* (Jewish law) when they planned to kill the inhabitants of Shechem because the people of Shechem were all deserving of capital punishment according to the Seven Laws of Noah. Shechem himself was liable to capital punishment for having kidnapped Dinah (the transgression of robbery). His fellow townspeople were also guilty since they knew of his deed but did not bring him to justice. According to the Seven Laws of Noah, they were obligated to administer justice. Since they refused to do so, Weissman argues, they deserved death.

The Seven Laws of Noah
The Seven Laws of Noah were considered by rabbinic tradition as the essential "moral laws" for all human beings. The rabbis believed that anyone who practiced them was "a righteous person." The laws prohibited idolatry, blasphemy, bloodshed, sexual sins, theft, and eating from a live animal; and they called for the setting up of a legal system of justice. (Sanhedrin 56–60)

Rambam (Maimonides)

Weissman's opinion is close to the views of both Moses Maimonides and Joseph ben Abba Mari Caspi. They also call attention to the failure of the inhabitants of the city of Shechem who knew that Shechem raped Dinah but refused to arrest and convict him for his evil deed. They believe that it was right for Simeon and Levi to take revenge since no one in Shechem had raised a protest on Dinah's behalf. Caspi writes, "They saw and knew and did not punish him." In other words, the people of Shechem were as guilty as Shechem because they stood by and did nothing to arrest and prosecute him. Consequently, they deserved the massacre inflicted by Simeon and Levi.

Hirsch

Samson Raphael Hirsch offers another point of view in support of Simeon and Levi. He points out that Jacob and his sons realized that they were a small, weak group by comparison with the strength of the people of Shechem. Any protest was futile. Any appeal to "human rights" or "justice" would not be heard. Shechem attacked an innocent, weak "Jewish woman" whose people were also weak. Now he was holding her captive in his city. It was an act of brute force, and the only response was brute force. Simeon and Levi are to be praised for seeking to rescue her and for seeking revenge against Shechem and Hamor.

Rabbi Hirsch, however, adds the following: "Had (Simeon and Levi) killed Shechem and Hamor there would be scarcely anything to say against it. But they did not spare the unarmed men who were at their mercy . . . and went further and looted (and) made the inhabitants pay for the crime of the landowner. For that there was no justification." Simeon and Levi, Hirsch explains, may have thought that they would teach all their enemies a lesson. They would show that, if others used force against their women, they would have to pay with their lives. "But they went too far," Hirsch concludes. "They took revenge on innocent people for the wrongs that their powerful leaders (Shechem and Hamor) had done." (*The Pentateuch*, Vol. I, L. Honig and Sons Ltd., London, England, 1959, pp. 517–524)

> ***Like a troop of murdering bandits***
> *The rabbis of the Midrash taught: "As bandits sit in the road, murder people, and seize their wealth, so did Simeon and Levi act in Shechem."*
> (Genesis Rabbah *80:2*)

In his commentary, Nachmanides also condemns Simeon and Levi for their massacre of the people of Shechem. He disagrees with Maimonides. He argues that the failure of the people of Shechem to prosecute Shechem for raping Dinah is no justification for the brutality of Simeon and Levi. Nachmanides declares: "It was not the responsibility of Jacob and his sons to bring them to justice."

Furthermore, Nachmanides speculates that, had Simeon and Levi not taken the law into their own hands, the people of Shechem, including Hamor and Shechem, might have lived alongside them as friends and as devoted followers of the one God. After all, they had willingly circumcised themselves. "They would have chosen to believe in God . . . thus Simeon and Levi killed them without cause for the people had done them no evil at all." (*Commentary to Genesis*, pp. 419–421)

Rabbi Joseph H. Hertz agrees. He comments that "the sons of Jacob certainly acted in a treacherous and godless manner, and Jacob "did not forgive [them] to his dying day." Hertz reminds us that, in the blessing that Jacob gave on his deathbed to Simeon and Levi, he said: "Simeon and Levi are a pair;/ Their weapons are tools of lawlessness./ Let not my person be included in their council,/ Let not my being be counted in their assembly./ For when angry they slay men,/ And when pleased they maim oxen./ Cursed be their anger so fierce,/ And their wrath so relentless." (Genesis 49:5–7)

Jacob's condemnation of Simeon and Levi for taking the law into their own hands, even to revenge the rape of their sister, seems clear enough. The answer to brute force, to violence, is not more violence, not the massacre of innocents. It is the pursuit of justice within the courts of society.

QUESTIONS FOR STUDY AND DISCUSSION

1. Apply the talmudic statement, "A person who acts like a goat will be eaten up by wolves," to Jacob and to Jewish history. Is that a fair assessment of what happened to Jews in Europe during Hitler's rise to power?

2. Does each individual need to "wrestle" with the meaning of life? What are the benefits of such a struggle?

3. Why was Jacob so upset with his sons when they took revenge against the people of Shechem for the rape of Dinah? Was it a matter, once again, of being a reed rather than a cedar or were there more significant issues involved in his decision?

PARASHAT VAYESHEV
Genesis 37:1–40:23

Vayeshev, which means "and he settled," contains the story of Jacob and his sons, who have settled in the land of Canaan. There is jealousy between the other brothers and Joseph, who dreams of ruling them. They plot Joseph's death, but Judah persuades them to sell him to a caravan of Ishmaelites heading for Egypt. Afterwards, they report to Jacob that Joseph was killed by a wild animal. Later, Judah's son Er dies, leaving his wife, Tamar, as a widow. Judah promises that his young son Shelah will marry Tamar, but Judah fails to keep his word. Therefore, Tamar disguises herself and tricks Judah into sleeping with her. When Judah is told that Tamar has "played the harlot" and is pregnant, he orders that she be put to death. Defending herself, Tamar reveals to Judah that he is the father of the child she is carrying. Realizing that he has not treated Tamar fairly, Judah declares: "She is more in the right than I, since I did not give her to my son Shelah." The Torah portion continues with the adventures of Joseph in Egypt, where he is sold to Pharaoh's chief steward, Potiphar, and quickly rises from being a slave to becoming manager of his master's house. Potiphar's wife is attracted to Joseph and tries to seduce him. Angry because Joseph refuses her advances, she reports to Potiphar that Joseph tried to force himself upon her. Potiphar has Joseph thrown into prison. There he meets Pharaoh's chief cupbearer and chief baker. They tell him of their dreams, and Joseph interprets them. (Later, as Joseph has predicted, the cupbearer is returned to Pharaoh's service, but the chief baker is put to death.)

OUR TARGUM

· 1 ·

Joseph, who is seventeen years old, helps his older brothers take care of their father's herds. Seeing that sometimes they are careless about their responsibilities, Joseph criticizes them to Jacob. Jacob favors Joseph and gives him a gift of an ornamented coat of many colors. Seeing that their father loves Joseph more than he loves them, the brothers resent Joseph.

One night, Joseph dreams that he and his brothers are binding sheaves in a field. His sheaf stands up and their sheaves all bow down to his. The next day he tells his brothers about the dream. "Do you mean to rule over us?" they ask him, hating him more because of his dreams.

Another night, Joseph dreams that the sun, the moon, and eleven stars are all bowing to him. He tells Jacob and his brothers about the dream. His father scolds him, "What do you mean by such a dream? Are we all to bow down to you?"

Later, Jacob sends Joseph out to bring him a report on how his brothers are caring for the herds. When his brothers see him coming, they plot to kill him. Reuben suggests that they throw Joseph into a pit rather than kill him, hoping that afterwards he might rescue Joseph.

The brothers strip Joseph of his colorful coat and throw him into a pit. As they sit down to eat, they see a caravan of Ishmaelites heading toward Egypt. Judah suggests that they sell Joseph. "What do we gain by killing him?" he asks his brothers. They agree and sell Joseph into slavery.

Reuben returns to find Joseph gone. He tears his clothes as a sign of mourning and says to his brothers, "The boy is gone! Now, what am I to do?" The brothers tear Joseph's coat, dip it in goat's blood, and take it to their father. They tell Jacob that Joseph has been killed by a wild beast. He weeps and tears his garments in mourning. Though his children try to comfort him, Jacob continues to cry over the loss of Joseph.

·2·

Soon afterwards, Judah marries Shua, a Canaanite woman. They have three sons, Er, Onan, and Shelah. Er marries Tamar but dies leaving no son. According to the tradition of the time, Judah asks Onan to marry Tamar and to continue his brother's line by having children with her. Although Onan marries Tamar, he refuses to father children. God punishes Onan for this by taking his life. So Judah now promises Tamar that, when Shelah matures, he will make sure that Shelah marries her and continues Er's line.

As the years pass, however, Judah does not keep his word. Since she is growing older and is still without children, Tamar decides to trick Judah. She dresses as a prostitute and sits by a road where she knows Judah will pass. When he sees her, Judah promises her a goat if she will sleep with him. When Tamar demands a guarantee until the goat is delivered, Judah gives her his seal, cord, and staff. Not knowing she is Tamar, Judah sleeps with her, and she becomes pregnant.

Three months later, Judah is informed that Tamar pretended to be a prostitute and is pregnant. He orders that she be put to death. Hearing this, Tamar sends Judah his seal, cord, and staff, telling him: "I am pregnant by the man to whom these belong."

Judah is shocked and realizes that he has wronged her. He declares: "She is more in the right than I, since I did not give her to my son Shelah."

·3·

Meanwhile, Joseph has been taken to Egypt where Potiphar, Pharaoh's chief steward, purchases him from the Ishmaelites. Seeing that Joseph is a talented manager, Potiphar appoints him to run his entire household. As a result, Potiphar's riches increase.

Potiphar's wife is attracted to Joseph and says to him: "Lie with me." When he refuses, she spitefully tells Potiphar that Joseph has tried to take sexual advantage of her. Furious, Potiphar has Joseph thrown into prison.

While in prison, Joseph impresses the warden with his abilities and is put in charge of all the prisoners. He meets Pharaoh's cupbearer and baker who are in prison for angering the king. Both of them have dreams and tell them to Joseph. He interprets them, predicting death for the baker and a second chance at court for the cupbearer. "Don't forget me," Joseph tells the cupbearer, hoping that he will one day be free.

The Torah portion ends with Pharaoh's cupbearer restored to his position at court, but forgetting all about Joseph.

THEMES

Parashat Vayeshev contains three important themes:

1. Suspicion and hostility among children.
2. Assuming responsibility for what we promise; refusing to demean or embarrass others.
3. Measuring loyalty and success.

PEREK ALEF: *What Went Wrong between Joseph and His Brothers?*

We have already seen the results of jealousy and hatred between Cain and Abel, and Jacob and Esau. Now, once again, the Torah returns to the theme of hostility between brothers. Clearly, problems of parental favoritism and sibling rivalry occur in every family and in each generation. By returning to these themes, the Torah emphasizes the need to deal directly and honestly with all their troubling aspects. We see something of ourselves and our own families in the story of Joseph and his brothers. Many questions emerge: What went wrong between Joseph and his brothers? Why did they feel such anger toward him? What did he do to make them want to kill him or sell him into slavery? What role did Jacob play in this grim drama?

Joseph's character
Elie Wiesel comments on Joseph's character: "Jacob refused him nothing. He owned the most beautiful clothes, for he liked to be regarded as graceful and elegant. He craved attention. He knew he was the favorite and often boasted of it. Moreover, he was given to whims and frequently was impertinent. Arrogant, vain, insensitive to other people's feelings, he said freely whatever was on his mind. We know the consequences: he was hated, mistreated, and finally sold by his brothers, who in truth were ready to kill him." (Messengers of God, pp. 145–146)

Joseph loved himself
Maurice Samuel in conversation with Mark Van Doren:

Samuel: Do you ever think of Joseph as a loving person?

Van Doren: No, he's a person who loved to be loved. He assumed that people loved him. (In the Beginning . . . Love, John Day Co., New York, 1973, p. 104)

Some biblical interpreters claim that Joseph was "spoiled" by Jacob. He was given whatever he wanted, including a beautiful coat of many colors. Because his father favored him, Joseph believed that he was superior to his brothers and, eventually, that he was even more important than his father.

Other commentators emphasize Joseph's immaturity. He was just seventeen, still a very self-centered young boy. He was concerned with how he looked to others. He used special brushes and pencils to color around his eyes. He curled his hair. He put high heels on his shoes so that he would appear taller and, perhaps, older than his age. (Genesis Rabbah, 84:7)

Furthermore, according to the rabbis, Joseph made up stories about his brothers and then told them to his father. He lied about his brothers in order to make himself look good. For example, he told his father that his brothers were eating meat that was not kosher and that they were insulting to one another. (*Genesis Rabbah* 84:7)

Rashi

Rashi claims that Joseph took advantage of every opportunity to gossip about his brothers to his father. Though he knew the truth about what they were doing, he deliberately misinterpreted whatever they said or did to his own selfish advantage. He slandered their intentions as well as their accomplishments. For these reasons, Rashi concludes, they mistrusted and hated him.

It is clear that most Jewish interpreters evaluate Joseph as an immature, self-centered gossip. Some even blame Jacob for spoiling him. Why, they ask, did Jacob single out Joseph for such special treatment and affection?

Rabbi Judah believed that Jacob favored Joseph because they looked alike. Rabbi Nehemiah thought that Jacob loved Joseph because Jacob spent more time teaching Joseph the fundamentals of his tradition than any of his other sons. Could that explain Jacob's preference for Joseph? Might this also explain why the brothers were jealous of him? (*Genesis Rabbah* 84:8)

Do not favor one child over another
Resh Lakish, quoting Rabbi Eleazar ben Azariah, said: "A person should not favor one child over another, for Joseph's brothers hated him because their father made him a coat of many colors." (Genesis Rabbah 84:8)

Morgenstern

Partiality is injustice
Jacob was at fault for manifesting greater love for Joseph than for his other sons and for spoiling him as he did. Partiality is always a form of injustice, and injustice is always wrong and

causes evil. We have seen this already in Isaac's greater love for Esau and in Rebekah's greater love for Jacob. (Julian Morgenstern, The Book of Genesis, Schocken Books, New York, 1965, pp. 264–265)

one who spreads lies or evil gossip is like one who shoots arrows."

Another brother said: "His tongue is like a poisonous snake. Let's throw him into a pit filled with snakes." (Genesis Rabbah 84:13)

Other interpreters express sympathy for Joseph, blaming his brothers for the hostility between them. Writer Elie Wiesel comments: "They should have felt sorry for their small orphaned brother, whose mother had died tragically; instead they pounded on him, harassed him. They should have tried to console him; instead they made him feel unwanted, an outsider. Their father favored him above all others, and why not? Jacob loved him best because he was unhappy. But they refused to understand and treated him as an intruder. He spoke to them, but they did not answer, says the Midrash. They turned their backs on him. They ignored him; they denied him. To them he was a stranger to be driven away." (*Messengers of God*, p. 153)

Wiesel's interpretation does not excuse Joseph's bad behavior, but it does explain Joseph's feelings. He lied to his father about his brothers because he felt rejected by them. By putting them down, he hoped that his father would love him more. Perhaps, had his brothers been concerned about him, Joseph would have been loyal to them.

Instead, he spied on them and spread evil reports about what they were doing. Joseph's brothers hated him for criticizing and ridiculing them. After he told them his dreams of how they would bow down to and be ruled by him, their hostility hardened into cruelty. They decided to kill him.

His dreams fanned their hatred
When he related his dreams, their hatred for him was fanned even more. This is the nature of hatred. Once a new motive for it is found, additional hostility is felt. (Gur Aryeh)

They decided to kill him
They saw Joseph coming, and one brother said to the other: "Let's shoot him with arrows, for

---

So what went wrong between Joseph and his brothers? Our interpreters offer several considerations: (1) Joseph's arrogance, his vanity, his self-centeredness, his lies about his brothers, his foolish declarations of superiority over his family; (2) Jacob's favoritism of one son over another; and (3) the brothers' isolation of Joseph, their insensitive treatment of a fearful and lonely young boy. Could it be that all these factors combined to spell tragedy for Jacob and his sons?

PEREK BET: *Judah and Tamar— Models of Moral Action*

Speiser

E. A. Speiser, the modern biblical scholar, calls the story of Judah and Tamar "a completely independent unit." It does not seem connected in any way to the story of Joseph and his brothers. In fact, it seems to interrupt the story. Once Joseph is sold as a slave, we are anxious to know what happens to him. Instead, we are given a story about Judah and his daughter-in-law, Tamar. Why? What is its message?

The Torah tells us that Judah and his wife, Shua, had three sons: Er, Onan, and Shelah. Er married Tamar but died before they had a son. According to Deuteronomy 25:5–10, if a man died leaving no male heirs, his brother was obligated to marry his widow and continue his line. The marriage was called a "levirate" marriage. In Latin, *levir* means "husband's brother."

Ancient peoples were concerned about producing children and assuring the future of their families and tribes. We see emphasis upon each marriage being "fruitful" in the first chapters of Genesis when God commands Adam and Eve:

"Be fertile and increase, fill the earth and master it. . . ." (Genesis 1:28) The rule of the "levirate marriage" was of great importance. To ignore it was to *deny* a future for your brother's name and line.

In this story about Tamar and Judah, God brings death to Onan because he refuses to impregnate Tamar, his dead brother's childless wife. Furthermore, when Judah does not give his surviving son, Shelah, to Tamar in marriage, he is not carrying out the responsibility he owes to his dead son Er and to the widow, Tamar.

Does that, however, justify the trick Tamar plays on Judah? Was Tamar "right" in disguising herself as a prostitute and allowing Judah to impregnate her? Do the ends justify the means here?

According to Rashi, "Tamar acted out of pure motives." She wanted to fulfill the commandment to have children for the sake of her first husband. Rashi also points out that she acted in a way that protected Judah from public shame. Instead of publicly revealing that he had fathered the child she was carrying, Tamar sent him a private message. Rather than declaring what Judah had done, she hired a messenger to deliver his seal, cord, and staff and to inform him that she was pregnant by the person who owned them. Although Judah declared publicly that Tamar should be put to death for prostitution, she chose not to embarrass him. Instead, she revealed the truth quietly and discreetly.

Rashi concludes that we learn an important lesson from Tamar's behavior. It is "far better for a person to risk death—as Tamar did—than to shame another person publicly." (*Sotah* 10b) Tamar's reward, Rashi suggests, was that future kings of Israel, among them King David, would be born from her line.

Ramban (*Nachmanides*)

Nachmanides agrees with Rashi's interpretation. He explains that, in her case, the ends justified the means. She was desperate. Judah was not fulfilling his responsibility and promise to her. Even he realized how wrong he had been when he admitted publicly: "She is more in the right than I. . . ." By that statement, Nachmanides explains

that Judah meant to say: "She acted righteously, and I am the one who sinned against her by not giving her my son Shelah."

Judah's use of power
Tamar, in her righteousness, does not accuse Judah of being the father but sends him a quiet, dignified message saying that the father is the one who is also the owner of the seal, cord, and staff. When Judah sees this, he has the option of carrying through with the cover-up by throwing away the symbols and letting Tamar be burned. Instead, however, he publicly acknowledges his mistake. . . . Judah shows that the proper exercise of power involves the capacity to admit when one is wrong and to act accordingly.
(*Reuven P. Bulka,* Torah Therapy, *pp. 24–25*)

Commenting on the dramatic events surrounding Judah's admission that Tamar was justified—and that he had wronged her—the fourteenth-century Aramaic translation of the Torah, called *Targum Yerushalmi*, claims that Judah was one of the judges before whom Tamar appeared when she was accused of being a prostitute. The *targum* imagines Judah, rather than remaining silent or condemning Tamar, rising to his feet and declaring:

With your permission, my brothers, I proclaim here and now that each human being is treated measure for measure, be it for good or for bad, and happy is the person who recognizes his sin. It is because I dipped Joseph's coat in the blood of a goat and brought it to my father, saying: "Please identify it. Is it your son's shirt or not?" that I must now identify before this tribunal to whom the seal, cord, and staff belong. . . . So, I acknowledge that Tamar is innocent. She is pregnant from me not because she yielded to any illicit passion but because I did not give her to my son Shelah."

This passage from the *Targum Yerushalmi* not only portrays Tamar as justified in what she did, but it also depicts Judah as courageously admitting that he has wronged Tamar and denied his son's rights.

Yet, as the *targum* claims, Judah also admits that he is guilty for having wronged his father, Jacob. In telling his father about Joseph, he misrepresented the facts. By lying, he abused his trust and power as a son. Now, in the case of Tamar, Judah uses his power and position as a judge to condemn his behavior with Tamar by attesting to her innocence.

This explanation of *Targum Yerushalmi* may help solve the question of why this story of Judah and Tamar is placed in the midst of the tale about Joseph.

Judah lied to his father. He told him that Joseph had been killed, not sold into slavery. As a result, he brought great sorrow upon Jacob. Now, in the case of Tamar, he was again deceptive. He lied to her, promising her a marriage to Shelah, which he failed to arrange. This time, however, when Judah is confronted with the truth about what he did to Tamar, he refuses to lie. Instead, he bravely takes the blame and saves Tamar from death.

This story of Judah and Tamar, coming as it does in the midst of the tale of Joseph, contains a significant lesson about how human beings can change and grow toward honesty. Judah is portrayed as a liar who fails to make good on his promises. But he is also a person who matures. He learns from his mistakes. When Tamar confronts him with the truth, he neither makes excuses for his behavior nor continues to call for her death. Instead, he courageously admits before all his townspeople that he is wrong. And Tamar, who has been treated unjustly, forgives him rather than publicly denouncing and demeaning him.

Both Judah and Tamar emerge as models of moral integrity and behavior.

PEREK GIMEL: *How Do You Measure Loyalty and Success?*

In the story of Tamar and Judah, Tamar acts like a prostitute and easily seduces Judah. By contrast, Potiphar's wife seeks to seduce Joseph but fails. In her disappointment and anger, she accuses Joseph of raping her, and Potiphar throws Joseph into jail.

Why did Joseph resist the flirtations of Potiphar's wife? No one was at home. Potiphar's wife is reported to have been beautiful and very much attracted to Joseph. So why did he turn her down? Why did he risk making her hostile and losing all that he had achieved?

According to an explanation in the *Sifre*, a commentary on Numbers and Deuteronomy, edited in the fourth century C.E., Joseph would not let his strong sexual desires get the best of him. He remained in control of himself. "As a righteous person, he told himself not to give in to the temptations Potiphar's wife was putting before him." (Deuteronomy 3:33)

In another interpretation, the *Tanchuma* explains that Joseph resisted her because he took an oath never to approach his master's wife. Putting words in Joseph's mouth, the author of the *Tanchuma* writes that Joseph said to himself: "How can I do such an evil thing as to sin against God by breaking my oath?"

A great hero
Is there among the virtuous a greater hero than a young seventeen year old surrounded by loose women who manages to keep himself from them? Because he did so, Joseph was rewarded when, much later, his children were blessed with the words of his father, Jacob. (Zohar, Genesis 48:19; also Pesachim 113a–b)

Steinsaltz

Joseph was a tzadik—a righteous man
The chief argument in favor of his being called a tzadik *is drawn from the climax of the story of the wife of Potiphar, whose temptations he firmly resisted. (Adin Steinsaltz, Biblical Images, p. 63)*

Other interpreters, however, do not view Joseph in such a positive way. They raise serious questions about his behavior. Rashi says that, as soon as Joseph was appointed by Potiphar to a position of importance, he began to eat and drink excessively like all the rest of the Egyptian ruling class. He curled his hair and lived lavishly. He forgot all about being a slave and assimilated into idolatry and the loose sexual practices of Egyptian society.

Modern writer Elie Wiesel raises a serious question about Joseph's character when he comments: "One does not provoke a woman unless one wants to. One does not love a woman—or a man—against one's will. Every relationship is a two-way affair." (*Messengers of God*, p. 148)

Adding to the suspicions about Joseph's behavior with Potiphar's wife, Rav Samuel says that Joseph "deliberately entered the house in order to be seduced by her." And Rabbi Abin says that "she chased him from room to room and from chamber to chamber until she brought him to her bed." It was only when they reached her bed, according to several interpreters, that Joseph began to question the morality of what he was about to do.

According to one version taught by the rabbis, Joseph is portrayed as saying to Potiphar's wife, "I am afraid that your husband will discover our affair." She answered him, "Then I will murder him." Joseph was shocked and answered, "Then I will not only be an adulterer but also the accomplice to a murder." (*Sotah* 36b and *Genesis Rabbah* 87:5)

Elsewhere, the rabbis say that Joseph looked up from the bed where he and Potiphar's wife were embracing and saw that she had placed a sheet over the head of an idol hanging on the wall. Suddenly he realized what a mistake he was making. "You have placed a sheet over the idol because you are ashamed of what we are about to do," he said to her. "How much more should I be ashamed before God, whose eyes are everywhere in the world?" To this version, Rabbi Huna commented that Joseph also declared: "By God, I will not do this wicked thing." (*Genesis Rabbah* 87:5)

Rabbi Huna taught that it was not an idol that Joseph had seen but rather the face of his father, Jacob. In that moment of temptation, just before he was about to sin and commit adultery, "Jacob appeared to him, and Joseph's passion immediately cooled." (*Genesis Rabbah* 87:7) Some interpreters speculate that Jacob said to him: "Do you want to be called an associate of prostitutes?" (*Tosafot* to *Sotah* 36b)

Joseph's moral victory

The vision of Joseph's venerable father appeared to him just as the will of the young man weakened, just as he was about to sin. Potiphar's wife believed she had at last charmed and seduced him. It was then that the sudden vision gave him the strength to control himself, to triumph over his moment of weakness, and to conquer his nature. . . . When a child's training and upbringing are such that even if he has long been separated from the family home and even if he is lost in the midst of licentious surroundings in a faraway country, his father's influence still guides him toward moral victory; then this training is the ideal Jewish upbringing." (Sefat Emet, *based on* Sotah 36a)

Do as Joseph did

When someone tries to talk you into sinning, the first thing you must do is refuse without going into details or engaging in debate on the reasons for your refusal. Only after having made it clear that you refuse to sin may you recite reasons for refusing. Do as Joseph did. He told her no, then he gave her the reasons: "Look, with me here, my master gives no thought to anything in this house, and all that he owns he has placed in my hands. He wields no more authority in this house than I, and he has withheld nothing from me except yourself since you are his wife. How then could I do this most wicked thing and sin before God?" (Sefat Emet)

Most of our commentators, it seems, conclude that Joseph came to his "moral senses" at the very last moment. Potiphar's wife offered powerful temptations. She was beautiful, alone, and anxious to make love to him. He was flattered, perhaps infatuated, by her. He nearly gave in to her flirtations and propositions. Yet, just as he was about to sleep with her, his *loyalty* to Potiphar, to the moral traditions that his father, Jacob, had taught him, and to God—all convinced Joseph to tell her: "How could I do this most wicked thing and sin before God?"

Like Judah his brother, Joseph grows and matures in his ethical sensitivity and ability to act justly. From the spoiled youngest son who lies about his brothers to win the attentions and affections of his father, Joseph becomes a person of loyalty and praiseworthy, ethical behavior.

For his decision, Joseph is called a *tzadik*—a "righteous person." It is a title he earns. He is not born to it. He becomes a "righteous person" through his struggle with temptations, with greed, and with selfishness. His achievement marks a turning point in his life.

Although Potiphar throws him into jail, Joseph's loyalty and morality are ultimately rewarded. First, he is given special privileges by the warden. Later, Pharaoh appoints him as the most powerful prince in Egypt.

QUESTIONS FOR STUDY AND DISCUSSION

1. Can parents be expected to treat their children equally? How can parents treat each child as an individual without showing favoritism?

2. What are some of the problems caused by teachers, counselors, judges, and bosses who show favoritism?

3. Levirate marriage seems to imply that the purpose of marriage is having children. Should marriage be more than that? What? How?

4. Do you agree with Elie Wiesel that "every relationship is a two-way affair"?

5. Some commentators argue that Joseph was weak and nearly seduced by Potiphar's wife. Others say that he was perfectly righteous in his responses to her. Which commentators have the most convincing case?

6. What role does guilt play in the transformation of both Judah's and Joseph's character? Is feeling guilty ever a good thing?

PARASHAT MIKETZ
Genesis 41:1–44:17

Miketz, which means "at the end of . . ." continues Joseph's adventure in Egypt. Pharaoh has two dreams that none of his advisors can interpret. The cupbearer remembers Joseph and tells Pharaoh about him. Joseph is brought from jail and interprets Pharaoh's dreams to mean that Egypt will have seven years of plenty and seven years of famine. Pharaoh puts Joseph in charge of his land. When the famine strikes, Jacob sends his sons, except for Benjamin, to Egypt. When they arrive, Joseph recognizes his brothers and accuses them of coming to spy in his land. They tell him that they have come for food and that they have an elderly father and one younger brother. Joseph seizes Simeon and tells the brothers that he will not go free until they return with their youngest brother. He takes their money and sends them off with sacks of food. Later, they discover that each of their sacks contains the money they had previously given to Joseph. As the famine worsens, Jacob tells his sons to return to Egypt. They remind Jacob that they cannot return without Benjamin. Judah pledges that Benjamin will be safe. When his brothers return to Egypt, Joseph frees Simeon and invites the brothers to his house for a banquet. He has yet to reveal his identity. When the banquet concludes, he orders that the brothers' bags be filled with food and that his wine cup be secretly placed in Benjamin's bag. After the brothers depart, Joseph sends his steward to pursue and arrest them for stealing his wine cup. They reply that they have taken nothing. When the wine cup is found in Benjamin's bag, the brothers are brought back to Joseph's house. He informs them that he will keep Benjamin as a slave but release the rest of them.

OUR TARGUM

· 1 ·

Two years after Joseph interprets the cup-bearer's dream and is restored to Pharaoh's service, Pharaoh has a dream. He is standing by the Nile River when out come seven large cows. They are followed by seven thin cows that eat up the seven fat ones. Then he dreams of seven ears of solid grain growing on one sturdy stalk and of seven scorched ears that swallow the sturdy ones.

When Pharaoh's magicians and advisors cannot interpret his dreams, the cupbearer tells him about Joseph.

Pharaoh sends for Joseph and tells him about his dreams. After listening, Joseph explains that both dreams carry the same message. They forecast seven years of plenty to be followed by seven years of famine. Joseph counsels the Egyptian ruler to appoint "a man of discernment and wisdom" who can manage Egypt's resources wisely.

Pharaoh asks Joseph to assume the responsibilities and presents him with his signet ring of authority, a house, a gold chain, a chariot, and a wife. Joseph organizes storage cities for Egypt's grain and carefully plans for the future. He fathers two sons. The first he calls *Manasseh,* meaning "God has made me forget completely my hardship and my parental home," and the second is named *Ephraim,* meaning "God has made me fertile in the land of my affliction."

· 2 ·

When famine sets in, Jacob instructs his sons to go down to Egypt to purchase food. When they arrive, Joseph recognizes them but acts like a stranger. They bow before him, and he recalls his dreams.

He speaks harshly to them, accusing them of coming to spy in his land. They tell him that they are ten brothers, sons of an old man, that they were once twelve but that their youngest brother has remained with their father, and that one brother "is no more."

Once again, Joseph calls them "spies." He puts them in jail for three days. Realizing that they are being punished for what they had done to Joseph,

Reuben tells them: "Did I not tell you, 'Do no wrong to the boy'? But you paid no attention. Now comes the reckoning for his blood."

Joseph overhears them but pretends not to understand their language. He orders Simeon seized and tells them to return to their land and not to come back without their youngest brother. Secretly, he instructs his servants to fill their sacks with grain and replace the money they have paid to him in each of their bags.

· 3 ·

The brothers return to Jacob and tell him about "the man" they met in Egypt, about Simeon, and about the money returned to them. They also share "the man's" demand to see Benjamin, but, fearing the loss of his youngest son, Jacob refuses. "My son must not go down with you," he says to them, "for his brother is dead and he alone is left."

As the famine becomes more severe, however, the brothers approach Jacob again. Judah promises to look after Benjamin, and Jacob finally agrees. Taking gifts and money with them, they return to Egypt. Joseph welcomes them and tells his steward to prepare a meal for them in his house. He returns Simeon to them and, greeting Benjamin, inquires about the health of their father. However, he does not reveal his identity to his brothers.

After the meal, he tells his steward to fill their bags with food and to return their money. Cleverly laying a trap for Benjamin, he instructs the steward: "Put my silver goblet in the mouth of the bag of the youngest one." When his brothers leave, he has them followed, stopped, and searched. They protest, declaring that they have taken nothing from Joseph. When the goblet is found in Benjamin's bag, the brothers are brought back to Joseph's house.

Fearing that returning without Benjamin will kill Jacob, Judah pleads with Joseph. He tells Joseph to take all of them as slaves, arguing that they are as guilty "as he in whose possession the goblet was found." Joseph refuses, telling them that he will take only Benjamin and that the rest of them can return to their father.

THEMES

Parashat Miketz contains three important themes:

1. Knowing what to do with dreams.
2. The choice between revenge and caring.
3. The choice between death and survival.

PEREK ALEF: *Joseph Knew What to Do with Dreams*

We have already encountered Joseph the dreamer. At seventeen he dreams about his brothers' sheaves bowing down to his and about the sun, moon, and eleven stars—his parents and brothers—also bowing to him. These dreams, as we have seen, anger his brothers and make Jacob suspicious about Joseph.

Some years later, while he is in prison, Joseph the dreamer becomes Joseph the interpreter of dreams. He accurately predicts the future for Pharaoh's former baker and cupbearer. The baker will die, and the cupbearer, he forecasts, will be restored to his position in Pharaoh's court.

Now, in our Torah portion, Pharaoh's cupbearer recalls Joseph's interpretive powers. Pharaoh has dreamed dreams that neither his advisors nor magicians can explain. The cupbearer informs his ruler about "the Hebrew youth" who understood his dream and predicted the future. Pharaoh is impressed. He frees Joseph and brings him to his court so that he can tell Joseph about his own dreams.

Hirsch

Joseph listened
Rabbi Samson Raphael Hirsch explained that Pharaoh said to Joseph: "I have heard of you that you listen to a dream in such a manner that you solve its meaning from its very contents." It all depends on listening to it correctly. Of ten people who listen to a speech or a story, often hearing it differently, only one hears it correctly. (The Pentateuch, *on Genesis 41:15*)

Listening
Human beings were endowed with two ears and one tongue that they might listen more than speak. (Abraham Hasdai, 13th century, translator and philosopher, Barcelona)

Listen and you will learn. (Solomon ibn Gabirol)

When two students listen patiently to each other in a discussion of Torah, God also listens to them.

And, if they do not, they cause God to depart from them. (Simeon ben Lakish, Shabbat 63b)

When Joseph arrives at court, Pharaoh greets him and says: "I have heard it said of you that for you to hear a dream is to tell its meaning." The Hebrew verb "hear" is *tishema*. It derives from the root *shema,* meaning not only "hear" but also "comprehend" or "understand."

Apparently, Joseph's success at interpreting the dreams that Pharaoh's wise men and magicians could not decipher had to do with his special listening skills. Some commentators speculate that Pharaoh's servants probably heard the king's description and then rushed off to consult their books on dreams. Instead of paying careful attention to Pharaoh's unique experience, they looked for an already accepted theory and explanation. As a result, they concluded that the dreams were two separate predictions of disaster. (*Genesis Rabbah* 89:60)

Joseph's approach was very different. He was ready to experiment with various original explanations. So he listened carefully to the dreams and to the varying shades and tones of Pharaoh's description in order to comprehend the emotion inside the words and to understand the subtle distinctions of each object Pharaoh mentioned and of every gesture made by the Egyptian ruler.

Because of his careful listening and openness to original insights, Joseph concludes that Pharaoh's two dreams are actually "one and the same." His ability to "hear" makes all the difference in his successful interpretation of Pharaoh's dreams.

But Joseph does more than offer interpretations. Psychologist Dr. Dorothy F. Zeligs, in her study of Joseph's personality, calls attention to the fact that he also presents Pharaoh with "a plan for dealing with the situation." Grain is to be stored throughout the land during the period of plentiful harvest in order to provide for years of famine. "Again," Zeligs writes, "Joseph the dreamer shows himself to be also a man of action. . . . Again he uses his very real abilities and his capacity for hard work to consolidate his position. His achievements therefore cannot be said to be based on fortuitous circumstances alone. For the rest of his life, Joseph remains in Pharaoh's favor. This

is no small accomplishment when one considers how fickle were the moods of those mighty potentates."(*Psychoanalysis and the Bible,* Bloch, New York, 1974, pp. 77–78)

Rabbi Mordechai Ha-Kohen, who lived in Safed during the seventeenth century, points out that Joseph did not delegate the responsibilities for distributing food to subordinate officials. Instead, he supervised all the storage and sales, personally making sure that no one was cheated. By the example of his own hard work and his compassion for the hungry and needy, he set a model of behavior for others. (*Siftei Kohen* on *Miketz*)

Dreamers and Dreams

Do not mock the words of our dreamers. Their words become the seeds of freedom. (Heinrich Heine)

If you will it, it is not a dream. (Theodor Herzl)

You see things; and you say, "Why?" But I dream things that never were; and I say, "Why not?" (George Bernard Shaw)

Other interpreters also emphasize that Joseph was not just an interpreter of dreams but a person of action as well. He established a careful plan for dealing with the seven years of plenty and the seven years of famine. Rather than procrastinating, he developed solutions to the problems facing Egypt. Nor did he lose time in implementing his design for saving the country from disaster. He planned and built storage cities, organizing an original system for collecting one-fifth of Egypt's produce during the years of plenty by storing it in silos.

Steinsaltz

"From being a dreamer of dreams," commentator Adin Steinsaltz observes, "Joseph became the person of the dream . . . a man who experienced the dream . . . as a burden and a responsibility and a course of action from which there could be no digression." (*Biblical Images*, p. 70)

Joseph's greatness, according to our interpreters, was not only that he developed a "sensitive ear," an ability to listen to what others were saying, but that he was also ready to assume responsibility for transforming dreams into reality. Pharaoh obviously sensed Joseph's leadership qualities and, therefore, immediately told him: "You shall be in charge of my court, and by your command shall all my people be directed. . . ."

It was a wise decision, for Joseph was a person who got things done. He was not a dreamer who shirked responsibilities. He was a hard worker who willingly used his skills for turning Pharaoh's dreams into a strategy for survival.

PEREK BET: *The Choice between Revenge and Caring*

Abravanel

In his commentary to our Torah portion, Isaac Abravanel asks: "Why did Joseph denounce his brothers? Certainly it was wrong of him to take revenge and bear a grudge against them. After all, while their intent had been evil, God turned it to good. It is true that he had suffered years in jail, but he had also emerged as one of the most important and powerful leaders of Egypt. None of his good fortune would have occurred had his brothers not sold him into slavery. So what justification did Joseph have for taking revenge after twenty years? Why did he not have compassion for them or at least show more concern for the feelings of his aged father?"

Bearing a grudge
"*You shall not take vengeance or bear a grudge. . . .*" (*Leviticus 19:19*)

Do not say, "I will do to him as he has done to me." (Proverbs 24:29)

Do not say, "Since I have been humiliated, let my neighbor be humiliated. Know that, when you humiliate another person, you are humiliating the image of God." (Ben Azai, Tanchuma, Genesis Rabbah 24:7)

If you refuse assistance to a neighbor because he had been unkind to you, you are guilty of revenge; if you grant him his request for aid and remind him of his unkindness, you are guilty of bearing a grudge. (Sifra to Leviticus 19:18)

Author Maurice Samuel is also bothered by Joseph's treatment of his brothers and father. He accuses Joseph of "cruelty" and "revenge." He calls Joseph "the brilliant failure" because of his success in reaching the pinnacle of power in Egypt and because of his insensitivity toward his brothers and father. Samuel writes:

He accused them of being spies. He watched their consternation, and he toyed with it while they, poor devils, stammered their protests at this unbelievable turn of events and argued with him, to no effect of course. It was like arguing with a lunatic—an omnipotent lunatic. They thought of their families at home, their wives and their little ones and old Jacob—very old by now—waiting for bread. And here was this mad governor of Egypt. . . . If you have forgotten some details of the story, if you think that Joseph is now satisfied, that, having had his innocent little revenge, he calls the shocking comedy off, then you do not know your man. The actor has an insatiable appetite for encores. . . . This wantonness of Joseph's, this frivolity, this cruelty, is particularly embarrassing.
(*Certain People of the Book*, Knopf, New York, 1955, pp. 312–326)

Ramban (Nachmanides)

Nachmanides disagrees with both Abravanel's and Maurice Samuel's criticism of Joseph. He maintains that Joseph is not guilty of cruel revenge but is simply carrying out the predictions forecast in his youthful dreams. He dreamed that "all the sheaves," and "the sun, moon, and eleven stars" would bow to him.

Joseph, Nachmanides argues, now recalled those dreams and believed that it was his duty to fulfill them. Therefore, he hid his identity from his brothers so that they would be forced to bring Benjamin and, ultimately, Jacob down to Egypt where they would all bow before him. "Joseph," Nachmanides writes, "carried out everything in the appropriate manner in order to fulfill his youthful dreams."

Rabbi Isaac Arama is shocked at Nachmanides' explanation and justification of Joseph's behavior. Not hiding his surprise, he comments, "I am astonished at Nachmanides' explanation that Joseph did what he did in order to make his dreams come true. What did such behavior benefit him? And, even if he benefited, he should not have sinned against his father with such cruel treatment of him." (*Akedat Yitzhak*)

Elie Wiesel agrees. Condemning Joseph's desire for revenge, he writes: "Later, when his brothers were brought before him, he sought only to ridicule them, to take his vengeance. Instead of inquiring about his father and his younger brother, he demanded hostages; instead of feeding them, he made them tremble with fear. Weeks and weeks went by before he deigned to reassure them. Ten times he heard his brothers refer to their father as *your servant Jacob* and, unmoved, neither protested nor betrayed himself." (*Messengers of God*, p. 160)

Hirsch

Clearly, many commentators criticize Joseph for mistreating his father and brothers. Like Nachmanides, however, Rabbi Samson Raphael Hirsch believes that Joseph acted neither out of revenge nor out of selfishness by seeking to fulfill the predictions of his youthful dreams. Instead, Hirsch argues, Joseph put his brothers to the test in order to determine two important matters: *First,* he wanted to know if they would do to Benjamin what they had done to him. If so, then he could neither forgive nor trust them. *Second,* he needed to test how they would react when, and if, he, as a ruler of Egypt, revealed himself as their brother. Would they trust him? Would they be loyal to him? Would they love him?

Hirsch calls Joseph's treatment of his brothers and father "unavoidable." He justifies Joseph's withholding his identity from his brothers, his accusing them of being spies, his forcing them to bring Benjamin to Egypt against their father's will, his planting of his goblet in Benjamin's sack and seizing him as hostage—as *necessary.* Joseph, Hirsch maintains, had to protect himself, his position, and his family. He had to be certain that his brothers could be trusted and that they were no longer out to destroy him. He had to test them. Joseph, says Hirsch, acted out of wisdom, not out of spite or revenge.

The differences of opinion remain about whether Joseph's behavior was justified or not. And so do the questions: Did he care about the feelings of his brothers or his aging father? Was he still angry about what his brothers had done to him? Was he determined to make them suffer as he had suffered? Did Joseph want revenge or reconciliation?

PEREK GIMEL: *Jacob's Choice— Risking Death for Survival*

Jacob's sons returned from Egypt with food but without Simeon. They explained to Jacob that "the lord of the land" spoke harshly to them, accused them of spying, and told them not to return unless they brought their youngest brother, Benjamin, with them.

Jacob responded with anger. "It is always me that you bereave: Joseph is no more and Simeon is no more, and now you would take away Benjamin." Hoping to win his father's trust, Reuben declared that if anything happened to Benjamin he would allow Jacob to put to death his own two sons. But Jacob refused. He would not allow them to take Benjamin to Egypt.

Months passed. Their food provisions began to run low, and famine threatened. So the brothers, once again, approached their father, hoping to convince him to send Benjamin with them back to Egypt. Judah spoke on their behalf, promising to care for Benjamin. This time, Jacob agreed. He sent them off with gifts and money. "As for me," he told them, "if I am to be bereaved, I shall be bereaved."

The incident is a dramatic illustration of family tension and parental love. And it raises important questions: What prompts Jacob's change of mind? Why is Judah able to convince Jacob to send Benjamin when Reuben's argument failed? Why is Jacob suddenly ready to risk Benjamin's life, with the potential of bringing great sorrow upon himself?

According to Rabbi Judah, Reuben demonstrated his moral insensitivity and stupidity when he tried to persuade Jacob to allow Benjamin to go down to Egypt with his brothers. His proposition to Jacob that, if anything were to happen to Benjamin, he could take the lives of his own sons was unacceptable. Jacob dismissed it by telling Reuben: "Fool! Do you not realize that your sons are my grandsons. How could I take their lives?" (*Genesis Rabbah* 91:8)

Rashi

On the other hand, Rashi believes that the real reason Jacob dismissed Reuben's argument but accepted Judah's was simply a matter of timing. Reuben approached Jacob just after returning from Egypt. Jacob was deeply upset that his sons had returned without Simeon and refused to place Benjamin's fate in their hands. Furthermore, because they had brought back plenty of food, he was not concerned with the danger of famine. He saw no reason, at that time, to risk losing another son.

Consequently, as Rashi points out, Judah waited until hunger finally threatened Jacob's entire family. Then, he came before his father and presented his argument. According to Rashi, Judah told Jacob: "You say that you fear for Benjamin. Well, none of us knows whether or not he will be seized by the Egyptian ruler. What we do know is that, if we do not return to Egypt with

Benjamin, all of us will die of starvation. Is it not better to let go what is doubtful and snatch what is certain?"

The worst decision

A story is told of two pious men who went on a sea journey. A huge wave threatened to sink their ship. One of them said: "This is the worst!" The other replied: "It could be much worse." "How is that possible?" asked the first. "We are at the gates of death. Can there be anything worse?" "Yes," explained the other. "We could be placed in the predicament of Jacob whose sons came to him seeking bread, and he had none to give them. Remember that choice. As long as he had food in the bin, he refused to allow Benjamin to go to Egypt. But, as soon as the bin was empty, he was forced to say: "Take your brother." (As related in Nehama Leibowitz, Studies in Bereshit, p. 474)

Can one life be sacrificed for many? *A group of people, walking along a road, are stopped by evil people who say to them: "Give us one of you, and we will kill him. If not, we will kill all of you." What shall be done? Rather than surrendering one person, let all of them be killed. But, if the evil people single out one person, as was the case with Sheba ben Bichri (who rebelled against King David), that person may be surrendered to them so that the others may be saved. Rabbi Simeon ben Lakish said: "Only someone who is under sentence of death, the way Sheba ben Bichri was, may be turned over."*

But Rabbi Yochanan disagreed. He argued that, if the evil people single out one person, then the others should save themselves by turning that person over to them. (Jerusalem Talmud, Terumot 8:12)

Nachmanides agrees with Rashi's view but extends it. He suggests that Judah wisely counseled his brothers to wait until there was no bread left in the house. Then Jacob would listen. He would make the difficult decision to risk one life in order to save many lives. (Nachmanides on Genesis 42:37)

Nehama Leibowitz wonders what it was that convinced Jacob to change his mind and agree to send Benjamin with his brothers. He does not seem to have been moved by either Simeon's imprisonment or by Reuben's appeal. Leibowitz believes that it was the hunger of his grandchildren that persuaded the patriarch. It was seeing the children wasting away, crying for food that moved him. "The hunger of the little ones finally broke his resistance. Judah meaningfully ended the first sentence of his appeal with the words: '. . . and also our little ones.' " (*Studies in Bereshit*, p. 474)

Jacob's refusal to go along with Reuben's suggestion that the brothers return immediately to Egypt with Benjamin in order to rescue Simeon raises several questions: Was it right for him to leave Simeon imprisoned and, perhaps, suffering for so long? Was he justified in delaying until they ran out of food, endangering the children?

Our commentators all suggest that the patriarch acted justly. He carefully weighed his options, waiting to see what events might bring. In the end, his difficult decision was based on compassion for all his children and upon what might guarantee their survival.

QUESTIONS FOR STUDY AND DISCUSSION

1. According to our commentators, what is the art of interpreting dreams? Are dreamers essential for human development?

2. Who has the better argument about Joseph's treatment of his brothers and father: Abravanel, Samuel, and Wiesel or Nachmanides and Hirsch? Was Joseph's motive innocent or deliberate revenge?

3. Should Jacob have rejected Reuben's plea to return immediately with Benjamin to Egypt? Was it just for him to wait until starvation threatened his grandchildren?

4. Are parents justified in taking any risk to prevent their children from starving?

PARASHAT VAYIGASH
Genesis 44:18–47:27

Vayigash, which means "and he approached him," begins with the confrontation between Judah and Joseph, whose identity is still unknown to his brothers. Judah tells Joseph that, if he refuses to allow Benjamin to return to his father, the old man will die. He pleads with Joseph to take him as a slave in place of Benjamin. Joseph hears Judah and then dramatically reveals his identity to his brothers. He instructs them to bring Jacob to Egypt and to settle there in Goshen. Pharaoh also invites Joseph's family "to live off the fat of the land." Jacob arrives in Egypt for an emotional reunion with Joseph and is welcomed as well by Pharaoh. The famine continues, and Joseph arranges for people to exchange livestock for food and, then, land for food. Controlling the land for Pharaoh, Joseph distributes seed for planting with the agreement that the people will give one-fifth to Pharaoh and keep four-fifths for themselves. Meanwhile, Jacob and his family increase in numbers and wealth in the area of Goshen.

OUR TARGUM

· 1 ·

Joseph arranges to have his goblet placed in Benjamin's sack and then arrests his brothers for stealing. His identity is still unknown to them. Now they appear before him falsely accused of a crime, fearful that he will enslave Benjamin. They know that, if they return without their youngest brother, the loss will kill their father, Jacob.

Judah approaches Joseph, reminding him of a previous conversation in which Judah told Joseph that, if the brothers returned without Benjamin, their father would die of sorrow. He pleads with Joseph to enslave him rather than Benjamin. "For how can I go back to my father unless the boy is with me? Let me not be witness to the sorrow that would overtake my father."

Joseph is moved and tells his attendants to leave the room. He then reveals his identity. "I am Joseph," he tells his brothers. "Is my father still well [alive]?" His weeping is so loud that the Egyptians in his house hear him and pass the news about his brothers to Pharaoh's court.

The brothers are stunned and afraid. Joseph assures them that, although they sold him into slavery, all has turned out well. "God," he explains, "has sent me ahead of you to insure your survival on earth and to save your lives in an extraordinary deliverance."

He tells them to hurry back to their father and to bring the entire family to Egypt. He promises to provide for them in the fertile region of Goshen, which is located today in the area between Port Said and the Suez. "You must tell my father everything about my high station in Egypt and all that you have seen; and bring my father here with all speed."

When Pharaoh and his court hear about Joseph's brothers, they are pleased. Pharaoh offers the brothers wagons with which to bring their households to Egypt and promises to give them "the best of the land of Egypt" as a place to dwell. They return to Canaan with bread, grain, and the fruits of Egypt, and they report to their father: "Joseph is still alive; yes, he is ruler over the whole land of Egypt."

Jacob is overjoyed with the news. He declares: "My son Joseph is still alive. I must go and see him before I die."

· 2 ·

Soon afterwards, they all set out for Egypt. Jacob travels to Beer-sheba where he encounters God in a night vision. God promises to be with him in Egypt—and that his people will become "a great nation."

Joseph and Jacob meet in Goshen. The old man embraces his long lost son. "Now I can die," he says, "having seen for myself that you are still alive."

· 3 ·

Joseph explains to his brothers that the Egyptians hate shepherds but that he has arranged for them to dwell in the area of Goshen where they can care for their livestock. Preparing them for a meeting with Pharaoh, Joseph counsels them that the Egyptian ruler will ask them, "What is your occupation?" He tells them to answer that they have been shepherds as their fathers before them were shepherds.

When Pharaoh meets with them and hears their response, he assures them of their safety. Pharaoh tells Joseph: "The land of Egypt is open before you . . . let them stay in the region of Goshen. And, if you know any capable men among them, put them in charge of my livestock."

After a conversation between Pharaoh and Jacob, the family settles in Goshen. Joseph cares for them, providing food for all. Through the years the family increases greatly in both numbers and wealth.

· 4 ·

With the famine increasing and the people without money to buy food, Joseph designs a plan, enabling the population of Egypt to purchase provisions in exchange for livestock. After the people have sold all their livestock, Joseph allows the people to trade their land for food.

Having gained control of all the land for Pharaoh, Joseph then offers the people a plan for production and taxation. At harvest time, they will pay Pharaoh with one-fifth of their produce and keep the remainder to feed themselves and their families. Only Pharaoh's priests are excluded from this arrangement since they already receive special payment from the Egyptian ruler.

THEMES

Parashat Vayigash contains four important themes:

1. The importance of speaking out for justice.
2. The difficulty and importance of achieving reconciliation.
3. Fear of the stranger.
4. Economic planning and justice.

PEREK ALEF: *Judah's Speech—A Plea for Justice*

Parashat Vayigash begins with Judah's plea for justice before the Egyptian head of state who has announced his intention to make a slave of Benjamin. The brothers are still unaware that it is Joseph with whom they are dealing, but they know that, if they return to Canaan without Benjamin, the loss will kill their father. As Judah steps forward, he realizes that everything now depends upon what he will say.

Interpreters of Judah's speech to Joseph call attention not only to the fact that it is the longest oration in Genesis but that Judah carefully calculates his arguments and even his tone of voice. His is not a spontaneous presentation. He is pleading for the life of his brother and father. Therefore, he measures every word, every gesture, every inflection.

Imagining Judah standing in Joseph's lavish court, the commentators provide us with a colorful portrait of their confrontation. Rabbi Onkelos, known as "the convert," who taught during the end of the first and the beginning of the second century, suggests that "Judah spoke with a pure, clear logic." Every point he made to Joseph was supported by facts and was impossible to refute. Another rabbi, perhaps a colleague of Onkelos, says that Judah diplomatically emphasized his concerns, arguing with Joseph until he was certain that he had penetrated his heart and turned his anger into compassion. (*Genesis Rabbah* 93:3–4)

What were the arguments Judah might have used in his plea for justice? How did he compel Joseph to reveal his identity and release Benjamin?

Hirsch

Rabbi Samson Raphael Hirsch believes that Judah decided to defend himself against Joseph's anger by flattering him. So he told him: "May that which I want to say not excite your sensitiveness for, see, you are as Pharaoh. I honor you as a pharaoh so, if anything that I say does not please you, do not think that I do it from lack of honor. What I say to you I would also say to Pharaoh." (On Genesis 44:18)

Rashi

Rashi speculates that Judah used a different approach. Rather than flattering Joseph, Judah attacked him. He told him: "You are as unreliable as Pharaoh. Just as he issues promises and does not carry them out, so do you. You promised that you only wanted 'to see' our youngest brother. Now you are making him your slave." In Rashi's view, Judah exposes Joseph's callousness. He tells him that he cannot be trusted, that he is a liar. (On Genesis 44:18)

Other interpreters say that Judah accused Joseph, not only of lying to them, but also of breaking Egyptian law. They explain that Judah confronted him with the fact that Egyptian law allows you to take from a thief everything he owns but does not permit you to make him your slave. "You are breaking your own laws," Judah complained to him. (*Midrash Tanchuma, Vayigash;* also Ba'al Ha-Turim on Genesis 44:18)

Abravanel

What Judah did not say
Abravanel asks: "Why is it that Judah did not criticize Joseph for falsely accusing him and his brothers of being spies?" Answering the question, Abravanel writes: "He did not mention it because he did not wish to give Joseph an opportunity to return, once again, to that subject."

Ramban (Nachmanides)

What really moved Joseph
Nachmanides suggests that it was not just Judah's speech that moved Joseph. "There were many people present in Pharaoh's house and other Egyptians pleading with Joseph to pardon Benjamin. Their compassion had been deeply stirred by Judah's plea, and Joseph could not overcome them all." (Nachmanides on Genesis 45:1)

Judah's offer
With Judah's selfless offer of himself as a substitute for Benjamin, Joseph finally had irrefutable proof of change in his brothers' old attitudes. Judah exemplified their devotion to Jacob, their love for Benjamin, and their sincere repentance for their crime against Joseph himself." Convinced of their love, Joseph reveals himself to them. (Meir Zlotowitz, trans., Bereishis, Vol. VI, Art Scroll Tanach Series, New Mesorah Publications Ltd., 1981, p. 1958)

Rabbi Judah comments that "Judah approached Joseph to do battle with him." Other interpreters agree, pointing out that Judah criticized Joseph for wrongly accusing him and his brothers of being spies. He also complained that Joseph had singled them out at the border for special questioning and harassment. "Thousands of others have come here seeking grain," Judah told Joseph. "Not once have you cross-examined any of them. So why did you treat us so meanly?"

Some commentators say that Judah became enraged as he spoke to Joseph. Shaking a finger at him, Judah declared: "If you do not release Benjamin, we will paint Egypt in blood. We will destroy its markets and cities."

Others say that Judah tried another tactic. Because he wanted to frighten Joseph, he told him that his father, Jacob, possessed the deadly power of cursing others. "If I return to him without Benjamin, he will lay a curse of destruction not only upon Egypt but also upon you." Joseph became terrified and immediately revealed himself to his brothers. (*Tze'enah u-Re'enah, Vayigash,* Genesis 44:19)

Other interpreters disagree. It was neither Judah's threat of violence against Egypt nor a curse by Jacob that persuaded Joseph to reveal himself to his brothers. Instead, it was Judah's willingness to offer himself as a slave in place of Benjamin, together with his plea for consideration of their father's feelings.

Jacob ben Isaac Ashkenazi of Yanof, the author of *Tze'enah u-Re'enah,* explains that Judah approached Joseph and said to him: "Take me instead of Benjamin. For I have guaranteed his life to my father. I have promised to bring him back home." Judah hoped to appeal to the Egyptian leader's sense of compassion. He wished to convince Joseph of his genuine concern for his brother and father.

Modern commentator Nehama Leibowitz points out that Judah uses the word "father" fourteen times in his speech to Joseph. The repetition, Leibowitz believes, is not accidental. It "is calculated to arouse compassion in the hardest of hearts, appealing to the most elemental of affections—parental love." Judah, Leibowitz argues, hoped that, by repeating the word "father," his plea for justice might touch the heart of the Egyptian leader with a sense of the pain that a loss of a child might bring to a parent.

The interpreters of Judah's plea for justice suggest a wide range of reasons that may account for Joseph finally revealing himself to his brothers: Judah's flattery of him, his attack upon him, his threat of Jacob's curse upon him, or his willingness to sacrifice his own life for Benjamin's. As with many interpretations of Torah, the challenge to uncover the reason—or combination of reasons—remains.

PEREK BET: *The Hard Way of Reconciliation*

The scene in which Joseph reveals himself to his brothers is a memorable and emotional one. Overcome with tears, he tells his brothers, "I am Joseph. Is my father still well?" His brothers are astonished; they are speechless. So he says to them: "Come forward to me. I am your brother Joseph, he whom you sold into Egypt." He then explains to them that God sent him to Egypt to save them, and he instructs them to return to Canaan to bring their father, Jacob, and the rest of the family down to Egypt to settle in Goshen.

For many centuries, Torah interpreters have wondered about how these brothers who hated one another could undergo such "dramatic" reconciliation. They had a long history of bitterness and suspicion to repair. Suddenly the man who treated them like spies, arrested them, and jailed them reveals that he is the brother they sold into slavery. How could they build trust and faith in one another? How would they be able to overcome the hostility between them?

Peli

Modern commentator Pinchas Peli believes that Joseph acted wisely in asking everyone to leave the court so that he and his brothers could be alone when he revealed his identity to them. Peli explains: "It was one of those moments when no outsider should be present, when deep feelings should be confined to the inner circle of the close family. Only there may one voice the grievances that demand expression."

Peli may be correct. The fact that Joseph chose to be alone with his brothers so that they could privately voice their accusations and hostility may have helped to speed their reconciliation. But was it enough? Might it even have been dangerous?

Two of the ancient commentators have a serious disagreement about how wise it was for Joseph to tell all of his servants to leave the court so that he could be alone with his brothers. Rabbi Hama ben Hanina believed that it was a serious mistake. "Joseph did not act carefully," he argues. "After all, the brothers could have attacked and killed him."

Rabbi Samuel Nachmani claims that Joseph acted with great sensitivity and wisdom. He did not fear his brothers. After overhearing them speaking to one another, he knew that they felt very guilty for selling him into slavery. Seeing how much they regretted what they had done to him, and how they feared now for the welfare of both Benjamin and their father, he was right to trust them. (*Genesis Rabbah* 93:9)

A later interpreter adds to Rabbi Samuel's argument. He explains that Joseph insisted on being alone with his brothers for two other reasons. First, he did not want them publicly humiliated at the moment when he revealed that he was the brother they had sold into slavery. It was now a private matter between them. Second, he was afraid that, if the Egyptians found out that his brothers had sold him into slavery, the Egyptians might never trust them or allow Joseph to settle them in Egypt. (*Tze'enah u-Re'enah, Vayigash*)

Other commentators speculate on additional factors that helped the brothers reconcile after years of hostility and separation. Some claim that, when Joseph asked his brothers to approach him, he opened his garment and showed them that he was circumcised. Seeking to prove that he was one of them, he also addressed them in Hebrew. Others add that he spoke to each of them, showing no preference between them and thus convincing them that he bore no grudge toward any one of them. (*Genesis Rabbah* 93:10; *Tze'enah u Re'enah* on Genesis 45:12)

Be forgiving

Rabbi Asher ben Yechiel taught: "Each night before going to sleep, forgive whomever wronged you." (Hanhaga, c. 1320)

Raba taught: "He who forgives . . . will himself be forgiven." (Yoma 23a)

The poet Heinrich Heine (1797–1856) commented: "Since I myself stand in need of God's forgiveness, I grant forgiveness to all who have wronged me."

Austrian psychiatrist William Stekel (1868–1950) once said: "To be able to forget and forgive is the prerogative of noble souls."

Basing herself on many traditional commentaries, Nehama Leibowitz claims that Joseph smoothed the way to reconciliation between himself and his brothers by offering an explanation for what they had done and what had happened to him. He told them to think of the "large picture" and to focus on the positive results of selling him into Egyptian slavery. On the surface it might appear as an evil act. Yet, considering the whole picture, their actions led to his becoming second in command in Egypt, a position from which he could save his entire family. Joseph told them: "Now, do not feel bad or guilty because you sold me into slavery. It was actually to save life that God sent me ahead of you."

Leibowitz's argument is that Joseph made the reconciliation possible by offering a new explanation for what had happened between the brothers. It was not the brothers, but rather God, who had directed all the events. Good had resulted from evil. Viewing events on a broader scale helped them heal their hostilities, overcome their guilt, and move on to saving their lives.

Good out of evil

Rabbi Samson Raphael Hirsch comments: "Joseph repeatedly points out to his brothers how this whole chain of events clearly stands out as Divine Management. . . . The great Master of the world achieves everything from the smallest beginnings. . . . God it is who brings everything to service. Without knowing it and without wishing it, folly and sin also are used to serve God's ends." (On Genesis 45:11)

Don Isaac Abravanel strongly disagrees with those who argue that "evil leads to good" or that evil should ever be excused because it led to a positive outcome. He condemns Joseph's brothers. He writes: "The fact that by a fluke the sale turned out well did not lessen their offense. A person is not judged by the accidental results of his deeds but by his intent. The accidental results are irrelevant to the moral dimension."

So far as Abravanel is concerned, offering excuses for the evil the brothers had intended to do—and actually did in selling Joseph into slavery—would not have led to their reconciliation. Instead, it might have brought about more suspicion and fear. They might have wondered: When will he turn the tables on us and pay us back for the suffering we inflicted upon him? In this regard, it is interesting to note that later, after Jacob dies, the brothers express their fear that Joseph will finally punish them for what they had done to him. (See Genesis 50:15ff.)

Other interpreters, agreeing with Abravanel, hold that Joseph insisted that he be left alone with his brothers because he realized that making peace required honesty. Neither he nor they could pretend that what they had done to him was "good." They had to face one another in the privacy of their family and talk out their differences and their hostility. They had to get rid of their anger and suspicions in order to reach new levels of understanding and commitment.

So, according to one interpreter, when Joseph saw that his brothers were terrified after he told them who he was, he calmed them by saying, "I am *your brother* Joseph." He emphasized the words *"your brother,"* making certain that they understood that their family bond made it possible for him to be honest with them and to forgive them.

Other commentators say that Joseph kissed each of the brothers, showing them genuine affection. Then he assured them that they were safe in his house and that he would make sure that they returned unharmed to their father. He comforted them by promising to save them from famine by settling them safely in Goshen. Joseph even pledged to them that he would never tell Jacob that they had sold him into slavery. It was to be their secret, not something he used against them. (*Tze'enah u Re'enah* on Genesis 45:3 and 11)

Jewish commentators through the centuries have tried to figure out Joseph's strategy for reconciling with his brothers. Some of their explanations excuse the evil intentions of the brothers; others describe Joseph as a kind, thoughtful, and caring brother and son. They claim he was a devoted Jew, anxious to forgive his brothers and forget the pain they had caused him. From the varying descriptions and disagreements among those who have studied Joseph's treatment of his brothers, we learn much about the difficulties of forgiveness and reconciliation.

PEREK GIMEL: *Strangers in the Land*

The Torah informs us that, after the brothers reconciled, Pharaoh invited Joseph's family to settle in Egypt. He sent wagons to Jacob to ease his journey, and he and his heads of state festively greeted Jacob and Joseph's brothers and families upon their arrival. The welcome appears to have been a very warm one. Pharaoh invited them all to settle in Goshen.

Interpreters of this part of the Joseph story are not satisfied with the Torah's "happy ending." They raise some significant questions: What was it like to be immigrants and strangers in a foreign land? Were Pharaoh and other Egyptians happy about welcoming Jews into their land? What about Jacob and his family? Did they fear being overwhelmed by Egyptian culture?

According to one interpretation, Pharaoh and the other leaders of Egypt were delighted to learn that Joseph—to whom they had given such high office and vast responsibilities—was not a common slave but the son of noble parents. They had been embarrassed by what they believed were his slave origins. In Egypt human beings were not judged by their talents and character but by their place in the social and economic order. Slaves were at the bottom of the society. The knowledge that Joseph was from distinguished parentage actually boosted his status and reputation among the Egyptians. (*Tze'enah u-Re'enah* on Genesis 45:14)

For some commentators that explains why Pharaoh welcomed Jacob so warmly. He considered him a "prince," a leader of another people. So he honored him with transportation, food, hospitality, and the generous offer of settlement in Goshen.

Other interpreters speculate that Pharaoh rushed out to greet Jacob and his family and offered them Goshen because he was afraid of losing Joseph as an advisor. He required Joseph's skills at administering Egypt's successful famine relief program. Joseph's leadership and knowledge were very valuable to the Egyptian ruler. Pharaoh reasoned that, if Joseph's father and brothers settled in Goshen, then Joseph would remain in Egypt. So he offered them the best of his land and assured them his protection. (*Midrash Tanchuma* to *Vayigash*)

Some commentators, however, do not agree that Pharaoh's welcome of Jacob and his sons was so enthusiastic. They say that many of Pharaoh's ministers complained that Jews, like Joseph, would compete with them for positions of leadership. "When Joseph came to power," they said, "we lost our positions. Now he will give positions to his brothers and make them lords over us." (*Midrash ha-Gadol* on Genesis 45:17)

Abravanel believes that Joseph was also concerned about the negative feelings of Egyptians toward Jews. He wanted it clearly understood that they were not arriving to take other people's positions or to be a burden upon Egyptian society. Abravanel says that Joseph told Pharaoh that his people would never require special support. They would always take care of their own needs.

Abravanel also explains why Joseph deliberately counseled his brothers to say that they were "shepherds." He knew that Pharaoh had a great need for shepherds because most Egyptians were farmers. So he reasoned that other Egyptians would accept them more easily if they seemed unlikely to compete for jobs with them.

Clearly, Abravanel believes that Joseph worried about the Egyptians accepting his family. He feared jealousy or an outbreak of suspicion and prejudice. Joseph sensed that as a minority their situation was precarious, even dangerous.

His family would be strangers in a new land. They would speak Egyptian with an accent; their names would be different. Their clothing and their preference of foods and styles might also be different from the Egyptian lifestyle. Joseph realized that their safety and success would depend upon how the majority population treated them.

Modern commentator Pinchas Peli raises another issue that he believes concerned Joseph. Peli explains that, just before Joseph sent his brothers back to the Land of Israel, he warned them to be very careful about how they treated any Egyptians they might meet on their journey. Joseph told his brothers to avoid all quarrels with the Egyptians and not to act superior because of their special relationship to him.

What Peli seems to be suggesting is that Joseph was worried that his brothers would call attention to themselves, embarrass him, or endanger themselves by arousing resentment. So Peli suggests that Joseph advised them that as strangers they should assume a "low profile." They should call as little attention to themselves as possible by always acting quietly and humbly. (*Torah Today*, pp. 47–48)

At least one commentator stretches this concern

of Joseph for the safety of his family to his land reforms. The author of *Lekach Tov* suggests that, because Joseph worried about the status of his family, he decided to relocate all the Egyptians from one city to another throughout Egypt. In this way, so the argument goes, he made every Egyptian a "stranger." He thought that, if the Egyptians experienced some of the problems and difficulties of starting all over again in a new place with new people, they might have a greater sensitivity to his family who were new settlers in Goshen.

Separate occupations

Joseph chose for his brothers a good, upright—but hated—public occupation. Had he wished, he could have appointed them to high positions but, instead, he had them say that they were shepherds. . . . The idea was to segregate them from the Egyptians . . . and to have Pharaoh settle them in Goshen. (Rabbi Isaac Arama)

Separate place

Joseph arranged matters to achieve the goal that they would live separately from the Egyptians in the area of Goshen. While this was contrary to what Pharaoh had wished, it was worth the sacrifice since it meant guaranteeing Israel's identity and traditions. (Rabbi Naphtali Zvi Judah Berlin, Ha-Emek Davar*)*

Assimilation

Rabbi Bechaye notes that Jacob wanted his sons to stay away from the royal court so that they would not be in danger of achieving high positions. He feared assimilation—that they might trade their loyalty to their people and traditions for the glory of high office.

Both Rabbi Isaac Arama and the modern Zionist writer Rabbi Naphtali Zvi Judah Berlin argue that Joseph was also very concerned with the difficulties of preserving Jewish tradition and culture. He feared that all the temptations of Egyptian life—riches, entertainments, sports, politics, and various religions—would eventually lead to assimilation and the end of Jewish family loyalties. So he convinced Pharaoh to segregate his people and to restrict them to the region of Goshen.

Rabbi Hizkiyahu ben Manoah, a thirteenth-century commentator who lived in France, also follows this line of reasoning. He explains that it was not only Joseph who worried about preserving Jewish identity. Jacob, he says, was also concerned that life in Egypt would become so comfortable and prosperous that Jews would forget their own history, language, land, and traditions. Therefore he told his son not to appoint his brothers to any high positions of government. He did not want them tempted by honors or by power. Instead, according to Hizkiyahu ben Manoah, Jacob told Joseph to send them off to Goshen where they might live separately and safely within Egyptian culture.

As the commentators point out, living as "strangers" or "immigrants" in a new land presents a number of difficult problems. While often newcomers are welcomed warmly, as Pharaoh greeted Jacob and his family, others in the settled population remain suspicious and hostile to aliens. They fear that their jobs will be taken, their neighborhoods changed, their schools invaded, and their economic situation endangered.

One of the most serious problems facing all immigrant groups is how to hold on to their traditions, language, and group identity. Interpreters of the Joseph story are correct when they point out two responses to the challenge of assimilation. One is to segregate into ghettos, to seal yourself off from the rest of society around you; the other is to participate fully in the society but also to work at retaining your historic traditions.

For centuries, Jews have struggled with the stress and strains of assimilation. In some places, they have flourished, contributing richly to the greater society while also preserving and advancing Jewish culture and faith. At other times, they have suffered the brutality of anti-Semitism or even the rejection and abandonment by some Jews of their own community.

The status of "stranger," "alien," or "newcomer" is a difficult one. Perhaps that is why the Torah constantly emphasizes sensitivity and compassion in our treatment of the stranger. Repeatedly we find the commandment: "You shall not wrong a stranger or oppress him, for you were strangers in the land of Egypt."

PEREK DALET: *Joseph's Economic Success*

Our Torah portion claims that Joseph not only saved his own family from famine but also brilliantly rescued Egypt from economic ruin. He designed and managed a series of strategies that guided the people through seven years of plenty and sustained them through seven years of famine.

What were these "strategies"? How did Joseph save Egypt and, some say, the entire world from the ravages of famine?

Nachmanides explains that Joseph did not allow individuals to build and operate private silos for food storage. Instead, he created public granaries. "He stored everything," Nachmanides writes, "and divided it out to the people in annual rations." By controlling the supplies, Joseph prevented private profiteering and selfish hoarding. By rationing and distributing foods fairly, he gained the confidence and support of the people.

Furthermore, Nachmanides claims that Joseph gave his own family the same rations as others received. Refusing to take advantage of his position or to grant special favors, he treated everyone equally. Joseph realized that only such fairness would guarantee the trust of those who depended upon him. In the absence of such trust people would begin to cheat and hoard supplies for themselves, and the cooperative effort for saving Egypt would collapse.

The Midrash comments on Joseph's wise policy of locating silos. Rather than putting them in one place, he built them in different cities throughout Egypt. With the distribution centers so near to to the population, the people felt secure. They did not have to travel long distances to find food for their families. Nor did they need to stand on long lines to receive their supplies. Joseph's plan was efficient. It promoted confidence in a time of potential panic.

According to the rabbis of the Midrash, Joseph also adopted special laws regulating the way in which aid was distributed to foreigners who entered Egypt for help. They were prohibited from entering without registering their family names. In this way the government could control how many times a foreigner visited the country and requested help. Visitors were also prohibited from entering with more than one donkey. This made certain that no food was later sold for profit and that each visitor received only that which his family required for survival. (*Genesis Rabbah* 91:4)

I'll take care of myself
When the public experiences a disaster, let no person say: "I shall take food and drink for myself. I can't be bothered about others." (Ta'anit *11a*)

Joseph could have given the members of his family more than everyone else in Egypt, but he did not. He supplied them with what they needed just as he supplied everyone else. (Sforno on Vayigash)

The most complex aspect of Joseph's economic plan unfolded in the midst of the years of famine. As the people ran out of money with which to purchase their rations, they began to sell off their land and themselves as slaves to Pharaoh. Again, Joseph responded with creative solutions. He moved whole towns of people from one place to another, and he promised the people that they would receive four-fifths of the harvest and Pharaoh would take only one-fifth.

Luzzatto

Commentator Samuel David Luzzatto explains the brilliance of Joseph's tactic. He points out that Joseph did not split the Egyptians into small groups and scatter them among many different cities and populations. Instead, he resettled them "city by city," preserving their bonds of trust, cul-

ture, family, and friendship. They were settled in a new environment, but they were not separated from their families, friends, old neighbors, and important sources of support. In this way, Joseph insured the high morale and positive feelings of the people for him, for Pharaoh, and for the stability of Egypt during difficult times of crisis.

Rabbi Samson Raphael Hirsch writes that Joseph also demonstrated strong leadership when the people became desperate and began offering to sell their lands and themselves as slaves to Pharaoh for continuing rations. Instead of accepting their offer, Joseph rejected it. Hirsch comments that Joseph opposed slavery. Rather than allow the people to sell themselves into bondage, he adopted a policy of purchasing the land for the central government. Then, he leased it back to the people.

The result, as Hirsch explains, was that "the ground belonged to Pharaoh for a fifth of the produce" while the farmer lived on four-fifths of the produce. The one-fifth, or 20 percent, was the citizen's tax to the state. The result of Joseph's plan, as Hirsch interprets it, was that, rather than making the people slaves, they became "tenant farmers." (Commentary on Genesis 47:26)

Hirsch's interpretation is close to an earlier view developed by Nachmanides who believed that Joseph's offer was exceedingly generous. Nachmanides speculates that Joseph told the people: "By rights Pharaoh, as lord of the land, is entitled to four-fifths and you as tenants to one-fifth. But I will treat you generously and give you the land-owner's share, and Pharaoh will take the tenant's share." In Nachmanides' view, Joseph's act was a demonstration of generosity, not simply clever economics. (Commentary on Genesis 47:26)

From the viewpoint of most interpreters, Joseph's economic revolution demonstrates sound planning, good management, and justice. At a time when it might have been easy for the rich to look out only for themselves and to profit from the poor, the commentators make clear that Joseph legislated laws guaranteeing equal distribution to all people. He even favored the poor when they lost their land and were about to declare themselves slaves.

Joseph also demonstrates a high level of moral leadership. He refuses to take profits for himself or offer preferential treatment to his own family.

For all these reasons, Joseph is known in Jewish tradition as a *tzadik,* a "righteous person."

QUESTIONS FOR STUDY AND DISCUSSION

1. The debate about the best way to achieve justice from individuals or from leaders in political power still remains. What approach should minority groups, such as Jews, take to confront government? Which of Judah's appeals or arguments might work best?

2. Does good result from evil? Could God have meant to have Joseph's brothers sell him into slavery so that he might later save them from famine?

3. Should there be such things as unforgivable offenses in a family? What might we learn from the story of Joseph and his brothers about reconciliation?

4. Must Jews maintain a "low profile" in order to succeed in societies where they are a minority? Would such a posture have been helpful during the rise of the Nazis in Germany?

5. The ancient rabbis suggest that the Israelites in Egypt prevented assimilation by four means: (1) They avoided sexual promiscuity with Egyptians. (2) They did not gossip about one another. (3) They did not change their names. (4) They did not change their language. Would such remedies work today? What other remedies might you suggest for stopping assimilation and guaranteeing Jewish survival?

6. What solutions for famine relief developed by Joseph might solve some of our modern problems today?

PARASHAT VAYECHI
Genesis 47:28–50:26

Vayechi may be translated "and he lived" and records the last years and death of Jacob. After living in Egypt for seventeen years, Jacob calls his son Joseph and his grandsons, Manasseh and Ephraim, to his bedside for a blessing. He asks Joseph to bury him with Abraham and Isaac at the cave of Machpelah. Afterwards he calls all of his sons to his side and blesses each one. When Jacob dies, Joseph and his brothers bury him in Hebron. After their father's death, Joseph's brothers begin to fear that Joseph will now punish them for selling him into slavery. He reassures them that they are safe and promises to care for them and their families. Joseph lives to the age of one hundred and ten. Just before he dies he tells his family that God will return them to the Land of Israel and instructs them to carry his bones up from Egypt at that time.

OUR TARGUM

·1·

When Jacob is one hundred and forty-seven years old and has lived in Egypt for seventeen years, he calls Joseph to him and makes Joseph take a vow. "Promise that when I die you will bury me with my fathers, Abraham and Isaac, in the cave of Machpelah." Joseph assures his father that he will carry out his wish.

Afterwards, when Jacob is ill, Joseph brings his sons, Manasseh and Ephraim, to him for a special blessing. Jacob reminds Joseph of God's promise to give the Land of Israel to his children and tells Joseph that Manasseh and Ephraim shall be counted as his own sons. He then blesses his grandchildren, placing his right hand upon Ephraim's head and his left hand upon Manasseh's head. Joseph notices that his father is blessing the younger with his right hand and the older with his left hand and tries to move his father's hands. Jacob, however, indicates that he knows what he is doing by putting Ephraim before Manasseh.

· 2 ·

Jacob calls his twelve sons to gather about his bed. He presents each of them with an evaluation of and a prediction for the future. He reminds them that they are to bury him in Hebron, and then he dies.

· 3 ·

Joseph weeps for his father and orders that he be embalmed. After a mourning period of seventy days, he requests permission from Pharaoh to take Jacob's body to the Land of Israel for burial. Pharaoh grants his wish, and Joseph, his brothers, and many Egyptians travel to Hebron for the burial. Once there, they observe a mourning period of seven days. Then they bury their father and return to Egypt.

· 4 ·

Upon their return, Joseph's brothers fear that he will now punish them for having sold him into slavery. So they send him a message indicating that, before he died, their father asked Joseph to forgive them. They tell Joseph: "We are prepared to be your slaves."

Joseph assures them that, while they might have intended harm for him, God intended what they had done for good. He promises to care for them and their families.

· 5 ·

After living to one hundred and ten years, Joseph is about to die. He gathers his family about him and tells them that God will one day return them to the Land of Israel. "When that day comes, carry up my bones from here." Upon his death, Joseph is embalmed and placed in a coffin in Egypt.

THEMES

Parashat Vayechi contains three important themes:

1. Burial and mourning traditions.
2. Making honest evaluations; defining "leadership."
3. Lying in the cause of peace.

PEREK ALEF: *Jacob's Death—Burial and Mourning Traditions*

Our Torah portion provides an important description of burial and mourning practices. Jacob requests that he not be buried in Egypt but rather in Hebron with Abraham and Sarah, Isaac, Rebekah, and Leah. At his death, we learn that Joseph orders Egyptian physicians to embalm Jacob, a process that takes forty days. The Torah also tells us that the Egyptians mourned for Jacob's loss for seventy days and that Joseph and his brothers mourned him for seven days before his burial in the cave of Machpelah.

Jewish burial and mourning customs have changed and evolved since biblical times. For instance, although embalming a dead body in order to prevent its decay was accepted during the time of Jacob and Joseph, later Jewish authorities opposed the practice.

Several reasons were given: First, embalming delays burial. Jewish tradition favored immediate burial most likely out of consideration for the health of the community. Some commentators also suggest that the rule of immediate burial may have been derived from God's statement to Adam: "Dust you are and to dust you shall return." (Genesis 3:19)

Second, embalming prevents the natural decay of the body and is actually a desecration of the body. Within Jewish tradition the human body is considered the sacred container for the soul. It should be buried with honor and without any mutilation or unnatural interference with its decomposition.

Third, embalming was opposed because it interfered with the mourner's necessary acceptance of the reality of death. Rabbi Maurice Lamm comments that "the art of the embalmer is the art of complete denial. Embalming seeks to create an illusion, and, to the extent that it succeeds, it only hinders the mourner from recovering from . . . grief." In other words, because the embalmer's job is to make the dead person appear "alive" and "beautiful," the result may be that mourners are actually prevented from accepting the finality of death. When that happens, a mourner often has difficulty getting on with all the responsibilities of life. (*The Jewish Way in Death and Mourning*, Jonathan David Publishers, New York, 1975, pp. 12–15)

Reform Judaism on burial
Since Judaism prescribes that the body should be returned to the dust from which it came, embalming is discouraged except when required by law or circumstances.

Burial is the most widely practiced method of disposition of the body among Jews and is, in fact, the only method allowed by tradition. However, it is clear that other methods (interment in caves) were practiced among Jews in ancient times. And so, while both cremation and entombment in mausoleums are acceptable in Reform Judaism, burial is the normative Jewish practice. (Simeon J. Maslin, editor, Gates of

Mitzvah, *Central Conference of American Rabbis, New York, 1979, pp. 52–57)*

Among the ancient commentators a serious disagreement developed over whether or not Joseph should have embalmed his father, Jacob. Rabbi Judah Ha-Nasi believed that Joseph had made a serious mistake and that his life ended early because he did not honor his father in death.

Other rabbis argue that Joseph honored his father by following his instructions to bury him in the Land of Israel with his family. By embalming him they prepared his body so that it could be taken on the long journey from Goshen to Hebron. (*Genesis Rabbah* 100:3)

Although Jewish tradition opposes embalming, or any delays in burial, it did allow room for special circumstances. Embalming was permitted in cases where public health was endangered. It was also permitted when it was necessary to send the body long distances for burial (as in the case of Jacob) or when there was a necessary delay in the burial because close relatives needed to travel to the funeral.

Reform Judaism on mourning
Jewish tradition prescribes several periods of mourning, differing in intensity and obligation, following the death of a loved one. These are:

Avelut: The name applied generally to the entire mourning period.

Aninut: The period between death and burial.

Shivah: The seven days of mourning following the funeral. Mourners are encouraged to remain at home during these days (except on Shabbat or festivals, when they should join the congregation in prayer), to refrain from their ordinary pursuits and occupations, and to participate in daily services in the home. . . . The first three days of the shivah period are considered the most intense and in Reform congregations are considered the minimum mourning period.

Sheloshim: The thirty-day period (including shivah) when normal life gradually resumes, and the mourners return to their daily activities while yet observing certain aspects of mourning. One should avoid joyful social events and entertainment during this period.

The First Year: *The period during which a mourner recites* Kaddish *for a parent.* (Gates of Mitzvah, *pp. 59–60*)

Our Torah portion makes it clear that it took forty days to embalm Jacob but that the Egyptians mourned him for seventy days. Afterwards, Joseph and his brothers took their father's body to Hebron. Once there, they mourned for seven days and then buried him in the cave of Machpelah.

The mourning period observed by Joseph and his brothers does not conform with what has evolved into accepted Jewish practice. The seven days (*shivah*) are observed after burial, not before it. However, if the burial is at a great distance, then it is permitted to begin the *shivah* period at the time the vehicle carrying the body sets out on the journey. (I. Klein, *A Guide to Jewish Religious Practice*, Jewish Theological Seminary, distributed by Ktav, New York, 1979, p. 286)

The *shivah* period of mourning and the other designated times for grief (*sheloshim* and the saying of *Kaddish* during the first year after the death of a loved one) are all meant to ease the pain of losing someone we loved. Visits from friends provide comfort at a time when loneliness and loss are felt most deeply. Prayers recited with others, especially the *Kaddish*, affirm that we are not alone. They remind us that death is a part of the pattern of life and that God is to be thanked for the gift of the loved one we have lost and whose memory we cherish.

Commenting on the Jewish periods of mourning, Rabbi Jack D. Spiro writes: "Judaism . . . recognizes that the difficult work of mourning takes time; there is no shortcut on the road to recovery." (*A Time to Mourn*, Bloch, New York, 1968, p. 138)

Through the centuries, Jewish tradition has developed a process for confronting death and mourning. The procedures for burial are ones that honor the body and spirit of the dead. The designated periods and rituals of mourning allow for a healthy—and necessary—expression of grief. Jacob's death and his children's mourning teach us that losing a loved one is a deep wound. It requires time, support, and care from others to heal.

PEREK BET: *Jacob and His Sons— Honest Evaluations*

Just before he is about to die, Jacob calls his twelve sons to gather about his bed. His words to them are a combination of blessing, criticism, and prediction.

The dying patriarch is bluntly honest in his evaluation of his sons. He tells Reuben that he is "unstable as water," accuses Simeon and Levi of "lawlessness" and "fierce anger," and assesses Issachar as a "strong-boned ass." He calls Dan a "serpent"; he tells Joseph that he is "a wild ass" and Benjamin that he is "a ravenous wolf."

Why, we might ask, was Jacob so harshly critical of his sons?

Peli

Modern interpreter Pinchas Peli believes that Jacob's evaluation was meant to be helpful to them. His honesty taught them important lessons about their strengths and weaknesses. As their father, he could say things that no one else would tell them. Peli argues that "our lives often become confused and entangled for lack of a precise definition of who and what we really are." He claims that Jacob's evaluation of his sons "was meant to help his children find their proper identity. Such a criticism of them," Peli comments, "would help them find their way towards the future, in which they were destined to assume the roles as heads of the tribes of Israel."

Peli's psychological approach has special appeal. A parent's role is to help children understand their strengths and weaknesses. Constructive criticism builds character. It can deepen sensitivity to one's self and to others and improve one's social skills.

But parental criticism can also undermine confidence or mislead children about their real talents. Perhaps, instead of being helpful, Jacob's last words to his sons were harmful. How were they to feel about themselves when their father on his deathbed characterized them with such negative descriptions?

Not all commentaries, however, agree that "improving character" was the reason for Jacob's critical evaluation of existence.

Abravanel

Don Isaac Abravanel offers a different answer. It is the one most accepted by Jewish interpreters.

Abravanel's theory is that, when it came time for Jacob to die, he decided to pass on the leadership (or rule) of his family to the son who was most qualified. He struggled with his decision because he realized that the future of the Jewish people depended upon his choice.

For that reason, he assessed carefully the strengths and weaknesses of each son. When he reached his conclusion about who was the most qualified leader, he then gathered his sons together and announced it to them. Because he wanted them to appreciate his conclusions, he honestly shared his evaluation with them. Jacob wanted each of them to understand why he had disqualified him for leadership of the Jewish people.

Whether or not Abravanel's view of what motivated Jacob is correct, his discussion of what qualifies or disqualifies someone for leadership is very valuable. The following summary presents what Abravanel believes Jacob was saying about his sons and the important qualities he took into consideration when he thought about each of them.

Jacob's Sons and Leadership

Qualities for leadership

Judah: Trusted and accepted by his brothers.
Brave and successful in battle.
Steady, thoughtful, and dependable.
Clear about his goals and determined to fulfill them.

Qualities that disqualified for leadership

Reuben: Unstable as water.
Simeon, Levi: Use of violence and force.
Zebulun: Always looking for profit.

Issachar: Use of others to fight his battles.
Dan: Snipes at others behind their backs.
Gad: Weakly gives in to his opponents.
Asher, Naphtali: Serve others but do not command respect.
Joseph: Hated and distrusted by his brothers.
Benjamin: Lacks balance of judgment and concern for others.

Abravanel's emphasis here is upon the important qualities that define leadership. Jacob, he argues, did not speak to his sons in order to hurt their feelings or to cause bitterness between them. His purpose was to clarify for them why Judah, above them all, qualified as the leader of the tribe that would produce King David and future rulers of Israel.

What makes a leader?

No fanatic can be a leader of the people of Israel. (*Rabbi Mendel of Kotzk*)

A gentle leader here on earth will also be a leader in the world to come. (*Rabbi Eleazar ben Pedat*)

A leader must always show respect for the community. (*Rabbi Nachman ben Jacob*)

God weeps over a community leader who is domineering. (*Hagigah 5b*)

Jacob's last words to his sons were neither a blessing nor a promise for a peaceful future. Instead, Jacob presented them with a blunt and honest evaluation of their behavior and personalities. Our interpreters believe that his purpose was to provide his sons with some critical insights into themselves and their motivations. In doing so, Jacob also created some valuable standards for defining the difference between good and bad leadership qualities.

PEREK GIMEL: *Are We Permitted to Lie in the Cause of Peace?*

The Torah reports that, after Jacob's death and burial in Hebron, Joseph and his brothers return to Egypt. The brothers, however, fear that they are in danger. They say to one another: "What if Joseph seeks to pay us back for all the wrong that we did to him?"

So they decide to send a message to Joseph. They tell him: "Before his death your father left this instruction: So shall you say to Joseph, 'Forgive, I urge you, the offense and guilt of your brothers who treated you so harshly.'" (Genesis 50:15–17)

The message is a strange one and raises many important questions. A bit of research reveals three important facts: First, Joseph never told Jacob that his brothers had thought to kill him and then sold him into slavery. Second, none of the brothers is reported to have told Jacob what they did to Joseph. Third, Jacob never indicates that he knew what the brothers had done to Joseph or gives any instruction about what they should say to Joseph after his death.

So why do the brothers make up such a story? Why do they lie to Joseph?

Many biblical interpreters have explored these questions. One of the first was Rabbi Levi, who lived in the Land of Israel during the third century. Rabbi Levi explains that, prior to Jacob's death, Joseph invited his brothers to dinner with him every evening. Suddenly, they were not invited, and they began to suspect that his attitude toward them had changed and that they were in danger.

Rabbi Isaac, who taught at the same time as Rabbi Levi, disagrees with his interpretation. The brothers, he suggested, suspected that Joseph was plotting to harm them because, on their way back to Egypt from Hebron, they watched Joseph stop at the pit into which they had thrown him before selling him into slavery. Rabbi Levi explains that, when the brothers saw him standing by the pit, they feared that he remembered how badly they had treated him and that he would soon seek revenge. (*Genesis Rabbah* 100:8)

The modern Torah commentator Nehama Leibowitz explains Joseph's behavior and his brothers' reaction to it in a slightly different way. She points out that, after Jacob's death, Joseph, who was still in mourning, was overwhelmed by the responsibilities of governing Egypt. His schedule did not permit him to see his brothers and family each day as he had when his father was sick. Jacob's illness and all the responsibilities of his burial no longer held the family together. As a result, the brothers may have suspected that Joseph's attitude toward them had changed and that he was about to harm them. Perhaps, that is why they decided to lie to him about what Jacob had said before his death. (*Studies in Bereshit*, pp. 556–558)

Nearly all commentators agree that the brothers lied to Joseph about Jacob's instructions to them. While commentators may cite different reasons for the behavior of the brothers, all conclude that the brothers were deliberately dishonest. That, however, is not the only instance of deception in our Torah portion. Joseph and his brothers also kept the truth from their father about how they had sold Joseph into slavery.

Some interpreters point out that the brothers said nothing because they feared their father would curse them. Other commentators claim that Joseph said nothing because he did not want to make trouble for his family. In other words, for the sake of peace, Joseph and his brothers did not reveal to Jacob what had happened between them in the distant past.

Others paint a slightly different picture. They maintain that Joseph visited his father only a few times after his arrival in Egypt. Joseph feared that, if he visited him often, Jacob would ask him embarrassing questions about how he had reached Egypt. Joseph preferred avoiding such discussions. He did not want to be forced into explaining to his father that his brothers had lied about what they had done to him. Joseph realized that his father might never forgive his brothers if he knew that they had plotted to kill him and then decided to sell him into slavery. So, for the sake of peace in the family, Joseph seldom visited his father and refused to speak with him about the past. (*Pesikta Rabbati* on Genesis 48:1)

If this explanation is correct, then another question should be asked. Does Jewish tradition justify lying—or avoiding the truth—for the sake of peace?

Peace and truth
Peace without truth is a false peace. (*Rabbi Mendel of Kotzk*)

Seek peace
"Seek peace and pursue it." That means, seek it in your own place and pursue it in all other places. (*Jerusalem Talmud*, Peah *1:1*)

Peace is more important than anything else. (Sifra Bechukotai)

Great is peace. Quarreling is hateful. (Sifre *to* Naso *2*)

According to most interpreters of our Torah portion the answer is yes. For example, the respected president of the Sanhedrin in Jerusalem during the first century, Rabbi Shimon ben Gamaliel, taught that peace was so important that it was permissible to lie for the purpose of promoting it. This great leader of the Jewish people justified his argument by using Joseph and his brothers as an example. "They lied about what their father had said to them in order to convince Joseph not to punish them but to accept them and live with them peacefully as his brothers." (*Genesis Rabbah* 100:9)

Other commentators not only agree with Rabbi Shimon ben Gamaliel's position, but they elaborate on it. Rabbi Ila'a, quoting Rabbi Eleazar ben Shimon, says that, when the brothers altered the facts for the sake of peace, they did the right thing.

Rabbi Ishmael notes that even God occasionally changes the facts for the sake of peace. He explains that, when God told Sarah that she would bear a child, she replied that it would be impossible because Abraham "is an old man." (Genesis 18:9–15) But, for the sake of peace, Rabbi Ishmael says that God lied to Abraham about Sarah's reaction. Instead of reporting that she had responded with the insult "Abraham is an old man," God reported that she had said, "I am old."

One of Ishmael's students summarized his teacher's attitude when he concluded: "For the sake of family peace, even the Torah allows for misquotes or a shaving of the truth." (*Yevamot* 65b)

In the same commentary, Rabbi Nathan holds that it is a mitzvah, "an obligation," to lie or to change the facts if it will bring about peace. Illustrating his position, he recalls the story of God's asking Samuel to appoint David in place of Saul as king of Israel. Samuel is frightened that Saul will kill him. So God tells him to make it look as if he were going to offer a sacrifice. Then Saul will be fooled, and Samuel will be saved and able to appoint the new king. Samuel lies and lives, and Rabbi Nathan concludes by teaching, "For the sake of peace, you can lie." (*Yevamot* 65b)

But this is not always so. The modern interpreter Rabbi Elie Munk reports an important exception that appears in *Sefer Hassidim* (426): "If a person comes to you for a loan, and you do not want to give the money to him for fear that he will not repay it, you *do not* have the right to lie and say that you *do not* have the money to give him for a loan. You must tell him the truth. For the permission to tell a 'white lie' in the interest of peace applies *only* to cases that have already happened, and which cannot be changed, but not to events that are in the future."

In summary, the rule of lying for the sake of truth is as follows: If you are faced with a situation that has already happened, then, for the sake of peace, you can alter the memory of it, as the brothers did about what their father had instructed them to say to Joseph. Creating trust and caring among family members is more important than recalling accurately all the facts of the past, especially when we know those facts will only hurt others and divide the family into angry factions. But, when dealing with others in business or in other negotiations, you must not lie or deal in falsehoods.

The present and future must be built on honesty. Jewish tradition teaches: "Every person shall speak the truth with his neighbor." (Zechariah 8:16)

QUESTIONS FOR STUDY AND DISCUSSION

1. If the body is merely a repository for the soul, why does Jacob request that his bones be brought back to the Land of Israel? What does it say about Jacob's view of Egypt? What might the biblical authors have intended by his request?

2. Should parents present their children with critical evaluations? What are the dangers of such evaluations? What are the dangers if they are not offered? What do we learn from Jacob's critique of his sons?

3. Is there a difference between lying about the past to foster family peace and rewriting, distorting, or avoiding history in order to further better relations between nations? Examples might include avoiding such subjects as the Holocaust with Germans, civil rights for Indians or Blacks with Americans, or terrorism with Palestinians.

4. Can you think of an example when, for the sake of family unity and peace, it would be better to lie?

Glossary of Commentaries
and Interpreters

(*For further information on those entries followed by an asterisk, see Introduction II in this book.*)

Abravanel, Don Isaac.*

Adani, David ben Amram (13th century). (See *Midrash ha-Gadol*.)

Akedat Yitzhak. A commentary to the Torah by Isaac ben Moses Arama. (See Arama, Isaac ben Moses.)

Alshikh, Moshe ben Adrianopolis (1508–1600). Lived and taught in Safed in the Land of Israel. His commentary to the Torah contains his Sabbath sermons.

Arama, Isaac ben Moses (1420–1494). Author of the Torah commentary *Akedat Yitzhak*. Spanish rabbi. Known for his sermons and allegorical interpretations of Torah. Defended Judaism in many public disputes with Christians and settled in Italy after the expulsion of Jews from Spain in 1492.

Ashkenazi, Eliezer ben Elijah (1513–1586). Lived in Egypt, Cyprus, Venice, Prague, and Posen. Died in Cracow. Emphasized the gift of reason and in his commentary, *Ma'aseh ha-Shem* (see below), urged students to approach the Torah with care and independence. Worked as a rabbi, Torah interpreter, and physician. (See *Ma'aseh ha-Shem*.)

Ashkenazi, Shimon (12th century). (See *Yalkut Shimoni*.)

Ashkenazi of Yanof, Jacob ben Isaac (13th century). Author of *Tze'enah u-Re'enah*. (See *Tze'enah u-Re'enah*.)

Astruc, Anselm Solomon. (See *Midrashei Torah*.)

Attar, Chaim ibn (1696–1743). Born in Morocco and settled in Jerusalem where he opened a school. His Torah commentary, *Or ha-Chaim* (see below), combines talmudic and mystical interpretations.

Avot or *Pirke Avot*, "Sayings of the Fathers." A book of the *Mishnah*, comprising a collection of statements by famous rabbis.

Avot de-Rabbi Natan (2nd century). Compiled by Rabbi Nathan, sometimes called "Nathan the Babylonian." Based on *Pirke Avot*.

Ba'al Ha-Turim, Yaakov (1275–1340). Born in Germany. Fled persecutions there in 1303 and settled in Spain. Author of the very important collection of Jewish law *Arba'ah Turim*, "Four Rows," the basis for the later *Shulchan Aruch*, "Set Table," by Joseph Karo. His Torah commentary known as *Ba'al ha-Turim* often includes interpretations based on the mathematical meanings of Hebrew words.

Bachya ben Asher (14th century). Lived in Saragossa, and Aragon. Known for his Torah commentary.

Bachya ben Joseph ibn Pakuda (11th century). Lived in Spain as poet and author of the classic study of Jewish ethics *Hovot ha-Levavot*, "Duties of the Heart." (See *Hovot ha-Levavot*.)

Bamberger, Bernard J.*

Berlin, Naphtali Zvi Judah (1817–1893). Head of the famous yeshivah at Volozhin. Supporter of early Zionism, his Torah commentary, *Ha-Emek Davar* (see below), is a record of his lectures on the weekly portions.

Bin Gorion, Micha Joseph (Berdyczewski) (1865–1921). Though a Russian citizen, spent most of his years in Germany. A Hebrew writer, his collection of Jewish folktales, *Mimekor Yisrael* (see below), is considered a classic.

*Biur.**

Buber, Martin Mordecai (1878–1965). Born in Vienna. Became renowned as a twentieth-century philosopher. With Franz Rosenzweig, translated the Bible into German. His *Moses* is a commentary on Exodus.

Caspi, Joseph ben Abba Mari (1280–1340). A philosopher and commentator who lived in France. His commentary seeks to blend reason with religious faith.

Da'at Zekenim mi-Ba'alei ha-Tosafot. A thirteenth-century collection of Torah commentaries by students of Rashi who sought to resolve contradictions found within the talmudic discussions of the rabbis.

De Leon, Moses. (See *Zohar*.)*

Deuteronomy Rabbah. One of the early collections of *midrashim*.*

Dubno, Solomon. (See *Biur*.)*

Ecclesiastes Rabbah. One of the early collections of *midrashim*.*

Edels, Shemuel Eliezer ben Yehudah Halevi (1555–1631). One of the best known and respected interpreters of Talmud. Born in Cracow. Also known as the *Maharsha*.

Epstein, Baruch (1860–1942). Murdered by the Nazis in the Pinsk ghetto. (See *Torah Temimah*.)

Genesis Rabbah. One of the early collections of *midrashim*.*

Gittin. A tractate of Talmud that discusses the laws of divorce.

Guide for the Perplexed. A philosophical discussion of the meanings of Jewish belief written by Moses Maimonides. (See Maimonides, Moses.)

Ha-Cohen, Meir Simcha (1843–1926). (See *Meshekh Hochmah*.)

Ha-Emek Davar. A Torah commentary written by Naphtali Zvi Judah Berlin. (See Berlin, Naphtali Zvi Judah.)

Ha-Ketav ve-ha-Kabbalah. A Torah commentary written by Joseph Zvi Mecklenburg.*

Halevi, Aharon (1230–1300). Born in Gerona, Spain. Served as rabbi and judge in Barcelona, Saragossa, and Toledo. Lecturer in Montpellier, Provençe, France, where he died. While *Sefer ha-Hinuch* (see below) is said to have been written by him, many doubt the claim.

Halevi, Isaac ben Yehudah (13th century). (See *Paneah Raza*.)

Halevi, Yehudah (1080–1142?). Born in Spain. Poet, philosopher, and physician. His book, *The Kuzari*, contains his philosophy of Judaism. It is a dialogue between the king of the Kazars and a rabbi who convinces the king of the superiority of Judaism.

Hallo, William W.*

Ha-Midrash ve-ha-Ma'aseh. A commentary to Genesis and Exodus by Yehezkel ben Hillel Aryeh Leib Lipschuetz. (See Lipschuetz, Yehezkel ben Hillel Aryeh Leib.)

Heinemann, Yitzhak (1876–1957). Born in Germany. Israeli scholar and philosopher. His *Ta'amei ha-Mitzvot*, "Reasons for the Commandments," is a study of the meaning of the commandments of Jewish tradition.

Hertz, Joseph Herman.*

Hirsch, Samson Raphael.*

Hirschensohn, Chaim (1857–1935). Born in Safed. Lived most of his life in Jerusalem. Supported the work of Eliezer ben Yehuda's revival of Hebrew. (See *Nimmukei Rashi*.)

Hizkuni. A Torah commentary by Hizkiyahu (Hezekiah) ben Manoah (13th century) of France.

Hoffman, David Zvi (1843–1921). A leading German rabbi. His commentary on Leviticus and Deuteronomy is based on lectures given in the 1870s, seeking to refute biblical critics who argued that the

Christian New Testament was superior to the Hebrew Bible.

Hovot ha-Levavot, "Duties of the Heart." A classic study of Jewish ethics by Bachya ben Joseph ibn Pakuda (see above). Concerned with the emphasis on ritual among the Jews of his times, Bachya argues that a Jew's highest responsibility is to carry out the ethical commandments of Torah.

Hullin. A tractate of Talmud that discusses laws dealing with killing animals for food.

Ibn Ezra, Abraham.*

Jacob, Benno.*

Kasher, Menachem. (See *Torah Shelemah.*)

Keley Yakar. A Torah commentary written by Solomon Ephraim ben Chaim Lunchitz (1550–1619) of Lvov (Lemberg) Poland.

Kiddushin. A tractate of Talmud that discusses laws of marriage.

Kimchi, David (RaDaK).*

Leibowitz, Nehama.*

Lekach Tov. A collection of *midrashim* on the Torah and the Five Scrolls (Song of Songs, Ruth, Lamentations, Ecclesiastes, and Esther), by Tobias ben Eliezer (11th century C.E.).

Lipschuetz, Yehezkel ben Hillel Aryeh Leib (1862–1932). Lithuanian interpreter of Torah and author of *Ha-Midrash ve-ha-Ma'aseh.* (See *Ha-Midrash ve-ha-Ma'aseh.*)

Luzzatto, Moshe Chaim (1707–1746). Known also as *Ramhal.* Italian dramatist and mystic whose commentaries were popular among chasidic Jews. His textbook on how to become a righteous person, *Mesillat Yesharim* became one of the most popular books on the subject of Jewish ethics. (See *Mesillat Yesharim.*)

Luzzatto, Samuel David.*

Ma'aseh ha-Shem. A commentary by Eliezer ben Elijah Ashkenazi published in 1583. (See Ashkenazi, Eliezer ben Elijah.)

Maimonides, Moses, Rabbi Moses ben Maimon (1135–1204). Known by the initials RaMBaM. Born in Cordova, Spain. Physician and philosopher. Wrote the *Mishneh Torah,* a code of Jewish law; *Guide for the Perplexed,* a philosophy of Judaism; *Sefer ha-Mitzvot,* an outline of the 613 commandments

of Torah; and many other interpretations of Jewish tradition. Famous as a physician. Served the leaders in the court of Egypt.

MaLBIM, Meir Lev ben Yechiel Michael.*

Mechilta. *

Mecklenburg, Joseph Zvi. (See *Ha-Ketav ve-ha-Kabbalah.*)*

Megillah. A tractate of Talmud that discusses the biblical Book of Esther.

Mendelssohn, Moses.*

Meshekh Hochmah. A Torah commentary published in 1927. Written by Meir Simcha Ha-Cohen, rabbi of Dvinsk. Combines insights from the Talmud with a discussion of the philosophy of Judaism. (See Ha-Cohen, Meir Simcha.)

Mesillat Yesharim, "Pathway of the Righteous." A discussion of how one should pursue an ethical life. Written by Moshe Chaim Luzzatto (see above).

Messengers of God. A study of several important biblical personalities, by Elie Wiesel. (See Wiesel, Elie; also Bibliography in this book.)

Midrash Agadah. A collection of rabbinic interpretations. (See discussion of *midrashim.*)*

Midrash ha-Gadol. A collection of rabbinic interpretations dating to the first and second centuries, by David ben Amram Adani, a scholar living in Yemen. (See Adani, David ben Amram.)

Midrash Sechel Tov. Compiled by Menachem ben Solomon in 1139. Combines selections of *midrash* and *halachah* on every Torah portion.

Midrash Tanchuma. Known also as *Tanchuma Midrash Yelamedenu.* A collection said to have been collected by Rabbi Tanchuma (427–465 C.E.). Many of the *midrashim* begin with the words *Yelamedenu rabbenu,* "Let our teacher instruct us. . . ."*

Midrashei Torah. A Torah commentary by Anselm Solomon Astruc who was murdered in an attack on the Jewish community of Barcelona in 1391.

Mimekor Yisrael. A collection of folktales from Jewish tradition by Micha Joseph Bin Gorion (Berdyczewski). (See Bin Gorion.)

Mishnah. *

Mizrachi, Eliyahu (1440–1525). A Chief Rabbi of Turkey during the expulsion of Jews from Spain.

Helped many immigrants. Wrote a commentary to Rashi's Torah interpretation.

Morgenstern, Julian.*

Nachmanides.* (See RaMBaN.)

Nedarim. A tractate of Talmud that discusses vows or promises.

Nimmukei Rashi. A commentary on Rashi's Torah interpretation by Chaim Hirschensohn. (See Hirschensohn, Chaim.)

Numbers Rabbah. An early collection of *midrashim.**

Or ha-Chaim. A Torah commentary by Chaim ibn Attar. Combines talmudic observations with mystical interpretations. (See Attar, Chaim ibn.)

Paneah Raza. A Torah commentary by Isaac ben Yehudah Halevi who lived in Sens. (See Halevi, Issac ben Yehudah.)

Peli, Pinchas Hacohen (20th century). Jerusalem-born scholar, poet, and rabbi. His "Torah Today" column in the *Jerusalem Post* seeks to present a contemporary view of the meaning of Torah.

*Pesikta de-Rav Kahana.** A collection of *midrashim* or early rabbinic sermons based on Torah portions for holidays of the Jewish year. *Pesikta Rabbati* is similiar in both content and organization.

*Pesikta Rabbati.** (See *Pesikta de-Rav Kahana.*)

*Pirke de-Rabbi Eliezer.** A collection of *midrashim* said to have been written by the first-century C.E. teacher Rabbi Eliezer ben Hyrkanos. Contents include mystic interpretations of creation, early human life, the giving of the Torah at Mount Sinai, comments about the Book of Esther, and the Israelite experience in the Sinai.

Plaut, W. Gunther.*

RaDaK, Rabbi David Kimchi.*

RaMBaM, Rabbi Moses ben Maimon. (See Maimonides.)

RaMBaN, Rabbi Moses ben Nachman.* (See Nachmanides.)

RaSHBaM, Rabbi Shemuel (Samuel) ben Meir.*

RaSHI, Rabbi Shelomoh (Solomon) Itzhaki.*

Reggio, Yitzhak Shemuel (1784–1855). Known also as YaSHaR. Lived in Italy. Translated the Bible into Italian. Created a Hebrew commentary that sought to harmonize science and religion.

Rosenzweig, Franz (1886–1929). German philosopher. Worked with Martin Buber in translating the Bible into German. Best known for book *The Star of Redemption,* which seeks to explore the meanings of Jewish tradition.

Sa'adia ben Joseph Ha-Gaon.* (See also Introduction I of this book.)

Sanhedrin. A tractate of Talmud that discusses laws regulating the courts.

Sarna, Nahum M.*

Sefer ha-Hinuch. Presents the 613 *mitzvot,* "commandments," found within the Torah. Divided according to weekly Torah portions. Said by some to have been written by Aharon Halevi of Barcelona. (See Halevi, Aharon.)

Sforno, Obadiah.*

Shabbat. A tractate of the Talmud that discusses the laws of the Sabbath.

*Sifra.** A *midrash* on Leviticus. Believed by scholars to have been written during the fourth century C.E.

*Sifre.** A *midrash* on Numbers and Deuteronomy. Believed to have been composed during the fifth century C.E.

Simeon (Shimon) ben Yochai.* (See *Zohar.*)*

Solomon, Menachem ben. (See *Midrash Sechel Tov.*)

Sotah. A tractate of the Talmud that discusses laws concerning a woman suspected of adultery.

Speiser, Ephraim Avigdor.*

Steinsaltz, Adin (20th Century). An Israeli Talmud scholar. His book *Biblical Images* contains studies of various biblical characters.

Ta'amei ha-Mitzvot. (See Yitzhak Heinemann.)

Ta'anit. A tractate of the Talmud that deals with the laws concerning fast days.

*Talmud.** Combines the *Mishnah* and *Gemara.* Appears in two versions: the more extensive *Talmud Bavli,* "Babylonian Talmud," a collection of discussions by the rabbis of Babylonia from the second to the fifth centuries C.E., and *Talmud Yerushalmi,* "Jerusalem Talmud," a smaller collection of discussions from the second to the fourth centuries C.E.

Tanna Debe Eliyahu. A *midrash* and book of Jewish philosophy and commentary believed by scholars to have been composed during the third to tenth centuries. Author unknown.

*Targum Onkelos.**

*Targum Yerushalmi.**

Toledot Yitzhak.

Torah Shelemah. A study of each Torah portion, which includes a collection of early rabbinic interpretations along with a commentary by Rabbi Menachem Kasher of Jerusalem, Israel.

Torah Temimah. A Torah commentary by Baruch Epstein. Includes a collection of teachings from the Talmud on each Torah portion. (See Epstein, Baruch.)

Tosafot. "Supplementary Discussions" of the Talmud. Collected during the twelfth and thirteenth centuries in France and Germany and added to nearly every printing of the Talmud since.

Tzedeh Laderech. An interpretation of Rashi's Torah commentary by Issachar Ber ben Israel-Lazar Parnas Eilenberg (1550–1623), who lived in Italy.

Tze'enah u-Re'enah. A well-known Yiddish paraphrase and interpretation of the Torah. First published in 1618. Written for women by Jacob ben Isaac Ashkenazi of Yanof. Divided by weekly Torah portions. One of the first texts developed to educate women. (See Ashkenazi of Yanof, Jacob ben Isaac.)

Wessely, Naftali Herz. (See *Biur*.)*

Wiesel, Elie (1928–   ). Nobel Prize-winning novelist. Author of *Messengers of God,* among other books. (See *Messengers of God*.)

Yalkut Shimoni. A collection of *midrashim.* Believed to be the work of Shimon Ashkenazi. (See Ashkenazi, Shimon.)

Yevamot. A tractate of Talmud that deals with laws concerning sisters-in-law.

Yoma. A tractate of Talmud that deals with laws concerning Yom Kippur.

*Zohar.**

Bibliography

Abbott, Walter M.; Gilbert, Arthur; Hunt, Rolfe Lanier; and Swain, J. Carter. *The Bible Reader: An Interfaith Interpretation*. New York: Bruce Publishing Co., 1969.

Adar, Zvi. *Humanistic Values in the Bible*. New York: Reconstructionist Press, 1967.

Adler, Morris. *The Voice Still Speaks*. New York: Bloch Publishing Co., 1969.

Aharoni, Yohanan, and Avi-Yonah, Michael. *The Macmillan Bible Atlas*. New York: Macmillan, 1976.

Alter, Robert. *The Art of Biblical Narrative*. New York: Basic Books, 1981.

Asimov, Isaac. *Animals of the Bible*. Garden City, New York: Doubleday, 1978.

Avi-Yonah, Michael, and Malamat, Abraham, eds. *Views of the Biblical World*. Chicago and New York: Jordan Publications, Inc., 1959.

Baron, Joseph L., ed. *A Treasury of Jewish Quotations*. New York: Crown Publishers, Inc., 1956.

Blumenthal, David R. *God at the Center*. San Francisco: Harper and Row, 1987.

Braude, William G., and Kapstein, Israel J., trans. Author unknown. *Tanna Debe Eliyahu*. Philadelphia: Jewish Publication Society, 1981.

Buber, Martin. *Moses*. New York: Harper and Row Publishers, Inc., 1958.

Bulka, Reuven P. *Torah Therapy: Reflections on the Weekly Sedra and Special Occasions*. New York: Ktav, 1983.

Chavel, Charles B., trans. *Ramban (Nachmanides) Commentary on the Torah*. New York: Shilo Publishing House, Inc., 1974.

Chiel, Arthur. *Guide to Sidrot and Haftarot*. New York: Ktav, 1971.

Chill, Abraham. *The Minhagim: The Customs and Ceremonies of Judaism, Origins and Rationale*. New York: Sepher-Hermon Press, 1979.

Cohen, Philip. *Rambam on the Torah*. Jerusalem: Rubin Mass Ltd. Publishers, 1985.

Culi, Yaakov. *The Torah Anthology, Yalkut Me'am Lo'ez*. Translated by Aryeh Kaplan. New York and Jerusalem: Maznaim Publishing Corp., 1977.

Danby, Herbert, trans. *The Mishnah*. London: Oxford University Press, 1933.

Deen, Edith. *All of the Women of the Bible*. New York: Harper and Brothers, 1965.

Doria, Charles, and Lenowitz, Harris, trans. and eds. *Origins, Creation Texts from the Ancient Mediterranean*. New York: Anchor Press, 1976.

Dresner, Samuel H., and Siegel, Seymour. *The Jewish Dietary Laws*. New York: Burning Bush Press, 1959.

Efron, Benjamin. *The Message of the Torah*. New York: Ktav, 1963.

Epstein, I., trans. and ed. *The Babylonian Talmud*. London: Soncino Press, 1952.

Fields, Harvey J. *Bechol Levavcha: With All Your Heart*. New York: Union of American Hebrew Congregations, 1976.

Freedman, H., and Simon, Maurice, trans. *Midrash*

Rabbah: Genesis, Vols. I and II. London: Soncino Press, 1961.

Friedman, Alexander Zusia. *Wellsprings of Torah.* Compiled and edited by Nison Alpert. Translated by Gertrude Hirschler. New York: Judaica Press, 1986.

Friedman, Rikchard Elliott. *Who Wrote the Bible?* New York: Summit Books, 1987.

Fromm, Erich. *You Shall Be as Gods.* New York: Holt, Rinehart and Winston, 1966.

Frye, Northrop. *The Great Code: The Bible and Literature.* New York: Harcourt Brace Jovanovich Publishers, 1981.

Gaster, Theodor H. *Festivals of the Jewish Year.* New York: William Morrow and Co., Inc. 1953.

Gilbert, Martin. *Jewish History Atlas.* New York: Macmillan, 1976.

Ginzberg, Louis. *Legends of the Jews.* Philadelphia: Jewish Publication Society, 1968.

Glatzer, Nahum N., ed. *Hammer on the Rock: A Midrash Reader.* New York: Schocken Books, 1962.

———. *On the Bible: 18 Studies.* New York: Schocken Books, 1968.

Goldman, Solomon. *In the Beginning.* Philadelphia: Jewish Publication Society of America, 1949.

Graves, Robert, and Patai, Raphael. *Hebrew Myths: The Book of Genesis.* New York: Greenwich House, 1983.

Greenberg, Moshe. *Understanding Exodus.* New York: Behrman House, 1969.

Herford, R. Travers. *Pirke Aboth, The Ethics of the Talmud: Sayings of the Fathers.* New York: Schocken Books, 1971.

Hertz, J.H., ed. *The Pentateuch and Haftorahs.* London: Soncino Press, 1966.

Heschel, Abraham J. *The Prophets.* Philadelphia: Jewish Publication Society, 1962.

Hirsch, Samson Raphael, trans. *The Pentateuch.* London, England: L. Honig and Sons Ltd., 1959.

The Interpreter's Bible. 12 vols. Nashville: Abingdon, 1951–1957.

Jacobson, B.S. *Meditations on the Torah.* Tel Aviv: Sinai Publishing, 1956.

Katz, Mordechai. *Lilmod Ul'lamade: From the Teachings of Our Sages.* New York: Jewish Education Program Publications, 1978.

Lamm, Maurice. *The Jewish Way in Death and Mourning.* New York: Jonathan David Publishers, 1975.

Leibowitz, Nehama. *Studies in Bereshit.* Jerusalem: World Zionist Organization, 1980.

———. *Studies in Shemot.* Jerusalem: World Zionist Organization, 1980.

———. *Studies in Vayikra.* Jerusalem: World Zionist Organization, 1980.

———. *Studies in Bemidbar.* Jerusalem: World Zionist Organization, 1980.

———. *Studies in Devarim.* Jerusalem: World Zionist Organization, 1980.

Levine, Moshe. *The Tabernacle: Its Structure and Utensils.* London: Soncino Press Ltd., 1969.

Maimonides, Moses. *The Book of Knowledge: Mishneh Torah.* Translated by Moses Hyamson. Jerusalem and New York: Feldheim Publishers, 1974.

Matek, Ord. *The Bible through Stamps.* New York: Hebrew Publishing Company, 1967.

Miller, Madeline S., and Lane, J. *Harper's Encyclopedia of Bible Life.* New York: Harper and Row Publishers, 1978.

Morgenstern, Julian. *The Book of Genesis.* New York: Schocken Books, 1965.

Munk, Eli. *The Call of the Torah.* Vols. I and II. Jerusalem and New York: Feldheim Publishers, 1980.

Neusner, Jacob. *Meet Our Sages.* New York: Behrman House, 1980.

Orlinsky, Harry M., ed. *The Torah: The Five Books of Moses.* A New Translation. Philadelphia: Jewish Publication Society, 1962.

———. *Understanding the Bible through History and Archaeology.* New York: Ktav, 1972.

Peli, Pinchas H. *Torah Today.* Washington, D.C.: B'nai B'rith Books, 1987.

Phillips, Anthony. Exodus Commentary. *The Cambridge Bible Commentary: New English Bible.* Cambridge, England: Cambridge University Press, 1972.

Plaut, W. Gunther, ed. *The Torah: A Modern Commentary.* Commentaries by W. Gunther Plaut and Bernard J. Bamberger. Essays by William W. Halls. New York: Union of American Hebrew Congregations, 1981.

Pritchard, James B., ed. *Ancient Near Eastern Texts Relating to the Old Testament.* Princeton, New Jersey: Princeton University Press, 1955.

Rabbinowitz, J., trans. *Midrash Rabbah* (Genesis, Exodus, Leviticus, Numbers, Deuteronomy). London: Soncino Press, 1961.

Rabinowitz, Louis I. *Torah and Flora.* New York: Sanhedrin Press, 1977.

Rad, Gerhard von. *Deuteronomy.* Commentary and translation by Dorothea Barton. Philadelphia: Westminster Press, 1966.

Reed, Allison. *The Story of Creation.* New York: Schocken Books, 1981.

Rosenbaum, M., and Silbermann, A.M., trans. *Pentateuch with Targum Onkelos, Haphtaroth and Rashi's Commentary.* Jerusalem: Silbermann Family Publishers, 1973.

Samuel, Maurice. *Certain People of the Book*. New York: Alfred A. Knopf, Inc., 1955.

Sandmel, Samuel. *Alone Atop the Mountain: A Novel About Moses and the Exodus*. New York: Doubleday, 1973.

Sarna, Nahum M. *Understanding Genesis*. New York: Schocken Books, 1966.

Schneerson, Menachem M. *Torah Studies*. London: Lubavitch Foundation, 1986.

Silberman, A.M., ed. *Pentateuch with Rashi Commentary*. Jerusalem: Silbermann Family Publishers, 1933.

Silver, Abba Hillel. *Moses and the Original Torah*. New York: Macmillan, 1961.

Simon, Solomon, and Morrison, David Bial. *The Rabbis' Bible*. New York: Behrman House, 1966.

Speiser, E.A., trans. *The Anchor Bible: Genesis*. New York: Doubleday, 1964.

Van Doren, Mark, and Samuel, Maurice. *In the Beginning . . . Love*. Edited by Edith Samuel. New York: John Day Company, 1973.

Wiesel, Elie. *Messengers of God*. New York: Random House, 1976.

Zakon, Miriam Stark, trans. *Tz'enah Ur'enah: The Classic Anthology of Torah Lore and Midrashic Commentary*. Brooklyn, New York: Mesorah Publications Ltd./Hillel Press, 1983.

Zeligs, Dorothy F. *Psychoanalysis and the Bible*. New York: Bloch Publishing Company, 1974.

Zlotowitz, Meir, trans. *Bereishis*. Art Scroll Tanach Series. New York: Mesorah Publications Ltd., 1977–1981.